Franchise Law Compliance Manual

Steven M. Goldman & Bret Lowell, Editors

ABA ◢

**Forum on Franchising
American Bar Association**

Cover design by Gray Cat Design.

© 2000 American Bar Association. All rights reserved.
Printed in the United States of America.

05 04 03 02 01   5 4 3 2 1

Goldman, Steven M., 1960-
    The franchising law compliance manual : keys to a successful corporate compliance program / Steven M. Goldman, H. Bret Lowell.
        p. cm.
    Includes index.
    ISBN 1-57073-773-8
        1. Franchise (Retail trade)—Law and legislation—United States. I. Lowell, H. Bret. II. Title.

KF2023.G65 1999
343.73'0887—dc21   99-59716

Discounts are available for books ordered in bulk. Special consideration is given to state bars, CLE programs, and other bar-related organizations. Inquire at Book Publishing, ABA Publishing, American Bar Association, 750 North Lake Shore Drive, Chicago, Illinois 60611.

www.ababooks.org

In Memoriam

In memory of Kathleen Callahan Anderson (1953 to 1998). Kathleen was a former Director of the Corporate Counsel Division and a member of the Governing Committee of the Forum on Franchising. She conceived of the idea of a compliance manual for franchise counsel and was always an inspiration to all who knew her.

Summary of Contents

Contents

CHAPTER 3:   **Franchise Records Management**   **141**
By Charles B. Cannon, Jerry Lovejoy, and Ken Minami

CHAPTER 4:   **Practical Considerations to Address Franchise
Agency Issues**   **175**
By Donnell J. McCormack, Jr. and Sheri A. Young

Foreword

The Mission Statement for the ABA Forum on Franchising is to be the preeminent forum for the study and discussion of the legal aspects of franchising. A primary goal we adopted to accomplish this objective is to provide high-quality educational programs and publications on the legal aspects of franchising. *The Franchise Law Compliance Manual* represents a giant step toward accomplishing this goal by combining the talents of skilled in-house counsel, as well as experienced outside counsel, to provide a user friendly and practical guide that will enable franchise companies to focus on a broad range of corporate functions related to franchising.

The Franchise Law Compliance Manual provides a ready resource to corporate counsel and their business clients with respect to the organization and implementation of standardized administrative systems and procedures for their franchise business. The initial idea for a compliance manual began with our late Governing Committee member, Kathleen Callahan Anderson, to whom this book is dedicated, who discussed her ideas with Steve Goldman. With the further help of Jeff Brimer and the members of the Corporate Counsel Division Steering Committee, Steve then designed the topics and structure for the manual, and the concept was initially tested at our 20th Annual Forum in Colorado Springs, which I had the privilege of chairing. All of the participants at a mini-program presented by the Corporate Counsel Division were encouraged to review written materials prepared on six topics ranging from establishment and protection of intellectual property rights to termination of the franchise relationship. Through roundtable discussions, the authors were able to solicit input from participants on new ideas, suggestions for change, and other recommendations to enhance the final product. During the next 18 months, comments from program participants were assimilated and incorporated by 13 authors into the final chapters which are produced in this book.

Our co-editors, Steven Goldman and Bret Lowell, brought together their vast substantive skills and editorial talents to pull together the various segments of the project into a comprehensive, enjoyable, and easy-to-understand volume. Throughout the process of developing this publication, there was always the desire to present a well-rounded viewpoint and to join an in-house counsel with a law firm practitioner for each chapter, thus assuring that practical business thoughts, as opposed to strictly legal positions, would be reflected in the final product. I was very excited about this project from its inception and was fortunate to have participated in many meetings of the Forum's Publications Committee as this monograph was being developed. I feel confident that you will agree with me that it represents an extremely invaluable addition to our Forum publications that will serve the needs of franchise practitioners and franchising companies.

On behalf of the Forum on Franchising, I want to thank Steve, Bret, and each of the 13 authors, all of whom are known to a wide number of our members as distinguished franchise attorneys, for their persistence and enormous energy expended in developing *The Franchise Law Compliance Manual.* Their dedication and hard work, together with the input and participation of the mini-program attendees, the Publications Committee of the Forum, the ABA staff, and a host of others who were actively involved along the way, have combined to make this a "must read" for our Forum members and their clients.

Richard M. Asbill, Chair
Forum on Franchising

Preface

The publication of *The Franchise Law Compliance Manual* marks a significant milestone in the growing field of franchise literature. The ABA Forum on Franchising's Corporate Counsel Division, under the leadership of its then-Director, Kathleen Callahan Anderson, first conceived of the idea for a compliance manual for franchise counsel. The idea was to focus on the general areas of corporate practice, such as labor and environmental law. When I became Director of the Corporate Counsel Division, Kathleen was a member of the Forum Governing Committee and encouraged me to pick up the project. I was not excited by the project initially, but Kathleen had a contagious enthusiasm.

As I thought about the project and discussed it with Kathleen, we realized that there was a need for a book specific to franchise law that would assist the lawyer new to advising a franchise company as general counsel or in-house counsel. That lawyer needed a guide not only on how to solve an *ad hoc* problem, but also on how to organize a company's compliance programs to proactively address the issues specific to franchising. There were compliance manuals for the generalist and, although other books on franchising have focused on specific issues such as registration and disclosure, mergers and acquisitions, and trademarks, there had not been a substantial treatment of the compliance aspects of franchise law. No single publication identified the scope of franchise law compliance issues, nor was there any uniform guidance on how these issues should be approached. The Steering Committee of the Corporate Counsel Division took up the challenge to fill this void. We agreed on the topics and, at the suggestion of Jeff Brimer, who was then a member of the Steering Committee, to give the project a "dry run" at the annual Forum program. Each of the chapters was presented as a series of papers and discussed at "roundtables" as a mini-program at the 20th Annual Forum of the ABA Forum on Franchising in Colorado Springs, Colorado. Entitled "How to Develop and Implement a Franchise Corporate Compliance Program," these papers formed the foundation for *The Franchise Law Compliance Manual.* From the outset of this project, we determined that this *Manual* should be a working reference for franchise lawyers to establish day-to-day compliance programs that would help protect the franchisor's property, limit liability, and prepare for and limit the inevitable tensions in a franchise system. To this end, we decided that this *Manual* could only be truly useful if it were prepared from the perspective of both in-house franchise attorneys and their outside corporate counsel, who must frequently work in tandem to achieve the legal and business objectives of franchisors. Similarly, the preparation of each chapter represented a collaboration between in-house and outside counsel (though, by the time this manual went to press, some of the authors' positions had changed).

We also realized that in preparing the *Manual* the editing needed the same outside counsel perspective as the authors, and we were fortunate enough to have

Bret Lowell, a former Chair of the Forum on Franchising, join as an editor. Our ongoing task has been to ensure that both perspectives are equally preserved in the ensuing work. With this in mind, we have both drawn on the diversity of our experience in counseling franchisors.

The Franchise Law Compliance Manual is thus the direct product of the ideas of the Corporate Counsel Division Steering Committee and the hard work of fifteen individuals, over the course of more than three years. It provides an in-depth, extensive view of franchise law compliance issues, offers countless forms and checklists which franchise attorneys will no doubt find indispensable in their daily practice, and it demonstrates the interplay of case law with compliance. With *The Franchise Law Compliance Manual,* franchise practitioners now have the keys to a successful corporate compliance program at their fingertips.

That said, this remains Kathleen's project and it is to her that this *Manual* is dedicated.

Steven M. Goldman

Acknowledgments

As editors of *The Franchise Law Compliance Manual: Keys to a Successful Corporate Compliance Program,* we would like to recognize the numerous individuals who contributed to this work and without whose efforts this publication would not have been possible. We would like to express our gratitude and appreciation to the following:

Chapter 1

William A. Finkelstein
Anthony M. Stiegler

Chapter 2

Mark B. Forseth
Grover C. Outland

Chapter 3

Charles B. Cannon
Jerry L. Lovejoy
Ken R. Minami

Chapter 4

Donnell J. McCormack
Sheri A. Young

Chapter 5

Raymond L. Miolla
Andrew C. Selden

Chapter 6

Lisa Pender Morse
Ronald T. Coleman, Jr.

We would also like to extend our appreciation to Frances S. Pelzman, Amanda L. Burt, and Amy K. Robinson of Piper Marbury Rudnick & Wolfe LLP (all of whom assisted with the proofreading and preparation of the monograph), to Leonard Vines, Chair of the Publications Committee of the Forum on Franchising (for his enthusiasm and persistence, which kept this project moving along), and to ABA Publishing (for bringing this project to its fruition).

Introduction

The Franchise Law Compliance Manual represents a long-overdue and essential addition to every franchise lawyer's library. Designed as a working tool for both corporate franchise lawyers and their outside counsel, *The Franchise Law Compliance Manual* is a practical, comprehensive guide to establishing and maintaining a successful corporate compliance program. From intellectual property to termination, this *Manual* covers every aspect of franchise law. To ensure complete, well-rounded coverage of the topics, each chapter was prepared by attorneys with experience as in-house corporate counsel, and experience working as outside counsel to franchisors. The same pattern was chosen in selecting the *Manual's* editors. The result of these collective efforts: a manual unparalleled in scope and breadth of coverage of franchise law from a compliance perspective.

A discussion of a corporate compliance program must first begin with intellectual property, the foundation of a franchise system. Chapter 1, *Proprietary Rights,* focuses on the importance of protecting a company's intellectual property rights. The authors, William Finkelstein and Anthony Stiegler, discuss the various types of intellectual property and show how best to obtain, maintain, and enforce these proprietary assets. The authors also provide numerous checklists and forms that the franchise law practitioner will find useful (for example, Intellectual Property Assets Inventory, Searching and Clearance of New Trademarks, International Protection, Trademark Infringement Report). In addition, the authors include several sample trademark provisions that are commonly found in franchise agreements.

As the system grows, franchisors must establish methods for easing compliance with federal and state laws that affect the franchise relationship. Chapter 2, *Franchise Sales and Managing Growth,* begins with a general overview of both federal and state laws and regulations on franchising. The authors, Mark Forseth and Grover Outland, offer tips on proper document filing and control, and then examine how to implement and monitor sales compliance policies. They also address how an effective compliance program can reduce the risk of litigation, especially in the context of non-traditional system expansion (for example, alternate channels of distribution, intra-brand competition). To supplement their discussion, the authors have included sample checklists and exhibits to help track the sales compliance process.

Chapter 3, *Franchise Records Managements,* embarks on a more detailed discussion of the importance of proper document control procedures. A records management program is integral to the success of a franchisor's overall compliance program. A properly designed records management system can increase employee productivity, facilitate access to important records, and protect records from theft. Charles Cannon, Jerry Lovejoy, and Ken Minami examine how franchisors can most effectively design and administer a corporate records management program. The authors explore different approaches to records management, as well as the benefits and disadvantages of each. Readers will find their Design Checklist for a records management program especially useful, in addition to the Sample Record Retention Schedule.

Another challenge a franchisor faces as its system grows is to ensure that both franchisees and the public receive the expected value, while not imposing on the franchisor undue hardships and risk. Chapter 4 focuses on *Franchisee Agency Issues* and explores how franchisors can establish and monitor system standards and procedures through the use of an Operating Manual. Donnell McCormack and Sheri Young begin their discussion with a recognition that protecting the quality of the system is much like a "balancing act." While the Operating Manual should be designed to protect the system, it should also protect franchisors from liability. To guard against liability—particularly vicarious liability—the Operating Manual should reflect that the franchised businesses are owned and operated by the franchise owner. To this end, the authors also offer detailed guidance on how to create, organize, update, and monitor an Operating Manual.

The authors in Chapter 5, *Franchise Relationship Management,* observe that a successful franchise relationship demands more than simply compliance with laws and contracts. It requires an approach that recognizes that the franchise relationship is a unique and long-term one. A corporate compliance program should therefore incorporate policies and processes that foster relations with employees and franchisees. The authors, Raymond Miolla and Andrew Selden, focus on the various ways in which communication can be enhanced throughout the franchise system (for example, advisory councils, franchisee associations, alternate dispute resolution). They also provide examples of different corporate models for enhancing communication in the system.

The final chapter in the book, *Termination, Nonrenewal, and Transfer* addresses the issues that most frequently give rise to litigation in the context of the franchise system. Authors Lisa Pender Morse and Ronald Coleman outline how franchisors can effectively implement and monitor procedures pertaining to termination, transfer, and renewal. As part of their chapter, they include a particularly useful summary of state franchise laws governing termination and nonrenewal. In addition, they have incorporated checklists that franchisors can use when assessing termination, transfer, and nonrenewal issues, as well as sample letters and agreements.

Together, these chapters unlock the secrets of a successful corporate compliance program. The work that follows is the product of three years of hard work, dedication, and commitment to the belief that this *Manual* would be a comprehensive reference tool for franchise law practitioners. As editors, we are confident that *The Franchise Law Compliance Manual: Keys to a Successful Corporate Compliance Program* has accomplished this goal. Indeed, it is the only such volume on the subject, and we expect that it will be *the* authority on franchise law compliance for many years to come.

Steven M. Goldman
H. Bret Lowell
Editors

CHAPTER 1

Proprietary Rights

William A. Finkelstein and Anthony M. Stiegler

Contents

Introduction: Intellectual Property and Franchising

Intellectual property—primarily trademarks, trade names, copyrights, patents, and trade secrets—is the cornerstone of the franchising concept. This property is created not with bricks or computer chips but with the human mind; it commonly includes names, symbols, designs, artistic creations, inventions, formulas, and methods of doing business. Proprietary rights in this property will generally be protected by law, but only under certain conditions and limitations. Moreover, there are very fundamental differences between the various types of intellectual property, giving rise to distinctively different legal relationships and requisites. On the other hand, there are many common themes and approaches to protecting intellectual property that should be the focus of a corporate compliance program.

Intellectual property rights are corporate proprietary assets with enormous value to a franchise business. In almost every instance, the bundle of proprietary rights developed by the franchisor and used by it and/or licensed to franchisees for their use, is the basis of the franchise system. It is often the reason why the business succeeds or fails and it is a prime factor in attracting franchisees and others, namely, shareholders, to invest in the business. Quite simply, the legal exclusivity that intellectual property rights can afford the franchisor and its franchisees quite often offers the competitive advantage that is essential to a successful franchising business.

The impact of failing to manage a company's intellectual property assets properly, thoroughly, and creatively can be substantial. On the business side, it can cause wasted investment, lost opportunity, or, worse yet, diminished or lost profits; from the legal perspective, uncertainty, expense, and significant risks and burdens of litigation. Proper management of intellectual property assets is a skill that should be a basic strategic objective of a franchise business, for which the underpinning is an active and pervasive corporate compliance program.

Setting Up the Intellectual Property Compliance Program

Corporate Commitment

The foundation for the program is having company management's belief in and recognition that intellectual property is important for the success of the business and then translating that into an ongoing commitment to a legal compliance program. Clearly, if the policies are put in a drawer and the procedures are given lip service only or ignored, the program will be ineffective. Management must forcefully communicate to every employee, franchisee, agency, and all others involved in the business that compliance with all policies and procedures, as well as total cooperation with counsel, who has a lead role in their execution, is essential. Thus, for example, use of a trademark without proper legal clearance can be a disaster; even an apparently routine matter like legal review of materials is rendered ineffective if items are submitted at the last minute with no time for adequate scrutiny or corrections. Management must buttress the commitment by allocating sufficient financial resources and manpower, either inside or outside counsel, or both, to ensure proper execution of the compliance program.

Identifying Sources of Conflict

The focus of the legal function within the corporate framework is to put the intellectual property assets into a position where their value can be exploited and maximized by the business free from (1) legal challenge by others and (2) injurious actions by others, that is, adverse registration or use. This goal can be achieved by implementing a corporate compliance program that anticipates the sources of litigation conflict. Generally, these fall into two categories. First, the company needs to be able to successfully defend its right to obtain, register, and use its own intellectual property assets. Second, the company's assets must be protected by the ability to take successful legal action against others who infringe rights, pirate assets, or seek to register adverse rights. Litigation arising in both categories, therefore, regularly reflects a common genesis: a failure to adequately or properly develop, maintain, and enforce strong, protectable rights. Unfortunately, this often is a result of an earlier failure to diligently implement an internal compliance program.

Intellectual Property Assets Inventory

The first step in determining the need for, or the current status of, a corporate compliance program is conducting an extensive and thorough inventory of the company's intellectual property assets (see Checklist No. 1-1). All assets in use must be identified and then compared with existing protection to isolate gaps or insufficiencies in such protection as well as underutilized or abandoned assets.

This process (sometimes more narrowly referred to as an "audit"), however, must encompass more than just a mere listing of specific intellectual property items, such as trademark registrations, patents, and so on.

It is also crucial to identify existing corporate policies, standards, and procedures for the maintenance, protection, and enforcement of the intellectual property and determine what may be missing or insufficient (see Checklist No. 1-2). The third facet of the inventory process, and perhaps the most difficult one, is to identify those areas where there has been inadequate implementation of existing policies, protection procedures, and actions. Only after this analytical process is completed can the next phase begin: remedying the gaps and insufficiencies identified in all three areas and, as part of a corporate initiative, prioritize and then protect those intellectual property assets that are considered the keys to business success.

Types of Intellectual Property

In a typical franchise business, trademark rights are most likely to be of paramount importance, followed by trade secret rights, which might cover methods of doing business and technical know-how. There usually are some copyright-related aspects to the business, such as advertising and other promotional and marketing materials as well as an operations manual. Occasionally, patents will be important. For example, utility patents might cover a proprietary piece of machinery and design patents might cover a building design. Although the focus of this chapter will be on trademarks, a brief discussion of the other types of intellectual property is necessary.

Copyrights

Copyright law protects original works of authorship that can be tangibly expressed, as opposed to a mere idea or concept. A copyright owner has the exclusive right to reproduce the work, distribute copies to the public, and to publicly perform and display the work. With franchises copyrightable material might include the operations manual, computer software programs, advertising (print, t.v., radio, music), architectural blueprints, and building designs.

Creation and authorship are key concepts in copyright law to which special attention must be paid. For example, many materials subject to copyright are created by outside parties retained by the franchisor (or the franchisees) and careful scrutiny must be exercised to make sure that these parties assign their copyright rights to the company or, if it fits into specific guidelines under the law, acknowledge that their work is a "work made for hire." Otherwise, valuable copyright rights could be lost. This facet of copyright law, among many others, must be part of a compliance program's policy and procedure.

Patents

A patent gives the owner an exclusive right to exclude others from making, using, selling, and offering for sale the patented invention. Utility patents cover new

and useful processes and machines; design patents cover new and original orna-
mental designs for articles of manufacture. While patent protection generally is
not a major factor in franchise businesses, it can occasionally provide a real
advantage, especially over the short term. There are very precise procedures and
technical requirements for obtaining patents that need to be covered by a compliance program. For example, since publicly using an invention for more than a
year eliminates the ability to obtain a patent, regular technology reviews and a
docketing system are essential.

In the franchise context, an important regular review process involves deciding whether to treat certain material as patentable or to retain it as a trade secret.
Once the patent route is chosen, the invention will be disclosed to the public and
the owner's protection will expire after a certain number of years. Trade secret
protection, on the other hand, can result in indefinite protection and often is a
vital, long-term element of a successful franchise business.

Trade Secrets

Trade secret law protects the owner's right to control and protect certain proprietary information under very limited conditions. A trade secret can include a formula, pattern, compilation, program, device, method, technique, or process that
is valuable because it is not generally known to the public and is maintained in
secrecy. This gives the owner the opportunity to obtain an advantage over competitors who do not know or use it.

The types of material that are subject to trade secret protection are often
found in the franchise business context. These include: technological know-how,
such as a cooking process; a method of doing business, such as teaching speed-
reading, instruction of ballroom dancing, or a program for quitting smoking; or
such items as customer lists, marketing and research information, and accounting and inventory management techniques. One particular advantage of a trade
secret over patent protection is that the standards of inventiveness and non-
obviousness are not as high. However, there are great risks in the decision not to
seek patent protection. If a strict corporate compliance program is not in effect
and properly executed, a trade secret could easily be lost without legal recourse
since by definition a trade secret only exists until it no longer is a "secret." While
loss of a trade secret from independent discovery or reverse engineering by others is out of the control of the trade secret owner, an owner can take steps to prevent accidental or intentional disclosure by his or her own employees, franchisees,
outside suppliers, and the like. Accordingly, while there can be an excellent competitive advantage to maintaining a trade secret, it is a perilous course which
needs extensive legal input and control.

Trademarks

In most franchising situations, trademarks represent the single most dominant
element and the focal point of the franchise package. Trademarks can be any
word or symbol used to identify one's goods or services and distinguish them
from those sold or offered by others. They can be designs, words, pictures, slo-

gans, colors, configurations, or three-dimensional manifestations of the site where the business is located, or any combination of these, which sometimes is termed "trade dress." The essence of trademark law is the protection of consumers from confusion between marketers as well as the protection of the franchisor's goodwill, which can be defined as favorable consumer recognition—the invaluable commercial magnetism of the mark.

In the United States, trademark rights arise from use and are confirmed by federal registration, which provides many substantial and procedural benefits. Trademark protection, unlike most other forms of intellectual property, will continue indefinitely if the mark is sufficiently protected, not abandoned, and used properly so that it does not become generic. It is compatible with parallel protection for all of the other forms of intellectual property and, in fact, a mark's goodwill is often associated with material that may be the subject of a trade secret, such as a method of food preparation, for example, Kentucky Fried Chicken and the secret fried chicken recipe.

Creation and Selection of Trademarks

The foundation of a trademark rights compliance program is the adoption of strong, distinctive, and protectable marks. The ramifications of proper trademark creation and selection will extend throughout the entire life of the mark and the history of the franchise. Selection of a good mark (see Checklist No. 1-3) will make searching and clearance smoother and more certain; registration easier; and protection more manageable as well as less costly and less burdensome. Indeed, perhaps the best result of proper selection is that very little litigation should occur.

Unfortunately, the selection of trademarks is often accomplished in the most casual and cavalier manner, often driven by marketing objectives to describe to the consumer a quality or characteristic of the goods or services, and often chosen as an afterthought at the last minute before launching the product or service. The proper compliance program will have guidelines for choosing the best marks and a procedure for the selection of new marks with sufficient time built into the process to allow for adequate legal consideration, research, and analysis. Counsel must be afforded the opportunity to be very involved in guiding the selection process toward trademarks that are both commercially viable and legally protectable.

Searching and Clearance of Trademarks

The next step in the adoption of a new mark is a comprehensive clearance search supervised and controlled by counsel. Prior to commencing searches, it is extremely helpful for marketing management to brief counsel (especially if outside counsel is used) on a variety of factors relating to the nature of the goods or services, the intended use, the competitive marketplace, and any industry-specific generic or descriptive terminology (see Checklist No. 1-4). The objective is to give counsel an understanding of where the mark fits in the business environment so that a reasoned analysis can be undertaken.

It is absolutely mandatory that new trademarks be searched and legally cleared by expert counsel prior to adoption (see Checklist No. 1-5). A failure to search is simply bad business judgment. Using a trademark before determining its availability could result in costly litigation, embarrassment and bad publicity, and lost investment; in the franchise context, this could and has resulted in litigation by franchisees for breach of contractual representations or rescission. In fact, many courts addressing the duty to search and clear trademarks have characterized the failure to do so as "willful ignorance" and "bad faith," which led to an adverse judgment.

Conducting a comprehensive search is an experience- and expertise-based skill. Sufficient lead time is necessary for completion of the process, which often includes extensive investigations and analysis of prior rights holders and resolutions of any potential conflicts with these parties. There are many potential risks in clearing trademarks, some of which cannot be resolved with absolute certainty. Thus, the adoption process for new marks must be a diligent and thorough undertaking.

Perfecting Trademark Rights

Once it has been determined that a new trademark appears to be available for adoption and management decides to go ahead, then applications for federal registration should be filed as promptly as possible (see Checklist No. 1-6). Even though in the United States priority rights are established either by the first use of a mark or the filing date of a federal application, there are many more benefits to obtaining a federal trademark registration. These include a presumption of the right to exclusive nationwide use and ownership of the mark as well as the furnishing of constructive notice to all others. Use-based rights only extend to a geographic area of use, reputation, and natural expansion; therefore, federal registration is highly recommended, especially for new, slowly growing franchise businesses that have a limited number of locations, to preserve the possibility of future expansion. Otherwise, the first party to use a mark in a particular area (prior to the company's federal application) will have superior rights that could block the company's expansion into that area.

Under U.S. law, if, prior to the filing of a federal application, a franchisor has not commenced use of a mark, it must be prepared to satisfy fairly stringent requirements regarding its allegation of a bona fide intent to use the mark in the future (see Checklist No. 1-7). These requirements cannot be taken lightly, because any registration that issues from an intent-to-use application where the facts do not support the original "intent" claim, could be invalidated. It should also be noted that continued bona fide intent to use a trademark is necessary throughout the application process until the trademark is used. The key compliance guideline is to confirm and then retain concrete manifestations of this intent to support the continued viability of the application.

Maintenance of Rights

The issuance of a federal registration is merely the beginning of the on-going protection and maintenance segment of the compliance program (see Checklist No. 1-6). The first step in the maintenance of the U.S. trademark protection portfolio is filing the appropriate use affidavits during the fifth year following registration (These should be filed as soon as possible in order to attain incontestability status, which is another benefit of federal registration.) and then filing renewal application and affidavits every ten years. (These require continued use of the trademark.) It is quite important to have a procedure in place to capture the appropriate use information and documentation. Maintenance of any international portfolio will require numerous filings, often with elaborate technical requirements.

In addition, there are many other procedures which need to be firmly established as part of the company's regular activities. The essential goal is making sure that trademarks are properly used since trademark rights can be lost if certain internal guidelines and standards are not followed. First, a detailed and well-illustrated trademark use manual or guide should be developed and widely circulated to all employees, franchisees, agencies, and others who develop materials using the marks, with company management's strong admonition that these guidelines be strictly followed. Indeed, this serves a concomitant and salutary business benefit since uniformity and consistency are the hallmarks of a franchise chain operation.

Next, a review and approval process must be established whereby all uses of the marks are submitted for legal review prior to dissemination to verify compliance with the company trademark use policy, its graphic identity standards, and all other company policies. Constant monitoring is usually necessary to ensure that timely and substantial compliance remains the norm.

All these maintenance activities need to be supported by an administrative infrastructure including an elaborate filing system and specialized software for managing all pertinent information regarding the company's trademark portfolio, including licenses, agreements, and conflicts with other parties (see Checklist No. 1-8). Especially important is using the system to maintain all pertinent date deadlines for administering the legal process involved in maintaining registrations. Such a system can be a very effective management tool for this function.

Trade Dress

Trade dress, a sub-category of trademarks, is generally protected under trademark law principles yet often requires its own special compliance guidelines (see Checklist No. 1-9), since it can be a very valuable proprietary element of a franchise business. Trade dress is the term given to a combination of elements that together represent the overall image of a product or business. For products, it can include the shape, layout, and color combination of packaging or labeling, or even the shape of the product itself. For services, it can include the shape of a building or specific architectural features, or the interior decor of a service establishment as well as signs, advertising, equipment, and uniforms.

Trade dress protection does not extend to vague images, themes, or concepts. Trade dress protection will only be granted to distinctive combinations of discreet characteristics that can serve to identify a particular business while not preventing competitors from using individual public domain elements that may be part of the protectable combination. The premise of trade dress protection is to protect and reward investment in unique and original identifying features, which, taken as a whole, are non-functional. Moreover, to be protectable, trade dress must be either inherently distinctive or subject to proof that it has acquired secondary meaning, that is, consumer recognition as an identifier, as a result of extensive use, advertising, and promotion.

Trade dress is often an extremely flexible yet fragile proprietary item that requires a great deal of attention from a corporate compliance program. If properly developed, nurtured, and protected, trade dress can become an extremely valuable asset in the franchise mix and is frequently worth the extensive work that is necessary to fashion it into a legally protectable entity.

Enforcing Trademark Rights

The franchisor needs to protect its system's intellectual property assets by taking vigorous and prompt action against the use and attempted registration of marks that are confusingly similar to the company's. Failure to prevent others from using or registering such infringements could result in a gradual diminution of the strength of the company's rights and potentially an eventual loss of exclusive rights. Worse yet, the resulting consumer confusion could translate into lost sales and diluted marketing efforts, followed by franchisee dissatisfaction and possible legal recourse.

First, company management must agree on a protection strategy emphasizing key marks, trade dress, and jurisdictions (see Checklist No. 1-10). Next, a policing system has to be set up so that regular surveillance of applications for registration and the marketplace is undertaken (see Form No. 1-1).

Analyzing whether to take action by way of an Opposition against an application for registration and/or by way of a court action for infringement, unfair competition, or dilution is an extremely fact-intensive and subjective undertaking (see Checklists Nos. 1-11 and 1-12). Proceeding with even a cease and desist warning letter without a thorough investigation and analysis is extremely risky. Some of the essential factors that must be considered before proceeding include: ascertaining that the company's priority of rights is clear; making sure that the company's rights are not vulnerable to counterattack; making a reasonable and balanced assessment of the chances of success; and knowing what the company's goals are in taking action. Moreover, this last one becomes important when the opportunity for settlement arises.

Settlement agreements for trademark matters require a great amount of thought and creativity to the extent that they seek to govern the on-going and future activities of two different parties. If the agreement contains any restrictions on the use of the company's marks, extreme caution must be observed due to the difficulty in anticipating the future direction of marketing activities (see Checklist No. 1-11 [5–6] and Form No. 1-2).

Franchise Agreement Trademark Provisions

An important part of a trademark protection program is controlling the licensing relationships involving the marks. The franchise agreement must contain a valid and enforceable trademark license. Moreover, it is imperative that franchisees not gain any rights in the marks by virtue of the franchise relationship and that the marks not be licensed absent proper quality control both in the documentation and in fact. Therefore, proper drafting and implementation of the trademark-related provisions in a franchise agreement are crucial (see Checklist No. 1-13 and Form No. 1-3).

Acquisitions of Trademark Portfolios

Proper and thorough legal due diligence before any acquisition as well as appropriate contractual provisions in the purchase documentation is crucial. This ensures that the trademark and related rights being acquired are what the company expected and that the company will be able to conduct the acquired business unimpeded by defects or gaps in its intellectual property portfolio or by clouds of potential litigation (see Checklist No. 1-14 and Forms Nos. 1-4, 1-5, and 1-6).

International Protection of Trademarks

U.S.-based franchisors frequently ignore international considerations such as language and culture when adopting new marks. Moreover, they often delay seeking protection for their marks in other countries. They then discover that their key marks are unacceptable or unregisterable, or that they have already been registered by another party, either coincidentally or with piratical intent. Therefore, it is imperative that foresight be exercised in developing an international protection strategy and extensive legal compliance procedures (see Checklist No. 1-15). It is important to note (1) the need in almost all instances to register marks country-by-country, (2) the variability of laws, regulations, and standards for both registration and enforcement, (3) the different laws and regulations regarding licensing, and (4) the substantial burdens of administration and expense in implementing an international trademark protection program.

Conclusion

As the cornerstone of the franchise system, intellectual property rights must be closely guarded. Failure to effectively protect those rights can result not only in substantial financial losses for franchisors, but also diminished brand recognition. A corporate compliance program that focuses on properly developing, maintaining, and enforcing a company's intellectual property rights will enable franchisors to maximize the value of their corporate proprietary assets. A properly implemented program will also minimize the risk of legal challenge by other parties, and it will guard against injurious actions by others, such as infringement.

CHECKLIST NO. 1-1:
Intellectual Property Assets Inventory

1. Objectives
   - Identify all corporate proprietary assets
     - identify unprotected assets
     - identify underutilized assets
     - identify abandoned assets
   - Identify corporate standards, procedures, and policies regarding the maintenance, protection, and enforcement of corporate proprietary assets
   - Remedy any gaps or insufficiencies so identified
     - insufficient protection
     - unnecessary protection
     - absence of appropriate standards, procedures, or policies
     - inadequate protection mechanisms and policies
     - inadequate execution of protection mechanisms and policies
   - Valuation of corporate assets
   - Identification/prioritization of key assets leading to strategic exploitation decisions and actions

2. Trademarks
   - Inventory existing registrations and applications worldwide
   - Inventory and review all marks in use and compare with existing portfolio
     - obtain current prioritization guidelines from management
     - review current usage of trade dress requiring secondary meaning to determine present availability of protection
     - identify slogans and other ostensibly short-term material to see if these have achieved longer term status requiring registration protection
     - review acquired portfolios to verify complete assimilation
     - review franchisee use
   - Review status of assigned assets to verify recordal and current status
   - Inventory and review all licenses
     - from the company
     - to the company
   - Internationally, review license recordal/registered user compliance where appropriate
   - Internationally, review new jurisdictions to verify appropriate applications
   - Inventory and review all pending conflicts
     - claims—actual and potential
       - by others
       - against others
     - litigation
       - by others
       - against others
     - opposition/cancellation
       - by others
       - against others
   - has insurance company been given notice

- Inventory and review all agreements
  - settlement of conflicts
  - coexistence
  - consents
- Review insurance coverage and procedures
- Review all policies and procedures regarding adoption and protection of trademark assets
  - selection, clearance, and acquisition of trademarks
  - applications for trademark registration
  - maintenance of trademark registration portfolio
  - proper use of marks
  - monitoring and review of franchisor and franchisee activities involving use of marks
  - insurance coverage
  - protection and enforcement of trademark rights
  - web site domain names
  - international protection

3. Trade names and corporate names
   - Review usage vs. incorporations, qualifications, assumed names
   - Review proper usage

4. Copyrights
   - Identify copyrightable material in use
   - Identify primary sources of material
     - employees
     - agencies, consultants, outside contractors
     - franchisees
     - licensed
   - Review policies and procedures for protection
     - "work for hire" vs. assignment
     - registration
     - review of materials
   - Identify potential compliance/avoidance issues
     - licensing agencies, for example, ASCAP, CCC
     - rights of others
       - copyright
       - publicity/privacy
   - Remedy gaps and insufficiencies
   - Identify all conflicts—pending or incipient

5. Patents
   - Review existing portfolio
     - time frames until expiration
     - pending applications
     - identify underutilized or unused patents
   - Identify new possibilities
   - Review procedures
     - internal development
     - licensed patents and know-how
     - avoiding rights of others

- Review policies
  - patents vs. know-how
  - patenting vs. trade secrets
  - design patents/trade dress
- Review enforcement policies and execution
- Remedy insufficiencies
- Dispose of unused patents
  - sell, license, or abandon
- Identify all conflicts—pending or incipient

6. Trade secrets
   - Identify protectable material in use
     - does it qualify
     - has it already been properly protected
     - is patent protection available
     - is it publicly known
     - can it realistically be protected
   - Review procedures for protection
     - notices and written agreements
     - employee agreements
     - employee "exiting" procedures
     - contractual relationships, for example, suppliers, contractors
     - franchisee use
     - franchise creation
   - Remedy insufficiencies in protective measures or their execution
   - Identify all conflicts—pending or incipient

CHECKLIST NO. 1-2: Corporate Policies Impacting Trademarks

1. Selection and clearance of new marks
   - Assist and guide proper selection (see Checklist No. 1-3)
   - Conduct and control searching and clearance (see Checklist Nos. 1-4 and 1-5)

2. Legal review and approval of materials and activities
   - Verify proper use of company marks
   - Verify compliance with company policies
   - Avoid prior rights of others
     - trademark
     - copyright
     - right of publicity
     - right of privacy

3. Trademark proper use guidelines
   - Create illustrated manual for dissemination (see Exhibit 1-A)
   - Basic marks and designs (need to keep updated)
   - Special guidelines for new slogans
   - Trade dress (see Checklist No. 1-9)

4. Corporate identity standards

5. Franchisee corporate and trade names

6. Quality control

7. De-identification of franchised business sites

8. Issuance of franchise agreements, offering circulars, disclosure documents

9. Copyright

10. Patent and trade secret

11. Computer systems
    - Software
    - Internet

12. Confidentiality
    - Research and Development
    - Employee agreements
    - Privileged communications
    - Agreements with outside agencies, consultants

13. Insurance
    - Coverage
    - Notice procedure

14. Unsolicited submissions

15. Record keeping and document retention
    - Systematized and accessible
    - Balance litigation risks with need for detailed essential history and substantiation of trademark and copyright rights

CHECKLIST NO. 1-3:
Selection of New Trademarks

1. Develop a corporate policy and procedure for the selection and adoption of new marks

2. Determine the intended function of the mark
    *   Primary brand or service identifier
    *   Secondary mark
    *   House mark
    *   Same as corporate name
    *   Logo or design
    *   Trade dress
    *   Slogan

3. Aim to adopt a strong, distinctive trademark
    *   Determines scope of legal protection
    *   Can be valuable marketing asset
    *   Need varies with intended function for the mark
    *   Determine business objectives—to be a distinctive identifier vs. describing or suggesting a quality or characteristic of the goods or services and/or conveying information about the product to consumers

4. Avoid adoption of generic terminology

5. Avoid adoption of descriptive terminology
    *   Note, however, that with exclusivity of extensive use and resulting consumer recognition, "secondary meaning" can be developed leading to protectability

6. Avoid surnames and laudatory, geographic, and non-registerable terminology

7. Choose a distinctive logotype or other presentation format
    *   Important for marks that are not strong
    *   Can develop independent significance apart from the word mark
    *   Can be beneficial internationally

8. Analyze business attributes for protectable trade dress elements (see Checklist No.1- 9)
    *   Two-dimensional, for example, packaging or labels
    *   Three-dimensional, for example, physical locations for service businesses
    *   Can be a combination or overall "package" of otherwise unprotectable elements
    *   Usually needs proof of secondary meaning for legal protection but can be inherently distinctive
    *   Must be non-functional
    *   Must not deprive competitors of public domain items

9. Adopt trademarks which can be both protected and commercially viable
    *   Suggestive, fanciful, or arbitrary
    *   Brief and easy to recall
    *   Readable and speakable, if words; recognizable and pleasing, if design
    *   Appropriate for use in advertising
    *   Without unpleasant or negative connotations
    *   Suitable for the intended audience
    *   Suitable for use in other countries
    *   Appropriate for future expansion, both geographically and into new types of products or services

CHECKLIST NO. 1-4: Prior to Searching New Trademarks

1. Goods, services, or both
    - What are the particular goods or services for which the mark will be used?
    - Is this for an existing product or service, or something new
    - Is the product or service unique and, if so, what would the generic terminology for the product or service be

2. Will this be a primary brand name, a house mark, a secondary mark, or is it intended solely for use in advertising and/or promotion, that is, a slogan

3. Is this a (line) extension of an existing mark
    - Need to check adequacy of current registrations
        - modification of presentation format
        - specification of goods or services broad enough
        - need to do current search, even if already registered

4. Meaning
    - Does the word mark have any meaning in any language
    - If a design mark, is there an apt description of it

5. In use
    - Is the mark already in use: (i) on this product or service (ii) on a different product or service
    - What is the approximate intended date of first use
    - Is there an estimated duration for the usage, especially if it is a slogan

6. Is the proposed use for a limited geographic area, nationwide throughout the United States, and/or for other countries

7. Type of use
    - Exactly how will it be used, for example, containers, labels, menus, signs, and so on
    - Are there any particular channels of trade in which the mark will be used
    - Could it be used as a domain name for a company Internet web site

8. Nature of use
    - If a secondary mark, with what primary or house marks will it be used
    - Will it be used with any design mark or logo
    - If a design mark, with what word marks will it be used
    - If a word mark, will it be used in a special format or logo
    - Will there be any particular colors used, for the words or for any design

9. Are any of the words or designs generic or descriptive with regard to the particular goods or services in this particular channel of trade or usage

10. Are any of the words or designs very commonly used in the particular channel of trade

11. Are there any competitors or others using any of the words or designs for similar or unrelated goods or services

12. What is the origin of the generation of this mark—internal sources, outside agencies or consultants, focus groups, and so on

13. Is there a strategy statement, proposed advertising theme or concept associated with the new mark

14. Are there any internal company policies that might bar the proposed mark

CHECKLIST NO. 1-5: Searching and Clearance of New Trademarks

1. A comprehensive search is essential before adoption
   - Using a trademark before determining availability could result in loss of investment and time, costly litigation, embarrassment and bad publicity, loss of confidence by franchisees and/or litigation by them for breach or rescission
   - Sufficient lead time is necessary for completion of the process, including investigations, due diligence, purchases, consents, negotiations of coexistence agreements
   - A follow-up search is necessary before adoption to reveal others who may have filed prior applications that were not previously available for searching

2. Duty to search
   - Constructive notice of prior registrations
   - Constructive use priority date of intent-to-use applications
   - Duty to avoid all existing marks, especially with actual knowledge
   - Presumption of bad faith or "willful ignorance" in case law for failure to conduct a complete search
   - Filing potentially fraudulent declaration of exclusive rights with new application

3. Failure to search is simply bad business judgment

4. Note different types and content of searches
   - Preliminary computer searches
     - only reveal federal and state registrations and applications
     - do not uncover common law references
     - do not use sophisticated strategy
     - only used for "knock-out" purposes
   - Full search
     - federal and state registrations and applications
     - common law references—directories, periodicals, trade listings, business names, and so on
     - Internet domain names
     - prior case law
   - Internal sources
     - company records and files
     - company employees
     - company market research
     - trade publications

5. Analysis of the search results
   - Strength of the proposed mark
   - Commonness of terminology or designs
   - Similarity of goods or services
   - Likelihood of confusion
   - Likelihood of dilution

6. Investigation and analysis of prior rights holder
   - Is the other mark in use or subject to a claim of abandonment
   - How is it actually used—in what form, with what goods or services

- What is the extent of its use, both geographically and volume
- What is the nature of the prior rights holder and the size and the strength of its business

7. Should the prior rights holder be approached for a consent, license, or possible purchase

8. Should the prior rights holder be challenged by way of, for example, a cancellation petition

9. Risks in clearance analysis
   - Is there a duty to investigate every potentially problematic reference uncovered in a search report
   - What is the appropriate depth of such an investigation
   - Is counsel's opinion about an absence of likelihood of confusion sufficient to establish "good faith"

10. Risks in searching process
    - Data bases could contain errors or omissions
    - Data bases, especially common law, may not contain all appropriate references
    - Data bases may not be up to date (especially federal trademark applications which have a lag-time of many weeks before appearing)
    - Subjectivity in categorization of references, especially designs
    - Difficulties in searching certain types of marks such as trade dress
    - Difficulties in investigating prior rights references with absolute certainty
    - Can't ignore abandoned applications or expired registrations—marks may still be in use

CHECKLIST NO. 1-6: Protection and Maintenance of Marks after Clearance and Adoption

1. File trademark applications as soon as possible
   - After clearance and before use or pre-use publicity
   - Assuming interstate commerce requirement satisfied (otherwise consider state registrations)
   - Assuming bona fide intent-to-use can be established (see Checklist No. 1-7)
   - Establishes constructive use priority date as of application date
   - Mark will appear in data base searchable by others

2. Designation of claim of trademark rights
   - Use of TM with new marks
   - Use of other notices and explanatory copy in advertising and other materials

3. Prompt prosecution of trademark applications
   - Proper drafting of application to anticipate issues
     - disclaimers
     - claim of ownership of other marks
   - Prompt response to Patent and Trademark Office objections, including telephone amendments
   - With intent-to-use applications, obtain specimens and file amendment to allege use as soon as use is made (prior to notice of allowance)
   - Obtain extensions of time to file Statement of Use, assuming continued bona fide intent can be established (see Checklist No. 1-7)

4. Defend against Opposition by other parties
   - Consider infringement threat
   - Consider coexistence agreement with consent
   - Consider abandoning application

5. Advise management of registration and need to use ® symbol

6. File affidavits between fifth and sixth anniversary of registration
   - To keep registration in force if mark in use (Section 8, Lanham Act)
   - To make registration "incontestable" if mark is in continuous use and not subject to adverse decisions or proceedings (Section 15)
   - File as soon as possible

7. File renewal applications
   - If mark in use (file accompanying "use" affidavit)
   - To perpetuate rights indefinitely (in ten-year increments)

8. Maintain detailed documentation evidencing history and use of marks
   - Samples or photographs of packaging, labels, signs, buildings, menus
   - Invoices, bills of lading, price lists
   - Sales records
   - Catalogs
   - Internal publications
   - Advertising and promotional materials

- Articles from magazines and periodicals
- Government regulatory compliance records

9. Develop and conduct educational activities for company personnel
   - Circulate use policies and graphic identity standards (see Exhibit 1-A)
   - Seminars

10. Review and approve all uses of marks for compliance with company policies and guidelines
    - Examples: adoption of new trademarks, slogans, logos, building designs; materials containing trademarks such as packaging, advertising, promotions, signs, trade pieces, publicity materials, stationery; communications to and with infringers; franchisee communications, franchisee generated materials; SEC documents; annual report; franchise disclosure and registration documents; internal publications

11. Docket all pertinent information regarding trademark portfolio, licenses, agreements, and conflicts, especially key follow-up dates into retrievable database (see Checklist No. 1-8)

12. Participate in and guide company restructurings involving trademark ownership
    - Tax-driven reorganization
    - Risks of naked licensing
    - Impediment to enforcement

CHECKLIST NO. 1-7: "Bona Fide Intent" Requirements for U.S. Trademark Applications

Filing New Applications

1. Who generated the new mark
    - Internal
    - External (ad agencies, name development houses, etc.)

2. Is this the exact mark that will be used

3. Will the mark be used in a stylized form or with graphic design elements

4. Does the product or service for which the mark is intended to be used presently exist

5. If not, is there on-going research and development

6. Are there any intended additional goods or services for which the mark might be used

7. What steps have been taken to launch the product or service
    - Product/service development
    - Market research
    - Package design/testing
    - Development/approval of advertising
    - Test marketing
    - Surveys/studies regarding customer acceptance
    - Is there a budget for launching this product or service
    - Is there a time frame for the launch
    - Have suppliers (of ingredients, packaging, and so on) been contacted yet
    - Have franchisees been advised
    - Have proposals been made to customers
    - Have sales materials been prepared or disseminated
    - Any press releases or other press reports
    - Any other steps to full-scale use
    - Is regulatory approval pending

8. Is there documentation supporting the above items

9. Are there any other alternative proposed marks intended to be used for this product or service
    - If so, have applications been filed or are such intended
    - How many

10. Was any application previously filed for this mark and then abandoned for any reason

Prosecuting Applications—When requesting extensions of time to file the Statement of Use, to determine continued bona fide intent review above points (especially no. 7) as applicable and consider the following additional points:

1. What progress has been made or obstacles encountered since the last claim of bona fide intent

2. If there were any contemporaneously filed intent-to-use applications for the same goods or services, how many (or what percentage):
    • Have proceeded to registration
    • Are still pending
    • Have been abandoned

3. Has the product or service for which this mark was originally intended been launched under a different mark

4. Have there been any decisions regarding narrowing the focus of the goods or services

5. Have there been any decisions regarding the exact form of the display of the mark?

CHECKLIST NO. 1-8: Portfolio Management Systems

1. Trademark searches and clearances

2. Trademark applications and registrations
    - Mark description
    - Owner
    - Country
    - Class and goods
    - Dates (application and registration)
    - Status
    - Assignments
    - Renewal and other maintenance dates
    - Docket and short-term, follow-up dates

3. Conflicts
    - Oppositions
    - Cancellations
    - Infringements

4. Agreements with other parties
    - Local
    - Worldwide

5. Franchise and license agreements
    - Links to other records
    - License recordal
    - Registered user

6. Miscellaneous
    - Report generation
        - regular
        - ad hoc
    - Link to word processing and form generation
    - Graphic images
    - Budget expense tracking
    - Outside counsel roster
    - Country law file

CHECKLIST NO. 1-9: Trade Dress Protection

1. Development stages
    - Survey the competition to determine what elements are in the public domain
    - Encourage distinctiveness and uniqueness during the development stages
      - Focus the development of distinctive elements toward items which are non-functional or merely incidentally functional
      - Analyze the core concept and draw the distinctive elements from it—do not depend on protecting the concept as a whole
      - Discourage copying—design away, not around
      - Narrow the protectable item(s) to as many distinctive and as few non-distinctive elements as possible
      - If possible, coin a term referring to the distinctive features that could and will become associated with them, as well as being a marketing and advertising tool
      - Perform trademark searches
      - Seek the advice of expert counsel

2. Consumer directed actions
    - Incorporate it in a two-dimensional logo
    - Develop and consistently use a term, for example, "The Golden Arches," for the design
    - Feature in advertising and call attention to it and its uniqueness
    - Display in business materials such as cards, stationery, invoices, manuals, trucks, telephone, and other directories
    - Use on packaging and in promotions
    - Explain the derivation, uniqueness, and proprietary nature of it when possible, for example, people read menus or table tents while waiting to eat
    - License as a mark on ancillary items such as toys, clothing, pens, and the like
    - Use in a consistent and precise manner pursuant to a company trademark and trade identity policy

3. Legal activities
    - Seek prompt and comprehensive trademark registration protection
    - Secure copyright ownership for any materials developed by parties outside the company
    - Seek copyright protection for architectural plans, all written materials, advertising, menus, packaging, and so on
    - Post conspicuous notices, both technical registration (®) and copyright (©) explanatory notices in narrative style
    - Take vigorous and prompt policing actions against third parties as well as ex-franchisees, choosing the circuit carefully
    - Draft the appropriate protection and de-identification language and insist on insertion in all franchise agreements; do not forget the preamble as an opportunity to obtain franchisee acknowledgment of your proprietary position

4. Other in-house compliance activities
    - Develop, disseminate, and implement policies for uniform and consistent materials, signs, buildings, and so on, throughout the system and deal carefully with the inevitable exceptions

- Involve and monitor (a) franchise development personnel—they must insist on the proper agreement language; (b) real estate personnel—they must insist on the proper lease language
- Develop a de-identification policy and an implementation kit
- Create franchisee and employee awareness in manuals, newsletters, awards, uniforms, and so on
- Solicit reports of possible third party infringing activity (see Form No. 1-1)
- Collect third party comments in periodicals, customer letters, and the like that indicate recognition
- Look for and collect market research that may be used to prove secondary meaning
- Be aware of the competition

CHECKLIST NO. 1-10: Policing Trademark Rights

1. Establish a protection strategy
    - Prioritize portfolio of marks
    - Prioritize geographic areas
    - Incorporate franchisee concerns and objectives
    - Budget balancing
    - Execute strategic marketing goals and objectives

2. Police promptly
    - Laches—unreasonable delay could impede the issuance of injunctive relief and preclude an award of damages
    - Dilution of the scope of legal protection
    - Consumer confusion and weakening of marketing efforts
    - Dissatisfaction and/or lawsuits by franchisees
    - Reduction in scope and extent of rights against other parties
        - goods and services
        - geographic

3. Surveillance of federal applications
    - Subscribe to service to uncover applications by others as soon as they are filed
    - Review *Official Gazette* for published applications

4. Surveillance of marketplace
    - Franchisees, company employees, distributors (See Form No. 1-1)
    - Trade publications and other advertising media
    - Investigators
    - Internet
    - Preventative advertising

5. Oppositions/cancellations
    - Need for extensive and careful investigation and analysis (See Checklist No. 1-11)
    - Protect against confusingly similar marks
    - Act against marks currently infringing
    - Protect against incursion into scope of exclusivity
    - Protect against dilution
    - Prevent others from gaining rights in descriptive or generic terminology

6. Infringement/unfair competition/dilution
    - Need for extensive and careful investigation and analysis (see Checklists Nos. 1-11 and 1-12)
    - Before taking action, establish with certainty the essential requirement of establishing priority/superiority of rights
    - Cease and desist warning letters
    - Preliminary injunctive relief or temporary restraining orders
    - Ex parte seizure orders
    - Injunctive relief
    - Monetary damages
    - Destruction of infringing goods
    - Attorneys' fees and costs

7. Other enforcement areas
    - Counterfeiting
    - U.S. Customs
    - Internet

8. Action against franchisees
    - Expired or terminated "holdover" franchisee
    - Breakaway franchisee
    - Consider infringement action as more expedient than breach of contract

9. Settlement (see Checklist No. 1-11(5.–6.))
    - Timing
    - Coexistence and other agreements (see Form No. 1-2)
    - Alternative Dispute Resolution

10. Insurance
    - Obtain defensive coverage
      - general liability coverage
      - advertising injury coverage
    - Obtain offensive (pursuit) coverage to fund enforcement
    - Notice issues—procedures in place
    - Element of litigation strategy

CHECKLIST NO. 1-11: Policing Trademark Rights—Deciding Whether to Litigate and/or Oppose

1. Identify objectives and develop strategy
   * Protection of your marks generally
   * Protection of the specific mark
   * Business posture versus the competition
   * Business posture versus the applicant
   * Preserving the company's right, as well as the competition, to use descriptive, generic, or commonly used terms or material

2. Gather and develop the facts
   * Identifying the importance of the company's mark
   * Identify current and future business plans
   * Establish the mark's history and current posture
     * origin—internal development or purchase
     * protective and/or enforcement efforts—any past court or Trademark, Trial and Appeal Board decisions
     * any restrictions on use or registration by prior agreements with others
     * use, sales figures, advertising, packaging, and so on
     * if based on prior intent-to-use application, is bona fide intent supportable
   * Verify the company's mark is up to date
     * validly registered, subsisting, and renewed
     * mark in use, that is, registration is not vulnerable to attack on the grounds of non-use or abandonment
     * goods or services description accurate vis-à-vis current use
     * presentation of mark accurate vis-à-vis current use
     * chain of title up to date and properly recorded
     * licenses, if any, accurate and up to date
     * license recordal and registered entries, if any, accurate and up to date
     * verify priority (absolutely essential)
     * prior registration
     * prior application
     * prior use
   * Confirm there are no limiting agreements with the applicant
   * Investigate the applicant in depth
     * application file history
     * was a citation of the company's mark or any other cite overcome during prosecution
     * were any descriptiveness or other objections overcome
     * other registrations, especially those which may be for a slight variation of the applied-for mark
     * nature and extent of business, for example, channels of trade, and so on
     * specific information about, and samples of, use of the apllied-for mark, advertising, packaging, and so on
     * license recordal/registered user applications, if any
     * any technical defects, for example, gap in title, improper assignment
     * strategies and psychological profile of other party

3. Evaluate the likelihood of a successful outcome
    - Evaluate legal strength of the case
    - Evaluate other party's commitment
        - application based upon proposed use or intent-to-use
        - application based upon foreign registration
        - is it a secondary type mark, a slogan, or other short-term material
        - extent of use, geographically or amount
    - Assess company's motivation
        - business issues
        - keeping register clean
            - to guard the company's mark against future progressive encroachment from third parties
            - to keep one competitor from gaining rights to material that is so descriptive, commonplace, or nondistinctive that competitors would be deprived
        - protecting the mark from an "infringement"

4. Evaluating the merits of an Opposition versus a court action
    - Advantages of Opposition (or threatened Opposition)
        - less expense
        - puts junior party on notice before its use commences or becomes extensive
        - simpler, more focused legal issues
        - may achieve very simple goal, for example, obtaining narrowing of the goods description
        - get junior party to bargaining table/settlement posture
        - obtain a favorable decision that may influence a court
        - could be dispositive in countries requiring a registration
        - keeping the register clean
        - may turn out to be quicker if interlocutory relief is not available and court dockets clogged
    - Disadvantages of Opposition only
        - only decides the right to register, not the right to use, depending on jurisdiction
        - narrow legal issues, not all evidence relevant
        - decision not binding on a court, depending on jurisdiction
        - loss of time
            - business effect—the junior mark has a chance to make its impact on the marketplace
            - legal effect
                - reduces the ability to get interlocutory relief
                - with the continued build-up of investment and goodwill a court may be reluctant to ultimately enjoin the junior party
    - Both at once
        - bring pressure on other party
        - expense for both parties
        - opens up discovery more quickly
        - obtain interlocutory relief
        - obtain damages
        - obtain precedent
        - publicity, that is, deterrence of other similar defendants

5. Settlement
   - Timing of approach to applicant/defendant
     - after filing of application but before use
     - after publication but during statutory or extended time to oppose (but note risk of applicant withdrawing application without prejudice)
     - after Opposition filed
     - after cease and desist letter sent (but note danger of declaratory judgment action)
     - after lawsuit filed
     - Benefits of settlement to opposer/plaintiff
     - certainty of outcome
     - avoid further expenditure of time, effort, and resources
     - protect business interests
       - ability to make/proceed with business plans
       - restrict activities of competitors
     - protect legal interests
       - avoid potential counterattacks on existing registrations
       - avoid adverse decision
         - allowing the other mark to be registered or used potentially broader ramifications, for example, a decision indicating weakness of the senior mark or other defects in the registration
       - the opportunity to resolve a wider range of issues beyond the specific issue of the mark, for example, use, trade dress, other potential conflicts
   - Downsides to settlement
     - eliminating the possibility of a complete victory
       - applied-for mark rejected
       - decision indicating strength of senior mark
       - decision indicating weakness of junior mark
       - psychological benefits vis-à-vis this competitor and others who will learn of the decision
       - in a settlement agreement opposer/plaintiff may have to agree to certain restrictions to which it was not previously subject
     - if the settlement includes allowance of registration and/or use by the junior party, it could dilute the senior party's position vis-à-vis present or future third parties
     - the inability to accurately predict the future—that the junior party's mark may become a significant competitive property

6. Settlement of Opposition agreement (see Form No. 1-2)
   - Structure of the relationship
     - application withdrawn but use of the mark will be allowed subject to limitations
     - application assigned to the senior party with license back to applicant
     - broadens scope of legal protection
       - but note issues of quality control and review, liability, registered users, effect on other licensees, dilution, goodwill, and reputation
     - application will be allowed to proceed to registration
       - with the consent of the senior party
       - with restrictions on the registration to be issued
       - with restrictions on use/coexistence

- Coexistence conditions
  - the presentation and display of the mark
  - the exact spelling
  - the exact manner or style
  - the exact design or device
  - the use of the word or design in combination with other words or designs (and then in a certain sequence)
  - the use of the mark in combination with a house mark or trade name
  - the precise trade dress
  - the language
  - the precise goods or services with which the mark can be used
  - the precise channels of distribution or method of offering the services
  - the methods of use: packaging, advertising, signage, etc.
  - restrictions on 'non-trademark' use, for example, "style" or "type"
  - limitations on geographic areas of use or locations
  - restrictions on registration
    - certain goods or services
    - disclaimers of descriptive or generic terms
    - generally track the use conditions
- Executional issues
- providing for the future
  - modifications of the mark
  - changes in the goods or services, channels of distribution, and so on
  - new applications
- covenants not to cancel or take other court action for infringement (but note distinction regarding abandonment or genericness)
- effect of abandonment, failure to renew, sale of business or mark
- assignability
- cooperation regarding third party applications or infringements

CHECKLIST NO. 1-12: Preparing for Trademark Enforcement

1. Analyze strength and scope of company's trademark rights

2. Analyze scope and strength of infringement
   - Similarity of marks
   - Consumer confusion
   - Dilution
   - Legitimate defenses
   - Infringer's market penetration and/or market share
   - Costs/benefits of litigation
   - Necessary to set example
   - Can the results be publicized to company's advantage

3. Gather evidence of infringement
   - Purchase products bearing infringing marks
   - Develop paper trail of custody and sales records
   - Engage investigator
   - Trace some of the infringing products to original supplier or as high up the chain as possible

4. Prepare evidence of company's ownership, use, and strength of mark
   - How strong is the company's mark
   - Secondary meaning
   - Affidavits and exhibits regarding duration of use, marketing dollars spent, revenues generated, and scope of consumer recognition of mark

5. Select venue
   - Home court favorable
   - Personal jurisdiction
   - Relative impact of costs on parties
   - Location of key witnesses and documents

6. Cease and desist letters
   - Gives notice
   - Achieve early settlement
   - May achieve results desired with minimal expense
   - Raises possibility of defensive "preemptive strike" in form of declaratory judgment action

7. U.S. Customs Service
   - Marks recorded with Customs
   - Customs provided with "enforcement notebooks" at key ports of entry
   - Photograph of actual goods, infringing goods, counterfeit goods
   - Customs provided with identities of suspected illegal importers
   - Trips made to key ports to educate import specialists and line officers

CHECKLIST NO. 1-13: Essential Trademark Provisions in Franchise Agreements

1. A valid and enforceable trademark license is an indispensable part of a franchise agreement (see Form No. 1-3)
   - To establish the rights and relationship of the franchisor and the franchisee
   - To establish the validity of the trademark license vis-à-vis third parties
   - To validate and support the franchisor's trademark rights

2. Quality control
   - The essential element and basis of the trademark license
   - The franchisor could lose its trademark rights if it fails to control the nature and quality or the goods and services sold by its franchisees
   - Quality control is mandatory so that the franchisor and franchisee can qualify as "related companies" under the Lanham Act
   - The mere recitation of a right to quality control is insufficient if not accompanied by actual exercise of this right.
   - Franchisor has a duty to reasonably police its franchisees
   - however the extent of the control could give rise to claims of vicarious liability and agency
   - Specific rights must be retained by franchisor to supervise and maintain quality control
     - specific procedures and requirements
     - reference to an operations manual
   - Naked licensing
     - failure to adequately provide for, or to exercise, quality control can lead to abandonment of trademark rights

3. Preamble clauses
   - Establish the special nature of the rights and business being licensed
   - Act as basis for fees, royalty payments, and post-termination injunctive relief

4. Granting clause
   - Exclusive vs. non-exclusive
     - must be extremely specific
     - must define any restriction upon the franchisor's activities, for example, channels of distribution
   - Right to sub-license
   - Specifying the marks vs. blanket grant of all present and future marks within the system
   - The ability to add or delete marks in the future
   - The need to define proprietary trade dress in great detail
   - Specifying the goods or services and/or defining the nature of the system being franchised
   - The precise geographic territory and/or location of site and any restrictions

5. Trademark relationship
   - Franchisee's acknowledgment that its use of the mark inures to the benefit of the franchisor

- Franchisee's acknowledgment of the mark's validity, the franchisor's ownership, and its goodwill
- Franchisee's acknowledgment that it acquires no rights in the mark or goodwill and will not contest the validity of the mark

6. Trademark use
   - Franchisee's acknowledgment to comply with franchisor's standards and guidelines
   - Franchisor's right to approve all materials and other uses of the mark

7. Trademark policing
   - Franchisor usually reserves the right to protect and defend the mark and control all enforcement decisions
   - Franchisee cooperation required
   - Assumption or allocation of costs and expenses

8. Rights upon termination and expiration
   - Immediate discontinuance of use of marks by franchisee
   - De-identification of proprietary trade dress at business sites
   - Transition provisions, such as changes to telephone directories

9. Miscellaneous provisions
   - Prohibitions or restrictions on assignments by franchisee
   - Indemnification by the franchisee
   - Prohibition against or restrictions on franchisee use of marks in franchisee trade names
   - Franchisor's ability to change or modify marks upon notice
   - Prohibition or restrictions on franchisee use of marks in Internet domain names
   - Indemnity by franchisor as to validity of the marks

CHECKLIST NO. 1-14: Trademark Portfolio Acquisition—Due Diligence

1. Determine the nature of the transaction
   - Acquisition or merger
   - Asset purchase (ownership will change)
   - Stock purchase (ownership need not change)

2. Identify and analyze the complete portfolio to be transferred
   - Obtain lists and files from seller
   - Verify key information by independent searches

3. Determine the scope of the acquired assets to make sure that the goodwill accompanies the trademarks

4. Verify ownership and status of registrations and applications
   - Closely examine chain of title and identify any gaps
   - Confirm that all renewals have been made and fees paid

5. Review all uses of marks by the seller
   - Confirm that appropriate protection has been secured for all marks in use or in pipeline
   - Identify registrations with vulnerability due to non-use

6. Review enforcement history

7. Verify scope and strength in key jurisdictions
   - Focus on important business areas
   - Focus on jurisdictions where there may be non-use vulnerability and therefore lack of past enforcement

8. Inventory and review all restrictions which could limit the buyer's rights or ability to use or expand use
   - Settlement agreements
   - Prior rights agreements
   - Consent agreements
   - License agreements

9. Identify jurisdictions of interest to the buyer where rights have not yet been protected by the seller

10. Identify jurisdictions where the coverage of goods or services by the registrations do not adequately encompass the buyer's business activities

11. Identify and review all jurisdictions with license recordal (registered user requirements)
    - Identify gaps and resulting contingent liabilities
    - Identify any impediments to obtaining transfer of such recordations

12. Identify and analyze any encumbrances, that is, security interests, liens, and so on.
    - That could block a transfer or must be dealt with prior to transfer
    - That will survive the transfer

13. Identify and review any limitations on marks being used but not owned by the seller
    - Trademark licenses
    - Franchise agreements
    - Distribution agreements
    - Must consent be obtained prior to transfer?
    - If transferable, what effect do these have on the buyer's business?

14. Identify and analyze all pending conflicts
    - Claims, challenges to registration, and/or claims of infringement against the seller
    - Claims, challenges to registration, and/or claims of infringement by the seller against third parties

15. Draft appropriate warranties and representations for inclusion in the purchase agreement
    - Requisite language can vary
        - asset purchase (see Form No. 1-4)
        - stock purchase (see Form No. 1-5)

16. Assignments
    - One blanket assignment recommended (see Form No. 1-6)
    - Blanket assignments will cover any unregistered assets
    - Specific assignments required for each jurisdiction
    - Special assignment form needed for intent-to-use applications in the United States, if a complete transfer of the business related to the trademarks is occurring; otherwise, these cannot be assigned without jeopardizing the validity of the assignment and any registration that thereafter will issue from the application
    - Identify those jurisdictions which will tax the value of the assets being assigned and assess the impact of the resulting contingent liability
    - Provide for (especially in an asset purchase situation) a post-sale procedure for executing assignment documents

17. Arrange for prompt transfer from seller
    - Files
    - Computer print-outs
    - Outside counsel roster

CHECKLIST NO. 1-15: International Protection of Trademarks

1. General principles
   - Be foresighted in developing an international filing strategy
     - It is imperative that foresight, long lead times, and the territoriality concept of trademark protection be integrated into the development of a global franchising strategy in order to successfully select, clear, and register trademarks in countries of commercial importance. Otherwise, successful and valuable trademark assets in one's home country may be useless for franchising in international markets.
   - Verify suitability and usability of marks
     - Never assume that an extensively used and successful trademark will be suitable for use in other countries. Localized market research will be necessary and a coordinated, cohesive approach between marketing personnel and attorneys is recommended in choosing the solution, for example, translations, transliterations, logos, and so on, which will work well across cultural and linguistic boundaries.
   - File early and as widespread as possible
     - Trademark rights are strictly territorial. They must be perfected on a country-by-country basis (with some limited exceptions) and the sooner the better since trademark piracy is an international fact of life. In most jurisdictions, the first party to file places itself in a superior position. Overcoming the prior registration of your own mark by another party based upon proof of your prior use or reputation will be based upon an extremely fact-driven and equity influenced analysis, thereby leading to an uncertain outcome.
   - Perform clearance searches
     - Clearance searches in each country prior to entering into franchise arrangements are essential: to avoid inadvertent infringements of another's coincidental prior right or to discover piracy of one's own mark.
   - Allocate sufficient budget and manpower
     - There are no easy or inexpensive ways to achieve blanket international trademark rights. The Madrid Protocol has promise (few countries now belong) enabling one filing to quickly preserve a priority date (and with savings at the "back end") but is only a filing mechanism subject to variable national laws and standards. The EC trademark system can be helpful but just covers 15 countries.

2. Registration
   - Registration is mandatory
     - Registration should be sought, as quickly as feasible, for every mark contemplated, for as broad a range of goods and services possible, in every jurisdiction considered for possible expansion. Relying on rights derived from use rather than registration is a poor basis for trademark protection for a franchising business.
   - Verify registrability
     - Trademark registrability standards vary greatly from country to country. Just because a mark is registrable in one's home country or other countries, does not mean it is necessarily registrable anywhere else. This could have a potentially serious impact upon the mark's value as a globally franchisable asset.

- Analyze classification issues
  - A filing strategy involving classification must be developed, taking into account varying standards in particular countries. Expense factors must be balanced against the necessity of full coverage for a franchise business which does not neatly fall into one particular class.
- Diversify registration portfolio
  - Since it is difficult to anticipate all future modes of use of a mark, all important marks should be registered in translations and transliterations to preempt pirates as well as to ensure that at least one registration will not be lost for failure to prove use.

3. Use Requirements
   - Be careful of non-use vulnerability
     - Most countries requiring use have specific non-use time periods which constitute a basis for invalidating trademark registration rights. It can be very difficult to overcome or excuse an allegation of non-use.
   - Use standards vary
     - The definition and extent of use needed to maintain a registration will vary widely. Most countries provide for the cancellation of registrations on the basis of non-use but the standards and procedures for achieving such cancellation vary from country to country.
   - Set up a use documentation system
     - It is recommended to anticipate proof of use requirements and to set up a system to capture and retain the necessary documentation.
   - Set up a re-filing program
     - Consider filing new applications to re-start the non-use time period for key marks but note loss of priority date and expense factors.
   - Draft franchise agreements carefully regarding non-use
     - Maintaining a registration can be a hyper-technical adventure, especially when use is through a franchisee. Registrations can easily be inadvertently lost even when the mark is in use, and care should be taken in drafting the franchise agreement so that the agreement does not automatically lapse if a registration is temporarily lost.

4. Enforcement of rights
   - Pursuing infringers varies by jurisdiction
     - Generally speaking, swift and broad civil relief for trademark infringement is difficult to obtain in many international jurisdictions.
   - Classification can be an impediment
     - It can be difficult to enforce a registration against similar or identical marks used in connection with different goods or services.
   - Verify availability of criminal action
     - Criminal remedies may be effective in those jurisdictions where civil proceedings are very slow, but the decision to request criminal remedies should be made with caution.
   - Non-use vulnerability a key factor in bringing action
     - Initiating offensive litigation when one's registration may be vulnerable due to non-use is not recommended unless the situation is so grievous that it is a chance worth taking.
   - Couple infringement action with attack on registration

- Oppositions and cancellation actions can be quite crucial in depriving the other party of the ability to use a registration as a defensive shield.

5. Licensing
    - Identify licensing laws and regulations early
        - It is imperative that franchisors seeking to expand to various international markets obtain advance advice as to the applicability of any local laws or regulations controlling the licensing of trademarks, especially those requiring the recordal of the license with a governmental entity.
    - Analyze the need for licensee recordal compliance
        - The trademark owner must carefully scrutinize the factual situation by which the goods are made and marketed, or the services performed, to determine which entities in the franchise relationship qualify as users that should be recorded. A trademark license is the best indication but related corporate entities without a formal license and joint ventures are among those users which sometimes escape attention.
    - Beware of technical compliance issues
        - Registered user requirements are most often merely routine, burdensome, and costly, but they can be a technical trap if not properly complied with and, occasionally, a difficult hurdle to overcome.
    - Local counsel advice crucial
        - Local counsel should be consulted to determine the need and method for compliance with license recordal requirements.
        - Noncompliance can jeopardize franchise system
        - Actively enforced license recordal requirements cannot be ignored due to the potentially disastrous consequences to trademark ownership and the validity of the license supporting a franchising structure in a particular country.

6. Administrative requisites
    - A portfolio management strategy
    - Specific procedures for filing and maintenance
    - A network of international counsel
    - A framework for balancing expense vs. protection issues
    - Centralized legal control
    - Adequate resources to handle a high volume, paper-intensive, technical practice

FORM NO. 1-1: Trademark Infringement Report

1. Name, address, and telephone number of infringing business.
2. How did this matter come to our attention: from a fellow employee, a customer, newspaper, t.v. or radio ad, telephone listing, or other?
3. How long has this business been in operation?
4. How long has the infringement situation existed?
5. If a service business, are there are other locations or branches? Is there a headquarters office?
6. Describe the nature, size, and scope of the infringing business.
7. Describe the infringement in detail, including which trademarks of the company are believed to be infringed.
8. Provide samples of the packaging and/or advertising or photographs of, for example, the signage or a building.
9. Is any connection known between the infringer's current management and our company or any of our former employees?
10. Please provide a copy of a yellow pages telephone book listing if available.
11. Does this business have a web site? If so, please provide the domain name.

FORM NO. 1-2: Prototype Contested Application Settlement Agreement

Agreement effective as of the _____ of _____, 20__, by ___Senior, Inc._____, located at _____ (hereinafter referred to as "**S**") and ___Junior, Inc._____, located at _____ (hereinafter referred to as "**J**").

WHEREAS, S is using and is the owner of the trademark _____ for "_____" as well as the owner of Trademark Registration No. _____. [or Trademark Application no. _____] for that mark as applied to those goods or services.

WHEREAS, J has adopted, subsequent to **S's** registration [application][use] the trademark _____ for "_____."

WHEREAS, J has filed trademark application no. _____ in the Patent and Trademark Office (hereinafter referred to as "PTO") on _____ 20__, to register its mark for "_____;" and **S** has threatened to file [has filed] an Opposition proceeding against **J's** application for registration [which Opposition is presently pending].

[or] **WHEREAS, J** has filed trademark application no. _____ in the PTO on _____, to register its mark for "_____;" and **S's** trademark as above was cited by the PTO as blocking said application.

WHEREAS, both parties are in agreement that there will be no confusion in the trade or in the marketplace by the concurrent use of their respective marks on their respective goods or services subject to the conditions and limitations set forth in this Agreement.

WHEREAS, the parties are desirous of settling this matter without further controversy.

NOW, THEREFORE, in consideration of the background stated above and the terms and conditions stated below, the parties hereby agree as follows:

1. (a) **J** agrees to promptly abandon its application no. _____ by expressly abandoning it and agrees not to use or re-file to register this mark for the same goods or services. [or]

    (b) **J** will file a new application for its mark as modified as set forth in Exhibit A.

2. **S** agrees to the use [and registration] by **J** of its mark on the following conditions:

    (a) that the use [and registration] of **J's** mark shall be restricted to _____.

    (b) that **J's** mark shall not be used [or registered] in connection with _____.

    (c) that the products sold under J's mark shall not be described as "_____;"

    (d) that clear and conspicuous use of the house mark _____ [or the design/logo] be used in conjunction with **J's** mark in all packaging and promotional materials with the _____ products or services;

    (e) that **J's** mark shall not be displayed in any manner of fashion similar to the manner or fashion in which **S** uses or displays its mark, and in no way shall imply any connection or relation to **S**; and

    (f) that the graphic display of **J's** mark shall always be as set forth in Exhibit A.

3.   **S** agrees to provide **J** in a form suitable for filing with the PTO an appropriate letter of consent to its application to register its mark for its goods as noted above and agrees to [refrain from filing Opposition] [withdraw its pending Opposition] against said application, refrain from taking any adverse action with respect to the validity of any registration which issues from the application, or taking any adverse action against the use of **J's** mark. [If the PTO fails to accept the consent, it shall not be considered a breach of this Agreement and **J's** obligations herein shall continue.]

4.   **S** and **J** agree to avoid using their respective marks in a manner which might cause consumers to mistakenly believe that the goods or services of one emanate from, are sponsored by, or otherwise associated with the other.

5.   **J** agrees to refrain from taking any adverse legal action against **S's** use of its mark or against any of **S's** registrations or subsequent applications for its mark.

6.   Provided **J** complies with all the terms and conditions of this Agreement, **S** shall not object to **J's** use and registration of its mark for its goods and services.

7.   This Agreement shall be without definite term, shall have effect throughout the [territory] and shall inure to the benefit of and shall be binding upon any related parties, subsidiaries, or affiliates owned or otherwise controlled by the parties and shall further be binding upon any successors in interest or assigns of the parties hereto. This Agreement constitutes the entire agreement between the parties and may be altered, modified, or amended only by an express declaration in writing signed by a duly authorized officer of each party and referring specifically to this agreement.

Senior, Inc.

By: _____

Title: _____

Junior, Inc.

By: _____

Title: _____

FORM NO. 1-3: Sample Trademark-Relevant Provisions in a Franchising Agreement

Recitals

1.1 Franchisor is the originator and owner of a unique, distinctive, and high quality type of _____ (the "Product") for which it has developed methods of manufacturing, marketing, and sales distribution (the "System").

1.2 Franchisor has developed and adopted for its own use and the use of its franchisees in performing _____ services (the "Services") a unique, distinctive, and high quality system of business operation (the "System"), consisting of certain business techniques, methods and procedures, distinctive features and characteristics, distinctive building designs, advertising signs, specially designed equipment and equipment layout plans, secret formulas, certain patents and proprietary technology, certain original and copyrighted materials, and a proprietary and confidential operations manual.

1.3 Franchisor owns valuable trademarks, service marks, and trade names, the primary ones of which are set forth on the attached Schedule, as well as various trademarks, service marks, trade names, slogans, designs, insignias, emblems, symbols, package designs, distinctive building designs and other architectural features, logos, and other proprietary identifying characteristics used in connection with the primary trademarks, service marks, and trade names (collectively the "Marks") all used in relation to and in connection with the Products and/or the System.

1.4 Franchisor has established a favorable and extensive reputation with the public as to the high quality of its Products and/or the Services provided and, as a result thereof, a goodwill of enormous value has developed in connection with Franchisor's System and Marks.

1.5 Franchisee recognizes the benefits of being associated with the System and being able to utilize the Marks and wishes to use the System and the Marks in the business of operating _____ to manufacture, market, and sell the Products and/or perform the Services at various locations in _____(the "Territory").

Grant of License

2.1 Franchisor grants to Franchisee for a period of _____ years commencing _____ (the "Term") and Franchisee hereby accepts upon the terms and conditions herein specified, the license, subject to 2.2 herein, without the right to sub-license, to use the Marks solely upon and in connection with the manufacture, marketing, and sale of the Products and/or performance of the Service in accordance with this Agreement.

2.2 This License shall be exclusive. Franchisor shall not itself, or license another to, manufacture, market or sell Products, or perform the Services in the Territory. [or]

2.3 This License shall be exclusive but Franchisor reserves the right to itself sell, or to license others to sell, Products within the Territory under the Marks through outlets other than Franchisee's locations. [or]

2.4 The License granted is non-exclusive and Franchisor reserves the right to operate or license others to operate locations to perform the Services under the Marks adjacent to, or in the vicinity of, Franchisee's location.

Marks

3.1 *Ownership.* Franchisee shall use the Marks only in connection with the System and agrees that all of Franchisee's use under this Agreement inures to the benefit of Franchisor. Franchisee acknowledges that Franchisor is the owner of the Marks and the goodwill associated therewith and the Marks are valid. Franchisee agrees not to contest the validity of the Marks during or after the Term. Apart from the right of Franchisee to use the Marks pursuant to this Agreement, Franchisee shall acquire no right, title, or interest of any kind or nature whatsoever in or to the Marks or the goodwill associated therewith.

3.2 *Approval.* Franchisee shall display the Marks only in such form and manner as is specifically approved by Franchisor and, upon request by Franchisor, affix thereto any legends, markings, and notices of trademark registration or Franchisor-Franchisee relationship specified by Franchisor or any other notice of Franchisor's ownership, including, without limitation, copyright, patent applications, and patents. Franchisor shall have the right to approve all advertising, displays, and other materials using the Marks prepared by Franchisee. Franchisee agrees to follow Franchisor's instructions regarding proper usage of the Marks in all respects.

3.3 *Franchisee Contributions.* Franchisee agrees that all artwork, graphics, layouts, slogans, names, titles, or similar materials incorporating, or being used in association with, the Marks which may be created by the Franchisee or its subcontractors pursuant to this Agreement shall become the sole property of Franchisor, including copyright rights; and Franchisee agrees on behalf of itself, its employees, its sub-contractors, and any other party with whom it may contract to create such materials, to promptly execute any and all appropriate documents in this regard.

3.4 *Protection and Defense.* Franchisor agrees to protect and defend the Marks. Franchisee agrees to cooperate fully with Franchisor in the defense and protection of the Marks and shall promptly advise Franchisor in writing of any potentially infringing uses by others in addition to any suits brought, or claims made, against Franchisee involving the Marks. Decisions regarding action involving the protection and defense of the Marks shall be solely in the discretion of Franchisor, and Franchisee shall take no action in this regard without the express written permission of Franchisor.

3.5 *Franchisee Cooperation.* Franchisee agrees to join with Franchisor in any application to enter Franchisee as a registered or permitted user, or the like, of the Marks with any appropriate government agency or entity. Upon termination of this Agreement, for any reason whatsoever, Franchisor may immediately apply to cancel Franchisee's status as a registered or permitted user, and Franchisee shall consent in writing to the cancellation and shall join in any cancellation petition. The expense of any of the foregoing recording activities shall be borne by Franchisor.

3.6 *Restrictions on Marks and Trade Names.*

(a) During the Term, Franchisee shall not use any trademarks or other identifying characteristics in connection with the System other than the Marks.

(b) During the Term, Franchisee shall not manufacture, market, or sell products nor perform services under the Marks which are not Products or Services approved by Franchisor.

(c) During or after the Term, Franchisee shall not use or register, in whole or in part, the Marks or Franchisor's name, or anything similar thereto, as part of Franchisee's name or as the name of any entity directly or indirectly associated with Franchisee's activities.

3.7 *Goodwill.* Franchisee acknowledges the tremendous value of the Marks and its significant responsibilities to the System, and Franchisee shall not use the Marks in any manner to disparage Franchisor or its reputation nor take any action which will harm or jeopardize the Marks, or Franchisor's ownership thereof, in any way.

3.8 *Changes to Marks.* Franchisor shall have the right at any time, upon notice, to make additions to, deletions from, and changes in the Marks at its complete discretion, and as soon as reasonable under the circumstances, Franchisee shall adopt and use any and all such additions, deletions, and changes pursuant to Franchisor's instructions.

Standards of Operation and Quality Control

4.1 In order to protect, preserve, and enhance the tremendous value of the Marks, the Products, and the System, the Franchisee agrees that it will manufacture, market, and sell the Products and/or perform the Services in strict accordance with the standards, specifications, requirements, instructions, procedures, and all other standards of nature and quality promulgated by the Franchisor (including those set forth in the Manual). Franchisee acknowledges and agrees that a uniform application and implementation of the Franchisor's standards of nature and quality is vitally important to the Franchisee, the Franchisor, and the collective success of all franchisees. Failure to adhere to Franchisor's standards shall be deemed a material breach of this Agreement.

4.2 All materials related to the marketing and sale of the Products and/or performance of the Services, including but not limited to packaging, advertising, signs, _____, _____, must meet the standards of nature and quality prescribed by the Franchisor.

4.3 Franchisee shall insure at all times that the Products/Services meet in fact Franchisor's standards, and Franchisee shall cooperate fully in all reasonable ways with Franchisor in enabling Franchisor to ascertain that all its standards are being met. By way of example rather than limitation, (a) the Franchisor's employees and agents shall have the right to enter upon any of Franchisee's premises where Products are being manufactured or offered for sale and/or Services are being performed at any reasonable time to determine whether Franchisee's business is being conducted in accordance with this Agreement and Franchisor's standards; (b) Franchisor's employees and agents shall have the right to request reasonable quantities of samples of Products, at Franchisee's expense, for the purposes of testing, inspection, and review; and (c) all advertising by Franchisee must be approved in advance by Franchisor.

4.4 [Deficiency and cure provisions specifically tailored to the particular business should follow.]

4.5 Franchisee shall fully comply with, adhere to, and abide by each and every rule, procedure, standard, specification, and requirement contained in Franchisor's Manual, which shall include Franchisor's sales guide and presentation book, as amended, modified, or supplemented from time to time and such other manuals and other written rules, procedures, standards, specifications, and requirements as Franchisor may promulgate or issue from time to time, as so amended, modified, or supplemented (the "Manual"). Franchisee expressly acknowledges that Franchisor may amend, modify, or supplement the Franchise Manual for the purpose of maintaining, improving, modifying, supplementing, or enforcing Franchisor's Methods. Franchisee agrees to keep Franchisee's copy of the Franchise Manual up to date. Franchisee acknowledges that the Franchise Manual is and shall remain the sole and exclusive property of Franchisor, shall not be reproduced by Franchisee, and upon expiration or termination of this Agreement, Franchisee shall immediately return the Franchise Manual to Franchisor.

4.6 Franchisee shall, in conducting its business, observe high ethical standards of operation reasonably calculated to maintain the uniformity of image, public goodwill, and reputation attached to the System and the Marks, and shall not engage in any activity which may harm the reputation of Franchisor or any other franchisee of Franchisor.

4.7 Franchisee warrants and represents that it will comply with all laws, regulations, ordinances, governmental standards, and the like applicable to the manufacture, sale, distribution, promotion, and advertisement of the Products and/or provision of the Services and agrees to indemnify and hold Franchisor harmless in this regard.

Proprietary Information

5.1 In addition to information contained in this Manual, Franchisor's proprietary formulations and secret formulas, all of which are highly confidential trade secrets, from time to time during the Term Franchisor may disclose to Franchisee certain confidential and proprietary information related to the Products and/or the System and Franchisee shall not reveal or disclose any such secrets or information during or after the Term of this Agreement. Franchisee further acknowledges and agrees that Franchisor is the owner of all rights in and to the System, and that the System constitutes a trade secret of Franchisor that is revealed to Franchisee in confidence, and that no right is given to or acquired by Franchisee to disclose, duplicate, license, sell, or reveal any trade secret to any person, other than an employee of Franchisee required by his work to be familiar with relevant trade secrets. Franchisee agrees to keep confidential such trade secrets, to obtain from each of its stockholders, directors, officers, employees, and agents an Agreement to keep and respect such confidences, and to be responsible for compliance by such stockholders, directors, officers, employees, and agents with such agreements.

5.2 If (a) Franchisee discloses any trade secrets to any person, or (b) one of the persons subject to Franchisee's control makes such a disclosure as a result of the failure of Franchisee to use its best efforts to take the necessary precautions to prevent such disclosure, then Franchisee and each of its officers individually shall pay to Franchisor for each and every breach of this covenant, the sum of _____ as liquidated damages and not as a penalty. The parties acknowledge that the precise amount of Franchisor's actual damages would be extremely difficult to ascertain and that the foregoing sum represents a reasonable estimate of such actual damages.

Copyrights

6.1   All copyrights in and to the Manuals and in and to any and all promotional, advertising, and other materials, in whatever medium, shall be the sole and exclusive property of Franchisor, expressly but without limitation including any advertising and/or new materials related to the System created by Franchisee and/or its agents which shall be deemed works made-for-hire by Franchisee for Franchisor or at Franchisor's option, Franchisee hereby assigns its copyright rights in all such materials to Franchisor. Franchisee agrees to execute whatever assignment or other documents are requested by Franchisor to evidence Franchisor's copyright ownership, and/or to assist Franchisor in obtaining copyright registration. During the Term of this Agreement, Franchisee shall use such copyrights or copyrightable material solely in connection with the promotion and sale of goods and services according to the System, and Franchisee shall not use such material for any other purpose, nor shall Franchisee use any other substantially similar material for any other purpose during the term, and/or after the termination or expiration for whatever reason, of this Agreement.

Termination or Expiration

7.1 Upon the termination or expiration of this Agreement or upon the closing of any site within the Territory, Franchisee shall immediately discontinue the use of the System and Marks. All rights granted herein with respect to the Marks shall revert to the Franchisor.

7.2 Franchisee shall immediately remove the Marks from all buildings, signs, fixtures, and furnishings, and alter and paint all structures and other improvements maintained pursuant to this Agreement a design and color which is basically different from Franchisor's authorized building design and painting schedule. In addition to and without limiting the generality of the foregoing, Franchisee shall make the following building alterations: _____.

7.3 If Franchisee shall fail to make or cause to be made any such removal, alteration, or repainting within ____ days after written notice, then Franchisor shall have the right to enter upon the site, without being deemed guilty of trespass or any other tort or civil wrong, and make or cause to be made such removal, alterations, and repainting at the reasonable expense of Franchisee, which expense the Franchisee shall pay Franchisor upon demand.

7.4 Franchisee shall not thereafter use any trademark, trade name, service mark, logo, insignia, slogan, emblem, symbol, design, package design, distinctive building design or other architectural feature, or other identifying characteristic that is in any way associated with Franchisor or similar to the Marks and Franchisee and those associated with Franchisee shall not operate or do business under any name or in any manner that might tend to give the public the impression that Franchisee, or its successor, is or was a licensee or franchisee of, or otherwise is or was associated with, Franchisor.

7.5 Immediately upon termination or expiration of this Agreement, Franchisee shall return to Franchisor all copies of the Manual received by Franchisee, together with any and all other materials containing trade secrets or other proprietary information.

7.6 Franchisee acknowledges that Franchisee's failure to abide by the foregoing termination provisions will result in irreparable harm to Franchisor and the System and that Franchisor's remedy at law for damages will be inadequate. Accordingly, Franchisee agrees that upon any breach by Franchisee of the foregoing termination provisions, Franchisor shall be entitled to injunctive relief or specific performance in addition to any other remedies available at law or in equity.

Indemnification

8.1 Franchisee agrees to indemnify and hold Franchisor, its subsidiaries, affiliates, franchisees, successors, and assigns harmless from any and all liabilities, damages, claims, judgments, awards, fines, penalties, or other payments (including reasonable counsel fees), that may be incurred by any or all of them arising out of any claims or suits which may be brought or made against Franchisor or those in privity with it, except for those arising directly out of the use of the Marks which are related to the Marks, for injuries resulting from Franchisee's conduct of business under this Agreement, or any unauthorized use by Franchisee by the Marks, or out of any breach by Franchisee of any provisions of this Agreement, provided Franchisor shall give prompt notice and reasonable cooperation and assistance to Franchisee relative to any such claim or suit brought to its attention. This provision shall survive indefinitely the termination or expiration of this Agreement.

FORM NO. 1-4: Sample Provisions
Asset Purchase Agreement

Seller possesses and agrees to convey all right, title, and interest in and to all of the Company's Marks, trade names, trade dress, labels, as well as the goodwill associated therewith, copyrights and patents and all registrations, renewals and applications therefor (the "Intellectual Property") owned by the Company and all licenses or agreements under which the Company has the right to use any of the Intellectual Property, each of which is listed and briefly described in Schedule [   ], in addition to the secret or confidential information, techniques, formulas, recipes, processes and related ancillary, and incidental know-how, standards and specifications relating to or essential to the manufacture and sale of products of the same characteristics and quality as now sold by the Company under the Company's Marks, and Seller represents these are valid and subsisting, are free and clear of any liens or encumbrances of any type, and are satisfactory and sufficient for the proper conduct of the Company's business under the Company's Marks.

To the best knowledge of the Company, except as set forth in Schedule [   ], there are no other persons with rights, or claims of rights, superior to or which restrict the right of the Company to use the Company's Marks or which may give rise to a claim of infringement against the Company nor are there any proceedings that have been instituted or are pending or threatened that challenge the validity of the ownership or the use by the Company of the Intellectual Property. Schedule [   ] contains a list of all licenses or agreements pursuant to which the Company licenses anyone to use any of the Intellectual Property or any other technical know-how or other proprietary rights of the Company, or pursuant to which the Company has consented, based upon its rights in the Intellectual Property, to any other person's use of a trademark, trade name, copyright, or patent. Except as set forth in Schedule [   ], Company has no knowledge of any use or any application for registration by any other person infringing any of the Company's Intellectual Property and there is no pending litigation based upon such use or application.

FORM NO. 1-5: Sample Provisions
Stock Purchase Agreement

All trademarks, service marks, trade names, symbols, logos, trade dress, all goodwill associated therewith, copyrights, and patents (collectively the "Intellectual Property"), whether registered or unregistered, and applications and registrations therefor, owned by the Company are listed and described in Schedule [   ]. The Company has good, valid, indefeasible, and marketable title to, and is the exclusive and unrestricted owner throughout the [territory] of, all the Intellectual Property listed on Schedule [   ], free and clear of any liens, claims, charges, pledges, security interests, options to purchase, encumbrances, or equitable interests of any nature whatsoever.

All franchises, licenses, consents, approvals, or authorizations that relate to the Company and to any of the Intellectual Property, including but not limited to all licenses and agreements under which the Company has the right to use or grants to any third party the right to use any of the Intellectual Property, are described in Section [   ] .

No claim has been received by the Company claiming that the Company's use of any of the Intellectual Property violates the rights of third parties.

To the best knowledge of the Company after reasonable inquiry: (a) neither the Company nor its operation as presently conducted infringes any of the Intellectual Property of any third party; (b) none of the Intellectual Property or registration listed on Schedule [   ] is void, invalid, or unenforceable; (c) there are no other persons with rights, or claims of rights, superior to, or which restrict the right of the Company to conduct its business as it is presently conducted or which may give rise to a claim of infringement against the Company nor are there any proceedings that have been instituted or are pending or threatened that challenge the validity of the ownership or use by the Company of the Intellectual Property listed in Schedule [   ] or the right to conduct its business as it is presently conducted; and (d) no third party by adverse use or application for registration is infringing the rights of the Company with respect to the use of the Intellectual Property listed on Schedule [   ].

Schedule [   ]
Trademarks, Service Marks, Trade Names, Symbols, Logos
(each being referred to below as "Mark"):

Mark	U.S. Reg. No.	U.S. Reg. Date	U.S. App. No.	R.S. App. Date	State App. or Reg. No. and Date: Name of State	Check here if no app. or regn.

Description of trade dress:

Copyrights:

Patents:

Description of all franchises, licenses, consents, approvals, or authorizations which relate to the Company and to any of the Intellectual Property, including but not limited to all licenses and agreements under which the Company has the right to use or grants to any third party the right to use any of the Intellectual Property:

FORM NO. 1-6: Blanket Assignment

WHEREAS, _____, a corporation of the State of
_____, with its principal place of business at _____,
has created, obtained, adopted, and otherwise owns intellectual and/or industrial property in connection with its _____ business (the "Intangibles");

    WHEREAS, _____, a corporation of the State of
_____, with its principal place of business at _____,
is desirous of acquiring all the said Intangibles;

    NOW THEREFORE, for good and valuable consideration, the receipt of which is
hereby acknowledged, _____ does hereby sell, transfer, convey,
and assign to _____ all right, title, and interest throughout
the world in or relating directly or indirectly to all the said Intangibles including, by way
of example and not limitation: trademarks, service marks, and trade names, together with
(a) the various symbols, designs, devices, logos, labels, trade dress, slogans, and other distinctive material used in association with, (b) the goodwill of the business symbolized
thereby, (c) the technology and trade secrets, including, but not limited to, formulas,
recipes, know-how, processes, techniques, methods, and specifications related to the manufacture and sale of the products and provision of services under the service marks and
trade names, and (d) all relevant trademark and service mark registrations and applications for trademark and service mark registration; patents and patent applications, inventions and designs; copyrights and applications for copyright registration; the right to
secure renewals, extensions, continuations, and re-issues to any of the foregoing, related
rights arising out of license or other contracts with third parties; and all pending or
inchoate causes of action or claims related to any of the foregoing, including the right to
sue and recover for past infringement or breaches of contract.

[Assignor]

_____
By:
Name:
Title:

STATE OF   }
                  } ss.
COUNTY OF   }

_____ being duly sworn, deposes and says that he is _____ of _____, and that he has executed the assignment for and on behalf of _____, being duly authorized to do so.

Subscribed and sworn to before me
this _____ day of _____, 19__

_____
Notary Public

CHAPTER 2

Franchise Sales and Managing Growth

Mark B. Forseth and Grover C. Outland, III

Contents

Introduction

In order to manage the franchise sales activity and the growth of a franchise system, a franchisor must establish internal policies and programs that facilitate compliance with federal and state laws and regulations applicable to the offer and sale of a franchise. Further, a franchisor must promote the franchise relationship and manage system expansion to control, or at least minimize, conflicts with franchisees. Effective implementation of such policies and programs dictates that *all* personnel of the franchisor who have contact with prospective and existing franchisees understand how the applicable legal and regulatory frameworks affect the franchisor's dealings with prospective and existing franchisees. While this chapter provides an overview of the applicable franchise relationship laws in connection with state registration requirements and issues related to system expansion, full discussion of such relationship laws is beyond the scope of this chapter.

Implementing the policies and procedures memorialized in an internal compliance program should lessen the franchisor's exposure for violations of state and federal laws. Further, the franchisor's adherence to an effective compliance program can provide the basis for a highly credible defense should any transaction be challenged, to the extent that the franchisor conducts its sales activity and business dealings in a manner consistent with its policies. The franchisor's failure to comply with announced policies and procedures, however, can be introduced as evidence in order to prove that the franchisor failed to meet its own minimum standards of conduct. Consequently, system policies (in particular, notification and/or impact policies) should establish standards that are achievable by the franchisor and consistent with its short-term and long-term expansion plans.[1]

Overview of Franchise Registration and Disclosure Laws

The offer and sale of franchises are regulated under both federal and state law. Such laws specify the form and content of the disclosure that must be made to prospective franchisees, the timing of delivery of such disclosure, and who must receive disclosure. On October 21, 1979, the Federal Trade Commission adopted the "FTC Rule" (formally titled "Disclosure Requirements and Prohibitions Concerning Franchising and Business Opportunity Ventures").[2] The FTC Rule requires delivery of the prescribed disclosure by a franchisor (and any franchise broker, if applicable) to prospective franchisees, in accordance with its timing requirements, prior to concluding the sale of a franchise, but does not require any filing or registration of the disclosure document with any federal agency. The FTC Rule applies in all fifty states and the U.S. territories.

In addition to the federal law, fifteen states specifically regulate the offer and sale of franchises.[3] On January 1, 1971, California became the first state to adopt a law specifically requiring registration and disclosure in connection with the offer and sale of a franchise.[4] The other 14 states enacted their laws prior to the enactment of the FTC Rule, with the exception of New York.[5] These states generally require the following: the registration (or filing) of the disclosure document with the state prior to offering and selling a franchise in that state (as defined by statute), the standards for and pre-use filing of all franchise sales advertising, and the registration of salespersons representing a franchisor in each state.[6] Further, 24 states have business opportunity laws or seller-assisted marketing plan practice acts that may impact a franchisor's ability to offer and sell franchises in a particular state.[7]

Most franchisors structure their franchise programs in order to qualify, where possible, for exemptions or to be excluded from such statutes. Several of these states, however, require franchisors to file a notice for, or otherwise to claim, the exemption under the law prior to offering and selling in that state (again as defined by statute). If a franchisor does not qualify for an exemption (or is otherwise excluded from coverage of the act), the franchisor may be required to register in accordance with the terms of such laws prior to any offer or sale of a franchise in that state. If the manner in which the franchisor offers its franchises falls within state statutory definitions of a business opportunity or a seller-assisted marketing plan, then the franchisor may face registration and disclosure obligations under these statutes that are similar to, or in addition to, those required under federal or state franchise laws. One of the most important things to communicate to business personnel involved in any franchise program is that violations of any of these laws can result in significant liability to the franchisor, as well as to the individuals responsible for the violation.

The FTC Rule

Generally, there are three common characteristics to product and package franchises that are covered by the FTC Rule: (1) distribution of goods or services using the franchisor's trademark, (2) significant control exerted by the franchisor or significant assistance given by the franchisor to the franchisee concerning the operation of the franchised business, and (3) the required payment by the franchisee to the franchisor of at least $500 prior to or during the first six months of operation.[8]

The FTC promulgated the Interpretive Guides to the FTC Rule to provide guidance and to assist franchisors in understanding their obligations under the FTC Rule.[9] The Interpretive Guides provide examples of conduct evidencing significant control or assistance elements. The term "significant" is defined by the degree to which the franchisee is dependent upon the franchisor's superior business expertise to reduce his or her business risk. Significant types of control over the franchisee by the franchisor include (1) site approval for unestablished businesses; (2) site design or appearance requirements; (3) hours of operation; (4) production techniques; (5) accounting practices; (6) personnel policies and practices; (7) promotional campaigns requiring franchisee participation or financial contribution; (8) restrictions on customers; and (9) location or sales area restrictions.[10] Significant types of assistance to the franchisee include (1) formal sales, repair, or business training programs; (2) establishing accounting systems; (3) furnishing management, marketing, or personnel advice; (4) selecting site locations; and (5) furnishing a detailed operating manual. To a lesser extent the FTC will also consider (1) requirements that a franchisee service or repair a product (except warranty work); (2) inventory controls; (3) required display of goods; or (4) on-the-job assistance in sales or repairs.[11]

The FTC intended the required payment element to be interpreted broadly and to include all sources of revenue which the franchisee must pay to the franchisor, or its affiliate, including initial franchise fees, rent, advertising assistance, amounts for required equipment and supplies, training, security deposits, escrow deposits, nonrefundable bookkeeping charges, promotional literature, equipment rental, payments for services, and continuing royalties. Any payments made by a purchaser at a bona fide wholesale price for reasonable amounts of merchandise to be used for resale will not be considered a "required payment."[12]

The trademark element is generally met when any of the following occur: (1) the goods or services distributed by the franchisee are associated with the franchisor's trademark, service mark, trade name, advertising, or other commercial symbol (for example, a product franchise); or (2) the franchisee is required to conform to quality standards prescribed by the franchisor where the franchisee operates under a name that includes, in whole or in part, the franchisor's trademark, service mark, trade name, advertising, or other commercial symbol (for example, a package franchise). If the franchisor wishes to avoid the trademark element of the definition of a franchise, and no mark is involved in the relationship, the FTC has indicated that an *express* prohibition against the use of any mark of the franchisor by the franchisee will avoid application of the FTC Rule.[13]

Unless a franchisor is exempt or excluded from coverage under the FTC Rule, the franchisor must comply with the FTC Rule's requirements for the delivery of offering documents to prospective franchisees, including those offers and sales made in the registration states. While each state statute sets forth the time frame for delivering an offering circular in that state (many of which are consistent with the FTC Rule delivery requirements, but some of which are shorter), the franchisor will meet all state delivery requirements by complying with the delivery requirements set forth in the FTC Rule.

There are two separate delivery requirements of the FTC Rule. An offering circular must be provided to a "prospective franchisee" at the earlier of (1) the "first personal meeting," or (2) the "time for making of disclosures."[14] These terms and others are defined in the following paragraphs.

First Personal Meeting

The FTC Rule defines a first personal meeting as a face-to-face meeting between a prospective franchisee and a franchisor, or a "franchise broker," or any such meeting between any agent, representative, or employee of such parties, held for the purpose of discussing the sale or possible sale of a franchise.[15] A first personal meeting is generally initiated by the franchisor, and thus is within the franchisor's control. Contact by telephone or through correspondence is not a first personal meeting requiring the delivery of an offering circular under the FTC Rule.[16] Most registration states, however, regulate correspondence and telephone contact regarding a franchise sale.[17] In the nonregistration states, before the delivery of the offering circular, contact through correspondence and telephone should be limited to general discussions of the franchise and the gathering of information concerning the prospect's qualifications to be a franchisee. As such, the franchisor may send the prospect a brochure that generally discusses the franchise and a franchise application or questionnaire to the prospective franchisee. Every time the franchisor has a brief, *general* discussion with an inquiring prospect concerning the franchise program (for example, every prospect that approaches the franchisor's booth at a trade show) the franchisor is not required to give an offering circular. Face-to-face meetings require delivery of the offering circular if the sale or possible sale of a franchise or earnings information related to the franchised business are to be discussed at the meeting. Franchisors are advised to delay all face-to-face meetings until such time as proper disclosure may be made.

Time For Making of Disclosures

The time for making of disclosures is defined by the FTC Rule as ten business days prior to the earlier of (1) execution by the prospective franchisee of any franchise or other agreement (such as a development agreement or option agreement) which imposes a binding, legal obligation on the prospective franchisee, or (2) the payment of any consideration for a franchise by the prospective franchisee.[18]

Franchise Broker

The FTC Rule defines a franchise broker as any person other than a franchisor or a franchisee (generally excluding employees of the franchisor or franchisee) who sells, offers for sale, or arranges for the sale of a franchise.[19]

The franchisor should note that the FTC definition of franchise broker is broad and somewhat ambiguous because it encompasses any person who "arranges for the sale of a franchise." Determining the types of activities that constitute arranging for the sale of a franchise is difficult and must be made on a case-by-case basis. As a general rule, the passive referral of a prospective franchisee to a franchisor will not constitute franchise brokering. On the other hand, any activity that may be interpreted as encouraging, enticing, or persuading a prospective franchisee to purchase a particular franchise is likely to be deemed the "brokering" of the franchise. If any non-franchisor individual or legal entity is participating in the franchisor's franchise sales process in any manner, the franchisor is urged to consult with its franchise counsel to address any brokering issues. As discussed earlier, registration, in addition to disclosure, of franchise brokers is frequently required in the states' registration/disclosure laws.

Prospective Franchisee

A prospective franchisee is defined by the FTC Rule as any person, including any representative, agent, or employee of that person, who approaches or is approached by a franchisor or a franchise broker, or any representative, agent, or employee of that franchisor, for the purpose of discussing the establishment, or possible establishment, of a franchise relationship involving such person.[20]

Each individual who is to execute the franchise, development, or other agreement (whether as the individual franchisee or as a guarantor of the obligations of a corporate or partnership franchisee) should also be provided appropriate disclosure as a prospective franchisee.

Business Day

The FTC Rule defines business day to mean any day other than Saturday, Sunday, or national holidays.[21] Each year the person charged with franchise sales law compliance should provide a list of national holidays to the franchise sales personnel to avoid violations of the business day requirement. The FTC Rule also requires a franchisor to provide the prospective franchisee with any agreement to be executed (with all blanks filled in) at least five business days prior to execution.[22]

Compliance with the FTC Rule's delivery requirements must be documented by use of franchisee-executed receipt form (Item 23 of the offering circular), as well as the franchisor's maintenance of its compliance records. The franchisor may also consider use of a Summary of Acknowledgments Form (see

Exhibit 2-H) or video or audio-taped closing procedures to further memorialize compliance with pertinent legal requirements.[23]

State Franchise Registration and Disclosure Laws

State franchise sales regulation imposes on franchisors various filing, registration, and pre-sale disclosure requirements concerning the offer and sale of franchises in certain states. For example, franchise offerings must be registered with state administrators (that is, filed with *and* made effective by the appropriate regulator) before the offer or sale of a franchise in the following states: California, Illinois, Indiana, Maryland, Minnesota, New York, North Dakota, Rhode Island, South Dakota, Virginia, and Washington.[24]

Hawaii law requires that an offering circular be filed with the state authorities prior to the sale of a franchise in Hawaii.[25] Although the statute does not expressly require review of the registration and declaration of effectiveness by the Hawaii Director of Commerce and Consumer Affairs before a franchisor offers the franchise for sale, as a practical matter, the current administration has a policy of requiring such review and effectiveness before such offer takes place. Generally, the review by the Division addresses a franchisor's compliance with certain procedural requirements of Hawaii (for example, compliance with state-specific disclosure requirements and inclusion of appropriate financial statements). Michigan requires only a one-page "Notice of Intent to Offer and Sell Franchises" to be filed with the state along with the annual payment of a filing fee before the offer and sale of a franchise.[26] Wisconsin requires the filing of a notification accompanied by the offering circular with the state authorities prior to the sale of a franchise.[27] Finally, Oregon requires only that pre-sale disclosure be made to a prospective franchisee and does not require that any filing be made with the state.[28] Each of the above states requires the offering circular to contain state-specific modifications reflecting particular aspects of state laws, and may require additional changes that have been requested by the state administrator during the registration process.

The right to offer and sell franchises under a registration (and in some cases, exemption from state registration) normally exists for one year from the time the registration or exemption is effective or, in other cases, until a few months (for example, ranging from two to four months) after the franchisor's fiscal year end. At that time the registration or exemption must be renewed or an annual report must be filed. In addition, both state law and the FTC Rule require that an offering circular be amended at any time there is a "material" change in the information presented. Please refer to Amendments and Renewals later in this chapter for a discussion of what constitutes a material change.

The Offer of a Franchise

Most state franchise statutes are triggered by specified *business activity* that takes place within state borders or involving state residents. While the jurisdictional scope of such laws varies, the following is a general statement of the various activities that may trigger application of a particular state franchise law:

1. The offer to sell originates in the state.
2. The offer to sell is directed by the franchisor to the state and is received at the place to which it was directed.
3. The offer to buy is accepted in the state.
4. The offer or sale is made to a franchisee domiciled in the state and the franchise is or will be operated in state.
5. The franchise will be operated in the state.
6. The offer or sale is made to a resident of that state.
7. The offer is to a person domiciled in the state.
8. The franchise contemplates or requires the franchisee to establish or maintain a place of business in the state.

The foregoing are general statements only. Please refer to Exhibit 2-A, Chart of State Franchise Law Jurisdictional Requirements.[29] All franchise salespersons must be trained to ask relevant questions and identify key jurisdictional elements in order to determine if registration is necessary and to ensure that disclosure is provided in accordance with applicable state law (see Multi-state Transactions in this chapter). At the outset of sales discussions, salespersons should be trained to obtain pertinent jurisdictional information such as that described below and in the sample checklist attached as Exhibit 2-B.

1. Where is the franchise business to be operated?
2. Who will be the franchisee (individuals, corporation, or other entity form)?
3. Where is franchisee's residence, principal place of business, and/or domicile (including all principal interest holders)?
4. Where will franchisor salespersons communicate with franchisee or its principals?

If the answers to any of those questions involve one or more of the fifteen franchise registration and disclosure states, the salesperson must consult with the franchisor's counsel or internal compliance officer to determine whether an offer or sale can be made.[30] All franchise salespersons should be provided with a summary of states in which the franchisor is authorized to sell and the dates of expiration of effectiveness, as well as a list of those states, if any, in which offer and sales activity may not be conducted until further notice. Please see the sample Registration Summary Checklist attached as Exhibit 2-C.

In each state requiring registration, it is unlawful to offer or sell a franchise prior to securing registration with the appropriate state authorities (except Wisconsin and Hawaii, which permit offers and only prohibit sales prior to registration). Additionally, in each state requiring registration and/or disclosure, it is unlawful to sell a franchise without providing the prospective franchisee with an offering circular containing the disclosure required for that state. Franchisors also must comply with the FTC Rule ten business day delivery requirement, as noted above. Practitioners differ on the manner in which state specific disclosures should be prepared for registration and delivery to prospective franchisees. Some practitioners prepare and use a separate offering circular for each registration state containing state-specific cover pages and receipt forms and substantive changes to the body of the offering circular. Other practitioners advocate use of a "roll-up" offering circular in which state-specific disclosures required by state regulators are included in addenda to reflect substantive provisions of state law that as a matter of public policy may override the terms of the franchise agreement described in the offering circular. The franchisor utilizing the roll-up approach will typically employ one offering circular in all registration and nonregistration states. The roll-up format thus insures that all prospects receive the correct disclosure for all states in which the franchisor does business. The franchisee would at closing be required to execute the applicable state amendments to the agreements (if any are required).

An important concept in franchise sales regulation is the "offer" of a franchise. Applicability of virtually every state's franchise law is triggered by sales activity constituting an offer, as that term is defined by the particular state's franchise law. Central to the analysis is the fact that most states' franchise laws will apply to an offer made to or from, or accepted in, a state, even though the prospective franchisee is domiciled in another state and the business may be operated in another state. State laws generally define the offer of a franchise to include "every attempt to offer or dispose of, or solicitation of an offer to buy, a franchise or interest in a franchise for value."[31] This broad definition of offer will generally include

1. oral or written contact with a prospective franchisee. Administrative interpretations suggest that any communication concerning a specific franchise opportunity may constitute an offer;
2. telephone communication to or from a registration/disclosure state;
3. newspaper, magazine, radio, or television advertising offering a franchise. However, if two-thirds of the circulation is outside the state,[32] then most states will exempt that advertisement from the definition of offer; and
4. promotional brochures and other franchise sales literature.

In contrast, the "sale" of a franchise generally refers to the execution of a franchise agreement or other binding contract (such as a development agreement, option agreement, or letter of intent), or the payment of consideration by the prospective franchisee to purchase franchise rights.[33] These events are particularly important as they also relate to the timing of disclosure as noted earlier.

All communications concerning the franchisor's franchise offering must be handled with great care. If the franchisor receives an inquiry from or relating to a registration state in which it is not yet effectively registered, franchisor representatives may not discuss the franchise program or send any promotional literature to that prospect until such activity has been cleared with counsel. The only acceptable response is to advise the person inquiring that the franchisor has not yet registered to sell franchises with the state in question and that the person's name and telephone number are being retained in the franchisor's files until such time as the franchise may be offered lawfully in that state. Such communication to the prospect should be in writing.

Once a franchise offering is registered with a state, the franchisor must take care that the sales presentation does not conflict in any way with the information in that state's registered offering circular. Salespersons should be familiar with state addenda attached to the offering circular.

It is critical to any compliance program that communication by franchise personnel with prospective franchisees be in accordance with state franchise laws. While telephonic or written communication (or advertising) may not trigger the FTC Rule disclosure requirements, such activity will likely constitute an offer of a franchise under state law, thus requiring registration prior to such communication (or advertising). Timely delivery of specified disclosure documents to the prospect is also crucial to compliance with state law (see discussion of delivery of offering documents under FTC Rule). Improper pre-sale communication and disclosure can result in sales that are subject to challenge.

Exemption from State
Franchise Registration Requirements

Most of the state franchise registration laws provide one or more exemptions or exclusions from registration that may be available to qualifying franchisors. While the nature and terms of such exemptions/exclusions vary widely from state to state, these provisions can typically be analyzed according to one of three criteria: (1) the nature of the offeror; (2) the nature of the offeree; and (3) the nature of the offer or transaction. Some common exemptions and exclusions that may be available in certain registration states are as follows: franchisor net worth and/or experience exemption; sales to existing franchisees; sales by franchisees; isolated sales; and franchisee net worth and experience.

State franchise registration laws vary widely in their treatment of exemptions, both as to number and type of exemptions granted, and the specific qualifications for obtaining the exemption. Determining whether the franchisor may qualify for a net worth or other exemption in a particular state depends upon the applicable law and the state's specific procedural prerequisites. It is the role of counsel to review the company's franchise program and applicable laws and then to provide the franchisor with a summary of the statutory exemptions and exclusions from state franchise laws that are applicable to its franchise program.

For example, the states of California, Indiana, Maryland, New York, North Dakota, Rhode Island, South Dakota, and Washington all have exemptions based on the net worth and/or experience of the franchisor.[34] California's net worth exemption requires the franchisor to (1) have a minimum net worth of $5,000,000, or a net worth of $1,000,000 and a parent (owning at least 80 percent) who has a net worth of $5,000,000 and guarantees the franchisor's performance (net worth to be determined based on most recent audited financial statements); (2) the franchisor or parent has either conducted, or has had at least 25 franchisees conducting, the business which is the subject of the franchise offering for a period of at least five years immediately prior to the offer or sale of the franchise; (3) the franchisor provides the required offering circular to the prospective franchisee; and (4) the franchisor files a notice with the state authorities.[35] Indiana has a similar exemption with no filing requirement.[36]

Maryland has a similar exemption, but the franchisor must have $10,000,000 in net worth, have had 25 franchisees operating during the five-year period, and file a copy of the most recent offering circular, along with other ancillary documentation, to claim the exemption.[37] Just having the franchisor or the parent conduct the business for the five-year period does not meet the experience requirements under the Maryland law. On the other hand, New York law does not require the franchisor to have any experience conducting, or having franchisees conducting, the subject business. New York law has two levels of net worth exemptions. The first requires (1) the franchisor to have a minimum net worth of $5,000,000, or a net worth of $1,000,000 and a parent (owning at least 80 percent) who has a net worth of $5,000,000 and guarantees the franchisor's performance; (2) the franchisor to provide full disclosure; and (3) the franchisor files a notice with the state agency. The second requires the franchisor to have a minimum net worth of $15,000,000, or a net worth of $3,000,000 and a parent (owning at least 80 percent) who has a net worth of $15,000,000 and guarantees the franchisor's performance. The exemption does not require the franchisor to file anything with the state and only requires disclosure of certain limited information to the prospective franchisee.[38] The other states with net worth exemptions have similar requirements with variations.

Exemption from registration under the laws of one registration state has no bearing on exempt status in any other registration state. As evidenced by the example above, counsel must individually review and consider exemptions and exclusions available under applicable law in each state where the franchisor plans to pursue its franchising activities, and a detailed analysis of all available exemptions is beyond the scope of this chapter. If the franchisor does not perfect an exemption under the laws of a particular state, registration and disclosure will be required under that state's laws. In addition, the substantive laws of the state applicable to franchising (for example, anti-fraud, unfair practices) generally will continue to apply to each offering regardless of any exemption or exclusion perfected or relied on by the franchisor.

State Business Opportunity Laws

In addition to the FTC Rule and the franchise laws of the fifteen registration/ disclosure states, the sale of a franchise may also be subject to state business opportunity laws and seller-assisted marketing plan acts, which for the purpose of this chapter we will refer to as "business opportunity laws." While state business opportunity statutes vary, these laws usually define a business opportunity so broadly that the typical franchise is covered by the definition, and under such statutes, it is generally unlawful to offer and/or sell business opportunities without appropriate pre-sale disclosure and (where required) registration.

Franchisors generally should be aware of these business opportunity statutes, although most franchisors are typically exempt or excluded from such laws based on either one of two exemptions or definitional exclusions: (1) offering a franchise in compliance with the FTC Rule; or (2) offering a franchise in conjunction with the licensing of a registered trademark or service mark. Further, a franchisor that registers a franchise offering (or is exempt from such franchise registration) in a state that has both a franchise law and a business opportunity statute typically will be exempt from any disclosure or registration provisions of the business opportunity statute. As with state franchise registration laws, an offering exempt from the registration/disclosure provisions of a business opportunity law will still be subject to any anti-fraud or other substantive provisions of that law. However, if the franchisor's offering is excluded from the definition of a business opportunity based on the statutory requirements, typically none of the provisions of the law will apply.[39]

Twenty-four states now have one of a variety of business opportunity statutes. These states are:

Alabama	Kentucky	Ohio
California	Louisiana	Oklahoma
Connecticut	Maine	South Carolina
Florida	Maryland	South Dakota
Georgia	Michigan	Texas
Illinois	Nebraska	Utah
Indiana	New Hampshire	Virginia
Iowa	North Carolina	Washington

Under the Texas Business Opportunity Act,[40] the definition of business opportunity generally includes the typical franchise, however, a franchisor offering its franchise in Texas that materially complies with the disclosure requirements of the FTC Rule may claim an exemption from the Act by filing a notice of exemption with the appropriate state authorities and paying the requisite fee (and complying with the FTC Rule). This one-time filing and fee payment must be made in order to rely upon the exemption. Similar to Texas law, the Nebraska Seller-Assisted Marketing Plan Act[41] requires franchisors claiming such exemption from the Nebraska Act to make a one time filing with the state and pay a filing fee.[42] The Kentucky Sale of Business Opportunities Act also requires franchisors to make a one time filing to claim the exemption, but does not require any filing fee.[43] In contrast, the Florida Business Opportunity Sales Act and the Utah Business Opportunity Disclosure Act[44] each require franchisors claiming an exemption from the Act based on the franchisor's compliance with the FTC Rule to file annually a notice with the state and pay a fee. However, both the Florida and Utah Acts specifically exclude from the definition of a business opportunity the sale of a marketing or sales program made in conjunction with the licensing of a registered trademark or service mark.[45] Therefore, unless the franchisor meets the other elements of the business opportunity definition, as described below, the franchisor may avoid the filing requirement in Florida and Utah if it has a registered trademark. The Michigan Business Opportunity Law has been incorporated in the Michigan Consumer Protection Act.[46]

Franchise counsel should be consulted immediately if any doubt or issue arises regarding the coverage of a particular business opportunity statute. For example, the existence of any provision in the franchise agreement granting the franchisee the right to a partial or total refund of the initial franchise fee at the franchisee's discretion, or the right to compel the franchisor to "buy back" certain equipment or inventory often triggers the applicability of a state's statute, even where the franchisor complies with the FTC Rule and/or offers the franchise in connection with the licensing of a registered mark. The FTC Rule also contains a definition of a business opportunity, but in most cases it is not applicable to a business format franchise. The elements that are required for the existence of a business opportunity venture (which are also designated as "franchises" under the FTC Rule) are (1) the franchisee sells goods or services that are supplied by the franchisor, (2) the franchisor secures or provides a third party to secure retail outlets or accounts for the goods or services, or locations for vending machines or racks, and (3) the franchisee is required to pay at least $500 prior to or during the first six months of operation to the franchisor. Examples of business opportunity ventures include distributorship, rack jobbing, and vending machine routes.[47]

Preparation of the Offering Circular

The disclosure document format used by most franchisors follows the Uniform Franchise Offering Circular (UFOC) Guidelines as amended by the North American Securities Administrators Association (NASAA) on April 25, 1993. Offering circulars prepared in accordance with the UFOC Guidelines will typically satisfy the requirements of the FTC Rule and of each individual state franchise law, after registration and inclusion of state specific disclosure, as applicable. The FTC Rule has its own specific format for preparation of a disclosure document, but most registration states will not accept a registration application using an FTC format offering circular.[48] The FTC in an Advance Notice of Proposed Rulemaking has requested comment on whether the FTC should replace its disclosure format with a format similar to the UFOC, and all preliminary indications suggest that the FTC will do so.[49]

The offering circular itself consists of twenty-three separate substantive categories commonly referred to as "Items" of information. The information in each Item must follow the specific UFOC Guidelines and instruments for that Item. Generally, the UFOC Guidelines are intended to provide the prospective franchisee with sufficient information about the franchise to enable the prospect to assess the terms and conditions of the franchise arrangements. The 23 substantive Items are as follows:[50]

Item	*General Description of Required Information*

1. Who the franchisor and its predecessor and affiliates are and a description of the franchise that is being offered
2. Biographical and professional information for the past five years pertaining to officers, directors, franchise executives, and brokers of the franchisor
3. Pertinent criminal and civil litigation history of the franchisor, predecessors, affiliates, and management for the past ten years
4. The bankruptcy history of the franchisor and its management
5. Description of the franchisee's initial fees (and other payments to franchisor and its affiliates prior to opening)
6. Description of all other fees that the franchisee will be required to pay to the franchisor or its affiliate during the term of the franchise relationship
7. Description of the franchisee's total initial investment
8. Description of any restrictions on sources of products and services
9. Description of the franchisee's obligations (as a cross-reference between the offering circular and franchise related agreements)
10. The terms of any financing arrangements offered by the franchisor or its affiliate (directly or indirectly)
11. All supervision, assistance, and services to be provided by the franchisor during the term of the franchise relationship
12. A description of any area or territory granted to the franchisee
13. Pertinent information concerning the franchisor's trademarks, service marks, and trade names
14. Pertinent information regarding any patents or copyrights and other proprietary information owned by the franchisor material to the franchised business
15. Description of any obligations of the franchisee to participate in the actual operation of the franchised business
16. Description of any restrictions on goods and services offered by the franchisee
17. Terms of renewal, termination, transfer, dispute resolution, and related matters
18. Any arrangements of the franchisor with public figures
19. Any representations of the franchisor concerning the financial performance of franchised or franchisor-owned outlets
20. Information regarding the numbers of franchised and franchisor-owned outlets
21. Financial statements of the franchisor
22. Any contracts that the franchisee must sign related to the franchise being offered
23. Two Receipts evidencing receipt of the offering circular

In order to prepare an offering circular that provides information sufficiently accurate to comply with the requirements of federal and state franchise laws, the franchisor will need the assistance and cooperation of all departments (and necessary personnel) to gather and assemble such information in the appropriate format. Such cooperation is necessary in the development of the background data to prepare the offering circular and must continue with the review of such information annually to confirm its continued accuracy and to update the offering circular with any changes when the disclosure is no longer accurate. Counsel should develop and circulate within the franchisor questionnaires that elicit and identify the key information necessary for compliance. Individual questionnaires should be completed and signed by each employee of the franchisor that has the responsibility for maintaining that particular information necessary for the offering circular. The entire questionnaire development and completion process, together with all other information gathering for initial preparation or updating of the offering circular, must remain under the supervision of in-house counsel or an in-house compliance coordinator (with the assistance of outside counsel, if applicable).

Attached as Exhibits 2-D-1, 2-D-2, and 2-D-3 are samples of questionnaires that are used to gather information necessary for Items 2, 3, and 4 (Identity and Business Experience, Litigation and Bankruptcy), Item 8 (Restrictions on Sources of Products and Services), and Item 11 (franchisor's Obligations, Training). Once the questionnaires are completed and returned to the in-house lawyer or compliance coordinator, such forms should be reviewed for completeness and accuracy with the applicable personnel and should be retained in the franchisor's due diligence file. Proper retention of this documentation will enable the franchisor to establish the appropriate legal defenses, should the franchisor later be challenged regarding the accuracy of any of the disclosures in its offering circular. The franchisor must be able to prove that it made reasonable inquiry concerning the accuracy of the information contained in its offering circular in order to establish its due diligence defense.

For example, with respect to the necessary disclosure for Items 2, 3, and 4, the process would involve circulating for review, completion, and execution Exhibit 2-D-1 to all directors, trustees and/or general partners, the principal officers, and other executives or subfranchisors who will have management responsibility related to the franchises offered under the offering circular. Once returned, the franchisor's in-house counsel or compliance coordinator should conduct interviews with each person to verify the information contained in the questionnaire. If the coordinator or in-house counsel has any concerns regarding the litigation or bankruptcy responses, independent computer checks should be conducted to verify accuracy and alleviate any concerns.

Exhibit 2-D-2, the questionnaire used for gathering information for Item 8, should be prepared and signed by the franchisor's personnel responsible for managing sourcing arrangements. The responsible employee will likely need the input of accounting personnel for the information concerning the precise basis of any revenue derived by franchisor and its affiliates from the franchisees' required purchases and leases, as well as the precise basis of any rebates the franchisor or its affiliates receive.[51]

Exhibit 2-D-3 is a sample questionnaire to be completed by the franchisor's training officer to provide the descriptions of the franchisor's training programs and the identity of training personnel for compliance with Item 11 of the offering circular. This Exhibit must be completed with careful scrutiny of the particulars of such programs because of the detail required to be disclosed under the UFOC Guidelines (that is, the subject matter, number of hours allocated to each subject, proposed classroom and on the job training).[52]

Periodic auditing, or other monitoring, of this information must be conducted by the franchisor at least on an annual basis. At a minimum, disclosure and questionnaire forms should be circulated to appropriate franchisor personnel for their review and signature confirming the accuracy of the information contained in the offering circular Items and there should be follow-up interviews and other checks by members of the legal department in connection with the annual update of the offering circular. For example, a legal department staffer could attend the training for franchisees once annually and record the time devoted to each subject, as well as the identity of each instructor. There is nothing more challenging for counsel than learning at a meeting of the franchisor's business personnel that the circular and the agreement do not reflect the way the company actually conducts business.

A master form of the disclosure document is used by the franchisor in all nonregistration states. The date of this disclosure document (set forth on the FTC cover page) is generally the date that the document is completed and ready for use by the franchisor.

For purposes of disclosure in the registration/disclosure states, each state requires the registration and/or disclosure of an offering circular that complies with its own "state" specific requirements. Each state disclosure document consists of the basic UFOC disclosure document with specified "state pages" incorporated into the basic document. For each registration/disclosure state, the additional state pages include a state cover page revised to reflect the date of the state disclosure document plus two receipt forms (Item 23 of the offering circular) revised to reference the state (unless you use a roll-up format offering circular). The state cover page(s) generally contain a description of the franchisor and the franchise, the amount of the franchisee's initial investment, rules for disclosure, the name and address of the state agency handling franchise sales, a disclaimer of state approval or endorsement and of accuracy of information, the prescribed risk factors, and any additional risk factors required by state administrators. In addition, in most registration states, the state pages also include state-specific "addenda" to the offering circular plus franchise and related agreements, as applicable. The addenda are attached to the end of the offering circular and each agreement, respectively, and modify each agreement (and the disclosure in the offering circular) to satisfy certain state franchise relationship laws (for example, restrictions on termination, nonrenewal, and transfer) or other state laws that affect the franchise relationship (for example, restrictions on noncompetition covenants, waivers and releases, liquidated damages, and choice of law or venue).

Most states will not require that any modifications be made to the actual text of the basic offering circular or agreements and will permit modifications by use of state addenda (which is one of the benefits of the roll-up format). The determination of which modifications should be set forth in each state's addendum is made by evaluating the state's franchise law and relationship law (if any), prior experience in registering in that state and knowledge of relevant non-franchise state law, and, to a limited extent, comments from the particular state examiner reviewing the disclosure document. No addenda are currently required for Oregon, Rhode Island, or Virginia. The date of each state disclosure document (except Michigan and Oregon, which are dated the effective date of the FTC disclosure document) is generally the effective date of registration or renewal, as applicable.

In order to obtain registration in all registration states, the franchisor initially submits a registration application to the particular state agency that reviews and acts on franchise registration applications. With a few exceptions, all of the registration states accept the uniform application forms prepared by NASAA. As described below, several of the states have sample forms appended to their franchise law or regulations which should be consulted. An application for registration consists of the offering circular containing the applicable state-specific disclosure (either one or two copies, depending on the state) and the registration fee, together with the following forms.[53]

1. Application or "facing" page—identifies the nature of the application (for example, initial registration, renewal, annual report, or amendment) and sets forth basic information about the franchisor and the contact person for the application.

2. Verification of application—executed by an authorized representative of the franchisor (preferably the president) and verifies that the contents of the application (including the offering circular) are true and correct. The verification must be notarized. The verification page for Hawaii is set forth at the bottom of the Hawaii application page (but Hawaii will accept the uniform form). The New York form requires verification of certain additional information. The person executing the verification may be held individually liable for misrepresentations in or material omissions from the offering circular.

3. Consent to service of process—executed by a representative of the franchisor and designates the appropriate state officer as the franchisor's agent for service of legal or other documents (typically, the Securities Commissioner, Attorney General, Secretary of State, or other specified person). This form must be accompanied by a notarized form of corporate acknowledgment which indicates that the individual executing the consent form has authority to designate the agent. Some states have their own form of consents (for example, Hawaii and New York).

4. Supplemental information page—required by several, but not all, registration states. Contains information regarding the franchisor's registration in other states and an estimate, by amount and source, of the funds the franchisor will expend in fulfilling its various pre-opening obligations under the franchise agreement.

5. Salesperson disclosure form—provides general information about each franchise salesperson. Please refer to "Registration of Salespersons and Franchise Brokers" below for further discussion.

6. Consent—executed by the auditor who prepared the franchisor's financial statements permitting the disclosure and distribution of its financial report in the disclosure document. There is no universal form for the auditors' consent.

Certain states also require other forms to be filed. For example, California requires the franchisor to submit a "Customer Authorization of Disclosure of Financial Records" that permits California to examine the franchisor's financial records,[54] and Maryland requires the franchisor to submit quarterly sales reports to maintain its registration.[55]

Upon filing, a registration application will be assigned to a franchise examiner from the particular state agency who will review the application for accuracy and completeness (that is, compliance with UFOC Guidelines and applicable state law). The state examiner's response is typically forwarded in a "comment letter" which details the application's "deficiencies" and requests additional information and/or revisions to the offering circular. Each comment letter is carefully evaluated by the franchisor's in-house or outside counsel, and state examiners are frequently confronted regarding requests that are not customary or are unsupported by state law. When all deficiencies are resolved, registration will be declared effective by the state.

As previously stated, in most registration states, registration is effective for one year from the effective date of registration. Registration is renewed by filing a renewal application that is substantially similar to the initial registration application with most of the above-listed forms as well as the new offering circular, accompanied by another copy marked to reflect the changes from the previously registered offering circular. The renewal application is required to be filed a certain number of days (generally 15 or 30 business days) prior to the expiration of the registration. If registration lapses before the renewal is declared effective, the franchisor may not sell franchises in that state during the "lapse" period. The renewal application is reviewed in the same manner as the initial registration. The renewal states are California, Indiana, Maryland, North Dakota, Rhode Island, Virginia, Washington, and Wisconsin (although Wisconsin's renewal is now essentially a notice filing).[56]

In other registration states, registration is effective until either 60 or 120 days following the expiration of the franchisor's fiscal year, by which time an "annual report" must be filed in the state. Usually the annual report is substantially similar to a renewal application and may contain a sales report. Illinois requires the filing of an annual report not later than one day before the anniversary date of the registration.[57] The annual report states are Hawaii, Illinois, Minnesota, New York, and South Dakota. While technically a renewal state, California requires the filing of a renewal application within 110 days after the franchisor's fiscal year end.[58]

The filings and disclosure required of a franchisor in any registration state in which the franchisor qualifies for an exemption from registration vary widely depending on the particular state and type of exemption claimed. In some states, an annual filing of a notice claiming the exemption is required for certain types of exemptions and not others (see discussion on Exemptions). In other states, the actual exempt offering circular to be used in the state must be filed (although it is not substantively reviewed as in the registration process). Alternatively, in several of the states, neither a notice of exemption nor the exempt offering circular must be filed (for example, Net Worth exemption in Indiana and New York).

Although a franchise offering may be exempt from registration in a particular state, comprehensive disclosure should still be given. The disclosure document for any state in which the franchisor is exempt is generally a state-specific exempt offering circular consisting of the basic FTC disclosure document with the above-described state cover page(s), modified to reflect an exempt transaction, together with an abbreviated form of the applicable state addenda for use in exempt circulars (or the roll-up offering circular). The date of any exempt state offering circular is the effective date of the FTC disclosure document. Exempt offering circulars should be amended at any time the FTC offering circular is amended (that is, at least annually to include the most recent audited financial statements and as necessary to disclose a material change).

Offering circulars for use by the franchisor in registration/disclosure states should always be clearly labeled if the franchisor does not use a roll-up format containing all state addenda. This applies to offering circulars used in states where the franchisor has obtained an exemption. If state-specific disclosure documents are used, then they may only be used in the appropriate states. Otherwise, the franchisor should use the master form of the FTC disclosure document that is prepared for use in nonregistration states (or a roll-up offering circular).

Inside or outside counsel should prepare a chart summarizing the franchisor's registration schedule for distribution to franchise sales executives so there is no confusion about the status of the franchisor's registrations or the states in which sales personnel may conduct business. The chart should be updated by the franchisor's counsel any time there is a change and an updated copy should be disseminated immediately.

Multistate Transactions

The franchisor will often be faced with a situation in which an entity residing in one state will seek to purchase a franchise that will be operated in a second state. To complicate matters, the franchisor may have made the offer in yet a third state. Since the offer of a franchise can only legally be made by delivering the correct offering circular to the prospective franchisee, great care must be taken to insure that the proper disclosure document is delivered when one or more state franchise disclosure laws may be applicable.

For example, the franchisor may be approached by representatives of an Indiana-based corporation interested in operating a franchise in Virginia, and representatives met with the franchisor's salesperson at a trade show or convention in Maryland. All three of these states potentially have some interest in the transaction: Maryland as the site of the offer,[59] Indiana as the residence of the prospective franchisee,[60] and Virginia as the location for the franchise.[61]

Each sales situation involving multistate transactions is unique and requires independent analysis and review. The interplay of state and federal franchise regulation is generally complex and far from uniform. In the area of multistate transactions, the complexity of these laws is further compounded. There are some exemptions under state law (for example, out-of-state sales exemption in California and Maryland)[62] that may alleviate to some degree the burden of multiple disclosure. Furthermore, the franchisor's use of a roll-up offering circular may substantially eliminate the complications inherent in offering and selling multistate transactions.

Immediately upon identifying any potential multistate transaction, the franchisor's counsel must be advised and responsive legal guidance must be obtained.

Registration of Salespersons and Franchise Brokers

The franchise laws of the registration/disclosure states generally require registration of franchise salespersons and franchise brokers. Some states, however, do not require the separate registration, or filing of salesperson disclosure forms for persons named in Item 2 of the offering circular. Although the laws may not specifically state the following distinction, a salesperson is generally considered an employee of the franchisor whose duties include solicitation of prospective franchisees, while a franchise broker or sales agent is generally an independent contractor retained by the franchisor for the purpose of securing prospective franchisees.

Virtually every registration state requires the identification of those persons who will be conducting franchise sales in that state. In every state except California and New York, identification is accomplished by filing a Uniform Salesman Disclosure Form, which contains personal information about the salesperson (such as address and social security number), as well as a summary of the salesperson's litigation and employment histories. California has a specific form that varies from the Uniform Salesman Disclosure Form in paragraph 2.A. The California form indicates that the disclosure does not include any pending proceedings involving an arrest of such person. New York requires that each sales agent be registered and upon the filing of the state-specific Supplemental Information form, New York will issue an order of registration. Attached as Exhibit 2-E is a copy of the Uniform Salesman Disclosure Form.

Franchise broker registrations often involve lengthy applications, particularly in California, Illinois, New York, and Washington. In addition, franchise brokers must be identified in the cover page of each disclosure document and in Item 2 of the offering circular, and included in the litigation disclosure set forth in Item 3 of the offering circular. In a multistate offering, the UFOC Guidelines permit a franchisor who uses a single offering circular to use an exhibit to refer to those personnel and brokers that differ from state to state.[63]

Advertising

As shown in Exhibit 2-F, most of the registration states require that any advertising for the sale of franchises, or other promotional materials used in conjunction with the offer or sale of franchises, be filed with state authorities before using such advertising or materials in that state (unless the franchisor has perfected an exemption from registration in that state).[64] While the states that require advertising to be filed generally do not issue formal approval of filed advertising, it is prudent for the franchisor to use an advertisement only after receiving a return file-stamped copy of the advertisement from the applicable state. Maryland[65] specifically requires clearance of the advertisement prior to use, and New York requires the filing of a verification by the franchisor that the advertisement is consistent with the disclosure statement. Several of the states also have requirements regarding the content of advertising (for example, disclosure of a disclaimer, the name of franchisor, and state registration number).[66]

It is important to remember that the state filing requirements apply to advertising for franchise sales; these restrictions do not apply to advertising for the goods and services offered by the franchisor or its franchisees. As with several other areas of franchise law, there may be applicable exemptions to the advertising filing requirements. If sales personnel have any questions in this regard, they should be encouraged to contact the in-house legal department or outside counsel, as applicable. The franchisor should require that all advertising or printed promotional material concerning franchise sales be approved by the franchisor's in-house legal department or outside counsel, as applicable, prior to use. In addition, the franchisor should maintain a schedule documenting the filing of all franchise sales advertising and promotional materials with the appropriate state agencies. Records of the filing of franchise sales advertising should be maintained. A sample tracking form is attached as Exhibit 2-G.

Amendments and Renewals

A franchisor is obligated to update its FTC and state franchise disclosure documents upon the occurrence of a material change. Additionally, as described above, in those states that require registration of the franchise offering, the registration must be renewed or an annual report must be filed on an annual basis.

Material Changes

Franchisors are obligated to amend their offering circulars immediately upon the occurrence of any material change to the information to ensure that the offering circular contains all pertinent and up-to-date information required for disclosure to prospective franchisees. The most common material change to occur for every franchisor is the annual issuance of its audited financial statements.

The FTC Rule defines a material change as "any fact, circumstance, or set of conditions which has a substantial likelihood of influencing a reasonable franchisee or a reasonable prospective franchisee in the making of a significant decision relating to a named franchised business or which has any significant financial impact on a franchisee or prospective franchisee."[67]

In addition, some state franchise laws specifically set forth events which constitute a material change in that state, some of which events may (arguably) *not* constitute a material change within the meaning of the FTC Rule.[68]

Types of changes that would generally trigger the need to amend the franchisor's offering circular include

1. terminating or failing to renew a substantial portion of the franchisor's franchisees;
2. a significant change in the franchisor's management;
3. an adverse change in the franchisor's financial condition;
4. a change in the terms of the offering itself (for example, a change in the fees imposed on franchisees);
5. a significant change in corporate structure; or
6. acquisition or franchising of competitive concepts.

The time within which registration states require the filing of an amendment for a material change varies from state to state and is generally measured by imprecise standards (for example, "promptly," or "as soon as reasonably possible").[69]

Commencement of Amendment and Renewal Process

As a practical matter, unless "interim" amendments are required because of a material change or because a renewal deadline in a particular state does not coincide with the issuance of a franchisor's financial statements, the franchisor will only amend its FTC and state disclosure documents on an annual basis. The annual updating and amendment process necessary to disclose the franchisor's most recent audited financial statements will generally commence upon the close of the franchisor's fiscal year. Upon issuance of the franchisor's annual audited financial statements, the updated offering circular is prepared for use in the nonregistration states, and necessary annual report, amendment, or renewal filings are made in the appropriate registration states. It is desirable that the renewal date for every renewal state occur within 90 to 120 days *after* the end of the franchisor's fiscal year, concurrent with the time the franchisor's audited financial report is released (60 days in Hawaii).[70] If the renewal date in any state does not coincide with the issuance of the audited financial report, the franchisor may effect a change in the renewal date for the next year by filing an early renewal application at the time of the issuance of the financial report.

Effect on Sales Activities

When a material change occurs (including the issuance of the franchisor's annual audited financial statements), all sales activities in the nonregistration states must cease until the nonregistration state offering circular (roll-up) is updated and ready for use by the franchisor. From a practical standpoint, however, because the disclosure document used in nonregistration states is not reviewed or registered by any federal or state regulatory body, any annual amendment and/or interim material amendment, with careful planning and prompt amending where required, should not halt the franchisor's sales activities in such states for a prolonged period of time.

In most registration states, a material change requires the cessation of all sales activities pending approval of an amendment. There are, however, exceptions to this general rule; California, Illinois, New York, Virginia, and Wisconsin allow for the continued offer of franchises pending effectiveness of an amendment so long as such offers are conducted in accordance with their regulations. The amendment and review process generally entails less time and fewer comments by a state regulator than initial registration or the renewal process. Because state law requires that an offering circular marked to show changes be included in the application, the examiner is typically reviewing only the changes to the documents, not the entire offering circular and exhibits.

Upon the filing of all renewal applications or annual reports in which a material change has occurred, as required by appropriate state registration laws, all offer and sales activities must cease. Currently, there are no provisions allowing continued offers and sales pending review and approval of the franchisor's renewal applications, with the exception of the states of California, Illinois, New York, and Virginia. In Illinois, an annual report must be filed not later than one day before the anniversary date of the registration, and the franchisor may continue to offer and sell unless notified by the Illinois Attorney General's Office that additional information or modification of the disclosure document is required. In Virginia, if the renewal (or amendment) application is accompanied by an executed Affidavit of Compliance, the application becomes effective upon receipt by the State Corporation Commission (or a date specified by the franchisor), unless (1) the franchisor has been convicted of any crime or been held liable in a civil action by final judgment since its last application; (2) the franchisor is insolvent or in danger of becoming insolvent; or (3) the revised offering circular submitted with the application is not in compliance with Virginia's franchise rules.[71] If the application does not qualify for automatic effectiveness in Virginia, it will become effective only upon the date granted by the Commission.[72] California and New York law permit the franchisor to continue to conduct offers, as specified under applicable law in the state, during the period when an amendment or renewal/annual report application is pending, but not to conclude any sales during that period.[73]

Document Use, Filing, and Control

The franchisor is encouraged to set up strict filing and control procedures that meet the following recommendations:

1. As described above, all disclosure documents will indicate on the cover page the appropriate state in which the document may be used and the

effective date, or in the case of a roll-up offering circular, in an addenda or exhibit to the offering circular. A master or roll-up offering circular will be used in nonregistration states. Each registration/disclosure state requires that the registered document be used for franchise sales in that state. An offering circular containing state-specific disclosures is also used for exempt offerings.

2. Central document control will be administered by the franchisor's counsel. When an amended disclosure document is forwarded to the franchisor, care must be taken to remove from salespersons and store or to destroy all outdated disclosure documents and to update the franchisor's current disclosure document files. Separate files should be maintained for each registration/disclosure or exempt state.

3. The appropriate documents will be forwarded to each person responsible for conducting franchise sales. Each salesperson should maintain adequate files so that the franchisor's current disclosure document is readily identifiable. The franchisor's legal department should monitor compliance with this practice.

4. If there is any question as to the appropriate document to be distributed at any time, each salesperson should contact the franchisor's counsel.

5. A disclosure document (including the offering circular and the completed agreement) should be given at the appropriate times to each prospective franchisee, or an authorized representative, if the franchisee is a corporation or other entity, and each principal who additionally is to execute the agreement as a guarantor. If there is any question regarding which individuals should receive disclosure in any proposed sales transaction, the salesperson should consult counsel.

6. Upon delivery of each disclosure document, an executed Receipt form should be obtained from the prospective franchisee and each principal or other person executing the agreement. A compliance tracking form should be prepared for each franchise sold. This form documents and tracks the various disclosure documents and completed agreements distributed to the franchisee and its principals, and dates of distribution, and signed receipt forms by the franchisee and its principals for the offering documents, as well as the completed agreements. As reviewed in Granting the Franchise below, the franchisor should also use and obtain signatures on a Summary of Acknowledgments form (or form similar to that attached as Exhibit 2-H) by the franchisee and each principal at closing. The executed Summary of Acknowledgments is used as an estoppel sheet to document franchisor's compliance. Further, if at the time such sheet is being completed instances of noncompliance come to light, the franchisor has the opportunity to postpone the sale and cure such deficiencies prior to completing the sale of the franchise (and creating a possible cause of action). Such forms must be submitted to the legal department and maintained in the franchisee's file.

7. The files of every salesperson or the central franchise sales file if all records are maintained by a department administrator must show that

appropriate disclosure was delivered. The liability for failing to disclose or delivering inappropriate disclosure is substantial. As discussed below willful violations of state and federal franchise laws carry criminal penalties, civil fines, and create causes of action by prospective franchisees for damages.

Attached as Exhibit 2-I is a sample form to use for each prospective franchisee to track compliance with federal and state franchise registration and disclosure laws.

Permissible Representations

The FTC Rule and all state franchise laws prohibit the making of oral or written representations to a prospective franchisee that are inconsistent with the information and representations contained in the offering circular, as well as any other document filed with the state franchise regulators. If such inconsistent representations are material, those representations may subject the franchisor to civil (and possibly criminal) liability under most franchise laws, and may permit a franchisee to recover substantial damages based on those misrepresentations.

For example, New York's franchise law specifically states:

> No sales literature shall include any representation or statement inconsistent with the prospectus on file with the Department and the franchisor shall verify in a writing submitted with the sales literature, that it is not inconsistent with the filed prospectus.

Moreover, under applicable federal regulations, unless the franchisor's offering circular contains a written earnings claim, no earnings claim or financial performance representations can be made. An earnings claim is defined as "any oral, written or visual representation to a prospective franchisee or for general dissemination in the media which states or suggests a specific level or range of potential or actual sales, income, gross or net profits." Proscribed by this definition are claims such as "earn a $10,000 profit" or a "sales volume of $250,000." Also prohibited are presentation of facts which suggest or from which a prospective franchisee easily could infer a specific level or range of income, sales or profits, such as "earn enough money to buy a new Porsche" or "100 percent return on investment within the first year of operation." Not included in the definition of earnings claim are mere puffery, such as "make big money" or "opportunity of a lifetime." An earnings claim made in connection with the offer or sale of a franchise must be included in full in the offering circular and must have a reasonable basis at the time it is made. The earnings claim must include a description of its factual basis and the material assumptions underlying its preparation and presentation.

If the franchisor includes an earnings claim in its offering circular, the franchisor may deliver to a prospective franchisee a supplemental earnings claim directed to a particular location or circumstance apart from the offering circular. A supplemental earnings claim must be (1) written, (2) explain the departure from the earnings claim in the offering circular, (3) be prepared in accordance with Item 19 of the UFOC Guidelines, and (4) be delivered to the prospective franchisee. The operating records of a franchisor-operated unit may also be provided to a prospective purchaser of that unit, if in addition to the operating records, the prospective purchaser is also provided the last known name and address of prior owners for the preceding three years.

It is therefore important that (1) franchisor personnel who will have direct contact with prospective franchisees have a working knowledge of the representations contained in the current offering documents, in all approved advertisements, brochures, and other promotional material, and in the manual; and (2) franchisees and developers and their principals acknowledge that all statements made to them were consistent with the representations contained in the current disclosure document. For further information see Summary of Acknowledgments form at Exhibit 2-H and the discussion in Granting the Franchise Legal Consideration.

Negotiation with Prospective Franchisees

Once the offering circular and franchise and related agreements are filed with the appropriate state regulator or have been delivered to a prospective franchisee in any other state, the range of permissible negotiation for the terms of the franchise relationship is narrowed. The registration process restricts much of the negotiation that exists in many other business relationships, unless the flexibility to negotiate is already made part of the agreement at issue. State franchise laws typically permit such negotiations, but may impose certain procedural requirements that make such negotiations impractical. For example, a franchisor must consider the duty it may have to disclose those negotiated changes to future prospective franchisees.

Accordingly, all franchisor personnel who will be in contact with prospective franchisees must make clear to those prospective franchisees that few, if any, amendments or clarifications to the agreements can be expected or will be permitted, and any such amendment must be cleared by the in-house counsel and may need to be discussed with outside counsel.

Private Rights of Action

Because of the litigious nature of franchisor-franchisee relationships, all franchisor personnel should be fully aware of the potential legal consequences of a failure to comply with franchise registration and disclosure laws or the terms of the franchise or related agreements. This section and the following section deal with certain kinds of legal actions that can be commenced by a franchisee (that is, private rights of action) and those that can be instituted by federal and/or state agencies (for example, stop orders, broad remedial powers, restitution, receivership, and criminal liability).

Most state franchise laws and certain state Little FTC Acts (which traditionally prohibit deceptive trade practices) permit franchisees and purchasers of "business opportunities" to seek one or more of the following remedies:

1. *Actual Damages*—All payments expended to acquire and implement the franchise; may also include damages to a franchisee's reputation and lost past and future profits and earnings.

2. *Injunctive Relief*—Preventing franchisor and sales personnel from offering or selling franchises, temporarily or permanently.
3. *Attorneys' Fees*—Related to litigation.
4. *Cost of Litigation*—Court costs and other administrative fees related to litigation.
5. *Treble Damages*—Punitive damages equal to three times a franchisee's actual damages.
6. *Rescission*—Requiring the franchisor to cancel the franchise agreement, to relieve the franchisee from all liability under that agreement and to restore the franchisee to the position he would have been in had the agreement not been executed (for example, return all initial franchise and royalty fees paid).
7. *Other Damages*—For example, punitive damages if permitted by statute.

Administrative Liability Under State and Federal Franchise Laws

In addition to private rights of action that can be brought under state law by a franchisee against a franchisor, its officers, directors, and employees, the state and federal franchise laws provide administrators with an arsenal of powers to regulate the offer and sale of franchises.

Common Characteristics of State Franchise Laws

Several characteristics are common to most state statutes.

1. *Definition of Fraudulent Practices*—Most franchise laws enumerate and define fraudulent and unlawful practices broadly. Any intentional making of an untrue statement of a material fact; any intentional omission of a material fact whose absence renders another statement misleading; any scheme or artifice to defraud; any act or practice which would or does operate as a fraud or deceit; any violation of any franchise law, or rules promulgated thereunder; and any attempt to compel waiver of any given statute's provisions are, in most states, declared fraudulent and unlawful practices.[74]
2. *Record Keeping*—Many state franchise registration statutes mandate that franchisors keep detailed records concerning their finances, franchise sales and expenditures of franchise fee proceeds in certain prescribed periods of time. These records are subject at any time to inspection by state franchise administrators.[75]
3. *Stop Orders*—Most states grant to their franchise administrators the power to issue ex parte stop orders prohibiting any franchise sales activities by individuals or entities who allegedly are violating the franchise statute in question, as well as the power to order the escrow or impound-

ment of franchise fees in instances in which franchisors are unable to demonstrate an ability to fulfill their contractual obligations.[76]

4. *Investigations*—All of the laws grant extremely broad investigative powers to franchise regulators.[77]

5. *Broad Remedial Powers*—Broad remedial powers are conferred upon state franchise administrators over and above their powers to deny registration—and thus franchise sales activity—in their respective states. Stop orders, injunctive relief, cease and desist mechanisms, and declaratory relief provisions are found in the majority of state franchise statutes.[78]

6. *Civil Proceedings*—Most franchise administrators are empowered to institute civil proceedings to seek restitution on behalf of those injured by practices declared fraudulent and illegal, including the right to seek such remedies against a broad range of individuals. Typically, state administrators have the power, at any stage of litigation, to seek and obtain a court-ordered receivership of any and all monies or property derived by a franchisor through fraudulent or unlawful means.[79]

7. *Criminal Liability*—Violation of state franchise laws can result in criminal liability, including felony exposure in many states. While many states can punish the willful violation of their respective franchise laws with substantial fines and/or imprisonment, an equal number can impose similar sanctions for the mere violation of those laws.[80]

8. *Persons Liable*—The number of persons who may be potentially liable for violating these statutes is extremely broad and can include officers, directors, and certain management personnel having responsibility for the administration of the franchise program.[81]

FTC Rule

There currently is no recognized private cause of action under the FTC Rule. The FTC may enforce the FTC Rule either (1) in an administrative proceeding leading to the issuance of a cease and desist order to halt an unfair or deceptive trade practice, with civil penalties of up to $10,000 (per violation) for any violation of such order, or (2) by legal action for an injunction and damages including freezing the assets of the franchisor and its principals.

Implementing Sales Compliance Policies

The purpose of any franchise sales compliance policy is to establish a practical system to facilitate the franchisor's compliance with the web of rather complex due diligence and registration and disclosure considerations discussed in detail earlier in this chapter. Effective implementation of such compliance policies requires a partnership or, at a minimum, extensive cooperation between the franchisor's legal and franchise sales departments. Several tensions are inherent in any implementation effort, including distilling complex due diligence and registration/disclosure considerations and terminology into a useable policy document readily understandable by any clerical employee in the franchisee sales department. Also inherent are those tensions that exist by reason of the often conflicting missions of the franchise sales and legal departments within the franchisor entity.

An effectively implemented set of franchise sales compliance policies balances these tensions and overcomes any conflicting objectives within the franchisor's departments to facilitate the sales process while minimizing the franchisor's liability for violations of state and federal laws and regulations. The franchisor's future success, if not its continued existence, depends on proper implementation of compliance policies throughout all departments and at all levels of the firm.

Role of In-House Counsel

At the outset, corporate counsel must recognize the competing missions of the franchise sales and legal department staffs. The primary objective of the franchise sales department in the start-up franchisor is typically to generate as much revenue as possible through the collection of initial franchise fees and signed franchise agreements. A complementary goal is to obtain as many qualified franchisees as possible so the franchisor can expand rapidly and reach "critical mass" leading to the public's acceptance of the franchisor's concept, products, and/or services. These objectives are typically present within the franchise sales staffs of established franchisors, too, but depending on the established concept's penetration and strategic plans, those efforts may be less intense than those of a start-up franchisor struggling for survival. Regardless of the size of the franchisor, it seeks to build, or improve upon, a base of franchisees for the collection of royalty fees and advertising contributions to enhance the franchisor's profitability, access to media and other marketing tools, and to promote the franchisor's concept in as many markets as possible.

The in-house lawyer (or legal department, if there is more than one lawyer, which is generally not the case in a start-up franchisor) often has a conflicting mission. As with all corporate counsel, and regardless of the financial strength of the franchisor, the goal is to create and preserve the net worth of the corporation, which, in the context of representing the franchisor, means tempering revenue and growth targets with considerations of the potential liabilities inherent in offering and selling franchises. Counsel should instinctively recognize the need for realistic compliance measures and should take the lead to formulate and implement sales compliance policies.

No aspect of the franchisor's sales practices should be immune from counsel's scrutiny in the formulation and implementation process. Compliance policies and programs establish, or, where existing policies are formally organized and adopted, memorialize the series of steps or routine tasks to be followed in selling franchises with due regard for the regulatory framework confronting franchisors. Effective utilization minimizes the in-house lawyer's need to review day-to-day details of the sales process on a regular basis. This in turn allows counsel to allocate more time to legal and business issues requiring expert analysis and recommendation.

Internal Compliance Manual

The most effective means of communicating due diligence requirements and registration and disclosure laws to all of the franchisor's personnel is to draft and circulate an internal compliance "manual" among all franchisor employees who have contact with prospective and existing franchisees. If the drafting or use of a manual is impracticable, then, at a minimum, supervisory employees within the franchise sales department and franchise salespersons should have a checklist, or series of checklists, available to them to assist in monitoring and documenting the process through which a prospective franchisee becomes an existing franchisee.

At the outset, the manual should summarize due diligence considerations and registration and disclosure requirements in the jurisdictions in which the franchisor offers or contemplates offering its franchises for sale. Rather than dwelling on the complexities inherent in the regulatory framework, the manual should focus on the staff's need to complete and document a series of routine tasks before the prospect becomes a franchisee. Where possible, simple steps and rules of thumb should be incorporated into the manual, and the various conflicts or inconsistencies between state and federal laws should be consolidated, if possible, into a single compliance regime. Administrative employees need a system under which pursuing and checking off a series of habitual assignments for each prospective franchisee will satisfy as many jurisdictions as possible. In this regard, as discussed earlier in the Preparation of the Offering Circular section, the franchisor and its counsel should give strong consideration to registering in all states (in which the franchisor has an interest in offering) and providing all prospects with a single roll-up or global Uniform Franchise Offering Circular that is valid in all jurisdictions.

Unfortunately, no manual immunizes the franchisor from all potential liabilities. In-house counsel must continually review the document as regulatory and due diligence requirements evolve based on legislative action and judicial decisions. Furthermore, counsel must monitor, from time to time, the manner in which franchise sales personnel adhere to sales compliance policies. The first step in emphasizing procedures for proper use of the manual, as well as educating sales personnel concerning the applicable regulatory framework, is sales compliance training.

Sales Compliance Training

The in-house practitioner should stress to officers and senior executives of the franchisor the relative cost-effectiveness of thorough, proactive training of the franchise sales force and administrative personnel versus the expense of litigating claims from franchisees or responding to complaints from franchise enforcement officials. Separate training should also be offered to the person charged with administering the franchise program, if such position exists, and any administrative staff in the franchise sales department. Training officers and senior executives of the franchisor should also be encouraged to attend, in order to buttress their understanding of the regulatory environment in which they do business.

Once counsel is generally comfortable with the franchise administrator or compliance officer's administration of the franchise sales department, the initial and continuing training for franchise salespersons and administrative staff should be addressed in detail. After reviewing existing disclosure documents, drafting or revising the manual, and attending at least a few franchise sales presentations to prospective franchisees, in-house counsel should be prepared to begin sales compliance training with franchise salespersons. Initial training of salespersons needs to be expanded from the role playing and recommended closing approaches, which are emphasized in many franchisors' informal training programs, into a thorough familiarization with the franchise offering circular, particularly items 1, 5, 6, 7, 9, and 11. The franchise agreement is the most important of the exhibits to the offering circular, and substantial time should be dedicated to reviewing the franchisor's approach to the underlying business, as reflected in the franchise agreement. Sales compliance training does not end when the new sales employee completes the initial compliance program offered by the franchisor; however, "refresher" training should be made available to, and required of, existing franchise salespersons on a regular basis.

If there are points in the franchise agreement that the franchisor is willing to clarify, or even negotiate, then these should be reviewed at the outset, first between in-house counsel and the franchisor's executives, and then as part of the initial training for franchise salespersons. Most franchisors choose not to negotiate for various legal and business reasons.[82] Counsel should recommend to the franchisor's management that any changes regularly negotiated by the franchisor be disclosed as part of the offering circular, because once the offering circular and any applicable franchise agreements have been filed with the appropriate state regulator, the scope of permissible negotiation narrows in terms of provisions that the franchisor may uniformly change per request by any prospective franchisee. This narrowing does not prohibit the franchisor from addressing a truly novel point raised by a prospect or from clarifying an agreement to reflect the particulars of a prospect's situation. In fact, Virginia law contains a provision requiring the franchisor to negotiate with the prospective franchisee. Nevertheless, the administrative burden placed on disclosure of the terms of the negotiation (by California[83] in particular—including the negotiated sales notice filing requirements), should be kept in mind. If the franchisor is willing to consider either negotiating or clarifying the franchise agreement, then an upper-level manager, such as the vice president of Franchise Sales, should be designated as a point of contact for such discussions. In any event, the franchisor's policies on the negotiation and clarification of franchise agreement provisions should be reviewed in detail as part of initial and refresher sales compliance training.

Counsel (or at least an experienced paralegal) should attempt to participate in the actual training of new franchise salespersons. The use of audio/visual materials and abstracts from the franchisor's actual documents, coupled with detailed review of manual procedures, should be included in all compliance training. From an administrative standpoint, the Legal Department representative in attendance should, prior to the end of the initial training, obtain from each new franchise salesperson an executed franchise salesperson disclosure form containing the background information on the salesperson required under the UFOC Guidelines for filing with the appropriate registration states. Consideration should be given to offering such refresher training to franchise salespersons contemporaneously with the annual renewal/updating process each franchisor undergoes pursuant to the FTC rule and applicable state laws following the end of the franchisor's fiscal year. If the opportunity for live refresher training is not available during this period, then, at a minimum, a memorandum describing changes in the offering circular and other franchise documents should be circulated among existing sales staff, together with a discussion of any other policy changes the franchisor intends to implement in the coming year. The salesperson must complete the new franchise salesperson disclosure form to be submitted to the state regulators with the franchisor's renewal packages. A sample of a memorandum on offering circular changes is attached as Exhibit 2-J to this chapter. If in-person attendance at a refresher course is not feasible, then the memorandum, salesperson disclosure form, and a certificate to be signed by the salesperson can be circulated and collected from the salesperson in the field in order to document the receipt of information on offering circular changes and the fact that the franchise salesperson has accurately updated his information on the salesperson disclosure form.

Internal Auditing and Monitoring Compliance

The drafting and circulation of a manual and the formulation and holding of sales compliance training sessions will provide limited value to the franchisor if the effectiveness of these tools is not monitored or otherwise evaluated. The franchisor should strongly consider monitoring parts of each franchise salesperson's telephone conversations with sales prospects in order to confirm adherence to compliance procedures. In doing so, the franchisor must comply with any applicable legal requirements in connection with such monitoring. A franchise sales executive or legal department employee can monitor all or part of such a sales presentation and then counsel the salesperson with any business or legal points.

Another means of monitoring available to the franchisor is the use of "shoppers," who have been sensitized to the particulars of franchise law. Those shoppers can call headquarters in response to advertising or appear at a trade show booth to engage in initial conversations with franchise salespersons, and to develop such contacts into first personal meetings with franchise salespersons. This tool enables the franchisor to gauge the effectiveness of its compliance programs, based on input from third parties in a simulated, real world sales environment. Written reports from these shoppers, with appropriate follow-up from the franchisor, can assist in documenting the franchisor's commitment to active monitoring and legal compliance.

As a result of these kinds of monitoring programs, or in connection with franchisee complaints or litigation, the in-house attorney will from time to time become aware of a need or opportunity to counsel a salesperson directly on a specific issue. The opportunity may arise based on counsel's general observations or monitoring of a sales presentation. On the other hand, the assertion by a franchisee of allegations that applicable laws have been violated demands immediate attention. Even if counsel's investigation of the facts produces no corroboration of the franchisee's claims, and the franchisor's management decides not to discipline the salesperson in question, the in-house practitioner should insist whenever possible on specific retraining or counseling in compliance procedures for the salesperson against whom such allegations are lodged, particularly where the salesperson has previously been the subject of similar complaints.

The opportunity for internal auditing of administrative personnel within the franchise sales department should occur at least once per year during the update of the offering circular, which is after the end of the franchisor's fiscal year. For example, for each franchise sold during the preceding fiscal year, the first page and signature page of each franchise agreement, together with a copy of the Receipt for the franchise documents signed by the then prospective franchisee, could be reviewed as part of the franchisor's annual update. Accordingly, all sales could be audited 30–60 days prior to fiscal year end in order to determine whether certain documents are missing from the file or additional documents are needed to complete the company's records of the transaction. If the volume of transactions prohibits a review of all files, minimally, a select number of transactions in each region (or market area, depending on how the company allocates its resources) should be audited to ensure that either the manual or compliance checklist(s) are being followed by the appropriate personnel. Deficiencies found in any franchisee's file should be addressed with the administrator of the franchise sales department in order to determine the cause and prevent recurrence. As discussed in the Preparation of the Offering Circular section, a legal department staffer could attend the initial training for franchisees in order to confirm the actual number of hours devoted to each classroom subject and the identity of those employees actually giving instruction in such training. Such an audit would help verify specific disclosures in the offering circular.

Curing Franchise Sales Law Compliance Violations

Establishment of and adherence to internal compliance procedures will substantially reduce the likelihood of franchise sales law violations. Nevertheless, instances of noncompliance may inadvertently occur even in the best-run systems. For example, consider the following scenario: Franchisor has properly disclosed to prospective franchisee the terms of development of unit that will be operated in registration state with franchisor's then-current effective offering circular. In the four months subsequent to the initial disclosure, franchisor's salespersons have had ongoing conversations with prospective franchisee concerning the terms of the franchise agreement and franchisee has been reviewing proposed sites for the unit. Also during that time, the franchisor is involved in litigation with another franchisee to collect royalties, and that franchisee files a counterclaim alleging fraud and state franchise law violations subject to disclosure in Item 3 of the offering circular. Upon the occurrence of this change, franchisor's legal department promptly files its amended offering circular with the appropriate state agencies.

Because of the length of time the parties have been negotiating, the franchisor's salesperson forgets to re-disclose the prospective franchisee with the amended offering circular and that sale closes. One week later the compliance coordinator is organizing the franchisee's files and reviewing the closing binder, or even auditing the files as discussed in the preceding section, and notices that there is a signed Receipt for the earlier offering circular in the file, but not one for the currently effective offering circular.

For purposes of our example, the franchise is to be operated in the state of California and the franchisee's principal place of business (and domicile) is Nevada, and all correspondence and contact with prospective franchisee have taken place either in franchisor's home state (Virginia) or in the state of Nevada. The first step is to determine the jurisdictional scope and applicability of state franchise laws to the transaction to determine which, if any, state law(s) have been violated. Section 31013 of the California Franchise Investment Law states that an offer or sale of a franchise has been made in the state when an offer to sell is made in the state, or an offer to buy is accepted in the state, or if the franchisee is domiciled in the state, and the franchised business is or will be operated in the state. Furthermore, the statute provides that an offer to sell is made in the State of California when the offer either originates from the state or is directed by the offeror to the state and received at the place to which it is directed.[84] In contrast, Section 13.1-599 B. of the Virginia Retail Franchising Act provides that the Act only applies to a franchise where the performance of which contemplates or requires the franchisee to establish a location or maintain a place of business within the Commonwealth of Virginia.[85]

In this circumstance, although there was contact with two registration states, there is no violation of the registration and disclosure laws of either state because neither the conduct of the franchisor and franchisee nor their domiciliary status or development plans trigger jurisdiction of the laws. But consider changing one variable of the scenario: Franchisor and franchisee negotiate and execute the final documents at a meeting in California approving the site for the franchised unit. In this case, the California Franchise Investment Law applies, and the franchisor has therefore violated the law.

In the first scenario, once in-house counsel has determined that no violation of a specific state franchise registration and disclosure law has occurred, the franchisor must determine whether there are any other sources of liability resulting from the franchisor's failure to provide the appropriate disclosure documents (such as, violation of the FTC Rule or state Little FTC Acts).

If there is an applicable Little FTC Act on which a franchisee could rely to bring an action for the alleged failure to comply with the UFOC Guidelines concerning litigation (and as a consequence, a violation of the FTC Rule) the franchisor has, depending on the provisions of the state law, a variety of options to attempt to reduce or eliminate future liability concerning such claims. The franchisor may do nothing and simply wait for the statute of limitations to run for a claim under the Little FTC Act, however such statutes of limitation typically run three to four years.[86] Further, it is better to attempt to limit liability early on while the relationship between the franchisor and franchisee is still in its honeymoon period. At this stage the franchisor should consider taking a more aggressive approach and either notify the franchisee of the inadvertent omission and provide the franchisee with the additional disclosure to review, or provide the additional disclosure and offer the franchisee rescission at this stage when the franchisee is least likely to accept it. Under the common law once the franchisee has notice of the violation or receives an offer of rescission, and fails to act within a reasonable period, the franchisee's causes of action may be barred.[87]

In the second scenario, the circumstances are somewhat more complicated because the inadvertent violation involves the registration and disclosure laws of a state where the franchisor is subject to registration. The approaches to cure will vary depending upon the state, its regulatory requirements, and even the administrator with whom you attempt to cure the breach. As in the nonregistration state where there was an applicable Little FTC Act, the franchisor has the option of doing nothing and waiting for the statute of limitations to expire. Most state franchise laws provide for a three- to four-year statute of limitation for civil liability.[88]

Failure to act poses the additional risk that the state administrator may become aware of the franchisor's violation through means other than those that the franchisor controls (for example, later the franchisee becomes aware of the violation and complains to the state agency, or at renewal time the state agency inquires about the date of sale because of the timing of the amendment). Assuming the franchisor makes the decision to address the situation while there is no other dispute between the franchisor and the franchisee, the franchisor would generally notify the state agency in writing of the inadvertent omission and provide a copy of a letter notifying the franchisee of such omission. If the violation involves California law, as in the example, the franchisor will not have to offer rescission but merely provide notice of violation in accordance with the respective states' requirements. Section 31303 of the California Franchise Investment Law provides that no action may be maintained under the civil liability section of the law unless brought within 90 days after delivery to the franchisee of a written notice disclosing any violation of Sections 31201 or 31202 of the law.[89] The form of notice of violation is prescribed by the California Department of Corporations.[90] With the exception of Illinois, none of the other registration states provide a specific format for issuing notice of violation.[91] In the other states, the franchisor will generally have some flexibility with the content of any notice.

For minor inadvertent infractions of the type described above, if brought to the state administrator's attention by the franchisor, the state administrator often will not require execution of any consent order that must be disclosed in the franchisor's offering circular, and will permit the franchisor to enter into an assurance of discontinuance or similar agreement with the state, which need not be disclosed in the franchisor's offering circular. If voluntarily brought to the administrator's attention, many times the administrator will also require the franchisor to pay little or no civil penalty. If any such penalty is charged, typically it will range between $1,000 and $2,500 per violation, in contrast to the $5,000 to $10,000 per violation a state may try to extract in connection with an enforcement action brought as a result of complaining franchisees.[92] Some administrators may, however, demand that the franchisor enter into a consent order that must be disclosed in the offering circular, regardless of the inadvertence or technicality of the violation. But in those circumstances where the franchisor has brought the violation to the state administrator's attention, there is generally greater flexibility in the description included in the offering circular. As a result, the franchisor can mitigate any negative impact it may have on its disclosure statement by drafting a disclosure in which the franchisor describes how it voluntarily brought the infraction to the administrator's attention and voluntarily offered rescission, rather than pursuant to an order of the state.

If an alleged violation is brought to the attention of franchise regulators, an investigation by state and federal agencies can take a variety of forms depending on the authority of the agency, the alleged conduct on the part of the franchisor, and the perceived threat of future consumer injury. Such action may range from a telephone call or a letter inquiring about the alleged conduct, to a civil investigative demand or subpoena accompanied by an order requiring the franchisor to cease and desist selling franchises or other specific conduct that is alleged to be in violation of a particular law.[93]

Granting the Franchise

Legal Considerations

Prior to execution of any of the binding franchise or related agreement by franchisor, the legal department must conduct its own due diligence to confirm compliance with all applicable franchise registration and disclosure laws. The franchisor's legal department tenders copies (as determined by franchisor procedures) of the franchise agreement and/or related agreements to the franchisor representative that is responsible for the execution of the agreement(s). No agreement will be so tendered, however, unless (1) the prospective franchisee and its principals have been given all disclosure documents in accordance with the FTC Rule and state law, if applicable; (2) the franchisor has received the fully executed receipt of the applicable offering circular from the franchisee and all principals named in the agreement; and (3) the appropriate time has passed between the date of the prospective franchisee's receipt of the offering circular and the date set for the agreement's execution. As stated previously, the agreement must be completed (with all blanks filled in) and provided to the prospective franchisee for at least five business days prior to execution. The delivery requirement of ten business days and the five business day requirement are separate requirements which must be independently satisfied; however, the former can run concurrently with the latter.

As part of that due diligence, the legal department should require that the franchisee and all of the franchisee's principals complete and sign the Summary of Acknowledgments form. All pages of the agreements must be reviewed prior to signature to determine that no changes or modifications have been made by the franchisee. The legal department must review all checks to confirm they are dated properly, to verify addresses, and to verify that the checks are signed by someone who is a party (or has the authority to sign on behalf of a party) to the franchise agreement and who has received proper disclosure. If money is being provided by a third person who is not a party to the agreements, a letter to the franchisor from the franchisee describing the nature and relationship of the person who is making the payment and identifying the nature of the payment (for example, payment is being made by the franchisee's father-in-law and the payment is a loan to the franchisee), and acknowledging that the payor is not a party to the agreement.

Business Considerations

Business realities often overshadow the legal considerations in the granting of a franchise. Because of state licensing requirements, certain franchisors may be compelled to require that the franchisee, or a majority owner of the franchisee, hold a valid state license for the business conducted under the franchisor's system. For example, real estate agency franchisors typically must require that the franchisee have a valid real estate broker's license in the state in which the franchisee intends to do business, and a pharmacy franchisor may need for the franchisee to be a licensed pharmacist in the state where the pharmacy franchise is to be established. Even if strict licensing requirements do not exist in a particular industry, the franchisor, depending on the business it franchises, may require a substantial background in its industry, or at least a demonstrated skill level in that type of business. On the other hand, restaurant franchisors often take the position that their franchisees do not have to be the chef or the cook; their criteria for potential success as a franchisee often include success in a business endeavor in another industry or in middle-management where systems or procedures must be followed in order to achieve business objectives.

Financial considerations are often paramount in reviewing the franchisee's qualifications. The franchisor may have only two or three financing programs available to its franchisees, and, if these are made available by outside lenders pursuant to an arrangement with the franchisor, then the lenders' criteria must be strictly followed. Accordingly, a franchisee with substantial cash and little home equity or other collateral may be a candidate for an equipment leasing program. Whereas a prospect with the minimum amount of cash required and substantial loanable equity in assets such as homes and other real estate may fit the profile of a U.S. Small Business Administration (SBA)-guaranteed loan applicant. A challenge most often arises from the standpoint of business considerations when the franchisor is presented with a marginal candidate based on financial qualifications.

The franchisor should follow established procedures when processing the franchisee's application, whether it appears qualified or not. Administrative personnel in the franchise sales department should approach this process in the same manner that the manual procedures are consulted in the processing of legal documentation with the initial disclosure and other follow-up concerning the prospective franchisee. One franchise sales clerical employee can be assigned the routine task of ordering credit and reference checks, or reference checks and employment history can be verified in-house by a mid-level administrative employee or executive. A candidate with minimal assets (according to a balance sheet and income statement) who has an acceptable credit report and a positive employment history may well be financeable under one or more of the franchisee financing programs. The franchisor should keep in mind that many franchisees understate their assets in the initial balance sheet; accordingly, administrative employees possessing a background in financing should interview each franchisee regarding his assets, liabilities, and employment history in order to maximize the likelihood of obtaining financing and establishing the unit.

To summarize the business considerations in granting the franchise, the franchisor must have established procedures, similar to the sales compliance policies embodied in the manual, for processing prospective franchisees from a financial and business standpoint. If the franchisor fails to organize itself in weighing business considerations in the grant of the franchise, then it potentially exposes itself to liability if many of its new franchisees fail. Moreover, one or more of the financing programs that the franchisor has worked hard to establish may be discontinued if there are repeated failures throughout the franchise system.

Coordinating Growth Strategies and Compliance for Litigation Avoidance

Traditional and Nontraditional System Expansion

As franchise systems mature and the marketplace and distribution methods become more sophisticated, disputes over inter-brand and intra-brand competition continue to provide fodder for lawsuits and law review articles.[94] Rather than provide an exhaustive analysis of the legal issues concerning claims of encroachment and the implied covenant of good faith and fair dealing, this section attempts to present a practical approach to assist in-house counsel in coordinating the franchisor's expansion plans; legal documents; and policies and procedures to manage risk; and the franchisor's exposure to claims involving such issues.

Systems expand and distribute their goods and services through a variety of means. Traditional expansion occurs through franchised and company owned units; nontraditional expansion includes kiosks, carts, food courts, and other alternative distribution sites. Further, cobranded or multibrand distribution relationships, distribution of product through retailers, catalog sales, infomercials, and even sales through the Internet are all commonplace today. The methods and means for distribution are limited only by the imagination and the ability of sales people. Of course, there are also practical constraints imposed by the terms of

existing and future generations of franchising, licensing, or distribution contracts, federal and state laws and regulation, case law, and economic matters
such as the need for the franchisor and franchisee to earn a reasonable return on
investment. When a company directly markets its products and services to its
ultimate customers, the company's ability to make decisions about whether or
not to (1) locate another unit in close proximity to an existing unit to prevent a
competitor from penetrating a given market, or (2) market its products through
retailers (for example, grocery stores or convenience stores) in direct competition with its company-owned outlets, is limited by its own business judgment
about what is the most effective means for marketing its goods or services, since
any negative impact by its decisions will only be felt by itself. Disputes tend to
arise when a company decides to segment or divide the manner in which its
products are delivered through the use of third parties (franchisees, distributors,
dealers, manufactures representatives, licensees). In a nutshell, system expansion and claims of "encroachment" only become a problem when, in so doing,
the company breaches a duty to, or violates a legally protected interest of, a third
party.[95]

Disputes generally occur when one party acts in a manner inconsistent with
the expectations of another party. Transactional costs in resolving such disputes
aside, from a legal perspective, those acts giving rise to disputes only become significant when they are inconsistent with the *reasonable* expectations of the other
party. One function of in-house counsel (or outside counsel), with the cooperation of the management and sales personnel, is to control, through the agreements, the disclosure in the offering circular, internal and external policies and
procedures, and the reasonable expectations of the franchisee with regard to the
rights that it is receiving. Franchisees typically bring claims for breaches of the
express terms of the contract, breaches of the implied covenant of good faith and
fair dealing (where the contract is silent or unclear on a particular issue, or the
conduct has been unconscionable, in bad faith, or in violation of stated company
policy),[96] and violations of specific state and federal laws and regulations.[97]

The implied covenant of good faith and fair dealing is universally described
to prohibit one party from acting in a fashion to prevent the other party from
enjoying the benefits the other is entitled to receive under the contract.[98] However, as a general premise, the courts have ruled that the implied covenant cannot be used to override the express terms of the agreement.[99]

In formulating its expansion plans and preparing contracts, together with
offering documents reflective of such plans, there are as many formulations as
there are subindustries and growth strategies in franchising. However, if there is
a common thread underlying the cases, it is that the franchisor should not attempt
to assert broad expansion rights by implication from a territorial or grant clause
in reliance on the clause's silence with respect to the rights granted to the franchisee or rights reserved to the franchisor. Instead, the franchisor should state all of
the various rights it plans to reserve to itself and not assume that the universe of
rights not expressly granted to the franchisee is expressly reserved to the franchisor
by implication. In order to illustrate the varying levels of complexity dictated by

industry considerations and the growth strategies of different franchisors, this chapter compares a number of clauses from franchise agreements that set forth the respective rights of the parties with respect to territorial protections and system expansion. Attached as Exhibit 2-E to this chapter are the actual pages from the agreements of those franchisors discussed and the Item 12 disclosure from their respective offering circulars. Item 12 is the section of the offering circular in which the franchisor must disclose the nature of any territorial protections that the franchisor grants to the franchisee, as well as the franchisor's rights to operate competitive businesses.

One common method used in describing the territorial rights (or lack thereof) granted to franchisees under the agreement is referred to as site specific franchising. Under this method the franchisee is granted the right to operate the franchised business only at the specific site where the franchised business has been approved to be located, and no other territorial protections are granted. Set forth in Appendices A and B, respectively, are excerpts from the McDonald's Franchise Agreement and Burger King Franchise Agreement detailing each franchisor's approach to site-specific grants of territorial rights. Each of these excerpts has been the subject of recent litigation involving alleged breaches of the implied covenant of good faith and fair dealing.[100]

In *Chang v. McDonald's Corp.*, the franchisee claimed that McDonald's had breached the express terms of the franchise agreement and the implied covenant of good faith and fair dealing by placing two new restaurants in the vicinity of Chang's business. In order to prevail under Illinois law on a claim that McDonald's had breached a duty under the implied covenant of good faith and fair dealing, Chang was obligated to prove that McDonald's had acted with an improper motive or inconsistent with the reasonable expectations of the parties. Absent evidence of any improper motive, the court held that:

> [Chang]'s reasonable expectations based on the express terms of the License Agreement . . . must have been that [McDonald's] could establish new restaurants. The License Agreement's express provision against territorial protection of [Chang] means that [Chang] could not have reasonably expected protection from [McDonald's] expansion.[101]

The language of the *Chang* contract is concise and simply indicates that the rights granted under the franchise agreement "are limited to the Restaurant's location only," and that no "exclusive," "protected," or other territorial rights are granted. Consequently, the provision at issue contains no express reservation to permit the franchisor to license or establish additional restaurants in the vicinity of the franchisee's restaurant. Nevertheless, the *Chang* court ruled in favor of the franchisor, finding the language to be clear on its face. The holding in *Payne v. McDonald's Corp.* was substantially the same. Applying Illinois law, the *Payne* court noted that in the absence of an ambiguity, Payne could not rely on the implied covenant of good faith and fair dealing, and that there "was no provision in the agreement that imposes a limitation on McDonald's right to open new restaurants near its existing franchisees."[102]

While the site-specific grant clause in the Burger King contract (see Appendix 2-B) is conceptually identical to that contained in its largest competitor's agreement, Burger King has experienced mixed results in litigation. In *Scheck v. Burger King Corp.*, the court, applying Florida law, ruled that:

> The express denial of an exclusive territorial interest to Scheck does not necessarily imply a wholly different right to Burger King—the right to open other proximate franchises at will regardless of their effect on plaintiff's operations. It is clear that while Scheck is not entitled to an exclusive territory, he is entitled to expect that Burger King will not act to destroy the right of franchisee to enjoy the fruits of the contract.[103]

In response to plaintiff's reliance on *Scheck*, the *Payne* court pointed out that the *Scheck* decision has been disavowed by other courts in the Southern District of Florida. Further, citing to several other decisions of the U.S. District Court for the Southern District of Florida,[104] the *Payne* court noted that the express terms of the Burger King contract permit Burger King to open additional restaurants in the vicinity of its existing franchisees, and that absent a breach of an express term of the contract, a claim for breach of the implied covenant of good faith and fair dealing cannot be maintained.[105]

The 11th Circuit Court also followed this line of reasoning in *Burger King v. Weaver*.[106] The court held that in Florida, there is no independent cause of action for breach of the implied covenant of good faith and fair dealing. In this case, Burger King established a restaurant near Weaver's two franchised locations, which he operated under two separate franchise agreements. One of the franchise agreements contained a statement clarifying that the franchisee was not granted any territorial rights, but neither agreement carved out explicit reservations of Burger King's right to locate additional restaurants. Weaver stopped paying Burger King amounts due, and Burger King consequently sued to recover those amounts. Weaver counterclaimed, but Burger King received summary judgment on all counterclaims, except for the claim of breach of the implied covenant. Several years later, though, the court granted the motion for summary judgment. Calling *Scheck* flawed and "unconvincing logically," the court stated that a claim for breach of the implied covenant cannot be maintained where it is contrary to the express terms of the contract, or in the absence of a breach of the express terms of the contract.

While *Scheck* and its progeny appear to have fallen out of judicial favor, at least temporarily,[107] the detailed grant and impact clauses Burger King uses in its Target Reservation Agreement (attached as Appendix 2-C) for developers establish a communication-intensive set of procedures for managing expansion. The specificity of the contractual terms outlining the placement of new locations in relation to existing units, method and content of notification, and the analysis of impact provides a stark contrast to the concise language of the franchise agreement.

In addition to traditional territorial expansion issues, the nontraditional expansion of many franchise systems through kiosks, carts, food courts, and other alternative distribution methods, together with cobranded or multibrand distribution relationships, has sparked further debate and the inevitable litigation that follows. Franchisors who contemplate such nontraditional methods as part of their expansion plans should expressly reserve such rights contractually. To avoid disputes, it is critical that the franchisee's expectations are consistent with the franchisor's expansion plans. Attached as Appendices 2-D and 2-E, respectively, are two excerpts from agreements used by Dunkin' Donuts, a franchisor at the forefront of nontraditional expansion, to illustrate how the company has contractually attempted to retain flexibility in its growth plans, while pursuing alternative distribution methods and cobranding.

As demonstrated in Appendix 2-D, the Dunkin' Donuts franchise agreement provides that the franchisee is not entitled to any territorial protections, and, moreover, expressly states that the franchisor may use the proprietary marks and/or system at shops and other locations that may compete for customers drawn from the same area. By implication, the franchisee may experience competition from any number of sources authorized by franchisor in the vicinity of franchisee's Dunkin' Donuts Shop. In its Store Development Agreement (excerpts attached as Appendix 2-E) for its joint Baskin Robbins/Dunkin' Donuts units, Dunkin' Donuts provides certain territorial protections by agreeing not to place any new units within a specified development area. The company also specifically outlines the limitations on the exclusivity provided in the development area and describes in detail a variety of "special distribution opportunities" that may arise within the development area that are excluded from such protections. Thus, when territorial exclusivity is granted, a franchisor should consider the nature of the exclusivity granted and the conditions for maintaining that exclusivity, while expressly identifying the type of activity the franchisor will not conduct within the territory (that is, Dunkin's refraining from opening new units). Additionally, the franchisor should identify any rights for other distribution methods that it wishes to reserve for itself (for example, special distribution opportunities).

The issues faced by a franchisor in drafting its contract provisions or territorial clauses will vary depending on the industry and the services offered, as well as the demand for territorial protections by its franchisees. The excerpt from the Cottman Transmission Franchise Agreement attached as Appendix 2-F is an example of the franchisor's straightforward grant of certain territorial protections to the franchisee. Because of the nature of the services provided under the Cottman Franchise Agreement, the franchisor has reserved few additional rights to itself.

In contrast to the relatively uncomplicated automotive aftermarket granting clause in Appendix 2-F, extensive language from the Ramada Franchise Systems, Inc. franchise agreement is attached as Appendix 2-G. Ramada is a subsidiary of Cendant (formerly HFS), which owns through its subsidiaries a variety of franchise brands in several different industries. Ramada reserves broad traditional and nontraditional expansion rights for not only the Ramada brand, but for the entire Cendant family of brands in its franchise agreement. For the new or seasoned in-house practitioner, the Ramada provisions stand as a benchmark in expansion rights draftsmanship.

Communication of Expansion Policies with Franchisees

As indicated above, the complexity of franchisor expansion policies varies from system to system. Start-up franchisors, and even many mid-size franchisors, particularly those in traditionally oriented industries have rudimentary expansion policies. In contrast, many larger franchisors with hundreds of units and multi-brand franchisors operating under diverse brands have elaborate notification policies and procedures.[108]

If the start-up franchisor has an expansion policy with notification provisions, such a policy is typically promulgated in the operations manual or monthly newsletter. After simple notification to existing franchisees within a certain distance of the proposed unit, the franchisor awaits franchisee input. The final decision generally remains with the franchisor for antitrust and business reasons. On the other hand, the multibranded franchisor Cendant has highlighted the essentials of the notification aspects of expansion policies for its brands as follows:

1. Publication of Policy
2. Franchisee Input
3. Triggering Event
4. Zone of Notice
5. Type of Notice
6. Response Period
7. Response Criteria
8. Evaluation Period
9. Decision Criteria
10. Referral to Independent Evaluator
11. Evaluation Cost Allocation
12. Ultimate Decision Maker
13. Notice of Decision
14. Appeal Process
15. Dispute Resolution Mechanism[109]

Franchisors establish and communicate expansion policies to franchisees for many reasons. First, franchisors with a long-term perspective seek orderly growth with minimal conflict. Second, a set of established procedures facilitates the exchange of information between the brand owner and its existing franchisees; and, even if the franchisee perceived to be most affected is not persuaded by the franchisor's rationale for the proposed expansion, the franchisee, and any supporters in the system, at least have the opportunity to express their concerns in an informal, non-adversarial setting. Finally, expansion policies with notification protocols may provide the franchisor with an effective shield against encroachment claims. Nevertheless, franchisors with thorough policies and procedures must remain cognizant of the fact that such programs, once communicated to franchisees, may be used as a sword against the franchisor, if the franchisor acts in bad faith or in a manner that is contrary to an established policy or procedure.

In *Century 21 Real Estate Corp. v. Hometown Real Estate Co.*,[110] a jury found that the franchisor's failure to abide by its unwritten policy was unconscionable under the Texas Consumer Protection Statute. The case involved a franchisor's unwritten policy of not placing a second franchise in an area served by an existing franchisee with at least 30 percent of the market (the "30 percent rule"). The existing franchisee (Hometown) had been a Century 21 franchisee for approximately 12 years when it sought to renew its franchise in 1992. Neither the franchise agreement nor the offering circular in the *Hometown* case referred to the 30 percent rule, which Century 21 acknowledged to be a company marketing policy. The franchise agreement, however, expressly stated that the franchisee received no territorial rights or protected area.

The appellate court in *Hometown* upheld the jury's verdict for the plaintiff, finding sufficient evidence to support the claim that Century 21 had engaged in an unconscionable action or series of actions with respect to the renewal. Accordingly, the finding that the franchisor took advantage of Hometown "to a grossly unfair degree" was sustained on appeal.[111] The *Hometown* court relied, among other things, on evidence that representatives of Century 21 stated to the franchisee that letter agreements memorializing the market share policy as an amendment to the franchise agreement were not available. Additionally instructive to the court was the admission by the franchisor's president that, had Century 21 known of Hometown's true market share (closer to 40 percent rather than the 9 percent to 18 percent that had been calculated in error), then the franchisor would not have proceeded with the second franchisee.

Likewise, in *Scheck,* a case recognized predominantly for the issue of whether the implied covenant of good faith and fair dealing can override the express terms of a written contract,[112] the franchisee introduced evidence that Burger King had failed to comply with its own policies. The *Scheck* court noted that "Burger King itself has developed specific policies and procedures to protect against the cannibalization and potential ruin of other Burger King franchises." The court found in part that Burger King's failure to comply with its own policies to protect against encroachment was one of the bases of the franchisee's claim.

In *Payne,* the court also reviewed McDonald's encroachment and "rewrite" policies on the operation of the license agreement in weighing various claims asserted by the plaintiff who had, for a number of years, owned several McDonald's restaurants in Baltimore, Maryland. To support his breach of contract claim in the face of Paragraph 28(e) included in part in Appendix 2-A, the plaintiff contended that McDonald's internal policy against encroachment was incorporated into the parties' license agreement. The court found, however, that the provision relied on by the franchisee to support his incorporation theory referred only to "operational obligations" and "the details of restaurant operations." Moreover, the *Payne* court held that "the integration clause contained in the License Agreement does not permit the [franchisee] to rely on documents not expressly incorporated therein." Persuasive to the court was the integration clause's clear statement that the agreement "contains all the terms, conditions and obligations of the parties." Finally, the complete and unambiguous license agreement evidenced no intent that any other extrinsic document be incorporated by reference to supply additional contract terms.

The integration clause at issue in *Hometown,* discussed above, was disregarded by the court in view of a jury finding that the franchisor and its wholly-owned subsidiary and subfranchisor had acted unconscionably under the Texas Deceptive Trade Practices Act (DTPA). The court found that "despite the integration clause and other contract provisions, Hometown believed that Century 21 would abide by its unwritten policy." Given that the "DTPA is to be liberally construed to effectuate its primary purpose: to protect consumers from deceptive business practices and to provide them with a cause of action without the numerous defenses found in common-law fraud, breach of warranty, or other contract actions," the court allowed the franchisee to recover under the statute.[113]

Conclusion

Managing the franchise sales activity and growth of a franchise system is a continuing challenge for legal counsel, as the methods through which systems expand continue to multiply and evolve. Internal policies and programs that facilitate compliance with regulatory requirements, promote the management of system expansion, and foster sound relationships with franchisees are necessary for the continued long term health of any franchise system. In the era of "managed" health care, a well managed franchise compliance program, organized and executed according to the best practices set forth in this chapter, should contribute significantly to the well being of the franchise system, while providing in-house counsel a means to avoid catastrophic injury.

Notes

The authors of this chapter wish to thank Kerry R. Jensen, University of Minnesota Class of 2000, Summer Associate with Gray Plant Mooty, for cite-checking.

1. Portions of this chapter were excerpted from an internal compliance manual prepared by Joyce Mazero, Ann Hurwitz, Jan Gilbert, Mark Forseth and other associates of Jenkens & Gilchrist; *See also* Grover C. Outland III, COUNSELING THE FRANCHISOR'S SALES AND OPERATIONS STAFF *presented at* 1996 American Bar Association Forum on Franchising (Mini-Program).

2. *See* 16 C.F.R. § 436, 2 Bus. Franchise Guide (CCH) ¶ 6090.

3. *See* 1 Bus. Franchise Guide (CCH) ¶¶ 3050 (Cal.), 3110 (Haw.), 3130 (Ill.), 3140 (Ind.), 3200 (Md.), 3220 (Mich.), 3230 (Minn.), 3320 (N.Y.), 3340 (N.D.), 3370 (Or.), 3390 (R.I.), 3410 (S.D.), 3460 (Va.), 3470 (Wash.), 3490 (Wis.).

4. *See* 1 Bus. Franchise Guide (CCH) ¶ 3050.

5. *See* 1 Bus. Franchise Guide (CCH) ¶ 3320. N.Y. Gen. Bus. Law, Art. 33, §§ 680– 695 became effective January 1, 1981.

6. These statements are generalities. It will vary from state to state, as described below, whether the offering must be registered or filed, whether and when advertising must be filed, and the circumstances and manner in which salespersons must be registered.

7. *See* 1 Bus. Franchise Guide (CCH) ¶¶ 3018 (Ala.), 3058 (Cal.), 3078 (Conn.), 3098 (Fla.), 3108 (Ga.), 3138 (Ill.), 3148 (Ind.), 3150 (Iowa), 3178 (Ky.), 3188 (La.), 3198 (Me.), 3208 (Md.), 3328 (Mich.), 3278 (Neb.), 3298 (N.H.), 3338 (N.C.), 3358 (Ohio), 3368 (Okla.), 3408 (S.C.), 3418 (S.D.), 3438 (Tex.), 3448 (Utah), 3468 (Va.), 3478 (Wash.).

8. *See* 2 Bus. Franchise Guide (CCH) ¶ 6204.

9. *See* 2 Bus. Franchise Guide (CCH) ¶ 5700 *et seq.*

10. *See* 2 Bus. Franchise Guide (CCH) ¶ 6206.

11. *See id.*

12. *See* 2 Bus. Franchise Guide (CCH) ¶ 6207.

13. *See* 2 Bus. Franchise Guide (CCH) ¶ 6205.

14. *See* 2 Bus. Franchise Guide (CCH) ¶ 6100.

15. *See* 2 Bus. Franchise Guide (CCH) ¶ 6183.

16. *See* 2 Bus. Franchise Guide (CCH) ¶ 6222.

17. *See id.; see also* "The Offer of a Franchise" on page 6 for more information on those states.

18. *See* 2 Bus. Franchise Guide ¶ 6172.

19. *See* 2 Bus. Franchise Guide ¶ 6178.

20. *See* 2 Bus. Franchise Guide ¶ 6170.

21. *See* 2 Bus. Franchise Guide (CCH) ¶ 6171.

22. *See* 2 Bus. Franchise Guide (CCH) ¶ 6149.

23. *See* 1 Bus. Franchise Guide (CCH) ¶ 3050.

24. *See* 1 Bus. Franchise Guide (CCH) ¶¶ 3050.29, 3130.10, 3140.09, 3200.14, 3230.02, 3320.04, 3340.03, 3390.05, 3410.06, 3460.04, 3470.02.

25. *See* Bus. Franchise Guide (CCH) ¶ 3110.03.

26. *See* 1 Bus. Franchise Guide (CCH) ¶ 3220.07a.

27. *See* 1 Bus. Franchise Guide (CCH) ¶ 3490.08.

28. *See* 1 Bus. Franchise Guide (CCH) ¶ 3370.01.

29. This Chart, and other similar charts showing state jurisdictional coverage, have been published in a variety of forms, including the Compliance Manual referred to in Endnote 1; Baer, Costello, Duvall, Mazero, and Wulff, "Application of U.S. Franchise Laws to International Franchise Sales," *International Bar Association,* May, 1996; Zeidman, Lowell, and Heller, *Franchising and Distribution* (materials furnished with ESI/George Washington University Course (1997–98)); and Zeidman and Lowell, *Franchising* (materials furnished with Federal Publications Course (1985–96)).

30. Salespersons should also determine whether a business opportunity state is involved. These states may require the franchisor to file, or otherwise be exempt or excluded from registration before the offer or sale of a franchise within their jurisdiction.

31. *See, e.g.,* 1 Bus. Franchise Guide (CCH) ¶¶ 3340.02(14), 3130.03(c)(iii)(12).

32. *See, e.g.,* 1 Bus. Franchise Guide (CCH) ¶¶ 3200.03, 3410.10.

33. *See, e.g.,* 1 Bus. Franchise Guide (CCH) ¶¶ 3140.01(d), 3130.03(c)(iii)(9).

34. *See* 1 Bus. Franchise Guide (CCH) ¶¶ 3050.25, 3140.03, 5200.11, 3320.05, 3340.04, 3390.06, 3410.12.

35. *See* 1 Bus. Franchise Guide (CCH) ¶ 3050.25.

36. *See* 1 Bus. Franchise Guide (CCH) ¶ 3140.03.

37. *See* 1 Bus. Franchise Guide (CCH) ¶ 5200.11.

38. *See* 1 Bus. Franchise Guide (CCH) ¶ 3320.05. Please also note that even though the statue does not specifically require an offering circular be provided, the FTC Rule disclosure requirements still apply.

39. *See, e.g.,* 1 Bus. Franchise Guide (CCH) ¶ 3338.01. The North Carolina Business Opportunity Sales Act defines a "business opportunity" to mean the sale or lease of any products, equipment, supplies, or services for the purpose of enabling the purchaser to start a business, and in which the seller represents: (1) That the seller will provide locations or assist the purchaser in finding locations for the use or operation of vending machines, racks, display cases, or other similar devices, or currency-operated amusement machines or devices, on premises neither owned nor leased by the purchaser or seller; or (2) that it may, in the ordinary course of business, purchase any or all products made, produced, fabricated, grown, bred, or modified by the purchaser using in whole or in part, the supplies, services, or chattels sold to the purchaser; or (3) the seller guarantees that the purchaser will derive income from the business opportunity which exceeds the price paid

for the business opportunity; or that seller will refund all or part of the price paid for the business opportunity, or repurchase any of the products, equipment, supplies, or chattels supplied by the seller, if the purchaser is unsatisfied with the business opportunity and pays to the seller an initial, required consideration which exceeds two hundred dollars ($200.00); or (4) that it will provide a sales program or marketing program which will enable the purchaser to derive income from the business opportunity which exceeds the price paid for the business opportunity, provided that this subsection shall not apply to the sale of a marketing program made in conjunction with the licensing of a federally registered trademark or a federally registered service mark, or when the purchaser pays less than two hundred dollars ($200.00).

If franchisor offers a marketing program in connection with the licensing of a federally registered mark and does not meet any of the other definitional elements of a business opportunity, then the act does not apply to the franchisor.

40. *See* 1 Bus. Franchise Guide (CCH) ¶ 3438.06.

41. *See* 1 Bus. Franchise Guide (CCH) ¶ 3278.22.

42. *See* 1 Bus. Franchise Guide (CCH) ¶ 3178.04.

43. *See* 1 Bus. Franchise Guide (CCH) ¶ 3098.026.

44. *See* 1 Bus. Franchise Guide (CCH) ¶ 3448.045.

45. *See* 1 Bus. Franchise guide (CCH) ¶¶ 3098.01 (Cal.), 3448.02 (Utah). Similar to the N.C. statute described *supra,* note 39, both the California and Utah Business Opportunity acts exclude from the definition of a business opportunity the offer of a marketing program in conjunction with a registered mark. Therefore, franchisors who do not meet any of the other required elements and have a registered trademark are excluded from the definition of a business opportunity under the acts. A franchisor that otherwise meets the definition of a business opportunity, but complies with the FTC Rule disclosure requirement, may file and claim an exemption from the registration and disclosure requirement of the Florida and Utah acts.

46. *See* 1 Bus. Franchise Guide (CCH) ¶ 3228.01.

47. *See* 1 Bus. Franchise Guide (CCH) ¶ 6208.

48. *See* 2 Bus. Franchise Guide (CCH) ¶ 6100.

49. 60 Fed. Reg. 17,656 (1995).

50. *See* 2 Bus. Franchise Guide (CCH) ¶¶ 5753–5775.

51. *See* 2 Bus. Franchise Guide (CCH) ¶ 5760.

52. *See* 2 Bus. Franchise Guide (CCH) ¶ 5763E.

53. *See* 2 Bus. Franchise Guide (CCH) ¶¶ 5776–5781.

54. *See* 1 Bus. Franchise Guide (CCH) ¶ 3050.30(b).

55. *See* 1 Bus. Franchise Guide (CCH) ¶ 5200.14.

56. *See* 1 Bus. Franchise Guide (CCH) ¶¶ 3050.40, 3140.18, 3200.19(b), 3340.07(5).

57. *See* 1 Bus. Franchise Guide (CCH) ¶ 3130.10.

58. *See* 1 Bus. Franchise Guide (CCH) ¶ 310.120.

59. *See* 1 Bus. Franchise Guide (CCH) ¶ 3200.03.

60. *See* 1 Bus. Franchise Guide (CCH) ¶ 3140.02.

61. *See* 1 Bus. Franchise Guide (CCH) ¶ 3460.03.

62. *See* 1 Bus. Franchise Guide (CCH) ¶ 3050.281.

63. *See* 2 Bus. Franchise Guide (CCH) ¶ 5902.

64. No advertising filing is required to be made in any state in which the franchisor is exempt. Of the 11 states that require the filing of advertising, California, Indiana, Maryland, New York, North Dakota, Rhode Island, and Washington provide that the franchisor does not need to pre-file advertising that is published in a newspaper or other publication that has had more than two-thirds of its circulation outside of the state during the past year. In addition, in South Dakota and Wisconsin, the franchisor does not need to pre-file advertising that is published in any newspaper or other publication that is not published in the state. Minnesota contains no comparable exemption from filing.

65. *See* 1 Bus. Franchise Guide (CCH) ¶ 3200.25.

66. *See, e.g.,* 1 Bus. Franchise Guide (CCH) ¶¶ 5200.09 (Md.), 5050.34 (Cal.).

67. *See* 2 Bus. Franchise Guide (CCH) ¶ 6182.

68. *See* 1 Bus. Franchise Guide (CCH) ¶ 5130.11. Illinois defines a material change to include *any* increase or decrease in the initial or continuing fees charged by the franchisor.

69. *See, e.g.,* 1 Bus. Franchise Guide (CCH) ¶ 3050.42, 3050.44 (Cal.) ("Promptly" after a material change in the information contained in the registered application, by application to amend. Application to amend must contain specified disclosure.); ¶ 3110.03 (Haw.) (If any material change occurs in the information contained in the offering circular, the offering circular must be amended before further sales of the franchise are made; ¶ 3130.11 (Ill.) ("Within 90 days of the occurrence" of any material change in the facts required to be disclosed. Re-disclosure required if material changes relates to or affects franchisor or the franchisee. Amendment not required if changes merely reflect negotiated changes.); ¶ 3140.20 (Ind.) ("Promptly" after a material change in the information in an effective registration, by application to amend.); ¶ 3200.20 (Md.) ("Promptly" after a material change in the information contained in the registered application, by application to amend.); ¶ 3220.19 (Mich.) ("Promptly" after any change in the information contained in the notice as originally submitted or amended.); 3230.07 (Minn.) (Within thirty (30) days after the occurrence of any material change in the information on file with the Commissioner, by application to amend.); ¶ 3320.04, § 683.9(a) (N.Y.) ("Promptly" after any material change, by application to amend.); ¶ 3340.07, § 51-19-07.6(a) (N.D.) ("Promptly" after any material change, by application to amend.); ¶ 3390.11 (R.I.) ("Promptly" after any material change, by application to amend.); ¶ 3410.40 (S.D.) (Within thirty (30) days after the occurrence of any material change in the information on file, by application to amend.) ¶ (Va.) ("Upon the occurrence" of any material change, by application to amend.); 3470.07(3) (Wash.) ("As soon as reasonably possible" after a material change in the condition of the franchisor or subfranchisor and after a material change in the information contained in the offering circular and in any case, before the further sale of any franchise, by application to amend.); ¶ 3490.13(1) (Wis.) (Within thirty (30) days after the happening of any material event affecting a registered franchise, by application to amend.).

70. *See* 1 Bus. Franchise Guide (CCH) ¶ 3110.03.

71. *See* 1 Bus. Franchise Guide (CCH) ¶ 5460.06.

72. *See id.*

73. *See* 1 Bus. Franchise Guide (CCH) ¶¶ 3050.283, 3320.04.

74. *See, e.g.,* 1 Bus. Franchise Guide (CCH) ¶¶ 3200.29–31, 3140.27, 3050.53.

75. *See, e.g.,* 1 Bus. Franchise Guide (CCH) ¶ 3200.24.

76. *See, e.g.,* 1 Bus. Franchise Guide (CCH) ¶ 3050.45.

77. *See, e.g.,* 1 Bus. Franchise Guide (CCH) ¶ 3050.34.

78. *See, e.g.,* 1 Bus. Franchise Guide (CCH) ¶ 3050.68–70.

79. *See, e.g.,* 1 Bus. Franchise Guide (CCH) ¶ 3050.725.

80. *See, e.g.,* 1 Bus. Franchise Guide (CCH) ¶ 3050.72.

81. *See, e.g.,* 1 Bus. Franchise Guide (CCH) ¶ 3050.62.

82. *See* A. K. Blair & L. D. Imber, COUNSELING TO AVOID SALES LAW VIOLATIONS, *presented at* Twenty-Fifth Annual Legal Symposium, International Franchise Association, at 12–13 (1992).

83. *See* 1 Bus. Franchise Guide (CCH) ¶ 3050.44.

84. *See* 1 Bus. Franchise Guide (CCH) ¶ 3050.15.

85. *See* 1 Bus. Franchise Guide (CCH) ¶ 3460.3.

86. *See, e.g.,* 1 Bus. Franchise Guide (CCH) ¶¶ 3017 (Ala.), 3447 (Utah), 3517 (D.C.).

87. *See* Bagel Enter. v. Baskin & Sears, 467 A.2d 533, 541 (Md. Ct. Spec. App. 1983).

88. *See, e.g.,* 1 Bus. Franchise Guide (CCH) ¶¶ 3050.725 (Cal.), 3130.24 (Ill.), 3140.30 (Ind.).

89. *See* 1 Bus. Franchise Guide (CCH) ¶ 3050.64.

90. *See* 1 Bus. Franchise Guide (CCH) ¶ 5050.37.

91. *See* 1 Bus. Franchise Guide (CCH) ¶ 3130.23.

92. *See, e.g.,* 1 Bus. Franchise Guide (CCH) ¶¶ 3050.725(a) (Cal.), 3078.14(b) (Conn.), 3098.08(2)(b) (Fla.).

93. *See, e.g.,* 1 Bus Franchise Guide (CCH) ¶¶ 3050.69 (Cal.), 3078.12 (Conn.), 3140.33 (Ind.).

94. Encroachment, and the implied covenant of good faith and fair dealing, have been the subject of numerous papers and articles. The following is a list several recent publications on the subject: Dienelt, Keyes, Lovejoy, Selden and Shapiro, *Expansion and Conflict: Issues That Arise As The Franchise System Grows,* 30th International Franchise Association Legal Symposium, Tab 17 (1997); Coldwell and Dienelt, *Gerrymandering: When Is System Expansion Encroachment,* 1996 American Bar Association Forum on Franchising Vol. 2; Dady, Goldman and Modell, *Encroachment: A Lyrical Look,* 29th International Franchise Association Legal Symposium, Tab 9 (1995); Dady and Giresi, *Encroachment: A Matter Of Good Faith,* 1995 American Bar Association Forum On Franchising Vol. 1.

95. See Coldwell and Dienelt, *Gerrymandering: When Is System Expansion Encroachment,* 1996 American Bar Association Forum on Franchising Vol. 2, at page 1, where the authors note that Black's Law Dictionary defines "encroach" as [to] enter by gradual steps or stealth into the possessions or rights of *another* (Emphasis added).

96. *See* Scheck v. Burger King Corp, 756 F. Supp. 543 (S.D. Fla. 1991), *on rehearing,* 798 F. Supp. 692 (S.D. Fla. 1992).

97. *See* Century 21 Real Estate Corp. v. Hometown Real Estate Co., 890 S.W. 2d 118 (Tex. App.—Texarkana 1994).

98. *See* Scheck v. Burger King Corp, 756 F. Supp. 543 (S.D. Fla. 1991), on rehearing, 798 F. Supp. 692 (S.D. Florida 1992); Vylene Enterprises, Inc. v. Naugles Inc., 90 F.3d 1472 (9th Cir. 1996).

99. *See, e.g.,* Domed Stadium v. Holiday Inns, 732 F.2d 480 (5th Cir. 1984); Burger King Corp. v. Weaver, Bus. Franchise Guide (CCH) ¶ 10672 (S.D. Fla. 1995); Chang v. McDonald's Corp., Bus. Franchise Guide (CCH) ¶ 10677 (N.D. Cal. 1995).

100. *See, e.g.,* Chang v. McDonald's Corp., Bus. Franchise Guide (CCH) ¶ 10,677 (N.D. Cal. 1995); Payne v. McDonald's Corp., Bus. Franchise Guide (CCH) ¶ 11,140 (D.Md. 1997); Scheck v. Burger King Corp, 756 F. Supp. 543 (S.D. Fla. 1991), *on rehearing,* 798 F. Supp. 692 (S.D. Fla. 1992); Burger King Corp. v. Weaver, No. 96-5438, 1999 U.S. App. Lexis 3635 (11th Cir. Mar. 9, 1999).

101. *See* Dienelt, Keyes, Lovejoy, Selden and Shapiro, *Expansion and Conflict: Issues that Arise as the Franchise System Grows,* 30th International Franchise Association Legal Symposium, at page 13, *citing Chang,* Bus. Franchise guide (CCH) ¶ 10,677 at 26,730.

102. *Payne,* Bus. Franchise Guide (CCH) ¶ 11,140 at 29,321.

103. *See* Coldwell and Dienelt, *Gerrymandering: When Is System Expansion Encroachment,* 1996 American Bar Association Forum on Franchising Vol. 2, at 7, *citing* Sheck v. Burger King Corp., 756 F. Supp. 543, 549 (S.D. Fla. 1991).

104. Barnes v. Burger King Corp., 932 F. Supp. 1420 (S.D. Fla. 1996); Burger King Corp. v. Holder, 844 F. Supp. 1528 (S.D. Fla. 1993); Burger King Corp. v. Weaver, Bus. Franchise Guide (CCH) ¶ 10,762 (S.D. Fla. 1995).

105. Bus. Franchise Guide (CCH) ¶ 11,140 at 29,322.

106. Burger King v. Weaver, No. 96-5438, 1999 U.S. App. Lexis 3635 (11th Cir. Mar. 9, 1999).

107. *See, e.g.,* Camp Creek Hospitality Inns, Inc. v. Sheraton Franchise Corp., 139 F. 3d 1396 (11th Cir. 1998); *Carvel Corp. v. Baker.,* Bus. Franchise Guide (CCH) ¶ 11,208 (D. Conn. July 22, 1997); *but see Davis v. McDonalds Corp.,* Bus. Franchise Guide ¶ 11,387 (N.D. Fla. March 30, 1998).

108. *See* Appendices C and E.

109. *See id.*

110. 890 S.W. 2d 118 (Tex.App.—Texarkana 1994).

111. *See id,* at 127.

112. Scheck v. Burger King Corp., 756 F. Supp. 543 (S.D. Fla. 1991) on *rehearing,* 798 F. Supp. 692 (S.D. Fla. 1992).

113. *See supra* note 110 at 130–131.

EXHIBIT 2-A: Chart of State Franchise Law Jurisdictional Requirements

As of September, 1998

Statute applies if one of the following are met:	CA[1]	HA[2,3]	IL[4]	IN	MD[1]	MI[3]	MN[1]	NY	ND	OR	RI[1]	SD	VA	WA	WI[1]
a. offer to sell originates in state	X	X	X[9]		X	X	X	X	X	X	X	X		X[5]	X
b. offer to sell directed by franchisor to state and received at place to which it was directed	X	X	X[9]		X	X	X	X	X	X	X	X		X	X
c. offer to buy accepted in state[6]	X	X	X[9]		X	X	X	X	X	X	X	X		X	X
d. offer or sale made to franchisee domiciled in state and franchise is or will be operated in state (regardless of site of offer/acceptance)[7]	X					X			X	X	X[8]	X			
e. franchise operated in state (regardless of site of offer/acceptance/operation)				X	X		X							X	
f. offer/sale made to resident (regardless of site of offer/acceptance/operation)				X	X									X	
g. offer to person domiciled in state (regardless of state in which business is to be located)			X												
h. franchisor contemplates/requires franchisee to establish or maintain a place of business in state													X		

NOTES

[1] The California statute exempts offers, sales or transfers to residents of another state or jurisdiction if the franchised business is located outside California. The Minnesota state registration statute/regulation exempts "out-of-state sales" in which:

a. the offer or sale is made to one who is not a resident of the state;

b. the offer or sale is made to a person who is not (to the seller's knowledge) domiciled in the state;

c. the offer or sale is made to a person who is not actually present in the state;

d. the franchised business is not to be operated in the state; and

e. the sale is not in violation of the law of any foreign jurisdiction.

The Rhode Island statutory exemption contains each of the above requirements, except b. The Wisconsin state registration statute/regulation which exempts "out-of-state sales" contains the elements provided in b, d and e. The Maryland state registration statute/regulation which exempts "out-of-state sales" contains the elements provided in a, d and e.

[2] In Hawaii, an "offer" or "offer to sell" includes every attempt or offer to dispose of and solicitation of an offer to buy a franchise or an interest in a franchise. No other jurisdictional provisions are provided.

[3] The Hawaii and Michigan statute exempt from coverage an offer or sale where the franchisee or prospective franchisee is not domiciled in the state and the franchised business will not be operated in the state.

[4] Illinois' antifraud provisions are broader in scope than the general jurisdiction provisions of the Act, and apply if (1) an offer to sell or buy is made in the state and accepted within or outside the state, (2) an offer to sell or buy is made outside of the state and accepted in the state, (3) the offeree is domiciled in the state, or (4) the franchised business is or will be located in the state.

[5] In Washington, an offer to sell that originates from the state is subject to the state's jurisdiction if it violates the franchise or business opportunity law of the foreign jurisdiction in which it is accepted.

[6] An offer generally is deemed to be accepted in the state when the franchisee directs it to the franchisor in the state, reasonably believing the franchisor to be in the state, and it is received in the state at the place (or by the franchisor) to which (or to whom) it was directed.

[7] The franchise may be deemed to be operated in the state if the franchise agreement simply provides for a sales territory in the state. It may not be necessary for the franchise to be located in the state.

[8] The Rhode Island statute applies if the offer is made to a resident of the state and is to be operated in the state.

[9] These criteria apply only if the franchise business is or will be located in Illinois.

Applicable Statutory and Regulatory Provisions

California	Secs. 31013, 31105; Reg. 310.100.1.
Hawaii	Secs. 482E-2, 4(a)(4).
Illinois	Secs. 3, 6, 10.
Indiana	Sec. 2.
Maryland	Sec. 14-203; Reg. 10.B.
Michigan	Secs. 445.1504, 1506(d).
Minnesota	Secs. 80C.03(h), .19.
New York	Sec. 681.12.
North Dakota	Sec. 51-19-02.14.
Oregon	Sec. 650.015.
Rhode Island	Sec. 19-28-4., 7.
South Dakota	Sec. 37-5A-7.1, 7.2.
Virginia	Sec. 13.1-559.B.
Washington	Sec. 19.100.020.
Wisconsin	Secs. 553.59; Reg. 32.05(1)(d).

EXHIBIT 2-B: Salesperson's Franchise Law Jurisdictional Checklist

1. Where is the franchise business to be operated?

State, City, or Metropolitan Area: _____

2. Who will be the franchisee?

Name (s) of Individual (s) _____

_____

_____

Name of Corporation/Partnership/LLC: _____

State of Incorporation/Formation: _____

Name (s) of Officers, Directors, Shareholders, Partners, Members, Interestholders

Name	Office Held (for example, Director, Gen Partner, Managing Member)	Percentage and Type of Ownership Interest
_____	_____	_____
_____	_____	_____
_____	_____	_____
_____	_____	_____

3. Where is franchisee's residence, principal place of business and/or domicile (including all principal interest holders)?

Name	Residence/Domicile	Principal Place of Business
_____	_____	_____
_____	_____	_____
_____	_____	_____

4. Prior to the closing of the sale, where will franchisor salespersons communicate with franchisee or its principals (for example, to which state or states will franchisor be sending information or making telephone calls)?

Name	Address
_____	_____
_____	_____
_____	_____
_____	_____
_____	_____

EXHIBIT 2-C: Registration Summary Checklist

[Company Name]
Fiscal Year End: [FYE1]   [CURRENT DATE]   **Maryland Quarterly Sales Reports:

Jurisdiction	Application Sent	Effective Date	Expiration Date	Amendment Sent	Amendment Effective Date	Advanced Renewal Filing Time	Renewal Filing Deadline	Comments
FTC						N/A	N/A	
California						15 business days		Annual Report
Hawaii						W/in 60 days of fye		Annual Report
Illinois			Anniversary Date:			1 day before anniversary date		
Indiana						30 days		
Kentucky (Business Opportunity State)			N/A	N/A	N/A	N/A	N/A	Exemption filing (1 time only).
Maryland								**
Michigan						15 business days		Notice of Intent Filing (annually)
						None		Annual Report
Minnesota						W/in 120 days after fye		
Nebraska (Business Opportunity State)			N/A	N/A	N/A	N/A	N/A	Exemption filing (1 time only). Seller Assisted Marketing Plan Act Section 59-1722
New York						W/in 120 days of fye		Annual Report
North Dakota						15 business days		
Oregon						N/A	N/A	Disclosure only
Rhode Island						30 days		Annual Report
South Dakota						W/in 120 days of fye		
Texas (Business Opportunity State)			N/A	N/A	N/A	N/A	N/A	Exception filing (1 time only).
Virginia						30 days		
Washington						15 business days		Notice filing (Prior to sale).
Wisconsin						1 day before expiration		1 year registration

107

EXHIBIT 2-D-1: Questionnaire for Directors, Trustees, General Partners, Officers, and Executives

INSTRUCTIONS FOR COMPLETION

1. THE FOLLOWING QUESTIONNAIRE IS DESIGNED TO PROVIDE INFORMATION FOR SEVERAL SECTIONS OF THE FRANCHISE OFFERING CIRCULAR AS WELL AS SALESMAN DISCLOSURE FORMS REQUIRED FOR FRANCHISE REGISTRATION IN MOST STATES. THE QUESTIONNAIRE IS DESIGNED FOR SIMPLICITY AND CLARITY; THEREFORE, THE QUESTIONS ASKED ARE AS INCLUSIVE AS POSSIBLE. PLEASE RESPOND TO EACH QUESTION EVEN IF THE RESPONSE IS NEGATIVE; YOUR COMPLETE RESPONSE WILL GREATLY ASSIST IN THE PREPARATION OF THE FRANCHISE OFFERING CIRCULAR.
2. PLEASE PROVIDE INFORMATION FOR THE PAST FIVE YEARS.
3. AN INDIVIDUAL MAY HAVE ONLY ONE "PRINCIPAL OCCUPATION" AT ANY GIVEN TIME. A DIRECTORSHIP OF A CORPORATION GENERALLY IS NOT CONSIDERED A PRINCIPAL OCCUPATION.
4. PLEASE TYPE, PRINT, OR WRITE CLEARLY.
5. PLEASE PRINT YOUR NAME AND SIGN THE QUESTIONNAIRE ON THE LAST PAGE.

Please fill in all information requested:

A.　1.　Name:
　　2.　Home address and telephone number:
　　3.　Date of Birth:
　　4.　Social Security Number:
　　5.　Are you a director of the Company?_____
　　6.　Is your current principal occupation as an officer or other employee of the Company?____If yes,
　　　　a.　what office or position do you currently hold with the Company?

　　　　b.　what is the beginning date (by month and year) of the position which you currently hold with the Company? _____

　　　　c.　will you be engaged in franchise sales for the Company? _____
　　　　　　If yes, please list the states in which you will engage in franchise sales for the Company, or note that it will be all states, if that is the case.)

　　　　d.　do you have management responsibility in connection with the operation of the Company's business relating to franchises? _____

7. If your current principal occupation is not a position or office with the Company, please provide:
   a. your current principal occupation or employment by title or description

   _____
   _____

   b. your current employer _____

   _____

   c. beginning date (by month and year) of your current position or employment

   _____

   d. city and state in which your employer is located _____

   e. city and state in which your employment is located, if other than (d).

   _____

8. Please provide the following information for the employment or position which you held immediately preceding your current principal occupation:
   a. principal occupation or employment by title or description _____

   _____

   b. name of previous employer _____

   _____

   c. beginning and ending dates (by month and year) of this position or employment _____

   d. city and state in which your employment was located _____

   _____

9. Please provide the information requested in paragraph 8 for each principal occupation which you have held for the last five full years. (If more space is needed, please attach a separate sheet.)

   _____
   _____
   _____
   _____
   _____
   _____
   _____

B. 1. Are you, at the present time
   • a defendant in a pending criminal action,
   • a defendant, or defendant to a counterclaim, in any pending civil matter, including any arbitration, or
   • a party to a pending administrative action, which alleges a violation of:
     • any franchise law _____
     • any antitrust law _____
     • any securities law _____
     • fraud _____
     • unfair or deceptive practices _____
     • or comparable allegations _____; or
     • a defendant or defendant to a counterclaim in any pending civil matter, other than the litigation noted above, involving more than one franchisee or having a potentially significant impact on the Company because of the size, nature or financial condition of the Company or its business operations _____

   _____

2. Have you ever
   - been convicted of any felony _____
   - pleaded nolo contendere to any felony _____, or

Within the last 10 years:

   - been held liable in a civil action by final judgment _____, or
   - been the subject of a complaint or been the subject of any other legal proceedings, involving a violation of:
     - franchise law _____
     - securities law _____
     - antitrust law _____
     - fraud _____
     - unfair or deceptive practices _____
     - or comparable allegations _____
   - been a defendant or defendant to a counterclaim in any civil matter, other than the litigation noted above, involving more than one franchisee or having a potentially significant impact on the Company because of the size, nature or financial condition of the Company or its business operations

If the answer to any of the questions in Section B.1. or 2. is yes, please provide the following information below:

a   Names of all the parties
b. Court in which action filed
c. Date of filing
d. Docket number
e. Legal and factual nature of claims asserted
f. Your relationship to defendant or party bringing the action (for example, former franchisee, supplier, and so on)
g. For pending actions, the current status of the action and the relief sought
h. For actions no longer pending, the disposition of the case, including the damages or penalties assessed and the specific terms of any conviction or settlement

_____
_____
_____
_____
_____
_____
_____
_____
_____
_____
_____

Note: If requested, provide copies of the pleadings to the Legal Department. Any determination about the "materiality" of any litigation will be made by the Legal Department. Use additional paper, if necessary, to fully describe this information.

3. Are you, at the present time,
   - subject to any currently effective injunctive or restrictive order or decree _____,

- subject to an effective injunction or restrictive order under any federal, state or Canadian franchise, securities, antitrust, trade regulation or trade practice law as a result of a concluded or pending action or proceeding brought by a public agency _____, or
- subject to any currently effective order of any national securities association or national securities exchange (as defined in the Securities Exchange Act of 1934) suspending or expelling you from membership in such association or exchange _____

If so, please provide the following information below:

   a. the name of the person subject to the order or decree

   b. the public agency and/or court

   c. a summary of the allegations or facts found by the court or agency, and

   d. the date, nature, terms and conditions of the order or decree

_____
_____
_____
_____
_____
_____
_____
_____
_____
_____
_____

Note: The terms of all confidential settlements entered into after April 25, 1993, must be disclosed.

C. *Bankruptcy*

  1. During the ten-year period prior to this date, did you ever

- file as a debtor (or had filed against you) a petition to start an action under the U.S. Bankruptcy Code _____
- obtain a discharge of your debts under the Bankruptcy Code _____
- reorganize due to insolvency _____
- serve as a principal officer of any company or general partner in any partnership that either filed as a debtor (or had filed against it) a petition to start an action under the U.S. Bankruptcy Code or obtained a discharge of debts under the Bankruptcy Code within one year after you held such position _____.

  2. Are you presently the subject of any pending bankruptcy or reorganization proceedings? _____

  3. If your answer to any of the questions concerning bankruptcy is affirmative, please provide the following information below:

    a. the name of the person or company that was the debtor and the debtor's relationship to the Company

    b. the date of the filing (if pending) or judgment (if discharged)

c. any other material facts or circumstances, including the court and the docket or case number

_____
_____
_____
_____
_____

Note: Cases, actions, or other proceedings under the laws of foreign countries should be disclosed, including any cases, actions or proceedings under the laws of foreign countries if such took place under the U.S. Bankruptcy Code.

_____
Signature

_____
Name (Printed)

_____
Date

EXHIBIT 2-D-2: Information for Item 8

Type: Restrictions on Sources of Products and Services (Item 8)

Department: _____

Contact Person: _____

(Person who will respond to preparer's questions or prepare the information needed).

Update Reporting Requirement: _____

Using the chart below, for each obligation describe:

1. The goods, services, supplies, fixtures, equipment, inventory, computer hardware and software, or real estate that a franchisee is required to purchase or lease from the Company or its affiliate. This includes a description of any purchases or leases a franchisee may make from the Company or its affiliate because the Company or its affiliate is an approved supplier. For all required purchases from the Company, describe the precise basis by which the Company will derive revenue from purchases by franchisees by stating the Company's total revenues and the Company's revenues from all required purchases and leases of products and services by franchisees. Also, state the percentage of the Company's total revenues represented by such required purchases or leases. For all required purchases from the Company's affiliates, state the affiliate's revenues from sales or leases to franchisees. These amounts should be taken from the Company's statement of operations (or profit and loss statement) from the most recent annual audited financial statement attached to the offering circular. If the Company's annual audited financial statement is not available, describe the source of the information. If any affiliate sells or leases required products or services to franchisees, disclose the sources of information used in computing revenues.

Product or Service	Total Amount Paid to the Company or Affiliate Last Fiscal Year for Product or Service	Purchased from the Company or Affiliate
_____	_____	_____
_____	_____	_____
_____	_____	_____
_____	_____	_____
_____	_____	_____
_____	_____	_____
_____	_____	_____

2. Other than the Company or its affiliates, the goods, services, supplies, fixtures, equipment, inventory, computer hardware and software or real estate that is required to be purchased or leased from suppliers approved or designated by the Company or in accordance with specifications of the Company. Describe the precise basis by which the

Company will derive revenue as a result of purchases by the franchisee. The basis of any payment includes any payments, rebates, fees, contributions of equipment or supplies, or lower prices made available to the Company or its affiliates as a result of purchases by franchisees.

Product or Service	Identify Name of Approved or Designated Supplier or Specification Requirements	Amount of Payment	Basis of Any Payment to the Company or its Affiliates (Include Formula or Flat Amount)	Total Payments to the Company or its Affiliates in Last Year

    a. What are the Company's total revenues? _____

    b. What is the Company's percentage of revenue from all required purchases and leases of products and services by franchisees as described in the foregoing charts?
_____
_____

    c. What are the total revenues from all required purchases or leases from affiliates? _____

NOTE: These disclosures may be made on an aggregate basis in the offering circular.

3. Describe the manner in which the Company issues and modifies specifications and standards or grants or revokes approval of suppliers:
_____
_____
_____

    a. Are specifications and standards issued to franchisees and subfranchisors?
_____

    b. Are specifications and standards issued to approved suppliers? _____

    c. Describe how suppliers are approved or disapproved. _____

    d. State whether criteria for approval is made available to franchisees, to suppliers proposed by a franchisee, or only to a limited number of suppliers selected by the Company in each market area? _____
_____
_____

e. Describe the procedures and fees to obtain approval of a product, service, or proposed supplier. _____

_____
_____
_____
_____
_____
_____
_____
_____
_____
_____
_____
_____
_____
_____
_____
_____

f. Describe the time periods for approval or disapproval. _____

_____
_____

4. List the categories of products and services for which the Company is an approved supplier. _____

_____
_____
_____

5. List the categories of products and services for which persons affiliated with the Company are approved suppliers. _____

_____
_____
_____

6. Underline the categories of products and services listed in paragraph 1. above for which the Company is the only approved supplier. Underline the categories of products and services listed in paragraph 1. above for which a person affiliated with the Company is the only approved supplier. If the Company and/or persons affiliated with the Company are the only approved suppliers, please state the reasons therefor: _____

_____
_____

7. State whether the Company negotiates purchase arrangements with suppliers (including price terms) for the benefit of franchisees. _____

_____
_____

8. State whether the Company provides material benefits (for example renewal or granting additional franchises) to a franchisee based on a franchisee's use of designated or approved sources. _____

_____
_____
_____

9. Estimate the percentage of the total goods and services necessary for the establishment of the business in relation to the cost of the goods and services required to be purchased or leased from the Company, its affiliates or other approved suppliers. _____

_____

_____

10. Estimate the percentage of the total goods and services required to continue the operation of the franchise in relation to the cost of the goods and services purchased or leased from the Company, its affiliates or other approved suppliers. _____

_____

_____

11. If any purchasing or distribution cooperatives exist, describe such cooperatives.

_____

_____

_____

Completed on the ___day of _____, 20 ____.

By: _____

Name: _____

(Contact Person)

EXHIBIT 2-D-3: Information for Training

Type: The Company's Obligations (Item 11)

Department: _____

Contact Person: _____
> (Person who will respond to preparer's questions or prepare the information needed).

Update Reporting Requirement: _____

Please describe the following information concerning the Company's training program:

1. Will the Company provide a training program? _____
   If so, describe the program _____
   _____
   _____
   _____

   Where will it be located? _____
   _____
   Who determines the location of the training? _____
   _____
   To whom is the training made available? _____
   _____
   _____
   _____

   Who is required to attend the training? _____
2. What is the length of time the franchisee will be trained at this location? _____
   _____
   _____

3. What instructional materials and procedures will be used? _____
   _____
   _____

4. Must the program be completed to the Company's satisfaction? _____
5. When and how often will the training program be conducted? _____
   _____
   _____

6. Does the Company maintain a training staff with franchise business operations and other relevant experience? _____
7. If so, state the position and principal duties of each member of the training staff.
   _____
   _____
   _____
   _____

8. Set forth the prior experience of each member of the training staff with the Company and any other relevant experience? _____
   _____
   _____
   _____
   _____

9. Will the Company charge for the training or any training materials? _____
   _____

If so, describe same. (These charges would also be disclosed in Items 5 and 6, as applicable.) _____

_____

_____

_____

10. Who pays the transportation charges of trainees to and from the training site?

_____

_____

11. Who pays for the living expenses of trainees? _____

_____

12. Will the Company pay any compensation to franchisee or his employees during training? _____

If so, please describe. _____

_____

_____

_____

_____

13. Is the training program mandatory? _____

14. If not mandatory, what percentage of new franchisees entered the training program during the 12 month period immediately prior hereto? _____

15. Does the Company plan to offer additional training and/or refresher courses?

_____

16. If so, will such courses be mandatory? _____

17. Will the franchisee have to pay for such courses? _____

18. Who pays transportation expenses and living expenses of trainees? _____

19. Where will such refresher courses or additional training be held? _____

_____

20. How long will such courses last? _____

21. What will be the content of such additional training programs? _____

_____

_____

Please complete the following table to state the subjects taught and the number of classroom and "on the job training" hours devoted to each subject.

Subject	Time Begun	Instructional Material	Hours of Classroom Training	Hours of on the Job Training	Instructor
_____	_____	_____	_____	_____	_____
_____	_____	_____	_____	_____	_____
_____	_____	_____	_____	_____	_____
_____	_____	_____	_____	_____	_____

NOTES:

Completed on the _____day of _____, 19/20__.

By: _____

Name: _____

Contact Person

EXHIBIT 2-E: Uniform Franchise Salesman Disclosure Form

1. As required by this state's statutes, list the persons who will engage in the offer or sale of franchises in this state and for each person list the following information:

    A. Name:

    B. Business address and telephone number:

    C. Home address and telephone number:

    D. Present employer:

    E. Present title:

    F. Social security number:

    G. Birthdate:

    H. Employment or occupation during the past 5 years. For each such employment state the name of the employer, position held and beginning and ending dates for each such employment.

        (1)

        (2)

        (3)

2. State whether any person identified in 1. above:

    A. Has any administrative, civil or criminal action pending against him alleging a violation of any franchise or securities law, fraud, embezzlement, fraudulent conversion, restraint of trade, unfair or deceptive practices, misappropriation of property or comparable allegations?

Yes _____   No _____

B. Has during the ten-year period immediately preceding the date of the offering circular:

    (1) been convicted of a felony or pleaded nolo contendere to a felony charge or been held liable in a civil action by final judgment if such felony or civil action involved a violation of any franchise or securities law, fraud, embezzlement, fraudulent conversion, restraint of trade, unfair or deceptive practices, misappropriation of property or any comparable violation of law?

    Yes _____   No _____

    (2) entered into or been named in any consent judgment, decree, order or assurance under any federal or state franchise, securities, antitrust, monopoly, trade practice, or trade regulation law?

    Yes _____   No _____

    (3) been subject to any order of any national securities association or national securities exchange (as defined in the Securities and Exchange Act of 1934, 15 U.S.C. 78a) suspending or expelling such person from membership in such association or exchange?

    Yes _____   No _____

C. For each question above that was answered "Yes" state:

    (1) the name of each person or entity involved

    (2) the court, agency, association, or exchange involved

    (3) a summary of the allegations

    (4) if applicable, the date of the conviction, judgment, decree, order or assurance

    (5) the penalty imposed, damages assessed and nature thereof, terms and conditions of the judgment, decree, order or assurance

EXHIBIT 2-F: State Advertising Filing Requirements

State Advertising Filing Checklist

State	Office of Filing	Number of Copies of Advertisement to be Filed	Time Period for Filing Prior to Use
California	Commissioner of Corporations	1	3 business days
Hawaii	N/A	No filing required	N/A
Indiana	Securities Commissioner	1	5 days
Maryland	Securities Commissioner (in office of Attorney General)	1	7 business days
Michigan	N/A	No filing required	N/A
Minnesota	Commissioner of Commerce	1	5 business days
New York	Department of Law	1	7 days
North Dakota	Commissioner of Securities	1	5 business days
Oregon	N/A	No filing required	N/A
Rhode Island	Director of Business Regulation	1	3 business days
South Dakota	Director of the Division of Securities	2	3 business days
Texas	N/A	No filing required	N/A
Virginia	N/A	No filing required	N/A
Washington	Director of Licensing	1	7 days
Wisconsin	Commissioner of Securities	2	5 days

EXHIBIT 2-G: Franchise Sales Advertising Tracking Chart

State	Name or Description of Advertisement	Date Received by State	Date of Approval/ Last Date of Review Period	Notes
California	_____	_____	_____	_____
Indiana	_____	_____	_____	_____
Maryland	_____	_____	_____	_____
Minnesota	_____	_____	_____	_____
New York	_____	_____	_____	_____
North Dakota	_____	_____	_____	_____
Rhode Island	_____	_____	_____	_____
South Dakota	_____	_____	_____	_____
Washington	_____	_____	_____	_____

Notes:

1. The advertisement may be used if you do not receive notice from the state within the time period for filing prior to use. Such time periods are detailed in the Advertising Filing Requirements Chart in Exhibit A. Please enter the last date of such period if no notice is received from the state by such date.

2. Of the registration states that require the filing of advertising, California, Indiana, Maryland, New York, North Dakota, Rhode Island, and Washington provide that the franchisor does not need to pre-file advertising that is published in a newspaper or other publication that has had more than two-thirds of its circulation outside of the state during the past year. In addition, in South Dakota, the franchisor does not need to pre-file advertising that is published in any newspaper or other publication that is not published in the state. Minnesota contains no comparable exemption from filing.

EXHIBIT 2-H: Summary of Acknowledgments Form

[CLIENT NAME]
SUMMARY OF ACKNOWLEDGMENTS

Franchisee: _____

(If corporation) State of Incorporation; _____

Address of Principal Place of Business: _____

_____

_____

Residence Addresses of undersigned individuals:

_____   _____

_____   _____

_____   _____

_____   _____

_____   _____

Indicate your acknowledgment of the following by initialing each statement and signing below:

_____ Franchisee acknowledges that it is not a domiciliary or a resident of any other state.

_____ Territory to be developed and/or location of franchised business:

_____

_____

_____

_____ Franchisee acknowledges that it has received Franchise Offering Circulars as follows:

Offering Circular required by Federal Trade Commission (nonregistration states) dated: _____.

Date of Receipt: _____

Offering Circular(s) required for the following registration states:

State	*Date of Offering Circular*	*Date of Receipt*
_____	_____	_____
_____	_____	_____
_____	_____	_____

Other (for example, offering circular(s) or other disclosure documents under applicable state business opportunity laws) and date(s) of receipt:

_____

_____

_____ Franchisee acknowledges that it has received the appropriate Franchise Offering Circular(s) at its first personal meeting with a representative of _____ (which meeting occurred on _____) or at least ten business days before execution of the Franchisee Agreement (which execution occurred on _____), or at least ten business days before making any payment for the license (which payment occurred on _____), whichever event first occurred.

_____ Franchisee has signed and returned to _____ the Acknowledgment of Receipt for each Franchise Offering Circular. Franchisee acknowledges that it has also retained an Acknowledgment of Receipt for its records. In addition, each of the undersigned Principles has signed and returned to _____ the Acknowledgment of Receipt for each Franchise Offering Circular and has retained a copy for his records.

_____ Franchisee acknowledges that it has had an opportunity to read each Franchise Offering Circular and that no representations have been made to Franchisee which are inconsistent with information presented in the Franchise Offering Circular(s), and Franchisee has not relied upon any representations inconsistent with or not contained in the Franchise Offering Circular(s).

_____ Franchisee acknowledges that it has had the opportunity to conduct an independent investigation of the licensed business offered and to seek independent counsel concerning the licensed business.

_____ Franchisee acknowledges that the licensed business, as any business venture, involves risks, and the success of the licensed business will depend largely upon the ability of Franchisee.

_____ Franchisee acknowledges that it not has received any warranty or guarantee, express or implied, as to the actual or potential volume, earnings, profits, or success of the licensed business.

_____ Franchisee acknowledges that no past or future oral representations made by any employee or other person speaking on behalf of Franchisor which are contrary to, or different from, the information contained in the Franchisee Agreement will affect Franchisor's obligations under the Franchise Agreement. The Franchise Agreement cannot be modified by Franchisor or Franchisee except in writing.

_____ Franchisee acknowledges that it has received the completed Franchise Agreement, with all blanks filled in, at least five business days prior to the date on which the Franchisee Agreement was executed (which execution occurred on _____).

                               _____

                               Franchisee

Attest: *Acknowledged by: _____

                               Title: _____

_____

Witness   Date: _____

Each of the undersigned has read this Summary of Acknowledgments and each individually acknowledges and states that each statement described above is true and correct:

Attest: Principal(s)

_____   _____
Witness   Name: _____
                                            Date: _____

_____   _____
Witness   Name: _____
                                            Date: _____

_____   _____
Witness   Name: _____
                                            Date: _____

_____   _____
Witness   Name: _____
                                            Date: _____

_____

*If a corporation, include the name and title of the officer signing on behalf of the corporation.

EXHIBIT 2-I: Franchise Sales
Compliance Tracking Form

Date: _____

Salesperson:_____

1. Name of Prospective Franchisee (if corporation or partnership, also list Principals guaranteeing performance):

   _____

   _____

   _____

2. Address of Prospective Franchisee: _____

   _____

   _____

3. State where the Prospective Franchisee is domiciled and/or incorporated or resides:

   _____

4. Telephone and fax number of Prospective Franchisee: _____

   _____

5. Proposed franchise location: _____

   _____

6. Telephone and fax number of franchise location: _____
7. State where business is to be located: _____

8. States where any part of assigned territory is to be located: _____

9. States where any territory in which Prospective Franchisee is to have any rights of first refusal is to be located: _____

   _____

10. State where offer to sell originated: _____

    _____

11. State where offer was directed and accepted, if different than (10) above: _____

12. Date of first contact with Prospective Franchisee (and name of individual contacted):

    _____

13. Was the contact made by telephone, letter or personal meeting?

    _____

14. How did Prospective Franchisee learn about the Company?

    _____

If referral, by whom? _____

15. What information was sent to Prospective Franchisee, if any? When was it sent?

    a. Promotional Brochures: _____

    b. Application and Request for Financial Information: _____

    c. Letters (attach copy): _____

    d. Other (describe or attach copy): _____

16. Date of first personal meeting with Prospective Franchisee and names of all individuals attending:

17. Date offering circular provided to the Prospective Franchisee and each Principal (Note: The Offering Circular should be provided at the earlier of the first personal meeting or ten business days before any agreement is signed or any payment is received from the Prospective Franchisee): _____

Acknowledgment of Receipt dated: _____

18. Prospective Franchisee approved by the Company

    a. Financial information verified: _____

    b. References verified: _____

    c. Employment history verified: _____

    d. Proposed site verified: _____

    e. Other: _____

19. Date Franchise Agreement (with all blanks filled in) provided to Prospective Franchisee and each Principal and any changes made from original offering circular:

    _____

20. Date of execution of Franchise Agreement:

    _____

List all State Addenda and other ancillary agreements (for example, Software License Agreement; Confidentiality Agreement) executed: _____

_____

_____

21. Date cash, check or other consideration received from Prospective Franchisee: _____

    _____

22. Date Summary of Acknowledgments received from Prospective Franchisee (executed by Prospective Franchisee and each Principal): _____

_____

EXHIBIT 2-J: Memorandum on Offering Circular Changes

MEMORANDUM

TO: All Franchise Salesmen
FROM:
RE: Changes in most recent Offering Circular (8/)
                   policy on earnings claims
         CORPORATE LEGAL ADVICE AT THE REQUEST OF   MANAGEMENT
DATE: November   , 19/20

This memorandum summarizes the changes implemented in the required annual updating of the generic Offering Circular (8/), typeset and 8-1/2" x 14", and discusses the prohibition on earnings claims. This memo is *required reading* for all franchise salesmen, and under no circumstances is it to be disclosed in whole or in part to any third parties outside of this company, including, but not limited to, franchise sales prospects.

For the first time in   history, the main body of the Offering Circular (which I refer to as the "UFOC" throughout this memo) is truly generic for all registration (for example, MD, IL, CA, NY, and so on) and nonregistration states. An addendum with information particular to each state (a "state-specific addendum") has been drafted for attachment to the UFOC based on the states for which a particular prospective franchisee must be disclosed.   and her staff have all of the details on single-state and multi-state disclosure with the new UFOC and state-specific addenda and look forward to working with you in what will hopefully be a more professional, sales-oriented package.

As of the date of this memo, MD, IL, and CA among the registration states have approved in writing the new UFOC with state-specific addendum approach. New York has given verbal approval, and applications are now pending in NM and WI. Applications will be filed between now and January for VA, RI, and IN.

Looking at UFOC 8/ on a page-by-page basis, two paragraphs have been added to the cover page (the FTC warning page) to indicate that state-specific addenda are now being used by   . Accordingly, the state-specific cover pages for the registration states have been moved to each state's addendum.

The table of contents on page 2 of the UFOC has been revised to reflect the new page references resulting from this company's having typeset the UFOC on a pre-printed form. At the middle and bottom of UFOC, p. 3, the personal histories in item II have been updated to reflect personnel changes among the officers and directors and to eliminate employment information before September 19.

In the middle of UFOC, p. 4, an insertion has been made to reflect that the $ balance of the franchise license fee is now payable *within seven days prior to Franchisee's beginning initial training* or within 120 days after the signing of the Franchise Agreement, whichever first occurs. Language has also been added to the last sentence of item V clarifying the basis for the non-refundability of the franchise license fee.

At the bottom of UFOC, p. 4 and the top of UFOC, p. 5, the *Advertising Fees* section of item VI has been revised to show that advertising is to be placed at the franchisor's discretion and that statements of receipts and disbursements from the advertising fund will be provided to the franchisee not more than once annually upon written request.

At the middle of p. 5, the *Payments In Conjunction With Assignments* section of item VI has been revised to delete references to commission and to provide for a $ transfer fee from the transferee franchisee and a $ transfer fee from transferor franchisee. Also in the middle of p. 5, a statement has been added in the *Late Fees And Interest On Late Payments* section that weekly royalty fees and advertising contributions are not subject to offset, set-off, counterclaim for any reason. Additionally, a sentence clarifying that the Franchise Agreement does contain a "time is of the essence" clause has been added to such Section.

In the first paragraph of item XI (middle of UFOC, p. 8), a sentence has been added clarifying that the Franchise Agreement disclaims the creation of a fiduciary relationship between franchisor and franchisee. At the top of p. 9, the *Training* section of item XI has been revised by an insertion clarifying that initial training is also known as the "franchise school" and that   has more than   years' experience as an   instructor.

Item XIII, near the middle of UFOC, p. 10, has been updated to reflect the fact that the mark "   " has been listed on the principal register with the Patent and Trademark Office during the previous year and giving the details of such registration. A sentence has been added to item XV on the same page clarifying that the franchisee will devote a minimum of   hours per week to the management of the franchised business.

In item XVII at the lower middle of UFOC, p. 11, a provision (ix) has been inserted clarifying that the franchisee's abandoning or vacating the Center for five or more consecutive days is a basis for terminating the Franchise Agreement.

In the paragraph at the bottom of UFOC, p. 12, the *Assignment (by Franchisee)* section of item XVII has been revised to reflect the restructuring of the transfer fees discussed earlier in this letter. Near the bottom of UFOC, p. 13, the *Governing Law and Arbitration* section of item XVII has been revised by the addition of two sentences which disclose the impact of certain provisions in the Franchise Agreement dealing with the injunctive relief and limitations on, and waivers of, certain rights by the franchisee.

In item XX on UFOC, p. 14, the appropriate numbers updating this company's growth over the past year have been inserted. Furthermore, references to "Schedule I" have been deleted in favor of references to the Addendum to Offering Circular. Item XXI on the same page now refers to audited financial statements for the years ending July 31, 19/20 , 19/20 , and 19/20 .

In closing, an IMPORTANT REMINDER about earnings claims—Any franchise salesman who makes "any oral, written or visual representation to a prospective franchisee which states a specific level of sales, income, gross or net profits of existing outlets . . . of the named franchise business or which states other facts which suggest such a specific level" (e.g. car counts and ARO) without providing the detailed disclosures required by the Federal Trade Commission *VIOLATES FEDERAL LAW* (See Trade Regulation Rule: Disclosure Requirements and Prohibitions Concerning Franchising and Business Opportunity Ventures, 16 CFR 436-sec. 436.1(c)).   under item XIX of the Offering Circular, states that no earnings claims are made, and all franchise salesmen are expected to comply strictly with this policy.

If you have any questions concerning this memorandum, please feel free to contact me.

CERTIFICATE

I,   , do hereby certify that (i) I have read the attached Salesman Disclosure form, (ii) that the information contained therein is correct in every material respect, and (iii) that I have this day received   memorandum dated November   , 19/20 regarding changes in generic Offering Circular 8/ .

_____

_____
Date

McDonald's Franchise Agreement

2. FRANCHISE GRANT AND TERM

(a)McDonald's grants to Franchisee for the following stated term the right, license, and privilege:

(i)to adopt and use the McDonald's System at the Restaurant;

(ii)to advertise to the public that Franchisee is a franchisee of McDonald's

(iii)to adopt and use, but only in connection with the sale of those food and beverage products which have been designated by McDonald's at the Restaurant, the trade names, trademarks and service marks which McDonald's shall designate, from time to time, to be part of the McDonald's System; and

(iv)to occupy the Restaurant as provided herein.

The rights granted under this Franchise are limited to the Restaurant's location only.

(b)The term of the Franchise shall begin on _____ and end on _____ , unless terminated prior thereto pursuant to the provisions hereof.

[Section 2 above must be read in conjunction with Section 28(e) of the McDonald's Franchise Agreement which provides:]

(e)This Franchise establishes a restaurant at the location specified on page 1 hereof only and that no "exclusive," "protected," or other territorial rights in the contiguous market area of such Restaurant is hereby granted or inferred.

Burger King Franchise Agreement

1. FRANCHISE GRANT: TERM AND LOCATION

BKC grants to FRANCHISEE AND FRANCHISEE accepts a franchise for a period of ____
( ) years to use the Burger King System and the Burger King Marks only in the operation
of a Burger King Restaurant on the Premises located at _____
(The "Franchised Restaurant") (the term "Franchised Restaurant" consists solely of the
shaded portions of the Premises as set forth on *Exhibit "A"*). The term of this Agreement
commences on the date the Franchised Restaurant opens for business (the "Commencement Date"), and shall expire _____ ( ) years thereafter (the "Term"), unless sooner terminated in accordance with the provisions of this Agreement. FRANCHISEE agrees to
operate the Franchised Restaurant at the Premises for the entire _____ ( ) year Term.
FRANCHISEE accepts this franchise with the full and complete understanding that the
franchise grant contains no promise or assurance of renewal. The sole and entire conditions under which FRANCHISEE will have the opportunity of obtaining a Successor
Burger King Franchise Agreement at expiration are those set forth herein in Paragraph
17. This franchise is for the specified location only and does not in any way grant or
imply any area, market or territorial rights proprietary to FRANCHISEE.

Burger King Target
Reservation Agreement

1.1.1 *Nonexclusive Rights.* Except as otherwise expressly stated on Exhibit "A" hereto, the Developer is hereby granted the nonexclusive right to develop and, subject to the full satisfaction of the terms and conditions of this Agreement, to be franchised to operate Restaurants at the Target Locations upon the terms and conditions of this Agreement and the franchise agreements which shall be entered into for each Restaurant. A Target Location is defined as a specific place with clear, describable boundaries that may be designated by an actual property description or address.

1.1.2 *Exclusive Target Location.* If the parties expressly agree to designate a Target Location as being exclusive to the Developer (the "Exclusive Target(s)"), as more particularly shown on Exhibit "A" hereto, then, subject to paragraphs 1.2, 1.3 and 1.5 herein, BKC agrees not to (i) grant to a third party an approval to develop a franchised Burger King restaurant on the Exclusive Target(s), or (ii) develop a BKC owned Burger King restaurant on the Exclusive Target(s).

1.2 *Institutional Locations.* Specifically excluded from these grants (unless the institutional Target Location has been submitted for approval by the Developer and is specifically designated on Exhibit "A" of this Agreement) are institutional locations such as, but not limited to, public buildings, schools, hospitals, airports, factories, turnpikes, toll roads, universities, and existing or hereafter established U.S. Military establishments. Developer acknowledges that BKC has no control over or ability to stop development of new Burger King restaurants on existing or hereafter established U.S. Military establishments, including their adjacent housing and support areas, and hereby releases BKC and its directors, officers, parent, subsidiaries, affiliates, employees, successors and assigns from all claims or liability relating to the existence or opening of a Burger King restaurant on such a U.S. Military establishment, including without limitation any claim of encroachment or breach of existing or future franchise agreements, from the date of this Agreement forward.

1.3 *Existing Approvals/Locations.* This Agreement is not intended to and does not diminish any rights or approvals previously granted by BKC to Burger King franchisees, their successors or assigns, or other persons or entities, whether granted by franchise agreement, development agreement, letter of intent or other written communication or agreement. In the event that such grant or approval includes a grant or approval to open Burger King restaurants within any Target Location described in this Agreement, such grant of right shall remain unaffected by this Agreement. Further, this Agreement shall not affect the ability of BKC or its franchisees to continue to operate existing Burger King restaurants, nor shall it affect or prevent BKC, in BKC's sole discretion, from issuing a grant of the right to continue such operations at the end of the term of an existing agreement. Further, this Agreement shall not affect the right of BKC to allow a franchisee or other person or entity to complete development of a Burger King restaurant at a location for which approval was granted by BKC prior to the date of this Agreement.

1.4   *Substitute Target Locations.* BKC shall allow the Developer to substitute a new Target Location (the "Substitute Target Location") for an existing Target Location set forth on Exhibit "A" hereto only on the following terms and conditions.

1.4.1   *Impacted Target Locations.* If BKC directly or indirectly develops, establishes and/or approves another franchisee to develop a Burger King restaurant (the "New Location") within a four (4) mile radius of any point within a Target Location or Exclusive Target granted to Developer pursuant to this Agreement, then BKC shall deliver written notice thereof to the Developer (the "Fifteen Day Notice"). The Developer shall have fifteen (15) days from actual receipt of the Fifteen Day Notice to deliver notice to BKC in writing that such New Location will, in the Developer's opinion, render the allegedly impacted Target Location (the "Impacted Target Location") no longer economically viable or profitable (the "Objection Notice"). In the event that the Developer fails to deliver an Objection Notice complying with the above requirement within the applicable fifteen (15) day period, the Developer shall be deemed to have elected to proceed, subject to the terms of this Agreement, with the development of the Impacted Target Location at the Developer's sole risk, responsibility, and expense. In the event the Developer delivers an Objection Notice within the applicable fifteen (15) day period, the Developer shall have Fifteen (15) days from the date of BKC's actual receipt of such Objection Notice to:

(a)   Provide BKC with evidence, including without limitation a written rationale and a pro forma income statement, supporting the Developer's belief that the New Location will render all reasonable sites within the Impacted Target Location no longer economically viable or profitable; and

(b)   Use its best efforts to locate and submit to BKC a Substitute Target Location for approval by BKC pursuant to BKC's then current approval criteria.

In the event that each of these conditions are met, the Substitute Target Location shall be substituted for the Impacted Target Location on Exhibits "A" and "B" hereto. In the event one or more of these conditions are not met, the provisions of Section 1.4.4 below shall apply.

1.4.2   *Possible Impact.* In the event that BKC denies Site Approval (as defined below) to the Developer for a specific site within a Target Location based on the belief that a new Burger King restaurant at that specific site would cause a material loss of sales at an existing Burger King restaurant, then the Developer shall have sixty (60) days from actual receipt of such denial to submit to BKC a Substitute Target Location for Site Approval. In the event the Developer obtains Site Approval for a Substitute Target Location within such sixty (60) day period, the Substitute Target Location shall be substituted for the original Target Location for Site Approval, or does not obtain Site Approval for a Substitute Target Location within such sixty (60) day period, the provisions of Section 1.4.4 below shall apply.

Dunkin' Donuts Franchise Agreement

SECTION 1. Grant of the Franchise

1.0 DUNKIN' DONUTS grants to FRANCHISEE for and during the term hereof and FRANCHISEE accepts a franchise to operate a donut shop utilizing the Dunkin' Donuts System in accordance with the terms, covenants and conditions of this Agreement, at one location only, described in Item "A" of the Contract Data Schedule of this Agreement (hereinafter called the "Site", "Dunkin' Donuts Shop" or "Shop", as the context permits). In connection therewith, this franchise includes the right to use at the Shop only, the trademark "Dunkin' Donuts", along with other Proprietary Marks owned and utilized by DUNKIN' DONUTS in connection with other Dunkin' Donuts Shops, and the right to use at the Shop only, the Dunkin' Donuts System including confidential and valuable information which now exists or may be acquired hereafter and set forth in DUNKIN' DONUTS' manuals or as otherwise from time to time disclosed to Dunkin' Donuts franchisees.

1.1 This franchise is specific to one location only. It grants no rights outside the Site, nor includes any territorial protection against competition. DUNKIN' DONUTS reserves the right to operate or permit others to operate Dunkin' Donuts shops or to otherwise use the Proprietary Marks and/or the Dunkin' Donuts System, in each case at locations which may compete for customers drawn from the same area as FRANCHISEE's Dunkin' Donuts Shop.

Dunkin' Donuts Store Development Agreement

1. Grant of License

Subject to the terms and conditions herein contained, Licensors hereby grant to Licensee (and Licensee hereby accepts) the license to develop within the Store Development Area during the term of this Agreement and to operate pursuant to Franchise and Ancillary Agreements (as defined in Section 5.A of this Agreement) between each Licensor and Licensee:

A. The number and mix of Dunkin' Donuts and Baskin-Robbins units specified in Schedule B attached hereto ("Specified Units"); and

B. Such additional number and mix of Dunkin' Donuts and Baskin-Robbins units ("Additional Units") as Licensee, with the prior written consent of Licensors, may thereafter elect to develop and operate within the Store Development Area. However, Licensee's right to develop and operate Additional Units shall be contingent upon Licensee's timely opening of all Specified Units in accordance with the Development Schedule set forth in Schedule C (the "Development Schedule") and compliance with the terms of this Agreement.

8. Limited Exclusivity

A. During the term of this Agreement, Licensors shall not operate or franchise any new Dunkin' Donuts and/or Baskin-Robbins units within the Store Development Area (except as set forth in Section 8.B. below), provided Licensee: 1) opens each Specified Unit in accordance with the Development Schedule; 2) complies with and does not breach or default under the provisions of this Agreement, or the Franchise and Ancillary Agreements for each unit; 3) continues to be qualified for expansion under Licensors' then current guidelines for multi-unit development and operations.

B. From time to time during the term of this Agreement, special distribution opportunities may arise within the Store Development Area that are not available to Licensee. Examples of such special distribution opportunities include, without limitation, hospitals, bus or train stations, limited access highway food facilities, office or in-plant food service facilities, department stores, mobile units, off-site sales accounts, convenience stores, supermarkets, restaurants, chain conversions, and other distribution opportunities which generally are not available to Licensors for franchising to Licensee.

Licensors shall have the right to pursue such special distribution opportunities either directly or by franchising to Licensee or to others. Where any such opportunity is available for Licensors to franchise to Licensee and Licensee meets the conditions set forth in Section 8.A. above, Licensors shall, to the extent practicable without diminishing the value of the opportunity, first offer Licensee the right to enter into Franchise and Ancillary Agreements, required by Licensors with respect to such opportunity. Such right of first refusal shall expire thirty (30) days after Licensors' offer to Licensee if Licensee fails to execute and deliver to Licensors all required documents within such thirty (30) day period.

The right of first refusal shall not apply to branded product routes, mobile units, off-site sales accounts and other product distribution programs. The rights reserved to Licensors, hereunder are intended to maximize potential distribution within the Store Development Area.

The phrase "chain conversions" shall mean conversion pursuant to an agreement by Licensors to acquire and/or convert to either of Licensors' Systems more than ten percent (10%) of the units of a chain of five (5) or more units operating under the same trade name, whether franchised or operated by the same entity or affiliated entities.

C.   Provided Licensee's rights under Section 8.A. are in force, if Licensors grant a franchise or operate directly within the Store Development Area pursuant to the rights reserved to Licensors under Section 8.B. the following provisions shall apply. If Licensors, in their sole and absolute discretion, determine that the potential development of the Specified Units has been or is likely thereby to be diminished, Licensors will offer Licensee one or more alternatives with respect to this Agreement. Such alternatives may include extending the term of the Development Schedule, reducing the Initial Franchise Fees for the Specified Units, changing the number or mix of Specified Units, expanding the Store Development Area, or such other alternative as Licensors, in their sole and absolute discretion, determine to be appropriate under the circumstances. Licensors, however, shall be under no obligation to offer alternatives to Licensee if Licensee has failed to open units in accordance with the Development Schedule, or is not in compliance with this Agreement, as well as the Franchise and Ancillary Agreements for each unit.

If Licensee does not accept the alternative offered by Licensors, Licensee may request that the issue be reviewed by Development Advisory Committee. The Committee's recommendations to Licensors shall be advisory only and not binding on either party.

If Licensee accepts the alternative offered by Licensors, Licensee shall execute agreement(s) prepared by Licensors to implement the arrangement within thirty (30) days after the agreement(s) have been submitted to Licensee; otherwise, Licensor's offer shall be deemed withdrawn.

9.   No Additional Rights

Licensee acknowledges and agrees that it is not hereby acquiring any rights with respect to the use of the name "Dunkin' Donuts", or "Baskin-Robbins" or any other rights constituting the Dunkin' Donuts and/or Baskin-Robbins System, except such rights as may be granted pursuant to the provisions of the Franchise Agreement entered into for each unit.

Licensee understands that Licensee's limited development rights as set forth herein relate solely to the Store Development Area. Licensee further acknowledges that Licensors and their affiliates, in their sole and absolute discretion, have the right to operate, franchise and license other units and all manner of distribution of products and services of every kind and nature in each case at such locations and on such terms and conditions as Licensors and their affiliates deem acceptable. These rights of Licensors and their affiliates apply fully and without condition to all areas outside the Store Development Area, including without limitation areas proximate or adjacent there to, and apply within the Store Development Area, subject only to the provisions of Section 8.

Cottman Transmission Franchise Agreement

Operator's Center shall be located within the following area:

S.M.S.A./COUNTY

The Center may not be relocated without the express prior written approval of [franchisor], which approval shall not be unreasonably withheld.

[Franchisor] reserves the right to establish other Centers within the same Standard Metropolitan Statistical Area or County. The number of Centers, however, shall not exceed one Center for each 50,000 motor vehicle registrations in the above named area. In areas which are not designated within a statistical metropolitan area, any Center established shall have exclusive territorial rights within a three-mile radius of the Center.

Ramada Hotels Franchise Agreement

We and our affiliates each reserve the right to own, manage, operate, lease, finance, sublease, franchise, license (as licensor or licensee), provide services to or joint venture, directly or indirectly:

(i) other franchise chains and systems in lodging, food and beverage and other businesses, with distinctive, separate marks and other intellectual property that are not part of the System, under separate agreements with you or others, for separate charges, for use of any such other marks or property,

(ii) other lodging and food and beverage facilities under the Marks utilizing modified System Standards, or other businesses utilizing the Marks and all or portions of the System, and

(iii) a Chain Facility at or for any location other than a location in the Protected Territory. You consent to our franchising another Chain Facility in the Protected Territory if you or your affiliate is the franchisee of the other Chain Facility.

(iv) You acknowledge that we are affiliated with, and in the future may become affiliated with, other lodging providers or franchise system that operate under names or marks other than the Marks. We and our affiliates may share, use or benefit from common computer hardware and software, communications systems, administrative

(v) systems and services for reservations, quality assurance, franchise application procedures, franchise committees, marketing and advertising programs, personnel, central purchasing, approved supplier lists, franchise sales personnel (including independent franchise sales representatives) and portions of the System that do not involve the Marks or Identity Program.

CHAPTER 3

Franchise Records Management

Charles B. Cannon, Jerry Lovejoy, and Ken Minami

Contents

Introduction

Various statutes obligate American companies to keep records of their business activities. The Internal Revenue Code compels every business to generate and retain tax records. The Securities Exchange Act requires that public companies develop and preserve detailed corporate and financial records. The Immigration Reform and Control Act forces American employers to obtain and preserve documentary evidence of their employees' nationalities. Examples of other such statutory record keeping requirements could fill an entire book.

Practical considerations also force companies to keep detailed records of their activities. Manufacturers can develop reliable production schedules only by knowing how many units they produced in the past and when customers wanted those units delivered. Sales representatives can keep track of their customers' buying habits only by developing customer profile databases. Franchise executives can determine which franchisees are complying with system standards only by referring to Quality/Service/Cleanliness (QSC) reports and notes of field representatives. People remember with their minds; corporations remember with their file folders and computer records.

No company can survive without business records. Without records, American businesses would grow blind and lose their institutional memories. But a company that continues to accumulate outdated, redundant and other unnecessary records can grow clumsy and sluggish. To be used effectively and reliably, records must not only be created, they must also be managed properly.

A recent study led by Pitney Bowes Inc.[1] demonstrates one reason why proper records management is imperative. The study examined the communications techniques that employees of America's Fortune 1000 companies use and found that these companies are approaching a communications gridlock. As employees rely increasingly on electronic communications technology, such as e-mail, intranets, and the Internet, they are not abandoning traditional paper-based ways of communicating. Rather than replacing the older methods with electronic means, employees are "bundling" electronic tools with paper-based media to ensure that messages get through.

The Pitney Bowes study was designed to determine whether a trend toward "paperless" communications is actually evolving and does not directly assess the stress that employee behavior is placing on records management. However, several implications from the study's conclusions are inescapable. In addition to creating an increasing volume of messages, these tendencies are creating more types of records with which corporate America must contend. As bundles of paper and electronic communicates proliferate, the logistics of storing, retrieving, and indexing these records grow enormously complex. Further, tracking these records to ensure that they are properly preserved and purged becomes increasingly complicated and tedious. To avoid gridlock in records management, corporate executives must continually monitor the type and volume of records their companies are creating and commit themselves to maintaining effective records management programs.

Records management programs vary widely in complexity and sophistication. Start-up companies usually depend on relatively simple arrangements; most use metal file cabinets for document storage and personal computers to store accounting records and databases. A mid-size company that is organized into departments may create a separate file storage area for each department and manage its file network through a manual or computer-based records retention program. A multi-national corporation with many regional and local offices may install a sophisticated computer network that serves both data storage and communications functions and complements (if not overshadows) its hard-copy records management system. A company's size, organizational structure, and sensitivity to record keeping issues all contribute to the type of records management program it adopts. Conversely, a company's records management system may influence its organizational structure to the extent the system constrains, or liberates, the way its departments access and share information.

Small companies often grow into mid-size organizations and beyond without carefully planning and monitoring the evolution of their records management programs. Most survive without dire consequences. Missing receipts sometime lead the IRS to disallow tax deductions; incomplete personnel records can result in fines by the Immigration and Naturalization Service; and a misplaced letter can undermine proof of a claim. These developments often prove frustrating and financially painful, but sloppy records management rarely surfaces as a principal cause of an enterprise's collapse.

Although records management may never rival other concerns with which a company must grapple in order to survive, timely attention to the logistics of records storage, retrieval, and retention can significantly reduce overhead and increase employee productivity. Companies with the foresight to include records management in their strategic planning can make seamless transitions from one growth phase to the next, while avoiding errors that waste corporate assets and contribute to employee stress.

Safekeeping of essential contracts, correspondence, and financial records, and sound administration of records retention policies lie at the heart of a records management program. These functions entail significant legal considerations, and many companies assign responsibility for the design and administration of their records management programs to their legal departments. This chapter examines the elements a comprehensive franchise records management program should include and explores the issues a legal department should address when chosen to serve as architect and gatekeeper of a franchise company's records management program.

What Are the Objectives of a Franchise Records Management Program?

A comprehensive franchise records management program accomplishes four objectives:

1. The program expedites access to files and records by employees who need to use them.

   For the sake of administrative efficiency, employees must be able to find the files they need speedily and with a minimum of effort. File rooms and file cabinets must be located conveniently to the people who use them. File cabinets, and the files they contain, must be arranged in a logical order. Otherwise, employees must commit too much detail to memory in order to find the files they need. Employees must be able to determine the location of files that others are using, so the program must include a checkout system that is simple and easy to use.

   A skillfully designed storage arrangement, coupled with user-friendly indexing and checkout systems, can dramatically increase employee productivity by eliminating wasted time; it can promote group harmony by reducing the emotional stress associated with long, sometimes fruitless, searches for misnamed or misplaced files.

2. The program protects the files from thieves and natural catastrophes.

    Industrial espionage can present problems even for smaller franchisors. Predatory competitors can wreck a company's fortunes by stealing secret recipes, proprietary formulae, and other trade secrets. Faithless employees can throw a company's profits into free fall by leaking its product development plans or by selling its marketing strategy to a competitor. Fires and floods can create equally devastating consequences by consuming a company's records and erasing its institutional memory.

    Thoughtful consideration to the measure of security particular records deserve can conserve corporate resources in both the near and long terms. Excessive security for routine documents that contain no sensitive or particularly valuable information depletes current resources that could otherwise be employed to produce revenue. Lax security for unique or highly sensitive records exposes the enterprise to unnecessary, and perhaps even life-threatening, risk.

3. The program ensures that records are preserved for an appropriate time, but are purged and destroyed after the appropriate retention period ends.

    Legal requirements and practical business considerations dictate that companies develop formal procedures to ensure that they maintain appropriate records. Federal and state regulations require that businesses retain tax, personnel, and other records to assist government agencies in conducting audits and investigations. Companies must also preserve records they may need to prosecute claims against franchisees, suppliers, and other adversaries, to defend themselves against claims their adversaries may lodge, and to establish their compliance with various laws and regulations.

    When records have exhausted their useful lives, formal procedures are also necessary to ensure that they are systematically purged and effectively destroyed. When a company cannot produce a document in response to a subpoena, it may be called upon to show that its document retention program was properly formulated and administered and that the document was not destroyed in anticipation of litigation. For defensive purposes, a company must be able to locate and destroy all copies and forms of a record when its retention period expires. A memorandum that remains in an executive's personal correspondence file is subject to production even if the official file copy of the memorandum was purged in accordance with the company's records retention guidelines. Also, if the memorandum was composed and saved on a computer, the disk drive on which the document was stored must be destroyed or magnetically cleansed.

4. The program conserves storage space.

    The most extravagant use of office and warehouse space is to store paper that contains outdated, redundant, or otherwise useless information—the equivalent of trash. The second most extravagant use of executive office space is to house inactive files that can be retained more economically in offsite storage. Space considerations relate to the storage of electronic records as well as the storage of paper. Electronically stored duplicates of correspondence, superseded contract forms, outdated offering circulars, and other historically relevant, but infrequently read, documents consume valuable computer memory. Companies that buy more and larger computer memories instead of managing their computer file space end up wasting corporate resources they could have devoted to income-producing activities.

Designing and Administering a Corporate Records Management Program

The architects of a records management program must attend to two sets of structural issues. One set concerns the elements and characteristics of the records storage and retrieval system. From a physical perspective, the architects must decide how and where to store different groups of records, and they must select the level of security best suited for various categories of records. From a system control perspective, they must devise an indexing system and check-out procedures that promote efficient work flow.

The other set of issues concerns the parameters and details of the records retention program. The architects must devise a document classification system that takes into account the organization's legal and practical needs to retain different kinds of documents for different periods. They must reflect this classification system in a formal records retention program that protects the company from fines, penalties, and court sanctions. They must develop procedures to purge and destroy outdated documents that are thorough and systematically administered. And they must install archiving procedures that minimize storage costs.

Records Storage and Retrieval

A paramount objective of a filing system is to allow employees to find the files they need speedily and with a minimum of effort. To achieve this objective, files must be conveniently located, they must be easy to identify, and they must be easy to trace when in use by a co-worker.

Different planning considerations bear on paper records than on electronic records. Paper records occupy physical space; they must be stored in file folders and file cabinets. They must be managed manually; paper documents move from place to place only when someone carries them. And they are subject to physical destruction; paper documents can be torn up, burned, shredded, and emulsified, both accidentally and intentionally. On the other hand, electronic records consist of electrical impulses that occupy no physical space. They reside on magnetic disks and move from place to place along cables. They can be "misplaced" if their document path code is corrupted or forgotten, and they can be "lost" if an electrical surge fouls the computer system or an operator fails to follow proper saving procedures. However, electronic documents cannot be destroyed except by magnetic erasure. These differences between paper and electronic records call into play different logistical considerations in developing a records management program that covers both types of records.

Paper Records

Initially, management of paper records involves space planning. Whenever possible, document files should be located conveniently to the people who use them. Legal files should reside in or near the legal department, real estate files should reside in or near the real estate department, and so on down the line. Oftentimes this simple objective proves difficult to accomplish. Complicating factors include overlapping user needs, constraints imposed by the size and layout of a company's offices, and security concerns.

In some instances, files have equal relevance to more than one department. Store lease files, for example, can be viewed as legal files from one perspective and as real estate files from another. Similarly, zoning records can be relevant to the legal, real estate, and construction departments, sometimes simultaneously. When two or more departments need the same information with relatively equal frequency and urgency, conflicts over file access can easily develop.

Thus, the size and layout of a company's executive offices can also undermine a filing system's efficiency. If two departments that routinely share files are located many yards, if not floors, apart, the staff of one or the other will invariably waste time traveling between departments or waiting for a messenger to complete the trip. Also, departments that accumulate more files than their allotted storage space can accommodate must either sacrifice work space to keep the files together or begin storing some of their files in remote locations.

Security concerns can also trump ease and convenience. Secret formulae, stock certificates, deeds to real estate, and personnel records rank among the documents that deserve special protection. Unless a company can afford to construct an appropriately secure storage area for each department, one or more departments will experience some degree of inconvenience in accessing necessary records.

These constraints can be alleviated to a degree with careful space planning. If the architects of a records maintenance program enjoy the luxury of designing their program around virgin office space, they can group department locations in ways that promote shared records usage. They can also anticipate each department's security requirements and its current and future needs for proximate and remote file storage space.

When space planning solutions reach their practical limits, organizational solutions become important. One such solution is the "office of record" approach. This solution involves designating the department that uses a particular group or type of documents most frequently, or that has the highest priority need to control them, as the office of record for these documents. The office of record retains custody of the originals, and other departments that have less frequent or compelling use for the documents retain photocopies for reference purposes. Management may decide, for example, that the real estate department reviews store leases more frequently than any other department and should serve as office of record for real estate leases. The real estate department would therefore retain control of the original, signed copies of all real estate leases, and the legal and operations departments would deal with photocopies.

In addition to improving access, this solution serves to alleviate a security concern. As the number of people who handle the original of a document increases, so does the risk that the document, or some of its pages, might get mislaid, destroyed, or stolen. If personnel in only one department can gain access to the original, accountability increases and risk of loss decreases.

Although efficient, the office of record solution involves several disadvantages. Even though it solves one security risk, it compounds another. As the number of photocopies of a document increases, so does the number of points at which industrial spies and faithless employees can access it. The office of record approach also complicates the records retention officer's job by increasing the number of copies of a document that must be accounted for and destroyed when the document's retention period ends. It also increases the amount of paper for which storage space must be allocated.

A variation on the office of record solution involves electronic duplication of the official documents. Instead of photocopying the official record and storing the copies in the file cabinets of junior user departments, electronic duplicates are stored in the company's computer database. When a need arises, employees retrieve the electronic copies and either read them on a computer screen or print out working copies. This solution saves office storage space, but potentially aggravates the records retention officer's task of locating all copies of a document when time comes to destroy it. Also, electronic records are more difficult and expensive to destroy than paper documents. These issues are discussed in greater detail in the "Records Retention" section of this chapter.

To be easily accessible, a file must not only be conveniently located, it must also be easy to identify once its general location is established. That is, it must be labeled and indexed in ways that enable staff to narrow their search to a precise location without undue effort.

A simple paper document filing system entails two dimensions: file naming and file arrangement. File naming involves manual labeling of file folders by document type or subject matter, usually with supplemental indexing information. For example, the file folder for a real estate lease will typically indicate the property's address; it may also indicate the landlord's name or other information relevant to the real estate department. File arrangement involves arranging the file folders in alphabetical, alphanumeric, subject matter, or some other logical order. For example, real estate lease files might be organized alphabetically by state, then by city, and then by street name. Employees must usually memorize the system their company or department uses to label, arrange, and store its files.

Simple two-dimensional filing systems prove inadequate when a company grows large enough to divide its files among numerous relatively autonomous departments. Employees need a better tool than memory to determine which department houses particular files and how each department organizes it files. Without this guidance, a paralegal who needs to review the building lease for a franchisee's third location might wander from the real estate department to the construction department and over to the franchise department before locating the appropriate file. The paralegal may discover that the franchise department organizes its files alphanumerically with a store code, whereas the real estate department organizes its files alphabetically by state, city, and street name, whereas the construction department organizes its files numerically with a project code. Unless the paralegal can turn to an index that provides a road map to the particular lease file, he or she will waste precious time browsing through at least one other department's file cabinets and disrupting its staff with requests for directions and assistance.

A reliable indexing system enables a user with different types of information about a file to trace it through the system. For instance, the paralegal in the prior example may know the name of the franchisee's principal operator, but not the name of the corporation that actually owns the franchise or the address of the franchisee's third location. A truly useful indexing system will allow the paralegal to key in the principal operator's name and, through cross-indexing, to locate the actual franchisee's name, the location of the franchisee's files and, if different departments house different types of franchisee files, the name of the department and file that contains the real estate lease.

A rational indexing system also standardizes the way different departments, and even individuals within a department, label and organize their files. If a particular department can justify a deviation from the company norm on functional or efficiency grounds, the master cross-indexing system should reflect the deviation. That way, employees need not memorize departmental variations, but can search effectively for particular files in any department through the central index.

Smaller companies can get by with a manual indexing system, provided someone in each department has responsibility for routinely updating the department's contribution to the departmental index and the master index. As companies grow larger and organizationally more complex, manual systems grow cumbersome and unreliable. Electronic indexes prove preferable in these environments, because they are easier to maintain and update. A new file can be logged into the index system at the same time it is logged into the records retention system, and the network server can be programmed to integrate the entry into the company's master and departmental indexes automatically.

In a perfect world, every file folder would always remain at home in its designated slot. In the real world, files frequently leave home in the hands of employees who need to read or copy them, and files migrate from desk to desk as other employees "borrow" them. Consequently, the job of a person who develops a filing system for paper records does not end with assigning each file a convenient, logically organized, and easily identified home. The architects must also establish a method for tracking and locating files that are in use. The tracking mechanism is a file check-out system.

Check-out systems can vary in formality. Some simply require a borrower to leave a card in the vacant folder space or in a separate box. The card contains space for the borrower to indicate his or her name and department. More formal systems require borrowers to check files out through a file librarian. The key to a successful check-out system is to ensure that it is either easy enough to use, or carries sufficiently painful penalties for nonuse, that employees will not try to circumvent it. Any system that achieves that objective will prove satisfactory.

Electronic Records

More sophisticated franchisors may also use an electronic means to retain records. The challenges involved in developing a filing system for electronic records focus primarily on indexing. Space planning and physical logistics play a lesser role than in paper filing systems because most companies provide each of their employees the equivalent of a departmental file room in the guise of a personal computer. Today, employees rarely need to leave their desks to find or use an electronic record; they simply instruct their computers to fetch it. A record may reside in the disk drive of an individual's desktop computer, or it may reside in a server—a more powerful computer with greater memory that distributes files through an electronic network. If the disk drive or network is properly configured, the location of an electronic file's residence creates no delays or logistical obstacles for the user; from the user's perspective, the challenge lies in finding the file once the user is inside the electronic file room.

An employee who does not know where to look for a paper file can go to a coworker, perhaps a records librarian, and provide a general description of the subject matter. If the first description is insufficient, the coworker can ask for details and, through a question-and-answer process, narrow the search to a particular file. Thus, an employee might ask for "Bob Johnson's real estate lease." The coworker might ask, "Who is Bob Johnson and where is the property located?" The employee might answer, "Bob is a franchisee and the property is at 1234 Avenue A in Everytown, Illinois." With this additional information, the coworker can probably direct the employee to the appropriate file cabinet.

But computers cannot yet engage in this kind of unstructured dialogue with an employee. To receive a useful answer, the employee must phrase the initial inquiry in a language and syntax the computer understands. Consequently, the most significant challenges the architects of an electronic filing system face in providing ready access to electronic records involve document typing, naming conventions, and related indexing issues.

Electronic indexing demands precise standardization and rationality in naming directories and, more important, in naming documents. Newer word processing and database programs allow for document names of unlimited length, but older programs constrain users to name their documents with 11 characters, eight in the first field and three in the second. Also, older word processing programs automatically capture the second, three-character field to designate the word processing application with which a document was created. WordPerfect automatically inserts "wpd" in the second field; many versions of Microsoft Word insert "doc" in the second field.

A user of Microsoft Word who is accustomed to naming the current version of a Store Franchise Agreement form "strfragm.doc" may experience infuriating frustration when searching for the same agreement his or her colleague has named "sfafrm99.doc." Users of these older programs can benefit immeasurably from a document naming manual that establishes uniform naming conventions and standards, and those responsible for developing an electronic document management program around older word processing applications should take the time to create such a manual.

These indexing challenges have been alleviated to a great extent through the introduction of document management software, such as PC Docs, Microsoft Express, and iMANAGE. Still, individuals responsible for developing an electronic filing system need to reinforce the reliability and utility of these programs by creating document naming conventions that departments throughout the organization recognize and use.

In addition to alleviating space planning problems, an electronic filing system makes documents easier to use and reduces the risk of their accidental damage or destruction. When an employee needs to examine an electronic document, he or she retrieves the document from memory instead of a file drawer. If the employee's assignment is to obtain information, he or she can glean the information directly from the computer screen, often with the assistance of a character recognition program that can rapidly sift through an entire document in search of particular words or phrases. This procedure not only saves time, it protects the original document from mishandling. Similarly, when an employee needs to create a new form or version of a document, he or she can retrieve the document from memory and assign it a new name (identifying code). The employee either modifies the new document directly on the computer screen or prints a working copy on which to make longhand notations. All the while, the originals of signed agreements and letters remain safely in their files, and the original of the electronic file the employee modified resides safely in his or her disk drive or the company's network server.

Electronic storage also facilitates communications between companies or branch offices. Lawyers and executives can share drafts of agreements and other documents by exchanging diskettes that contain the documents. They can communicate even quicker by transmitting the documents as attachments to e-mail messages, either internally through a network server or externally via the Internet. Companies that use optical scanning equipment enjoy similar capabilities for documents they receive as hard copies. Scanning equipment creates electronic duplicates of paper documents that can be stored in computer memory and later manipulated like any other electronic record.

Electronic databases represent a variation of electronic records storage that has proven essential for larger franchisors. As franchise companies grow from local and regional players to national and multi-national enterprises, they find increasing need to provide their employees with shared access to data that is used frequently or is needed for statistical or comparative purposes. They satisfy these needs with system-wide databases that networks of departments and satellite offices can access and use simultaneously. In many organizations, databases of selected franchisee and site-specific information can evolve into the primary component of a records management program. Use of databases can eclipse previous concerns regarding the accessibility and physical location of hard copy franchise files within the confines of a corporate headquarters. As reliance on paper records diminishes, the debate within the corporation can focus on the type and scope of information the various departments desire to capture in the database.

For franchisors that lease or sublease real estate to their franchisees, or buy property to construct company-owned stores, the interrelationship among the franchising, operations, and real estate sectors of the business increases the need for the coordination of information availability and accessibility. For example, upon the opening of a new franchise location, a franchisor's legal, field services, and rental accounting departments all need and rely on common information about the franchisee and the site. In order for the franchise system to operate efficiently and in harmony, this information must be entered into the database accurately for viewing and use by these and other departments.

The legal department is typically responsible for the generation of legal notices arising out of a franchise agreement, sublease, and other contracts. The accuracy of the franchisee database is critical to the legal department, since these notices, including default and termination notices, must be delivered to the proper parties. In situations where the legal department is charged with the responsibility of ensuring that all franchisees and stores within a system are properly documented, an updated and accurate database is crucial both for the timely renewal of franchise documents before their expiration, and for the assignment or execution of new documents upon the transfer or sale of an existing franchise.

The collections department plays an elevated role in most franchise companies, based on the fact that the primary source of income for these companies is a royalty stream. In many companies, the accounts receivable database is managed and updated independently of the store and franchisee information databases or the property management information system. However, the accounts receivable database is often linked in some manner to the company's other information systems. The collections department monitors the payment by franchisees of all fees and charges accruing in connection with the franchise agreement, including all royalty and advertising fees. If the company subleases store premises to its franchisees, the role of the collections department is extended to oversee collection of past due rent and other lease related charges. Close interaction with the rental accounting department becomes necessary due to the collection administrators' dependency on the delinquency information transferred to them from rental accounting. Companies that also manufacture products or supplies for the franchise system require the collections department to wear yet another hat in adding to their rent collector and franchisor duties.

Another heavy user of information databases within franchise organizations is the rental accounting department that performs a property management function. Strong ties to the rental accounting department become essential to the accounts payable department for the timely payment of rent and other prime lease charges to landlords. The level of interface with the legal and collections departments also surges upward as disputes arise among and between landlord, franchisor, and franchisee.

In summary, an organization composed of a matrix of interdependent sectors is held together to a large degree by the information glue that takes the form of one or several interrelated, system-wide databases. World class franchising organizations have been able to leverage these databases to enhance interdependency within their companies, and even smaller franchisors are growing increasingly dependent on them.

Protecting and Safeguarding Records

Whether a company relies primarily on paper records or electronic files and databases, it must remain vigilant against a variety of security risks. Even start-up companies routinely protect their records from casualty loss by storing duplicates of sensitive documents in remote locations and by backing up their computer files with commercially available software programs.

Businesses also need to remain vigilant to risks of theft and pilferage. When a company grows large enough to have employees with no personal relationship with the founders and no equity stake in the company's ownership or fortunes, it needs to begin developing policies and procedures governing records access. These policies and procedures should be appropriate to the company's size and structure, and grounded in an expectation they will evolve into more sophisticated forms as the company adds employees and becomes more organizationally complex.

Access restrictions serve the purpose of ensuring that employees and visitors cannot intentionally or inadvertently gain access to records they have no business seeing. Trade secrets retain their monopoly value only so long as the owner maintains their secrecy. A company that relies on trade secrets must take care to shelter them from predatory competitors and dishonest employees. Similarly, contracts such as test agreements with cobranding partners often impose restrictions on the use of confidential information, requiring the recipient to provide access only to employees who need to use the information in performing their assigned jobs. Other types of records also require discrete handling for legal and competitive reasons, such as personnel files, customer lists, and strategic planning files. A company that handles sensitive records lackadaisically risks liability for breach of contract or invasion of privacy, as well as loss of the competitive advantages business secrets provide.

When the authors presented a roundtable discussion of records management programs at the 1997 ABA Forum on Franchising, a participant shared a story that illustrates the importance of maintaining appropriate, sensible file room security. The story involved a franchisor that was engaged in a running dispute with a franchisee over system standards. While the parties were staking their positions and talking reconciliation, the franchisee visited the franchisor's headquarters. During the visit, someone in the company's franchise department allowed the franchisee to examine his own franchise file without supervision. Some months later, the franchisor sued the franchisee. When the franchisee subpoenaed his file, the franchisor discovered several documents beneficial to the franchisee's position that the franchisee had apparently placed in his file during the unsupervised visit. The franchisor could not establish that the franchisee himself embellished the file and found its case weakened by the suspect documents' contents.

Some may shrug this story off as "The Case of the Foolish (or Lazy) Franchisor," assuming that few companies would countenance such obviously flawed security procedures. Perhaps that assumption is valid insofar as conscious behavior is concerned. However, abuses of confidence and trust potentially plague every franchisor, and no franchise company can safely assume that it will never become a target of unauthorized incursions into its records.

Franchisors can employ a variety of physical and procedural measures to secure their facilities. Some deposit secret formulae and other trade secret records in a bank safe deposit box; some isolate their sensitive files in separate rooms that are equipped with fireproof safes and padlocked file cabinets. They either lock these rooms and provide keys or combinations only to authorized personnel, or they restrict entry by posting a records librarian outside the door. Some larger companies house their sensitive records in facilities comparable to bank vaults that are fortified with electronic sentries, motion detectors, time locks, and similar high-tech devices. Employees who need access to a file may be required to identify themselves by signing a log, using an electronic key or, in extreme cases, having their identities and security clearance verified by finger, voice, or retina prints.

Companies also employ sophisticated measures to protect their electronic records as they grow in size and organizational complexity. Computer networks can be configured to make particular files accessible only to individuals or work groups with required security clearance. Qualified users must log into their personal computers or into particular file directories with passwords that indicate their clearance status. Some users may have the ability only to read a file; others may have limited manipulation capability (such as the ability to fill out a form); still others may have the ability to edit and modify a file.

Companies that communicate with the outside world via the Internet or their own intranets also employ special precautions to protect sensitive data from industrial spies. One technique involves the networking of server computers in a way that routes all external communications through a server that cannot communicate directly with the computers on which accounting and other sensitive data is stored. Even if a spy infiltrates the communications server, he or she cannot penetrate into the data storage computers absent extraordinary luck or extraordinary competence in computer programming. A complementary technique involves the use of sophisticated "firewall" programs that screen incoming inquiries and messages for proper access authorization, thereby protecting against viruses that can corrupt or erase an entire computer system's memory. Some companies even encrypt their messages with codes that can only be deciphered with the corresponding decoding software.

Appendix 3-A to this chapter contains a checklist that reprises the logistical and systems control features that a sound records management program must encompass. The checklist suggests questions that people who are charged with designing a records management program might ask to test their program's suitability and adequacy.

Records Retention

The second set of structural issues with which the architects of a records management program must contend is records retention. A records retention program serves dual purposes. Properly designed and administered, it ensures that a company's records are safely preserved for an appropriate time. It also ensures that the records are purged and destroyed after their useful lives expire. A by-product of conscientious purging is that it frees valuable storage space for repeat use.

A carefully designed classification system lies at the heart of a sound records retention program. Such a classification system takes into account three of a record's characteristics: its legal retention period, which is the time a law or regulation prescribes for a record's retention; its legal consideration period, which relates to a record's potential offensive or defensive use in litigation and the consequences of its discovery by an adversary; and its practical (or user) retention period, which is the period employees are likely to refer to a document or electronic file for information they need to perform their jobs.

Typological Approach

American companies traditionally base their records retention programs on a typological classification system. That is, they sort their records by subject matter or document type and assign a separate retention period to each type of record. A franchise company, for example, might separate its franchise documents by reference to their title or type, such as development agreements, franchise agreements, personal guaranties, confidentiality agreements, store leases, construction documents, offering circulars, and so forth; and assign a specific retention period to each type of document on the basis of that classification.

The typological approach works in theory, but involves several practical drawbacks. First, and most significant, it is tedious and time-consuming to administer, especially for companies that accumulate significant volumes and varieties of files. The major categories of documents can easily be identified and typed. But unique or infrequently used documents invariably aggravate the process. One-off license agreements, test agreements, and vendor contracts, for example, require the same depth of analysis as do franchise agreements and offering circulars.

Second, the documentation of a typological retention program (a process addressed later in this section) can involve significant duplication of efforts. The number of record titles and document types may run into the hundreds, and the same regulatory retention requirements and statutes of limitations may apply to many of them, necessitating repeated citation of the same statute or regulation in the legal requirements section of the program's documentation. Often, the priority and enthusiasm that staff members initially devote to a typological records retention project wanes long before the less significant document groups are analyzed and the program's documentation is completed. Unless management doggedly presses the process to conclusion, the more obscure documents will receive superficial attention, if any.

Further, the accuracy and efficiency of a typological analysis depends on a high degree of consistency in document naming. If different authors randomly use "Confidentiality Agreement," "Non-Disclosure Agreement," and "Secrecy Agreement" to title substantively identical documents, the staff assigned to categorize the documents may treat them as three distinct types. Unless an attorney carefully reviews their preliminary efforts, the staff may conduct three separate analyses and mistakenly establish three separate retention categories. More troublesome, if different types of documents have received identical titles, serious classification errors can result. If a company's franchise agreements, trademark license agreements, and software license agreements are indiscriminately titled "License Agreement," misclassification by a clerk or administrative assistant becomes a significant risk.

In addition, the typological approach can result in different retention periods being mistakenly assigned to documents that are practically related, but fall into different legal categories. Franchise agreements and personal guaranties are integrally linked at the practical level; franchisors typically want to sue on owner guaranties if the franchisee defaults on a monetary obligation. In some jurisdictions, franchise agreements and personal guaranties may be subject to different statutes of limitations, and the two types of documents may therefore be assigned different retention periods by clerical and administrative personnel. Absent care by legal counsel in reviewing the retention program's documentation, the franchisor may learn of the error only when preparing for a multipronged collection action and discovering that the personal guaranty files have been destroyed.

Finally, the maintenance of a typologically designed retention program can prove unwieldy. Legal retention requirements and statutes of limitations may change, necessitating continual review, and sometime wholesale revision, of the program's documentation. Also, every time a franchisor acquires a competing system or consolidates with an independently managed affiliate, the acquired entity's records must be painstakingly integrated into the acquirer's retention program. Depending on the circumstances, the integration process can require as much effort and expense as the company devoted to its original records retention program.

Functional Approach

The authors of *Legal Requirements for Business Records* suggest a less cumbersome approach to records retention. They call it the functional approach.[2]

Under the functional approach, records are grouped and analyzed by reference to the major functions they perform for the organization, not by document title or type. *Legal Requirements for Business Records* explains the approach with an example based on accounting records:

> . . . An accounting department consists of a great number of different records: ledgers, journals, invoices, statements, vouchers, canceled checks, bank statements, bills, payroll, etc. Realistically, all these records serve *one major function: to ensure that the organization's income and expenses are handled and accounted for appropriately* [emphasis supplied]. . . . Although many different record titles are involved and different groups within the accounting department or the entire organization use these records, all these different records are maintained to support the singular functional purposes stated above.[3]

Like the typological approach, application of the functional approach involves a three-step process to determine a record's retention period. However, the first step differs radically from the first step in the typological approach. The first step in the typological approach involves separating records into categories by reference to title or type. The first step in the functional approach involves separating records by reference to the functions they perform for the organization. In practice, a franchise company might view its franchise records as serving two major functions: to ensure that franchisee relationships are managed appropriately, and to demonstrate compliance with applicable franchise registration and disclosure requirements. In assigning functional retention periods to its franchise records, this company would start by sorting them into one or the other of two categories that correspond to these functions: franchisee relations and sales compliance.

Records that relate to the first function, franchisee relations, might include development agreements, franchise agreements, personal guaranties, confidentiality agreements, franchise store leases, construction documents, default and termination notices, general correspondence, and all other records that relate to the life-cycle of a franchise relationship. Records that relate to the second function, sales compliance, include offering circulars, advertising materials, state registration records, offering circular receipts, foreign disclosure statements, and all other records that demonstrate compliance with the various statutory and regulatory requirements. Instead of each document's being assigned to a category by reference to its title or type, all the franchise life-cycle records would be assigned to a common category and all the sales compliance records would be assigned to another common category. Whereas the typological approach might produce scores of document groupings for a company's franchise records, the functional approach produces only a handful.

A more detailed examination of the functional approach must take into account the second and third steps in developing a sound records retention program. As indicated earlier, those steps are to analyze the legal and user requirements for each group of records, and to assign a retention period to each group.

Length of Time to Retain Records

The period a company should retain a record depends on a combination of two factors: the legal requirements that apply to a record's retention and the practical business uses an organization has for a record, which are called its user requirements.

A legal requirements inquiry divides into two branches: legal requirements and legal considerations. Legal requirements relates to mandatory legal requirements that apply to a record's retention. The franchise statutes of Minnesota, North Dakota, and South Dakota, for example, all require that a franchisor maintain offering circular receipts for a period of three years.[4] A company must satisfy this mandatory requirement to avoid fines and penalties for failure to maintain a record long enough. The second branch relates to legal considerations—the offensive and defensive uses a company may have for a document in dispute resolution proceedings. A company should take these uses into account in deciding how much longer, if any, a document should be retained beyond its mandatory retention period.

A company's legal department should always have responsibility for identifying a record's legal retention period. Proper discharge of this function depends on the ability to locate and interpret sometimes obscure or ambiguous statutes and regulations. To complicate matters, mandatory retention periods are frequently buried under generic or obscure captions. The Minnesota requirement for offering circular receipts, for example, appears under the caption "Public Offering Statement." Unless a researcher knows of these kinds of requirements in advance and pointedly searches for their source, he or she can easily overlook pertinent information. Fortunately, useful research materials are available. *Legal Requirements for Business Records* contains an extensive survey of federal and state requirements that apply to various industries and types of records. CCH also publishes a useful resource called the *Guide to Record Retention Requirements.*

Many statutes do not contain express record retention requirements, and those that do often fail to state a definite retention period. The authors of *Legal Requirements for Business Records* suggest that, when research uncovers no mandatory retention period, a three-year retention period usually applies.[5] Their suggestion is based in part on a statement in the guidelines that implement the federal Paperwork Reduction Act of 1980. The guidelines state, in effect, that a federal agency may not impose a records retention period of longer than three years, unless the requirement relates to health, medical, or tax records, or unless the agency demonstrates that a longer period is necessary to satisfy statutory requirements or another substantial need.[6] The publication's authors also point out that the Uniform Preservation of Private Business Records Act allows businesses to destroy records after three years, unless a longer retention period is designated by law.[7] Although the three-year presumption appears reasonable, it does not carry the force of law, and legal counsel should examine its merits before proposing its adoption as company policy.

Legal considerations, the second branch of a legal retention inquiry, involves consideration of the ways a class of records might be used in dispute resolution proceedings. The statutes of limitations that apply to various types of actions are especially pertinent to this inquiry, but not as a talisman by which to decide how long a record should be retained. Instead, the inquiry should be framed in terms of whether a particular class of records would more likely prove helpful or harmful to the company in arbitration or litigation. If a company is more likely to be the plaintiff in certain types of actions, it may want to retain its records beyond their mandatory retention period to ensure their availability to prove a claim. Conversely, if a company is susceptible to claims that plaintiffs typically establish through discovery of a defendant's records, the company may want to destroy its records soon after their mandatory retention period ends to protect the company against adverse discovery consequences. A rule of thumb that many records administrators follow is that a record should be kept beyond its legal retention period only if its contents have greater offensive utility than potential for mischief if proffered or discovered in litigation.

An effective limitations period cannot be assigned to some types of common law and statutory tort claims, such as pollution and product liability claims. A company that is subject to these kinds of claims may wish to retain records that support its defense against these kinds of claims indefinitely. In this context, legal considerations dominate over legal requirements, and the company should set its retention policy without regard to mandatory legal retention periods.

Before a company makes a final decision about the retention period it will apply to various categories of records, it should also determine their user retention requirements. This inquiry involves an evaluation of the reasons employees typically access particular records and the period during which access is important for employees to do their jobs. User retention questions relate to the period after a record is no longer the subject of routine activity, but may be needed for occasional reference. With respect to contracts, user retention questions focus on the period after a contract has been fully performed. For example, a vendor contract may expire in the middle of a franchisor's fiscal year, but the authors of the company's franchise offering circular may need to access the contract well into the next fiscal year for purposes of drafting Item 8 of the offering circular. Similarly, user retention questions about franchise sales compliance materials relate to the period after a registration has expired, an offering circular has become outdated, or the legal retention periods for offering circular receipts have expired.

An organization's age, organizational complexity, and style bear on user retention issues, and the user retention time allocated to different types of records tends to be organization-specific. Although employees in each department must participate in the user requirements evaluation of the records they use, *Legal Requirements for Business Records* recommends that legal counsel head the inquiry and make the final determination. The reason is that employees are prone to request unnecessarily long retention periods that may conflict with the most sensible retention period that legal requirements and legal considerations indicate.[8]

After the architects of a functional records retention program have assigned various records to functional categories and have analyzed the legal and user retention questions pertinent to each category, they are prepared to assign specific retention periods to each document category. A previous example dealt with a company that assigned one major block of its franchise records to a functional category called "franchisee relations." In the example, this category included development agreements, franchise agreements, personal guaranties, confidentiality agreements, store leases, construction documents, default and termination notices, general correspondence, and all other records that relate to the life cycle of a franchise relationship.

To carry the example forward, suppose that counsel has determined that three years represents the longest mandatory retention requirement to which any document in the company's "franchisee relations" category is subject. Suppose also that counsel has assigned legal consideration and user retention periods to the category as a whole of four years. Based on these conclusions, the ultimate retention period for all the records in functional category "franchisee relations" would equal the life (or term) of each such contract, plus four years. Assuming that the company's development agreements run for periods of three years, subject to renewal for so long as the developer remained active, the company would retain each of these agreements for four years after it expires or is terminated. Similarly, if the company's franchise agreements carry terms of 15 years, subject to one ten-year renewal, the company would retain each of its franchise agreements, as well as related personal guaranties, confidentiality agreements, and other ancillary documents, for four years after the franchise agreement expires or is terminated.

The authors of *Legal Requirements for Business Records* point out the advantages of the functional approach over the typological approach with these observations:[9]

1. The functional retention schedule is relatively easy to develop.

   Most functional areas can be determined basically by examining an organization chart, interviewing people within each functional group, and through experience from a knowledge of an organization.

2. The functional retention schedule can be developed with a minimal inventory.

   Most traditional, detailed records retention schedules can only be developed after an extensive inventory of company records. . . . A functional retention schedule uses the inventory only to ensure that all categories have been included. . . . [M]any functional categories can be developed without even using an inventory.

3. The functional retention schedule is more consistent since a large number of record titles are grouped into one functional category.

   In a traditional, detailed records retention schedule, the different record titles must be listed and a retention schedule assigned to each. Since these records may appear anywhere within the retention schedule, it is difficult to check one against the other to ensure that the retention period assigned is consistent.

4. The functional retention schedule is easily maintained.

    Since the functional retention schedule affects the legal and user require-
    ments for many related records, these requirements will rarely have to be
    changed in the future. When appropriate, a few exceptions may be added
    to the functional categories to provide for special circumstances.

In addition to being appropriately structured, a company's records retention
program should be carefully documented. Documentation serves both to ensure
that records are safely maintained for the appropriate time and to rebut charges
of improper document destruction by opponents in litigation. The necessary documentation includes several elements:

1. A Memorandum of Legal Authorities that summarizes the results of the
    research on the legal retention requirements applicable to each category
    of records the company maintains.
2. A Records Retention Schedule that assigns a retention period to each cat-
    egory of records (functional or typological) the company maintains. A
    Sample Records Retention Schedule is attached as Appendix 3-B.
3. A Records Review Calendar that establishes the dates when various depart-
    mental files and records libraries will be examined and purged of docu-
    ments whose retention period has ended.
4. An Exceptions Schedule that identifies documents that must be rescued
    and segregated for use in pending or threatened litigation, audits, and
    investigations.
5. A Records Disposition Log that contains a Certificate of Destruction for
    each set of records that has been destroyed, indicating the date and man-
    ner of destruction and the name of the person who conducted or super-
    vised the destruction.

After a company's legal department has finished structuring a proposed
records retention program, senior management should carefully review and
approve the records classification scheme and retention matrix that legal counsel recommends. This is a wise procedure for two reasons. Unless department
heads agree with the classifications assigned to records they control, they may be
reluctant to cooperate in the purge and destroy process. Also, if a document's
destruction is ever challenged by an adversary, the company may be called on to
prove that it adopted and administered its records retention program in the ordinary course of business.

Administering a Records Retention Program

Proper administration is also critical to a records retention program. Even if a
program is properly structured and documented, its integrity can be compromised if its administration proves deficient. Although the administration practices vary among companies, the process can be grouped into three broad
functions: archiving, purging and destruction, and rescue.

Companies typically store files in their corporate offices during their active lives, and then transfer them to remote, offsite storage for the remainder of their retention periods. For example, a franchisee's contract and correspondence files will usually remain in the company's Franchise Department until the franchisee sells the business or the agreement expires. After transfer or disaffiliation procedures are completed, the Franchise Department will transfer the files to a warehouse or other remote storage facility. The files can be recalled if needed; otherwise, they simply occupy relatively inexpensive warehouse space until the time arrives for their destruction.

Archiving is the process by which files are prepared for storage, both short term and long term. Preparation for short term storage involves a scavenging process that involves the elimination of redundant copies and informal, work-in-progress records from the filing system. A company is not obligated to keep informal records that do not document actual transactions or reflect its official positions. However, even informal records must be produced if they reside in the files when a company receives a discovery request. Consequently, companies are well advised to discard informal records as soon as they are incorporated into or superseded by a formal, official record. This process usually occurs at the point a transaction or project is completed, or on a routine schedule if a relationship is not characterized by identifiable episodes.

Interim archiving procedures are especially useful for files that contain records of transactions, such as franchise sales, business or asset acquisitions, and debt financings. These projects frequently span weeks or months, during which the working file accumulates phone message slips, longhand notes on deal points, and scraps of paper containing names, numbers, and random entries that have meaning only to their authors. The document and computer files also grow thick with drafts of various agreements and closing documents. Once the transaction closes, these documents lose value to the company. Drafts are superseded by the formal closing documents, which usually contain merger clauses that negate the utility of prior drafts. Names, telephone numbers, and personal notes that have lasting importance are transferred to permanent records, rendering the original notes redundant. A company that fails to purge its transaction files of these kinds of documents not only stores trash in valuable file space, it risks retaining ambiguous or visceral notations that may later prove damaging in litigation.

Archiving's second stage involves timely movement of inactive document files out of prime office space into less expensive warehouse space. The need to access and examine a file on a frequent basis usually ends before the retention period assigned to its contents ends. A company that is sensitive to the cost of document storage will systematically transfer inactive files into sturdy file boxes, mark and index them for easy retrieval, and transport them to an offsite facility. Companies that do not maintain warehouses can hire independent document storage companies to store and manage their inactive files.

Archiving is equally important for electronic records. Personal computers designed for business use now come equipped with hard drives that can store several gigabytes of data. Network servers contain even greater memory capacity.

The amount of electronic storage space available to even the smallest company exceeds by several magnitudes the amount available a dozen years ago, except on giant mainframe computers. Companies are therefore tempted to regard their electronic storage space as unlimited—until their computers grow sluggish, or even crash, because their memories are nearing capacity.

Computers usually develop tell-tale signs of memory stress before disastrous failures occur, and support staff can delete or compress data to avoid calamity. However, the Peter Principle dictates that memory overload will occur during the most intense point of a project cycle, when those in charge of archiving decisions have no time to think clearly and those responsible for executing archiving and data transfer programs have more pressing duties to discharge.

Companies with sensitivity to records management issues resist tempting fate by developing archiving routines for their electronic records. These routines are based on principles and procedures similar to those involved in a hard copy archiving. For short-term storage, the process can involve the deletion of drafts and document inserts when a transaction closes. For correspondence and internal memoranda, the procedure might involve a one-month retention period, after which a secretary verifies that a hard copy of the document resides in the appropriate document file, and deletes the electronic version from memory. For short-term storage, the process might involve the use of compression software that removes formatting codes and other material, but preserves the base data. It might also involve deletion of all but a record copy of the record, which itself is transferred to a floppy disk library for permanent storage.

The purging and destruction process should be handled as routinely and systematically as the intake process in order to avoid charges of capricious administration by government investigators or private litigants. Senior management should establish a fixed date, either annual or semi-annual, on which all departments should begin their purging routines. Usually, clerks or junior level administrators have responsibility for identifying and marshaling the records that become eligible for destruction in a particular cycle. The staff should not only search departmental and central files for copies of pertinent records, but should also circulate memos among executives and other employees who might have had reason to place duplicates of particular records in their personal files. After the staff has completed the task of identifying, gathering, and listing the records destined for destruction, a senior administrator or department head should review the list to verify its accuracy and completeness.

During the purging process, the company's legal department should prepare or update lists of the documents and computer records the company must preserve for purposes of pending or threatened litigation. Records a company knows or has reason to believe may be included in a discovery request cannot be destroyed with impunity once a claim has been asserted or a suit filed. These records should be rescued from the destruction process and set aside for future use.

Records can be destroyed in several ways. Some companies simply discard outdated documents as they would ordinary rubbish. More cautious companies shred or emulsify paper records in order to prevent their pilferage by competitors or disloyal employees. Most companies remove electronic records from floppy disks by reformatting the disks. Many remove files from their hard drives by simply following the programmed delete routine. This procedure is not effective to destroy an electronic file, and companies that truly want to cleanse their hard drives either destroy them or subject them to repeated magnetic erasure.

Individuals who conduct or supervise record destruction procedures should routinely complete a Certificate of Destruction for each batch of records that is destroyed. These certificates become part of the company's permanent records retention files. They serve to establish that particular records perished in compliance with the company's records retention program and thus in the ordinary course of business. For companies that rely on warehousemen or other outside services to destroy their records, these certificates also provide verification that the destruction process was actually carried out in accordance with the company's instructions.

To review, the authors of *Legal Requirements for Business Records* observe that a records retention program must address each of these points in order to withstand judicial scrutiny:

1. The records retention program must be systematically developed.

    A records retention program is systematically developed if the program is developed in the ordinary course of business, the various records' values have been properly determined, the program is documented, and the program has been properly approved [by management]. This requirement ensures that all retention requirements . . . have been provided for in the program. It also establishes the fact that the retention program has been well conceived and executed . . . , rather than developed to deliberately destroy unfavorable documentary evidence prior to litigation or government investigation.

2. The records retention schedules must cover all records, including all reproductions.

    Many records retention programs do not contain provisions for "information copies" or "personal copies" of records. . . . During litigation or government investigation, these copies may be subpoenaed and used against the organization, even though the original records were properly destroyed under the records retention schedule.

3. The records retention schedule must also include provisions for records maintained on other media, especially microfilm and data processing media.

4. Written approvals must be obtained for each records retention schedule and for the entire program.

    Upon completion of each records retention schedule, one version of the schedule must be reviewed and signed by the [responsible department head and by legal counsel]. . . . These approvals again indicate that the . . . program was systematically developed in the ordinary course of business, instead of in anticipation of litigation or government investigation.

5. Records should be systematically destroyed as specified by the records retention program.

   Generally, the procedures should specify that, once a year, the records manager provide each department, the legal counsel, and the tax manager, with a listing of records that can be destroyed. After review, destruction can be halted for records related to litigation or government investigation; other records can then be destroyed in an orderly basis at the designated time.

6. Program controls and management must be provided.

   At least one person in the organization must be responsible for managing the . . . program to ensure . . . that destruction proceeds in an orderly manner. This person [should also be prepared] to testify in court, if necessary, regarding [development and operation of] the program.

7. Procedures must be provided for the suspension of records destruction in case of foreseeable, pending, or actual, litigation or government investigation.

8. Documentation relating to the development and implementation of the . . . program, including records retention schedules, procedures, changes in procedures, approvals, legal research, and listings of records destroyed must be maintained.[10]

Conclusion

A comprehensive records management program accomplishes four objectives: (1) it expedites access to files and records by employees who need to use them; (2) it protects the files from thieves and natural catastrophes; (3) it ensures that records are preserved for an appropriate time, but are purged and destroyed after the appropriate retention periods ends; and (4) it conserves storage space.

To accomplish these goals, the architects of a records management program must attend to several basic structural issues. From a physical perspective, they must decide how and where the company should store different groups of records, and they must select the level of security best suited for various categories of records. From a system control perspective, they must devise an indexing system and check-out procedures that promote efficient work flow.

Other issues also influence the creation and administration of a suitable records retention program. The program's designers must devise a document classification system that takes into account the organization's legal and practical needs to retain different kinds of documents for different periods. They must reflect this classification system in a formal records retention program that protects the company from fines, penalties, and court sanctions. They must develop procedures to purge and destroy outdated documents and make certain that these procedures are thorough and systematically administered. Finally, they must install archiving procedures that minimize storage costs.

A records management program that embodies appropriate solutions to these issues generates benefits at several levels. A skillfully designed file storage arrangement, coupled with user-friendly indexing and checkout systems, can dramatically increase employee productivity by eliminating wasted time; it can promote group harmony by reducing the emotional stress associated with long, sometimes fruitless, searches for wayward files. A thoughtfully designed document security system can promote institutional stability and financial security by sheltering sensitive records from theft or tampering, while at the same time allowing employees the least encumbered access to the records they need to perform their jobs.

A carefully designed and administered records retention program can produce substantial financial benefits. A program that gives due consideration to the utility of a functional classification system (as opposed to a more traditional typological classification system) can significantly reduce the time, effort, and expense required to establish and document appropriate policies and procedures. A program that is conscientiously administered reduces the risk that a company will be fined or sanctioned for failure to safekeep a required record or to produce it in response to a discovery request. A conscientiously administered program also reduces the risk that production of an informal, unofficial record, or a record that has outlived its legal and practical usefulness, can be compelled in response to a subpoena. Last but not least, a conscientiously administered archiving program can significantly reduce a company's expenditures for storage space.

A franchise company can realize immeasurable benefit in terms of employee productivity and expense reduction by implementing a comprehensive records management program. Over time, these benefits far outweigh the effort and inconvenience that a sound program's development entails. The earlier in its life a company becomes cognizant of these benefits and begins to incorporate records management considerations into its strategic planning, the greater the benefits it will derive.

Notes

1. *Managing Corporate Communications in the Information Age,* a study conducted by Pitney Bowes Inc., the Institute for the Future, the Gallup Organization, and San Jose State University (May 1997).

2. "The Functional Records Retention Schedule . . . An Alternative That Works!", *Legal Requirements for Business Records,* Information Requirements Clearinghouse ¶ 020-2030-00.

3. *Id.*

4. Minnesota Statutes, Sec. 80C.05, Subdiv. 5, Bus. Franchise Guide (CCH) ¶ 3340.08; North Dakota Franchise Investment Law, Sec. 51-19-08.6, Bus. Franchise Guide (CCH) ¶ 3340.08; South Dakota Codified Laws, Sec. 37-5A-48, Bus. Franchise Guide (CCH) ¶ 3410.48.

5. "Legal Requirements for Records Retention . . . the Three-Year Presumption!", *Legal Requirements for Business Records,* ¶ 020-1050-00.

6. 5 CFR §1320.6.

7. Uniform Preservation of Private Business Records Act, Sec. 2.

8. See "User Requirements for Records Retention Programs," *Legal Requirements for Business Records,* ¶ 020-2040-00.

9. *Id.*

10. "Legal Issues in Records Retention and Disposition Programs," *Legal Requirements for Business Records,* ¶ 020-1030-00.

Design Checklist for a Records Management Program

Following is a list of questions that an individual who is charged with designing a records management program can ask to determine whether his or her program accomplishes all the goals a comprehensive records management program envisions.

1. Can people who need particular records find and retrieve them easily?
   a. Are document files and records stored closest to the employees who use them most often?
   b. Have the needs of routine users, occasional users, and common users been taken into account in making decisions about document storage locations and file room/file cabinet configurations?
   c. If remote storage is necessary on account of space constraints or security precautions, is an appropriately staffed, cost-effective file retrieval and delivery system in place?
   d. Has the most appropriate "office of record" been designated for each category of record, and have all department heads been notified of the designations?
   e. Is the filing system organized into alphabetical, subject matter, or other logical patterns that employees can easily understand and remember?
   f. Is there a document indexing system that employs readily understandable codes or symbols and that provides several ways to inquire where a particular file resides?
   g. Is there a file check-out system in place that employees find easy and convenient to use?
   h. Are computer records named and indexed through an electronic document management program?
   i. Has a naming convention for computer documents been adopted that allows occasional users to search for particular documents efficiently?
   j. Has someone in the department or document library received enough training about the system's organization to provide effective assistance to people who have difficulty locating particular files or documents?

2. Does the program include a security system that prevents access to sensitive files by people who lack authority or legitimate reason to read or peruse them?
   a. Are security precautions adequate to deny access to file cabinets and storage areas by outsiders and curious insiders with no legitimate reason to know a particular file's contents?
   b. Do the security precautions provide adequate levels of security for the kinds of records that are being maintained? For example, are secret formulae provided tighter security than routine correspondence files?
   c. Is access to computer records appropriately restricted through passwords, "read only" codes, and similar devices?

3. Does the program ensure that records are safely preserved?
   a. Are unique and sensitive documents (proprietary formulae, for example) adequately shielded from theft, fires, floods, and other casualties?
   b. Are duplicates of unique and sensitive documents kept in a different location than the primary records?
   c. Are computer records routinely backed up?
   d. Are the back-up tapes or disks kept either in a different location than the primary records, or in a fireproof vault or other especially secure environment?

4. Does the program ensure that records are preserved for an appropriate time?
   a. Is the records retention program based on a classification system that is rational, comprehensive, and efficient?
   b. Does the records retention program entail appropriate documentation, such as:
      1) A Memorandum of Legal Authorities that summarizes the results of the research on the legal retention requirements applicable to each category of records the company maintains.
      2) A Records Retention Schedule that assigns a retention period to each category of records the company maintains.
      3) A Records Review Calendar that establishes the dates when various departmental files and records libraries will be examined and purged of documents whose retention period has ended.
      4) An Exceptions Schedule that identifies documents that must be rescued and segregated for use in pending or threatened litigation, audits, and investigations.
      5) A Records Disposition Log that contains a Certificate of Destruction for each set of records that has been destroyed, indicating the date and manner of destruction and the name of the person who conducted or supervised the destruction.
   c. Does the program assign documents and records a retention period that ensures they remain available for the time the law and sound business practice requires? (For more on this subject, refer to the Sample Record Retention Schedule in Appendix 3-B.)
   d. Are procedures in place to exempt documents and records that are identified for use in litigation, tax audits, or similar proceedings from normal purge and destroy processes?

5. Does the program ensure that files and records are purged and destroyed after the appropriate retention period ends?
   a. Does the program include guidelines to distinguish formal business records that must be maintained from informal records (such as document drafts, duplicate copies, and personal notes and reminders made by employees for their own use) that can be assigned discretionary retention status?
   b. Are procedures in place to identify and ensure that informal records are removed from a folder before it undergoes transition from working file status to permanent file status?
   c. Are routines in place to ensure that the locations of permanent files, including those sent to off-site storage and those that employees maintain by preference or company policy (such as personal correspondence files), are identified and tracked?
   d. Is time set aside on a periodic basis to allow employees to purge the files in accordance with corporate records retention policy?

    e. Has senior management assigned sufficiently high priority to the purging process and are department heads accountable for ensuring that departmental files are examined and purged in accordance with corporate records retention policy?

    f. Do contracts with independent off-site storage facilities provide for compliance with the company's records retention policy, and are procedures in place to ensure actual compliance?

    g. Are documents destroyed in an appropriate fashion, such as shredding, burning, or emulsification?

    h. Are computer files destroyed by magnetic erasure of disk drives and either magnetic erasure or physical destruction of floppy disks?

6. Does the program conserve storage space?

    a. Is office storage space reserved for files and records that employees use often enough to justify the dedication of relatively expensive office space to that purpose?

    b. Are older, inactive files sent to warehouse storage?

    c. Are inactive computer files compressed and archived?

    d. Are samples of outdated contract forms, manuals, and similar materials sent to historic form files, and are excess supplies of these materials discarded?

    e. Are paper copies of documents with no historic significance destroyed after they are scanned or copied and stored electronically?

Sample Record Retention Schedule

Overview

Following are excerpts from a sample "functional retention schedule" that covers the franchise documents a hypothetical franchise company might use. Rather than assigning individual records retention periods to thousands of record titles, this approach simplifies the process by grouping records into functional categories. In this example, the "functions" that particular records serve are designated as "franchise relations" and "sales compliance." Documents are listed by type under one of those two functions, and subheadings have been included to facilitate locating a particular record category.

The sample retention schedule is presented as a finished product. It assumes that senior management and departmental representatives have already decided how to combine legally required retention periods with practical business considerations to determine total retention periods. Decisions have also been made as to which department will maintain the records and serve as the Office of Record.

Information Fields

The Records Retention Schedule contains several fields of information. The titles and contents of these fields are:

Record Title: A brief label identifying the basic content of the record group.

Description: A brief label identifying the types of records in the record group.

Office: The period during which the records will be kept in a departmental or central storage area in the company's offices.

Records Center: The period during which the records will be kept in an off-site storage facility.

Total: The total retention period for particular categories of official records.

Unofficial Records: The period for retaining copies of unofficial records, including photocopies, microfilm, etc.

Office of Record: The office or department responsible for maintaining particular categories of official records during the retention period.

Abbreviations

ACT: Active—retain record while matter is active or in force
P: Permanent—retain record indefinitely
S: Superseded—retain record until replaced by more current version (applicable to forms)
+   Plus. Some retention periods consist of two or more components. For example, records with the period ACT+3 should be kept while the matter is active, plus three years.

RETENTION PERIODS OF OFFICIAL RECORDS

Record Title and Description	Office	Record Center	Total	Unofficial Records (duplicates)	Office of Record
FRANCHISE RELATIONS					
CORE CONTRACTS	ACT	4	ACT+4	ACT	Legal

Master Franchise Agreements
   for U.S. master franchisees
   (subfranchisors)
Development Agreements for
   U.S. area developers
Franchise Agreements for
   traditional units or outlets
   in the United States
Franchise Agreements for
   special purpose/special
   venue units or outlets in
   the United States
Master Franchise Agreements
   for foreign master franchisees
Development Agreements for
   foreign area developers
Joint Venture Agreements for foreign
   venture partners
Franchise Agreements for units/
   outlets operated outside the
   United States by franchisees or
   subfranchisees of foreign master
   franchisees
Guaranties of payment/performance
   by owners of domestic and
   international franchisees
Alliance Agreements governing
   cobranding alliances
Trademark licenses for
   nontraditional units/outlets
Standard amendments and addenda
   to core contracts

ANCILLARY CONTRACTS	ACT	4	ACT+4	ACT	Legal

First refusal options
Building leases and subleases
Equipment leases

ANCILLARY CONTRACTS	ACT	4	ACT+4	ACT	Legal
Assignments of building and equipment leases					
Loan agreements					
Security agreements					
Promissory notes					
Software licenses					
Confidentiality agreements					
Product/service test agreements					
Advertising co-op agreements and bylaws					
Franchise broker and sales agent/ representative contracts					
Standard amendments and addenda to ancillary contracts					
Site/location approval forms					
Construction document approval forms					
Required real estate lease provisions for U.S. Franchisees					
UCC financing statements					
Financial reporting forms (royalty statements, P&Ls, and so on)					
Operations report forms (QSC evaluations, local area marketing reports, equity ownership reports, and so on)					
Preauthorized payment (direct debit) agreements					
Assignments of telephone numbers					
Transfer approval forms					

RETENTION PERIODS OF OFFICIAL RECORDS

Record Title and Description	Office	Record Center	Total	Unofficial Records (duplicates)	Office of Record
SALES COMPLIANCE					
CURRENT DOCUMENTS	S	4	S+4	S	Legal
Franchise Offering Circular (Federal Trade Commission version for nonregistration states)					
State Specific Records:					
Franchise Offering Circular, w/State Specific Addenda, for each state in which the program is registered					
Registration Applications and Orders					
Exemption notices					
Advertising copy and approvals					
Correspondence with administrators					
Disclosure statements for foreign transactions (France, Mexico, and so on)					
Brochures and information kits					
Franchise Application forms					
Earnings Claims Statements					
Back-up for Offering Circular and Earnings					
Claims statements (questionnaires, calculations, projections, and so on)					
HISTORICAL DOCUMENT LIBRARY		P	P		
Core contracts—samples of all generations and versions					
Ancillary contracts and forms— samples of all generations and versions					
Franchise Offering Circulars—copies of prior year circulars for all jurisdictions					
Registration Applications and Orders—prior year documentation for all jurisdictions					

HISTORICAL DOCUMENT *LIBRARY*	*P*	*P*	
Exemption Statements and Orders—prior year documentation for all jurisdictions			
Operations Manuals—samples of all generations and versions			
Bulletins, newsletters, and other communiqués—copies of all issues			

RETENTION PERIODS OF OFFICIAL RECORDS

Record Title and Description	Office	Record Center	Total	Unofficial Records (duplicates)	Office of Record

CHAPTER 4

Practical Considerations to Address Franchise Agency Issues

Donnell J. McCormack, Jr. and Sheri A. Young

Contents

Portions of this chapter are based on the article "Evolution of Vicarious Liability as Applied to Franchise Law" authored by Sheri A. Young and Jonathan Solish and published in the American Bar Association materials for the 1993 Forum on Franchising.

Introduction

Franchise systems have unique value for the franchisor, the franchisee, and the public. A franchise system enables a franchisor to increase distribution and grow its brand more rapidly than it could through company-owned outlets. One of the fundamental sources of value for the franchisee is the investment in a business with a recognized name and a pretested and established product and operating method.[1] For the public, the value lies in being able to readily identify and obtain a product with a consistent character and quality.

The franchisor has the challenge of ensuring that both its franchisees and the public receive the value expected by them. To meet this challenge, the franchisor must establish and monitor system standards and procedures (the "operating manual" or "manual"). While doing so, the franchisor must ensure that it protects itself from liability under vicarious liability and similar theories. This chapter discusses the creation and enforcement of an operating manual, the legal risks involved, and the methods for avoiding these risks.

Protection of the System: The Balancing Act

As Chapter One illustrates, intellectual property (the trademarks, service marks, logos and trade names, and the goodwill associated with these) is one of the two primary elements of a franchise. The second consists of the system—the product, along with the operating method and standards for delivering the product to the public. A franchisor's primary activities should be focused on defining, protecting, and enhancing its intellectual property and its system. These efforts in relation to the franchisee are threefold. First, the franchisor must create an appropriate franchise agreement. Second, the franchisor must create an appropriate operating manual; and third, it must enforce the operating manual and otherwise act in a manner consistent with the manual.

The franchisor's creation of standards is not optional. The Lanham Act requires a franchisor to protect its intellectual property through issuance of an operating manual. Specifically, the act provides that a franchisor must control the nature and quality of the goods and services used with the mark if it licenses another to use the mark.

The act and the franchisor are in sync in this regard. The franchisor wants to ensure that its system is followed and receives the many benefits of an operating manual. By carefully describing the requirements of its system to franchisees in the manual, the franchisor protects and enhances its intellectual property and the system. Franchisees know the specific criteria with which their performance will be evaluated. Clear standards lead to consistency. Consistency promotes public consumption, revenue, and market share. Thus, the requirement of the Lanham Act to control the use of the franchisor's intellectual property has significant and essential benefits for the franchisor.

The Vicarious Liability Theory

The description and exercise of the right to control a franchisee's activities is not without challenges and risks. Drafting a manual that accurately describes the franchise system is challenging and time-consuming. In addition, the franchisor must circumscribe its requirements of the franchisee to reflect that the franchised business is owned and operated by the franchise owner, not the franchisor. The operating manual should contain requirements only to the extent necessary to protect the intellectual property and system.

Extending beyond this level of control may create a basis for a claim that the franchisee is the franchisor's agent. If a court concludes that the franchisee is the franchisor's agent, the franchisor is at risk of being held liable for third party claims arising from the franchisee's actions. Since the reality is that the franchisor is not at the franchisee's location making the day-to-day decisions regarding the franchised business, this creates an unknowable and untenable risk to the franchisor. Federal case law states clearly that the "control" required by the Lanham Act does not create a federal law of agency. See *Oberlin v. Marlin Am. Corp.,* 596 F.2d 1322, 1327 (7th Cir. 1979). The franchisor needs to ensure that by its own actions it does not create an agency relationship which would not otherwise exist.

In addition to a court concluding that a franchisee is an actual agent of its franchisor because the franchisor has exerted, or reserved the right to exert, too much control, a court may conclude that a franchisee is an apparent agent of its franchisor if a franchisor fails to enforce standards that require a franchisee to indicate its separate identity. Specifically, courts find apparent agency when (1) the franchisor acts in a manner that represents to a third party that the franchisee is the agent of the franchisor, and (2) the third party justifiably relies on these representations.

The courts will not find reasonable reliance when evidence establishes that (1) the franchisee made the plaintiff aware of its independent status, or (2) the plaintiff was drawn to the franchisee for a reason other than the franchisor's trademark. Similarly, if the plaintiff's injury resulted from an act, circumstance, or event unrelated to the plaintiff's reliance on the franchisor's trademark, the court will not find reliance. In contrast, the courts are particularly unsympathetic to a franchisor when it (1) fails to ensure that a franchisee discloses its independent status in a conspicuous and meaningful manner, or (2) should have known about and could have controlled the risk arising from its franchisee's conduct. Some courts believe that the franchisor should bear the risk because the franchisor (1) can select and influence its franchisees and therefore control the risk, (2) has drawn the public to the risk, or (3) can theoretically spread the risk.

Sample Cases

Reasonable Reliance

In *McDonald v. Century 21 Real Estate Corp.,* Bus. Franchise Guide (CCH) ¶ 7975 (Wis. Ct. App. 1983), the appellate court concluded that the evidence regarding whether the plaintiff had reasonably relied on the appearance of agency was subject to conflicting interpretations which required reversal of the grant of a motion for summary judgment.

The court noted the following facts: A plaintiff claimed that he had seen commercials which represented that Century 21 was the largest real estate company in the country with a nationwide referral service and "neighborhood professionals" to assist consumers; the franchisee real estate company displayed the Century 21 logo on signs and forms, and "advertised as a business containing a 'neighborhood professional' belonging to a nationwide organization that more people have put their trust in." *McDonald, Bus. Franchise Guide* at 13,628.

In contrast, the franchisee's signs and printed materials contained the statement: "[e]ach office is independently owned and operated" and the Century 21 warranty form that the plaintiffs signed contained three statements that the franchisee was an independent operator. *Id.* at 13,629. The plaintiff explained that he thought that the language "independently owned and operated" referred to that particular office's responsibility for a particular territory, but generally believed that he was dealing with a real estate broker who was part of a national company. From this combination of evidence, the court concluded that apparent agency may have existed. This case indicates that franchisors should require clear disclosure of the franchise relationship in national advertising in addition to a franchisee's individual signs and forms. Ensuring proper disclosure in one aspect of a franchisee's business, while ignoring other aspects of the business, leaves the franchisor vulnerable to losing summary rulings and to liability.

In some cases, courts have concluded that injured plaintiffs have presented convincing showings of reliance upon apparent authority. In *Crinkley v. Holiday Inns, Inc.,* Bus. Franchise Guide at 18,817, the plaintiffs, who were robbed and beaten in their hotel room, brought suit against Holiday Inns. Their claim of apparent agency was supported by the manner in which they booked their room. The plaintiffs initially attempted to book a room at the Charlotte Holiday Inn. When they learned there was no room at that hotel, they consulted a Holiday Inn directory and booked a room in the Concord Holiday Inn, 20 miles down the road. The plaintiffs testified that they had previously stayed at Holiday Inns, were familiar with the system's national advertising, and "would be greatly surprised to find out that Holiday Inns was not involved in the operation of the Holiday Inn-Concord. . . ." *Crinkley,* Bus. Franchise Guide at 18,817.

A similar holding in *Holiday Inns, Inc. v. Shelburne,* 576 So. 2d 322 (Fla. Dist. Ct. App. 1991) noted that the franchisee was allowed to use the Holiday Inns reservation center, logo, and signs "in order to draw customers through name recognition." *Shelburne,* 576 So. 2d at 334. The court concluded that the testimony demonstrated "Holiday Inns, Inc.'s extensive efforts to have its franchisee recognized by the public as part of its system . . .", from which the jury could find reliance. *Id.* This case has had disturbing implications for franchisors who commonly seek to draw the public to their franchisees' locations through the franchisors' name recognition, including at reservation centers.

Florida later modified its opinion in *Shelburne* in the case of *Dalia v. Electronic Realty Associates, Inc.,* 629 So. 2d 1075 (Fla. Dist. Ct. App. 1994). Electronic Realty Associates, Inc. (ERA) was the franchisor in *Dalia.* Its franchisee was Northgate Realty, Inc. The franchise agreement required the franchisee to hold itself out as an independently owned and operated business. The franchisee did business as Northgate Realty, Inc. The *Dalia* court decided that the *Shelburne* opinion applied to franchisors that required use of a single trade name throughout their chains so that the public might assume that all properties were operated by the same organization. *Dalia,* 629 So. 2d at 1075. In contrast, the court found no evidence of this approach by ERA and therefore a lack of reasonable reliance on the plaintiff's part. Summary judgment was affirmed. *Id.*

Because a strict interpretation of *Shelburne* would unfairly impose sweeping liability upon a franchisor, when it has little ability to affect the event from which a claim arises, courts likely will find that the *Shelburne* opinion is limited to its specific facts. Nevertheless, franchisors should establish and enforce standards that require clear and conspicuous identification of the franchise relationship to the public in all instances to avoid liability for the acts of franchisees. The holding of *Dalia* assists franchisors who use a common trademark to identify their franchisees to defeat a claim of apparent agency if they follow such a practice.

Conspicuous Identification

An example of a franchisor that failed to do this is found in *Beck v. Arthur Murray, Inc.* 54 Cal. Rptr. 328 (Cal. Ct. App. 1966). The appellate court affirmed the trial court's finding that the plaintiff, a purchaser of dance classes, reasonably believed that the dance studio franchisee was an agent of its franchisor. The plaintiff presented evidence of a collection of phone calls, mailings, signs, and cards, all of which referred to "Arthur Murray" or "Arthur Murray Dance Studio." The court found that these communications misled the plaintiff to believe that the franchisor, Arthur Murray, Inc., was the operator of the dance studio rather than merely the franchisor of the true operator. The contract between the dance studio and the plaintiff was also misleading as it identified the dance studio contracting party as "Arthur Murray School of Dancing." 54 Cal. Rptr. at 330.

None of the representations by the dance studio included a word like "dealer" to indicate to the plaintiff that the dance studio was independently owned. In fact, the plaintiff testified that she focused completely on the trade name and that no one informed her that the particular dance studio was owned by someone other than Arthur Murray.

Arthur Murray, Inc. contractually required its franchisee to conspicuously display a sign identifying itself as a separate entity. This disclaimer sign, however, was inconspicuous and was not brought to the plaintiff's attention. The court concluded that apparent authority existed and suggested that the franchisor "could have easily protected itself by requiring that its franchisee inform the public of his franchisee status in more effective ways than the one inconspicuous sign that was in fact required." *Id.* at 331.

No Causal Link between Reliance and Injury

Even if an injured plaintiff demonstrates that it relied on the franchisor's trademark and the lack of notice of the franchisee's independent status in conducting business with the franchisee, a court may still require the plaintiff to prove that his or her injury was caused by this reliance. In *Little v. Howard Johnson Co.* 455 N.W.2d 390 (Mich. Ct. App. 1990), the court denied plaintiff's apparent agency claim, stating that the plaintiff's belief that Howard Johnson operated the restaurant could not have reasonably led her to expect that the sidewalk would be free of ice and snow.

Similarly, the causal link was found missing in *Frey v. PepsiCo, Inc.,* 382 S.E.2d 648 (Ga. Ct. App. 1989). The plaintiffs brought suit against, inter alia, PepsiCo, Inc. to recover for injuries caused by a bottler's delivery truck. PepsiCo's motion for summary judgment was granted and the plaintiffs appealed. The court found that PepsiCo retained control over the bottler's manufacturing and packaging, but had not "retained or exercised any supervisory control over the hiring and firing of the bottler's route salesman or over the time, manner, and method of their performance." *Frey,* 382 S.E.2d at 650. The fact that the bottler's trucks and employee uniforms bore the PepsiCo trademark and that the trucks carried only PepsiCo products was not sufficient to find actual agency. In addition, the court concluded that the plaintiff could not succeed on an apparent agency claim, stating, "[u]nless the appellants chose to be hit by the bottler's truck, that doctrine has no application under the present circumstances, inasmuch as it requires reliance on the apparent agency relationship." *Id.* at 650–51.

Vicarious Liability in Employment Matters

Employee-plaintiffs have sought recovery, based on employment claims such as discrimination and wrongful discharge, from franchisors due to the actions of the plaintiffs' employer-franchisees. In these employment-related cases, plaintiffs make, among others claims, two types of arguments. One is that the franchisor is vicariously liable for the franchisee's actions because the franchisee is the franchisor's agent; the franchisor has the means to control the methods of operation of the franchisee's business. A second argument is that the franchisor is actually the plaintiff's employer jointly with the franchisee.

The first argument of agency requires a careful analysis of the facts and is less likely to be dismissed with a summary judgment motion, except in constructive discharge cases. A successful claim of constructive discharge requires a finding that the employer "intentionally created or knowingly permitted working conditions that were so intolerable or aggravated" that the employee was compelled to resign. *Garcia v. Midas Int'l Corp.,* 29,354 Bus. Franchise Guide (CCH) ¶11,149 (Cal. Ct. App., 2d App. Dist., 1997). (Opinion not for publication.)

A third party, including a franchisor, who is not an employer of the employee cannot be held liable for constructive discharge, even if the franchisee-employer is found to be the franchisor's agent. As the court in *Garcia* explained:

> [Plaintiff] ignores the differences between an agency relationship and the employment relationship. They are not synonymous. While it is true that an employment relationship ordinarily creates a principal-agent relationship between the employer and employee, the converse does not apply: agency does not necessarily create an employer-employee relationship. . . .

Id. The court noted that while a principal is usually responsible for its agent's tortious acts, this rule does not apply to the tort of constructive discharge. For a franchisee's employee to win a constructive discharge claim against a franchisor, the employee has to prove that the franchisor is also an employer.

The question of whether a franchisor is an employer of its franchisee's employee has been addressed in various Title VII cases. Title VII addresses unlawful employment practices of employers. Thus, a franchisee's employee has to prove that he is also the employee of the franchisor as a threshold to a successful claim. As noted in *Lockard v. Pizza Hut,* Bus. Franchise Guide (CCH) ¶11,553 (10th Cir. 1998), 162 F. 3d 1062, courts have used several different tests to determine whether an apparent third party is an employer.

In *Lockard,* where the plaintiff employee of a franchisee brought a Title VII sexual harassment claim against the franchisor, the court identified three common tests to determine employer status. The common law agency test examines whether the defendant controls the "means and manner by which the work is accomplished." *Lockard,* Bus. Franchise Guide at ¶11,553. As noted above, this test, if passed, will not be persuasive in constructive discharge cases. A second, hybrid test combines the first test with a look at the economic dependence of the person on the third party. The third test is the single employer or economic reality test. This test requires an examination of (1) the interrelation of the operations; (2) centralized control of labor relations; (3) common management; and (4) common ownership or financial control. *Id.* at 11,553.

The *Lockard* court noted that the single employer or economic reality test is the most favorable to plaintiffs and the common law test is the most favorable to defendants. Under the single employer test, the plaintiff-employee has to have a justified belief that the franchisor is jointly responsible with the franchisee for the franchisee's acts. According to the *Lockard* court, "[t]he critical question is, [who] made the final decisions regarding employment matters related to the person claiming discrimination?" *Id.* at ¶11,553. With respect to this question, the *Lockard* court held that the fact that the franchisor's policies were used at the franchisee company, and even the fact that the franchisor had an ownership interest in the franchisee, did not overcome the lack of evidence that the franchisor had a role in implementing the policies at the franchisee location.

A franchisor should be very careful when it receives notice that one of its franchisees has engaged in employment discrimination or other employment-related torts. A creative plaintiff, although unsuccessful, asserted a claim that a franchisor should be held to have conspired with its franchisee's alleged race discrimination since the franchisor failed to terminate the franchisee upon learning of the alleged discrimination. *See Barnett v. Doctors Associates, Inc.,* Bus. Franchise Guide (CCH) ¶11,061 (S.D. Fla. 1996). A person can be held liable for another party's Title VII civil rights violations if the person has actual knowledge that a civil rights violation is about to occur, can prevent the violation with reasonable diligence, fails to do so, and the violation occurs. *See* 42 U.S.C. section 1986 (1996).

The question arose in *Barnett* as to what constitutes actual knowledge. The court held that "notice of isolated events or acts of discrimination is insufficient as a matter of law to impose liability." *Id.* at ¶11, 061. The plaintiff's alleged making of an anonymous telephone call and sending of a letter to a company that provided franchise services to the franchisor failed to constitute sufficient notice of an ongoing civil rights conspiracy. However, if a franchisor has notice of ongoing discrimination activities and fails to investigate or take appropriate action based on the investigation results, it may place itself at risk of liability. Note that the term "ongoing" is important; a franchisor should not pursue franchise agreement default and termination procedures unless the default is material.

In *Barnett,* the court found in essence that the franchisor could not prevent the violation with reasonable diligence, in addition to concluding that there was no actual notice of the violation. The plaintiff asserted that the franchisor was part of a conspiracy to discriminate because it failed to terminate the franchise agreement following notice of the allegations. The court concluded that it would be unreasonable to require a franchisor to terminate a franchisee based only on complaints of discrimination. "[I]f Plaintiffs' theory were accepted, it would impose liability on any company that did not immediately terminate its contracts with other businesses based upon unsubstantiated allegations that those businesses are discriminating against their own employees."

The discussion provides a sampling of the issues that arise in franchisee-employee claims against franchisors. Although the particular cases discussed were favorable to the franchisors, they emphasize the need for franchisors to structure their franchise systems to avoid an agency relationship with their franchisees and to be proactive when presented with complaints that their franchisees are violating employment law.

Liability for Voluntary Undertaking

Courts have imposed liability upon franchisors on negligence theories where the franchisor voluntarily undertook responsibility for aspects of a franchisee's business and then failed to fulfill its obligations. This theory has been applied, for example, where the franchisor set standards for, or actually controlled, security at franchised locations and failed to ensure the security standards were followed. In *Martin v. McDonald's Corp.,* 572 N.E.2d 1073 (Ill. App. Ct. 1991), McDonald's appealed from an adverse judgment arising from a murder and robbery which took place at a franchised McDonald's location. The plaintiffs, who were the franchisee's employees, alleged that McDonald's voluntarily undertook to provide for the security of the employees at the McDonald's franchise and was negligent in providing security.

McDonald's created a corporate branch to address franchisee security problems and prepared a security operations manual. It also assigned a regional security manager to communicate security policies, to check for franchisee security problems, to correct problems, and to follow up on implementation of recommended security procedures. McDonald's security program recommended that the back door of stores remain locked after dark. Store employees failed to keep the door locked at the franchisee crime scene and an intruder gained access through the unlocked back door. It was alleged that McDonald's security personnel failed to ensure compliance with the programs they recommended.

Although McDonald's asserted that it was only the franchisor and did not employ the injured employees of its franchisee, the court noted that "[n]o matter what legal relationships existed, it was McDonald's Corporation which undertook to provide security and protection to plaintiffs." *Martin,* 572 N.E.2d at 1077. The McDonald's franchisee did not have its own security supervisor, relying instead on employees of McDonald's. From this, the court concluded:

> Once McDonald's Corporation assumed the duty to provide security and protection to plaintiffs, it had the obligation to perform this duty with due care and competence, and any failure to do so would lead to a finding of breach of duty.

Id. at 1078 (citation omitted).

In the *Shelburne* case discussed in the Reasonable Reliance section above, the appellate court also found that Holiday Inns was negligent in fulfilling duties it had undertaken to maintain security at the franchise location.

Holdings of negligent undertaking by franchisors also have occurred when franchisors have specified equipment for franchisees and failed to ensure the safety of the specified equipment or failed to change the specifications when safety issues arose. In *Papastathis v. Beall,* 723 P.2d 97 (Ariz. Ct. App. 1986), the plaintiff brought a wrongful death action against the Southland Corporation after the plaintiff's decedent had been struck by a soda can which fell from a soft drink rack in a franchised store. The decedent had reached into the cooler to make a selection just as the franchisee's employee was loading soft drink cans into the rack. The lower court found for the plaintiffs and the defendants appealed, with the appellate court affirming.

On appeal, Southland did not dispute that the franchisee's employee had been negligent, but contested its vicarious liability. The facts demonstrated that Southland requested its franchisee's permission to allow Coca-Cola to install the racks, and that Southland's regional manager chose the rack and did little to check the safety of the rack. Southland argued that it did not own or maintain the rack or require its franchisee to use the rack, that it did not know of any defect in the rack, and that, therefore, it had acted reasonably in offering the rack to its franchisee. Finding no Arizona case law on the issue, the court decided to follow Section 324(A) of the Restatement (Second) of Torts (1986), which states:

> One who undertakes, gratuitously or for consideration, to render services to another which he should recognize as necessary for the protection of a third person or his things, is subject to liability to the third person for physical harm resulting from his failure to exercise reasonable care to protect his undertaking, if (a) his failure to exercise reasonable care increases the risk of such harm, or (b) he has undertaken to perform a duty owed by the other to the third person, or (c) the harm is suffered because of reliance of the other or third person upon the undertakings.

Beall, 723 P.2d at 100. The court held that Southland had negligently selected, recommended, and inspected the rack and that, therefore, there was a jury issue as to Southland's negligence.

In *Whitten v. Kentucky Fried Chicken Corp.,* 570 N.E.2d 1353 (Ind. Ct. App. 1991), an employee of a Kentucky Fried Chicken franchisee brought suit against, inter alia, the franchisor (KFC) for injuries he suffered while cleaning some cooking equipment. The case against KFC was dismissed on summary judgment, but the judgment was reversed on appeal.

Prior to signing a franchise agreement with KFC, the franchisee purchased a large quantity of pressure fryers for its restaurants. The franchise agreement specifically required the franchisee to use equipment approved by KFC. The franchisee instructed its employees to clean the fryers by releasing the steam pressure through vents in the fryers. Apparently, the pressure had not been released when the plaintiff opened the lid of the fryer, and the plaintiff was severely burned. The court examined two potential bases for liability against the franchisor. The first was Section 414 of the Restatement (Second) of Torts (1965), which provides:

> One who entrusts work to an independent contractor, but who retains the control of any part of the work, is subject to liability for physical harm to others for whose safety the employer owes a duty to exercise reasonable care, which is caused by his failure to exercise his control with reasonable care.

Whitten, 570 N.E.2d at 1356.

The court of appeals found a question of fact as to the extent of KFC's ability to control the operations of the franchisee, noting that "[t]he amount of control sufficient to impose liability must consist of something more than a general right to make suggestions or recommendations or to order the work stopped or resumed." *Id.* at 1356. The court found that because KFC acknowledged in its franchise agreement that some franchisees were using earlier model fryers, and because the renewal franchise agreement specifically required the franchisee to use approved equipment, KFC could have required new equipment as a condition of renewal. Thus, the court found that there were material issues of fact as to whether KFC could be held liable under Section 414 of the Restatement (Second) of Torts.

The court also concluded, as in *Beall,* 723 P. 2d 97, *supra,* that the jury could find under Section 324A of the Restatement (Second) of Torts:

> that KFC undertook to recommend or select a safe fryer for the use of the employees of its franchisees, and increased the risk to Whitten due to KFC's failure to exercise reasonable care. A jury could also find, pursuant to subsection (b) of the Restatement that KFC undertook to perform a duty owed by Wheeler to Whitten, i.e., the recommendation or selection of safe equipment to be used by Wheeler's employees. In addition, the franchise contract provided for the right to inspect to determine compliance with the contract specifications. KFC admitted in its answer that it had exercised that right of inspection.

Whitten, 570 N.E.2d at 1357.

Vicarious Liability and the Americans with Disabilities Act

A franchisor must give serious consideration to the Americans with Disabilities Act of 1990, 42 U.S.C. §§12101–12213 (1997) (ADA), in developing and enforcing standards. To comply with federal law and the terms of the typical franchise agreement, a franchisee must comply with the ADA. However, the ADA is extremely vague in its requirements. The franchisor faces the dilemma of how to monitor compliance within its system without mandating activities that will subject the franchisor to direct or vicarious liability.

Since the passage of the act, disabilities' rights groups have vigorously pursued the act's enforcement through publicity and civil lawsuits. The United States Department of Justice (the DOJ) has been equally aggressive. The DOJ even attempted to make a franchisor responsible directly for ADA compliance at its franchisees' premises but failed in its attempt. *Neff v. American Dairy Queen Corp.,* 58 F.3d 1063 (5th Cir. 1995) arose from an action wherein a wheelchair-bound customer complained of numerous barriers that made American Dairy Queen (ADQ) stores in San Antonio, Texas, inaccessible to the disabled. *Id.* at 1064. The district court granted summary judgment for ADQ, concluding that ADQ only had the power to veto modification of the franchise store's facilities, and that this amount of control was insufficient to bring ADQ within the scope of the ADA. Neff appealed on the ground that a question of fact existed in determining whether ADQ operated its franchised stores. The Fifth Circuit affirmed the order granting summary judgment. *Id.* at 1070.

The *Neff* court examined the ADQ franchise agreement in detail and held that the relevant inquiry was whether ADQ specifically controlled the modification of the franchised facilities to improve accessibility to the disabled. *Id.* The court pointed out the provision of the franchise agreement requiring the franchisee to establish, equip, and operate the stores as part of the franchise system; the provision mandating that the store be constructed and equipped in accordance with ADQ's specifications and standards; the requirement that modifications to the building or equipment must be approved by ADQ; the provision for maintaining the building and equipment according to ADQ's standards and ADQ's right to inspect for compliance; and the requirement that the licensee use the ADQ management system as its continuing operational routine. The court found that such requirements demonstrate only that ADQ sets standards for buildings and equipment and for approving or disapproving structural changes. Such supervisory authority did not constitute sufficient control over the franchisee's business to conclude that ADQ operated the business within the meaning of the ADA. *Id.* at 1068, 1069.

The opinion of the *Neff* court was clear and reasonable. Yet the DOJ continues to pursue franchisors for purported ADA violations at franchise locations. In response to a DOJ investigation, Days Inn of America, Inc. (Days Inn) filed suit against the DOJ in the Western District of Texas, the venue of the district court in *Neff.* Days Inn asked the court to determine whether Days Inn or its franchisees were responsible for complying with the ADA. Buffalo News, February 9, 1996 (no citation available). In presumed retaliation for filing in that venue, the DOJ filed five suits in different states against Days Inn, its parent, Hospitality Franchise Systems (HFS), and individual franchisees in those states. The DOJ asked the court to hold Days Inn and HFS liable for civil penalties and to require them to refurbish the franchisees' buildings to meet federal standards. *Id.* The court dismissed the lawsuit filed by Days Inn in Texas.

In September 1998, a federal district court in Kentucky ruled on one of the actions brought by the government against Days Inn. The court held that Days Inn was not responsible as a franchisor for its franchisees' compliance with the ADA. *United States v. Days Inn of America, Inc.* 22 F.Supp.2d 612 (1998). This case involved modifications to a hotel constructed prior to enactment of the ADA. The court predicated its holding on language in the ADA that defined potentially liable parties as owners, operators, lessors, and lessees. *Id.* at 614. The court found that the license agreement, operating manual, training programs, and quality assurance inspections, neither individually nor collectively, made Days Inn an operator within the definition of the statute. In order to leave no doubt about the interpretation of its decision, the court stated that Congress did not intend to make franchisors such as Days Inn liable under the ADA. This court's reasoning is consistent with the practicalities of the franchise relationship.

The government was successful in prosecuting Days Inn for ADA violations in a case involving the new construction of a franchise hotel in Illinois. See *United States v. Days Inn of America, Inc.* 997 F. Supp. 1080 (1998). The court noted that Days Inn's license agreements require franchisees to obtain franchisor approval prior to commencing construction of a hotel. Days Inn inspects hotel properties several times a year to ensure consistency within its system. It provides operating manuals to its franchisees that include planning and design standards. The manuals require corporate approval of individual plans to ascertain compliance with

Days Inn's standards. With regard to this Illinois hotel, Days Inn made suggestions about the plans and engaged in an interactive relationship with the franchisee during the course of the design and construction of the hotel. Days Inn argued these facts were not relevant because it did not own, lease, or operate the hotel and therefore it could not be held liable under the ADA, as stated in *Neff, supra.* This court rejected *Neff.* It found that the "own, lease, or operate" language did not apply to new construction because that language is not contained in the new construction section of the statute. The court stated that Days Inn, through its license agreements and manual, had a supervisory role in the design of the hotel and could be held liable for ADA violations. This court's reasoning regarding new construction was fairly compelling. However, it added that if its reasoning regarding the inapplicability of the "own, lease, or operate" language to new construction was erroneous, then Days Inn should be considered an operator of the hotel. The court mentioned there was ample legislative history to support this conclusion, but it did not cite such history. Instead, the court cited from a House of Representatives committee report that sought to clarify that the owner of public accommodations could be liable for discrimination under the ADA. The report stated that if a corporate headquarters of a chain of restaurants designed new restaurants that contained barriers to access, the headquarters could be enjoined from making the construction inaccessible. The report made no mention of franchising. The court erroneously assumed that a franchisor was in the same position as the owner of a chain of outlets. Because the court questioned its own reasoning in ignoring *Neff* and then made an unsupported conclusion regarding Days Inn's status as an operator, this case should not be widely followed.

The Eighth Circuit Court of Appeals rejected a franchisor agency liability claim under the ADA in *Pona v. Cecil Whitaker's, Inc.,* 155 F. 3d 1034 (8th Cir. 1998). In *Pona,* a restaurant franchisee required a disabled person to leave its premises because a service dog accompanied her. Pona argued that the franchisor had sufficient control over the premises to make it an operator within the meaning of the ADA or, at a minimum, that the franchisee had apparent authority to act on behalf of the franchisor because the franchisor's signs were on the building and the franchisee's employees wore uniforms bearing the franchisor's logo. The court rejected both arguments. The court used the same reasoning as in the *Days Inn* case from Kentucky above to find that the franchisor was not an operator. The court stated that the plaintiff's agency argument was entirely without merit. It reasoned that the question of the franchisor's liability under the ADA "depends on its actual connection to the premises, not on Ms. Pona's belief about that relationship." *Id.* at 1036.

It is impractical and unreasonable for a franchisor to actively supervise ADA compliance throughout a franchise system. Further, a franchisor should oppose becoming an investigative arm of the DOJ. Therefore, a franchisor should take steps proactively to demonstrate that it follows reasonable procedures to monitor compliance.

The ADA requires owners or operators of property to make their premises accessible to and functional for the disabled, if the necessary changes to the property are readily achievable. While the "readily achievable" standard will vary with each property depending upon age, building type, and solvency of the franchisee, certain obvious requirements of the ADA should be required by the franchisor. Ramps, barrier-free restrooms, Braille elevator buttons, designated parking spaces, and visual fire alarms are examples of items that a franchisor could incorporate as specific standards that the franchisor can inspect for compliance. Enacting such standards demonstrates an effort to monitor ADA compliance. A franchisor should consider retaining a consultant for assistance in identifying and drafting these standards. A statement that meeting the standards does not necessarily fulfill the requirements of the ADA or other federal, state, or local laws also is necessary.

To address the subjective judgment calls required by the act, a prudent franchisor also should place a plain statement in the operating manual requiring compliance with the ADA. The franchisor should add to that requirement a suggestion that the franchisee should consult with its legal counsel and/or appropriate expert on the ADA to determine whether it is in compliance. Such statements emphasize that the responsibility for compliance is that of the franchisee.

Finally, a franchisor should treat a finding by the DOJ or the courts that a franchisee is not in compliance with the ADA or other law as a default under the license agreement and terminate, if necessary, for failure to cure. Such action is harsh but necessary for protecting a franchisor from action by the DOJ and civil lawsuits by the disabled.

Training of appropriate personnel of the franchisor is required for a meaningful ADA compliance program. Reservations personnel, in particular, should become familiar with accommodations for the disabled available throughout the system. If an individual has special needs, a reservation person should know or have the ability to learn whether a franchisee can meet those needs. Those in charge of franchise administration, quality, and compliance should be aware of the requirements of the franchisor and the general issues surrounding the ADA. Any person who deals with the media should receive training on this subject.

Needless to say, the franchisor should lead its system by example and take reasonable action to ensure its offices and company-managed locations comply. A corporate policy statement expressing a commitment to serve disabled employees and customers of the franchise system further assists in ensuring compliance.

The best and most cost-effective strategy for franchisors is to take reasonable action over a planned time period to demonstrate a good faith effort in ensuring compliance of the franchise system.

Practice Tips

There are numerous methods by which a franchisor can improve its chances of avoiding vicarious liability, many of which are reflected in the cases discussed above. The following section discusses, in summary form, some of these methods from a practitioner's perspective.

The Franchise Agreement

The franchise agreement and any accompanying operating manual are the first documents a court should examine to determine if the franchisor has reserved the right to exert control over the method by which the franchisee conducts its business in excess of the control required and therefore allowable under the Lanham Act. While oral statements and conduct may also be considered in a vicarious liability action, the franchise agreement is of particular significance.

Disclaim Agency

The franchise agreement should explicitly state that the franchisee is not an agent of the franchisor but, instead, is an independent operator. Although the stated contractual characterization of the parties' relationship is not considered determinative of whether agency has been created, its absence may be. In addition, the franchisor has to decide on the restrictions or reservations of control to be placed in the franchise agreement. The goal is to achieve uniformity among the various businesses using the franchisor's registered marks and to protect the mark's goodwill, while avoiding the assertion of control over daily operations, particularly employee hiring, firing, and supervision.

Require Conspicuous Franchisee Disclosure of Independent Status

In all instances, the franchisor should require and ensure that all franchisees have conspicuously displayed signs and conspicuously displayed statements in all forms, advertisements, and other documents exposed to the public (including on the Internet) that clearly identify the franchises as independently owned and operated businesses. This is especially important on any document a customer signs, such as bills of sale, or other documents confirming a transaction. The courts are often not sympathetic to franchisors who do not avail themselves of this simple protection.

State Only Standards or Rights the Franchisor Intends to Enforce

The franchise agreement should contain a statement incorporating the manual as a part of the agreement. If a franchisor does not intend to exercise a right or enforce a particular standard, it should not be mentioned in the franchise agreement or operating manual. Similarly, if the franchisor does not intend to enforce compliance with a particular method of operation, the franchisor should not retain a right to do so and should not raise an issue regarding it during any inspection.

Require Indemnification from Franchisee

The franchise agreement should contain a specific provision requiring the franchisee to indemnify and defend the franchisor and any parent, subsidiary, affiliates and their respective officers, directors, employees, agents, successors, and assigns. These parties are often sued when the franchisor is intended or sued in addition to the franchisee. The provision should allow the franchisor to retain its own counsel and conduct its own defense if the franchisor deems it appropriate. The indemnification provision should state further that the franchisor is entitled to indemnity, even when punitive damages are allowed or awarded against the franchisor. Certain insurance policies prohibit such coverage unless such protection is required by the franchise agreement. A minority of jurisdictions prohibit coverage for punitive damages due to public policy, but such language should be stated as a matter of form.

To make the indemnification provision meaningful, the franchise agreement should also contain a provision requiring insurance in the amounts necessary to properly cover all potential claims. The franchisor and its affiliates should all be included as additional named insureds. The protection of an insurance policy should exceed the protection of an indemnification clause. Insurance companies usually make liability coverage for franchisors available to franchisees for no additional premium cost.

See *Murray v. Wilbur Curtis Co. Inc.,* 592 N.Y.S.2d 837 (N.Y. App. Div. 1993), in which the appellate court held that a Burger King franchisee had to defend and indemnify Burger King since the franchise agreement required the franchisee to name Burger King as an additional insured on its comprehensive general liability policy. The franchisee had declined the tender on the grounds that the franchisor had acted negligently in designating defective equipment. It relied upon a provision of the agreement which required indemnity unless Burger King was negligent. Despite this, the court held for the franchisor, determining that the comprehensive general liability policy would have covered "all liability arising out of the activities contemplated by the agreement, including liability based upon [Burger King's] own alleged negligence." *Murray,* 592 N.Y.S.2d at 839.

Create an Operating Manual

Getting Started

Once the franchisor determines that a manual must be created, a Manual Committee should be formed. This committee will require the full endorsement of the senior management of the franchisor because significant resources in time, personnel, and costs will be required to complete the project and address franchisee concerns.

The Manual Committee will need to identify the fundamental elements of the franchised business to be covered by the manual, which may change as the needs of the franchise system change. The committee will also need to identify work teams who will work with subject matter experts to develop the manual. The manual will likely address two different categories of information.

The first category will consist of mandatory standards of the franchise system that a franchisee must follow to comply with its franchise obligations. These mandatory standards should set forth *what* a franchisee must do to maintain its operations, not *how* to conduct its operations. For example, a standard could require a franchisee's employees to greet customers in a courteous and friendly manner but should not mandate exactly what the franchisee's employees say. Similarly, an appropriate standard may require a franchisee to provide reasonable security for its premises but should not dictate the path for the security guard's rounds.

Personal injury plaintiffs attempt to use a standards manual against franchisors in almost every lawsuit. The "what-not how" approach helps protect against a plaintiff's claim that a franchisor controls a franchisee sufficiently to establish actual agency or a claim of independent negligence by the franchisor. Thoughtful drafting of standards to place clear responsibility for operations on the franchisee will help avoid franchisor liability and the attendant costs.

The other category of information in the manual will consist of suggested, but not required, procedures that the franchisee may follow to improve business and more closely meet the standards. For example, the franchisor may require as a standard that the franchisee complete a certain type of customer transaction in two minutes. The suggested procedure may propose a method for completing that transaction which the franchisee may, in its discretion, decide to follow.

These suggested procedures should answer for the franchisee the questions of "what," "how," "who," "where," "when," and "why." If the franchisee decides to follow the procedures, it will then have a clear understanding of what the franchisor is suggesting. Recommendation of tools to assist in following the procedure will also be helpful.

Establishing the Basics

Work teams will determine the standards and procedures for the manual related to the various fundamental areas of the franchised business identified by the Manual Committee. The work teams may suggest further refinement of these areas as the manual develops.

To enhance consistency and efficiency, the Manual Committee or the work teams should develop an agreed process for creation and communication of the manual, as well as for the format for the manual and the individual standards and procedures.

Figure 4-1 is a sample format for manual standards and procedures. This format includes a section to describe the policy reason for the standard or procedure. The policy statement will help the franchisee understand the reason for and accept the standard or procedure. The standard or procedure will then inform the franchisee how the policy objective is expected to be or can be accomplished.

The format in Figure 4-1 directs the franchisee to related topics in the manual and informs the franchisee which job functions will find the information useful. The format also provides for a reference number, date, and other information to guide the reader.

Developing Standards and Procedures

The work teams will need to follow the same process to develop standards and procedures. To start, each work team will want to follow these general steps:

1. Determine the current standards and procedures—what is in writing, what is understood, and what is really being practiced at both franchised and company locations.
2. Evaluate these current standards and procedures—what is problematic, relevant, effective, efficient, competitive, practical, and the best practice.

Figure 4-1

Subject: Inventory Accounting   Date:
No.   A 1.96.1 Tab: Chart of Accounts   Replaces:
Other References: Accounting Bulletin for Inventory   Maintenance Accounting

Distribution: Inventory Accounting, General Accounting,
                            Accounts Payable, and Financial Analysis and
                            Reporting

Purpose:
                            To communicate:
 	
Policy:
 	
Procedure:
 	
Contact for information and feedback:
 	
                            Title of Contact, (xxx)yyy-zzzz

3. Determine what niche and image the franchisor wants for the franchise system. For example, does the franchisor want to provide the best service or the best value?

4. Determine root causes of circumstances that are preventing the franchised system from operating in accordance with the franchisor's realistic vision of the franchised system.

5. Develop revised standards and procedures as needed to address these causes and the stated goals. The franchiser should only implement what it is prepared to enforce and justify. As the saying goes, "If you are going to count it, make sure it counts." Develop standards that are repeatable, measurable, and realistic.

6. Develop measurements and measurement tools for assuring that the franchise system follows the standards and procedures. This should include the development of an audit checklist that will measure whether the standard or procedure is being followed correctly. The audit checklist should mirror the manual and be updated when the manual is updated. As with all standards and procedures, all checklists will need to be monitored by the Manual Committee to ensure consistency in format and content.

7. Identify any technology, marketing program, modernization program, and other system changes that may be required to perform the standards and procedures. Confirm the ability of the franchisor to make these changes and evaluate the ability of the franchisees to comply prior to issuing the standards and procedures.

8. Document the new standards and procedures.

9. Test the new standards and procedures, and revise as necessary. The franchisor will get the greatest benefit from a test if it is conducted in operations with varying characteristics that will challenge the standard or procedure. Also, testing in a franchisee's operation may ultimately give the standard or procedure more credibility.

10. Communicate the new standards and procedures. A communication action plan should be established to ensure that interested parties are informed about the progress of the project and any critical issue that may arise. Interested parties will include the franchisor's senior management, the franchise department, the franchisee advisory committee, and the franchisees. Obtaining everyone's agreement and support in the order listed above should help with obtaining the next group's support.

The work teams should not only agree on the above steps, but also should agree on how to maintain their files so that the work can be readily reviewed and accessed. For example, some of the work team files may include the following:

- Current practice on Standard XYZ
- Interview notes on Standard XYZ
- Measurement of Standard XYZ
- Drafts of Standard XYZ
- Comments on Standard XYZ
- Changes to Standard XYZ
- Final Standard XYZ
- Issued updates to Standard XYZ
- Quality inspection checklist for Standard XYZ

Team Membership

Membership on the work teams should be carefully considered to ensure the best product and the least resistance to the changes. Each work team will require a highly organized leader and a detailed action plan identifying (1) the key objective, (2) the actions to be taken to meet the objective, (3) the responsible parties, (4) the date the action must be completed by, (5) the current status of the project, and (6) whether the status has been communicated to the proper parties.

Using work teams with members from different functional areas will help minimize the likelihood that a standard or procedure will have an unexpected detrimental effect on the business. In addition, a franchisee advisory subcommittee should be developed to work closely with the franchisor's Manual Committee. It may be helpful, and even more efficient, to have a franchisee member on each of the work teams. The franchisee work team members can report to the franchisee advisory subcommittee on the manual progress and obtain suggestions regarding particular issues. This process should allow for the raising of troublesome issues along the way, so that when the franchisor is ready to publish the manual, it will already have addressed any material issues with the franchisees.

The franchisor should be careful to preserve the attorney-client privilege regarding documents and communications that involve adoption of a standard or procedure that relates to pending or anticipated litigation. A lawyer should coordinate the team's communications regarding all such matters.

Once the manual is completed, the work teams should deliver their proposed manual sections to the Manual Committee. All of the work teams' standards and procedures should be reviewed by the Manual Committee to ensure that the standards and procedures are consistent, complete, and accurate.

Tips on the Creation and Organization of the Manual

1. Use a structure that is user friendly.
2. Write in plain English.
3. Use short, concise sentences written in the active voice.
4. Use abbreviations, acronyms, or industry terms only if a glossary is provided.
5. Do not use clichés.
6. If multiple binders are used for separate topics, clearly label each as part of the manual and identify what part each binder is.
7. For each binder, use a table of contents and use an index for the entire collection of binders.
8. Limit the number of type faces and sizes on each page of the binder.
9. Use the same format on each page so the reader can easily find the needed information.
10. Use subheadings and an outline form to facilitate ease in information retrieval and a better understanding of the relationships among the information provided.
11. Use clearly understandable charts as a reference tool, but also explain the charts in plain English.
12. Date each page and give each topic a series number.
13. Use three-ring binders to ease inserting and deleting pages.
14. Use separate sections or binders for required standards and for suggested procedures.

Distribution of Operating Manual

The original copy of the manual should stay at the franchisor's headquarters. The franchise agreement should have a provision that states that the manual located at the franchisor's main office will be the governing manual in the event of a dispute. Also, providing the manual and updates electronically in "read only" form can decrease the cost of distribution.

When the franchisor distributes the manual to its franchisees, it should number each copy and obtain a receipt for the manual from the recipient. The receipt should include an acknowledgement and agreement by the franchisee that all rights, title, and interest in the manual are owned by the franchisor; that the manual is a confidential document; and that the franchisee will not disclose the information in the manual other than to those who need to know the information to operate the franchised business, or use it for any purpose other than to conduct its franchised business.

Franchisor's franchise sales department should maintain a manual distribution log. The Manual Committee should maintain a copy of all revisions to the manual dated as they occur. The Franchise Department should also keep a list of the serial number of the manuals for which franchisees are sent updates.

When a franchisee transfers its franchise, the transfer document signed by the transferee should contain an acknowledgment of receipt of the manual.

Updating the Manual

A procedure should be developed for incorporating changes into the manual on a semi-annual basis (or more often if there is a critical need). The Manual Committee should distribute the various sections of the manual to the work teams with the request that the teams review the sections and identify any changes, additions, or deletions that need to occur. The same method for approving original standards and procedures should be used to evaluate and include changes, unless the change is not material.

Updates should be made easily recognizable by presentation with either different colored cover pages or pages with, for example, "updates" printed across the cover page in bold, large print. A cover page that explains the updates or provides a redlined version of changes in addition to the page to go in the manual will help the reader identify and understand the change quickly.

Examining Internal Actions

Assuring Franchisee's Status as an Independent Contractor

Maintaining the independent contractor status of the franchise relationship requires the franchisor's constant vigilance and training on a companywide basis. Many of the documents that a franchisor produces may be relevant to a court's determination of apparent or actual agency, in addition to the key document, the franchise agreement. Many departments produce these documents. Each of the relevant franchisor departments should be trained so that they fully understand the nature of the relationship between the franchisor and its franchisees, and can conduct their relationships with the franchisees and the rest of the outside world accordingly.

Public Relations Department—This department often provides information about the franchisor and its franchisees to government agencies, news reporters, and the general public. Inquiries may relate to the ownership of a particular location, the identity of the purchaser of assets of a franchised business, the requirements regarding operational policies, and many other topics that relate to who owns and governs the daily business decisions of a franchised business. Public relations employees should have an understanding of the critical elements and boundaries of the franchise relationship, so that they can provide accurate information without the need to refer to others for time-sensitive inquiries.

To educate public relations personnel, it is useful to provide them with a list of the operating locations worldwide that identifies the full name, address, and telephone number of the principal contact for each franchisee. In addition, summary information that lists the total number of the franchised and nonfranchised locations will give the department an overview.

In addition to general information about the franchisees, it is helpful to review a sample franchise agreement and a disclosure document with the public relations department so that its members can better understand the respective rights and obligations of the franchisor and franchisee. Moreover, they should be educated about the importance of avoiding suggestions that the franchisor has a right to control aspects of a franchisee's business where it has no such control.

A franchisor's public communications sometimes mistakenly refer to the franchisor as the "parent company" of its franchisees, or to the network of company-owned and franchise-owned stores as "company-owned stores" or "the company's network of stores." Not only are these terms contrary to the franchise relationship, they mislead the public. "Parent company" indicates a direct corporate affiliation between the franchisor and its franchisees and encourages the belief that the franchisor has ownership and control over its system's stores. Referring to the franchise system's network in any manner as company stores also gives the public the impression that the franchisor owns all the system's locations. When a franchisor continually uses these terms in presentations, press releases, and published materials, a court may consider an explanation of the true franchise relationship irrelevant in a defense to a claim of apparent agency.

In the 1980s, many corporations began to use the term "partnering" when describing business relationships. The term is meant to describe a coordinated effort to pursue a common purpose. Using the term "partner" is admirable symbolism, but it creates risk in the franchising context. When franchisors must fight daily legal battles over agency and apparent authority issues, using words that promote their adversaries' arguments negatively affects the bottom line. If a franchisor feels it must use terms like "partner" to convey an idea, it should make certain that written materials containing the term also explain its use or define the franchise relationship.

Referencing the franchise relationship accurately should become part of the corporate culture. To help ensure this, in-house counsel should review all public communications (including on the Internet) that describe the franchise system.

Publicized emergency situations are another area where it is important to understand and properly handle the boundaries of the franchise relationship. Franchise systems are periodically exposed to difficult events such as explosions, violent crimes, discrimination claims, and food contamination. These are the types of events that attract public attention, create rumors, and can result in litigation for both the franchisor and franchisee.

Contingency plans for emergencies, along with related training, should be developed at franchisee locations. Practicalities of the franchise relationship render it inadvisable for the franchisor to assume any duties related to the immediate handling of an emergency at a franchise location. Nevertheless, it is advisable to request each franchisee to refer all questions concerning the franchise system and standards to a specific employee of the franchisor. In situations attracting intense media interest, it could be necessary for a franchisor to send a representative to the affected franchise location to respond to media inquiries. If a franchisor retains persons with expertise in handling the emergency at hand, an offer of assistance to the franchisee should be made. If a claim of franchisee wrongdoing is made, a franchisor should immediately commence an investigation to determine if the franchisee has violated system standards or the law. If the franchisee has, the franchisor should ensure that the franchisee remedies the situation quickly. If the franchisee fails to do so, at the very least, it risks a claim of franchisor negligence, in addition to vicarious liability if the franchisee engages in the same conduct in the future. A franchisor that appears knowledgeable and responsive in the face of a franchisee crisis will reduce the likelihood and amount of any damages against it if a lawsuit results.

Marketing Department—This department will be involved in referencing the franchisor and franchisee operating locations on a regular basis—for example, in ad copy for direct mail, the Internet, television, radio, and print; and in material used for joint marketing programs and in joint marketing contracts. In-house counsel should work with the marketing department to establish standard language to be included in ad copy. An example of appropriate language is "Burger House is a network of independently owned and operated franchisees." The language should be conspicuous in the ad both in type size and placement. Additional or different language may be needed depending on the nature of the ad and the nature of the franchise system.

Providing Form Contracts as a Service to Franchisees

Some franchisors sell or gratuitously provide their own form contracts to franchisees or their store managers and assume that the form will be redrafted to delete the franchisor as a party. Experience indicates that franchisees do not always follow this practice. Occasionally, the franchisor's name is printed as the contracting party, but the document is signed by the franchisee or the franchisee inserts its name as an additional party and signs on behalf of both. Usually, the franchisee is not intending to commit fraud, but sloppy practice creates a risk that the franchisor will be found liable for permitting the franchisee to hold out the franchisor as a party to the transaction. Form contracts delivered to franchisees should delete the franchisor's name and contain a blank for the franchisee's name or be printed with the franchisee's name only, while leaving the franchisor's trademark on the form.

Employee Training

A franchisor should explain thoroughly the franchise relationship in employee orientation. This not only ensures that employees recognize franchisee agency issues when they start work, it also should deepen their understanding of the business and lessen their learning curve. Those employees who deal directly with franchisees and vendors or are involved in litigation or dispute resolution should be retrained periodically. Including franchisee agency issues as part of a routine business seminar is a good retraining vehicle. A method for making retraining more interesting and meaningful is to raise issues that have arisen in the franchise industry as a result of noncompliance with the basic rules. During training, care must be taken not to disclose privileged or confidential information related to pending disputes, settlements, or sensitive issues.

Monitoring and Enforcement

The manual will have limited value if the franchisor fails to ensure that the members of the franchise system comply with the manual. Three steps should be taken to ensure that franchisees comply with the manual. The first involves communicating with franchisees about the purpose, importance, and content of the manual through mailings and meetings. Second, the franchisor should provide training on the manual's content, in both initial orientations and retraining. For each standard and procedure, the franchisor will want to identify the tools that the franchisee currently has that will help them meet the standard or follow the procedure. Further tools, such as software programs, may need to be developed by the franchisor for the franchisee to be able to comply. Additionally, the franchisor may need to train its franchisees on how to use the tools.

The third step toward getting value from a manual is to monitor and enforce compliance. While several franchise companies are moving toward statistics-based quality evaluations, on-site quality inspections are vital in defending tort claims and minimizing exposure to punitive damages. To ensure objective enforcement of standards, a group in the franchisor company that is separate from the franchise sales group should be responsible for monitoring the franchisee operations. Quality inspectors should have a good understanding of the business so they can more quickly identify problems of, and solutions for, the franchisee. A franchisor's staff who have successfully operated company stores are good candidates for the inspector position, because they have more credibility with franchisees.

Quality inspectors should be trained together so that they learn the same approaches for interpreting and measuring standards, and assessing what is a material variance from a standard. Quality inspectors will benefit by periodically auditing different franchisees or regions. This will eliminate biases that may develop with particular franchisees and allow auditors to identify regional variances that need to be considered when evaluating a franchisee's compliance. Monthly meetings to review questions of interpretation or evaluation will help ensure that the quality inspectors continue to approach inspections consistently. Mystery shoppers and customer surveys may also be helpful to add to the neutrality of the inspection results.

Training for quality inspectors should emphasize the importance of each inspection in minimizing liability for the franchisor. Most franchise agreements require, at a minimum, that franchisees operate safe premises and comply with federal, state, and local laws. Such language is sufficient to justify inclusion of a checklist in the quality evaluation forms addressing blatant safety and security issues.

Quality inspectors usually are not trained to conduct loss prevention surveys, but they have the common sense necessary to recognize an obvious issue. They are also in the best position to notice obvious defects that might result in safety problems. The first, and often overlooked, item on the checklist is an examination of the permits and certificates required to keep the franchise property in operation. The inspection should note only whether the certificate appears on its face to be current and valid. Such certificates include verifications that the property has undergone governmental inspections of fire equipment, kitchens, elevators, and any other certification applicable to the franchisee's operation.

The quality inspector should also note obvious safety issues, which would include leaks, blatantly inadequate lighting, holes or tears in the floor covering, faulty doors or door locks, furniture in disrepair, and other issues that would be apparent to most people. Failure to take action over such matters sets the stage for large punitive damage verdicts. The inspector must be trained to decide whether a condition presents such a large risk or can be fixed so quickly that he or she should require the franchisee to cure the problem immediately while still on-site.

If the inspector determines that an immediate cure is neither reasonable nor practical, then the franchisor should monitor the situation to make certain the franchisee makes the cure as soon as reasonably possible. In the event the franchisee fails to cure the problem by the anticipated date, either a reasonable basis for extending the date should be recorded or the franchisor should issue an immediate default with an accelerated termination date. If appropriate, the franchisor should require the franchisee to post warnings of any hazards and restrict public access during the cure period or until the property is terminated from the system.

The franchisor should designate a supervising employee to answer questions and handle disputes between the inspector and the franchisee over any matters concerning these serious issues. The inspector should try to obtain the franchisee's signature on any report written at the franchisee's location identifying serious problems. If the problems are significant, and in particular if the franchisee refuses to sign the on-site report, some franchisors have their inspectors videotape the "evidence." This approach is risky as the videotape may be used as evidence against the franchisor as well as the franchisee.

A standard inspection report form should be developed to ensure that the same information is obtained for each inspection and is communicated uniformly. Quality inspectors should avoid subjective comments, such as "the franchisee seems to be trying very hard" or "the franchisee is fighting hard against competition and therefore is doing. . . ." A lawyer should review all reports prior to their issuance. Draft reports should be distributed to the franchisor's attorney with a cover memo requesting the lawyer's advice to identify any legal problems. Once the lawyer has approved the report, the quality inspector can send the draft report to the franchise department and any other department that is responsible for an area that may be violated. Any action that a department agrees to take in relation to the franchisee—for example, that a particular department will review the issues with the franchisee—should be included in the report. Once all groups to whom the report is routed confirm their agreement to the report, it may be sent to the franchisee. All reports issued and any responses should be filed in the franchisee's main legal file.

Reports of on-site quality inspections will provide evidence of the condition of a franchisee's premises at the time of the most recent inspection prior to an event giving rise to a lawsuit. If the inspector performed a thorough job, recorded conditions, objectively addressed any deficiencies causally related to the subsequent event, and the franchisor had no actual or imputed notice of a subsequent problem, then a court should find that the franchisor acted in a reasonable and prudent manner. The franchisor should be able to defeat any asserted negligence claim that the franchisor failed to fulfill the duties of a reasonable franchisor. Punitive damages also should be eliminated based upon such claims.

Loss Prevention Programs

Traditional loss prevention at franchisee locations is not the responsibility of a franchisor nor should a franchisor undertake this duty. Nevertheless, certain types of knowledge may give rise to specific loss prevention duties. A franchisor's quality department should coordinate with the insurance and loss prevention efforts of the company. The inspector should route safety concern findings to a central source to determine whether common safety trends or issues exist throughout the system.

In addition, because injured parties often make claims against both the franchisee and franchisor, the franchisor may unwillingly become a central repository of the facts regarding the cause of many claims and suits. Repetitive injuries caused by conditions or equipment in widespread use throughout a franchise system probably give rise to a duty to warn franchisees about the risk. A responsible franchisor should take the further step of requiring its franchisees to investigate their premises to determine whether the problem exists, make necessary changes, and provide written certification to the franchisor that the required action was completed. Conditions at individual franchise properties could also give rise to a franchisor duty to demand that a franchisee cure a defect in the premises if a claim or suit of which the franchisor receives notice makes it apparent to a reasonable person that allowing the condition to continue creates a risk of harm to others.

The franchisor should designate one or more individuals to review claims and suits for such issues. The task ought not to be time-consuming because only obvious conditions are at issue. The task does not require an expert analysis of each matter. Loss prevention programs concerning franchisees should be limited to obvious or repetitive situations. Such programs are designed only to convey relevant knowledge to franchisees and demand correction. If a franchisee permits the defective condition to reoccur without the knowledge of the franchisor or deceives the franchisor about the cure, the paper trail created by this compliance process should help exculpate the franchisor from liability.

Conclusion

Establishing operating manuals and related compliance programs is important generally to the long-term success of franchisors. Such actions promote consistency and integrity in the corporate culture. A franchisor's employees know the practices and philosophies that should guide their decision making. The franchisee may conduct business with full awareness of the franchisor's criteria for satisfactory performance. This should lead to more efficient dealings between the franchisor and franchisee, fewer franchise disputes, and reduced risks for the franchisor of uncontrollable liability. Most importantly, such an approach and program should improve the image of the brand to the public. The small investment in manpower for monitoring of the program will pay substantial dividends.

Notes

1. References to products in this chapter are intended to include services.

CHAPTER 5

Franchise Relationship Management

Raymond L. Miolla, Jr. and Andrew C. Selden

"We must indeed all hang together, or, most assuredly, we shall all hang separately."

Benjamin Franklin: remark to
John Hancock, at signing of the
Declaration of Independence,
4 July 1776

Introduction

A successful franchisor/franchisee relationship requires more than strict compliance with laws and contracts. It also requires acknowledging that the franchisor/franchisee relationship is a uniquely long-term relationship where the ultimate success of both parties depends upon mutual cooperation and a shared sense of responsibility. Accordingly, the goal of a corporate compliance program should not be limited to ensuring that corporate employees follow the letter of all applicable laws and contracts. It should also provide a framework for ensuring that corporate employees are acting in accordance with the policies and values of the franchisor. This chapter will explore the importance of good franchisor/franchisee relations and examine ways to build into your corporate compliance program the institutions, processes, and guidelines necessary to encourage corporate employees and franchisees to value good relations and avoid unnecessary conflict.

Why Good In-System Relationships Matter

Interests of System Participants

Good in-system relations are much more than a moral objective. Business is, after all, business, and the objective of a franchise-based business is no different from any other: outrunning the competition to anticipate and serve customers' needs, and to make money doing it. Good relations within a franchise organization are necessary, not simply desirable, because competing profitably in the marketplace cannot be pursued successfully by a franchise organization riven by internal strife.

Although franchisors and franchisees share this general economic interest, the structure of the traditional franchise relationship often sends them in different directions. Traditional franchisors and franchisees both benefit from sharing a strong, competitive system, but they also make their profit in different ways. The franchisor often runs its own outlets, but it may also be a licensor, a vendor, a service provider, a lender, and/or a landlord. The franchisee is usually engaged in a retailing business and, relative to the franchisor, may be a buyer, a tenant, a borrower, and/or a licensee. These differing roles create an inherent divergence of interest in even the best run and most benign franchise organizations. For a franchise-based business to function up to its full potential, this divergence of interest must be reconciled with the parties' shared interest in the success of the system.

Franchise organizations flourish when the participants recognize the significant advantages to be derived by all of them from bridging (or occasionally even just overlooking) the differences and exploiting the commonalities. Franchise organizations that fail to reach that understanding will never realize their full potential. In those cases, shareholders of the franchisor will be every bit as frustrated and disappointed as will the franchisee/investors in the system.

What are the investment objectives of parties to a franchise-based business? From the perspective of the franchisee, the objectives include both capital leverage and information leverage: purchasing from the franchisor the know-how that would otherwise be developed at presumably greater cost through trial and error, combined with the (presumably favorable) goodwill associated with use of the franchisor's methods and trademarks. The franchisee expects to use this leveraged capital and information base to run a successful business, to earn a positive return on investment in the business, and to achieve a level of personal satisfaction in doing so. In pursuing these goals, franchisees certainly expect to have to function in a competitive environment, but few, if any, genuinely expect their own franchisor to be a significant competitive threat in terms of "encroaching" locations it sponsors, or unnecessarily expensive equipment or supplies it sells. This expectation exists empirically irrespective of the contents of the franchisor's UFOC. These are prime examples of areas where a franchise relationship can become strained when the two parties pursue their own individual goals without due regard for the interests of the other, or of the system as a whole.

The franchisor's objectives in building a franchise-based business organization also include capital leverage, but beyond that, particular objectives of individual franchisors vary globally. The franchisor most often undertakes a franchise-based form of business in order to recruit into the enterprise the capital, both financial and human, of the franchisee/investor. This leveraging allows rapidity of expansion, facilitates penetration of distant or foreign markets, and in some cases allows more rapid accretion of market share than would otherwise be the case. The franchisor's goals can be threatened, and the relationship strained, however, when a franchisee deviates significantly from system requirements, perhaps by refusing to contribute to or participate in system marketing initiatives, or perhaps cutting costs by purchasing substandard supplies or deferring facility repairs.

The multiple roles that franchisors and franchisees take on within the ongoing franchise are represented by a variety of more traditional common law relationship models. These include landlord-tenant, licensor-licensee, lender-borrower, vendor-vendee, and others. These component relationships usually do not include master-servant (employer-employee) or fiduciary relations, but the franchise relationship itself—representing an accumulation of component relationships set forth in the franchise agreement and collateral contracts, and filtered through traditional common law principles for interpreting and enforcing private contracts—certainly is much more than the sum of those component relationships. The common law has yet to evolve a fully satisfactory single legal model for the *combination* of traditional business relationships embraced by most business format franchises, so the challenge remains for parties and their lawyers to find workable solutions to system conflict arising from a variety of sources without sacrificing the parties' respective investment objectives.

Within the component relationships of the franchise contracts are the seeds of dissension. Each of these component or subordinate relationships involves an element of adversarial relations. Certainly a seller and buyer have conflicting interests relative to price and terms of sale, as do a landlord and tenant. If a franchise devolves into only one of these relationships, the inherent adversarial character of that relationship is likely to come to the fore, damaging the prospects for cooperation and collaboration that drives success of a franchise-based business network, viewed as a whole. And this is true even in benign or ideal circumstances because the friction of divergent or conflicting economic interests is intrinsic in these component relationships. Where either party to a franchise relationship exploits power or position in one of the component relationships to obtain opportunistic advantage, a breakdown in the umbrella franchise relationship is all but certain. This breakdown can certainly impair the working relationship between the franchisor and that franchisee, but the strain and collateral damage can also injure the entire system.

Thus, the success of the franchise-based enterprise, involving efforts of both the franchisor and the franchisee in a "Shared Business Enterprise," depend on identifying and exploiting the parties' shared interests in their common objectives, which usually involve competitive success of the system as a whole, appropriate research and development, marketing and advertising campaigns, adherence to system norms, and fair allocations of growth opportunities, as well as reconciling sometimes divergent or conflicting partisan economic interests.

Parties who act opportunistically in a franchise relationship to exploit their individual interests in the component or subordinate relationships usually end up doing so at the expense of undermining their ability to achieve success in the broader franchise enterprise. For example, franchisors who so exploit their franchise networks, perhaps through inappropriate sourcing restrictions, unduly restrictive system governance procedures, or the like, certainly should not then wonder why franchisees do not respond enthusiastically to "company" marketing initiatives, or may even resist forcefully, in legal and even legislative channels, franchisor activities (such as encroachment, or monopolization of sourcing) that franchisees perceive as threatening to their core investment interests. Similarly, franchisees who consistently ignore system-wide marketing programs, or let their outlets deteriorate, should not complain when their franchisor denies them expansion opportunities in favor of other franchisees who more fully embrace shared system initiatives and values.

Franchisees are increasingly sophisticated, well educated, well advised, and demanding in their franchise relationships. Franchisors who fail to respect the symbiotic nature of the franchise relationship and the investment objectives of their franchisees (in the eyes of their franchisees, irrespective of what the parties' technical legal rights might be) should not wonder why their systems become unmanageable as franchisees become alienated, resentful, and fearful. Franchisees, by the same token, should not wonder why their franchisor becomes alienated, hostile, and suspicious if they exploit opportunistically their relative individual advantage, perhaps by pursuing individual, local, business initiatives at the expense of system integrity or uniformity of brand development.

Public and Regulatory Perspective

Because franchising is an important economic force in the U.S. economy it should be little wonder that public policy addresses itself to the franchise relationship. Legislatures and even most administrative bureaucracies take seriously the public objectives of promoting economic stability, encouraging growth in employment, conserving judicial resources, pursuing efficiency of public agency operation and administration, and protecting the public from misrepresentation.

Politically, more than one legislator has observed that for every franchisor in the United States, there are hundreds of franchisees. Franchisees tend to be local small business owners, and voters. Franchisors tend to be remote corporations. Since "all politics is local," it should surprise no one that when state legislatures are motivated to investigate franchise relationships, the tendency is to protect the interests of the local investor, business owner, and voter.

What most legislators hear about franchising seems to come more from franchisees whose businesses have failed for one reason or another. This incomplete factual understanding of franchising makes a volatile mix with the political environment in which those grievances are voiced.

For franchisors who oppose public legislative intervention into franchise relationships, the imperative of maintaining good in-system relations is self-evident.

Role and Responsibilities of Franchise Lawyers

The rules of professional responsibility recite that a lawyer has a duty to be a zealous advocate of the lawyer's client's interests. Every business lawyer knows that the lawyer's role in a business transaction is to provide the best advice possible, attempt to maximize the clients' position in negotiations, and then facilitate a closing.

The business lawyer is accustomed to dealing with distinct transactions, where the parties will have little or no continuing relationship. If a bridge needs to be burned, it is a regrettable but profitable necessity. A trial attorney is even less concerned with preserving a relationship between two combatants.

The problem with these traditional roles is that they seldom make sense in the franchisor/franchisee context. In most cases, the franchisor and franchisee will remain in business together long after the transaction or dispute is forgotten. For example, if the franchisor's lawyer adequately disclaims on paper an equipment warranty but does not ensure that the franchisee understands the existence or meaning of the disclaimer, the lawyer has done his client no good service when the equipment fails. All the lawyer has done is left the franchisor with an unhappy, aggrieved business associate. Similarly, if a trial lawyer for a franchisee alienates the franchisor with baseless claims of "bad faith" in a lease dispute at one site, the franchisor is unlikely to be responsive to the franchisee's later attempt to find a "business solution" to an issue at another location.

This does not mean that franchisees must stoically suffer abuse at the hands of the franchisor, or vice versa. What it does mean is that lawyers (for either side) can add value and well represent their own client's best interests by tempering their approach, to remember at all times that the franchisor and franchisee will probably remain in business together at the conclusion of the transaction or dispute and that both share an interest in a healthy and productive system. Transactions can be an opportunity to build trust and cooperation if handled correctly, and disputes can be handled professionally and without personal recrimination in order to minimize the damage to the relationship and collateral damage to the system. Later in this chapter Alternative Dispute Resolution discusses how various procedures can further this goal.

The challenge to the lawyer representing the franchisor, the franchisee, or a group or association of franchisees, is to observe that the client's interests in a franchise business, even in the event of a particular transaction or a dispute, include an overriding interest in the success and growth of the system as a whole. This interest of the client may cause the lawyer to adopt a strategy in advising and representing the client that differs from what "zealous advocacy" of partisan interest might call for outside of an ongoing business relationship. A lawyer must recognize that the client has a material interest in acting in a manner consistent with the best interests of the system.

How to Go About Achieving Good Relationships

Methods of Identifying Common Ground

Good franchise relationships are an ongoing *process* more than a particular *result*.

Franchisors and their franchisees can employ effective methods of identifying what the common ground is in each franchise system. Continuous, open, substantive, professional, and copious communication is a necessary foundation. A full discussion of communication issues in franchise systems is found later in this chapter.

The first, easiest, and most important method of identifying common interests is to establish, collaboratively, what the goals of the system are. Certainly in a start-up franchise organization this responsibility will fall entirely or disproportionately on the franchisor. But in a mature organization, system goals may have never been concretely articulated, or have changed (or become obsolete) over time or in response to market conditions. In those circumstances, there is every reason for a franchisor to work collaboratively with its franchisees to identify and articulate shared system goals. It does no good for a franchisor to prescribe goals or strategies to which its franchisees do not subscribe.

Different means can be employed to achieve this. If a franchisee association exists, the franchisor can ask it to form a task force to work with representatives of the franchisor to develop such a "mission statement." If there is no independent representative of the franchisee community, perhaps the franchisor can help organize, or use an existing, franchisee advisory council or independent association. Franchisee opinion and participation in this effort can also be pursued through the use of focus groups or other recognized, objective, methods of gathering opinion data.

Participants in the process of articulating shared system objectives all must understand, recognize, and respect the investment interests of other parties to the system. Without reciprocal understanding and respect for the other participants' investment interest, this process cannot be successful.

Paramount in the articulation of shared objectives is the ongoing mutual responsibility of the various participants for the success of the system. This is an area that may be challenging for some lawyers, who may be more focused on preserving and enforcing the "rights" of their clients, but the client certainly did not invest in the franchise system in order to establish and exercise its "rights," but to achieve its business objectives. Both the franchisor who solicited sales of franchises, and the franchisee who by buying into the system became a member of the team, share a business responsibility to their respective owners to work towards the success of that shared business enterprise. For a franchised business organization to flourish, both the franchisor and the franchisees—and their lawyers—must continuously ask, "What is best for the *system*?"

Methods of Communication

Methods of Communication between Franchisor and Franchisees

Good communication is key to a good franchisor/franchisee relationship. How much communication is necessary will depend on the nature of the franchise. Choices of methods of communication are increasingly complex. The traditional systemic approaches include monthly mailings to franchisees and annual or quarterly meetings at the national or regional level. Another traditional practice is "polling" or surveying franchisee support for various franchisor initiatives. For example, if a franchisor wants to initiate a national price point promotion, it can poll its franchisees to evaluate the level of franchisee support. Commercials advertising a 99¢ price point product promotion will be counterproductive if two-thirds of the franchised outlets decline to participate.

Still another traditional communication tool is training provided by the franchisor, both in the classroom and at the franchised outlet. Franchisors who approach training as a "policeman" miss an important opportunity to set a tone of cooperation and mutual investment. Approaching training and operations support as a teacher may not put you in the best position to take legal action against an isolated nonperforming franchisee, but it will maximize the performance of all of the other franchisees. The value of maximizing the performance of the entire system vastly outweighs the extra effort required to prepare an isolated enforcement action.

Less traditional yet potentially efficient methods of communication also are available. For example, if the franchisor has a voice mail system, it can assign a mailbox to each franchisee. This allows the franchisor to send broadcast messages to the franchise community and also allows franchisees to respond with questions or comments in an easy and efficient manner. It also has an intangible benefit in that it can help to create a sense of integration and incorporation on both sides. The franchisor should, however, make sure that appropriate safeguards and firewalls are built into the system to ensure that confidential messages are not inadvertently delivered to unintended mailboxes.

A more recent method of communication is the Internet. Although more expensive and complicated than a voice mail system, establishing the franchisor's web site as a communication vehicle has the added advantage of allowing the franchisor to present more detailed information. It is even possible for the franchisor to make documents such as applications or polling forms available to franchisees through the web site.

Practical and technical limits exist. Not all franchisees are willing to pay the cost of their own computer access to the Internet. Recruiting franchisees who feel comfortable using the Internet may be even harder. Moreover, there are obvious security issues. Web sites may be designed with restricted access and each franchisee can receive a security password. That said, the franchisor still needs to consider whether highly confidential information such as marketing plans belongs on the Internet.

It is also possible to connect web sites belonging to the franchisor, franchise association, and suppliers through various "bridges."

The subject of franchisee web sites is a separate issue, raising similar questions of content and security. A copy of the policy on franchisee web sites used by Burger King Corporation (BKC) is attached as Exhibit 5-A.

For a useful discussion of communication generally between a franchisor and its franchisees, see "Plain Talk," the coursebook of a separate Forum program, available from the Forum or the American Bar Association publications office in Chicago.

Communication Among Franchisees

Franchisees have both a need and various opportunities to communicate amongst themselves for purposes of participating in system decision-making and governance. Franchisees who volunteer to serve in leadership capacities in the franchisee association or advisory council take on a somewhat anomalous position of responsibility for the success of the system which sometimes has the practical effect of aligning them more with the franchisor than with the views of some individual members of the franchisee community. Franchisee leaders are no more omniscient or possessed of perfect foresight and judgment than are the franchisor's officers. Thus, franchisee leaders have both a practical and a political need to stay in close touch with the constituents they represent.

Communication within a franchisee community must be bilateral. Association meetings must occur with sufficient frequency to assure informed decision-making within the franchisee ranks. Newsletters, opinion surveys, and independent professional advice are all part of the process of informing franchisee leaders in their role in system governance.

For franchisees to participate effectively, responsibly, and professionally in system decision-making sometimes requires that franchisees engage their own independent experts, whether legal, marketing, financial, or other, at their own expense, to inform them in areas that may be beyond their individual experience or competencies. There is nothing inappropriate about franchisees, for example, engaging expert legal counsel to advise them on the laws relating to the franchise relationship, or marketing experts to advise them on consumer preferences and advertising strategies. Some of this information must be shared within the franchisee community, and some with the franchisor and some of it must be kept confidential; franchisee leaders must draw wise divisions. Franchisees often will find that hiring an expert consultant will refine and validate their opinions, as well as adding great weight to their opinions when shared with the franchisor. Occasionally, expert advice may be grounds for reconsideration of franchisee opinion on a matter, and franchisees must be open to that possibility as well.

Finally, it is every bit as incumbent on franchisees as it is on the franchisor to share information responsibly and appropriately within the system. This does not mean that franchisees have a legal or practical duty to share everything they know with their peers or the franchisor, but it does mean that the franchisees should not withhold material information when disclosure to the franchisor would enhance system decision-making, or business growth.

Methods of Communication with External Constituencies

In addition to communicating with each other, franchisors, franchisee associations, and individual franchisees must also communicate with external constituencies who affect the franchisor/franchisee relationship. The most obvious examples are the government and the press.

In the governmental arena, franchisors and franchisees will have some areas of common interest (for example, minimum wage legislation) and some areas of complete disagreement (for example, some franchising regulations). Although lobbying activities are for professionals, franchisors and franchisees can add value by identifying the areas where franchisor and franchisee have common interests. By combining their efforts in these areas they can both build a spirit of cooperation and trust, and also present the most effective case.

For franchisors and franchisees, communicating with one voice in the legislative and regulatory arenas is critical. It's the most sure-fire way to affect successfully the outcome of important public policy issues. Obviously, that means the franchisor and franchisee need to have the same (or largely similar) positions on the same issues. Generally, this consensus is not difficult to achieve.

Issues about which franchisors and franchisees tend to care most are those that affect their businesses. For regulatory issues that affect the system as a whole, finding common ground in identifying and prioritizing issues is often surprisingly easy. In a few cases the nature of the franchisor-franchisee relationship makes achieving consensus more difficult. Some types of franchise relationship legislation provide a good example. However, if the legislation would have a negative or positive impact on the franchise system as a whole, agreement can be reached even here.

Once both parties clearly understand the potential impact of proposed policy, they will share a common interest. Franchisors often have the resources to analyze the impact of proposed policy, and they can involve franchisees in the analysis in order to help develop consensus. At the same time, franchisees can be excellent conduits of information to franchisors, particularly on state and local policy issues. They are the eyes and ears of the system throughout the country. There are, therefore, excellent synergies inherent in the franchise relationship.

Once issues are identified and prioritized, the focus turns to strategy to affect outcomes, and orchestrating the tactical lobbying campaign accordingly. Again, franchisees can play a critical role. Legislators care most about one issue: re-election. Only their constituents can vote for them, and the constituents are therefore who they want most to please. Franchisees, then, are the perfect contacts to do the grassroots lobbying, while franchisors are most often best at coordinating the political process. This is yet another example of franchise synergies.

With regard to the press, leadership responsibility in building and managing the brand usually should fall to the franchisor. With this comes the responsibility of hiring a professional public relations advisor and incorporating franchisees into the process. Franchisees must in turn view the franchisor's public relations representative as an asset and commit to the brand that they will work with that representative to ensure that the brand is presented in a way that is consistent with the system's marketing strategy. If both sides work collaboratively in public relations rather than unilaterally, then the system as a whole is most likely to benefit.

Cooperation on public relations is especially important in a crisis involving public health or allegations of wrongdoing such as racial discrimination. The franchisor can facilitate cooperation and damage control in these instances by establishing a clear program for crisis management, and ensuring that all franchisees have a clear understanding of which franchisor executive or system spokesperson should be contacted in the case of a crisis.

Franchise systems increasingly must interact with another external constituency: third party interest groups. Whether those groups are the National Association for the Advancement of Colored People, Christian Coalition, or handicapped rights organizations, it is in everyone's interest that the system speak with one voice. From the franchisors' perspective, this will be possible only if the franchisees and their associations are involved in initiatives like minority recruiting or compliance with the Americans With Disabilities Act (ADA). Burger King Corporation, for example, has a "Diversity Action Council" including BKC executives, prominent franchisees, and community leaders to advise BKC on diversity issues. Again, the key is active collaboration for the benefit of the system.

Means of Interaction

Councils and Associations

There are as many means of interaction between franchisors and their franchisees as there are systems. The most effective, both from the franchisees' perspective and from the perspective of the system as a whole, is the independent, autonomous franchisee association funded and operated by franchisees. A franchisee association is a trade association representing the interests of its members in a common area, in this case system governance and system success. The next most effective is the franchisor-sponsored, but franchisee-elected, advisory council. Usually unincorporated, the advisory council serves to provide a forum for bilateral communication between the franchisee community and the franchisor.

Systems that are too young or too small to function effectively with an advisory council or autonomous association, or a larger or older system with a specialized need for one-time interaction, might form some type of ad hoc task force or advisory body with both franchisor and franchisee members to deal with a specific issue over a limited period of time.

In this regard, some systems use advisory groups or standing committees that are focused on specific issues, such as marketing or advertising, or distribution, sometimes over long periods of time, or which exist only for a limited period of time.

Franchisee associations themselves can exist in a variety of different forms: some may be a single national organization, others may be discrete geographic regional associations, or there may be some combination of the two, with discrete regional organizations participating in a national umbrella organization. Associations usually engage in a scope of activities that transcends interaction with their franchisor. A growing number of franchise systems have associations. When the association is truly representative of its constituent franchisee community and professionally run, it can be a real asset to the system and a benefit to the franchisor. An association does not, of course, eliminate or preclude problems or friction in the system, but it can go a long way to solve relational problems as well as business problems in the system when they arise. For a comprehensive treatment of the role of autonomous associations, and how to organize and manage them, see "The Dynamics of Franchisee Associations." (Gerald T. Aaron, Anita K. Blair, Andrew C. Selden, Mitchell Shapiro, Alan Silberman, Mary Beth Trice, ABA 1991 Forum on Franchising, San Francisco).

Special Function Bodies: Co-ops

Purchasing Co-ops   In many business format franchise systems, the franchisor is also a manufacturer and/or distributor of goods to the franchise system. This may be a function of the franchisor's desire to regulate the nature of the goods being used or sold at the franchised outlets, and/or the need to maintain proprietary information. Or, it may reflect the franchisor's desire to develop a separate source of additional income.

Franchisors sometimes receive secondary benefits from the supply and distribution channel, even if they are not the direct manufacturer or distributor. The franchisor may receive various types of fees, rebates, or allowances from suppliers or distributors. Such arrangements often distress franchisees, who see them as merely adding cost.

These franchisor goals will sometimes conflict with the goals of the franchisee, who is interested in minimizing its cost of goods sold. This will create an inherent conflict if the franchisor is indeed seeking a second source of income, or if the franchisor simply cannot provide the goods at the lowest possible price. Some less obvious considerations can also come into play. Obtaining the lowest possible price is not the only goal of a supply and distribution system. A supply and distributor system must also ensure a continuous and reliable supply of goods that meet the specifications of the franchise system. These goals often require that franchisees compromise their attempts to obtain goods at the lowest possible price.

The idea of a joint purchasing cooperative for the entire system is sometimes the best way to balance a franchisor's need to assure system-wide reliability of delivery and quality, against the franchisees' desire to obtain the lowest possible price.

A purchasing cooperative is the pooling of purchasing requirements by a group of individual businesses with common needs to achieve lower delivered costs and more favorable terms. Of course, skilled, professional management is usually necessary to achieve efficient volume purchasing. In a fast food chain which has 2,000 units, averaging $1 million of sales annually per unit and incurring food costs equal to 30 percent of revenues, total purchases for food items will be $600 million annually. If a 1 percent savings in food costs can be achieved, the system saves a staggering $6 million per year, which translates to $3,000 per unit on average.

There is no precise formula for achieving this type of savings, but it is clear that volume purchasing and distribution open up many options. Even suppliers benefit from a system which purchases through cooperatives. Among other things, it allows suppliers to (1) plan production more effectively, thereby reducing manufacturing costs; (2) purchase raw materials in larger quantities, which usually leads to better unit prices for those raw materials; (3) take advantage of volume freight rates and other distribution efficiencies; and (4) reduce credit risk and cost of sales.

All of this translates into lower cost for the supplier, which should in turn be passed on to the franchise system. Volume purchasing may also result in improved distribution methods and allow the system to coordinate and more effectively use marketing allowances.

The Burger King system offers a good model for capturing these values. In the early 1990s purchasing had become a difficult issue within the Burger King system. Most of the system-wide purchasing was being managed by the distribution arm of Burger King Corporation (BKC). The balance of the products were purchased by independent, BKC-approved distributors. This arrangement was disliked by the Burger King franchisees for several reasons: (1) the franchisees had minimal ability to affect purchasing decisions; (2) BKC was not able to obtain the best available prices because, among other things, purchasing was fragmented; (3) vendors mistakenly viewed distributors as the buyer and thus distributors retained much of the economic benefits; (4) franchisees questioned whether BKC had committed adequate financial and personnel resources to purchasing; and (5) the franchisees believed, mistakenly, that BKC was making a lot of money on this part of its business.

From BKC's perspective, it was struggling to make a profit and deal with a credit risk which was substantially larger than the credit risk present in the balance of its business. Both parties agreed, however, that the purchasing responsibilities were distracting BKC from its other activities and promoting friction between BKC and its franchisees.

Recognizing the existing problems in purchasing, BKC and its franchisees agreed to the creation of a joint purchasing cooperative which would assume all responsibilities with respect to purchasing for the Burger King system. The plan for the co-op, called Restaurant Services, Inc. (RSI), included the following elements:

1. BKC would provide the start-up capital for RSI out of dollars it would save from eliminating the general and administrative costs associated with providing purchasing functions.

2. RSI's board of directors would be controlled by 19 democratically elected franchisee representatives. BKC would be entitled to only one seat on the board, even though all of its stores (approximately 16 percent of the system) would be purchasing substantially all of their food, paper, equipment, and other items from RSI.

3. Outside professional management would be hired to manage RSI, and certain BKC employees who had been involved in purchasing would be transferred to RSI.

4. All franchisees would buy substantially all of their food, paper, and equipment products through RSI, thereby giving RSI significant cost savings opportunities.

5. Patronage dividends would be paid annually by RSI to its members (that is, BKC and the Burger King franchisees), based upon the ratio of their respective purchases made through RSI to RSI's total volume of sales.

6. BKC retained sole and absolute responsibility for establishing specifications for the products, quality controls, and supplier approvals and disapprovals. This meant that RSI would negotiate price only with vendors previously approved by BKC as capable of meeting quality specification and delivering goods in a reliable, consistent fashion.

Although there have been some bumpy moments between RSI and BKC, and also between RSI and the National Franchise Association, Inc. (NFA), the independent franchisee association for the Burger King system, RSI has nevertheless been an enormous success. Its creation has resulted in millions of dollars of savings to its members (which include the BKC franchisees and BKC itself). More importantly, it has created a higher level of trust in the purchasing process by virtue of the fact that franchisees were allowed to participate and manage the overall domestic purchasing function, and eliminated most of the strife between BKC and its franchisees that resulted from the prior arrangement.

For a complete discussion of the technical legal issues relating to the establishment of a purchasing cooperative, see "Franchise-Related Purchasing Cooperatives," Andrew C. Selden and Rupert M. Barkoff, *Charting the Course for Franchising,* ABA 1992 Forum on Franchising, Volume I. In summary, however, the basic decisions revolve around (1) choosing the best form of legal structure for the organization; (2) federal income tax considerations; (3) securities law considerations; (4) antitrust law considerations; (5) sourcing restrictions in the franchise agreement; (6) resolving trademark usage issues; and (7) vicarious liability considerations.

Marketing Co-ops   In addition to cooperatives designed to purchase goods for use at the franchised outlet, franchise systems occasionally also include an arrangement whereby franchisees pool their efforts in advertising, promotion, and marketing activities through cooperative efforts or organizations, either on their own initiative or in a franchisor-sponsored program. Franchisors are often very reluctant to cede control over brand identity and brand development to the franchisees. The brand itself is the most valuable asset owned by the franchisor and its development, and promotion is the principal activity of most franchisors.

In a typical franchisor-administered advertising program, the franchisor sets up the fund, sets up franchisee contributions, and controls expenditures. The franchisor may retain total control over creative concepts and media allocation, or may permit franchisees to participate in the decision-making to some degree, perhaps by way of a franchisee advisory committee. The franchisor may or may not create a separate legal entity, such as a trust or nonprofit corporation, to administer the funds.

The franchisor may not have the resources to perform the advertising function effectively, or is required to share control of this activity in order to keep the franchise system alive. In some systems, the national advertising function is funded and controlled by franchisees, or by a franchisee-dominated co-op. Franchisees may wish to form a local advertising cooperative to coordinate local spending above and beyond the local spending done by the franchisor, or even to form a national franchisee cooperative advertising program which is committed to national "investment spending" by the franchisees above and beyond their commitment to the franchisor.

Cooperative advertising programs such as these, in which franchisees pool their financial resources, sometimes with those of the franchisor, to promote the brand at a local, regional, or national level, allow franchisees to achieve economies of scale through coordination of franchisee advertising and promotion efforts. Participating franchisees benefit from the use of uniform, consistent, coordinated advertising and from access to more sophisticated research, creative, and production resources than would be available to individual owners, as well as the ability to afford to use broadcast media. The national advertising co-op functions in a way as a national purchasing co-op for advertising, and can have the same systemic and relationship benefits (in addition to purchasing efficiencies) as a joint purchasing co-op.

Organizing and operating an advertising cooperative raises many of the same legal and business issues and choices present when considering a more traditional purchasing cooperative. Again, see "Franchise-Related Purchasing Cooperatives," Andrew C. Selden and Rupert M. Barkoff, *Charting the Course for Franchising,* ABA 1992 Forum on Franchising, Volume I, for a detailed discussion.

External Trade Associations

Franchisors and their franchisees may occasionally interact through external trade associations, such as a state or local restaurant association (or similar industry association), a Chamber of Commerce, or a Better Business Bureau committee. Jointly sponsored political action committees exist in some organizations. Some systems may sponsor on a joint basis an off-shore, captive insurance organization. Still others may share ownership or participation in a purchasing and distribution cooperative, or advertising cooperatives.

All of these "external" organizations afford opportunities for the franchisor and its franchisees to interact constructively, although usually on a specific topic, rather than on the broad range of issues affecting the franchise organization generally.

Resources

Use of Experts   Conventional wisdom holds that few if any franchisors possess the level of perfect information, perfect foresight, and perfect judgment to enable them to act unilaterally with any effectiveness in managing the ongoing affairs of the franchise organization.

The same is true of franchisees. Franchisees often collectively have more experience than the franchisor in the day-to-day operation of the franchised business, and therefore have a "street wisdom" that transcends anything available at the franchisor's headquarters. The other side of that coin, however, is that franchisee perspectives tend sometimes to be too parochial to be effective in system-wide decision-making.

Both sides are well advised in many cases to engage the services of outside consultants or experts on any of a range of issues that the franchise system must deal with in order to succeed. Ideally, a franchisor and its franchisees will act jointly to engage the services of experts so that the result of the expertise can be shared by the collaborative decision-making mechanism in each system. Maximizing the efficiency and effectiveness of system advertising, marketing, procurement, and distribution functions can often benefit from joint procurement of expert advice and information. Those engagements should be jointly funded in most cases to reflect the joint benefit to be derived from the engagement.

Failing that, however, there is nothing inappropriate about either the franchisor or the franchisee body independently engaging experts to advise it and to assist in system decision-making. If the results of such an engagement are shared with the other party for the benefit of the system, it is also not inappropriate to expect the other party then to reimburse a proportionate share of the expense of the engagement reflecting the benefit to the system.

The benefit lies in the efficient collection, sharing, and use of information. Decisions affecting system welfare cannot be made in a vacuum, or on the basis of only one party's information and interests. It is to the advantage of all participants in a franchise organization that information concerning the performance of the system or the opportunities available to the system be collected and shared appropriately to facilitate collaborative decision-making. Some franchisors control the availability and use of information to further a purely parochial interest in maintaining (at least the illusion of) control within the organization. The best franchisors understand that this sophisticated form of corporate "hide the bean" management is usually counterproductive. Franchisees also have a corresponding interest in sharing with the franchisor information they have that would be useful to system decision-making.

Codes of Behavior and Training   Certain external codes of behavior affect the interaction between franchisors and franchisees. Federal and state laws and regulations govern sales activities, franchise transfers, termination, and certain other activities. Some professional and trade associations have their own codes. The most prominent code is the "Code of Principles and Standards of Conduct" of the International Franchise Association (IFA). A copy of the IFA Code of Principles and Standards of Conduct is attached as Exhibit 5-B. Although the IFA Code may not provide franchisees with a legal remedy, it must certainly be generally respected by franchisors who wish to maintain their IFA membership, avoid bad press, and maintain good relations with franchisees.

More effective than the IFA Code is a franchisor-initiated code of ethics for its own employees. Although franchisors are often painted as monolithic and controlling, the truth is that all large companies struggle to balance employee empowerment and minimum standards of conduct. A franchisor can help minimize problems created by individual conflict or misdeeds by clearly communicating to its employees the company's expectations regarding relations with franchisees. A good code of ethics will go beyond legal obligations relating to franchising and deal with a broader range of topics such as: sexual harassment, conflict of interest, or limits of employee authority. A copy of the Code of Business Ethics and Conduct used by BKC is attached as Exhibit 5-C.

If such a code of ethics is to be most effective in disciplining and regulating employees, it should be countersigned by each employee and returned to the franchisor. There should also be a franchisor employee (often the General Counsel) designated and available to answer questions and provide advice.

Most franchisor employees want to be fair to franchisees and do the right thing. The more guidance they receive, the better equipped they are to avoid mistakes that will hurt the franchisor/franchisee relationship.

Another important element of maintaining a good relationship with franchisees is employee training. Well-trained employees are better respected and add more value to system and the franchisor/franchisee relationship. In large franchise systems, however, the franchisor should not miss the opportunity to expand its employee training beyond the nuts and bolts of the franchise system. Courses in leadership, conflict resolution, negotiation, diversity, etc. will all help minimize conflict and enhance the franchisor/franchisee relationship.

Finally, the franchisor can reinforce important topics through the use of pocket guides and other easy reference tools. Copies of BKC's pocket guides on antitrust, trademarks, and sexual harassment are attached as Exhibits 5-D, 5-E, and 5-F.

ADR/Conflict Resolution

Some form of conflict and dispute is inevitable in every franchise system. Both sides should remember to keep that conflict in context and find a way to resolve the dispute in the manner that does the least damage to the system generally and the ongoing business relationship between the parties to the dispute. Because of the context, franchise disputes are uniquely well suited for the use of out of court procedures generally referred to as alternative dispute resolution (ADR). Of course, the best way to handle disputes is to avoid them before they occur. Good communication and training, and adherence to company policies and procedures, will always help minimize disputes.

To minimize or control disputes a franchise organization can (1) institute a formal system of *objective* measures, (2) provide a business process for franchisee appeals, and (3) establish a system of checks and balances before legal action is taken.

The task of establishing objective performance criteria will differ in each franchise system and is probably best viewed as a goal. Complete objectivity is seldom possible (for example, how clean is clean?), but if the franchisor strives to be as objective as possible in its standards (for example, "no rodents, no mold"), then the objectivity will benefit both franchisor and franchisee by clearly setting forth both duties and obligations. This will make both performance and enforcement easier.

Given the ongoing business relationship between franchisor and franchisee, it is also important that the franchisee understand the franchisor's chain of command so that "appeals" may be directed to the appropriate executive. This also benefits the franchisor, which does not want all disputes immediately escalating to the office of the CEO. Indeed, some large franchisors have sought to protect the CEO from day-to-day disputes and give the franchisees a formal forum for complaints by establishing an ombudsman whose sole duty is to review franchisee/franchisor disputes. The ombudsman is usually a well respected senior or retired executive of the franchisor.

All franchisors should have some formal legal review before deciding to take legal action against a franchisee. This review should not be limited to an analysis of the legal rights of the franchisor. The franchisor's goal is not to win a lawsuit, it is to solve a business issue and to protect the business of the system. Thus, the legal review should also ask whether the field staff has worked with the franchisee to solve the problem, whether the franchisee has any valid complaints of its own, and whether settlement options such as a buy-out, sale, or remediation plan have been discussed. A copy of the checklist used by BKC before taking legal action to terminate a franchisee is attached as Exhibit 5-G. If all of these measures fail to avoid or resolve the dispute, then ADR should be considered.

Traditional litigation can be especially destructive in a franchise environment. Courts are overcrowded, parties are angry, litigation costs are astronomical, and franchise relationships are being destroyed. The entire system can be adversely impacted by an individual dispute that is not resolved quickly and fairly. Business people are frustrated with lawyers who are too busy addressing procedural issues, posturing for purposes of personal ego, or foot-dragging. They are angry with protracted negotiations, long court delays, and discovery processes that consume huge chunks of time and legal budgets. The appeal of ADR is that it can help resolve conflicts quickly and fairly, and with the minimal possible damage to the franchise system and the franchise relationship. ADR is a collection of strategies for resolving disputes outside the usual process of litigation and confrontational negotiations. It can be formal or informal.

The most common types of ADR are facilitated negotiation, mediation, and arbitration. There are dozens of variations including neutral evaluation, summary jury trial, mini-trial, and judicially hosted settlement conferences. Indeed, one reason for ADR's attractiveness is its flexibility.

ADR is not always preferable to litigation. Litigation offers full discovery, trial by jury, the opportunity to establish precedent, and appellate review. Additionally, litigation tends to level the playing field for disputants who have a wide difference in power. That said, ADR has a number of significant advantages over traditional litigation.

1. ADR often reduces legal costs. Pretrial settlement often occurs "on the courthouse steps" or in a judicial settlement conference held within weeks or days of trial. This occurs only after the parties have expended considerable sums on discovery and trial preparation. Since most lawsuits tend to settle, ADR simply helps them to settle sooner and more economically.

2. ADR generally reduces the time spent on disputes. Many ADR processes involve summary or abbreviated procedures, and virtually all ADR processes take less time than trial. For example, the American Arbitration Association's Rules for Expedited Commercial Arbitration provide for the arbitrator's award to be rendered within 60 days of the initial demand for arbitration. Because ADR can operate outside the court system, a dispute does not need to wait its turn in an overcrowded court docket, a result that can lead to a prolonged period of poisoned or deteriorating relations between the franchisor and the franchisee.

3. ADR allows the parties to control who decides the dispute. Thus, the parties can agree on a mediator or arbitrator who has expertise, either legal or business, in the franchising industry.

4. ADR allows for increased participation by business representatives. The constraints of typical courtroom procedures often reduce meaningful,

problem solving communication. ADR, on the other hand, allows for more informal communication, reducing posturing and procedural rules. It also allows the business representatives to talk directly and bypass the escalation of hostilities often associated with American trial lawyers.

5. ADR also facilitates creative communicative problem-solving. Courts can provide only a limited range of remedies, usually involving an exchange of money. Often the business representatives have a continuing business relationship and can fashion a solution that revolves around a "win-win" proposition such as a commitment from the franchisee to build additional units, or a commitment by the franchisor to deploy additional training or marketing resources.

6. ADR also makes it easier to keep the dispute confidential, as almost all litigation is public.

7. ADR also allows the parties to tailor their approach to the nature of the dispute. For example, they can agree to involve a third party, allow for a binding or nonbinding decision, limit discovery, relax evidence rules, or take whatever other steps they deem appropriate. BKC's ADR policy for resolving encroachment disputes is attached as Exhibit 5-H.

8. ADR also allows each party to fashion a settlement which will not only deal with the problem at hand, but also improve relations going forward and avoid similar disputes. Litigation generally breeds only resentment and bitterness which can lead to additional conflict.

On the other hand, there are also some disadvantages to overcome when using ADR:

1. Many business representatives are unfamiliar with ADR and some short-sighted trial lawyers are reluctant to leave the familiar and high-paying courtroom environment.

2. ADR works best where the parties have essentially equal bargaining power, which is often not the case in the franchisor/franchisee relationship. A neutral party, like a judge, can provide some balance, but if one side can overwhelm the other, the weaker party may need the protection of a courtroom setting.

3. Most ADR proceedings require some minimum amount of cooperation and good faith effort—a mutual desire—to resolve the dispute. If the franchisor/franchisee relationship is so poisoned that neither party can speak directly in a rational manner, then litigation may be the only workable solution.

4. The very efficiency of ADR may encourage a party to a dispute to pursue additional claims against the other or resort to an adjudicative process too hastily.

Determining the most appropriate form of ADR is probably the most important decision made in the efficient and least destructive resolution of a franchise dispute. The Center for Public Resources Inc. (CPR) in New York, (212) 949-6490, operates a franchise-specific mediation program which includes a panel of neutrals who purport to have franchise related expertise. A copy of their Procedure for Resolution of Franchise Disputes is attached as Exhibit 5-I.

Conclusion

Good relations drive good business results. Indeed, empirical experience in franchise organizations over the past thirty years suggests that sustained success for franchisors and franchisees alike requires good relations between the parties.

The keys to good relations and franchise success are a focus on shared interests of the participants, emphasis on what is good for the system as a whole (a "system view"), ample communication, participation of franchisees in system governance, leveraging system resources through advisory councils, constructive representation by franchisee associations, and parties playing their appropriate roles in system operations, and use of ADR.

Finally, franchisors and their franchisees should seek to exploit their common interests and goals as a means to avoid conflict that naturally arises by virtue of each parties' respective, and often differing, role in the franchise system. Otherwise, franchisors and franchisees may, as the chapter's epigraph warns, "hang separately."

EXHIBIT 5-A

MEMO

TO: All Franchisees Worldwide

FROM: Paul Clayton, Senior Vice President, Worldwide Marketing

DATE: November 15, 1996

SUBJECT: FRANCHISEES' MARKETING ON THE WORLD WIDE WEB

As you all should know by now, Burger King Corporation ("BKC") has set up a home page on the World Wide Web (the "Web"). It can be found at *http://www.burgerking.com.* It is my understanding that several franchisees have set up home pages on the Web and that many others are considering doing so in the near future. The Web has the potential, if exploited properly, to be a powerful tool for marketing the Brand. So as to bring some order and common sense to the process, BKC has developed this policy statement regarding franchisees' use of the Internet and the Web.

POLICY GOAL:

To allow BKC and its franchisees to exploit the unique marketing benefits of the World Wide Web in a manner that maintains a consistent worldwide Brand image without creating incremental legal risk to the Burger King System.

POLICY:

Trademarks: A franchisee's Web page that utilizes Burger King trademarks, such as the marks BURGER KING®, HOME OF THE WHOPPER® and the Burger King BUN HALVES logo, is a form of advertising and, pursuant to the Franchise Agreement, must be reviewed by BKC before it is disseminated to the public. All franchisees interested in setting up a Web site should send copies of the prototype pages to their BKC Marketing Manager before going live. Those franchisees who have already set up Web pages should provide their Marketing Manager with the address of the site so that a review can be done. Each time you make a material change to your Web page you must run the text through your Marketing Manager for approval.

Hyperlinks: No franchisee should "hyperlink" or "hot link" their sites to the BKC Web page or the Web page of any of BKC's promotion or marketing partners (i.e., Coca-Cola and Alcone Marketing Group) without BKC's and the relevant marketing partner's consent. Requests for these consents should be processed through your Marketing Manager.

Domain Names: No franchisee should use any of the Burger King trademarks or variations of the marks in their domain names. BKC has registered *burgerking.com, whopper.com* and *bk.com.* Do not attempt to register variations such as *burgerking.net, bkkidsclub.com* or *bkburgers.com* with the Internet registration agency, InterNic. The same can be said for *haveityourway.com* and *getyourburgersworth. com.* These type of Web addresses infringe and dilute the trademarks, will confuse customers as to the source and location of the official Burger King Web site, and create potential liability for BKC. Before you seek registration of an address that you think might be a problem, please call your Marketing Manager.

Disclosures: All franchisee's Web sites should disclose to the viewer, on the first screen page and in appropriate size type, that the Web site is "operated by ABC, Inc., a franchisee of Burger King Corporation." This is similar to the disclosure signs that are required in all Burger King restaurants.

Finally, it should be noted that there are many legal risks involved in setting up and maintaining a Web site and all franchisees are encouraged to seek the advice of competent legal counsel before doing so.

The technology and the law in this area will surely evolve over the next several years and this policy will evolve with it. If you have any questions or suggestions regarding this policy, please call Melanie Wisniewski in Brand Strategy at (305) 378-7579 or Craig Prusher in the Law Department at (305) 378-3066.

EXHIBIT 5-B: International Franchise Association

Code of Principles and Standards of Conduct

SECTION I: PREAMBLE

Franchising is a business relationship utilized in more than 65 different industries. A wide variety of franchise relationships exists between thousands of franchisors and hundreds of thousands of franchisees. Franchising offers an excellent opportunity for individuals who are seeking to enter into business for themselves, by providing a framework for a mutually beneficial business relationship. In recognition of the increasing role of franchising in the marketplace and the very beneficial and positive contributions of franchising to the American economy, the franchisor and franchisee members of the International Franchise Association ("IFA") believe that franchising must reflect the highest principles and standards of fair business practices. The IFA seeks to promote this objective by means of a strong and effective *Code of Principles and Standards of Conduct (the "Code")* that is applicable to its franchisor and franchisee members. To protect and promote the interests of consumers, franchisees, and franchisors, and to ensure that this unique form of entrepreneurship continues to flourish with a high degree of success and security, we, the members of the IFA, do hereby set forth the following principles and standards of conduct. The policies and practices of members of the IFA shall not be inconsistent with the *Code.*

SECTION II: PRINCIPLES

Franchisors and franchisees shall conduct their businesses professionally, with truth, accuracy, fairness, and responsibility.

Franchisors and franchisees shall use fair business practices in dealings with each other and with their customers, suppliers and government agencies.

Franchisors and franchisees shall comply with all applicable laws and regulations in all of their business operations. Franchisors and Franchisees shall not engage in any activity that will bring discredit to their business, industry or their franchised network.

Franchisors and franchisees shall recognize the interdependence of the franchisor and franchisees of a franchised network and the responsibility of the franchisor and each franchisee of the network to every other franchisee in the network.

Franchisors and franchisees shall offer opportunities in franchising to minorities, women and disabled persons on a basis equal to all other persons.

SECTION III: APPLICABILITY AND INTERPRETATION

1. Applicability. The *Code* shall be applicable to all franchisor and franchisee members of the IFA in their United States operations. These principles and standards of conduct reflect the collective beliefs of the franchisor and franchisee members of the IFA with respect to the manner in which franchise relationships generally should be established, structured and implemented. Franchise relationships should be established by the delivery of clear and complete disclosure documents, as required by law, and by clear and unambiguous franchise agreements. A franchise relationship is governed by the franchise agreement. The principles and standards of conduct contained in the *Code* do not substitute for or supplement the franchise agreements between franchisors and their franchisees or create any rights for either franchisors or their franchisees. Franchise agreements entered into before these principles and standards were adopted may not be in accord with all of these principles and standards. Some franchise relationships, due to their structure, product or service, may not be able to be implemented in complete accord with these principles and standards. Therefore, these principles and standards must be applied with flexibility, taking into consideration the wide range of structures, forms of agreement and reasonable business practices used to document and implement franchise relationships in the past and currently.

2. Interpretation. Developing and applying standards to a wide variety of franchised businesses is a challenging undertaking. For this reason, changes to the *Code* and interpretative releases may be issued from time to time. Interpretations of the *Code* will be made by the Board of Directors of the IFA and its interpretations will be final and binding on the franchisor and franchisee members of the IFA. The Board of Directors will consider the interpretations recommended by the Standards Committee of the IFA. With respect to all matters relating to the *Code*, whenever the Board of Directors is not meeting, the Executive Committee of the Board of Directors may act for and on behalf of the Board of Directors. To the extent that applicable law imposes standards of conduct that are different from those contained in the *Code*, franchisor and franchisee members shall comply with both such applicable law and the *Code*, except to the extent that compliance with the *Code* might constitute a violation of such law.

SECTION IV: ENFORCEMENT
The IFA's enforcement philosophy, summarized below, has been shaped by its recognition that in most instances it is not possible for the IFA itself to engage in fact finding in the context of franchisor-franchisee disputes and that negotiation, franchised network dispute settlement procedures and/or nonbinding mediation are generally preferable to litigation and should be encouraged.

1. **Enforcement Philosophy:** The *Code* enforcement philosophy of the IFA is:
(a) To educate franchisor and franchisee members of the IFA regarding the *Code* and to assist members to comply with the *Code*.
(b) To require franchisor members to develop fair and effective dispute resolution procedures, to publicize the existence of these procedures within their respective franchised networks and to make a good faith effort to resolve disputes by use of such procedures and/or third party mediation whenever practicable. Such dispute resolution procedures need not involve any specific format, but they should be designed to be fair and effective in resolving disputes. Examples of dispute resolution procedures include the evaluation and resolution of a dispute by a senior officer of the franchisor member, an ombudsman, a panel composed of franchisor management personnel and franchisees or a neutral person or panel of neutrals. The procedures should afford each party to the dispute an opportunity for a full and fair hearing of its view of the relevant facts. If the franchised network has a franchisee advisory council, such procedures should be supported by such council.
(c) To rely on third party fact finding, since the IFA does not have investigative resources and, therefore, will generally limit its role to application of the *Code* to facts determined by courts, arbitrators and administrative agencies. Exceptions may be made when the facts of a dispute are agreed upon by the parties to the dispute, or are readily determinable by the Standards Committee.
(d) To require members who in isolated cases have violated the *Code* to adopt procedures and policies that will reduce the likelihood of future violations and to reserve sus-

pension or termination of IFA membership for members whose policies and practices reflect systemic disregard of the *Code*.

2.   Enforcement Policies and Procedures

(a)   A complaint to the IFA alleging facts that may constitute a violation of the *Code* by a franchisor or franchisee member must be in writing. While no form of complaint is prescribed, the facts and the relief sought by the complainant should be clearly stated. The complainant should also indicate the extent to which the internal dispute resolution procedures of the franchised network, negotiation and/or mediation have been utilized, and the results thereof. The complaint should also indicate whether litigation or arbitration relating to the complaint has previously occurred or is currently pending.

(b)   In consideration of the IFA's efforts to facilitate a resolution of a dispute, and in the interest of full and open disclosure and discussion by all parties to the dispute, such parties, on behalf of themselves and their respective shareholders, members, partners, directors, officers, employees, and agents, must agree in writing to waive any and all claims that any such person or entity may have against (1) the other parties to such dispute, and their respective shareholders, members, partners, directors, officers, employees and agents and (2) the IFA, any director, officer, employee, attorney or agent of the IFA, any officer or member of a committee or advisory group of the IFA or any person occupying a similar position, that may arise out of any IFA investigation, discussion or disciplinary action, or statements made incident thereto, including, without limitation, claims for defamation of character and trade libel. The parties to a dispute, on behalf of themselves and their respective shareholders, members, partners, directors, officers, employees and agents, must acknowledge and agree in writing that statements made by any such person in relation to such investigation or disciplinary action shall have an unqualified privilege. Such waivers do not, of course, include any claims that any such party may have against another party that are not related to the IFA investigation or disciplinary action with respect to the complaint.

(c)   The IFA will send the complainant's written complaint to the other parties to the dispute and request that such other parties submit written replies to the IFA responding to the factual allegations contained in the complaint, describing any claims that any such other party has against the complainant and describing any dispute resolution, negotiation and/or third party mediation procedures that such party believes to be applicable to the dispute, their prior use and/or future availability to resolve the dispute and such party's willingness to make a good faith effort to resolve the dispute. The IFA will send such written responses to the complainant.

(d)   A relatively small category of disputes between a franchisor and its franchisee involve issues so fundamental to the franchise relationship that such disputes cannot practicably be resolved by negotiation, internal dispute resolution procedures or third party mediation. The great majority of disputes between franchisors and franchisees do not fall within this category and are susceptible to resolution by such techniques. If a complaint, or a party's response to a complaint, indicates the existence of a dispute that may be resolved by such techniques, a franchisor and/or franchisee member are obligated to make a good faith effort to resolve the dispute by means of (1) negotiation, (2) dispute resolution procedures available within the franchised network and/or (3) third party mediation.

(e)   If litigation or arbitration involving the principal issues of a dispute is pending, the IFA will, as a general rule, take no further action with respect to the dispute until the conclusion of such litigation or arbitration. If no such litigation or arbitration is pending, and if a member fails to respond to a complaint that complies with these enforce-ment procedures, and the parties do not resolve the dispute, or the Standards Com-mittee believes that the facts are determinable from the letters and documents in its possession, the Standards Committee will determine whether a violation of the *Code* has occurred and will report its findings to the Board of Directors. Failure of a mem-ber, without good cause, to make a good faith effort to resolve a dispute is grounds for disciplinary action against the member or dismissal of the complaint, as appropriate.

(f)   If the parties fail to resolve their dispute, and subsequently the dispute is resolved in litigation or arbitration, or by an administrative agency, with findings of fact that are publicly available, the Standards Committee will, at the request of any party to the dispute, evaluate such findings of fact to determine whether a violation of the *Code* has occurred, and will report its findings to the Board of Directors.

(g)   The final determination of whether the *Code* has been violated by a member will be made by the Board of Directors. If the Board of Directors determines that the *Code* has been violated, it may (1) issue a warning to the member, (2) suspend the membership of the member for a period of time deemed appropriate by the Board of Directors or (3) terminate the membership of the member. All proceedings shall be private and confidential, except for the final written decision of the Board of Directors. It shall be within the discretion of the Board of Directors to include in or exclude from its writ-ten decision the reasons for its decision and disciplinary action, if any.

SECTION V: STANDARDS OF CONDUCT APPLICABLE TO FRANCHISOR AND FRANCHISEE MEMBERS

1. Franchise Sales and Disclosure. The sale of franchises is heavily regulated in the United States under federal and state law and may be subject to regulation in other coun-tries. Franchisors that comply with such regulation disclose an extensive body of informa-tion to prospective franchisees regarding the franchisor, the nature and costs of an investment in its franchise and the franchise relationship that it offers. Therefore, in the advertisement and grant of franchises, a franchisor shall comply with all applicable laws and regulations. Disclosure documents shall comply with all applicable legal requirements. A franchisor shall advise prospective franchisees to seek legal or other professional advice prior to the signing of a franchise agreement and to contact existing franchisees to gain a better understanding of the requirements and benefits of the franchise and the business.

All matters material to the granting of a franchise shall be contained in or referred to in one or more written documents, which shall clearly set forth the terms of the relation-ship and the respective rights and obligations of the parties. (A franchisor may establish and periodically modify system standards and policies and prescribe such standards and policies in a separate document, such as an operations manual.) Disclosure documents shall be provided to a prospective franchisee on a timely basis as required by law. A fran-chisor that complies with applicable federal and state laws relating to the grant of fran-chises will be in compliance with this paragraph.

Prior to entering into franchise relationships, franchisees have a responsibility to effectively utilize the information made available to them and to undertake the due dili-gence necessary to a full understanding of the business segment of the franchisor, the his-tory and status of the franchisor in its business segment, the investment requirements and terms of the franchise and the effort required to operate the franchised business success-fully. This responsibility includes a thorough reading of the offering circular, franchise agreements and other documents furnished by the franchisor and consultation with exist-ing franchisees of the franchised network and professional advisors.

2. Good Faith Dealing. In the United States, many jurisdictions imply in every contract an obligation of good faith on all parties to the contract. However, the good faith obligation does not supersede, enlarge or diminish the rights and obligations contained in an agreement.

Therefore, franchisors and franchisees shall deal with each other fairly and in good faith, which means dealing honestly, ethically, and with mutual respect, in accordance with the terms of their franchise agreements. A franchisor and a franchisee that act in compliance with the terms of their franchise agreement are dealing with each other fairly and in good faith. Franchisees and franchisors shall conduct their relationships with other franchisees, suppliers and customers fairly and with respect.

3. Franchisor-Franchisee Cooperation. Cooperation between a franchisor and its franchisees promotes a healthy, competitive and financially sound franchised network. Effective communication between a franchisor and its franchisee also promotes a healthy franchise relationship. Many franchisors have established advisory councils to which franchisees elect and/or the franchisor appoints franchisees. A number of franchised networks have associations that represent a majority or a minority of their franchisees. Some franchised networks have both an advisory council and an association that represents some of the network's franchisees. Franchisors have increasingly utilized advisory councils and franchisee associations to improve communication between the franchisor and its franchisees and as the mechanism to foster discussion and exchange of ideas that enhances the competitive capability of the network and its ability to deal efficiently and effectively with any problems or disagreements that arise in the franchise relationship. The effective operation of a franchised network and cooperation among the franchisor and the franchisees of the network requires the dissemination of substantial information within the network. Much of this information is confidential and may include trade secrets of the franchisor.

Therefore, the franchisor and franchisees of a franchised network shall foster open dialogue within their network by such means as they determine to be most effective, including one or more franchisee advisory councils, an association of franchisees or other communication mechanisms. A franchisor shall not prohibit a franchisee from forming, joining, or participating in any franchisee association. A franchisor and the franchisees of a franchised network should at all times endeavor to work together cooperatively to advance the interests of the network and to protect the interests of the franchisor and each franchisee of the network. Franchisees of a franchised network and their advisory councils and associations shall support and assist other franchisees of the network that experience problems in the operation of their businesses. Franchisees shall comply with the confidentiality requirements of their franchise agreements and maintain the confidentiality of the information circulated within their networks that is indicated to be confidential or subjected to disclosure restrictions.

4. Termination of Franchise Agreements. Termination of franchise agreements before their expiration is a rare occurrence. Such terminations are initiated by both franchisors and franchisees. Terminations by a franchisor are usually the result of the franchisee's failure to pay fees in compliance with the franchise agreement. Terminations by a franchisor also occur when a franchisee has failed to comply with system standards or other obligations set forth in the franchise agreement or collateral documents and has failed to remedy such defaults after notice and an opportunity to do so. Terminations by franchisees are usually the result of the franchisee's belief that the franchisor has failed to comply with its obligations or, occasionally, a desire by the franchisee to avoid paying continuing fees to the franchisor. Termination may be costly to both the franchisor and the franchisee.

The franchisor and the franchisees of a franchised network work together to maintain the competitiveness of the network. A franchisor and its franchisees have a strong interest in diligent enforcement by the franchisor of (1) franchisees' payment obligations, which support a wide range of franchisor activities that maintain and enhance the competitiveness of the franchised network and (2) system standards, which are the foundation of the goodwill of the network. A franchisee who attempts to unilaterally disaffiliate from its franchised network, in violation of the terms of its franchise agreement, harms the other franchisees of the network as well as the franchisor.

Therefore, franchisors and franchisees shall apply the following standards in connection with the termination of franchise agreements:

(a) Franchisees shall comply with the requirements of their franchise agreements relating to maintaining standards of appearance, product and service quality, health, safety, cleanliness, customer service, advertising and financial reporting and payment to their franchisor. Franchisees shall endeavor in good faith to avoid acts or omissions that constitute noncompliance with their obligations to their franchisor and that may lead to termination of their franchises. Franchisees shall not commit any act or engage in any activity that may cause adverse customer, public or government reaction with respect to their franchised network.

(b) A franchise agreement may only be terminated for good cause, which includes the failure of a franchisee or franchisor to comply with any lawful requirement of the franchise agreement. Some franchise agreements permit franchisees to terminate the agreement without cause and a termination by a franchisee of a franchise agreement pursuant to such a contractual right shall not violate this *Code*.

(c) A franchisee and a franchisor shall be given notice and a reasonable opportunity to cure breaches of the franchise agreement that are curable under the terms of the franchise agreement. The cure period shall be consistent with the nature of the breach.

(d) A franchise agreement may be terminated immediately, without prior notice or opportunity to cure, in the event of a franchisee's abandonment of the franchised business, repeated breaches of its franchise agreement, material dishonesty, criminal misconduct or endangerment of public health or safety.

(e) A franchise agreement may be terminated pursuant to an express provision in the franchise agreement providing for a reciprocal right to terminate the agreement without cause.

5. Expiration of Franchise Agreements. Most franchises are granted for a specific term. Some franchise agreements grant qualified renewal rights to the franchisee and others do not address the issue of a franchisee's post expiration rights to continue to operate as a franchisee. The continuation of a franchise relationship subsequent to the expiration of a franchise is an element of the franchise relationship that each franchisor must determine and express in its franchise agreement. However, expiration of a franchise need not necessarily deprive a franchisee of the value of his or her business (as distinct from the value of the expired franchise). This value can be preserved by giving a franchisee reasonable advance notice that his or her franchise relationship with the franchisor will not continue subsequent to the expiration of the franchise and an opportunity to sell his or her business to a successor franchisee (who will acquire a new franchise from the franchisor). Alternatively, the franchisee can be granted the right to continue in the same business at the same location or in the same market or otherwise be able to realize the value of his or her business (as distinct from the value of the expired franchise).

Therefore, a franchisor shall apply the following standards in connection with the expiration of franchise agreements that provide for a specific term:

(a) A franchisee shall be given notice, at least 180 days prior to expiration, of a franchisor's intention not to grant a new franchise agreement to the franchisee.

(b) The franchisor may determine not to grant a new franchise agreement:
    (1) for good cause, which includes the failure of the franchisee to comply with any lawful requirement of the franchise agreement; or
    (2) if the franchisor permits the franchisee to:
        (i) during the 180 days prior to the expiration of the franchise, sell the business to a purchaser meeting the then-current qualifications and requirements specified by the franchisor; or
        (ii) continue to operate the business under a different trade identity at the same location or within the same trade area; or
        (iii) if the franchisee is otherwise permitted to realize the value of the business (as distinct from the value of the expired franchise).

(c) The franchisor may determine not to grant a new franchise agreement to a franchisee, without prior notice, in the event of the franchisee's abandonment of the franchise business, repeated breaches of its franchise agreement, material dishonesty or bad faith, criminal misconduct or endangerment of public health or safety.

(d) The franchisor may exercise any right to purchase the franchisee's business as provided in the franchise or other agreement.

(e) The franchisor may determine not to grant a new franchise agreement to a franchisee if the franchisor is withdrawing from the market area.

A franchisee shall comply with the terms of the franchise agreement relating to expiration. Such requirements may include diligent efforts to sell his or her businesses to a successor franchisee or to the franchisor or the deidentification of his or her business.

6. Transfer of Franchise. The great majority of franchise agreements grant to the franchisee a qualified right to transfer the franchise in connection with the sale of his or her business. Transfer rights are important to franchisees, because transferability is an important element of the value of the franchise and the franchisee's business. Restrictions on transferability are equally important to the franchisor, which has a compelling interest in the right to determine the persons who operate under its franchise and the terms on which its franchises are acquired.

Therefore, except with respect to franchises that are expressly nontransferable personal service contracts, a franchisor shall not withhold approval of a proposed transfer of a franchise when the following criteria are met:

(a) The transferring franchisee is in compliance with the terms of the franchise agreement;

(b) The proposed transferee meets the then-current qualifications of the franchisor;

(c) The terms of the transfer meet the then-current requirements of the franchisor and the transfer provisions of the franchise agreement;

(d) The franchisor determines not to exercise a right of first refusal in accordance with the franchise or other agreement.

A franchisee shall fully comply with the transfer restrictions of the franchise agreement, including without limitation the required advance notice to the franchisor, cooperation in furnishing information to the franchisor about the proposed transferee and the terms of the transfer, and cooperating with the franchisor if it exercises a right of first refusal to buy the franchisee's business.

7. System Expansion. The granting of territorial protection to franchisees varies widely among franchised networks due to differing business and competitive considerations. Accurately predicting the competitive impact of establishing an additional outlet (whether a fixed location or mobile facility) in a market already served by one or more franchisees may not be possible. Nevertheless, in addition to respecting the legal rights of a franchisee, sound franchising practice requires a franchisor to consider those factors relevant to its business that will determine the impact of an additional outlet on the business of an existing franchisee and to balance the projected impact with the needs of the franchisor's network to expand, gain market share and meet competition.

Therefore, in determining whether to open, or to authorize the opening of, an outlet in close proximity to an existing franchised outlet, that will offer products or services similar to those of the existing outlet, a franchisor shall take into account the factors that are relevant to its business, which may include any or all of the following:

(a) Territorial rights of existing franchisees contained in their franchise agreements.
(b) The similarity of the new outlet and the existing outlet in terms of products and services to be offered and the trademarks to be used.
(c) Whether the new outlet and the existing outlet will sell products or services to the same customers for the same occasion.
(d) The competitive activities in the market.
(e) The characteristics of the market.
(f) The ability of the existing outlet to adequately supply anticipated demand.
(g) The positive or negative effect of the new outlet on the existing outlet.
(h) The quality of operations and physical condition of the existing outlet.
(i) Compliance by the franchisee of the existing outlet with the franchise agreement.
(j) The experience of the franchisor in similar circumstances.
(k) The benefit or detriment to the franchise system as a whole in opening the new outlet.
(l) Relevant information submitted by existing franchisees and the prospective franchisee.

A franchisor and its franchisees should work cooperatively to develop systems and procedures for dealing with potential system expansion conflicts in a manner that is effective in terms of network expansion and fair to both the franchisor and its franchisees. Any program, method or procedure agreed to by a franchisor and its franchisees to resolve system expansion issues will comply with this *Code*.

8. Supply Sources. A franchisor has a compelling interest in maintaining system standards and protecting its trademark. Controlling the sources of operating assets, goods sold and materials and supplies utilized by its franchisee in developing and operating his or her business is an effective method of policing system standards compliance. Such controls can also protect a franchisor's trade secrets and other confidential information and can constitute a valuable service to franchisees by assuring sources of high quality goods and services at competitive prices. Franchisors that derive their principal revenue by selling goods to their franchisees for resale must be able to be assured that their franchisees will not buy such goods from other sources, thereby impairing the franchisor's revenue base. Restrictions on the suppliers from which franchisees may buy goods and services used in the establishment and operation of their business is comprehensively regulated under federal and state antitrust and trade regulation laws.

Therefore, with respect to the formulation and implementation of designated and approved supplier programs and other restrictions on the suppliers from which franchisees are permitted to purchase goods and services, franchisors shall comply in all respects with applicable franchise disclosure laws and antitrust and trade regulation laws. Franchisees shall comply with the restrictions contained in supply programs established by their franchisor that are in compliance with applicable franchise disclosure, antitrust and trade regulation laws.

9. Disputes. Litigation between franchisors and franchisees has frequently been costly and antithetical to productive franchise relationships. Franchisors and franchisees should resort to judicial dispute resolution only after other methods have failed to resolve a dispute.

Therefore, whenever practicable, a franchisor and its franchisee shall make a diligent effort to resolve disputes by negotiation, mediation, or internal appeal procedures. A franchisor and its franchisees shall consider the use of additional alternative dispute resolution procedures in appropriate situations to resolve disputes that are not resolved by negotiation, mediation or internal appeal.

10. Discrimination. Discrimination is not consistent with fair and sound franchising practices. A franchisor should make its franchises available to the widest possible spectrum of individuals. Many franchisors have adopted programs to assist minority and other disadvantaged persons to become franchisees. Both franchisors and franchisees should make employment opportunities available to the widest possible spectrum of individuals.

Therefore, a franchisor shall not discriminate in the operations of its franchised network on the basis of race, color, religion, national origin, gender, sexual preference or disability. Franchisors and franchisees shall not discriminate in hiring, other aspects of their employment relationships or otherwise in the operation of their businesses on the basis of race, color, religion, national origin, gender, sexual preference or disability. Franchisors and franchisees may utilize reasonable criteria in determining eligibility for its franchise and employees and may grant franchises to some franchisees and hire some employees on more favorable terms than are granted to other franchisees or employees as part of a program to make franchises and employment opportunities available to persons lacking capital, training, business experience or other qualifications ordinarily required of franchisees and employees. A franchisor and its franchisees may implement other affirmative action programs.

EXHIBIT 5-C: The Code of Business Ethics and Conduct

Contents   **Page**

THE CODE OF BUSINESS ETHICS AND CONDUCT

To All Company Employees:

Over the years, the Company has earned a global reputation for the highest standards of integrity and quality. Our Company continues to grow and succeed because of the relationships we develop and maintain with our customers, fellow employees, franchisees, vendors, suppliers, and other business sources.

The Code of Business Ethics and Conduct (The Code) provides guidelines for your business practices. As a Company employee, you must comply with all laws and regulations and must conduct yourself and any business activities with the highest ethical standards.

You are responsible for knowing and complying with the information in *The Code.* This is a very serious matter, and it is important to know that anyone violating *The Code* will be subject to disciplinary action, including the possibility of dismissal or imprisonment for criminal violations.

Much of the information included in *The Code* is common sense, but occasionally something that seems right and fair may not comply with regulations. We have attempted to cover most situations, but there will no doubt be unique circumstances that need to be addressed individually. If you have any question or even a doubt about a situation, you should check with your supervisor, the General Counsel or the office listed in the sections throughout *The Code.* If you suspect or learn that someone else is violating *The Code,* you must report your suspicions.

If we all perform our jobs according to these standards, the Company will remain a good place to work, thus enhancing the services we provide, sharpening our competitive edge, and increasing our profitability.

Chief Executive Officer

April 1997

REPORTING VIOLATIONS

If you have any questions about the Company's* policies or standards, or if you think that ethical standards have been compromised by an employee, business source or any agent of the Company, you must contact your supervisor, the General Counsel or the offices listed throughout *The Code.* You will find the phone numbers for those offices in your Company phone book.

Be assured that you will not be penalized for reporting information in good faith. All questions and comments will be confidential and can remain anonymous if you would like; only those who have a need to know will be informed.

Burger King Corporation
General Counsel/Law Department
Miami, Florida
(305) 378-7132

We encourage you to call the General Counsel or Law Department or you may call the toll-free number posted in your workplace. All calls will be taken seriously and acted upon, as appropriate.

---

*Where Company is used throughout *The Code,* it means Burger King Corporation and its subsidiaries.

EQUAL OPPORTUNITY AND DIVERSITY

Every employee is entitled to equal opportunity regardless of sex, race, color, religion, national origin, age, disability, veteran's status or any other protected status. Our goal is to provide a work environment free from any form or unlawful discrimination or harassment.

For the Company to grow and succeed, we must recognize and encourage diversity in our employees, franchisees, business sources, community involvement and sponsorships.

The Company expects you to support and facilitate these policies in your day-to-day responsibilities. If you become aware of any violation of these policies, immediately notify Human Resources.

HEALTH AND SAFETY

You and our customers are entitled to a safe and healthy workplace. You are responsible for preventing accidents by following safe work procedures, complying with the Company's safety programs and strictly adhering to occupational safety and health regulations, including work restrictions applying to minors.

If you have questions about, or know of any safety, health or environmental issues, contact your supervisor or the Safety and Risk Department.

You must immediately report any unsafe or potentially dangerous condition.

Environmental Responsibility

The Company is committed to operating in an environmentally responsible manner. Company activities must comply with applicable environmental law and minimize any adverse consequences to our natural environment. The Company has adopted worldwide guidelines designed to protect the environment and add value to our business.

You must take great care, for example, to dispose of any waste materials in accordance with proper procedures. You must also provide complete and accurate information to government authorities when applying for any environmental permit. If you are uncertain about what is required, contact the Law Department before taking action.

Product Quality

Burger King® customers expect high quality products and services. In addition to meeting all quality standards, our products must be formulated, prepared and served in full compliance with food safety, health and consumer protection laws. Be sure that all product inspections, testing and related documents are accurate, timely and complete.

CONFLICTS OF INTEREST

When you are hired, you agree to be a loyal employee and to act exclusively in the Company's best interest. You have a conflict of interest any time your business judgment may be influenced or *appear to be influenced* by personal or financial gain. There are many areas of business where a conflict of interest may occur.

You are responsible for ensuring that you (and your employees, if applicable) do not have a conflict of interest. If you have any doubt about a situation, contact the Law Department or General Counsel for advice.

The following sections provide guidelines for avoiding conflicts of interest with non-governmental business sources. Business sources include vendors, suppliers, franchisees, cooperatives, distributors, consultants or others doing business with the Company. Specific rules that apply to government interactions are discussed in "Relationships with Governments and Government Representatives," beginning on page 239.

Financial Compensation

You may not accept **any** financial compensation (e.g., salaries, fees, commissions, rebates or monetary rewards) from any business source.

Business Meals

You are encouraged to maintain cordial business relationships. When conducting business, you may accept or pay for meals and refreshments within reason. You should avoid excessive or unreasonably priced items. Also, you should limit the number of business meals you furnish to or accept from a particular business source.

Gifts and Entertainment

Acceptable Practices

You may, occasionally, give and receive modest gifts and entertainment in connection with your business relationships, such as:

- Sporting or theatrical events.
- Advertising or promotional items, such as pens, note pads, calendars, paperweights and other similar items.

If you are in a position to entertain or buy gifts for a business source, be sure that you comply with our policies as well as the policies of your business source's company.

Unacceptable Practices

You **may not** give or accept expensive gifts or entertainment to or from any business source (see below for exceptions in foreign countries).
In addition, **you may not:**

- Ask business sources for gifts or favors for personal or family use or gain (e.g., asking a vendor to donate to a charitable organization in your name).
- Accept bribes or kickbacks, or any gift or favor that may be perceived as such.
- Accept personal discounts that are not generally available.
- Accept cash or cash equivalents from business sources.
- Give, solicit or receive favors that violate any law, or generally accepted ethical standard or business practice.
- Condition the purchase of goods or services on whether the business source buys our Company's products.
- Accept an all-expense paid trip to a supplier's annual picnic or golf outing.
- Accept or purchase unreasonably priced meals or refreshments.
- Request a vendor to fund a Company function unless the vendor receives some value from the funding, such as an opportunity to sell its goods to franchisees.
- Compromise the ethics of business sources by putting them in a situation that might place their personal interests above their company's or violate their firm's policies.

Reporting Gifts or Entertainment

If you or your family receives more than $100 worth of gifts or entertainment (not including meals) in any 12-month period from a single business source or more than $250 in a 12-month period from all combined sources, you must disclose the source and circumstances of the gift/entertainment in the manner prescribed by the Company (see attached Certificate of Compliance).

Gifts in Foreign Countries

As a global operation, the Company is attuned to, and respects cultural practices that exist in the countries in which we do business. The Company expects you to be aware of and comply with *The Code,* as well as the legal and ethical requirements of each country in which you do business.

For example, in some countries it is lawful, as well as good business manners, for senior executives to give or accept expensive gifts, entertainment or gratuities. Failing to do so may be a serious breach of etiquette with adverse business and social consequences.

If you receive an expensive gift, you must notify the head of your operating unit and/or the Chief Executive Officer (CEO). Depending on the gift and the circumstances, you may have to give the gift to the Company.

If you are in a position to give an expensive gift, your operating unit head and/or CEO and Law Department must approve the item beforehand.

For more information about foreign business practices see "Relationships with Governments and Government Representatives," beginning on page 239.

Conducting Business with Family Members and Relatives

Conducting Company business with a family member or relative creates a potential conflict of interest and should be avoided. Situations may occur in which you unknowingly or unintentionally have a conflict of interest. It is important to be aware of any relative's business dealings that may involve the Company so that there is no actual or suggested impropriety.

For example, you may not:

- Hire or pressure another employee to hire a family member or relative (or close friend) in any capacity.
- Hire a contractor who employs, or is owned or controlled by a family member or relative.
- Have job duties directly related to a restaurant franchised to, or who employs a family member or relative.
- Supervise, review or have any influence on the job evaluation, pay or benefits of any family member or relative.

Personal Business Ventures

You (and in some cases, family members) may not have any financial or other personal interest in a firm that does business with the Company if you represent the Company in, or have authority over, those business dealings.

For example, **you may not:**

- Take advantage of an opportunity you may have learned about through your job that would be to the detriment of the Company (e.g., buying land that the Company may be interested in acquiring).
- Have a financial or professional relationship (e.g., consulting) with a supplier or competitor.
- Be employed by a competitor or supplier.
- Negotiate for any financial or ownership interest in a franchisee or joint venture partner.
- Borrow from or lend money to a competitor, franchisee, joint venture partner or a business that supplies the Company with goods or services.
- Hire a contractor who does business with the Company to make repairs or improvements to your or a family member's home if you have any control over the contractor's relationship with the Company.

Note: If you do not have control over the contractor, you or a family member may hire the contractor for personal business as long as you pay the fair market value for the work, and do not receive special consideration because you are a Company employee.

- Engage in any outside activity or *moonlighting* that interferes with you fulfilling your job responsibilities for the Company.
- Own any stock or have any ownership interest in a competitor of, or any firm having a financial relationship with Grand Metropolitan PLC or any of its affiliates, such as a supplier, franchisee, joint venture partner or customer.

Note: As an exception, you *may* own up to 10% of issued and outstanding shares of stock of a firm worth $500 million and traded on a nationally recognized stock exchange.

Summing Up Conflicts of Interest

The examples in these sections are not all-inclusive. Keep in mind that if a family member or relative is involved in any of the situations discussed in this section, it will probably create a conflict of interest for you.

Contact the General Counsel if you think you, a family member or relative may have a conflict of interest. Also, if you anticipate conducting Company business with a family member or relative or with a business associated with your family member or relative, contact the General Counsel before taking any action.

In some cases, the conflict may be excused if it does not compromise our standards, is lawful, and is in the best interest of the Company.

CONFIDENTIALITY

Proprietary Information

Our trade secrets and other proprietary information set us apart from the competition. These trade secrets and all confidential information belong to the Company and must be safeguarded during and after your employment. Examples include, but are not limited to:

- Marketing strategies and plans
- Product formulations
- New product or equipment technology
- Restaurant development plans
- Unpublished financial reports
- Personnel and salary data
- Operations manuals
- Training materials

Confidential information will be communicated on a need-to-know basis within the Company. If you are in a position to know any confidential information, you may not provide this information to anyone inside the Company who does not need the information to perform his or her job, or to anyone outside the Company. Be careful to avoid inadvertent disclosures in your routine business dealings and in social conversations with friends and relatives.

The Law Department may approve disclosing information in conjunction with a confidentiality agreement.

Trademark Protection

Our Trademarks (e.g., BURGER KING® and WHOPPER® are among the most important Company assets. They distinguish us from our competitors and represent our hard-earned reputation for quality products and services. It is up to you and other authorized users to protect our trademarks.

All trademarks (registered and unregistered) must be accompanied by their appropriate designations. Contact the Law Department for guidance on the proper use of trademarks.

Competitor Information

You may not accept confidential information about anyone, including a competitor, without prior authorization from the Law Department. This applies whether the information comes from the owner, ex-employee, former franchisee of another chain or consultant. Examples of confidential information include, but are not limited to:

- Marketing strategies and plans
- Product formulations
- New product or equipment technology

Additionally, you are expected to respect the confidentiality of your former employers, just as you are expected to protect the Company's information after you leave.

Inside Information

You may have information about the Company that is not generally known to the public. This is what is commonly referred to as "inside information." You may not profit from inside information about the Company or any company with which we do business. This means that you may not buy or sell Company stock (Grand Metropolitan PLC) or tell this information to another person (including family and friends) until the information is made public.

If you trade Company securities or exercise stock options based on non-public, material information, or if someone you know trades Company securities because of information you have disclosed, you will violate insider trading laws. The penalties for insider trading are serious for both you and the Company, and may result in civil and criminal penalties including fines and imprisonment.

If you think you have inside information, contact the General Counsel before trading any Company securities.

Talking to the Media

If the media or any outsider contacts you for information about the Company (e.g., position on a public issue, Company activities, legal matter or financial information), explain that Company policy does not permit you to comment, and direct them to the Diversity and Corporate Affairs Department.

RELATIONSHIPS WITH GOVERNMENTS AND GOVERNMENT REPRESENTATIVES

We encourage you to be a politically involved private citizen, but be aware that when you represent the Company, you must adhere to the laws governing political and lobbying activities.

Contributions

You may not make any contributions to political parties or candidates on behalf of the Company without prior authorization from the Diversity and Corporate Affairs Office. If you choose to make a private donation, do not do anything to imply that you are acting on behalf of the Company such as using Company facilities, property or logos.

Lobbying

The Company may legally lobby to support or oppose issues pertinent to our business, but only as approved by the CEO or authorized representative of the CEO. You may not lobby on behalf of the Company or lobby for any personal issues while on Company time.

Government Contracts

If your job involves business with the government, including the military, you must know the rules regulating these business arrangements. If you are unsure about any of the rules, ask your supervisor or call the Law Department.

Government Investigations

The Company will fully cooperate with any appropriate government investigation. You must follow established Company procedures regarding routine inquiries such as tax audits, OSHA inspections or wage and hour audits.

    If you receive any other inquiries, requests or subpoenas at work or at home, explain that Company policy requires you to notify the Law Department before responding. Be aware, there are civil and criminal penalties for you and the Company if you furnish untrue or misleading information, destroy or alter records or do anything to obstruct a government investigation.

Foreign Governments

The Company requires that all business dealings comply with all applicable laws and regulations everywhere we operate.

The Foreign Corrupt Practices Act

Under the U.S. Foreign Corrupt Practices Act, you may **not** offer or make any payments or give gifts or favors of any value to any foreign government official or politician (including political parties or candidates for office), or to a member of their staff in exchange for or in an effort to obtain favorable business treatment for the Company or any other person, or to affect any government decision. This also includes government agencies or departments, any foreign government monopoly or corporation, political candidates and any intermediaries or third-parties who may influence or transfer the gift to someone in the government.

    Any violation could subject you and the Company to civil and criminal sanctions. There are exceptions to this law. However, only the CEO, with written approval from the General Counsel, may approve any exceptions to these prohibitions.

COMMERCIAL TRANSACTIONS

All commercial agreements should be completed according to Company guidelines. You should avoid oral contracts, letters of understanding or intent, handshake deals and *gentlemen's* agreements. Examples of commercial agreements are: real estate transactions, franchising agreements, intellectual property transfers, supplier or distributor arrangements, joint ventures, acquisitions and divestitures.

    You should always act within your level of authority and never make unauthorized promises or assurances to others. If you are considering terminating a relationship with a business source, discuss the situation with the Law Department before a final decision is made, letters are sent or plans are communicated.

Trade Regulations and Antitrust Laws

Fair and open competition is the foundation of a free-market economy. *Antitrust* is a blanket term for the laws and regulations that protect businesses and individuals from unfair trade practices and ensure the right for all to compete for business to their utmost abilities.

The laws pertain to every phase of our operations, and affect our relationships with suppliers, distributors, customers, competitors, cooperatives, franchisees and almost all others with whom we deal in our day-to-day business.

The Company's policy is to fully comply with antitrust laws. Companies or individuals may be fined, face heavy penalties and restrictions, or be imprisoned for violations.

If you have responsibilities in areas affected by trade regulations or antitrust laws, you must be knowledgeable of all applicable laws in order to identify and avoid any unlawful conduct that may be detrimental to the Company.

Antitrust Guidelines

Here are some guidelines (although not exhaustive) to ensure compliance with antitrust laws. If you have any questions, contact the Law Department.

- We do not discuss prices or agree to fix prices with any competitor, nor do we set prices at a point designed to destroy a competitor.
- We do not collude with any competitor to divide the market in order to limit the competition in certain locales, nor do we restrict the amount of service each will provide in the same market.
- We do not use tying devices. A tying device forces a customer to buy a product or service from us that it does *not* want in order to get a product or service it does want and cannot obtain somewhere else at a competitive price.

Expanding Our Global Business

The Company is interested in growing our world market, but you may not expand restaurant operations or contractual relationships into any new foreign country without first having received commercial approval for the transaction from the Company's CFO and CEO. You should then contact the Law Department for the proper procedure and approval.

Acting without the proper authority could lead to serious legal and tax consequences.

RESTAURANT FRANCHISES

Burger King® franchised restaurants are owned and operated by independent business persons. They are key to the Company's success, and our relationship with our franchisees is critical. Franchisees are not Company employees or captive customers. While the Company must maintain enough control over franchises to protect our trademarks and reputation, it is important not to exercise more control than is allowed by law.

- In certain jurisdictions, the Company is held to strict regulations when a franchise is offered, terminated or transferred. If your position includes dealings with franchisees, you must be knowledgeable of and comply with these and all related regulations. If we do not comply, it may result in costly lawsuits by franchisees, civil fines and perhaps, criminal prosecution.
- The Company does not make earnings claims or provide estimates of potential sales or profits to existing or prospective franchisees.
- Decisions regarding franchisee development, credit, collections, terminations and other internal matters must be the Company's sole decision.
- Our franchises are granted for specific locations. No one below the CEO may grant exclusive territorial rights. You must not discuss exclusive area, market or territorial rights with franchisees or prospective franchisees.

The basis of a franchising relationship is recognizing each party's rights and duties under the existing franchise agreements and laws. If you have any questions, call the Law Department.

ACCOUNTING AND FINANCIAL REPORTING

The Company keeps records in accordance with generally accepted accounting principles and governmental reporting requirements. You must record payments, receipts, and other transactions accurately and promptly.

You may not:

- Make false, incomplete or misleading entries.
- Establish or maintain secret or unrecorded funds or assets.
- Administer an account or funds for the benefit of others (e.g., franchisees).
- Sign, or ask another employee to sign, documents you know to be inaccurate, untrue or misleading.

Report any financial irregularities or improprieties to your supervisor or the appropriate Company representative immediately.

CONSULTANTS, AGENCIES, AND NON-EMPLOYEES

Occasionally, the Company hires outside consultants, agencies or other non-employees. In some cases, these representatives may be considered legal agents of the Company. Since the Company can be held accountable for the actions of its agents, it is our policy that anyone we retain comply with our *Code of Business Ethics and Conduct.*
If you hire outside representatives, be sure they are aware of and adhere to *The Code.*

MANAGEMENT RESPONSIBILITY

Because a corporation acts only through its employees or agents, a manager may be held personally liable under civil or criminal law for the Company's wrongful acts. In some cases, a manager can be held responsible for the actions of his or her employees, even if the manager has no knowledge of the wrongdoing.

If you are accountable for any Company activities and operations, you must ensure compliance by knowing:

- The law related to your area of responsibility.
- Company policies relative to such activities and operations.
- How the activities and operations are conducted.

You must also report any suspected or detected violations of the law and Company policies.

CONCLUSION

As stated at the beginning, *The Code* is a general guide for you and should not be considered all-inclusive.

You are responsible for knowing the policies and regulations that affect your job, and we encourage you to re-familiarize yourself with *The Code* from time to time. Adhering to the principles of *The Code* and complying with the law are conditions of your continued employment. Failure to do so may result in disciplinary action, suspension, salary reduction, demotion, dismissal, fines or imprisonment.

If you have any questions or concerns about a situation, contact the General Counsel or appropriate department before taking any action.

EXHIBIT 5-D: Burger King Corporation Pocket Guide to Antitrust & Franchising

Five Fundamental Antitrust Rules Competitors May Not Agree:

1.   on the **prices** they charge for goods or services.
2.   on **terms of sale.**
3.   to **allocate markets, customers, or territories.**
4.   not to compete or otherwise agree on bids—**bid-rigging.**
5.   to join in a **boycott** of suppliers or customers to accomplish anti-competitive ends.

Avoid Contact with Competitors—Agreements between Competitors Can Be Prosecuted Criminally.

Four Other Antitrust Areas—Possible Civil Suits/Treble Damages

Liability will be determined by factual circumstances and reasonableness of restrictive behavior, but legal advice must still be sought in each instance.

1.   Tying: Making a product or service available on the condition that the purchaser must accept another, perhaps unwanted, product or service.
2.   Unfair competition: Some actions may be classified as unfair competition, such as hiring an employee of a competitor as a way of gaining access to trade secrets.
3.   Exchanging information: Certain types of information may be exchanged between competitors <u>under very limited circumstances</u> but should be done only with prior consultation with Company lawyers.
4.   Terminations: Terminating Suppliers, Distributors or Franchisees requires careful legal analysis. The situation should be discussed thoroughly with Company lawyers before any decision is made, letters are sent or plans are communicated.

When in Doubt Contact Your Attorney

Eight Fundamental Franchising Considerations

1.   The hallmark of the relationship between BKC and its franchisees should be the recognition of each parties' rights and duties under existing agreements as well as applicable law.
2.   Remember that there is a Burger King® <u>**SYSTEM**</u>—"special deals" can create serious problems.
3.   **DON'T SAY OR WRITE IMPRUDENT THINGS**—What you say and write IS important. Remember that in your dealings with people, you are viewed as a corporate representative. Be clear and objective in what you write and say.
4.   Franchisees are independent businesspersons—they are not our "employees", or our "captive" customers; nor are they our "partners" in a legal sense.
5.   BKC does <u>not</u> make **earnings claims** or provide estimates of sales or profits to existing or prospective franchisees regarding prospective restaurant performance. Refer existing and prospective franchisees to the information contained in the UFOC.

6. Decisions regarding franchisee expansion, development, credit, collections, termina-
    tions and other internal matters must be the **UNILATERAL** decision of BKC—Fran-
    chisees may be useful sources of information regarding market conditions but don't
    "<u>conspire</u>" or side with one franchisee (or a group of franchisees) against another
    franchisee.
7. Our franchises are granted for the specified location only. No one below the CEO of
    BKC is authorized to discuss or grant exclusive territorial rights and such rights will
    only be granted in writing after careful consideration. **DO NOT discuss exclusive
    area, market or territorial rights with franchisees.**
8. Don't cause, encourage or induce one party to breach a contract which it has with
    another party.

Your Attorney Can Help You with Specific Problems

EXHIBIT 5-E

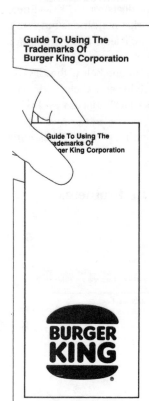

Guide To Using The Trademarks Of Burger King Corporation

Some Of Our Trademarks

BURGER KING®

HOME OF THE **WHOPPER**®

WHOPPER JR.®

HAVE IT YOUR WAY®

CROISSAN'WICH®

BK BROILER®

CHICKEN TENDERS®

BURGER KING.®

WHOPPER.®

Let's Protect Our Trademarks.

Our trademarks are among the most important assets of Burger King Corporation. They distinguish us from our competitors and represent our hard earned reputation for quality products and services. It is up to each Burger King Corporation employee, franchisee, restaurant employee and other authorized users to protect our trademarks!

The words yo-yo, aspirin, cellophane, and even shredded wheat were once well-known trademarks. Misuse by the companies who owned these marks led to their loss of trademark status. Therefore, we should be on guard against all misuse of our trademarks.

Fortunately, it's very easy to protect our trademarks. Just follow these simple rules:

---

1. Let Others Know Our Trademarks Belong To Us.

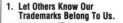

The ® notice means that the trademark is registered by the owner with the U.S. Patent and Trademark Office. Place the ® symbol after all registered trademarks. In printed material, the notice should appear the first time the trademark is used. BURGER KING®, WHOPPER®, HOME OF THE WHOPPER®, and the Bun Halves Logo are some of our most frequently used trademarks.

When the ® symbol is not available or when the registered trademark is frequently used in the text, you may identify the trademark by placing an asterisk after the trademark, which refers to a footnote stating the trademark is registered.

A ™ notice generally means the word, symbol or device is not registered, but is being used as a trademark. It puts others on notice that we claim trademark rights.

CORRECT:
Come to a BURGER KING® restaurant.
or
Enjoy a hot WHOPPER* sandwich.
*Reg. U.S. Pat. & TM. Off.

---

2. Yes, Even Memos Should Follow The Rules.

Bad trademark usage often begins with the trademark owner. Improper usage in memos and correspondence has a way of being picked up by suppliers and creeping into advertising copy. Be sure to follow the rules of proper usage in all your communications — whether it's a mass mailing to franchisees or an internal memo to another employee.

CORRECT:
The test kitchen is initiating a new series of taste tests for the WHOPPER® sandwich.

INCORRECT:
The test kitchen is initiating a new series of taste tests for the Whopper.

---

3. Don't Confuse Our Trademarks With Our Trade Name.

A TRADEMARK can be a word, name, symbol, device (or a combination of these) that is used to identify a product or service. It is a brand name. The words BURGER KING® form a trademark, a brand name which identifies the consistent quality behind our restaurant products and services. It describes a restaurant system and an image.

A TRADE NAME is the name under which a company does business. "Burger King Corporation" is our trade name. It does not require a ®.

Our trademark should not be substituted for our trade name.

CORRECT:
There are over 7,000 BURGER KING® restaurants worldwide.
The headquarters of Burger King Corporation is located in Miami, Florida.

INCORRECT:
There are over 7,000 Burger King® Corporation restaurants worldwide.
The headquarters of BURGER KING® is located in Miami, Florida.

4. Be Exact.

PMS 1235
(PROCESS 94%
OF YELLOW
30% OF MAGENTA)

PMS 485
(PROCESS 90%
OF YELLOW
100% OF MAGENTA)

Use our trademarks exactly as specified, since changing the appearance of a trademark suggests to the public that it's just another word or slogan. Don't vary or change the appearance of our trademarks. And, avoid exaggerations, abbreviations and changes in form or color. The spelling, contents and words should not be altered. And, you must not combine two marks into one.

Our trademarks may be printed in black or white. The bun halves logo may also be printed in the familiar red and orange combination. When color is used in print, the bun halves must be printed in the orange color PMS #1235 (Pantone Matching System). The red letters and ® mark must be printed in PMS #485.

CORRECT:
Enjoy a WHOPPER® sandwich at a BURGER KING® restaurant.

INCORRECT: (colors reversed):
Enjoy a BURGER KING WHOPPER® sandwich.

5. Emphasize Our Trademarks.

A trademark is not an ordinary word. It should not "blend-in" with typography or photography. Give it special treatment. The mark should be shown in all caps, in italics, in quotes or in bold-face type.

CORRECT:
The WHOPPER JR.® sandwich is a smaller version of the WHOPPER® sandwich.

INCORRECT:
The whopper jr.® sandwich is a smaller version of the whopper® sandwich.

6. Never Let Our Trademarks Stand Alone.

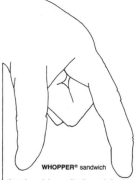

WHOPPER® sandwich

A trademark is an adjective and should be used with the common name of the product or service it identifies, at least once in every piece of printed material. There is no such thing as a WHOPPER®; there is only a WHOPPER® sandwich.

CORRECT:
Visit your local BURGER KING® restaurant and enjoy a WHOPPER® sandwich.

INCORRECT:
Visit your local BURGER KING® and enjoy a WHOPPER®.

7. Forget The "S".

"S"

Never use a trademark in either the possessive or the plural form. Remember, the trademark is not a noun and should not be used as such.

CORRECT:
Enjoy one of our great WHOPPER® sandwiches at this BURGER KING® restaurant's anniversary celebration.

INCORRECT:
Enjoy one of our great WHOPPERS at this BURGER KING's anniversary celebration.

8. Other Rules

Do's & Don'ts

a.   Always make sure the trademark is spelled correctly.
CORRECT:
WHOPPER® sandwich.
INCORRECT:
WHOPER® sandwich.

b.   Never hyphenate the trademark.
CORRECT:
WHOPPER JR.® sandwich.
INCORRECT:
WHOPPER-JR® sandwich.

c.   Never use the trademark with the word "type."
CORRECT:
We make many WHOPPER® sandwiches.
INCORRECT:
We make many WHOPPER® type sandwiches.

d.   Avoid combining a trademark with another trademark.
CORRECT:
Try a WHOPPER® sandwich from a Burger King® restaurant.
INCORRECT:
Try a Burger King® WHOPPER® sandwich.

e.

SUBMIT ALL COPY TO THE LEGAL DEPARTMENT FOR APPROVAL OF CORRECT USAGE OF OUR TRADEMARKS.

9. Don't Confuse ® With ©.

Trademark law protects short titles, words, phrases, symbols and designs; copyright law protects works such as books, advertising copy, artwork and music.

CORRECT:
© 1994 Burger King Corporation

INCORRECT:
® 1994 Burger King Corporation

10. The Trademarks Of Other Companies Deserve Our Respect.

Always use the same care with trademarks of other companies as you do with our own. Make sure you have written authorization to use their marks and that you use them in the form specified and approved by the owner.

Additional Information.

For more detailed information about proper use of the trademarks appearing in this booklet, or any other trademarks of Burger King Corporation, contact the Law Department.

Notes

_____
_____
_____
_____
_____
_____
_____
_____
_____
_____
_____
_____
_____
_____
_____
_____
_____
_____
_____
_____
_____
_____
_____
_____
_____
_____

BURGER KING

©1994 Burger King Corporation
Printed in U.S.A.

EXHIBIT 5-F

BURGER KING CORPORATION
POCKET GUIDE TO ANTI-HARASSMENT

All BKC employees have the right to work in a harassment-free work environment and to be treated with dignity and respect. As part of BKC's policy to provide a harassment-free work environment, BKC requires its supervisors and managers to prevent and eliminate all forms of harassment within their respective departments. Failure to do so may result in liability for BKC _and_ personal liability for the supervisor or manager.

Why Harassment is Unacceptable

Sexual harassment has no place at our workplace for three simple reasons:
- sexual harassment is wrong
- sexual harassment is costly
- sexual harassment is illegal

The Law and Sexual Harassment

Title VII of the Civil Rights Act of 1964 prohibits discrimination on the basis of sex. Sexual harassment is a form of unlawful sex discrimination.

IMMEDIATELY REPORT HARASSMENT TO YOUR SUPERVISOR, HUMAN RESOURCES OR VIA THE BKC TOLL FREE TELEPHONE LINE 1-888-880-8020

EEOC Guidelines

The Equal Employment Opportunity Commission has stated that unwelcome sexual advances, requests for sexual favors or other verbal or physical conduct of a sexual nature constitute sexual harassment when:
1) submission to such conduct is made either explicitly or implicitly a term or condition of an individual's employment;
2) submission to or rejection of such conduct by an individual is used as the basis for employment decisions affecting such individual; or
3) such conduct has the purpose or effect of unreasonably interfering with an individual's work performance or creating an intimidating, hostile, or offensive working environment.

"Quid Pro Quo"

There are two basic kinds of sexual harassment. The first type is called **quid pro quo** which means trading "this for that". Sexual favors are demanded in exchange for job benefits. This type of behavior would be generally engaged in by the individual's supervisor.

Hostile Environment

The second kind of sexual harassment is called **hostile environment** which consists of unwelcome sexual conduct that unreasonably interferes with an individual's job performance or creates an intimidating, hostile, or offensive working environment. This

behavior may be committed by supervisors, colleagues, customers or workers outside the Company.

Business Related Functions

Employees are expected to conduct themselves in a professional, business-like manner. Under no circumstances should an inappropriate entertainment venue (e.g., restaurant concept based on sex appeal or adult entertainment club) be selected which would create an intimidating, hostile or offensive environment for any BKC employee.

What to Look For

Sexual harassment may include:
- unwanted physical conduct
- indecent gestures
- off-color jokes
- sexually suggestive pictures
- demeaning comments about an individual's gender
- crude or offensive language
- questionable or inappropriate compliments

If you find the conduct offensive, you should make your displeasure clearly and promptly known to the harasser.

BKC PROHIBITS HARASSMENT OF ITS EMPLOYEES IN ANY FORM

Reporting

If you experience harassment, you should promptly report the incident to BKC Management. Information provided by employees will only be shared with those who have a need for the information, or when required in the course of investigating the complaint. No retaliation of any kind will be taken against an individual filing a good faith complaint. If investigation confirms that harassment has occurred, the responsible individual will be subject to disciplinary action up to, and including, dismissal. For additional information, please refer to the BKC Anti-Harassment Policy.

IMMEDIATELY REPORT HARASSMENT TO YOUR SUPERVISOR, HUMAN RESOURCES OR VIA THE BKC TOLL FREE TELEPHONE LINE 1-888-880-8020

EXHIBIT 5-G

PRIVILEGED AND CONFIDENTIAL
IN ANTICIPATION OF LEGAL ACTION

DATE: **May 8, 1997**

TO: V.P. Operations Name

CC: Attorney Name, Law Department

FROM: Finance Manager

SUBJECT: **Franchise Default/Termination Checklist—Franchisee Name**

We have discussed with (Attorney Name) of the Law Department the possibility of placing the above franchisee in default for reasons outlined below. At (Attorney's Name)
request, in anticipation of the possibility of taking legal action, we are requesting certain
information and approval from you as indicated below. Please complete and return to me,
and I will follow up with the Law Department.

(Items 1-7 to be completed by Corporate)
1.   Why is the franchise being reviewed for default and potential termination?

2.   What is the personal financial strength of each franchisee/owner?

3.   Why hasn't the franchisee paid?

4.   Has repayment plan been implemented? Explain:

5.   Detail financial viability of the business:

6.   Has BKC guaranteed any loans for the franchisee? _____ Yes   _____ No
     If yes, for what amount?_____

7.   Are there any loans outstanding through the FAC Finance Program?   _____Yes
     _____ No   If yes, what is the total amount of the loans? _____

(Items 8-13 to be completed by FM)
8.   Outline the performance of the franchisee in the following areas:

     Operations:

     Competition:

     Facility/Image:

     P&L Management:

     Other comments:

9. Has franchisee been advised how to improve sales? What was the franchisee's response?

10. Has the franchisee been advised to try to sell the restaurant(s)? What was the franchisee's response?

11. Could another franchisee operate the restaurant(s) more effectively than this franchisee?

12. What could another franchisee do differently to improve the business?

Operations:

Competition:

Facility/Image:

Other comments:

13. Is there an existing or new franchisee who might be interested in acquiring this restaurant(s)? Who?

(Items 14-15 to be completed by FM and VP)
14. Would the company be interested in acquiring these restaurants?

15. FM to complete Exhibit A regarding Current Operational Rating. FM and VP to complete Exhibit B regarding potential counterclaims.

PLEASE SIGN BELOW TO AUTHORIZE THE LAW DEPARTMENT TO PLACE THE FRANCHISEE IN DEFAULT AND INSTITUTE LEGAL PROCEEDINGS TO COLLECT AMOUNTS DUE BKC:

_____   _____
XXXXXXXXXXX, Director   DATE
Regional Finance

_____   _____
XXXXXXXX, Franchise Mgr.   DATE
XXXXXXXX Region

_____   _____
XXXXXXXX, V.P. Operations   DATE
XXXXXXXX Region

_____   _____
Clyde Rucker, V.P.   DATE
Diversity Business Enterprises

PRIVILEGED AND CONFIDENTIAL

EXHIBIT A
DETAILED ADDRESSES/SALES INFORMATION

TO BE COMPLETED BY CORPORATE AND FM

FRANCHISEE

Restaurant(s) to be placed in Default:

			Current	*Last 12 months sales ended:*				
						95-96		*96-97*
BKC Rest.	*Opening Date*	*Location*	*Operational Rating**	*Month/95*	*Month/96*	*Comp%*	*Month/97*	*Comp%*

* Current Operational Rating to be completed by Franchise Manager

Other Restaurants owned by franchisee:

PRIVILEGED AND CONFIDENTIAL

EXHIBIT B
POTENTIAL COUNTERCLAIMS

(TO BE COMPLETED BY FRANCHISE MANAGER AND VP)

1.　Please check the appropriate box and identify any complaints, disputes, or issues that this franchisee has or has had with BKC that may form the basis for a claim by the franchisee against BKC:

❏　No potential claims known to Franchise Manager

❏　No potential claims known to Regional Vice-President

❏　Potential claims by franchisee are described below:

2.　The following individuals have been involved with **_Franchisee Name_** and may be aware of other potential counterclaims:

NAME	CURRENT POSITION	PAST RELEVANT POSITIONS

**COMMITMENT TO CPR—
PROCEDURE FOR RESOLUTION OF
FRANCHISE DISPUTES**

COMPANY

ADDRESS

CITY, STATE, ZIP

TELEPHONE

We recognize that for many franchisor/franchisee disputes there is a less expensive and more efficient means to resolve the issues than litigation. For a two year period commencing on the date set forth below, we commit to use, at a franchisee's request, the *CPR Procedure for Resolution of Franchise Disputes* ("Resolution Procedure") in an attempt to resolve any dispute with a franchisee covered by the Resolution Procedure. The two-year commitment does not apply to (i) a request for mediation from a franchisee who has voluntarily withdrawn from a mediation concerning the same issue, or (ii) if there has been a completed mediation or final court decision on the same issue involving the same franchisee. We also hereby confirm that we will not penalize any franchisee or withhold any right or privilege accorded to other similarly situated franchisees by virtue of a franchisee seeking to resolve a dispute in accordance with the Resolution Procedure.

Chief Executive Officer

Chief Legal Officer

Date

(Note: Please send a signed copy of your commitment to Center for Public Resources, Inc., 366 Madison Avenue, New York, NY 10017, Attention Franchise Panel Management Group)

EXHIBIT 5-H: Procedures for Resolving Development Disputes ("JENNIFER")

1. General Purpose

1.1 Burger King Corporation ("BKC") recognizes that disputes have arisen, and are likely to continue to arise, concerning the development of new restaurants by BKC and its franchisees which are near existing Burger King® restaurants. Many of these disputes have resulted in mutually destructive litigation. The purpose of these procedures is to implement a more efficient and less adversarial process for reconciling such disputes by utilizing alternative dispute resolution ("ADR") procedures.

1.2 BKC believes that these disputes may be reconciled by a procedure that opens the process, improves communication and acknowledges the parties' mutual interests. The goals of these procedures are first to open communication between BKC and its franchisees in order to avoid disputes; and secondly, to reconcile disputes that cannot be avoided, without resorting to litigation. Accordingly, these procedures are private and consensual. Therefore, nothing in these procedures or in any communication sent pursuant to these procedures shall be deemed to constitute an admission of encroachment, or a waiver of any defenses, claims or legal rights BKC or any franchisee may have now or in the future in any court or other forum.

2. Targeting

2.1 *Procedures.*

    2.1.1 In order to avoid potential disputes before they start, it is the intention of BKC to establish a process of communication between BKC and potentially affected franchisees early in the targeting, site selection and approval process. The following procedures are intended to supplement and coordinate with BKC's then existing development procedures (the "Development Procedures"). To the extent these procedures and the Development Procedures are inconsistent, the provisions of these Procedures for Resolving Development Disputes shall be controlling. The sequence of these procedures would be as follows:

    2.1.2 A potential target location is identified by BKC. A "Target Location" is defined as a specific place with clear, describable boundaries.

    2.1.3 BKC notifies all company-operated restaurant managers and franchisees and operators of restaurants (a "Potentially Affected Franchisee" ["PAF"]) which may be affected by a restaurant located in the intended new Target Location ("New Restaurant"). A PAF means all franchisee operators who own and operate one or more restaurants ("Affected Restaurant") located within a four (4) mile radius of the Target Location, unless the Target Location is located in a Metropolitan Statistical Area which has a population of 2,000,000 or more as defined by the U.S. Government Bureau of Census, in which case a PAF means all franchisee operators whose restaurants are located within a two (2) mile radius of the Target Location. Provided, however, that if there are no restaurants within a four (4) or a two (2) mile radius of the Target Location, whichever is applicable, then such notice shall be sent to the franchisee(s) who own and operate the two (2) restaurants nearest to the Target Location, each of which also must be, in any event, within a fifteen (15) mile radius of the Target Location.

2.1.4   If any PAF wishes to object to the New Restaurant to be located within the Target Location on the grounds of "unreasonable encroachment," it shall so advise BKC of its objection within fifteen (15) days of its receipt of the notice given pursuant to paragraph 2.1.3 above. The objection must specifically state reasons why the New Restaurant will encroach and unreasonably impact the PAF's restaurant, and the PAF's estimate of the amount by which the new restaurant will encroach on the sales and profitability of the PAF's restaurant.

(a)   Any PAF serving objections and appropriate representatives of BKC, including the applicable Franchise Manager ("FM"), shall meet at the PAF's offices or at such other location as is mutually agreed upon, within fifteen (15) days of receipt of the PAF's objection. At this meeting ("Initial Meeting") the parties shall review the objections, discuss the issues, address concerns and attempt to reconcile any potential disputes. No less than five (5) business days prior to the meeting with BKC, the PAF shall deliver to BKC a summary report in the form attached hereto as Exhibit "A," which shall set forth site information and other data which the PAF believes is relevant to BKC's decision on whether a New Restaurant should be developed in the Target Location.

(b) (i)   If, at or after the Initial Meeting between BKC and the PAF, BKC elects to continue with the intended Target Location, a PAF may request that a Sales Transfer Study ("STS") be performed by an independent vendor and the results of the STS be considered by BKC prior to it making a final decision with regard to the Target Location. BKC shall determine who shall have initial responsibility for the cost of the STS. The PAF shall cooperate with all reasonable efforts of BKC and the STS vendor to perform the STS.

(ii)   If the PAF requests the STS and BKC has not otherwise agreed that either BKC or the developing franchisee ("Developer") shall bear the cost of the STS, the PAF shall deposit with BKC, within five (5) days of the Initial Meeting, the sum of Five Thousand ($5,000) Dollars ("STS Deposit") to be held in escrow by BKC and used for the payment of the STS and all related costs of the STS. BKC shall, upon receipt of the STS deposit, order an STS from a vendor of BKC's choosing. Failure to provide the STS Deposit within the allotted time frame will relieve BKC of any obligation to order the STS or delay its decision with regard to the Target Location as provided below. A copy of the results of the STS shall be forwarded to the PAF and BKC directly by the STS vendor. Acceptable vendors shall be designated by BKC and the Franchisee Advisory Council, as that term is defined in the current Franchise Agreement.

(iii)   Upon receipt of the STS deposit, BKC shall withhold making any decision to proceed with the Target Location until the STS results have been received by BKC and the PAF and duly considered.

(iv)   In the event the results of the STS show a projected impact on the PAF's restaurant of ten (10%) percent or more, BKC shall refund the

STS deposit to the PAF. If the projected impact is less than ten (10%) percent, the STS deposit will be applied against the cost of the STS, and any balance left over after payment of the STS will be returned to the PAF, if the PAF paid for same.

(v) The ten (10%) percent threshold specified in paragraph 2.1.4(iv) above is not intended to be evidence of anything other than determinative of which party bears the cost of the STS or whether the PAF qualifies for royalty deferment and additional interim funding as set forth in Paragraphs 3.2 and 3.3.2 below.

2.1.5   After consideration of the information obtained by and/or provided to BKC relative to the Target Location, including the STS, if applicable, and before BKC approves the site for development ("Site Approval") is granted for a specific site ("Development Site") within the Target Location ("Development Decision"), BKC shall notify all PAF's and the Developer that BKC will either:

(a) not approve the Target Location; or

(b) grant to an approvable PAF the right to develop a New Restaurant in the Target Location (the "Development Right"), or

(c) approve the proposed development of a New Restaurant in the Target Location, as proposed.

2.1.6   In the event BKC elects to continue with the Target Location despite an STS which predicts that ten (10%) percent or more of the PAF's restaurant sales may transfer to the New Restaurant in the proposed Target Location, the PAF shall have the right to request a conference with the Chief Executive Officer ("CEO") of BKC, or the designee of the CEO [the designee shall be in a position outside the development department and shall be authorized to discuss the issues and address any concerns]. If requested, the conference, via telephone or personal meeting, shall, to the extent possible, occur within five (5) business days, or such later date if the CEO or the designee is unavailable, of the Development Decision. All action on the Development Decision shall be suspended pending the outcome of the CEO/PAF conference. BKC's CEO will consider the input from the PAF as well as other relevant data concerning the Target Location. If the CEO overrules the Development Decision, the Target Location as previously proposed will be disapproved. If the CEO approves the Development Decision, BKC may, in its discretion, proceed with the development of the Target Location.

2.1.7   If BKC grants to the PAF the Development Right, the PAF shall have fifteen (15) days after receipt of the notice given under paragraph 2.1.5(b) above together with the Target Reservation Agreement to accept the Development Right by executing and delivering to BKC BKC's then existing Target Reservation Agreement ("TRA"). Upon the PAF receiving Franchise Approval (as that term is defined from time to time by BKC), the original proposed Developer shall be treated as a PAF if it operates a restaurant meeting the criteria of paragraph 2.1.3 above; however, while the original Developer shall have the right to participate in the Mediation and Arbitration Processes (collectively the "ADR Processes"), it shall not have the right to call for an Initial Meeting. The PAF shall have the right, but not the obligation, to accept the Development Right. If the PAF declines to develop the Target Location, or if the PAF is unable to obtain control of a site in the Target Location, the PAF shall not be deemed to have waived any rights to participate in the ADR Processes.

2.2 ***Initiation of ADR Processes.***

2.2.1   If BKC decides to approve the Target Location, then any such objecting franchisee ("OF"), BKC and the Developer, may, at the OF's option, proceed to participate in the ADR Processes set forth in Section 5 which are initiated as set forth in 2.2.2. If BKC is the Developer, then BKC and the OF shall be the only parties to the Arbitration Agreement described in paragraph 2.2.2 below. As a condition to proceeding in the Arbitration Process described in Section 5 below, the OF shall first participate in the Mediation Process set forth in Section 4.

2.2.2   If the OF elects to proceed with the Arbitration Process, the OF, BKC, and the Developer shall sign an Arbitration initiating agreement ("Arbitration Agreement"), substantially in the form attached hereto as Exhibit "B", under which all parties shall agree to resolve the dispute ("Development Dispute") through the Arbitration Process set forth in Section 5 of these procedures. Failure of the Developer to sign the Arbitration Agreement will not relieve BKC or OF from proceeding with the Arbitration Procedure. The Arbitration Agreement shall be signed by all participants not later than thirty (30) days before the New Restaurant on the Development Site (defined below) is scheduled to open for business. On signing the Arbitration Agreement, the OF shall deposit with BKC the sum of $2,500.00 (the "Arbitration Deposit") to be held in escrow. The Arbitration Deposit shall be applied against the costs of the Arbitration Meeting, or be returned to the OF pursuant to the Neutral Advisor's decision, or applied pursuant to the agreement of the parties. If the OF elects to withdraw from the Arbitration Procedure at any time prior to the retention of the Neutral Advisor, the Deposit (less any sums expended or committed to be expended by BKC in connection with these Arbitration Procedures) shall be returned to the OF. Failure of the OF to execute the Arbitration Agreement or place the Arbitration Deposit with BKC in a timely manner shall relieve BKC of any obligation to resolve the dispute through the Arbitration Process.

2.2.3   After the New Restaurant on the Development Site is opened, BKC and the OF shall each independently track the performance of any OF's restaurant at their own cost. This tracking of performance shall not exceed a period of twelve (12) months after the New Restaurant is open ("Tracking Period").

2.2.4   If, at the time of filing an objection to a Development Site, the OF has a Multiple Franchise Application ("MFA") in process, or subsequent to the filing of an objection, the OF files an MFA, provided all other current requirements for franchise expansion approval are fully satisfied, the TRA will be conditionally issued ("Conditional Issuance") to the OF upon the occurrence of either of the following events:

(a) the execution and delivery to BKC by the OF of BKC's then current Limited Release relating to specific claims of encroachment asserted by the OF relative to the Development Site, or

(b) the election by the OF to participate in the ADR process and to fully comply with the requirements set forth in this Section 2.2.

In the event the OF elects to withdraw from the ADR process prior to the rendition of a decision or award by the Neutral Advisor and does not provide the Limited Release described in 2.2.4(a), the Conditional Issuance of the TRA shall be automatically withdrawn and deemed void from its inception. All costs and expenses, if any, incurred by the OF pursuing the development of a site, pursuant to the Conditional Issuance, or otherwise, will be the sole responsibility of the OF.

2.2.5 The OF may, at any time, withdraw from these procedures upon execution and delivery to BKC of a Limited Release, in form and content acceptable to BKC, as to the claims relating to or arising out of the proposed Development Site.

2.3 ***Target in Jeopardy.***

2.3.1 On occasion, a Developer must commit to acquire a site prior to the time in which the results of an STS can be obtained. In such cases the site may be considered by BKC to be "in jeopardy."

2.3.2 A Target Location shall be considered "in jeopardy" if the ("Development Site") identified by the Developer is a specific site in the Target Location and if, in the reasonable discretion of BKC, it is determined that the Target Location is:

(a) available for development by others for uses other than a Burger King® Restaurant;

(b) likely to become unavailable for development as a Burger King® Restaurant due to a delay in decision-making caused by the need to wait for results of an STS; and

(c) unique in that there is not an economically comparable alternative site available within the Target Location.

BKC may also consider any other relevant information in making its determination.

2.3.3 If BKC determines that a site is "in jeopardy," BKC may elect to proceed with a Development Decision without waiting for the results of an STS. In such cases, the OF shall be treated as if an STS had been conducted showing results in excess of ten (10%) percent and the OF shall be entitled to: (a) a conference with the CEO or his designee as described in paragraph 2.1.6 above, (b) Conditional Royalty Deferral, as defined in paragraph 3.2 below and (c) Quarterly Status Meetings and, if applicable, additional financial support as described in paragraph 3.3 below.

2.3.4 BKC shall provide the Franchisee Advisory Council with a quarterly report as to the number of sites classified as being "in jeopardy" for which BKC granted approval for any site before receiving an STS, together with the names of the Developing Franchisees for such sites or in the case of a Company-developed restaurant, the location thereof.

3. Interim Compensation

3.1 ***Conditions Precedent.*** The following provisions of this Section 3 shall apply only if all of the following "conditions" have been met:

3.1.1 The OF requests an STS and timely delivers the STS Deposit to BKC, if BKC decides the OF must pay for the cost of the STS.

3.1.2 The STS results predict that ten (10%) percent or more of the sales of the OF's restaurant will transfer to a New Restaurant in the proposed Target Location.

3.1.3 BKC elects to proceed with the development of a site in the Target Location with a party other than the OF.

3.1.4 The OF elects to proceed with the Arbitration Process.

3.1.5 The Development Site opens for business.

3.2 ***Royalty Deferral.*** In the event each of the conditions listed in paragraph 3.1 above has been met, commencing on the tenth (10th) day of the first (1st) calendar month following the opening for business at the Development Site, the OF shall be permitted to defer payment of BKC Royalty charges payable under the Franchise Agreement for the OF's restaurant ("Affected Restaurant") on a conditional basis (the "Conditional Royalty Deferral"). This Conditional Royalty Deferral shall continue for so long as the ADR Processes for the Development Site continue, until such time as a decision is rendered by the Neutral Advisor, or until the ADR Processes are otherwise concluded through mediation or other mutual agreement of the parties, whichever occurs first.

3.3 *Quarterly Status Meetings.*

3.3.1 At three-month intervals following the commencement of the Conditional Royalty Deferral, the OF, FM and a designated BKC controller ("Controller") shall meet to discuss the status of the Affected Restaurant ("Quarterly Meeting"). At least five (5) business days prior to the Quarterly Meeting, the OF shall provide the FM and Controller with an up-to-date profit and loss statement and balance sheet for the trailing 12-month period. The OF shall provide to the FM and Controller all information and data relevant to the operation of the Affected Restaurant, including any sales promotion activity or other matter affecting the sales and/or profits of the Affected Restaurant.

3.3.2 If it is determined by the FM and Controller that additional financial support is necessary to enable the OF to generate additional net cash flow in the current year from the operation of the Affected Restaurant, BKC shall loan to the OF, with no interest, amounts to be determined by BKC to be sufficient to assist the OF to achieve such additional net cash flow but not to exceed the net cash flow level obtained in the preceding year for the comparable periods. The OF shall execute Demand Promissory Notes evidencing the loan amounts in the form attached as Exhibit "C."

3.3.3 If the OF receives an award pursuant to paragraph 5.7.3 below or if the parties reach an agreement as set forth in paragraph 4.7.2 or 5.5.3 below, the amount to be paid to the OF shall be decreased by (a) the amount of Conditional Royalty Deferral pursuant to paragraph 3.2 above plus (b) the amount of any loan made pursuant to paragraph 3.3.2 above.

4. Negotiation/Mediation Procedures

4.1 *Negotiation Phase.*

4.1.1 BKC and OF shall attempt, in good faith, to resolve any Development Dispute by discussion and negotiation (the "Negotiation Phase") with the other party prior to the commencement of the mediation process as discussed in paragraph 4.2 below.

4.1.2 If the Development Dispute has not been resolved in the Negotiation Phase by the time the mediation process ("Mediation Process"), as described below, is scheduled to commence, the parties shall submit the Development Dispute to Mediation in accordance with the following procedures.

4.2 *Mediation Process.*

4.2.1 The Mediation Process shall be mandatory and non-binding.

4.2.2 The Mediation Process shall be deemed initiated by an OF advising BKC in writing that it wishes to object to the decision to develop a new restaurant in accordance with paragraph 2.1.3 above. If the Development Dispute is resolved at the Initial Meeting, in the Negotiation Phase or otherwise, Mediation Process shall be deemed unnecessary. If, however, the Development Dispute remains unresolved, the Mediation Process shall commence automatically following the opening of the New Restaurant.

4.3 *Selection of Mediator.*

4.3.1 A panel of Mediators shall be created by The Center For Public Resources, Inc. ("CPR"), a nationally recognized not-for-profit corporation dedicated to resolving business disputes without resorting to litigation, or such other third party dispute resolution organization qualified to create a panel of Mediators (collectively and individually the "ADR Organization").

Unless otherwise agreed to by the parties to the Mediation Process, no person selected as a Mediator shall:

(a) have been a BKC franchisee during the preceding five (5) years;

(b) have been an officer, director or employee of BKC or any affiliate of BKC, or any BKC franchisee or such franchisee's affiliate during the preceding five (5) years; or

(c) have performed significant professional services for BKC, one or more BKC franchisee(s) or any BKC franchisee organization during the preceding five (5) years.

4.3.2 A Mediator shall be selected by the parties from a panel of three (3) candidates identified to the parties by the ADR Organization from the region where the development site is located, not later than one hundred eighty (180) days after the opening of the New Restaurant. If the parties cannot agree on the selection of the Mediator from the originally proposed panel, then the ADR organization shall select the Mediator at random from the other members on its panel but not from the original three (3) member panel.

4.3.3 The Mediator's per diem or hourly charge shall be established at the time of selection. Unless the parties otherwise agree, or except as provided in the following sentence, fees and expenses of the Mediator and any other expenses of the Mediation Process shall be shared equally by the parties. Each party shall bear their own expenses in preparing for and participating in the Mediation Process. If an STS is conducted prior to a Development Decision being rendered which predicts that ten (10%) percent or more of sales will transfer to the new restaurant, and BKC elects to approve the Development Site, BKC shall pay all fees and expenses of the Mediator and other expenses of conducting the Mediation excluding Franchisee's expenses.

4.4 *Mediation Session.*

4.4.1 The mediation session shall be conducted by and held before a Mediator at an informal exchange (the "Mediation Session") held in the locale of the OF's principal office at a place and time agreeable to BKC, OF and the Mediator. The Mediator shall determine the format of the session which shall be designed to insure that both the Mediator and the parties have an opportunity to hear an oral presentation of the other party's views on the Development Dispute and that the parties attempt to reach a resolution of the Development Dispute, with or without counsel or others, but with the assistance of the Mediator.

4.4.2 The Mediation Session shall be conducted not less than sixty (60) days, nor more than one hundred twenty (120) days following the first (1st) anniversary of the opening of the New Restaurant.

4.4.3   The Mediator shall control the procedural aspects of the Mediation Session in accordance with these procedures and the parties shall cooperate fully with the Mediator.

4.4.4   The Mediator shall be free to meet and communicate separately with each party.

4.4.5   In the event that either party has, in order to prepare for the mediation, substantial need for information in the possession of the other party, the parties shall attempt in good faith to agree on procedures for the expeditious exchange of such information, with the help of the Mediator, if necessary.

4.4.6   BKC and OF may be represented by more than one (1) person, such as a business person, an attorney and an accountant or other financial consultant. At least one (1) representative of BKC and OF must be authorized to negotiate a settlement of the Development Dispute.

4.4.7   Each participant involved in the Mediation Process has a privilege to refuse to disclose, and to prevent any person present at the proceeding from disclosing communications made during the proceedings. The entire Mediation Process shall be considered settlement negotiations. Except as otherwise provided in 4.4.9 below, all offers, promises, conduct and statements, whether oral or written, made in the course of the proceedings by way of the participants, their agents, employees, experts and attorneys and by the Mediator, shall be confidential. Such offers, promises, conduct and statements are privileged under any applicable mediation privilege, and shall be inadmissible and not discoverable for any purpose, including impeachment.

4.4.8   The Mediator shall be disqualified as a witness, consultant, or expert for any participant, and in rendering a decision or award as is hereinafter provided, the Mediator's oral and written opinions shall be inadmissible for all purposes in this or any other dispute involving the participants.

4.4.9   Notwithstanding the provisions of paragraphs 4.4.7 and 4.4.8, nothing contained in these procedures shall be deemed to prohibit any BKC franchisee or its counsel or representative from disclosing or sharing with another BKC franchisee exhibits, strategy, tactics, information, or documents which the franchisee participant has developed or submitted during the Mediation Process; nor shall these procedures be deemed to preclude the disclosure of the proposed settlement offer of the Mediator or the terms of any settlement arrived at through the Mediation Process.

4.5 *Restrictions on Mediator.*

4.5.1   If the Mediation Process does not result in a resolution of the Development Dispute and the matter proceeds to Arbitration as described in Section 5 below, the Mediator shall not serve as the Neutral Advisor unless the parties specifically agree.

4.5.2   The Mediator may freely express his views to the parties on the legal issues unless a party objects to his doing so.

4.5.3   The Mediator may obtain assistance and independent expert advice with the agreement of the parties and at the parties' expense.

4.5.4   The Mediator shall not be liable for any act or omission in connection with the role of mediator.

4.6 *Submissions to Mediator.*

4.6.1   The Mediator may request the parties present a written summary of the Development Dispute to the Mediator with such other additional information as the Mediator deems necessary to become familiar with the Development Dispute.

4.6.2 The Mediator may raise legal questions and arguments.

4.7 *Settlement.*

4.7.1 If the parties have failed to reach an acceptable settlement, prior to the end of the Mediation Session, the Mediator, before concluding the Mediation Session, may submit to the parties a settlement proposal which the Mediator deems to be equitable to both parties. Each of the parties shall carefully evaluate the proposal and discuss it with the Mediator.

4.7.2 If a settlement is reached, the Mediator, or one of the parties at the request of the Mediator, shall draft a settlement agreement for execution which shall be edited as necessary by all parties until it is mutually acceptable.

4.8 *Conclusion of Mediation.*

4.8.1 The parties shall cooperate and continue to mediate until the Mediator terminates the procedures. The Mediator shall terminate the procedures upon the earlier of: (i) execution of a settlement agreement, (ii) a declaration by the Mediator that the Mediation is terminated, or (iii) completion of a full day Mediation Session unless extended by agreement of the parties.

4.8.2 If the OF has elected to proceed to Arbitration ("Arbitration Process"), the parties shall proceed according to the procedures set forth in Section 5 below.

4.8.3 Even if the Mediation Process does not resolve the Development Dispute, the parties shall refrain from instituting legal procedures regarding the Development Dispute for a period of five (5) business days following the conclusion of the Mediation.

5. Arbitration Procedure and Rules

5.1 *Institution of Proceeding.*

5.1.1 The Arbitration Process shall be formally initiated by the execution of the Arbitration Agreement as previously set forth in Paragraph 2.2.2 above. The participants in the Arbitration Process shall be BKC, all OF's with respect to the Development Site, and the Developer. Each OF shall have a separate Arbitration Meeting as defined in Paragraph 5.4.1. The Neutral Advisor for each Arbitration Meeting relating to a particular Development Site shall be the same.

5.2 *The Neutral Advisor.*

5.2.1 A panel of three (3) proposed Neutral Advisors shall be submitted to the participants not later than ten (10) days after the conclusion of the Mediation Process by the ADR Organization from the region where the Development Site is located. The Neutral Advisor shall be selected by the parties from the panel. The final selection of the Neutral Advisor shall be completed not later than thirty (30) business days after the conclusion of the Mediation Process referenced in Section 4 above. If the parties cannot agree on the selection of the Neutral Advisor from the originally proposed panel, then the ADR Organization shall select the Neutral Advisor at random from the other members on its panel but not from the original three (3) member panel. If there is more than one OF per Development Site, and the OF's cannot mutually agree on their selection of a Neutral Advisor, each OF shall select one Neutral Advisor from the panel and the ADR Organization shall make a random selection from those individuals selected by the OF's. The individual selected by the ADR Organization shall be the OF's selection.

5.2.2 The Neutral Advisor may not be the same individual as the Mediator chosen and utilized in the Mediation Process described in Section 4 above unless specifically agreed to by the parties.

5.2.3 The Neutral Advisor shall assume the duties described in this Section 5 and perform them in accordance with the procedures set forth herein. The Neutral Advisor shall sign a "Neutral Advisor Retention Agreement" in substantially the form attached hereto as Exhibit "D." The Neutral Advisor shall perform any additional functions on which the participants may hereafter agree.

5.2.4 No participant, nor anyone acting on its behalf, shall unilaterally communicate with the Neutral Advisor on any matter of substance, except as specifically provided for herein or as agreed upon by the participants. Not later than forty-five (45) days after the conclusion of the Mediation Process, each participant shall send a summary of its position to the Neutral Advisor for the purpose of familiarizing the Neutral Advisor with the facts and issues in the dispute with a copy being provided simultaneously to the other parties. The participants shall comply promptly with any requests by the Neutral Advisor for additional documents or information relevant to the dispute.

5.2.5 The Neutral Advisor's per diem or hourly charge shall be established at the time of selection. Unless the participants otherwise agree, fees and expenses of the Neutral Advisor and any other expenses of the proceeding shall be taxed as costs and paid as determined by the Neutral Advisor.

5.2.6 Unless otherwise agreed to by the parties to the Arbitration Process, no person selected as a Neutral Advisor shall:

(a) Have been a BKC franchisee during the preceding five (5) years;

(b) Have been an officer, director, or employee of BKC or any affiliate of BKC, or any BKC franchisee or such franchisee's affiliate during the preceding five (5) years; or

(c) Have performed significant professional services for BKC, one or more BKC franchisee(s) or any BKC franchisee organization during the preceding five (5) years.

5.2.7 The panels of Neutral Advisors created by the ADR Organization shall be updated as necessary by the ADR Organization to maintain a panel of at least five (5) persons in each BKC region.

5.2.8 The Neutral Advisor shall notify the participants to the ADR Agreement and the ADR Organization of his/her unavailability to conduct the Arbitration Meeting, in which case a replacement Neutral Advisor shall be selected by the parties or, if the parties cannot agree within the time specified by the ADR Organization, then the ADR Organization shall select the Neutral Advisor from the remaining members of the panel, but not from the originally proposed three-member panel.

5.3 *Pre-Meeting Disclosure.*

5.3.1 It is anticipated that the participants may have a need for discovery to prepare for the Arbitration Meeting. Each participant shall have the right to depose each expert witness designated under paragraph 5.3.2 and all other witnesses, who shall be identified by each participant. The participants shall attempt, in good faith, to agree on a plan for reasonably necessary, expeditious discovery. If they fail to agree, any participant may request a joint meeting (by telephone) with the Neutral Advisor, who shall assist the participants. In the absence of an agreement, a discovery plan shall be implemented by the Neutral Advisor.

5.3.2   Before the Arbitration Meeting, at a time mutually agreed upon by the participants but not later than thirty (30) days prior to the date set for the Arbitration Meeting, all participants shall exchange, and submit to the Neutral Advisor, all documents or other exhibits on which the participants intend to rely during the Arbitration Meeting. In addition, the participants shall exchange, and submit to the Neutral Advisor, a brief that shall include the following: (a) a summary of all expert witness opinions to be expressed and the basis and reasons for those opinions, including the data or other information relied upon in forming such opinions; (b) the qualifications of any expert witness, including education and employment history and a listing of other matters in which the expert witness has testified as an expert; and (c) a summary of the statements to be made by such participant during the Arbitration Meeting. The brief shall not exceed fifteen (15) pages, single-spaced or thirty (30) pages double-spaced.

5.3.3   Each participant is under a duty to reasonably supplement or correct its disclosures if the participant obtains information on the basis of which it knows that the information previously disclosed was either incomplete or incorrect when made, or is no longer complete or true. The Neutral Advisor shall, upon request of an aggrieved participant, grant such appropriate non-monetary relief to assure that these disclosure procedures are followed and that adequate pre-Arbitration Meeting disclosure is made.

5.4 *Arbitration Meeting.*

5.4.1   Each participant shall make an oral presentation and present proofs to the Neutral Advisor at an informal information exchange conducted by the Neutral Advisor (the "Arbitration Meeting"). No later than forty-five (45) days after the close of the Mediation Session, the participants and the Neutral Advisor shall establish the date and time of the Arbitration Meeting. The Arbitration Meeting shall be set to commence not later than ninety (90) days from the close of the Mediation Session. The Arbitration Meeting shall be held before the Neutral Advisor in the locale of the OF's principal office and at a location agreed to by the participants and the Neutral Advisor.

5.4.2   During the Arbitration Meeting each participant shall make a presentation of its best case, and each participant shall be entitled to a rebuttal.

5.4.3   The Neutral Advisor shall consider evidence from the participants as to what percentage decrease, if any, in the annual gross sales and profits of the OF's restaurant was reasonable under the circumstances (the "Reasonable Impact Percentage"). The participants may agree on a Reasonable Impact Percentage to be applied by the Neutral Advisor in rendering a decision under paragraph 5.7.2 below.

5.4.4   The order and permissible length of presentations and rebuttals shall be determined by agreement between the participants, or failing such agreement, by the Neutral Advisor. It is the intention that the Arbitration Meeting be as brief as possible, but to allow each participant reasonable opportunity to present his position. Each participant's initial presentation shall not exceed two (2) hours and shall not be interrupted except by the Neutral Advisor. Each participant shall have no more than one (1) hour within which to question the other participant and its witnesses. Each rebuttal shall not exceed one (1) hour. As long as each party is treated equally, the Neutral Advisor may extend or shorten such time periods, provided that the Arbitration Meeting shall not exceed two (2) days unless otherwise agreed to by the parties.

5.4.5   The Neutral Advisor shall moderate the Arbitration Meeting. The presentations and rebuttals of each participant may be made in any form, and by any individuals, as desired by such participant. Presentations by fact witnesses and expert witnesses shall be permitted. No rules of evidence including rules of relevance, shall apply at the Arbitration Meeting, except that no witness or participant shall be required to divulge privileged communications or the advice and/or work product of an attorney. Witnesses shall be required to testify under oath or affirmance.

5.4.6   Following each initial presentation, the Neutral Advisor may ask questions of counsel or other persons appearing on that participant's behalf. Following the Neutral Advisor's questions, any other participant or its representatives, including counsel, may ask questions of such counsel, participant or other persons.

5.4.7   Each participant shall be represented by at least one (1) member of its management and, at its option, legal counsel, at the Arbitration Meeting. Members of the management of each participant, and their counsel, may ask questions of opposing counsel and witnesses during the open question and answer exchanges.

5.4.8   At the election of any party, and subject to the provisions of paragraph 5.6 below relating to confidentiality, the Arbitration Meeting may be tape recorded. In the event the Arbitration Meeting is recorded, then the tape shall be retained by BKC. The OF shall have access to the tape recording.

5.4.9   In addition to legal counsel, each participant may have advisors in attendance at the Arbitration Meeting, provided that notice is given to all participants and the Neutral Advisor of the identity of such advisors at least five (5) days before commencement of the Arbitration Meeting.

5.5   *Negotiations Between Management Representatives.*

5.5.1   At the conclusion of the rebuttal presentations, the management representatives of each participant shall meet one or more times, as necessary, and shall make all reasonable efforts to agree on a resolution of the dispute.

5.5.2   The Neutral Advisor may meet with each participant's management representatives, jointly or, with agreement of the parties, separately, at the Neutral Advisor's discretion, in an attempt to facilitate the negotiations and propose settlement terms. The Neutral Advisor shall control the procedures to be followed in this facilitated negotiations phase. Counsel shall be permitted to communicate privately with their clients. At the discretion of the Neutral Advisor and with the agreement of the participants, negotiations may proceed in the absence of counsel.

5.5.3   If an agreement is reached, it shall be reduced to writing and signed by the participants and their counsel, if any. Once the written settlement agreement is signed, it shall be legally binding on the participants and specifically enforceable by any court of competent jurisdiction.

5.6   *Confidentiality.*

5.6.1   Each participant involved in the Arbitration proceeding has a privilege to refuse to disclose, and to prevent any person present at the proceeding from disclosing, communications made during such proceedings. The entire Arbitration Process shall be considered settlement negotiations. Except as otherwise provided   in paragraph 5.6.3 below, all offers, promises, conduct and statements, whether oral or written, made in the course of the proceedings by way of the participants, their agents, employees, experts and attorneys and by the Neutral Advisor, shall be confidential. Such offers, promises, conduct and statements are privileged under any applicable mediation privilege, and shall be inadmissible and not discoverable for any purpose, including impeachment.

5.6.2   The Neutral Advisor shall be disqualified as a witness, consultant, or expert for any participant, and in rendering a decision or award as is hereinafter provided, the Neutral Advisor's oral and written opinions shall be inadmissible for all purposes in this or any other dispute involving the participants.

5.6.3   Notwithstanding the provisions of paragraphs 5.6.1 and 5.6.2, nothing contained in these procedures shall be deemed to prohibit any BKC franchisee, its counsel or representative, from disclosing or sharing with another BKC franchisee exhibits, strategy, tactics, information, or documents which that franchisee participant has developed or submitted at the Arbitration Meeting; nor shall these procedures be deemed to preclude the disclosure of the decision or award of the Neutral Advisor rendered as a result of the Arbitration Meeting.

5.7 *Decision of the Neutral Advisor.*

5.7.1   If the participants do not reach an agreement as to any matter as a result of the negotiations between management representatives as facilitated by the Neutral Advisor, then the Neutral Advisor shall declare an impasse and render a decision or an award as provided in these rules. The declaring of an impasse shall be within the sole discretion of the Neutral Advisor. The decision or award of the Neutral Advisor shall be in writing and shall be signed by the Neutral Advisor. The Neutral Advisor shall deliver a copy to each participant either personally or by registered or certified mail, or as provided otherwise by these rules, not later than thirty (30) days after conclusion of the Arbitration Meeting. The decision of the Neutral Advisor shall be dated and shall identify the prevailing participant and the amount of the award, if any, due to the OF.

5.7.2   The decision or award of the Neutral Advisor shall be one of the following:

(a) A decision that the New Restaurant on the Development Site has not directly or proximately caused a reduction in the annual gross sales or profits of the OF's restaurant; or

(b) A decision that no compensation is due an OF based on a finding that the OF has failed to prove that the New Restaurant on the Development Site has directly or proximately caused a reduction in the annual gross sales of the OF's restaurant in an amount in excess of the Reasonable Impact Percentage as determined by the Neutral Advisor or agreed to by the participants under paragraph 5.4.3 above; or

(c) A decision that compensation is due an OF based on a finding that the OF has proven that the New Restaurant on the Development Site has directly or proximately caused a percentage reduction in the gross sales of the Affected Restaurant in excess of the Reasonable Impact Percentage, if any, as determined by the Neutral Advisor or agreed to by the participants under paragraph 5.4.3 above. The compensation to the OF shall be calculated in accordance with the following steps:

STEP 1:   The Neutral Advisor makes a finding that the New Restaurant on the Development Site directly or proximately caused a decrease in the gross sales of the Affected Restaurant by a certain percentage. Such percentage amount shall be for the first 12-month period following the opening of the New Restaurant on the Development Site.

STEP 2: The Neutral Advisor shall subtract the Reasonable Impact Percentage, if any, from the percentage amount, found by the Neutral Advisor in Step 1 (the "Compensation Percentage").

STEP 3: The Neutral Advisor shall multiply the "gross sales" of the Affected Restaurant for the 12-month period immediately preceding the opening of the New Restaurant on the Development Site by the Compensation Percentage to determine the "Lost Sales."

STEP 4: The Neutral Advisor shall multiply the Lost Sales times thirty-five percent (35%) to determine the "Lost Annual Profit."

STEP 5: The Neutral Advisor shall multiply the Lost Annual Profit figure by an amount selected by the Neutral Advisor (the "Multiple"), which shall be either (a) not less than one (1) nor (b) greater than eight (8) years.

5.7.3 The total award shall be paid to the OF within ten (10) business days of the date of the Neutral Advisor's award subject to the following limitations:

(a) In those instances where the Neutral Advisor selects a Multiple which is greater than the number of years remaining on the term of the Franchise Agreement ("Term") for the Affected Restaurant as of the date of the opening of the New Restaurant, the award will be divided into an "Initial Installment" which is the portion allocated to the "Term" and the balance will be placed in escrow ("Escrowed Balance") and disbursed as set forth below. The Initial Installment to be paid to the OF shall be the total award proportionately reduced by an amount equal to that portion of the award applicable to the number of months in excess of the remaining Term of the Franchise Agreement.

(b) The Initial Installment shall be paid to the OF within ten (10) business days of the date of the Neutral Advisor's award.

(c) The Escrowed Balance shall be held by BKC and shall accrue interest from the date of the award at a rate equivalent to the average money market deposit rate being paid on the date of the award by 100 large banks and thrifts in the 10 largest metropolitan areas as compiled by Bank Rate Monitor.

The Escrowed Balance together with accrued interest shall be disbursed to the then current owner of the franchise for the Affected Restaurant upon the issuance and execution by BKC of the Successor Franchise Agreement for the Affected Restaurant. If a Successor Franchise Agreement is not granted for the Affected Restaurant, BKC may withdraw the Escrowed Balance plus any accrued interest and use such sums for its own purposes.

By way of illustration only, if it is determined that the New Restaurant directly or proximately caused a reduction of the Affected Restaurant's gross sales in the amount of ten percent (10%), and if the Reasonable Impact Percentage is determined to be six percent (6%), and the Affected Restaurant's gross sales reported to BKC for the twelve-month period immediately preceding the opening of such New Restaurant were $950,000, then the Compensation Percentage would be four percent (4%) (i.e., 10% minus 6% Reasonable Impact Percentage). The

Compensation Percentage of 4% is then multiplied by the gross sales of $950,000 to determine the "Lost Sales." The Lost Sales of $38,000 ($950,000 times 4%) is then multiplied by 35% to determine the Lost Annual Profit for the twelve month period following the opening of the New Restaurant. The $13,300 in Annual Lost Profit ($38,000 times 35%) is then multiplied by a number which is not less than one (1) nor greater than eight (8) (as selected by the Neutral Advisor at his/her sole discretion) to determine the total award payable to the OF. In this example the total award would be $26,600 based on a multiple of 2, $66,500 based on a multiple of 5 or $93,100 based on a multiple of 7. Or, by way of illustration, if it is determined that the New Restaurant directly or proximately caused a reduction of the Affected Restaurant's gross sales in the amount of eight percent (8%), and if the Reasonable Impact Percentage is determined to be zero percent (0%), and the Affected Restaurant's gross sales reported to BKC for the twelve-month period immediately preceding the opening of such New Restaurant were $600,000, then the Compensation Percentage would be eight percent (8%) (i.e., 8% minus 0% Reasonable Impact Percentage). The Compensation Percentage of eight percent (8%) is then multiplied by the gross sales of $600,000 to determine the "Lost Sales." The Lost Sales of $48,000 ($600,000 times 8%) is then multiplied by 35% to determine the Lost Annual Profit for the twelve-month period following the opening of the New Restaurant. The $16,800 in Annual Lost Profit ($48,000 times 35%) is then multiplied by a number which is not less than one (1) nor greater than eight (8) (as selected by the Neutral Advisor at his/her sole discretion) to determine the total award payable to the OF. In this example, the total award would be $16,800 based on a multiple of 1, $67,200 based on a multiple of 4, $134,400 based on a multiple of 8.

In the case of a successor term, by way of illustration only:

If the Neutral Advisor multiplied the "Lost Annual Profit" by 4 x and made a total award of $240,000 to an OF whose Franchise Agreement for the Affected Restaurant has a remaining Term of 3 years, 7 months and 15 days from the date of the opening of the New Restaurant on the Development Site, then:

1. The remaining Term of the Franchise Agreement for the Affected Restaurant is 43.5 months. The number of months in the Multiple is 57.
2. Amount of Award / Multiple (mos.) $240,000 / 57 = $4,210.53 (monthly award)
3. (Monthly Award × Term) − Initial Installment $4,210.53 × 43.5 = $183,158.05
4. Amount of Award − Initial Installment = Escrowed Balance $240,000 − $183,158.05 = $56,841.95

5.7.4   The Neutral Advisor shall provide reasons or an explanation for the decision or award and shall file the same with BKC. Copies of such decisions or awards shall be provided to all franchisees upon reasonable request.

5.7.5   If necessary, the decision or award of the Neutral Advisor shall be binding. The decision or award of the Neutral Advisor shall be confirmed and enforced as an arbitration award in accordance with the law of the appropriate court of competent jurisdiction.

5.7.6   Unless otherwise agreed to by each of the participants to the ADR process, if the Developer is a franchisee, the Developer will not be liable for any compensation due to an OF.

6. Reopening of Closed Restaurant(s)

6.1   *Reopening of Closed Restaurant(s)*
The reopening of a closed Burger King® restaurant (a "Closed Restaurant") shall not be subject to these procedures, and franchisees claiming encroachment from a reopened Closed Restaurant shall not be entitled to participate in these procedures, except as specifically set forth in this Section.

6.2   *Definitions:*
The following definitions shall apply to this Section 6 only:

6.2.1   Determination Date: The date upon which BKC determines whether a Burger King® restaurant is an Affected Restaurant under these procedures.

6.2.2   Excluded Restaurant: A Burger King® restaurant that has been closed for less than 12 consecutive months as of the Determination Date or temporarily closed longer than 12 consecutive months for the following reasons:

(a)   condemnation/street widening;

(b)   fire;

(c)   force majeure; or

(d)   other temporary closings due to reasons beyond the control of the restaurant operator.

The reopening of an Excluded Restaurant shall not be subject to these procedures or Section 6.3.3 below.

6.3   *Notification; Availability of the ADR procedures:*

6.3.1   Before reopening a Closed Restaurant, BKC shall send written notice (the "Reopening Notice") to any adjacent franchisee who would have qualified as a PAF if the Closed Restaurant was treated as a Target Location under Section 2.1.3 hereof. For purposes of this Section only, such franchisee shall also be referred to as a PAF. In addition, for purposes of this Section only, such franchisee's restaurant shall also be referred to as an Affected Restaurant. The Reopening Notice shall state that BKC or a franchisee may reopen the Closed Restaurant in the near future.

6.3.2   After receipt of the Reopening Notice, if a PAF wishes to object to the reopening of a Closed Restaurant on grounds of "unreasonable impact", it shall advise BKC of its objection in writing within 15 days of its receipt of the Reopening Notice (the "Reopening Objection"). The Reopening Objection must specifically state reasons why the reopening of the Closed Restaurant will unreasonably impact the Affected Restaurant. The Reopening Objection shall also state the PAF's estimate of the amount by which the Closed Restaurant will unreasonably impact the sales and profitability of the Affected Restaurant. BKC agrees to meet with the PAF within 15 days after receipt of the Reopening Objection to discuss the issues raised in the Reopening Objection. After reviewing the information supplied by the PAF at the meeting, BKC shall notify the PAF that BKC will:

a)   proceed with the reopening of the Closed Restaurant;

b)   permit the PAF the opportunity to reopen the Closed Restaurant; or

c)   not reopen the Closed Restaurant at this time.

6.3.3   If and only if the PAF (or its predecessor) was not notified of the possible reopening of a Closed Restaurant before BKC granted site approval for the Affected Restaurant, then the PAF is entitled to participate in these procedures with respect to reopening of the Closed Restaurant. The PAF must state in its Reopening Objection that the Affected Restaurant is entitled to participate in these procedures. In accordance with the foregoing, if an Affected Restaurant was open or had received Site Approval before the date a Closed Restaurant closed, then the PAF for the Affected Restaurant is not entitled to participate in these procedures.

6.3.4   BKC reserves the right, in its sole discretion, to subject the reopening of a Closed Restaurant or an Excluded Restaurant to these procedures.

7. Miscellaneous

7.1   These procedures shall become effective October 1, 1995.

7.2   If the Affected Restaurant is subject to an exclusive territorial agreement, then the Affected Restaurant and the PAF for the Affected Restaurant shall be precluded from participating in these procedures.

7.3   These procedures do not amend any franchise or other agreement to which BKC is a party, except to the extent they are incorporated by specific reference into a Franchise Agreement and these procedures may only be modified in accordance with the procedures described in any such Franchise Agreement, which Franchisee acknowledges may not require a specific or individual franchisee's consent or concurrence. These procedures shall not create any third party beneficiary rights.

7.4   These procedures shall be available to franchisees in the Burger King System for Affected Restaurants which are operating pursuant to the form of Burger King franchise agreement offered after October 1, 1995 regardless of whether they have received or are eligible to receive formal notification pursuant to paragraph 2.1.3.

7.5   A franchisee that has raised an objection to the development of an intended Target Location shall not be denied expansion approval solely because of said objection provided the franchisee is otherwise fully approved to expand to new Burger King locations and the franchisee has formally entered the Arbitration Process described herein, executed the Arbitration Agreement and placed the Arbitration Deposit with BKC.

7.6   Unless otherwise provided herein, the time periods provided in these procedures may be shortened, extended, or enlarged only by mutual written agreement of the participants.

EXHIBIT "A"
DEVELOPMENT DISPUTE ANALYSIS DATA FORM

General Instructions
A. Complete a separate form for each existing Burger King® restaurant (the "Existing Restaurant") you believe may be adversely affected by the proposed new restaurant site (the "Development Site"). At a minimum, one form must be submitted for each Existing Restaurant located within a four (4) mile radius of the Development Site, unless the proposed Development Site is located in a Metropolitan Statistical Area which has a population of 2,000,000 or more, as defined by the U.S. Government Bureau of Census, in which case you must submit one for each Existing Restaurant within a two (2) mile radius of the Development Site.
B. Attach a street map of the area surrounding the Existing Restaurant and the proposed Development Site (scale of the map should be approximately 1" = 1 mile or larger).

Specific Information
A. Answer each of the following questions. Answers must be specific and not contain any general or conclusory statements. Designate *all* the information described in items 1–17 which follow.

   1. **EXISTING RESTAURANT**
       Burger King® Restaurant #_____
       Cross Streets _____ and _____
       Address _____
       _____

   2. **PROPOSED SITE**
       Cross Streets _____ and _____
       Address _____
       _____

   3. Shortest driving distance and travel time between Existing Restaurant and proposed Development Site

       Distance   _____
       Time of Day _____ Minutes _____ Breakfast
       Time of Day _____ Minutes _____ Lunch
       Time of Day _____ Minutes _____ Dinner

   Describe roads driven to obtain above distance and time

   _____
   _____
   _____

   Shortest distance between Existing Restaurant and proposed Development Site "as the crow flies" (straight line)

   Distance   _____

4. From what geographic area do you think the Existing Restaurant currently is drawing customers? Define the trade area and be specific—include street names, radius, distance and traffic generators (i.e., a mall or schools).

_____

_____

_____

_____

_____

5. What areas described in #4 do you think the proposed Development Site's trade area will encroach upon? Be specific.

_____

_____

_____

_____

_____

6. In your opinion, what is the trade area of the proposed Development site? Be specific—include street names, radius, distance and traffic generators.

_____

_____

_____

_____

7. Which arteries provide the main flow of traffic to the Existing Restaurant? Include street names and directional flow.

_____

_____

_____

_____

_____

8. From which arteries that are serving the Existing Restaurant do you feel the proposed site will siphon off? Include street names and directional flow.

_____

_____

_____

_____

_____

9. Which main arteries do you think will be feeding traffic flow to the proposed Development Site? Include street names and directional flow.

_____

_____

_____

_____

10. Are there any natural or man made barriers which separate the Existing Restaurant from the proposed Development Site? If yes, please describe.

_____
_____
_____
_____
_____

11. How would you rate the physical appearance of the Existing Restaurant compared to a "New Burger King Restaurant?" Better than, equal to, or not as good as a new facility (choose one). Give reasons for your opinion.

_____
_____
_____
_____
_____

12. What is the date of the last remodel at the Existing Restaurant and what was the scope of work? Be specific.

_____
_____
_____
_____
_____

13. Does the franchisee currently have any plans to upgrade the Existing Restaurant? If so, what are the proposed upgrades? Be specific, include scope of work and dates.

_____
_____
_____
_____
_____

14. What percentage of the Existing Restaurant's sales do you think the proposed site will cannibalize if it's built?
_____%

15. Which day parts would be most affected? Why?

_____
_____
_____
_____
_____

16. What marketing activities have taken place at the Existing Restaurant in the past six (6) months other than national promotions? Please be specific. How successful were they?

_____
_____
_____
_____

17. Do you believe the market can support a Burger King Restaurant at the proposed Development Site but only if it is owned by the operator of the Existing Restaurant? If so, please explain your reasons.

_____

_____

_____

_____

_____

BY: _____   DATE: _____, 19____

            Development Manager

EXHIBIT "B"

ARBITRATION INITIATING AGREEMENT

For valuable considerations, the receipt of which each party to this agreement acknowledges, the undersigned agree to resolve the following described dispute by using the Procedures and Rules for Resolving Development Disputes ("the Arbitration procedure") promulgated by Burger King Corporation:

Nature of Dispute:

The parties agree to forego the filing of any lawsuit or legal action relating to the dispute and agree to be bound by the decision or award of the Neutral Advisor under the Arbitration procedure.

The Neutral Advisor conducting the Arbitration procedure shall be selected in accordance with Section 5 of the Arbitration procedure. The time and place of the ADR meeting shall be as selected in accordance with Section 5 of the Arbitration procedure. The rules and provisions of the Arbitration procedure are incorporated herein by reference and the parties agree to be bound by same.

DATED this _____ day of _____, 199__.

BURGER KING CORPORATION

By: _____
          Vice President

Attest: _____
          Assistant Secretary

                    (Corporate Seal)

By: _____

By: _____

EXHIBIT "C"
DEMAND PROMISSORY NOTE

$_____   _____

FOR VALUE RECEIVED, we, the undersigned ("Makers"), jointly and severally, promise to pay to the order of BURGER KING CORPORATION ("BKC"), a Florida corporation, 17777 Old Cutler Road, Miami, Florida 33157, ON DEMAND the principal sum of _____ DOLLARS ($_____).

Until demand for payment is made, this Note shall not accrue interest.

The Makers hereby waive presentment, notice, protest and all other notices required or permitted hereunder and by law in connection with the delivery, acceptance, performance, default or enforcement of this Note, and assent to any extension or postponement of the time of payment or of any other indulgence, substitution, exchange or release of collateral, and/or to the addition or release of any other party or person primarily or secondarily liable on this Note.

This Note is being given to evidence the loan by BKC to Franchisee of Interim Compensation pursuant to the Procedures for Resolving Development Disputes, the terms of which are expressly made a part of this instrument. The Makers hereof acknowledge that payment may be demanded by BKC upon the earlier to occur of: (i) settlement of the Development Dispute through Mediation or otherwise, (ii) Conclusion of the Arbitration Procedure, or (iii) any default by the Makers of the terms of any Franchise Agreement, Lease Agreement, or the occurrence of an event of default by which there is a violation of the terms and covenants of any other contractual obligation by the Makers hereof to BKC. The terms, covenants and conditions of agreements between the Makers and BKC are expressly made a part of this instrument.

This Note is payable by mail or in person at the office of BKC or such other place as BKC may designate.

In the event of delinquency in the payment of any principal or interest payment due on this Note or in the event any default be made and it becomes necessary to retain an attorney for collection or to enforce the terms and conditions hereof, the Makers agree to pay reasonable attorney's fees, whether suit be brought or not.

The enforceability of the terms of this Note and the legality of the interest rate specified herein shall be interpreted in accordance with and governed by the laws of the State of Florida. In the event of litigation involving this Note, Makers agree that this Note shall be construed in accordance with Florida law or in the law of any other jurisdiction which has any relationship to the transaction and under whose laws the Note would be enforceable.

In the event payment in full is not made within thirty (30) days of demand, interest on the unpaid balance shall accrue at the maximum rate allowed by Florida law, or if no maximum rate relating to this promissory note is in effect in the State of Florida, eighteen (18%) percent per annum.

During the term of this Note, and upon ten (10) days written request by BKC, Maker agrees to give BKC adequate assurances as to Maker's ability to comply with the terms of this Note. Such assurances shall include, but not be limited to, Maker's then current financial statement, which BKC may require be certified by a Certified Public Accountant. Maker agrees that BKC may disclose such financial statements, or any other financial information pertaining to Maker which BKC may possess, to any potential buyer, assignee or holder in due course of this Note.

This Note is personal to the Makers and is not assignable. In the event Makers sell, assign or transfer their interest in the Franchise Agreement or Lease/Sublease Agreement for Burger King® Restaurant #_____ , the entire principal amount then outstanding on this Note shall immediately become due and payable. This provision shall not apply to an assignment to a corporation in which Makers own one hundred percent (100%) of the issued stock, in accordance with the terms of the Franchise Agreement, so long as Makers retain personal liability on the Note. This Note is assignable by BKC.

The Makers acknowledge that a default under the terms of this Note shall constitute a default under the terms of the Franchise Agreement between Makers and BKC for Restaurant #_____ . Should Makers fail to cure said default within fifteen (15) days of receipt of written notice, BKC shall have the right to terminate said Franchise Agreement and all post-termination obligations of said Agreement shall apply.

_____

EXHIBIT "D"
NEUTRAL ADVISOR RETENTION AGREEMENT

This agreement is made this _____ day of _____, 199__.

A dispute involving the development of a new restaurant by Burger King Corporation has arisen between Burger King Corporation ("BKC") and _____ ("OF"). BKC and OF have agreed to participate in an Alternative Dispute Resolution Procedure ("Procedures") pursuant to the "Procedures For Resolving Development Disputes" procedures, a copy of which is annexed hereto. _____ ("Neutral Advisor") has been chosen as the neutral advisor for the Procedures. BKC, OF and the Neutral Advisor accordingly agree as follows:

1 . The Neutral Advisor agrees to be bound by and to use his best efforts to comply faithfully with the Procedures, including without limitation, the provisions regarding confidentiality.

2. The Neutral Advisor and the Neutral Advisor's employees, agents, partners and shareholders, if applicable, shall not be liable for any respective act or omission in connection with the Procedures other than as a result of fraud or an intentional and willful failure to comply with the material provision of the Procedures after having received written notice of such failure and refusal by the Neutral Advisor to correct such failure. Exercise of discretion shall, by itself, in no event result in any liability.

3. The Neutral Advisor has made a reasonable effort to learn and has disclosed to the parties in writing:
   (a) All business or professional relationships the Neutral Advisor has had with the parties or the parties' law firms within the past five (5) years, including all instances in which the Neutral Advisor has served as an attorney for any party or adverse to any party;
   (b) Any financial interests the Neutral Advisor has in any party;
   (c) Any significant social, business or professional relationship the Neutral Advisor has had with an officer or employee of any party or with an individual representing a party; and
   (d) Any other circumstances that may create doubt regarding a Neutral Advisor's impartiality.

4. Neither the Neutral Advisor nor the Neutral Advisor's firm shall undertake any work for or against a party regarding the subject matter of the alternative dispute resolution.

5. Neither the Neutral Advisor nor any person assisting the Neutral Advisor with the Procedures shall personally work on any matter for or against any party or its affiliates regardless of the subject matter, prior to six (6) months following cessation of the Neutral Advisor's services in this proceeding other than as a Neutral Advisor in this or another proceeding.

6. The Neutral Advisor's firm may work on matters for or against a party during the pendency of the Procedures if such matters are unrelated to the subject matter of the Procedures, have been disclosed in advance to all parties hereto, are discussed to all of the parties hereto, and are expressly consented to in writing by such parties ("Unrelated

Approved Activities"). The Neutral Advisor shall establish appropriate safeguards to ensure that other members or employees and the Neutral Advisors firm working on the Procedures do not have access to any confidential information obtained by the Neutral Advisor during the course of the Procedures. Neutral Advisor hereby represents that there are no Unrelated Approved Activities as of the date hereof.

7.   The Neutral Advisor shall be compensated for services performed in connection with the Procedures in accordance with paragraph 5.2.5 of the Procedures. The Neutral Advisor's fee shall be taxed as costs and paid as determined by the Neutral Advisor.

8.   Counsel representing each party is as follows:

Counsel for OF: _____

_____

_____

_____

Counsel for BKC: _____

_____

_____

_____

BURGER KING CORPORATION

By: _____

Its: _____

Attest: _____

Its: _____

(Corporate Seal)

NEUTRAL ADVISOR

By: _____

Name: _____
(print)

[OBJECTING FRANCHISEE]

By: _____

Name: _____
(print)

EXHIBIT 5-I: A Dispute Resolution Process for Franchising*

Endorsed by the International Franchise Association

National Franchise Mediation Program

CONTENTS

Rev. February 1996

CPR Institute for Dispute Resolution

*©2000 **CPR Institute for Dispute Resolution,** 366 Madison Avenue, New York, NY 10017-3122; (212) 949-6490. This **excerpt** from **National Franchise Mediation Program** reprinted with permission of **CPR Institute.**

The **CPR Institute** is a nonprofit initiative of 500 general counsel of major corporations, leading law firms, and prominent legal academics whose mission is to install alternative dispute resolution (ADR) into the mainstream of legal practice.

NATIONAL FRANCHISE MEDIATION PROGRAM

Early in 1993 an ad hoc group of major franchisors joined forces to find a way of resolving disputes between franchisors and franchisees without the rancor of litigation where possible. Their goal was to create an alternative dispute resolution (ADR) process that would resolve conflicts quickly, amicably, and cost-effectively.

The result was the establishment of the National Franchise Mediation Program, designed in collaboration with the CPR Institute for Dispute Resolution (CPR), a nonprofit alliance of more than 500 corporations and law firms organized to develop alternatives to the high costs of litigation. The program has been endorsed by the International Franchise Association.

Franchisors joining the program agree to comply with program procedures for an initial term of two years by signing the Commitment Form, which follows. Participation by franchisees is entirely voluntary. All franchise companies are welcome to join the program.

Detailed ground rules are set forth in the CPR Procedure for Resolution of Franchise Disputes (the "Procedure"), which follows the Commitment Form. The Procedure is initiated by a Dispute Letter (Appendix 1) sent by the franchisor or the franchisee to the other party and CPR. The Procedure requires the parties first to attempt to resolve their differences through negotiations between senior representatives without the intervention of a neutral third party. A majority of franchise disputes are resolved at this stage.

Unless CPR is notified within a specified time period that negotiations were successful, CPR provides the parties with names of five mediators located in the franchisee's region. If the parties cannot agree on a mediator, they are asked to rank order the candidates and CPR appoints the candidate with the lowest combined score.

Mediators are selected from the CPR Franchise Panel of Neutrals, consisting of more than 140 prominent attorneys, located throughout the United States, who are well qualified to mediate franchise disputes.

Since the Program's inception, disputes have involved the following issues:

- Impact/encroachment
- Under-reporting of sales or other financial violations of the franchise agreement
- Development rights of franchisee
- Termination of franchise
- Renewal of franchise
- Customer service

Through Dec. 31, 1997, a 90% success rate was achieved in cases in which the franchisee agreed to participate, with many cases resolved without intervention of a mediator. Franchisors also report that as a result of the program they are resolving substantially more disputes with franchisees through informal negotiations without either party needing to submit a Dispute Letter invoking the program. For program statistics, see Appendix 4.

THE MEDIATION PROCESS

Mediation is a nonbinding form of negotiation facilitated by a neutral third party. Mediation should not be confused with binding arbitration or private judging. In mediation a third party—the mediator—holds a series of joint sessions and separate caucuses with the parties in an effort to assist the parties in reaching an agreement. The mediator is not empowered to impose a settlement.

Mediation is private, voluntary, nonbinding, and confidential. The most widely used ADR process, mediation is highly flexible and informal. Typically, it is concluded expeditiously at moderate cost. The subject matter can be large and complex or modest. The number of parties can be few or many. The process is far less adversarial than litigation or arbitration, and therefore less disruptive of business relationships. Since other options are not foreclosed if mediation should fail, entering into a mediation process is essentially without risk.

In fact, failure is the exception. Time and again, with the assistance of a skillful mediator, parties to a great variety of business disputes have succeeded in bridging wide gaps in their positions and often in developing creative, mutually advantageous business solutions. The principal pre-condition is that the parties share a genuine desire to resolve the dispute promptly in an equitable manner.

Mediation is result-oriented. Each party is given an opportunity to state its legal position and its views regarding the rights and wrongs of past conduct. However, the primary focus is on solving problems and developing a mutually acceptable solution.

One of the important benefits of mediation involves the ability of each party to disclose in confidence to the mediator certain matters that the party would not disclose to the other party in settlement negotiations. Armed with such information, a skillful mediator is often able to identify hidden interests and settlement alternatives that would not have been considered in conventional negotiations.

Once parties to a dispute agree to engage in mediation, they frequently arrive at a resolution of their dispute even before the mediation process has begun. This has occurred in a majority of cases submitted under the program.

The most frequently cited advantages of mediation include:

- substantial savings in legal fees and other litigation expenses
- promptness of resolution
- preservation of business relationships
- creative, business-driven results not available in a court of law
- privacy and confidentiality

There are two fundamentally different approaches to mediation: "interest mediation" and "evaluative mediation." In the former, the mediator, usually meeting separately with each party, first explores with the parties their underlying interests. Having identified these interests, the mediator and the parties explore opportunities for a creative "win-win" solution, such as a mutually advantageous new business arrangement. This approach is likely to be applicable when a business relationship already exists between the parties, as in the franchisor-franchisee situation. The mediator ordinarily will not offer opinions on the merits of the case or the positions of the parties.

In evaluative mediation the focus is on the parties' legal rights and obligations, the strengths and weaknesses of their positions, the likely outcome if the case were tried in court, and what represents a fair settlement. Structuring a settlement other than an immediate lump sum payment by one party to the other is by no means ruled out. This approach is likely to be used if the case does not present opportunities for interest mediation or if the interest mediation approach has been unsuccessful.

ROLE OF THE MEDIATOR

The mediator, skilled in sophisticated communication and negotiation techniques, assists the negotiations in important ways:

- Works to improve communication among the parties
- Helps each party clarify its own underlying interests and concerns as well as gain an understanding of those of the other party

- Probes the strengths and weaknesses of each party's legal positions
- Explores the consequences of not reaching agreement
- Generates options for mutually agreeable resolution of the dispute

By interpreting the positions and interests of the parties in an adroit way, the mediator can promote understanding and empathy and facilitate the exchange of necessary information. Although the mediator does not make decisions, he or she may identify or evaluate legal or factual positions of the parties.

Skilled mediators will identify and address barriers to settlement such as differing perceptions, communication problems, internal and external pressures, and delay considerations. An effective mediator must be absolutely impartial and fair, able to instill trust and confidence in the parties, a quick study, an excellent communicator, and a creative problem solver. The mediator can help the participants understand the problems and "face the facts," function as a communication channel, and develop solutions. Finally, the mediator may persuade the parties to accept a particular settlement.

On a practical level, the mediator facilitates the administration of the process by scheduling, arranging, and chairing the meetings, and setting the agenda.

The mediator does not negotiate for the parties, although mediators may instruct parties how to negotiate more effectively. The mediator serves as a catalyst for negotiations by suggesting, interpreting, advising, raising alternatives, and testing each party's perceptions. Through probing and questioning, the mediator must induce each party to think through and justify its acts, demands, and positions, and look at the case from the other side's point of view, while maintaining each party's confidence.

ROLE OF THE INVOLVED PARTIES

In a mediation, understanding is best promoted when business executives or managers explain their positions directly to their counterparts, rather than communicating indirectly through surrogates. These executives have the best understanding of their company's interests and are the most likely to embrace creative, business-oriented solutions.

Counsel to the parties, who may be in-house or outside lawyers, also have important roles to play:

- Counseling on the advisability of settlement and mediation
- Persuading parties to agree to the process
- Educating the executive about the legal issues
- Drafting statements for submission to the mediator
- Preparing for an effective presentation
- Serving as a sounding board for the client and discussing settlement options as the mediation progresses
- Assuring confidentiality of the proceeding and avoiding compromise of the client's litigation position should the mediation fail
- Drafting the settlement agreement and assuring its enforceability

A TYPICAL MEDIATION

A typical mediation progresses through the following stages:

- **Preparing for Mediation.** To educate the mediator about the dispute, the parties submit key documents and short written statements shortly before the first mediation session. These materials are returned to the parties at the conclusion of the process.

- **Location.** Mediation is generally conducted at the offices of the mediator, in the same geographic region of the U.S. as the franchisee.
- **Initial Joint Session.** A typical mediation consists of joint and separate sessions between the mediator and the parties. At the initial joint session, the mediator usually explains the mediation process, hears short presentations from each side, and asks open-ended questions to clarify positions and interests.
- **Initial Separate Sessions (or Caucuses).** The mediator often then meets privately with each party to explore in a confidential setting each party's underlying interests and concerns, both legal and nonlegal, and determine their priorities.
- **Subsequent Separate and Joint Sessions.** The parties are helped to develop options and alternative proposals that will result in a mutually acceptable resolution. At this stage, the mediator may help the parties generate ideas, evaluate alternatives realistically, and consider the consequences of not settling.
- **Completing the Process.** When the parties reach agreement, the mediator or other designated person will record the terms. If complete settlement is not possible, the mediator will seek partial agreement and/or help the parties consider other dispute resolution options.

The length of a mediation varies with the complexity of the dispute. Mediation of a typical franchise dispute may take 10–15 hours and involve two or three sessions.

WHY MEDIATION WORKS

A high percentage of mediations of franchise and other business disputes results in a resolution. Even when agreement does not occur during the proceeding, the greatly enhanced mutual understanding substantially improves the prospects for a later agreement. Satisfaction with the process on the part of users is also high.

What are the reasons for the dramatic success of the process? Each case has unique aspects, but the following factors are common:

- Disputes ostensibly between dispassionate corporate entities involve human beings endowed with emotions. When they face each other at a conference table in the presence of a mediator, direct discussions tend to reduce misunderstandings and antagonism frequently subsides. Concerns beyond legal issues are discussed. The process itself presents a joint challenge to all participants to devise solutions. The momentum of mediation leads to accommodation.
- The mediator can establish ground rules designed to maximize the chances of success. Settlement represents success for all involved.
- The mediator typically will first urge discussion of non-controversial subjects or those for which agreement is readily achieved, and postpone consideration of difficult issues. These early discussions help build a spirit of cooperation.
- The mediator can help identify and overcome barriers to settlement. Mediation provides the parties with an opportunity—at little or no risk—to crystallize issues and learn more about the other party's perceptions of the pertinent facts.
- In caucusing with each party, the mediator will diplomatically urge that party to face facts and dispel unrealistic expectations such as over-optimism regarding chances of prevailing in court. The mediator, if a lawyer, can point to the weaknesses of each party's case, as well as to the costs and burdens of prolonged litigation.
- Just as an impending trial often induces litigants to stop posturing and seriously seek a settlement, commitment of the parties to a mediation is likely to motivate

them to "bite the bullet" rather than to postpone unpleasant decisions. The mediator will reinforce this motivation.

- Once the mediator understands the true interests of each party, he or she can recommend opportunities for common gains. Many franchise disputes are resolved through innovative business arrangements not previously contemplated.

'SELLING' MEDIATION TO THE OTHER PARTY

The other party may well have to be "sold" on mediation, especially if it lacks prior experience. A suggestion or offer to mediate may not suffice. The advantages of mediation to both sides should be carefully explained. The proposer should emphasize that:

- this particular dispute is well suited to mediation
- the procedure is voluntary, nonbinding, and confidential
- the parties retain control over the outcome
- the mediator must be acceptable to both parties
- the ground rules must be acceptable to both parties
- a franchisee may withdraw at any time, and there are time limits after which either party may withdraw
- the cost of the procedure is likely to be relatively modest
- experience shows that the chances of success are very high
- the proposer will negotiate in good faith and trusts the other party will do likewise
- even if the procedure should not succeed, something will be gained through better mutual understanding

CONFIDENTIALITY

The Procedure provides that the entire process is confidential. There exists a high level of protection against disclosure.

- A mediation is a settlement negotiation and as such is entitled to the protection accorded by Rule 408 of the Federal Rules of Evidence and state counterparts. Rule 408 is couched in terms of admissibility in evidence. Courts are split on whether to apply Rule 408 in the discovery context.
- The legislatures of more than 40 states, wishing to encourage disputants to mediate rather than litigate, have enacted statutes broadening the protection given by Rule 408 and its counterparts. These statutes differ from each other and many are limited to particular kinds of mediation. Typically they are designed, inter alia, to assure that the mediator will not be compelled to testify as to the mediation process.*
- Rule F-8 of the Procedure provides contractual assurance of confidentiality between the parties. Rule F-4(b) provides that there will be no record of any meeting; and Rules G and H require the mediator and each party to return all written materials to the originating party.
- Rule F-10 prohibits the mediator from serving as a witness, consultant, or expert in an action relating to the subject matter of the mediation.

---

*Rogers and McEwen, *Mediation Law, Policy, Practice* (1989, Cum. Supp. 1990 and 1991) contains a detailed treatment of the subject of confidentiality and summaries of all state laws protecting the mediation process. See also *CPR's Confidentiality* (Rev. 1998).

Only rarely have mediators been compelled to testify or disclose materials as to a mediation proceeding, and then usually for reasons of overriding public interest, e.g., knowledge of a felony.

HOW TO PARTICIPATE IN THE PROGRAM

Any franchise company may join the National Franchise Mediation Program by executing the Commitment Form that follows, thereby agreeing for a period of two years to use the Procedure to attempt to resolve any dispute with any of its franchisees. The procedural ground rules of the process follow the Commitment Form. Appendix 1 is a form of the Dispute Letter, and Appendix 2 is a form of an agreement to submit a dispute for resolution under the Procedure.

There is no charge for joining the program. When parties enter into a mediation, they will engage a mediator from the CPR Franchise Panel, Appendix 3. CPR panelists usually charge their normal rates. CPR charges a flat fee per case. Fees are divided equally between the parties.

For more information, please contact the Panel Management Group, CPR Institute for Dispute Resolution, 366 Madison Avenue, New York, NY 10017-3122; (212) 949-6490.

**CPR FRANCHISE INDUSTRY
DISPUTE RESOLUTION COMMITMENT**

_____

COMPANY

_____

ADDRESS

_____

CITY, STATE, ZIP

_____

TELEPHONE/FAX

We recognize that for many franchisor/franchisee disputes there is a less expensive and more efficient means to resolve the issues than litigation. We commit to use, at a franchisee's request, the **_CPR Procedure for Resolution of Franchise Disputes_** in an effort to resolve any dispute with a franchisee covered by the procedure. This commitment is for an initial period of two years. Thereafter, the commitment may be terminated on 90 days' written notice to CPR without affecting pending cases.

_____

CHIEF EXECUTIVE OFFICER

_____

CHIEF LEGAL OFFICER

_____

DATE

Note: Please send a signed copy of your commitment to CPR Institute for Dispute Resolution, 366 Madison Avenue, New York, NY 10017-3122, Attention: Panel Management Group.

CPR PROCEDURE FOR RESOLUTION OF FRANCHISE DISPUTES

INTRODUCTION

Disputes between franchisors and franchisees continue to arise. On occasion, those disputes have resulted in mutually destructive litigation. The signatories to this Resolution Procedure believe that those disputes can be more effectively and efficiently reconciled by an alternative dispute resolution (ADR) process.

The CPR Institute for Dispute Resolution (CPR), a nationally recognized not-for-profit corporation, is dedicated to resolving business disputes without the undue expense, time, and animosity inherent in litigation. CPR has designed the following Resolution Procedure to help franchisors and franchisees address individual disputes through a process which encompasses open communication and identifies the interests of all parties without unnecessary litigation. To assist in resolving disputes, CPR has formed a Franchise Panel consisting of retired judges and attorneys who are experts in mediation and are prepared to serve as mediators in franchisor/franchisee disputes.

As a condition to agreeing to abide by this Resolution Procedure, each franchisor has affirmed that it will not penalize a franchisee, or withhold any right or privilege accorded to other similarly situated franchisees, by virtue of a franchisee seeking to resolve a dispute in accordance with this Resolution Procedure. As with any mediation process, the parties' willingness to negotiate in good faith is crucial to the success of this Resolution Procedure.

A. REASONS TO INITIATE A RESOLUTION PROCEDURE

If either party to a franchisee/franchisor dispute believes the matter has not been satisfactorily resolved in the normal course of business, that party can initiate a Resolution Procedure under these rules. Although either a franchisee or franchisor can initiate a Resolution Procedure, participation is mandatory only for those franchisors that have signed the CPR Franchise Industry Commitment. Franchisee participation is entirely voluntary.

B. INITIATING A RESOLUTION PROCEDURE

A Resolution Procedure is initiated by a Dispute Letter from the franchisor or the franchisee addressed to the other party and CPR. (A model Dispute Letter is attached as Appendix 1.)

Within 10 business days after receiving the Dispute Letter, senior representatives of the franchisee and franchisor will meet, or speak by telephone, concerning the issues. (If the franchisor has an ombudsman or other nonbinding resolution program in place, those procedures should be followed.) The parties will negotiate in good faith in an attempt to resolve the issues.

C. COMMENCING MEDIATION

Unless CPR has been notified that the dispute has been successfully resolved through negotiation, within 20 business days following CPR's receipt of the Dispute Letter, CPR will begin selecting mediator candidates.

D. SELECTING THE MEDIATOR

Within 25 business days following receipt of a Dispute Letter, and no receipt of a notice that the dispute has been resolved through negotiation, CPR will submit to the parties the names of 5 mediator candidates from the region in which the franchisee is located, with their resumes and hourly rates. If the parties are unable to agree on a candidate from the list within 5 business days following receipt of the list, each party will, within 10 business days following receipt of the list, send to CPR a list of candidates ranked from number 1 to number 5 in descending order of preference. The candidate with the lowest combined score will be appointed as the mediator by CPR.

Any mediator candidate will promptly disclose to both parties any circumstances known to him or her which would cause reasonable doubt regarding the candidate's impartiality, including any relationship of the individual with franchising or the franchise industry during the past ten years. If such circumstances are disclosed, the individual will not serve, unless both parties agree.

E. MEDIATOR EXPENSE

The mediator's compensation rate will be determined before appointment. The parties will each pay 50% of the compensation and any other costs of the process, including CPR's $1,200 administrative fee for each mediation.

F. GROUND RULES

The ground rules of the mediation will be:
1.   The process is non-binding.
2.   The mediator will be neutral and impartial.
3.   The parties will cooperate fully with the mediator.
4.   The mediator controls the procedural aspects of the mediation.
     (a) The mediator may meet and communicate separately with each party.
     (b) The mediator will hold an initial joint meeting with both parties and then decide when to hold joint and/or separate meetings. The mediator will fix the time, place, and agenda for each session. There will be no record of any meeting. Formal rules of evidence will not apply.
5.   At least one representative of each party who is active in the mediation will be authorized to negotiate a resolution of the dispute.
6.   The process will be conducted expeditiously. Each representative will make every effort to be available for meetings.
7.   The mediator will not transmit information received from any party to another party or any third party unless authorized to do so by the party transmitting the information.
8.   The entire process is confidential. Unless otherwise agreed to in writing, the parties and the mediator will not disclose information regarding the process, the information disclosed by the other party, the Neutral Evaluation described in paragraph J, or the terms of a proposed resolution. The entire Resolution Procedure shall be treated as an offer to compromise under the Federal Rules of Evidence and state rules of evidence and is therefore inadmissible in any subsequent court or administrative proceeding.
9.   The parties are encouraged to refrain from pursuing judicial and/or administrative remedies during the mediation. However, whether before or during the mediation, either party may seek a preliminary injunction or other provisional judicial relief if, in its sole judgment, such action is necessary to avoid irreparable damage or preserve

the status quo. Despite any such action the parties will continue to participate in good faith in the procedures specified herein.

10.   The mediator will be disqualified as a witness, consultant, or expert in any pending or future investigation, action, or proceeding relating to the subject matter of the mediation.

11.   The mediator, if a lawyer, may freely express views to the parties on any legal issues underlying the dispute.

12.   The mediator may obtain assistance subject to the agreement, and at the equal expense, of the parties.

13.   Unless the parties agree otherwise, the procedure will be deemed terminated without any agreed upon resolution if:

    (a) After 60 business days from the date the Dispute Letter is received by CPR, a written resolution has not been agreed upon by the parties and a party has given written notice to the mediator of its intention to withdraw and the mediator has provided the parties with the Neutral Evaluation described in paragraph J, below, or

    (b) The mediator concludes that further efforts would not be useful and has provided the parties with the Neutral Evaluation described in paragraph J, below, or

    (c) The franchisee withdraws from the procedure.

14.   Neither CPR nor the mediator shall be liable for any act or omission in connection with the mediation.

15.   At the beginning of the mediation, each party will agree in writing to all provisions of this procedure, as modified by agreement of the parties. (A model Submission Agreement is attached as Appendix 2.)

G. PRESENTATION TO THE MEDIATOR

Upon entering into mediation, and at least 5 business days before the first mediation conference, each party will deliver to the mediator a statement summarizing the dispute's background and such other information it deems necessary to familiarize the mediator with the dispute. The parties will submit jointly their franchise agreement and any other materials they agree upon. The mediator may request that each party provide clarification and additional information, and present its case informally to the mediator at the initial joint meeting or at later separate meetings.

The parties are encouraged to exchange all information submitted to the mediator to further each party's understanding of the other's viewpoint. Except as the parties otherwise agree, the mediator shall keep confidential any information submitted. At the conclusion of the mediation, the mediator will return to each party all written materials which that party provided to the mediator.

H. EXCHANGE OF INFORMATION

If either party has a substantial need for documents or other material in the possession of the other party, the parties will attempt to agree on the exchange of requested documents or other material. Should they fail to agree, either party may request a joint meeting with the mediator to assist the parties in reaching agreement. At the conclusion of the mediation process, the recipient of documents will return them to the originating party without retaining copies.

I. NEGOTIATION OF TERMS

The mediator may promote a resolution in any manner the mediator believes is appropriate. The parties are expected to initiate proposals for resolution. If the parties fail to develop mutually acceptable settlement terms, before terminating the procedure the mediator shall submit to the parties a final settlement proposal which the mediator considers fair and equitable. The parties will carefully consider the mediator's proposal and, at the mediator's request, discuss the proposal with the mediator. If a party does not accept the final proposal, it will advise the mediator of the reasons why the proposal is unacceptable.

J. NEUTRAL EVALUATION

If the mediator concludes that mediation techniques have been exhausted and the parties have not reached agreement, or either party has given written notice of its intent to withdraw, the mediator will give both parties a written evaluation of the issues. (If a party has given written notice of an intent to withdraw, the written evaluation shall be given to the parties within 10 business days of the mediator's receipt of the notice.) The evaluation may recommend compensatory or equitable relief but will not recommend action that would require either party to breach a contract with third parties. Shortly following delivery of the evaluation, the mediator will call another mediation conference, in the hope that the mediator's evaluation will lead to a resumption of negotiations.

K. RESOLUTION

If a resolution is reached, the mediator, or a representative of a party, will draft a written settlement agreement incorporating all terms, including mutual general releases from all liability relating to the subject matter of the dispute. This draft will be circulated among the parties, amended as necessary and formally executed.

If litigation is pending regarding the subject matter of the resolved dispute, the settlement will provide for dismissal of the case with prejudice promptly upon execution of the settlement agreement with each party bearing its own costs.

APPENDIX 1

DISPUTE LETTER

[Name and address of franchisee/franchisor]

     Attention [Officer of franchisee/franchisor]

CPR Institute for Dispute Resolution
366 Madison Avenue
New York, NY 10017

     Attention Franchise Panel Management Group

Dear Sirs:

I request commencement of a *CPR Procedure for Resolution of Franchise Disputes* to address the following issue: [brief description of the issue or issues].

     I understand I will be contacted by a senior representative of [franchisee/franchisor] within 10 business days after this letter is received by [franchisee/franchisor]. If the issue is not resolved by direct negotiation between the parties, I [or we] understand that CPR will forward to the parties a list of mediator candidates.

     I [or a senior representative] will personally participate in any negotiation or mediation conference.

                                             Sincerely,

                                             [Franchisee/Franchisor]

APPENDIX 2

**SUBMISSION AGREEMENT PURSUANT TO
CPR PROCEDURE FOR RESOLUTION OF FRANCHISE DISPUTES**

AGREEMENT made _____, 20__ between

_____

of _____ _____

("Franchisee"); and _____ of

_____ ("Franchisor");

    An issue has arisen between the parties regarding (describe briefly).

    Both wish to dispose expeditiously of their differences without resorting to litigation. The parties hereby agree to private and confidential mediation of their differences pursuant to the *CPR Procedure for Resolution of Franchise Disputes,* a copy of which is attached hereto. The parties hereby adopt and agree to all provisions of the Resolution Procedure.

    The Resolution Procedure shall be conducted before _____

_____, who has agreed to serve as Mediator and whose compensation has been agreed to between the parties and the Mediator. Franchisee and Franchisor shall each pay 50% of Mediator's compensation and expenses and CPR's administrative fee. Neither party knows of any circumstances which would cause reasonable doubt regarding the impartiality of the Mediator.

                                 _____

                                         [Franchisee]

Signed by: _____

                                       Representative

                                 _____

                                         [Franchisor]

Signed by: _____

                                         Representative

APPENDIX 3

CPR FRANCHISE PANEL OF NEUTRALS

The CPR Franchise Panel of Neutrals, consisting of leading members of the bar, has been organized to implement the National Franchise Mediation Program. The Panel is divided into five regions. A current list of Panel members is available from CPR or on the CPR Web site at www.cpradr.org (click on *neutrals*).

CPR will submit to parties the names of five mediator candidates from the region in which the franchisee is located. Insofar as possible, CPR will propose candidates based in reasonable proximity to the franchisee.

Members of the CPR Franchise Panel are also available to arbitrate disputes in which mediation under the CPR Procedure was unsuccessful. They are additionally available to serve as neutrals in franchise or similar disputes not subject to the CPR Procedure. To retain a Panelist for such cases, the parties to the dispute should contact the CPR Panel Management Group.

CPR has also established other panels of outstanding lawyers and former judges available to serve as neutrals in a great variety of disputes.

Fees and Costs

Franchise Panelists usually charge their normal hourly rates. Fees and payment procedures are agreed to in advance of finalizing neutrals in each case. As to cases falling under the CPR Procedure, CPR currently charges $1,200 per case for its services in administering the program. This fee normally is divided equally between the parties and becomes payable when the procedure is initiated.

APPENDIX 4

CPR FRANCHISE DISPUTE RESOLUTION REPORT
(As of April 1998)

Summary	
Total Matters Filed, Prior to Current Period	110
Matters Filed this Month	4
Total to Date	114

Involving 23 franchise companies
    71 filed by franchisees; 36 filed
    by franchisors; 7 filed jointly	

Matters in Which Franchisee Would Not Participate	12
Matters Closed this Month	00
Total Matters Closed	75
Matters Pending	27

Breakdown of Total Matters Closed   **75**

Matters Closed Successfully 40 through mediation; 25 direct negotiation	66
Unresolved Matters	9
TOTAL	75

Subject of Disputes

Impact or Encroachment	34
Development Right of Franchisee	7
Customer Service	2
Termination, Rescission, or Non-Renewal of Franchise	11
Underreporting of Sales or Other Financial Violations of Franchise Agreement	14
Lease-Related Claims	4
Miscellaneous Violations of Franchise Agreement	40
Purchase/Sale of Franchise	2
TOTAL	114

SELECTED BIBLIOGRAPHY

"Code of Ethics." International Franchise Association, Washington, D.C. (Undated).

"Franchise Agreement Arbitration Clauses Are Here To Stay . . . Or Are They?" *World Arbitration & Mediation Report* 172 (July 1996).

Ninth Circuit Strikes Down Arbitration Clause Waiving Statutory Rights, *Graham Oil Co. v. Arco Products Co., World Arbitration & Mediation Report* 37 (February 1995).

Goldberg, Stephen B., Frank E. A. Sander, and Nancy H. Rogers. "Dispute Resolution: Negotiation, Mediation, and Other Processes." (Little, Brown and Company, Second Edition, 1992) (1995 Supplement).

International Franchise Association. "The National Franchise Mediation Program" (1994).

Bogard, Donald. "Relationships: Joint Ventures, Franchises, and Partnerships." The Conference Board, Presentation Materials (May 1994).

Kaufmann, David J. "A New Mediation Program." *New York Law Journal* (April 28, 1994).

Reno, Barbara M. "Burying the Hatchet: Using Mediation to Resolve Disputes and Get On with Business." *Franchising World* 49–50 (March/April 1994).

"Wisconsin Enacts Mandatory ADR for Auto Franchise Disputes." *World Arbitration and Mediation Report* 266 (Transnational Juris Publications, Inc., November 1993).

Giresi, Mark A. "Burger King Encroachment Procedures." CPR Award Program Submission, November 1993. (Obtainable from CPR).

Seidler, Mark P. and John F. Verhey. "The Case for Alternative Dispute Resolution." 11 *Franchise Law Journal* 107–111 (Spring 1992).

Davis, Michael R. "The Perspective of In-House Counsel: Organization, Compliance/ Enforcement Program, Negotiated Sales, Transfer, Termination, and Advertising and Franchisee Councils." In *Corporate Counsel's Guide to Distribution Counseling.* Edited by William Hancock. (Business Laws, Inc., 1991).

"Lawyers Differ Sharply on Merits of Arbitrating Franchise Disputes." *ADR Report* 300–302. (The Bureau of National Affairs, Inc., September 13, 1990).

Ury, William L., Jeanne M. Brett, and Stephen B. Goldberg. "Getting Disputes Resolved: Designing Systems to Cut the Costs of Conflict." (Jossey-Bass Publishers, 1988).

SELECTED ARTICLES FROM *ALTERNATIVES*

Alternatives is a national ADR newsletter published by the CPR Institute for Dispute Resolution since 1983. *Alternatives* focuses on cutting-edge trends and information, and acts as a practice guide for companies, firms, and the courts. Copies of the *Alternatives* articles listed below are available on Westlaw and LEXIS-NEXIS. From the Westlaw directory screen, enter <db ALTHCL>. On LEXIS, select the <ADR> library, then enter <altern>. Contact CPR for subscription information at (212) 949-6490 or by e-mail at Alternatives@cpradr.org.

"CPR News: Franchise Update," 15 *Alternatives* 70 (May 1997).

"Court Voids Employment Arbitration Clause," 15 *Alternatives* 51 (April 1997).

"Briefs: Justices Dissent Over Arbitration Decision," 14 *Alternatives* 143 (December 1996).

"Mediating in Cyberspace," 14 *Alternatives* 117 (November 1996).

"Drafting Arbitration Clauses," 14 *Alternatives* 2 (January 1996).

"Court Limits Requirement to Arbitrate," 13 *Alternatives* 13 (February 1995).

"An ADR Arena Suits Davids and Goliaths," 12 *Alternatives* 17, 20, 27 (February 1994).

"Franchisers Form Special ADR Vehicle," 11 *Alternatives* 37, 42 (March 1993).

"ADR Well-Suited to Handle Franchise Cases," 10 *Alternatives* 131–133, 140 (September 1992).

"Fifth Circuit Panel Decides Franchise Arbitration Case," 5 *Alternatives* 139, 142 (September 1987).

"Ten Years and 1500 Cases Later, McDonald's Ombudsman Continues to Flourish," 2 *Alternatives* 1, 3–4 (September 1984).

A Retrospective on Franchisee Associations

by

Rupert M. Barkoff*

I can't honestly say that I was "there" at the birth of franchise law. As most of us know, this occurred around 1970 with the enactment of the California Franchise Investment Law. I was beginning my study of law at the time.

But I can claim to have been present during most of the growth of franchise law as a discipline. It's hard to put an exact date on when franchising first became a recognized, distinguishable area of the law, but my guess would be 1976 to 1977, after the enactment of all of the state franchise registration acts (except New York's), and just prior to the adoption of the Federal Trade Commission's Disclosure Rule in 1978. Coincidentally, the birth of the American Bar Association's Forum on Franchising effectively occurred that same year, when it held its first Annual Program in Chicago that Fall.

What has gone unnoticed, however, is that the growth of franchisee associations rides almost precisely parallel to the Forum's. The first Forum attracted 150 persons, more or less—small by today's standards; now attendance exceeds 700. Franchisee associations were also for the most part in their incipient stage in 1978. Just prior to the Forum on Franchising's First Annual Program, a small group of representatives from the existing independent franchisee associations also gathered in Chicago to discuss common problems. I have often referred to that meeting as a gathering of a ragtag army. There were three strong franchisee associations represented at that meeting—associations representing Midas, AAMCO and KFC. There were representatives from other fledgling groups, including IHOP and a rump group representing McDonald's franchisees. And there were a few of the "Granddaddies" of franchise law: Tim Fine, Myron Gordon and Harold Brown. The leader of the gathering was a gentleman named Gil Meisgeier, who was Executive Director of a group called the National Association of Franchisees—a quite weak counterpart to the International Franchisee Association, and the precursor of the two franchisee-oriented trade associations of today—the American Franchisee Association and the American Association of Franchisees and Dealers.

I have gone through this exercise not to demonstrate my uncanny recall of these almost prehistoric events, but to show how young franchising is, at least in its commercial form, and that franchisee associations are really a Johnny-come-lately.

Interestingly enough, I doubt that anyone has a good handle on how many associations there may be today, and, as in the early days, there are several strong ones, and a host of those which are in fact not very representative of their systems, or poorly funded, or managed by inexperienced leaders, or simply dysfunctional. But there is no doubt about their growth in numbers and strength, and the crystal ball suggests that there may be no end to this growth in sight. In fact, if growth has continued during the boom years of the 1990s, what level of growth can be expected when the economy cools and the harmony in many franchise systems that exists today turns into discomfort and perhaps even hostility, as sales dollars run flat or decline and franchisors cut back services to maintain profit levels?

---

*Partner, Kilpatrick Stockton LLP, Atlanta, Georgia.

If the rise of the franchisee association is a phenomenon of the last two decades, so too, is the proliferation of legal literature that has addressed this subject. To my recollection, the first programs on franchisee associations were held in San Francisco in 1979 and in Orlando in 1980—at the Second and Third Annual Forums on Franchising. At the San Francisco Forum, a panel discussion, led by myself, Mark Rodman (another attorney in private practice) and Ed Ellis, General Counsel of Holiday Inns, proved one of the controversial programs at that meeting. Ironically, the controversial part of the presentation came from Mr. Ellis, who spoke of how franchisee associations could be positive factors in franchise system development. During those days, when the world was either black or white, this was heresy. Even today, many franchisors do not buy into this proposition.

After the Orlando program, the subject of franchisee associations became a more common topic for legal franchise seminars. The I.F.A. Legal Symposium first addressed the subject at the 1985 program. The ABA Forum on Franchising has held six programs on franchisee associations over its twenty-one year history, including two at this year's program.

The seminal program on franchisee associations, in this author's opinion, was held in San Francisco in 1991, when a panel comprised of Gerald Aaron, Anita Blair, Andrew Selden, Mitchell Shapiro, Alan Silberman and Mary Beth Trice held what I think was the first plenary program on the subject. Of particular note from that program was the paper prepared by the presenters. It is, in my mind, the foremost authority on the subject and for that reason I and my fellow panelists for this program—Bill Darrin from Subway and John Regnery from Snap-on Incorporation—have reproduced it in its entirety with this piece.

Given the rise of franchisee associations since this piece was first published, one would expect there to be a developing body of law covering franchisee associations. But there is not. To this author's knowledge, only two cases since 1991 have mentioned franchisee associations in connection with legal principles.

In *Queen City Pizza, Inc. v. Domino's Pizza, Inc.,* [1] the Third Circuit noted that before the district court, the defendant had argued that IFAC (the system's franchisee association), a named plaintiff in the action, was without standing. The trial court "found it unnecessary to address this issue in light of its order dismissing the case for failure to state a claim."[2]

In *Dunafon v. Taco Bell Corp.,*[3] the plaintiff, a Missouri based franchisee, claimed that it was entitled to the protection of the right to associate provisions of the California Franchise Investment Law since the franchise agreements provided that California law applied. The court, however, noted that the choice of law provision only applied to the construction and enforcement of the franchise agreement, and therefore, rejected the plaintiff's claim.

You will find attached to this retrospective:

(1) a piece written by John Regnery, covering franchisee advisory councils.
(2) a bibliography of articles addressing franchisee associations. Interestingly, there seems to be more commentary than case law on the subject!
(3) *The Dynamics of Franchisee Associations,* the article written for the 1991 Forum on Franchising's Annual Program and referred to above.

There is also in the course materials for this year's (1998) Forum on Franchising Annual Program, an excellent article by co-panelist Bill Darrin and Erik Wulff and Seth Stadfeld on franchisee associations.

With this retrospective, the San Francisco publication, the Darrin-Wulff-Stadfeld paper and the articles listed in the attached bibliography, you have before you a directory of substantially all of the legal literature on franchisee associations. The world is now your oyster!

---

[1] 124 F.3d 430 (3d Cir. 1997).

[2] 124 F.3d at 434, n. 3.

[3] Bus. Franchise Guide (CCH) ¶10,919 (WD. Mo. 1996).

Franchise Advisory Councils

by

John W. Regnery*

I. *Introduction*

As a franchise system grows, it becomes more and more of a challenge to maintain effective means of communication between the franchisor and franchisees in the system. Given the "partnering" nature of the franchise relationship, effective lines of communication are essential. One such mechanism is through the establishment and use of a franchisee advisory council, whether established early on in the life of a system or later when a system has matured, in which franchisees can meet with franchisor management on a regular basis to discuss issues of system-wide significance. Depending on the system, topics can include product development, marketing programs, advertising initiatives, operational issues and franchise concerns—whatever topics need an open forum within a given system.

Many companies find advisory councils valuable because they provide a sounding board for review of new programs as well as feedback on issues within the system that may need to be addressed on an ongoing basis. One should remember, however, that with this benefit comes a cost that needs to be considered, both in terms of money and management time and commitment that needs to be spent in order to maintain a meaningful and effective council.

II. *Purpose*

When considering an advisory council, the overall reason for establishing the council must be considered. The purpose may be as basic as a general need for a mechanism to enhance system communication or it may be in order to respond to specific issues that have surfaced in a particular system.

In order to obtain feedback and generate meaningful dialogue within the system on the subject of the proposed advisory group and its structure, an initial advisory meeting could be held between management and selected franchisees to consider certain current issues within the system and to allow both parties to have input on the desirability of such a group and its structure. Although a high level of franchisee participation in the group is recommended, as discussed below, other options exist, such as management calling meetings when it feels the need with franchisee participants selected by the franchisor. Whatever structure is decided upon, formal rules should be adopted which can be referred to as the by-laws, charter, articles, advisory rules or whatever is deemed appropriate to accomplish the goal of setting up parameters, or rules of the road, within which the group will operate. Although a draft of the by-laws will likely be prepared by the franchisor, franchisee advisors should be given time to provide meaningful input both to make it the best product possible and to avoid the appearance of rules that were dictated by management. The first meeting would be the time to consider that document.

*Associate General Counsel, Snap-on Incorporated, Kenosha, Wisconsin.

Consideration should be given to establishing an advisory council prior to significant issues surfacing in a system as a way to proactively and effectively deal with system issues and enhance system communication. If an advisory group is viewed by franchisees as an established, effective means for dealing with system-wide issues, franchisees may use that group to raise concerns and provide input to management instead of taking other less desirable action.

In establishing the purpose of the council, thought should be given to including provisions covering that topic in the by-laws (or whatever the rules are called), which can be as general or specific as the situation requires. It could be as broad as the following:

(1) To establish an open forum for communication between franchisees and franchisor to discuss issues that are of a broad mutual interest and concern.

(2) To increase awareness about market issues and conditions from both a franchisor and a franchisee perspective.

(3) To evaluate and formulate policies, procedures and programs that may affect franchisees and to make recommendations to franchisor management on behalf of the franchisee group.

(4) To promote a spirit of cooperation between franchisor and franchisee and to work together as a team to resolve concerns before they become problems.

Some council members may want to spend time on problems they have individually or that are faced by a small number of franchisees. These issues need to be dealt with, but should be handled through other means within the company and not at council meetings. Consider putting provisions in the by-laws to exclude issues that are relevant only to an individual or a small group of franchisees, or issues that relate personally to individuals or that deal with personality conflicts between individuals. As a result, situations can be handled in a non-personalized manner by referring to the by-laws which prohibit such topics.

III. *Council Credibility*

Most often an advisory council will be started on the initiative of the franchisor. An issue and a challenge is to make the council the franchisees' council as soon as possible. Franchisee acceptance of the council must be obtained. Establishing the credibility of the council early on is a must in order for it to thrive. It must be viewed as being of real benefit to franchisees and something in which individuals will be willing to spend time and energy as members. In order for it to be successful, the system must believe that the council can provide meaningful input and affect change within the company. If council input is not viewed to be taken seriously by management and addressed promptly, the system may seek other means to remedy any problems that may exist.

No matter how the council is structured, franchisor management must pay attention to issues raised, respond candidly regarding whether or not the concerns will be dealt with and why or why not, deal with the issues on a timely basis and communicate to the advisors as well as the system, generally, how the issues are being handled. To enhance credibility, it is important to acknowledge the role of the advisory council in bringing issues to the attention of management, that are then dealt with in a manner that is win-win for the franchisor and franchisee. Moreover, timely and effective communication to franchisees about the activities of the council is critical. Communications to franchisees must be prepared and sent out to the system as soon as possible after any meeting. Moreover, a system for effective ongoing communication to the system needs to be established and utilized. A franchisor representative, likely the council secretary, must be responsible for this activity to ensure that follow up occurs.

The initial members could be appointed by the franchisor, but thereafter a representative selection process must be established with advisor input. Options include national or regional elections or, perhaps in smaller systems, rotating everyone in the system as council members. If franchisees are not involved in the process of selecting their representatives, it is doubtful that the council's activities will be viewed seriously. Even though the goal is to make it the franchisees' council, the franchisor must help facilitate that goal, providing support in the areas of, elections, meeting planning, agenda development, communications, etc.

IV. *Membership*

The number of franchisee members is an important consideration. One must strike a balance between a group that is too large to be effective and one that is too small to represent the interests of the franchisees in the system. Many franchisors are divided up geographically from a business organization perspective; this structure could dovetail into the basis for franchisee representation. For example, if a company were divided into 6 geographically based regions, 2 or 3 members (plus an alternate who would serve if a member in the region was unavailable) from each of the regions could provide a convenient way to achieve system-wide representation with a workable number of franchisee advisors, 12 to 18. Whatever is decided upon, one must strive for as meaningful cross-section of franchisees as is possible to deal with issues important to the system as a whole.

Also important is the issue of franchisor representation. Who should participate as a management member of the group must be thought out. The council should include a sufficient number of individuals to be able to deal quickly and effectively with issues at a meeting, based on agenda items as well as those that are brought up during the course of the meeting, yet at the same time not have so many franchisor members that the meeting becomes franchisor out-of-balance. Serious consideration should be given to membership and participation by the president or CEO of the franchise side of the company. The ability of a franchisor to deal with issues and communicate to the franchisees, as well as adding credibility to the council, will be enhanced by such participation.

V. *Qualifications and Term*

Another consideration is who will be eligible to serve on the council and length of service. Is it necessary to have been with the system for any length of time or are new franchisees eligible to participate? Should performance levels be a consideration? The first thought may be to only allow high level performers to be eligible, feeling that that group will be the most serious about the business and successful enough to have the most meaningful input regarding the system and related issues; consider, however, that adding lower achievers may result in input regarding system issues that a franchisor may not get from any higher achieving group. Wherever one comes out on that issue, though, requiring members to have spent some time in the system in order to be eligible is a good idea. One approach is requiring that advisors be franchisees for at least three years, be at average level in terms of financial performance and be in good standing under the franchise agreement. Having such a requirement may enhance the perception of the council since franchisees must at least meet certain requirements to "earn" eligibility to be on the council.

Consideration should be given to the length of time advisors will serve prior to the next election. Relatively short terms and some type of term limits should be considered in order to maintain an influx of fresh new members and ideas into the council. This will ensure that certain franchisees do not get entrenched as "permanent" council members;

changeover can help enhance credibility with the system since all qualified franchisees will have a better chance to participate. A council could be structured with two-year terms, and a ban on consecutive terms. However, two years may not be a sufficient time to deal effectively with council issues and continuity may be lost with turnover occurring every two years. Three-year terms with, for example, one-half of the advisors being replaced each year with no elections every third year might be more effective. Random but not consecutive terms could be allowed. This could provide sufficient council tenure and continuity to deal effectively with agenda topics yet provide sufficient turnover to ensure new and fresh ideas being brought to the council meetings.

VI. *Agenda Development and Meeting Preparation*

There will invariably be topics that the franchisor will want to be included on any meeting agenda; however, a means needs to be put in place to have franchisees give ownership to agenda topics and have issues of concern and interest to franchisees in the system be included. A franchisee advisory chairperson should be appointed to take charge of this and related issues. A franchisor representative, possibly the secretary or franchisor chairperson of the council, needs to work with the franchisee designate, likely the chairperson, in developing the agenda. Critical to this will be the establishment of a mechanism for franchisees to communicate their concerns to their franchisee advisors so that issues can be placed on the agenda for consideration, keeping in mind that system-wide, and not individual, issues should be dealt with at the advisory council level; individual concerns should be dealt with through other avenues within the company. The goal should be significant franchisee input into meeting agendas. Company support in setting up dealer advisory e-mail systems, voice mail ability and fax access as a means for advisors to receive input from their franchisee constituents is important. It may take some time for this to develop, but the sooner the issue is dealt with the more likely that goal will be met in a timely fashion.

The frequency of meetings must be established. One may want to start with having the first few meetings every six months and annual meetings thereafter, although, semi-annual meetings may work effectively initially and continue longer than initially contemplated. Meetings could be held over a weekend in the spring and fall of the year. In this structure, consider having advisors arrive Friday morning, with an afternoon meeting by franchisees to discuss the upcoming meeting and agenda topics amongst themselves. Initially, the importance of this preparation time may not be appreciated; it will, however, soon be recognized as an important element of the process. Franchisee advisors need time amongst themselves to review agenda items and prepare for meetings. This is particularly important for new members who have not yet experienced a council meeting, and leads to much more effective and efficient use of actual meeting time.

There will be times at which non-member franchisor (and franchisee) representatives will participate in a meeting to make presentations related to agenda topics; this makes development of the meeting agenda early on very important so that these resources have time to prepare. Consider having meeting presenters participate in their portion of the meeting and leave shortly thereafter in part to avoid over attendance by the franchisor.

As far as meeting location is concerned, if a franchisor has facilities that may be of benefit for franchisees to experience, some short facility tour can be part of the meeting itself. Otherwise, some change of location to various parts of the country, for convenience sake if for no other reason, is a good idea.

Unless justification can be made in a particular system, the company should pay meeting related expenses. Compensation for lost time in the business is likely not necessary. There may be systems that could require advisors to pay expenses and still maintain an effective advisory council, but it is doubtful that that is generally the case.

VII. *Officers*

Officers should be appointed on both the franchisor and franchisee side. A franchisor chairperson should be appointed to at least run the meetings from the perspective of facilitating such things as starting and ending the meeting on time and following the agenda. However, a significant role should be played by the franchisee chairperson in dealing with substantive issues. In addition to being meeting coordinator, the franchisor chairperson should coordinate and preside over the elections, help develop the final meeting agenda and develop, along with the secretary and the franchisee chairperson, communications to franchisees concerning council activities.

The franchisee chairperson should also work with the advisors to develop the franchisee meeting agenda, be responsible for making sure that advisors attend scheduled meetings and appoint advisor committees, as needed, to carry out any such council requests.

The council should also appoint a secretary to be responsible primarily for keeping the minutes and working with the franchisee chairperson to develop franchisee communications. Franchisee members typically will not want this position and the company will likely be in a better position to devote a resource to taking responsibility for this function. The council should determine to whom the minutes will be distributed, and establish a procedure for their review so that the final minutes accurately reflect what occurred at the meeting.

VIII. *Conclusion*

Many of the above issues should be covered by some form of rules, such as by-laws, that can be initially prepared by the franchisor but reviewed and approved by advisors at the first or second meeting. Amendments can then be made over time to accommodate changing conditions. By-laws should be adopted since they help provide order and formality to the council and a skeleton of operating rules which will most definitely be referred to with some regularity. Topics to cover include:

1. Name.
2. Purpose and objectives.
3. Membership, eligibility and selection process.
4. Officers and their duties.
5. Agenda Development.
6. Meeting Expenses and Quorum.
7. By-law Amendment Procedure.

An advisory council can provide an effective means for two-way communication between franchisor and franchisees. The time to establish such a council is before system-wide issues of significance arise. It should be a proactive and not a reactive step taken by franchisors as one of a number of techniques to enhance system communication. Advisors will often provide very meaningful input on ways to structure new programs being considered by a franchisor to make them better for both franchisor and franchisee alike. In addition, although advisory group approval or endorsement of program changes is not binding on the system, such advisor endorsement, if council credibility is high, can aid in acceptance by franchisees of those new programs.

APPENDIX 5-B

Dynamics of Franchisee Associations

Contributing Authors:

Gerald Aaron   Mitchell Shapiro
Anita Blair   Alan Silberman
Andrew Selden   Mary Beth Trice

1991 ANNUAL FORUM
ABA FORUM ON FRANCHISING
San Francisco, California
October 17, 1991

TABLE OF CONTENTS

Dynamics of Franchisee Associations

Gerald Aaron   Mitchell Shapiro
Anita Blair   Alan Silberman
Andrew Selden   Mary Beth Trice*

1991 Annual Forum—San Francisco

Introduction

The term "franchisee association" encompasses any group of operators within a single franchise system, whether the group consists of franchisees only or admits franchisor representatives, whether it is a formal or informal organization, and whether it was constituted for general or specific purposes. Although the impetus to form a franchisee association often does not occur until the franchise system arrives at a certain size (or crisis), many smaller franchise systems have franchisee associations.

It is difficult to generalize about franchisee associations, which are at least as varied as franchise systems themselves. One general rule seems to apply: A franchisee association behaves and operates differently depending on whether the franchisor actively interacts with it. When franchisees form their own group without consultation with the franchisor, they often call it an "association" or use some other term that connotes a separate, exclusive and independent business group. On the other hand, if the franchisor helps found or organize the group or provides financial or administrative support for it, the group often becomes known as the "franchisee advisory council" or some similar name that suggests certain limitations on the group's functions. As used in this paper, "association" will be used in the sense defined above.

The primary reason why franchisees decide to form an association is to be able to interact with, or confront, the franchisor as a group over one or more issues. If several franchisees unilaterally form an association as a result of some grievance, it is not necessarily unhealthy for the franchisor or the system. It is true that a franchisee association may provide a useful vehicle for litigation or for stirring up strife within a system. It is also true that a franchisee association can serve both franchisees and franchisors as a tool for communication and compromise, leading to a more effective and successful system.

Other common sources of discontent that often underlie franchisees' decision to act collectively include declining sales or profitability, a change (or anticipated change) in ownership or management of the franchisor, an unsuccessful new product or service introduction, or a franchisor's attempt to execute unilaterally a significant change in direction for the system or a significant change in the franchise contract.

Many franchisors not only do not object to the establishment of a forum in their system for franchisee representation, they actively encourage it. The existence of a franchisee association in a system can help moderate the effects of controversies in the system. If a problem arises, the association gives the franchisees a ready outlet for expressing their views and the franchisor a protocol for receiving them. Having a franchisee association in a system also can be an attractive selling point to prospective franchisees. Therefore, some franchisors seize the initiative in forming a franchisee association, and even begin planning for it at a very early stage in the growth of the system.

---

*Authors' contributions are indexed at the foot of the paper.

I. ORGANIZATION OF THE ASSOCIATION

A. Forms of Organization.

1. *Business and Tax Planning.* All of the considerations that militate towards incorporation of a business or non-profit organization operate to suggest that a franchisee association should be incorporated unless it is intended to address a single issue over a very short period of time. As it is extremely rare for the association to be engaged in any business activity for its own account, the choice of form ordinarily will be a non-profit corporation formed under a convenient state law.

The main tax issue affecting a franchisee association is its not-for-profit status. Section 501(c)(6) of the Internal Revenue Code and related regulations establish the qualifications for tax exemption for business leagues and commercial trade associations organized for educational and other purposes and operated on a nonprofit basis. Franchisee associations normally do not engage in for-profit activities. Income to the association usually only covers expenses and is not distributed to the members in any way. The franchisee association need not be incorporated to maintain its nonprofit status, although the members may want to incorporate for other reasons. Nevertheless, an association within a single-brand system cannot qualify as a tax-exempt organization under I.R.C. § 501(c)(6). *National Mufflers Dealers Assn. v. United States* 440 U.S. 472 (1979).

One reason for incorporation of an association might be to insulate members from individual liability for claims against the association. This might be of interest to a franchisee association, for example, to avoid having trade debts charged directly to members, or to insulate themselves from exposure to claims of defamation resulting from publications of criticism of the franchisor. Even if the association is incorporated, however, the members may not be able to shield themselves from some types of claims, such as liability for business torts or violation of antitrust laws.

Several options exist for the form of organization of a franchisee association. Most state laws provide for nonstock nonprofit corporations, which could be a suitable form of organization for a franchisee association. Some states also have statutes providing specific rules for the establishment of cooperative associations, which might apply to a franchisee association.

If the members wish to minimize expenses and paperwork, but still retain a certain amount of procedural formality, they may adopt a charter and bylaws similar to a corporation but operate as an unincorporated association. Finally, if the group is small or has a very limited mission, it might decide to operate on a very informal basis as an ad hoc committee.

If an informal committee involves a number of people or may outlive its original mission, the organizers would be well advised to adopt some minimal bylaws or rules of order at the outset. If the members defer this task too long, the group may grow to include different constituencies, which are harder to control. At that point it may be impossible to reach agreement on any ground rules at all.

2. *Choosing the Form of Organization.* A range of organizational options, from corporation to committee, is available to franchisee associations. There are no hard and fast rules for selecting one form over another, except that the appropriate form of organization usually depends on the degree of formality that the members want or need for effective operation of their association and its anticipated duration. A member-owned co-op may be desirable. See Part I.D., below.

The larger the membership or the broader the mandate of the association, the more likely it is that the association will need well-defined rules. Likewise, the association may need a more formal level of organization if the membership includes different classes of franchisee-members or franchisor representatives. At a minimum, every franchisee association should have discernible policies concerning its purposes, membership, voting, administration, and finances.

(a) *Purposes.* The organizers of any franchisee association should consider carefully what their basic purposes are and whether an association is the appropriate vehicle to accomplish their aims. For example, if the association claims general jurisdiction over all issues of interest to franchisees, it may discover that (a) franchisees have a very broad range of interests, and (b) franchisees do not necessarily share the same opinions about issues of interest to them. An association that purports to be all things to all franchisees will not succeed. Indeed, one of the critical, early needs of the organizers is to identify those objectives that represent the broadest possible consensus within the membership.

Unless the franchisee association is truly an *ad hoc* committee dedicated to one issue, the purposes of the association should not be too narrow. Both franchisors and franchisees should guard against the needless proliferation of organizations within the franchise system. At best, allowing numerous organizations to exist within the system will drain the energy of the participants. Even if each group starts out with a limited mandate, sooner or later their interests will overlap. The resulting conflicts and confusion will be harmful to the system, as well as outside parties with whom they may deal. If multiple associations are allowed to exist, politics will take precedence over pragmatism, as the various groups compete for the title of "official" or "authorized" or "primary" franchisee association. In that process, the groups may make unrealistic promises to franchisees, or cause unnecessary strife within the system.

This is not to say that each franchise system should tolerate no more than one association, council, or committee that represents the franchisees. In some cases, a franchisee association, which normally would be organized somewhat democratically, might not be the most effective body to advise or act on a particular issue. For example, if the goal is to obtain more effective advertising, a group of self-selected or elected franchisees might not have the necessary expertise in advertising to make their efforts credible or useful. It is often more effective for the franchisor, the franchisee association, or both, to appoint a committee of knowledgeable, experienced individuals to address specialized or technical issues.

(b) *Membership.* Most franchisee associations encourage participation by as many franchisees as possible. Nevertheless, several issues typically arise in connection with defining the qualifications for membership in the franchisee association, especially if the association was not organized by or in conjunction with the franchisor. In that case, the franchisees must decide whether, and on what terms, the franchisor, including its company-owned units, should participate in the association.

The primary advantages of including the franchisor in some role in the association are improved access and communication between the franchisor and franchisees and financial and administrative support (or control) by the franchisor. Excluding the franchisor may cause or exacerbate bad relations between franchisor and franchisees.

The primary disadvantages of including the franchisor in the association are that the franchisees may find it awkward to confront the franchisor representatives in person with criticism about the system, and they may prefer to conduct some or all of their proceedings on a confidential basis. Also, franchisees might be concerned that, once admitted into the association, the franchisor will try to take over its operations in some way.

Another membership issue is whether to allow outside parties, such as vendors, to participate in the association in some way. If properly managed, this can provide financial and other benefits to the association and the franchise system. The association can create classes or categories of membership (such as "associate member") for this purpose. Both the franchisor and the franchisees should take care to define the limits on participation by outsiders, including express restrictions on their ability to claim a connection with the association or the franchise for any purpose (including any display of the franchisor's marks).

In some systems, membership in the "association" is effectively mandatory, in the sense that all franchisees are deemed to be voting members. Some franchisors require franchisees to be in good standing under their franchise agreements before they can vote or serve on a franchisee council. Associations organized by franchisees tend to make membership voluntary, but tie it to payment of dues or meeting other qualifications.

(c) *Voting*. If the association has no real power or authority, voting may not be an important issue. But most associations serve at least in an advisory role, and to that extent, members will be interested in the standards for electing representatives or officers and voting on referenda.

The first issue is whether voting is direct or through election of representatives. If a franchise system is large enough to consider having an association, it is probably too large to be effective under a direct voting system by all franchisees. Each system may have different requirements for achieving fair representation of franchisees. Representatives can be elected from different classes of members, different geographical regions, or a combination of these or other factors. Officers or directors of the association may be elected directly by the membership at large or indirectly by the representatives. A compound structure of membership meetings and an elected Board conducting separate meetings, patterned after a normal business corporation, is often the best choice.

Next the association must determine whether to establish different voting rules for different types and classes of members. For example, if company-owned units are included in the association, will they be permitted to vote for representatives on the same basis as franchisee members? May employees of company-owned units run for office? Under what circumstances may franchisor representatives, associate members, or others, be excluded from meetings?

Even more controversial in systems where there are many multi-unit owners is the "one unit/one vote" issue. Multi-unit owners prefer to have a separate vote for each of their franchise locations, while single unit owners prefer the "one owner/one vote" approach. Franchisees also may endorse the latter approach as a means of reducing the influence of company-owned units.

The association should consider whether there are any potential resolutions that should require a super-majority vote before adoption. If the association is a corporation or other creature of statute, statutory requirements for voting may apply.

Finally, the franchisor may determine that it needs a veto power over resolutions by the franchisee association that might adversely affect the system or the franchisor's marks. Although the franchisee association might desire to have a veto power over some decisions by the franchisor, most franchisors would regard it as extremely inadvisable to cede any part of their authority in that fashion.

(d) *Administration*. Even an informal franchisee association needs someone to call meetings, contact members, and follow up on action items. Most franchisee associations also require accounting services and access to copying and mailing facilities.

In many cases, the franchisor offers to perform some or all of these functions for the association. This may be a cheap and easy way for the association to operate, but it also gives the franchisor the benefit of additional control over and knowledge about the association.

If the association handles its own administrative functions, it may do so through the volunteer efforts of members or through a hired staff, either on a clerical or executive level. The association should adopt a policy for reimbursing members who incur costs and expenses in association administration. The policy should not only set forth procedures for reimbursement but also specify whether indirect costs (e.g, overhead) may be reimbursable.

Sometimes associations use a law firm for considerable administrative work as well as legal services. Lawyers will be glad to be reminded that ethical rules generally discourage or prohibit the advancement of costs and expenses on behalf of clients. The Association likely will find it to be less costly to provide for its own clerical and administrative needs through employees rather than a law firm.

(e) *Finances.* Some franchisee associations operate on a very small budget based on nominal dues from franchisees. Other associations have a substantial portion of their financial requirements underwritten by the franchisor as a goodwill gesture. Special projects are often financed by one-time special assessments.

Other than franchisees and the franchisor, there are few other possible sources of income for a franchisee association. The primary outside source would be vendors to the system. As a matter of ethics and legal compliance, the association should have policies for dealing with third parties, especially those who are seeking to influence franchisees' purchasing decisions or to gain by a presumed connection with the system or the franchisor's marks. Traditional and almost presumptively lawful means of obtaining revenue from vendors include registration and booth-rental fees at franchisee-sponsored conventions and selling ads in newsletters. See Part I.B., below.

An association may also be able to raise money by selling goods or services. Any use of the franchisor's mark or logo in that connection by the association must be authorized by the franchisor as unauthorized use in a "trademark usage" without authority would almost certainly constitute infringement. The members' individual franchise agreements alone ordinarily would not constitute a license for the association to offer similar or different goods or services under the franchisor's trademarks. See Part II.C., below.

If the association collects dues, the bylaws of the association should specify the requirements for payment and the consequences of nonpayment. Collection efforts will be simplified if all members sign a written agreement to pay. Similarly, it will be easier to impose and collect special assessments if there is a pre-existing provision for them in the bylaws.

B. Financing An Association Through Supplier Contributions.

Financial support for a franchisee association may be sought from suppliers or potential suppliers to the franchise system. Where suppliers are approved by the franchisor, their loyalty is likely to be directed to the franchisor, rather than to franchisees and financial support for an association which is adverse to the franchisor will probably not be forthcoming. But, even if dollars are available, federal (and state) price discrimination laws may make supplier financing of the association a subject for careful planning.

"Price discrimination" is not a common law concept. Illegality thus depends on the precise terms of the statutory prohibition—(in the federal context, the Robinson-Patman Act, 15 U.S.C. § 13 (1987)). The principal prohibition, contained in § 2(a) of the Act (15 U.S.C. § 13(a)) makes it unlawful for a "person engaged in commerce in the course of such commerce . . . to discriminate in *price* between *different purchasers* of like grade and quality," where either purchase is in interstate commerce, and where there is a reasonable possibility or probability that the discrimination may substantially injure competition (emphasis added). Thus § 2(a) requires sales, at different price terms, to different purchasers, of products which are considered like kind and quality before any issue is raised. Financial aid to a franchisee association may, or may not, involve these elements.

Other price discrimination provisions (§§ 2(d) and (e), 15 U.S.C. §§ 13(d) and (e)), focus on allowances and services. These provisions apply to payments, of something of value to *or for the benefit of* a customer for customer-furnished services or facilities, where the payment is related to the resale of the seller's product, if the payment is not available on proportionally equal terms to all other customers competing in the distribution of those products. Robinson-Patman Act § 2(c), 15 U.S.C. § 13(c) prohibits commission or brokerage payments to a third party, with respect to sales, except for payments made for services rendered by the third party.

By its terms, "price" discrimination requires a *difference* in the *price* at which commodities or products are *sold* to two different purchasers. Two sales are required before any further analysis is needed. Supplier support for a franchisee association may occur without any such two-sale price difference, in which case no price discrimination issue is present. For example, where a supplier sells an item exclusively to the franchise system and not to others, a payment to a franchisee association—even if it were deemed to be a reduction in "price"—may involve no discrimination at all. If Supplier A sells product X only to Distributors A, B and C (or direct to franchisees A, B and C) and charges all of them the same price, and there are no sales at different prices unless the "benefit" is received by some stores in the franchised system and not others (or unless the "benefit" is received by one set of purchasers not by others), there is no illegal price discrimination. If that same "Supplier A" also funds a franchisee association at a product purchase-related rate (e.g, $1.00 per case sold), has there been a discrimination in "price"? The payment to the association may displease some franchisees or company-owned outlets who do not favor the association, but unless the conduct can be called a reduction in *price* for one purchaser as opposed to another, there is no § 2(a) price discrimination.

Where a product is sold on the basis that an amount per unit will be paid to an association, it is not difficult to see the payment as a reduction in price (even though the funds are being paid to the designated third party). Thus, if sales are made direct to the franchisee (with a $1.00 per case contribution to the franchisee association) and direct to company stores (with no $1.00 per case allocation), a differential is plainly present.

In many supply systems, a distributor, rather than the franchisee, is the supplier's customer. If that distributor can be seen as the franchisee's agent, rather than as an independent seller, the contribution to the association might also be seen as a reduction in "price" to the purchaser, but usually there is no such agency relationship.

If a supplier sells product for $10.00 per case to the franchise system and contributes $1.00 to the association, and it sells the same (or like kind and quality) product to others for $9.00, there is no illegal price difference (even if one assumes that the $1.00 payment is a reduction in price paid to the purchaser—an issue discussed *infra*). That practice, however, may introduce another problem: if the supplier sells to a third party for $9.00 net, must it not also sell at "$9.00 net" (with no $1.00 to the association) if a franchisee requests those items? The answer would appear to be "yes."

The initial question will always be "Are there discriminatory sales and is any discrimination legally a discrimination in price?"

Given the specificity of these provisions, funds received by a franchisee association from a franchise system supplier may be structured so as to avoid condemnation as price discrimination.

Even if there are sales at different prices, it only means that the analysis must proceed to the next § 2(a) element: "Is there a basis for saying that the discrimination may substantially injure competition?" This question can be examined at three different levels: the "primary line" (where the competitive effect is on those who compete with the discriminating seller); the "secondary line" (where the effect is on competition between the beneficiaries of the discrimination and those competing with it); and the "tertiary line" (where the effect is on the customers of those purchasing from the seller's customers). There is usually no factual basis (much less any legal support) for claims of competitive injury involving secondary or tertiary line discrimination. Dollars flowing from a supplier to an association ordinarily would not make the franchisee more competitive with its competitors, nor would it lead to any pricing strategy which disadvantages the franchisee's customers. As a legal matter, any inference of competitive injury can be rebutted. *J. Truett Payne Co. v. Chrysler Motors Corp.,* 451 U.S. 557 (1981); *Short Oil Co. v. Texaco, Inc.,* 799 F.2d 415 (8th Cir. 1986); *Reserve Supply Corp. v. Owens-Corning Fiberglass Corp.,* 639 F. Supp. 1457 (N.D. Ill. 1986). On the primary line level, pricing which is not predatory is generally incapable of producing competitive injury in a market where there are substitute suppliers. *Ashkanazy v. I. Rokeach & Sons,* 757 F. Supp. 1257 (N.D. Ill. 1991).

Moreover, there is no reason why a supplier's financial support should be treated as a payment linked to purchase. A supplier may be asked to make a voluntary (one-time or annual) contribution to the association. The association is not a purchaser (unless it is, or also controls, a purchasing co-op). Its receipt of funds should not, therefore, be seen as a price reduction. Whether a payment is (or is not) a reduction in price may involve a question of fact. However, a payment which does not appear to be contingent on or related to purchases will probably avoid categorization as a price reduction, avoiding the price discrimination label entirely. Evidence which tends to establish that such payments are unrelated to sale transaction could include (a) a contribution whose amount is totally unrelated to transactions (e.g. $10,000 per supplier); (b) a payment which is not contingent on sales (e.g, a commitment made on a set date as opposed to one which turns on sales made); (c) an amount which reflects status rather than sales volume; (d) solicitation of the contribution by association personnel rather than franchisee-purchasers; (e) use of the funds for associational purposes rather than as a pass-through to individual franchisee-purchasers.

Can the franchisee-purchaser and the franchisee association be viewed as affiliates or as each other's agents in the product sale transaction? The association has no right to control individual members' purchases, nor does any individual member have a right to control the association's solicitation of financial support in its own name. "Control" is used as the test where a manufacturer is related to an intermediate distributor (*See, e.g., Barnosky Oils, Inc. v. Union Oil Co.,* 665 F.2d 74, 83-84 (6th Cir. 1981).) Presumably, the same test would be applied where a purchaser and an association are involved. If, however, the funds are provided to the association subject to direction given by the franchisee-customer, it is more likely that the payment would be viewed as a reduction in the price charged to the franchisee-buyer, making the question of discrimination turn (as noted above) on whether or not there are sales at two different prices and whether or not there may be substantial competitive injury.

The fact that the franchisee association is neither the purchaser nor the party designating or approving suppliers becomes particularly significant. To the extent a Court is confused about price discrimination precedents, it can rely on the practical distance between the franchisee association and a seller's customer to conclude that contributions to the association are simply not within the intended scope of price discrimination laws since the payment is not an integral part of the sales relationship.

As an alternative to outright contributions, a supplier may be more willing to provide more indirect financial support: e.g., to sponsor a dinner at the association's convention;

to bear the cost of a seminar; or to pay fees for participating in a "supplier's showcase" at an association meeting. For the reasons discussed above, such payments escape categorization as price reductions.

Price discrimination prohibitions, however, also extend to promotional allowances and services. Here, too, the price discrimination issue will turn on whether or not the payments are being made to or for the benefit of the customers in connection with the sale of the supplier's product. The analysis, in the first instance, is similar to that described above.

Unlike a price differential, where a promotional payment or allowance is at issue, proof of "competitive injury" is not required. On the other hand, promotional payments or allowances are not prohibited; the seller is obligated to offer competing buyers—including buyers from the supplier's distributor—proportionally equal treatment.

When structured properly, payments made by a supplier to a franchisee association for support of the association's activities should escape the scope of §§ 2(d) and (e) of the Robinson-Patman Act. Those provisions are limited to promotion, advertising or similar activities connected with the *resale* of goods. *Motive Parts Warehouse v. Facet Enterprises,* 774 F.2d 380 (10th Cir. 1985). A supplier's support of a franchisee association is undoubtedly the payment of something "of value" and, possibly, it is "for the benefit of a customer"—*Nuarc v. F.T.C.* 316 F.2d 576 (3d Cir. 1963)—although that would be subject to factual dispute. It is not, however, generally thought of as a payment being used for promotion of the resale of the manufacturer's goods. Thus, for example, payments made for booths at a wholesaler's trade show are viewed as payments which relate to the original sale of goods; not to resale. *Herbert R. Gibson,* 95 F.T.C. 553 (1980). *A fortiori,* expenditures for supporting an association which is not involved in the chain of distribution at all would not appear to be susceptible of classification as a resale promotional payment.

If payments and association were viewed as payments for the benefit of a customer in connection with the customer's resale of goods (as, for example, might occur if the association engaged in advertising activity and the payments were earmarked for advertising), the supplier would be subject to compliance with the "availability to competing customers on proportionately equal terms requirement." As noted above, there may be a serious question as to whether there are any competing customers. Analysis of that question requires examination of the geographic boundaries of competition and the functions being performed. *See, generally, F.T.C. Advertising Guides,* 6 Trade Reg. Rep. (CCH) ¶ 39,035. Moreover, claims made by private plaintiffs in such cases are subject to significant defenses. If the plaintiff did not purchase directly from the defendant, it cannot maintain a claim for the supplier's failure to meet proportionate equality standards. *H.A.B. Chemical Co., Inc. v. Eastman Kodak Co.,* 1981-1 Trade Cas. (CCH) ¶ 63,912 (C.D. Cal.). Competing manufacturers do not have a right to assert treble damage claims, *Frito-Lay, Inc. v. Bachman Co.,* 1986 2 Trade Cas. (CCH) ¶ 67,384 (S.D.N.Y.), and a private plaintiff must show actual competitive injury in order to recover damages, *World of Sleep, Inc. v. La-Z-Boy Chair Co,* 756 F.2d 1467 (10th Cir.), *cert. denied,* 106 S.Ct. 77 (1985).

In addition, associations sometimes receive payments from suppliers based on services provided (e.g, market research and similar functions) by the association. Such transactions may arguably be related to the "resale" of product, but they would still escape §§ 2(d) and 2(e) because they are not payments for the benefit of the actual customer. In addition, to the extent they are payments for services rendered, they are expressly authorized by the "anti-brokerage" provision (§ 2(c)).

In some situations, the franchisee association (or its affiliate) earns its funds by actually being part of the distribution system—purchasing product for resale to its customers by functioning as a purchasing cooperative. If the association functions in this manner, its supplier-originated earnings are, simply, profit. No price discrimination issue is presented (unless the association-distributor is also the beneficiary of illegal discriminatory prices). In these situations, the association is no different than any other purchaser. If the association receives discriminatory treatment with respect to its purchases as compared to contemporaneous purchases of the same products by others, there is a price discrimination. On the other hand, given the unique status of the association, it is highly unlikely that competitive injury is present. The Robinson-Patman Act exempts a cooperative association's return of net earnings to its members. *Mid-South Distributors v. F.T.C.*, 287 F.2d 512 (5th Cir.), *cert. denied*, 368 US. 838 (1961). It follows that if those earnings are not returned, but are used to further the activities of the association, no price discrimination claim could be sustained. *See, generally,* Selden, *An Analysis of Cooperative Buying Associations—Including New Concerns For Franchise Systems,* The Business Lawyer, Vol. 37, No. 4 (July 1982) ABA.

C. Statutory Protection of Franchisee Associations.

General statutory protection of franchisee associations is provided by nine states,[1] including one which provides such protection by administrative regulation.[2] Essentially, these statutes forbid franchisors from restricting or inhibiting the right of franchisees to form and/or enter franchisee associations.

1. *Arkansas.* The Arkansas Franchise Practices Act (1977) provides that:

> It shall be a violation of this chapter for any franchisor, through any officer, agent, or employee to engage directly or indirectly in any of the following practices . . . [t]o prohibit directly or indirectly the right of free association among franchisees for any lawful purpose. Ark. Stat. Ann. § 4-72-206(2) (1987).

2. *California.* The California Franchise Investment Law (1970) provides:

> It shall be a violation of this division for any franchisor, directly or indirectly, through any officer, agent or employee to restrict or inhibit the right of franchisees to join a trade association or to prohibit the right of free association among franchisees for any lawful purpose. Cal. Corp. Code § 31,220 (West 1977 & Supp. 1990).

---

[1] Proposals have been introduced in other states, including Iowa in 1991.

[2] In addition to these statutes, the proposed "Iowa Franchise Investment Act" provides that:

> A franchisor shall not restrict a franchisee from associating with other franchisees or from participating in a trade association, or retaliate against a franchisee for engaging in these activities. S. 522, 74th Gen. Assem., (1991).

Twenty-eight states provide statutory protection for industry-specific franchisee associations. Those industries include motor vehicle dealerships, gasoline distributors, and breweries, beer wholesalers and suppliers, wineries, wine wholesalers, and other liquor distributors. *Ricky Smith Pontiac v. Subaru of New England,* 14 Mass. App. Ct. 396, 440 N.E.2d. 29, appeal denied, 441 N.E.2d 260 (1982) is the only reported case discussing such statutes.

Although franchisee associations are similar in many ways to collective bargaining units, there is no federal statutory or administrative protection for franchisee associations similar to those federal labor laws protective of employee associations. Emerson, *Franchising and the Collective Rights of Franchisees,* 43 Vand.L.Rev. 1503 (1990).

3. *Hawaii.* The Hawaii Franchise Investment Law (1974) provides that:

    > [I]t shall be an unfair or deceptive act or practice or an unfair method of competition for a franchisor or subfranchisor to . . . [r]estrict the right of the franchisees to join an association of franchisees. Haw. Rev. Stat. §48E-6(2)(A) (1988).

4. *Illinois.* The Illinois Franchise Disclosure Act of 1987 provides that:

    > It shall be an unfair franchise practice and a violation of this Art for a franchisor to in any way restrict any franchisee from joining or participation in any trade association. Ill. Ann. Stat. ch. 121 1/2, para. 1717 (Smith-Hurd Supp. 1990).

5. *Michigan.* The Michigan Franchise Investment Law (1974) (amended 1984) provides that:

    > [T]he following provision is void and unenforceable if contained in any documents relating to a franchise: A prohibition on the right of a franchisee to join an association of franchisees. Mich. Comp. Laws § 445.1527(a) (1989).

6. *Minnesota.* Minnesota is the sole state to have established a general right of association through administrative regulation.

    Minnesota law states that no person "shall engage in any unfair or inequitable practice in contravention of such rules as the commissioner may adopt defining as to franchises the words 'unfair and inequitable.'" Minn. Stat. Ann. § 80C.14, Subd.1 (West 1986 & Supp. 1990).

    Pursuant to this section, the Securities Division of the Minnesota Department of Commerce established that:

    > It shall be 'unfair and inequitable' for any person to . . . restrict or inhibit, directly or indirectly, the free association among franchisees for any lawful purpose. Minn. R. 2860.4400 (1975); Bus. Fran. Guide (CCH) ¶5230.31.

7. *Nebraska.* The Nebraska Franchise Practices Act (1978) provides that:

    > It shall be a violation of [the Nebraska Franchise Practices Act] for any franchisor, directly or indirectly, through any officer, agent or employee, . . . [t]o prohibit directly or indirectly the right of free association among franchisees for any lawful purpose. Neb. Rev. Stat. § 87-406(2) (1987).

8. *New Jersey.* The New Jersey Franchise Practices Act (1971) provides that:

    > It shall be a violation of this Act for any franchisor, directly or indirectly, through any officer, agent or employee . . . [t]o prohibit directly or indirectly the right of free association among franchisees for any lawful purpose. N.J. Stat. Ann. § 56:10-7(b) (West 1989).

9. *Washington.* The Washington Franchise Investment Protection Act (1972) provides that:

    > [I]t shall be an unfair or deceptive act or practice or an unfair method of competition and therefore unlawful and a violation of this chapter for any person to . . . [r]estrict or inhibit the right of the franchisees to join an association of franchisees. Wash. Rev. Code Ann. §19.100.180(2)(a) (1989).

Only *McAlpine v. AAMCO Automatic Transmissions, Inc.*, 461 F. Supp. 1232 (E.D. Mich. 1978) has examined any of these statutes. In *McAlpine*, a group of former franchisees brought suit against their former franchisor, AAMCO for breach of the franchise agreement and violation of antitrust laws. Upon filing, the franchisees broke away to form Interstate Transmissions, a competing transmission repair business. AAMCO counterclaimed, alleging that the franchisees had conspired in secret meetings to breach their franchise agreements, and start up a competing business.

The *McAlpine* court held that the franchisee "gatherings, and joint activities which do not violate the law" are protected by force of law. Franchisees, "like all other persons in the United States," enjoy the First Amendment right to assemble. Additionally, the court cited the 1974 Michigan Franchise Investment Law which provided that a franchisor could not restrict the right of franchisees to join an association of franchisees.

The court noted:

> One of the traditional control mechanisms of a franchisor has been to keep its franchisees disorganized. Franchisees, by necessity, must have access to the franchise group in order to act together to deal with common problems, whether those problems be the oppressiveness of the franchisor or some less momentous concern. The fact that a contract might have been breached as a direct result of franchisee organization means nothing more than that the franchisor would have a cause of action for breach of contract.

The court concluded that the franchisees' secret meetings, "begun as a lawful vehicle for discussing legitimate business concerns, cannot rise to a level of a tortious conspiracy. . . ." *McAlpine,* 461 F. Supp. at 1274.

Professor Emerson suggests that *McAlpine* may prove to be important in that it places a judicial imprimatur on franchisee associations.[3] No reported case has cited *McAlpine* for this proposition.

The "restriction" or "inhibition" of the franchisees' right to associate includes the physical disruption of franchisee meetings. In *State of New York v. Carvel Corp.* (N.Y. Sup. Ct., App. Div. 1981), 1982 Trade Cases ¶ 64,533; 186 N.Y.L.J. No. 102, p. 13; Bus. Fran. Guide (CCH) ¶ 7787, New York brought a state antitrust action against the franchisor based on the intimidating and harassing behavior of the franchisor at an association meeting organized to gather support for pending legislation.

The franchisor had disrupted a meeting of Carvel franchisees by entering the meeting place with two other men, demanding to be heard, attempting to obtain the names of the franchisee-organizers of the meeting, and threatening suit to discover these names. His two companions warned franchisees entering the meeting that they risked losing their franchises if they attended. On an appeal, the Appellate Division of the New York Supreme Court upheld the lower court's decision to deny the franchisor's motion for summary judgment.

Nothing in any of these statutes or in the bare handful of reported cases to date suggests that a franchisor is subject to an enforceable duty to bargain collectively with an association representing its franchisees. The business wisdom of doing so has not risen to the level of a legal duty. Moreover, there is no counterpart in franchising to the National Labor Relations Act. *See* Part I.D.7, below; Emerson, *Franchising and the Collective Rights of Franchisees,* 43 Vand.L.Rev. 1503 (1990).

---

[3] Emerson, *supra,* Note 2.

D. Cooperative Association Law.

A franchisee association can be organized in any of a number of different forms. *See* Part I.A., above. Anticipated activities of the association may suggest that the entity be organized as a cooperative under state law.

Cooperative associations in most states (other than some special category cooperatives, such as agricultural marketing organizations) actually are organized under the state's business or nonprofit corporation statute. Outside of some of the special categories, such as agricultural co-ops, there is no technical legal definition of a "cooperative," and in most cases a franchisee association is organized in the same fashion as would be a trade association under a state nonprofit corporation act. Most such statutes afford sufficient flexibility to the management, ownership and control structures of a nonprofit corporation that a cooperative association can easily be structured under the statute.

One treatise defines a "cooperative" association under a corporation statute as a corporation created by a banding together of persons for their common advantage or advancement, financial or otherwise, organized for the mutual benefit of the members, without gain to itself. 18 AmJur2d, Cooperative Associations, § 1.

In most cases, a franchisee association would be organized on a membership basis rather than on the basis of shares, certificated or non-certificated. Members would elect directors, possibly divided by geographic regions, and possibly providing for staggered terms (not as a "poison pill" but to provide continuity of management). Use of a non-stock membership structure could avoid possible applicability of federal and many states' securities laws to the distribution of shares in a stock-based association.

Although the association even if set up as a co-op would be organized in most cases under a state nonprofit corporation act, the association in all likelihood still would not be able to qualify as a tax exempt organization for purposes of the U.S. Internal Revenue Code under § 501(c). Single-brand trade associations cannot qualify under the "trade association" authorization in § 501(c)(6), because the benefits of that subsection are available only to interbrand associations of competitors organized to advance the interests of a particular industry or sector, rather than organizations formed to advance the more parochial interests of a single competitor, even on a collective basis. *National Mufflers Dealers Ass'n, Inc. v. United States,* 440 U.S. 472 (1979).

Notwithstanding the restrictive definitions of the Internal Revenue Code, a cooperative association of franchisees could be considered a trade association as a matter of state law. A trade association may be defined as a:

> . . . nonprofit, cooperative, voluntarily-joined organization of business competitors designed to assist its members and its industry in dealing with mutual business problems in several of the following areas: accounting practices, business ethics, commercial and industrial research, standardization, statistics, trade promotion, and relations with Government, employees and the general public.

Antitrust Advisor, § 7.02 (C. Hill, Third Ed. 1985) (quoting 1984 Directory of National Trade and Professional Associations of the United States, at 5).

If organized under a state nonprofit corporation act, the franchisee association organized as a cooperative association is a complete and separate legal entity, distinct from its members and subject to general state laws relating to corporations (unless it falls into a special statutory category that may be provided by state law). *See* 18 AmJur2d, Cooperative Associations, § 1.

While franchisees as such have a legal right to associate, either by statute (*see* Part I.C, above), or by common law (*see* State of New York v. Carvel Corp. (N.Y. Sup. Ct. 1981), Bus.

Fran. Guide (CCH) ¶ 7787), that does not mean that the association thereby achieves any special status under the law vis a vis the antitrust or securities laws, for example, or other state or federal trade regulation statutes. Some special types of cooperatives (e.g., agricultural marketing cooperatives) are specifically exempted from antitrust laws, but that exemption does not extend to other trade association-type cooperatives. Indeed, trade associations have been a ripe source of antitrust litigation over the years. Because the existence of a franchisee association derives from its members, who in many systems are at least nominally competitors acting in a horizontal alignment, the association not only all but automatically fulfills the "conspiracy" jurisdictional requirement for an action under the Sherman Act, it does so in an area (horizontal conspiracy) that has historically been dealt with on a *per se* basis of liability. Older antitrust cases dealing with horizontal action by members of cooperative associations are still valid law, and could be applied, given similar fact patterns, to a franchisee association that engaged in anticompetitive behavior, including boycott-type actions directed against the franchisor. *See, e.g., United States v. Sealy*, 388 U.S. 350 (1967) (horizontal price fixing); *United States v. Topco Assocs.*, 405 U.S. 596 (1972); *American Motor Inns, Inc, v. Holiday Inns, Inc.*, 521 F.2d 1230 (3rd Cir. 1975) (horizontal market allocation arising out of franchisees' collective exercise of veto over siting new franchised outlets). *See* Part II.G., below.

Under the Robinson-Patman Act, there was at one time concern based on several FTC enforcement actions that cooperative purchasing organizations organized by retailers (an increasingly common phenomenon among organized franchisee associations) constituted illegally discriminatory pricing under either § 2(a) or § 2 (f) of the Act. *See, e.g., American Motor Specialties Co. v. FTC*, 278 F.2d 225 (2d Cir. 1960); *Mid-South Distribs. v. FTC*, 287 F.2d 512 (5th Cir. 1961); *Alhambra Motor Parts v. FTC*, 309 F.2d 213 (9th Cir. 1962).

More recent cases, however, combined with a much more politically and economically conservative Federal Trade Commission, suggest that where a cooperative purchasing organization functions as a legitimate, independent business operation, rather than as a sham for collective, collusive action by competitors, it will be treated no differently from any other wholesaler for Robinson-Patman purposes. *See, e.g., Central Retailer-Owned Grocers, Inc. v. FTC*, 319 F.2d 410 (7th Cir. 1963). *See* Part I.B., above.

To summarize, an association of franchisees may be organized along any of the traditional bases under which any business organization, or trade association, is organized. The ordinary considerations that dictate incorporation for purposes of limiting liability apply with equal force to a franchisee trade association. Caution must be exercised, nevertheless, because in most cases a franchisee association, even if organized as a nonprofit, membership cooperative, will not be exempt from ordinary principles of antitrust law relating to collusive activity by competitors.

II. ASSOCIATION REPRESENTATIONAL ISSUES

A. Do Franchisee Associations Have Standing to Assert Claims?

In a franchise context, an association will seek to augment its power vis-a-vis the franchisor and its leadership position vis-a-vis franchisees by being able to take legal actions in its own name. Ultimately, the franchisee association seeks the ability to litigate—if litigation becomes necessary—in the name of the association. The benefits to those in control of the association's affairs are obvious: by creating an institutional plaintiff, less-aggressive franchisees are able to participate "under cover," providing financial and informational support without being seen as a chief antagonist. Also, association positions can usually be advanced by a small group of zealots. Thus, a decision made by a majority of the Board, or even a majority of members actually voting an a proposition, can be effective even though a substantial number of association members are silent. In addition, an "association as plaintiff" brings an aura of equity, if not selflessness, to the claims; a sense that the merits have been "pre-tested" (albeit not by a disinterested group) and have passed muster. In a litigation context, associational standing can circumvent many of the challenging prerequisites to class action certification under Rule 23 of the Federal Rules of Civil Procedure, and save the time and expense that might otherwise be consumed in technical class action issues before ever reaching the merits of the case.

1. *Standing.* The path toward associational standing in franchise litigation, however, is far from smooth. Most often such efforts have failed, unless the association itself has a contract right against a franchisor.

The rules applied to test an association's standing to bring a cause of action on behalf of its members in its own name are no different for a franchisee association than they are for any association. The test of "standing" is "whether the plaintiff has alleged such a personal stake in the outcome of the controversy as to warrant *his* invocation of federal court jurisdiction and to justify the exercise of the court's remedial powers on his behalf." *Warth v. Seldin,* 422 US. 490, 498-499 (1975) (emphasis in original). To satisfy the "case or controversy" requirement, a plaintiff "generally must assert his own legal rights and interests, and cannot rest his claim to relief on the legal rights or interests of third parties." *Id.* at 499.

By definition, a franchisee association, bringing an action as a would-be representative of its members, is seeking to assert the legal rights and interests of third parties—its members. Associations have been allowed to assert the third party rights of its members only if the three tests for associational standing set forth in *Hunt v. Washington-Apple Advertising Com.,* 432 U.S. 333, 343 (1977) are satisfied:

> [A]n association has standing to bring suit on behalf of its members when: (a) its members would otherwise have standing to sue in their own right; (b) the interests it seeks to protect are germane to the organization's purpose; and (c) neither the claim asserted nor the relief requested requires the participation of individual members in the lawsuit.

The first criterion looks to the rights of the individual franchisee against the party being sued. In a franchise context, the claim being asserted is most often against the franchisor; in such cases the terms of the franchise contract are usually sufficient to establish the requisite, individual member standing. However, associations may attempt to bring other types of actions against third parties. If, for example, a franchisor elects to license its marks to a manufacturer of collateral products, the individual franchisee will usually *not* have standing to bring a direct action against the manufacturer, the franchisor having reserved those rights to itself. If so, having an "association" assert the claim will be of no benefit.

The second criterion—whether the interests sought to be protected in litigation are germane to the association's purpose—is similarly of little moment in a franchising context. Even if a corporate charter is not drafted specifically to meet this requirement (a fact which seems highly unlikely), it is probable that an association of franchisees will have been formed to voice common concerns over franchise contract terms and performance, franchisor policies and matters affecting the economic vitality of the franchise system and, particularly, its franchisees. It is difficult to envision a serious franchisee issue which will not be germane to such a statement of purpose.

The third criterion for standing—a showing that the issues may be fully and properly adjudicated without participation of individual association members—is, on the other hand, far more problematic. The "no individual participation" requirement is derived (as regards federal court litigation) from constitutional principles limiting the exercise of judicial power to cases or controversies. State law restrictions are similar. To justify relief the association must either show that *it* has suffered harm, or the association must be able to show that one or more of its members has been injured. *See Warth v. Seldin,* 422 U.S. 490, 515 (1975); *Sierra Club v. Morton,* 405 U.S. 727 (1972). When the requisite proof of injury cannot be offered by the association in its own name (but would have to come from an individual member speaking in his or her own right) the association is not itself party to any justiciable "case or controversy" and there is no basis for the exercise of judicial power vis-a-vis a claim made by the association *Pesticide Public Policy Foundation v. Wauconda,* 622 F. Supp 423 (N.D. Ill. 1985), *affirmed,* 826 F.2d 1068 (7th Cir. 1987). Stated somewhat differently, the case or controversy principle seeks to insure that litigation will be maintained and controlled by that party (or those parties) whose interests are actually at stake rather than by an entity whose interest is less immediate.

2. *Relief.* What kinds of association claims fit within this framework? In general, claims for prospective equitable relief are likely to qualify. On the other hand, associational standing is universally denied when claims for damages are asserted. Between these two poles, litigants will find substantial room for argument.

The dichotomy between claims for prospective equitable relief and claims for damages appears to be comparable to distinctions between class actions under Rule 23(b)(2) and Rule 23(b)(3), Federal Rules of Civil Procedure. Under the former rule, a single litigant can maintain an action seeking to establish a standard of conduct applicable to an entire class (indeed, participation in such an action may be mandatory for all class members, while under the "(b)(3)" subdivision evidence that individualized proof will be required will support an order denying class certification and, at the minimum, requires a decision as to participation through the "opt-out" mechanism. The principle, in both class actions and associational standing, is the same: a limitation on the ability of a representative (whether an association or a class representative) to use judicial power for a claim which is perceived as one which, by its nature, should be pursued as a matter of individual choice.

These principles were most recently applied in *Independent Popeye's Franchise Group v. Al Copeland Enterprises, Inc.,* Civil Action No. 90-4572 (E.D. La., March 27, 1991) (see 60 ATRR (BNA) 519). While the ruling was made without formal opinion, it appears that the court accepted the principle that the nature of the claims—involving antitrust, unfair competition and breach of contract allegations—made in the individual participation of each injured party indispensable to proper resolution of the case. *See also AM/PM Franchise Association v. Atlantic Richfield Co.,* 584 A.2d 915 (Pa. 1990).

Claims for damages under individual franchise contracts are plainly of an individual nature and thus not appropriately asserted by an association. An association does not have standing to seek money damages on behalf of its members. *Warth v. Seldin, supra,* 422 U.S. at 515-16, *See also Contractors Ass'n. v. City of Philadelphia,* 735 F. Supp. 1274, 1286 (E.D. Pa. 1990); *United Steelworkers of America, AFL-CIO v. University of Alabama,* 599 F.2d 56 (5th Cir. 1979); *Newton v. Kroger Co.,* 501 F. Supp. 177, 179 (E.D. Ark. 1980); *International Woodworkers of America, AFL-CIO v. Georgia-Pacific Corporation,* 568 F.2d 64 (8th Cir. 1977); *Organization of Minority Vendors, Inc. v. Illinois Cent. G. Railroad,* 579 F. Supp. 574 (N.D. Ill. 1983). As the Supreme Court explained:

[T]he damages claims are not common to the entire membership, nor shared by all in equal degree. To the contrary, whatever injury may have been suffered is peculiar to the individual member concerned, and both the fact and extent of the injury would require individualized proof. Thus, to obtain relief in damages, each member of Home Builders who claims injury as a result of respondents' practices must be a party to the suit, and Home Builders has no standing to claim damages on his behalf.

Warth v. Seldin, supra, at 515-16. *Warth* involved constitutional challenges to a town's zoning practices as excluding the existence of low and middle income housing. Suit was brought by several individuals and associations. Home builders moved to intervene on behalf of firms involved in the construction of residential housing alleging that its members had been precluded from building appropriate housing in the town.

To recover damages, the harm to the individual members of an association would have to be proven on an individual basis. *Neighborhood Action Coalition v. Canton,* 882 F.2d 1012 (6th Cir. 1989) (diminished value of property as result of city's allegedly discriminatory conduct requires individual proof). The need to offer individual proof to prove such damages dictates that individual association members must participate in the litigation. *See, e.g. Rockford Principals & Supervisors Association v. Board of Education,* 721 F. Supp. 948, 951 (N.D. Ill. 1989) ("The form of the individualized proof, be it in-court testimony, affidavits or mathematical calculations, is not dispositive; rather, the existence of such proof is."); *Telecommunication Research v. Allnet Communication Services., Inc.,* 806 F.2d 1093, 1095 (D.C. Cir. 1986) (association lacked standing to sue on behalf of members allegedly injured by unlawful utility rate structure because damages to overcharged subscribers would require individual proof even though association claimed the damages could be "calculated by applying a simple formula. . .").

In *Telecommunication Research v. Allnet Communication Service, Inc.,* supra, Judge Bork concurred in the denial of standing to the association and stressed how absolute the rule that an association may not seek to recover damages on behalf of its members is:

> In *Hunt v. Washington State Apple Advertising Commission,* 432 U.S. 333, 97 S.Ct. 2434, 53 L.Ed.2d 383 (1977), the plaintiff association sought injunctive and declaratory relief, but not damages. The Supreme Court set out a three-part test for associational standing in such cases, the third part of which requires that "neither the claim asserted *nor the relief requested* requires the participation of individual members in the lawsuit." *Id.* at 343, 97 S.Ct. at 2441 (emphasis added). The Court made no suggestion that relief in damages could ever satisfy this part of the test, and indeed reiterated that it has *never* granted standing to an association seeking to press the damage claim of its members. *Id.* Quoting *Warth,* 422 U.S. at 515, 95 S.Ct. at 2213.

Emphasis in original. (806 F.2d at 1097).

The "no damages" principle cannot be evaded by artful pleading. In *Pesticide Public Policy Foundation v. Village of Wauconda,* 622 F. Supp. 423 (N.D. Ill. 1985), *affirmed,* 826 F.2d 1068 (7th Cir. 1987), a foundation challenged a village's ordinance regarding pesticides. Rather than allege that the village was liable to the foundation's members for the costs and expenses incurred in complying with the challenged statute, the foundation sought "only a declaration from this Court that defendants are liable to its members for the costs and expenses of compliance with the Wauconda ordinance." *Id.* at 434.

The District Court refused to accept the plaintiff's arguments:

Such a declaration cannot be categorized as prospective relief because its purpose is to compensate plaintiff's members for the past effects of an invalid ordinance. It would not, however, require the participation of individual members in *this* lawsuit.

Plaintiff has not cited, and this Court has not found, a single case where an association has sought this hybrid form of relief. In essence, plaintiff has fashioned its request for relief in a novel manner in order to circumvent the associational standing requirements of *Warth v. Seldin* to assert a claim for damages. If this Court were to issue a declaration of defendants' liability, plaintiff's members would be in a position where they would be entitled to receive damages from defendant upon the production of individualized proof. That the members would be required to go into another court to actually obtain the money judgment is a distinction that violates the spirit of the Supreme Court's holding in *Warth v. Seldin* and its concern that "absent the necessary allegations of demonstrable, particularized injury," *Id.* 422 U.S. at 508, 95 S.Ct. at 2210, no "case or controversy" exists. This Court therefore holds that the Foundation may not circumvent the standing requirements by seeking a declaration of entitlement to money damages. *The Foundation has standing to sue only for prospective relief; it lacks standing to sue for a declaration that its members are entitled to damages.*

622 F. Supp. at 434-435 (emphasis added).

Declaratory actions which assert prospective-only claims do not automatically involve issues which call for individual facts, assuming they involve only performance standards which are not linked to individual interests or facts. Application of the principle is not precise. For example, a claim by an association that a franchisor cannot use its authority to approve a franchise transfer as a means of obtaining new contract terms not provided for in the contract might be seen as a claim capable of being adjudicated without any individualized evidence, on the theory that the claim involves a question of law standing alone. However, an action that seeks to list the types of franchisor concerns which may justify disapproval and list those which do not justify disapproval can easily be seen as one which must be adjudicated in the context of an individual factual setting and the parties' specific concern leaving possible future claims to be resolved on the basis of *res judicata,* collateral estoppel or precedent (to the extent applicable). To the extent that cases contain language referring generally to the propriety of associational standing when a prospective declaratory judgment is being sought (*see, e.g., International Woodworkers of America v. Georgia Pacific Corp.,* 568 F.2d 64 (8th Cir. 1977) ("an association may only seek injunctive or declaratory relief")), reliance on such quotations out of context does not appear to be reasonable.

Even if a complaint makes no explicit reference to an award of damages for association members, the complaint may nonetheless be classified as one whose ultimate aim is the awarding of individual money damages, thereby precluding associational standing.

Prohibiting associational standing where damages are being sought is, however, only one facet of the "no individualized proof" rule. Some courts have described the rule as one designed to "assure that the most effective advocate of the rights at issue is present to champion them." *Mountain States Legal Foundation v. Dole,* 655 F. Supp. 1424, 1431 (D. Utah 1987) (quoting *Duke Power Co. v. Carolina Environmental Study Group, Inc.,* 439 U.S. 59, 80 (1978)). Other cases assert that the prohibition on associational standing where individualized proof is required guards against the danger that an association will choose to litigate disparate grievances of its members, which each member considers to be minor (and thus not worthy of utilizing judicial resources). *See Telecommunications Research v.*

Allnet Communications, 806 F.2d 1093, 1095 (D.C Cir. 1986). In a broader sense, there are claims which, by their very nature, are seen as claims which call for individualized proof, individual plaintiff participation and, ultimately, individual plaintiff control over the litigation process.

Many contract claims may fall into this category, either because they raise issues concerning each party's state of mind; or because they involve plaintiff's judgment as to whether there was any injury which should be asserted; or where the prospect of counterclaims means that individual participation will, at the end of the day, be required.

The issue was addressed in *Rockford Principals and Supervisors Ass'n v. Board of Education,* 721 F. Supp. 948 (N.D. Ill. 1989), in which an association of school administrators brought an action against a school board alleging wrongful rescission of a promised salary increase and seeking reinstatement. The plaintiff association in *Rockford Principals* sought to raise the contractual rights of its individual members.

In response to the defendant's contention that these claims required individualized proof as to, for example, the parties' state of mind, the plaintiff argued that:

> [N]o "state of mind" and therefore no individualized proof is necessary to establish the existence of the parties' contractual obligation. All that needs to be established, according to the plaintiffs, is that the salary increases contained in the [salary] Package were communicated to all the members of the Association.

Id. at 950.

Plaintiff in *Rockford Principals* argued that the factual element common to all of its members was defendant's "unilateral" action in communicating to the association's members a change in the members' contractual agreements and that this common factual element made associational standing appropriate. In *Rockford Principals,* the allegedly improper unilateral action was the school board's rescission of a prior across-the-board pay raise.

The *Rockford Principals* Court rejected this attempt to circumvent the rule of *Warth v. Seldin, supra,* holding that:

> *Individualized proof will be necessary to prove the existence of the alleged contractual-type relationships whether termed as "mutually explicit understandings" or implied employment contracts.* The unilateral action of the Board approving and "communicating" the Package to the administrators is certainly not enough to show the formation of a contractual relationship nor even an informal understanding. Formation of a contractual relationship requires mutual assent on the subject to which the parties are contracting. Even in the context of an implied employment contract, the requirements of formation are not present unless both parties intended to contract, in other words, an offer and acceptance. Determining whether the plaintiffs were aware of and accepted the defendants' offer requires that the individual circumstances of the Association's members be revealed. For contrary to the plaintiff's argument, proof of the plaintiff's blanket offer is insufficient to prove the existence of the alleged contracts or even "understandings" without proof of the individual member's acceptance.

Id. (citations omitted) (emphasis supplied).

The same result was reached in *Reid v. Dept. of Commerce,* 793 F.2d 277 (Fed. Cir. 1986), where the Court denied a trade union standing to pursue the reinstatement claims of its discharged members *even though no money damages were sought.* After noting that *Warth v. Seldin* bars associational standing whenever "both the fact and extent of injury would require individualized proof," 793 F.2d at 279, *quoting, Warth v. Seldin,* 422 U.S. at 515-16, 95 S. Ct. at 2214, the Court observed that:

> The Union here, if permitted to enter as petitioner, would similarly be seeking particular-ized relief dependent on the individual circumstances of each employee. While damages are not sought, reinstatement relief (and concomitant back pay) similarly requires that the injured union members be parties to the action.

793 F.2d at 279-80.

The same result was also reached in *Terre Du Lac Ass'n, Inc. v. Terre Du Lac, Inc.,* 772 F.2d 467 (8th Cir. 1985), *cert. denied,* 475 U.S. 1082 (1986), where the Court upheld the denial of standing to an association of home purchasers allegedly injured by the defendant's violation of the Land Sales Act. The Court denied standing despite the plaintiff's protestations that it was *not* seeking money damages but only specific per-formance.

> We reject the Association's arguments. In order to determine whether a specific perfor-mance remedy is appropriate, the court would have to receive substantial evidence relating to the individual claims and damages of members of the Association in order for it to determine whether specific performance, as opposed to a damages remedy, would be "fair, just, and equi-table." 15 U.S.C. § 1709(a). Further, the fact that much of the proof could be submitted by writ-ten rather than testimonial evidence does not help the Association's cause. The Association's argument boils down to the proposition that the rule against granting associational standing where the "participation of individual members" is required in the lawsuit, *Hunt v. Washington Apple Advertising Commission, supra,* 432 U.S. at 343, 97 S.Ct. at 2441, refers solely to partici-pation in the form of in-court testimony. Such a narrow reading of *Hunt* is unfounded. Associa-tional standing is properly denied where, as here, the need for "individualized proof," *id.* at 344, 97 S.Ct. at 2442 so pervades the claims asserted that the furtherance of the members' interests requires individual representation.

772 F.2d at 471.

In other words, the case law demonstrates that when the individual members of a plaintiff association must someday, somehow introduce some sort of evidence unique or peculiar to them in order to prevail, standing must be denied.

An association claim involving the implied duty of good faith performance—more and more common in franchise litigation—would appear to make association standing even more problematic. Where there is room for an implied obligation of good faith, the implication is based on the principle that the parties will not perform their contract obli-gations in a manner which defeats the parties' reasonable expectations as of the time the contract was made. *See Dayan v. McDonald's Corp.,* 125 Ill. App. 3d 972, 989-90, 466 N.E.2d 958, 972 (1st Dist. 1984). This standard may automatically involve the trier of fact in an inquiry concerning reasonable expectations which may (or may not) vary from licensee to licensee; the problem is that the Court may not know whether or not there are such variances until *after* individualized proof has been sought.

While an association may assert that all of the interests of its members are in complete harmony, that is often not the case. Where contractual rights and obligations are disparate and possibly conflict, or where certain franchisees would not benefit from an assertion of their rights because of other factors, associational standing may also be inappropriate. For example, in *Associated General Contractors v. Otter Tail Power Co.,* 611 F.2d 684 (8th Cir.

1979), the Court refused to grant an association standing to pursue a claim that the defendant violated the antitrust laws where the members' interests were too diverse and some members actually stood to benefit by the alleged conduct.

> Moreover, the claim asserted requires the participation of the individual members of the association. The association is clearly not in a position to speak for its members on the question of whether the Stabilization Agreement is violative of antitrust laws. Their status and interests are too diverse and the possibilities of conflict too obvious to make the association an appropriate vehicle to litigate the claims of its members. Some members are not qualified and others are not willing to work on the project; some stand to benefit from working on the project under the Agreement and still others will be hurt by not being able to do so. The fact that the association voted unanimously to bring the lawsuit sheds little or no light on the germaneness of the lawsuit to the organization's purpose. It is for the court, not the members of the association, to determine whether their interests require individual representation. Here, in view of the actual and potential conflicts, they clearly do.

Id. at 691 (footnote and citations omitted). *See also Mountain States Legal Foundation v. Dole,* 655 F. Supp. 1424, 1431 (D. Utah 1987) (denying association standing because it was "entirely conceivable" that many of the association's members would oppose the litigation or benefit from the challenged action). *See also NCAA v. California,* 622 F.2d 1382 (10th Cir. 1980) (one factor weighing heavily against the recognition of associational standing as evidence of serious disagreement among the alleged beneficiaries of the litigation); *Telecommunications Research v. Allnet Communications,* 806 F.2d 1093, 1095 (D.C. Cir. 1986) ("the number of members in an organization with a concrete stake in the outcome may be so small that the theoretical identity between the organization and its members disappears"), *quoting, International Union v. Brock,* 477 U.S. 274, 297, 106 S. Ct. 2523, 2536-37, 91 L.Ed. 2d 228 (1986) (Powell, J., dissenting).

B. Third Party Beneficiary Rights.

Does the third party beneficiary doctrine provide an alternative means by which a franchisee association can gain the ability to assert contract rights of its members? The answer in the typical case would appear to be "No."

In order to qualify as a "third party beneficiary," the contract must have been made and entered into with the intent to benefit the third person. *Chitlik v. Allstate Ins. Co.,* 34 Ohio App. 2d 193, 299 N.E. 2d 295 (Ohio Ct. App. 1973). The third party need not be named in the contract, nor accept the contract, or even be aware of it, as long as he is contemplated by the parties to the contract and sufficiently identified. *Id.* at 297. However, a mere incidental or indirect benefit is not sufficient to give the third party a right of action. *Visintine and Co. v. New York, C. & S. L. R.R. Co.,* 169 Ohio St. 505, 9 Ohio Ops 2d 4, 160 N.E.2d 311 (1959). Before recognizing such rights in a third party, it must be established that, not only did the parties to the agreement intend to benefit the third party, but also that the agreement contains all the elements of an enforceable contract.

Associations are traditionally *not* referenced in franchise contracts. Accordingly, the usual prerequisites for asserting third party beneficiary status would not be present. Where, on the other hand, the association is referenced in the contract (as in the case where a franchisor decision must be presented to or received by a franchisee association), performance rights pertaining to that process are the right of each franchisee. In addition, any issues concerning performance standards would appear to meet associational standing criteria, so that the association would be able to assert a claim regardless of whether it also met the requirements for a third party beneficiary claim.

Regardless of whether there is a franchise contract reference to a franchisee association, the franchisor may have a long-standing practice of dealing with an association—consulting on a regular basis and possibly using the association as a means for efficiently discharging the franchisor's obligation to provide information to (or consult with) its franchisees. Such courses of conduct do not by themselves create contract rights in any party. Still, if they reflect generally used means for performance of a contract obligation, the course of conduct may be evidence of a reasonable interpretation of the parties' respective performance obligations. What, then, if the franchisor decides to change its approach? As noted above, the association is generally not entitled to require that the franchisor serve *its* interests. Also, typically, franchise agreements leave the right to select alternative means of contract performance (individual advice; written communication, etc.) to the franchisor.

There may, nevertheless, be instances in which a traditional contract claim relating to association rights may be put forward. If, for example, a franchisor has provided information required by contract to be provided to franchisees, and has done so through presentations at association meetings, a franchisee could assert that a change in the practice (e.g., refusing to continue dealing with the association in this manner because the franchisor wishes to undermine its significance) works a qualitative change in the level of performance (e.g., information provided subject to the give-and-take of group discussion is more beneficial). Arguably, such a shortfall in performance could be treated as a material breach of rights held by the association as a beneficiary of the individual franchise agreements of its members.

Franchisees and their associations would be well-advised, however, not to introduce such rigidity into their systems through "course of dealing" arguments that the system itself becomes unable to adapt or react to changing competitive circumstances.

If the franchisor and the franchisee association have a contractual relationship, the third party beneficiary doctrine can arise in a somewhat different context. A franchisee, as a member of the association, may claim that he or she is entitled to assert the association's rights on the theory that the franchisee is the intended beneficiary of any franchisor-to-association obligations.

C. Trademark Law Issues.

One of the most persistent, perplexing and so far unanswered areas of the law as it relates to franchisee associations is the extent to which an organized group of franchisees, presumably all of whom are duly licensed to use the franchisor's trademarks, may use those marks or derivations thereof in connection with their association activities.

The easiest example is the choice of the name for the association. The association itself almost invariably does not have a license from the franchisor to use the franchisor's trademarks. Nevertheless, each of its members has such a license, although in most cases the license will be restricted in its permissible field of use to the establishment and operation, including the marketing and promotion, of the franchised business. May franchisees, for example, name their association the "Association of ALDO'S Franchisees, Inc." without thereby infringing the franchisor's "ALDO'S" trademark? Does the answer change if the name of the association instead is the "ALDO'S Franchisee Association, Inc."?

The question becomes more challenging still when the association uses its name, and possibly the franchisor's actual trademark, or perhaps some derivative trade identification or trade dress, on the masthead of the association's newsletter, on news releases, or even on promotional or novelty materials produced for use by members of the association (rather than for display or resale to the public).

At the far end of the spectrum, it is indisputable that absent a license from the franchisor a franchisee association may not, without infringing the franchisor's trademark, employ the trademark or any other mark or device confusingly similar to the franchisor's trademark, as brand identification of a product or service that the association might produce or have produced for its account for sale to member franchisees, even in circumstances where the product is for the internal consumption of the franchised business, rather than for resale to the consumer.

A long recognized common law defense to a claim of infringement is the "fair use" doctrine. Under this doctrine, a junior user is entitled to use a trademark, which is itself descriptive, in a non-trademark manner of use in its ordinary descriptive property without infringing the rights of the senior user, even if the descriptive mark has acquired secondary meaning and thereby become registerable on the principle register. McCarthy, *Trademarks and Unfair Competition*, Second Edition (Lawyers Co-Op Pub. Co., 1984) § 11:17. McCarthy explains:

> It is obvious that this "fair use" defense for descriptive marks is founded upon much the same principles as the defenses of freedom to describe geographical origin. . . . In considering this defense, one starts with the supposition that the mark in question has been determined to be "descriptive."

Id. at 475.

Thus, the "fair use" doctrine is properly thought of as a specific instance of the more general defensive argument that the junior user's use is not likely to cause confusion with the senior user's trademark. Illustrative, but non-franchise, cases include: *Beer Nuts, Inc. v. Clover Club Foods Co.*, 805 F.2d 920 (10th Cir. 1986) (defendant used the words "Brew Nuts" pictured with an overflowing stein to introduce and sell a product similar to plaintiff's Beer Nuts; held, that defendant was using "Brew Nuts" as trademark and therefore the fair use defense was inapplicable); *Zatarain's, Inc. v. Oak Grove Smokehouse, Inc.*, 698 F.2d 786 (5th Cir. 1983) (defendants used the words "fish fry" to describe the coating mix they manufactured; the court upheld defendant's fair use defense to allegations of infringing plaintiff's "Fish-Fri" trademark. The court found that the defendants had used "fish fry" descriptively, not as a trademark, and in good faith); *Leathersmith of London, Ltd. v. Alleyn*, 698 F.2d 27 (1st Cir. 1982) (defendant's use of the term "leathersmith" to describe his trade did not infringe on plaintiff's "Leathersmith" trademark); *Boden Prods., Inc. v. Doric Foods Corp.*, 552 F. Supp. 492 (N.D. Ill. 1982).

The cases draw the distinction sharply between use of a descriptive term in its primary, descriptive sense, on the one hand, from, on the other, "trademark use" by a junior user of a senior user's originally descriptive trademark. In those cases, the manner of use as a trademark negates any possibility of a meaningful defense based on absence of a likelihood of confusion, and the "fair use" doctrine is unavailable. *See e.g., U.S. Shoe Corp. v. Brown Group. Inc.*, 740 F. Supp. 196 (S.D. N.Y. 1990).

An association's use of a descriptive (or other) mark as or as part of its trade name, or as part of the association's own corporate name, may constitute "trademark use" of the franchisor's mark, depending upon the facts and circumstances of the case. McCarthy states:

Even though a defendant may make fair use of a protectible descriptive mark by using it merely to describe its business or services, use of the mark as part of a corporate name of the defendant may or may not amount to a "trademark" usage so as to be likely to cause confusion and not to be a "fair use".

McCarthy at 478 (citation omitted). *See, e.g., Service Merchandise Co. v. Service Jewelry Stores, Inc.,* 737 F. Supp. 983 (S.D. Tex. 1990).

The "fair use" doctrine is reflected in the Lanham Act. Lanham Act § 33(b)(4) (15 U.S.C.A. § 1115(b)(4)). "Fair use" appears in the statute as a defense to an infringement action even where the senior user's registration of its trademark has become incontestable. In its statutory manifestation, it is clear that the defendant who relies on "fair use" must establish:

- Defendant is not using the term or device in a "trademark" manner
- Defendant is using the term "fairly and in good faith"
- Defendant's use is "only to describe" its goods or services.

Courts have not been consistent in whether (in using the statutory doctrine) the junior user-defendant must also establish that the senior user's mark is "descriptive." *Compare Institute for Scientific Information, Inc. v. Gordon and Breach,* 743 F. Supp. 369 (E.D. Pa. 1990) and *International Order of Job's Daughters v. Lindeburg Co.,* 633 F.2d 912 (9th Cir. 1980), *with Cullman Ventures, Inc. v. Columbian Art Works, Inc.,* 717 F. Supp. 96 (S.D. N.Y. 1989).

The "fair use" defense is also available in respect to good faith, non-trademark, use of geographic names and personal surnames. Lanham Act § 33(b)(4). *See, generally, McCarthy, supra,* § 13:3 (surnames), and § 14:7 (geographic names). Courts have not been consistent in whether (going beyond the face of the statute) the junior user-defendant must also establish under the statute that the senior user's mark is itself "descriptive."

The difficulty for most franchisee associations with the "fair use" doctrine at common law is that it presupposes that the franchisor's trademark is "descriptive." If the franchisor's trademark is, instead, "arbitrary" or "coined," the defense is not likely to be available. On the other hand, read literally, the "fair use" defense as it appears in the Lanham Act turns not on the "descriptive" classification of the senior user's mark but on the manner of use by the junior user. Consider a group of service station dealers who, for example, named their association "Exxon Dealers Association, Inc." The underlying trademark, "EXXON," is a fanciful or coined mark, not a "descriptive" mark that took on secondary meaning. The dealer association's use in its corporate name is probably defensible under the Lanham Act as a "fair use" against a claim of infringement, but would not constitute "fair use" under the common law doctrine. This conclusion does not mean, however, that as a matter of common law the dealers might not still be able to argue that their association name was in fact a descriptive use, albeit of a non-descriptive mark, and prevail on a more general defense showing that there was no likelihood of confusion as a general proposition. If established, that defense should prevail even though the manner of use might not qualify for the "fair use" subspecies of the defense at common law.

To illustrate, it is substantially more likely that, "fair use" aside, an association could establish the absence of likelihood of confusion if its chosen corporate name were "Association of ALDO'S Franchisees, Inc." than "ALDO'S Franchisee Association, Inc." The latter form of use, unlike the former, carries with it some vague connotative implication of official recognition, sanction or sponsorship by the franchisor, which is the owner and senior user of the "ALDO'S" trademark. False indication of sponsorship is a species of "palming off" and constitutes an infringing use, and may also violate § 43(a) of the Lanham Act (the broad federal false advertising prohibition). *See, generally, McCarthy* at § 27; Gilson, *Trademark Protection and Practice*, § 5.05[10], § 5.09[3] (Bender, 1991). The former example, "Association of ALDO's Franchisees, Inc." is more descriptive in its manner of use and less suggestive of some official sanction by the owner of the mark.

The same general considerations concerning likelihood of confusion would also apply to the association's use of its name, and possibly the franchisor's (logo) trademark itself, on the masthead of its newsletter. If both usages were clearly descriptive and conspicuously disclaimed as to affiliation with the franchisor, it is quite possible that the association would be able to establish a defense of absence of likelihood of confusion. That defense is harder to establish with usage of a logo trademark as compared to clearly descriptive use of a word-mark. The association would still have to take care to avoid use (regardless of likelihood of confusion) that might constitute dilution or tarnishment (disparagement) of the system marks. *Gilson, supra,* § 5.05[2][b]; *McCarthy, supra,* at §§ 24:13-24:16.

Different franchisors have varying policies concerning their franchisees' collateral use of system trademarks. Unless reflected in clear contractual commitments, however, such policies may be no more than a statement of enforcement intention by the franchisor without binding legal effect. For example, if the franchise agreement licenses the franchisee to use the system's trademarks to advertise and promote the franchised business, the franchisee could make a very powerful argument that he or she is free to use the marks in a variety of applications intended to promote the business, such as billboards, handbills, promotional novelties, and local sports team sponsorships. In each of those instances, the franchisee's use of the mark would almost certainly come within the express scope of the license in the franchise, and the franchisee would be equally entitled to delegate the right to use the mark to an agent, such as an advertising agency, or a quasi-licensee, such as a local sports team. That being the case, it is only a small logical progression to conclude that the association might achieve agency status on behalf of the franchisee/licensee in those forms and manners of use of the system marks that "advertise and promote" the franchised business in ways that the franchisee itself would be permitted to do under the license in the franchise.

On a practical level, it would rarely if ever make sense for a franchisor to go out of its way to penalize an association of its franchisees who are generally in good standing for responsible and descriptive use of the franchisor's trademarks as part of the association's name, or in low-key, "internal" media such as system newsletters. While it might be appropriate for the franchisor to insist upon a license arrangement with the association, it should be done on a perfunctory, non-royalty bearing basis (if only to avoid the applicability of franchise registration and disclosure requirements to the transaction between the franchisor and the association). The franchisor has a much more legitimate objection to uses of its marks that go much beyond that, such as use of the association's name (including the mark) as a brand on the label of products it sponsors for sale to its members.

D. Strategies of an Association.

How can a franchisee association operate most effectively, becoming effective not only with its members, but effective in its interaction with the franchisor? Can an association represent its members' interests without assuming an adversarial posture towards the franchisor?

The association must represent a sufficient number of members of the system to be able to claim a mandate in order to be effective with the franchisor. In order to have impact with its members and the franchisor, it is imperative that the initial Steering Committee be representative and comprised of both the principal "movers and shakers" in the franchise system and have some representation of the "little guy."

At a very early stage, the interim Steering Committee should develop a Mission Statement and Key Strategies to guide the association. The association should strive to have a positive focus. Negative reasons may be the original impetus for formation—but negativity usually won't sustain itself for long. It's too easy for the franchisor to eliminate the irritant and pull the rug out from under the association. Positive focus can include proactive, self-help initiatives on behalf of the members, such as formation of franchisee-owned Co-ops—to provide purchasing, advertising, insurance or other needed benefits.

The following is an example of a Mission Statement and Key Strategies for a new association which was recently formed:

Mission:

To protect the common franchise rights, interests and investments of all Company franchisees who are Association Members.

Key Strategies:

To take all reasonable steps to maintain and enhance the profit, quality and image of the system units;

To communicate franchisees' viewpoints and interests to (franchisor) in order to facilitate effective systemwide communication network;

To ensure effective utilization of the National Advertising Fund with a defined process for franchisee input/approval/audit of marketing/advertising support/materials;

To explore quality of products, equipment and supplies at favorable prices;

To explore various insurance alternatives; e.g., health and casualty.

Note that the Mission and Strategy statements are written in a positive tone, yet enumerate the primary direction of the association. A positive tone does not preclude directly addressing the problems that instigated formation of the association, and some very challenging relationship or leadership issues could easily be subsumed within the objectives as articulated.

It is important to hire outside professionals who have had experience in the establishment of franchisee associations and who will have standing with the franchisor and the franchisor's outside professionals. Despite the cost, the investment is worthwhile because of the avoidance of trial and error in both internal organization and initial contacts and dealings with the franchisor.

The Steering Committee should develop a membership solicitation package. Typically, the package would include:

- Mission Statement/Key Strategies;
- Benefits to accrue to franchisor, such as more effective communications, a better cross section of franchisee representatives (better than the current franchisor-sponsored advisory council), commitment to system-wide perspective;
- Benefits to accrue to franchisees, such as having a dedicated group on particular issues, providing comfort in the event of acquisition, financial difficulty, etc., of the franchisor; offers a forum for monitoring local store marketing; vehicle for interchange of information; ability to pool financial resources to hire professional advisors, etc.

- Information describing members of Steering Committee, Chairman, Secretary, Treasurer;
- Description of professional advisors;
- Description of dues structure—used for interim period until approved by franchisees.

Once the membership solicitation package has been mailed to the franchisees, the Chairman should contact the franchisor, advise it of the association objectives and request a face-to-face meeting between the franchisor and the Steering Committee. This action represents the first step toward being effective with the franchisor. However, once contact is made, the association will often be in a responsive mode if the franchisor responds alertly and aggressively. And the franchisor's response will be the primary determining factor in whether relations will be constructive or hostile. There is no better way to induce membership growth and emotional solidarity in an association than to do things the franchisees perceive as threatening their interests, and then stonewalling their association's attempt to redress the situation.

Ultimately, the effectiveness of the association in interacting with the franchisor (assuming an intelligent response by the franchisor) will be determined by the proportion of members the group garners, whether the primary franchisees are involved, and the focus the group can maintain. If the franchisor is willing to meet and discuss issues and needs of the system with the association, that fact will help recruit association members. Of course, the franchisor may fear that establishing dialogue may legitimize the association with the franchisees. Conversely, the franchisor may stonewall and/or play hardball with individual franchisees or members of the Steering Committee. Unfortunately, while the latter course of action in too many instances is the franchisor's instinctive response it is usually counterproductive. The refusal of the franchisor to recognize the association—to refuse to meet—often is the impetus for moderate franchisees to elect to join the association. Again, once contact is made with the franchisor, the association's efforts will often primarily be responsive to franchisor's lead.

Utilization of co-ops and establishing various task forces to study specific issues help ensure a positive focus. Several franchisee associations that initially were formed under adversity thrive today because they evolved into purchasing/distribution co-ops or general purpose franchisee representatives.

Initially, the primary focus will be on franchisor communications. However, the style and tone of communications with franchisees is equally as important. Members of the association and its board need to have a positive attitude and treat their constituents with respect, in the same manner as they expect from their franchisor. It is vital that the Steering Committee/Board understand the legal restrictions that are imposed upon them. Associations do not have the same rights and powers as labor unions. Emerson, *Franchising and the Collective Rights of Franchisees,* 43 Vand.L.Rev. 1503, 1519 (1990). The outside professional must counsel the client to refrain from any discussions seeking to restrain free trade or competition among the franchisees. *See* Part II.G., below.

In communicating with the franchisor, associations should strive to identify system-wide issues and concerns, and avoid personal attack. The real enemy is the competition—not other members of the same system.

E. Strategies of a Franchisor.

1. *Effective System Management.* Before addressing what a franchisor's strategy should be once confronted with a franchisee association attempt, it is worth noting that

the following suggestions (if implemented independently) likely could have avoided an association effort in the fast place.

The franchisor has several interests to protect. It wants to prosper. It wants to facilitate growth of the system and minimize conflicts with franchisees. The system will be faced with major challenges and changes over time and the franchisor wants the system to be able to move, and to do so in a coordinated, rather than fragmented, effort. Communications are most important—both style and tone. Perception is reality. The franchisor does not want seeds of friction to fester, or early franchisee failures. The franchisor needs to understand, and respect, the investment interests and aspirations of its franchisees.

The use of a Franchisee Advisory Council ("FAC") (as a franchisor-sponsored advisory group, as distinguished from an autonomous franchisee-sponsored association) at the inception of franchising is advisable. The franchise agreement should contain procedures and systems for implementing major changes to the system to the extent possible. The guidelines contained in the booklet *How to Organize a Franchisee Advisory Council* (International Franchise Association, Washington, D.C.) are helpful in this area. One of the reasons for an effective FAC is to assure the upward flow of information from the field— where the best source is the franchisee. The FAC should be organized by region, type, or size of franchisees, with representatives elected rather than appointed and the council must be representative of the franchisee community. The franchisor does not want franchisees on the council who will quickly be labeled "company lackeys."

The FAC should meet on a regular basis (at least quarterly) and allow the franchisee Chairman to select its own agenda items. Additionally, the Council should spend time alone developing alternatives and attempting to arrive at balanced, effective solutions— thereby experiencing the difficulty of making decisions that are in the best interest of the system. The franchisor must foster two-way communications and treat franchisees as business associates, not serfs. Through the FAC, it would collaborate with them on issues that affect them. The franchisor should adopt a philosophy statement that sets a standard for interaction by its employees with franchisees, and attempt to understand the needs/concerns of the franchisees and to understand how those needs/concerns change as the franchisees evolve and mature. The franchisor should actively solicit franchisee input and participation in a manner that makes clear that it respects the franchisees' interests and ideas. The franchisor must be aware, and periodically acknowledge, that franchisees need to make a fair return on their investment. Awards programs and recognition for franchisees' achievements are one way to address this. Whether they like it or not, and justified or not, franchisors should be mindful that franchisees often muse about the value being derived in exchange for system royalties.

By following these simple guidelines, the franchisor can minimize the likelihood of being confronted with a hostile franchisee association.

2. *Responsive Strategy.* The franchisor's strategy when first confronted with an autonomous and possibly hostile franchisee association will depend upon the facts, circumstances and who is involved on behalf of the franchisee association.

Competent, experienced advisors can be retained to help guide the franchisor through the process.

The franchisor's initial strategy is to find out as much information as possible without committing to a position. The focus will be to learn why this has happened. What is the franchisees' major complaint? What is the reaction of the FAC members? Does the FAC feel that the effort is unnecessary, or are they a part of the Steering Committee? What is the current overall relationship with franchisees? Is the system doing well from a sales/profit standpoint? Are lines of communication open and do the franchisees share that perception? Do franchisees feel they can address issues, or has the system evolved to where it shoots the messenger? Are growth opportunities being thwarted? In other words, learn all you can. In some cases, the franchisor may be asking questions for the first time—questions that should have been asked years ago. Do the causes represent new issues or rehashing of existing/old issues?

Should the franchisor meet with the association as a group? Certainly, but not before the franchisor completes its due diligence. A vice president of the franchisor could meet preliminarily with a representative of the association to better understand the issues and learn all he or she can while preserving the company's options, before it "legitimizes" the association by meeting with its Board. Depending upon the issue, and the reaction of the FAC, the franchisor may want to work through the FAC to address the issue(s). Membership on the FAC may need to be quickly adjusted. If the FAC can be a part of resolving the issue, the impetus for the association may dissolve.

One thing the franchisor does *not* want to do is stonewall the association and cut off communications, although many franchisors will do exactly that. Hardball tactics can serve to galvanize the franchisees.

Who are the organizers of the association? Do they represent mainstream franchisees or a splinter group? Again, what is the reaction of FAC? Is the FAC doing its job by identifying issues and raising them? How has the franchisor responded in the past?

Perhaps there is a genuine need for the association. The franchisees may want health insurance, or car and travel discounts. They may want to establish a purchasing cooperative. Perhaps the franchisor can support their cause. What is the association promising franchisees? How can the franchisor make the FAC a hero? The franchisees' problem can, perhaps, be resolved by agreeing to delay rolling out a specific new product or new service—and give the FAC credit.

The franchisor may conclude that the existence of the association is a foregone conclusion, and therefore, that its strategy should be to support it (but not financially) and focus on attempting to help shape it to some extent. As to the steering committee, the franchisor's focus may be to assure that key franchisees, the system's opinion leaders, become involved, in order to reduce the likelihood of overt antagonism.

In many cases, an association may evolve in response to a franchisor's efforts to make changes in the system. In those circumstances, if the association can be incorporated into the process, its presence can become a substantial asset to the franchisor in defining and accomplishing its own goals in ways that would not be possible without active franchisee cooperation and participation. To achieve this, however, the franchisor must overcome its own ego and its not inconsiderable fear of loss of (or even sharing of) "control." If the franchisor can make a persuasive business case for change, franchisees more often than not will line up to follow the company's leadership. But to make that showing, franchisees must be brought into the decision-making process in a meaningful role, even if the franchisor reserves the ultimate decision-making authority.

3.   *Trying to Block the Association: Theories and Answers.*

(a) *Tortious Interference Claims.* By definition, the members of a franchisee association are persons or entities which have an existing contractual relationship with a franchisor. As a result, in addition to possible antitrust considerations (discussed elsewhere in these materials), franchisee associations must consider the prospect of potential claims of tortious interference with contractual relations (or interference with prospective business advantage—where that tort is recognized) brought against the association by a non-participating franchisee. Such claims could potentially arise where the association seeks to enlist the aid of the franchisor in dealing with its own troublesome member. Such claims are most likely to be a matter of concern where the franchisee association is engaged in group activities (e.g., advertising and promotion) which benefit the franchisor.

If, in such cases, a franchisee elects not to participate, the franchisee association may attempt to use the franchisor to compel participation (or financial contribution) by the non-competing franchisee or to deprive the non-participating "free rider" of the benefits produced by the association's dealings with the franchisor.

In general, tortious interference claims require the existence of an actual or prospective contract or business relationship; an action by a defendant which is not legally justified which results in a third party's action to breach the contract or discontinue the actual or prospective relationship. *See, generally,* Restatement (Second) of Torts § 766.

With respect to a franchisee association, the most significant element in the analysis is likely to be the element of causation: the franchisor is likely to be in a position where it will make its own decision for its own business interests; the notion that the franchisee association "caused" a franchisor to take action against a franchisee who was acting contrary to the interests of both the franchisor and the franchisee association seems highly unlikely. Put simply, if a franchisee is taking action which damages the interests of the franchisee association and the interests of the franchisor, one would expect that the franchisor will act on its own to protect its interests. The fact that the association may have passed along information (for example, identifying the names of franchisees not participating in supporting advertising and promotion activities) is not likely to constitute, by itself, an inducement of action by the franchisor.

To the extent, however, that an act of inducement by an association could be viewed as a cause of the franchisor's conduct, the franchisee association can benefit from principles of "privilege" or legal justification which are applicable to interference torts. *See, generally,* Restatement (Second) of Torts § 768. In general, an association may be privileged to engage in acts which otherwise constitute "interference" when it is protecting its own contractual and/or financial interests in a proper manner. Thus, the association (both in its own right and as representative of its members) has both its own business relationships to maintain and an economic interest in maintaining the vitality of the franchise system for the benefit of its members generally.

In the end, however, all claims of legal justification are subject to an "unlawful means" test—a principle which looks at the overall context of the activity in question. *See, e.g., Engine Specialties, Inc. v. Bombardier, Ltd.,* 330 F. Supp. 762 (D. Mass. 1971). Thus, while tortious interference claims would not appear to be a principal area for association concern, they underscore the principle that, as regards relationships between a franchisor and an association, both parties should carefully analyze (and where appropriate, articulate) their respective roles and the facts that justify actions taken with respect to individual franchisees.

(b) *Challenging Litigation Support Activity.* Franchisors may, from time to time, be confronted by franchisee associations whose agendas involve aggressive non-cooperation with the franchisor: encouraging litigation, advancing funds for individuals who are willing to file suit, or assisting in the prosecution of litigation. Words such as "barratry," "champerty" and "maintenance" are bandied about and franchisor's counsel are asked to opine that an association has committed actionable misconduct. A successful (indeed, a proper) legal challenge to such activity, however, is highly doubtful.

Barratry is the crime of frequently stirring up suits and quarrels between individuals, an offense recognized at common law. *See State v. Batson,* 220 N.C. 411, 17 S.E. 2d 511 (N.C. 1941). The court defined "barratry" as conduct in which a person solicits a large number of claims of the same nature, and charges a fee for his services in connection with the claims contingent on the amount recovered. (Citing 10 *Am. Jur.* Champerty & Maintenance, p. 551.)

Champerty is a slightly different pattern of conduct. An illustrative case discussing champerty is *Schnabel v. Taft Broadcasting Company Inc.,* 525 S.W. 2d 819 (Mo. Ct. App. 1975). The *Schnabel* court held that under Missouri and Kansas law the

> . . . constitutive elements of champerty [were] (1) an agreement by one with no interest in a suit of another (2) to support or maintain the litigation at his own expense (3) in exchange for a part of the litigated matter in the event of a successful conclusion of the cause.

Id. at 825. The *Schnabel* court noted that the scope of champerty had been ". . . narrowed, tempered and mellowed in modern times." *Id.* According to the *Schnabel* court the modern doctrine exempts from the rule against champerty ". . . those who interfere in litigation in which they have, or honestly believe they have, an interest." (emphasis added). *Id.,* citing *Breeden v. Frankfort Marine Accident & Plate Glass Ins. Co.,* 220 Mo. 327, 119 S.W. 576 (1909).

The doctrines of champerty and maintenance developed at common law to "prevent officious intermeddlers from stirring up strife and contention by vexatious and speculative litigation which would disturb the peace of society, lead to corrupt practices, and prevent the remedial process of the law." *Id.* at 823, citing 14 C.J.S. Champerty & Maintenance § 3.

Association activities, aimed at promoting member franchisees' legal or business interests, are not likely to fit these definitional requirements.

(c) *Challenging Cooperation With Other Franchise Associations.* There is no reason to assume that the interests of a franchisee association are limited to matters relating to the specific franchisor-franchisee relationship or the concerns of the one system. On the contrary, some statutory provisions expressly guarantee the right of association for any lawful purpose. For example, Arkansas Franchise Practices Act, Ark. Ann. Stat. § 4-72-206(2); California Franchise Investment Law, Cal. Corp. Code § 31220; Nebraska Franchise Practices Act, Neb. Rev. Stat. § 87-406(2); New Jersey Franchise Practices Act, N.J. Ann. Stat. § 56:10-7(b). Regulations established by the Minnesota Department of Commerce are to the same effect. Moreover, these statutes are not limited to associational rights within a franchise system. In applicable states, franchisees are protected in their rights to associate with all other franchisees. *See, e.g.,* Arkansas Franchise Practices Act, Ark. Ann. Stat. § 4-72-206(2); California Franchise Investment Law, Cal. Corp. Code § 31220; Hawaii Franchise Investment Law, Haw. Rev. Stat. § 48E-6(2)(A); Michigan Franchise Investment Law § 445.1527(a); New Jersey Franchise Practices Act, N.J. Ann. Stat. § 56:10-7(b); Washington Franchise Investment Protection Act, § 19.100.180 (2)(a). Other statutes refer to any "trade association". For example, California Franchise Investment Law, Cal. Corp. Code § 31220; Illinois Franchise Disclosure Act, Ill. Ann. Stat. Ch. 121 1/2 ¶1717. *See* Part I.C., above.

Even where there is no statutory protection for franchisee associations, franchisors cannot prevent lawful franchisee conduct without being able to point to an enforceable right. There is no abstract right to prevent joint action between, e.g., the franchisees of the Eat-Em-Up Restaurant System and the franchisees of Get-Up-And-Go Vitamin Store System and, even if there were a contract provision prohibiting free association as such, one would quickly question the propriety of judicial enforcement of a private contract in derogation of a constitutional right. Indeed, private conduct designed to deprive individual franchisees of civil rights leads to a potentially-serious cause of action.

There may be inter-system association activity which is problematic for a franchisor, but no reported case has explored the contours of this issue.

On the other hand, a franchisor has various contract rights—for example, a right to have the confidential and proprietary information of the franchise system maintained in confidence or a right to prevent franchisees from involvements in other businesses. Where an individual franchise breaches those obligations, the fact that he or she has done so through associational activity would hardly seem to create an excuse for activity which is otherwise improper. Likewise, an association which fosters such activity is itself subject to challenge by applying principles of tortious interference with contract. Note, however, that both claims—against the individual and against the association—are grounded in a contract right whose purpose is entirely independent of any effort to impair the association.

F.   Registration and Disclosure Issues.

1. *Disclosure of the Existence of a Franchise Association.* The existence of a franchisee association is not a fact which must be disclosed to prospective franchisees under either the UFOC[4] or FTC disclosure requirements.[5] For a reasonably diligent prospective franchisee, the information about franchisees and former franchisees of the system required by Item 20 of the UFOC Guidelines could lead to discovery that an association exists.

A franchisor who is concerned about what its franchisees may tell a prospect about an association or its agenda might consider putting the prospect on notice of the facts. Such a disclosure could minimize the negative impression the prospect may get by learning of these matters independently. Including such a disclosure in the offering circular may be difficult as there is no section of the accepted disclosure formats which directly relates to the subject. Arguably, a franchisor using the UFOC format could put this information in Item 1 describing the franchisor and the franchise generally or in Item 20 describing the franchisees of the franchisor. The FTC Rule nominally does not permit the inclusion of additional information beyond what is required to be stated in the circular. Because offering circular disclosure is not expressly required (and may not be permitted), a disclosure made orally or in a separate writing might be preferable, especially since it would not need to be registered.

2. *Disclosure Beyond the FTC Rule and UFOC Guidelines.* When a franchisee association or its constituent members threaten to file suit against the franchisor, may the franchisor continue to sell new franchises without disclosure of the threatened action to

---

[4] Uniform Franchise Offering Circular Guidelines prepared by the Midwest Securities Commissioners Association, whose former responsibilities now lie with the North American Securities Administrators Association. Referred to herein as the "UFOC Guidelines." Bus. Fran. Guide (CCH) ¶ 5700.

[5] Federal Trade Commission's trade regulation rule entitled "Disclosure Requirements and Prohibitions Concerning Franchising and Business Opportunity Ventures." CFR, Title 16, Chapter I, Subchapter D, part 436. Referred to herein as the "FTC Rule." Bus. Fran. Guide (CCH) ¶ 6000.

prospects? If the association organizes a buying cooperative which competes with the franchisor in the distribution of goods to the chain, is this a disclosure issue? What if the association or its members advise the franchisor that it is in breach of contract, that its covenants not to compete are unenforceable, and the franchisees intend to repudiate their contracts and adopt a new trade name?

Threatened legal action, threats to repudiate contracts, royalty strikes and other activities taken by or pursuant to the agenda of a franchisee association are not circumstances which are specifically required to be disclosed under the letter of the UFOC Guidelines, the FTC Rule or any state franchise statute. However, like Rule 10b-5 of the Securities and Exchange Commission's rules under the Securities Exchange Act of 1934, most state franchise statutes prohibit in generalized terms omission of a material fact necessary to make other statements made not misleading.[6]

The failure to mention the mere existence of a franchisee association is not likely to distort the meaning of other disclosures made by the franchisor. However, if activities of the association, such as those mentioned above, would have a material, adverse effect upon the franchisor's financial position, upon its ability to continue providing critical services to the franchisees, or upon the viability of the franchise system, the franchisor may need to disclose this possibility to prospective franchisees in order not to present a misleading picture of the franchise opportunity being offered.

The possibility also exists for common law fraud or misrepresentation claims based upon non-disclosure of material facts relating to threatened action by a franchisee association. Under the prevailing view at common law, non-disclosure of material facts is not actionable absent special circumstances such as the existence of a fiduciary relationship

---

[6]

State	Statute §	Bus. Fran. Guide (CCH) ¶
California	31201 & 31202	3050.54 & 3050.55
Hawaii	482E-5(b)(1)	3110.05
Illinois	6(b)	3130.06
Indiana	27(2)	3140.27
Maryland	347(b)(2)	3200.03
Michigan	445.1505(b)	3220.05
Minnesota	80C.13 Subdiv. 2	3230.13
New York	687.2(b)	3320.08
North Dakota	51-19-11	3340.11
Oregon	650.020(1)(b)	3370.04
Rhode Island	19-28-7	3390.07
South Dakota	37-5A-43	3410.42
Virginia	13.1-563 (b)	3460.07
Washington	19.100.170(1)	3470.17
Wisconsin	553.41(4)	3490.14

Item 3 of the UFOC Guidelines, which could be applicable by analogy, defines a matter as "material" if there is a substantial likelihood that a reasonable prospective franchisee would consider it important in making a decision about the franchise, or it would have or has had any significant financial impact on the franchisor.

between the parties, which most courts have declined to find in the relationship between a franchisor and its franchisee.[7]

Two fairly recent decisions in states which do not require the "10b-5" type of disclosures noted above support the proposition that the franchisor has no affirmative duty to disclose facts to a prospective franchisee beyond what is required by the FTC Rule in the absence of a fiduciary duty.[8] It has also been held a franchisor has no affirmative duty to disclose information to its existing franchisees.[9] In the absence of a 10b-5 type of disclosure requirement as noted above, or in the absence of specific facts giving rise to a fiduciary relationship, it appears there is no explicit duty to disclose to prospective or existing franchisees any information about a franchisee association, regardless of its materiality.

3. *Disclosure of Pending and Concluded Litigation.* Pending claims against the franchisor for fraud, violation of franchise law or comparable allegations, under Item 3 of the UFOC Guidelines, must be disclosed if the actions are material, or numerous regardless of materiality. Where the claims are brought by numerous franchisees or an association purportedly on behalf of numerous franchisees, the complaint will probably include some causes of action covered by Item 3 requirements and should be disclosed.

If a judgment is entered against the franchisor on "Item 3" claims it must be disclosed regardless of the economic materiality of the action. The disposition, whether adverse or not, of all concluded material actions alleging such claims must also be disclosed. However, the disposition of non-material actions by an association or its members not involving an adverse ruling against the franchisor would not have to be disclosed under the letter of the UFOC Guidelines.

The fact that a franchisor is being or has been sued by a group of franchisees or a franchisee association may in itself be considered material by a prospective franchisee and its omission could give rise to claims under the "10b-(5)" sections of state franchise statutes noted above. To avoid these claims, the franchisor may want to disclose all such actions, pending and concluded, regardless of the nature of the claims or a precise determination of their materiality.

4. *Material Modifications of Existing Franchises.* The franchisor who decides to negotiate contract changes in response to the demands of a franchise association should be mindful that franchise registration and disclosure requirements may be applicable.

---

[7] See, e.g.: *McGuirk Oil Co. v. Amoco Oil Co.*, Bus. Fran. Guide (CCH) ¶ 9505 (6th Cir. 1989) (Tennessee law); *Rosenberg v. The Pillsbury Co.*, Bus. Fran. Guide (CCH) ¶ 9445 (S.D.N.Y. 1989) (Massachusetts law); *Avery v. Solargizer International, Inc.*, Bus. Fran. Guide (CCH) ¶ 9189 (Minn. App. 1988); *Wallach Marine Corp. v. Donzi Marine Corp.*, Bus. Fran. Guide (CCH) ¶ 9014 (S.D.N.Y. 1987) (New York law); *Groseth International, Inc. v. Tenneco, Inc.*, Bus. Fran. Guide (CCH) ¶ 8893 (S.D. 1987); *Premier Wine & Spirits v. E. & J. Gallo Winery*, 644 F.Supp. 1431 (E.D.Ca. 1986); *Bain v. Champlin Petroleum Co.*, 692 F.2d 48 (8th Cir. 1982).

[8] *Scarlata v. Siegel Business Services, Inc. and Dunkin' Donuts of America, Inc.*, Bus. Fran. Guide (CCH) ¶ 9466 (Penn. Ct. Com. Pleas 1989); *Norman v. Amoco Oil Co.*, Bus. Fran. Guide (CCH) ¶ 9603 (Ala. 1990).

[9] *Carter Tire & Auto v. The Goodyear Tire & Rubber Co.*, Bus. Fran. Guide (CCH) ¶9312 (S.D.Ind. 1988); *Vaughan v. General Foods*, 797 F.2d 1403, Bus. Fran. Guide (CCH) ¶ 8630 (7th Cir. 1986) *cert. denied,* 479 U.S. 1087 (1987).

Offers of material modifications of existing franchises are subject to all registration/disclosure requirements under some state laws,[10] and, arguably, the FTC Rule.[11]

Negotiations directly with franchisees about the restructuring of any material aspect of the franchise or the franchise agreement, before amending offering circulars and franchise registrations to reflect these changes, could constitute the offer of a modified franchise. The nature of the negotiation process will usually make it impossible to comply with laws possibly requiring that every change of the offer is subject to *prior* registration and disclosure. However, negotiations with a franchisee association might not create "offers" to the individual members of the association, and in that respect collective bargaining with the association could sidestep the risks of noncompliance with registration and disclosure laws inherent in one-by-one negotiations with individual franchisees.

5. *Suspension of New Franchise Sales.* When material modifications of the franchise agreement and the franchise are contemplated as a means of settlement with an association, or as a necessary component for the future success of the system, the franchisor should consider putting system expansion on hold. For many reasons, including the possibility of multiple amendments of franchise registrations, it may be unwise to offer a revised franchise to prospects until existing franchisees have concurred in the changes. It may be equally troublesome to perpetuate the old deal through new sales as that may create inconsistent and conflicting contract rights and obligations. Inviting new franchisees into the confusion can complicate an already bad situation and create claims against the franchisor for misrepresentation (by material omission) in connection with those franchise sales.

G. Antitrust Aspects of Concerted Action by Franchisees.

In order to obtain such objectives as better products, more operating support, territorial protection and the like, franchisees frequently resort to concerted action. Concerted action may assist franchisees in gaining recognition as an association, obtaining reduced

---

[10]

State	Statute §	Bus. Fran. Guide (CCH) ¶
California	31125	3050.44
	31101(c)(2)	3050.25
Hawaii*	482E-4(a)(5)	3110.04
Michigan*	445.1506(1)(e)	3220.06
North Dakota*	51-19-04(1)(d)	3340.04

*Express exemptions from registration requirements for non-material changes in existing franchises suggest material modifications *are* subject to registration and disclosure.

Even in states where the franchise registration statutes do not expressly address the matter, state regulators may take the position that the offer to materially modify an existing franchise is an "offer" of a franchise subject to registration.

Whether a new franchise, or the material modification of an existing franchise, has been offered may turn on the presence of a combination of factors including the requirement of new or different fees, a significant additional investment, changes in territory provisions, licensing of new trademarks, or the creation of new or different contractual rights and duties.

[11] Statement of Basis and Purpose Relating to Disclosure Requirements and Prohibitions Concerning Franchising and Business Opportunity Ventures, Chap. V., J. Definition of "Sale of a Franchise," Section 436.2(k); Bus. Fran. Guide (CCH) ¶ 6359. Selden, *An FTC Post-Sale Material Modification Disclosure Requirement?* Franchise Legal Digest, Vol 3 (May/June 1988) (Intl Franchise Assoc.)

royalties, new products, more aggressive management and better advertising. However, concerted action immediately raises the specter of Section 1 of the Sherman Act which provides: "Every contract, combination . . ., or conspiracy, in restraint of trade . . . is declared to be illegal." Sherman Antitrust Act, 15 U.S.C.A. § 1.

There is a dearth of reported cases involving concerted action by franchisees; specifically, only *McAlpine v. AAMCO Automatic Transmissions, Inc.,* 461 F. Supp. 1232 (E.D. Mich 1978), and *In Re Arthur Treachers,* [1980-1083 Transfer Binder], Bus. Fran. Guide (CCH) ¶ 7696 (E.D. Pa. Aug. 3, 1981) focus on this issue. There are, however, many antitrust cases involving concerted action by groups, from which we can analogize. These cases may be categorized into two types: (1) professional association cases; and (2) consumer boycott cases.

1. *Permissible Activities.* For group action to avoid antitrust exposure, it is imperative that associations distinguish programs designed to collect and disseminate information—activities permissible under the Sherman Act—from those designed to fix prices, allocate territories, and the like.

Although not a franchise association case, the status of the doctrine of concerted action can perhaps best be understood by a review of the recent *Monsanto* decision. In *Monsanto Co. v. Spray-Rite Serv. Corp.,* 465 U.S. 752 (1984), plaintiff Spray-Rite alleged that Monsanto and some of its distributors had conspired to fix the resale prices of Monsanto herbicides. Spray-Rite alleged that Monsanto terminated Spray-Rite's distributorship, adopted compensation programs and shipping policies, and encouraged distributors to boycott Spray-Rite in furtherance of the conspiracy. The Court held, *inter alia,* that there was sufficient evidence for the jury reasonably to have concluded that Monsanto and some of its distributors were parties to an "agreement" or "conspiracy" to maintain resale prices and to terminate price cutters. Further, the Court found that Monsanto had reacted to numerous complaints from its distributors about Spray-Rite's low prices, and that termination was imposed to enforce the conspiracy's prices.

The Court affirmed that while concerted action to set prices is *per se* illegal, nonprice restrictions are subject to the rule of reason, which requires a weighing of the relevant circumstances of a case to decide whether a restrictive practice constitutes an unreasonable restraint on competition.

The *Monsanto* Court held that a manufacturer may choose—or refuse—to deal with whomever it likes, as long as that decision is made independently. Accordingly, a manufacturer may announce its resale prices in advance, and refuse to deal with those who fail to comply, and a distributor is free to acquiesce in the manufacturer's demand in order to avoid termination. *Id.* at 760, citing *United States v. Colgate & Co.,* 250 U.S. 300, 307 (1919). However, a manufacturer may not act *in concert* with its distributors in terminating another distributor. Monsanto's actions were not independent, and as such in violation of the Sherman Act.

In *American Motor Inns, Inc. v. Holiday Inns, Inc.,* 521 F.2d 1230 (3d Cir. 1975), a franchisor was held to have violated the Sherman Art by permitting its existing nearby franchisees to determine whether a new hotel—potential competitor—would be established at a particular location.

It was Holiday Inns' practice to send written notices of a new application to at least the three Holiday Inns nearest the proposed location. The recipients were invited to forward their comments on the application. If any objection was received in response to the notice of application, the only action which could be taken by the franchisor's committee authorized to grant franchises would be to deny the application.

The court determined that Holiday Inns treated its franchisees' objections to American Motor Inns' application as dispositive and thus allowed its franchisees to determine whether the applicant would be allowed to compete with them. This, the court continued, enabled the franchisees already in that market to divide the area between themselves, thus precluding further intrabrand competition. This concerted action constituted a horizontal market allocation violative of the Sherman Act

American Motor Inns relied on *U.S. v. Topco Assoc.,* 405 U.S. 596 (1962) in reaching its conclusion. In *Topco,* a number of grocery chains formed an association to manufacture a line of private-label grocery products that the member chains could then retail. Each of the participating grocers was assigned a territory in which it had the exclusive right to market the products. If an additional grocer applied for permission to market the products, the existing member whose operations were closest to those of the applicant, or any other member within 100 miles of the applicant's stores, had a right to object to the licensing of the applicant. The power of existing members to lodge such an objection, the Supreme Court said, operated as "a veto of sorts" over the approval of the application. The Court held that these features of the Topco plan constituted a horizontal restraint of trade and therefore a *per se* violation of the Sherman Act.

2. *Consumer Boycotts.* Protest boycotts have traditionally been accorded some measure of protection by the courts. In *NAACP v. Claiborne Hardware,* 458 U.S. 886 (1982), the Supreme Court held that a consumer boycott to obtain a civil rights objective fell outside the scope of the antitrust laws. In *Claiborne,* a group of black citizens organized by the NAACP refused to patronize white merchants in Claiborne County, Mississippi. The boycott was designed to make white government and business leaders comply with a list of demands for equality and racial justice. The affected merchants sued under state law to stop the boycott.

The Supreme Court held that boycott activity which was not itself violent was protected under the First Amendment and therefore could not give rise to liability under state law. "The right of the States to regulate economic activity could not justify a complete prohibition against a nonviolent, politically motivated boycott designed to force governmental and economic change and to effectuate rights guaranteed by the constitution itself." 458 U.S. at 914.

The Eighth Circuit held similarly in *Missouri v. National Organization for Women, Inc.,* 620 F.2d 1301 (8th Cir. 1980). In *National Organization for Women* (NOW), various organizations, including NOW, agreed to boycott the convention facilities of states that had not yet passed the Equal Rights Amendment. The Eighth Circuit held that the boycott was privileged on the basis of the First Amendment right to petition the government, and was not subject to antitrust scrutiny.

In *Allied International, Inc. v. International Longshoremen's Assn.,* 640 F.2d 1368 (1st Cir. 1981), *cert. denied,* 458 U.S. 1120 (1982), longshoremen protesting the invasion of Afghanistan by Soviet armed forces agreed with each other not to work for ships engaged in trade with the Soviet Union. The First Circuit held:

> We think this limited refusal to handle goods, undertaken as a political protest by a labor union acting on its own, and ill-designed as a means of gaining a competitive advantage for the union or its members, is not the sort of evil at which the Sherman Act is aimed.

The cases cited above had provided an umbrella of protection for protest boycotts. However, in *Federal Trade Commission v. Superior Court Trial Lawyers Assn.,* 110 S. Ct. 768 (1990), the Supreme Court placed into question the protections such boycotts had enjoyed. In *Trial Lawyers,* a group of attorneys who represent indigent criminal defendants in the District of Columbia jointly refused to accept new cases from the city government until such time as the city agreed to raise the fees it paid lawyers who accepted such work. The Supreme Court affirmed the FTC's holding that the lawyers' boycott violated the antitrust laws.

The Court held that, although the Sherman Act cannot be violated merely by an attempt to influence the passage of legislation, *see Eastern Railroad Presidents Conference v. Noerr Motor Freight, Inc.,* 365 U.S. 127 (1961), the activities of the Trial Lawyers were nevertheless subject to antitrust scrutiny. It ruled that the concerted refusal to accept any further assignments without a compensation increase was motivated by the desire of an economic advantage for those who agreed to participate, and as such was a violation of the Sherman Act. "The social justifications proffered for [the Trial Lawyer's] restraint of trade . . . do not make it any less unlawful." 110 S. Ct. at 777.

Claiborne was distinguished because, although it also involved a boycott, the boycotters sought no special advantage for themselves. The Claiborne campaign did not intend to destroy legitimate competition, whereas the Trial Lawyers stood to profit financially from the lessening of competition in the boycotted market.

Taken to its logical conclusion, this holding could subject to antitrust scrutiny collective direct action in the marketplace designed to inflict economic injury, irrespective of motive. If social and political justifications no longer immunize boycotts as they did in *Claiborne,* then all boycotts are potential antitrust combinations. While *Trial Lawyers* may be distinguished on the ground that the lawyers sought a special commercial advantage for themselves, it may be argued that the objectives in *Claiborne* were economic as well as social and political. In most cases, the line between the existence of an economic and noneconomic motive will be unclear.

Franchisees' concerted action, such as withholding royalties in order to obtain recognition, will probably be considered more akin to the *Trial Lawyers* case, as the association's objective often is economic benefit for its members rather than a political objective. The association's objective must be scrutinized carefully to determine if the activity is free from antitrust exposure.

What if franchisees joined together to affect price—are they competitors? Activities such as promotional advertising by franchisees involve the substantial risk of running afoul of antitrust laws. *See United States v. Pittsburgh Area Pontiac Dealers, Inc.,* 1978-2 Trade Cases ¶ 62,233 (1978) (automobile dealers permitted to advertise the manufacturer's suggested retail price of automobiles so long as it was clearly identified as such in each advertisement, and to advertise average price, provided it was determined by an independent surveyor in a confidential manner, it was clearly identified, and dealers surveyed were unaware of information's intended use). Such activities may be characterized as price-setting agreements between competitors. However, it may be argued that the purpose of such advertising is not to stifle intrabrand competition but to promote interbrand competition with other brands. Still, the antitrust implications remain. *See* Zeidman, *The Rule of Reason in Franchisor-Franchisee Relations,* 47 Antitrust L. J., 873, 886-7 (1978).

3. *Compilation of Information.* Is the franchisees' purpose legitimate if their goal is simply the compilation of information? In general, the compilation and dissemination of industry statistics is permissible so long as reports concern only past transactions, figures are in composite form so that the identity of individual businesses or transactions is not revealed, and the information is available to non-participants. *See Wire Mesh Prods. Inc. v. Wire Belting Assn.,* 520 F. Supp. 1004, 1008 (E.D. Pa. 1981) (trade associations which compile industry statistics in composite form do not violate antitrust laws).

In *Cement Manufacturers Protective Association v. United States,* 268 U.S. 588 (1925), the Supreme Court held that an association's gathering and dissemination of information regarding specific job contracts was not an unlawful restraint of trade in violation of the Sherman Act. The association was comprised of nineteen corporations engaged in the manufacturing and shipping of Portland cement, formed with the purpose of collecting and disseminating information concerning credit, freight rates, and the price of cement in existing contracts.

The Court held that the association's gathering and reporting of this information did not rise to the level of an unlawful restraint of trade, "even though it be assumed that the result of the gathering and reporting of such information tends to bring about uniformity in price." *Id.* at 604. *See Maple Floorings Manufacturers Association v. United States,* 268 U.S. 563 (1925) (members of a trade association do not become conspirators in restraint of trade merely because they gather and disseminate trade information as to cost of production, freight rates, and amount of sales and prices, or make use of it in management and control of their individual businesses); *see also Sugar Institute v. United States,* 297 U.S. 553 (1936) (reporting by sugar refiners of information as to current or future prices was not a violation of the Sherman Act, as such reporting permits voluntary price announcements by individual refiners, in accordance with trade usage).

However, in *United States v. Container Corporation of America,* 393 U.S. 333 (1969), the Supreme Court held that an agreement between competitors in the corrugated container market to furnish its most recent price charged or quoted established a combination or conspiracy in violation of the Sherman Act. The Court held that in some markets, such exchange would have no effect on a truly competitive price. However, since the market in corrugated containers is dominated by relatively few sellers, the product is fungible and the demand is inelastic, the exchange of price information tends to stabilize prices.[12]

4. *Ethical Codes.* What if the purpose is to develop ethical code or other guidelines for the group? Such actions may violate antitrust laws where the effect is to persuade members to engage in anticompetitive practices.

In *Fashion Originators' Guild of America, Inc. v. Federal Trade Commission,* 312 U.S. 457 (1941), an association of designers, manufacturers and distributors of women's garments and manufacturers and dyers of textiles agreed not to sell their products to retailers who sold garments of other manufacturers copied from the designs of association members. The agreement was held to be in violation of both the Clayton and Sherman Antitrust Acts. The combination exerted sufficient power to exclude from the industry those manufacturers and distributors who did not conform to the rules and regulations of the association, and as such tended toward a monopolization of the industry.

5. *Penalties.* Penalties imposed by ethical codes must be "reasonable" and provide for due process. The FTC test for reasonableness is whether the penalty would "unreasonably affect a businessman's ability to compete." FTC Advisory Opinion No. 119 (April 6, 1976). *See also* Herold and Webster, *Antitrust Guide for Association Executives,* p. 109 (American Society of Association Executives, 1986). Thus, penalties may not take the form

---

[12] Typical franchisee collective information gathering and disseminating activities include marketing research and planning, local advertising cooperatives, and local or national purchasing organizations.

of price fixing, allocation of territories, limitation of production, blacklists, boycotts, etc. Very limited approval has been given by the FTC and the Justice Department to liquidated damages provisions in codes of ethics. (*See* Paid-During-Service Agency Committee, File No. 673-7038 (FTC, May 1967); BNA, Antitrust & Trade Reg. Rep. No. 307, May 30, 1967, p. X-1; BNA, Antitrust and Trade Rep. No. 154, June 23, 1964, p. X-23.)

6. *Membership.* The greater the economic advantage to membership in a trade association, the less restrictive the association may be in its membership policies. Denial of membership may reduce the competitiveness of that applicant, and thus violate antitrust law as a combination which reduces competition.

In *Associated Press v. United States,* 326 U.S. 1 (1944), a provision in the association's bylaws allowed those members who had been in the association for more than 5 years to block nonmember competitors from membership. Further, members were prohibited from selling any part of their news to nonmember competitors. The Court held that such a provision violated the Sherman Act as a restraint of trade:

> Inability to buy news from the largest news agency, or any one of its multitude of members, can have most serious effects on the publication of competitive newspapers, both those presently published and those which but for these restrictions, might be published in the future. . . . The net effect is seriously to limit the opportunity of any new paper to enter these cities.

Franchisees should be exceedingly careful about adopting membership guidelines that restrict membership. This is usually not a problem because most associations want as large a membership base as possible so as to maximize their financial strength and their negotiating leverage with their franchisor. However, compulsion to join trade associations may be illegal under antitrust laws. *United States v. Fish Smokers Trade Council, Inc.,* 183 F. Supp. 227 (S.D.N.Y. 1960) (association of fish processors was prohibited from agreeing to induce or compel jobbers to join any union or association); *Leonard v. Abner-Drury Co.,* 25 U.S. App. D.C. 161 (Sup. Ct. 1905). Associations may adopt guidelines for expulsions and may expel members "for cause." 7 C.J.S. Associations § 23 (1980); *Elfer v. Marine Engineers Beneficial Association No. 12,* 179 La. 383, 154 So. 32 (1934). Expulsion proceedings must provide due process and be conducted in accordance with the association's rules. *Silver v. New York Stock Exchange,* 373 U.S. 341 (1963).

May an association force a member to adhere to the terms of its membership, e.g., can association sue to have a "free rider" contribute to cooperative advertising program? While the association may expel such a recalcitrant member in accord with the association's rules, no reported case has examined whether a member of a franchisee association may be forced to perform the obligations of its membership.

A franchisee association which expels members may be held to violate antitrust principles if the expulsion indeed has an anticompetitive effect. In *Northwest Wholesale Stationers, Inc. v. Pacific Stationery and Printing Co.,* 105 S.Ct. 2613 (1985), a retail office supply store, Pacific Stationery, brought suit against a non-profit cooperative buying association, Northwest, alleging that the Pacific's expulsion violated the Sherman Act as a concerted refusal to deal. The Court narrowed the question to whether Northwest's decision to terminate Pacific amounted to a group boycott, and determined that Northwest's activity could not conclusively be presumed anticompetitive per se.

> Unless the cooperative possesses market power or exclusive access to an element essential to effective competition, the conclusion that expulsion is virtually always likely to have an anti-

competitive effect is not warranted. . . . Absent such a showing with respect to a cooperative buying arrangement, courts should apply a rule-of-reason analysis. *Id.* at 2614.

Therefore, expulsion of a franchisee from a cooperative does not necessarily imply an illegal boycott. The actual anticompetitive effect of the expulsion must be examined before
such an act will be invalidated.

7. *Collective Bargaining.* Collective bargaining with franchisors on issues of concern
to franchisees can, if intelligently pursued, be the most effective tool of franchisees. It can
facilitate the negotiation of changes in franchise agreements, the establishment of cooperative advertising programs and the implementation of programs beneficial to both franchisors and franchisees. In many circumstances, collective bargaining can be a uniquely
effective and efficient way for a franchisor to accomplish some of its own objectives, even
though there is no statutory or (apparently) common law duty to bargain on the part of the
franchisor. Emerson, *Franchising and the Collective Rights of Franchisees,* 43 Vand.L.Rev.
1503 (1990).

Because franchisees are independent business persons, agreements resulting from collective bargaining in theory can be horizontal restraints of trade, particularly if the agreements result in establishing exclusive territories. *See, e.g., GTE Sylvania, Inc. v. Continental
T.V.,* 1976-1 Trade Cases ¶ 60,848 (9th Cir. 1976). On setting prices, *see, e.g., United States
v. Sealy,* 388 US. 350, 87 S. CT. 1847 (1967).

In *Sealy,* the U.S. alleged that Sealy violated § 1 of the Sherman Act by conspiring
with its manufacturer/licensees to fix resale prices charged by the licensees' retail outlets,
and to allocate exclusive territories among licensees. The District Court found a conspiracy to fix prices and enjoined Sealy from engaging in the violative conduct. However, the
court's order specifically permitted Sealy to disseminate and use *suggested* retail prices
for national advertising purposes. With respect to the charge regarding territory allocation,
the District Court applied the "rule of reason" and held that the government had not
proved that Sealy's conduct unreasonably restrained trade (it was undisputed that Sealy
had allotted exclusive territories to its licensees).

The Supreme Court found it unnecessary to inquire into the reasonableness of Sealy's
conduct, since territory allocation amounted to a horizontal restraint, a *per se* violation of
the Sherman Act. This was so because the 30 Sealy licensees owned nearly all of Sealy's
stock, and Sealy's business was managed by a board of directors, all of whom were
required by the bylaws to be stockholders, and by an executive committee comprised
exclusively of licensee-stockholders. *See also, United States v. Topco Associates,* 405 U.S.
596, 92 S. Ct. 1126 (1972); and *American Motor Inns, Inc. v. Holiday Inns, Inc.,* 1973-2
Trade Cases ¶60,390 (3rd Cir. 1975) (franchisor's practice of permitting franchisees to veto
proposed new franchises was a horizontal restraint on competition in violation of the
Sherman Act).

In *De Filippo v. Ford Motor Co.,* 516 F. 2d 1313 (3d Cir. 1975), eight Philadelphia area
Ford dealers successfully combined to persuade Ford not to give other Ford dealers special terms for a new dealership. In ruling for the dealer group, the Third Circuit looked at
the rationale for the combination and concluded that the collective action was not a group
boycott constituting a *per se* unreasonable trade restraint. Inasmuch as the plaintiffs still
were able to become Ford dealers and otherwise conduct business on the same terms as
the other dealers, there was no Section 1 violation.

If franchisees collectively and directly confront the franchisor over competitive
issues, there is a strong risk that the combination may be an illegal horizontal conspiracy.

In *United States Audio & Copy Corp. v. Philips Business Systems, Inc.*, 1983-1 Trade Cases, ¶ 65,364 (N.D.Ca. 1983), dealers in office dictation equipment combined to convince their supplier to restore exclusive territories. They withheld payments, filed lawsuits, interfered with the appointment of new dealers, encouraged dealers to switch to competing products, and pressured the dealer trade association to encourage dealers to use another supplier. The trial court, in denying the defendant dealers' motion for summary judgment, found that these activities could establish a horizontal conspiracy to divide markets, an unlawful boycott, a concerted refusal to deal with the supplier, an attempted monopolization, or perhaps even a conspiracy to fix prices. For a case illustrating the risk of boycotting a discounter, *see Lovett v. General Motors Corp.*, Antitrust and Trade Reg. Reptr. (BNA) Vol. 61, p. 193 (D. Minn. 1991).

8. *Concerted Action By Franchisee Associations.* Although franchisee associations generally have not had noticeable success, industry specific groups have had some success in obtaining protective federal and state legislation. Automobile dealers were instrumental in obtaining passage by Congress of the Automobile Dealers Day in Court Act, 15 U.S.C.A. § 1221, which provides a federal cause of action for retention of the franchise for a dealer claiming the franchisor failed to act "in good faith and without coercion" in terminating the franchise. Also, gasoline dealers have been quite successful in several states with industry-specific "fairness" legislation.

Largely as a result of action by franchise associations, several states have laws limiting the ability of franchisors (not limited to franchisors in the automotive area) to *terminate* a franchisee, or which provide a cause of action for unjust termination. *See e.g.,* California Franchise Relations Act, Cal. Bus. & Prof. Code §§ 2000-20043.

9. *Lobbying.* In general, lobbying by associations to enact, broaden, or retain state franchisee protection statutes, or pursue administrative remedies against franchisor abuses is protected by the First Amendment from antitrust attack. *See Eastern Railroad President's Conference v. Noerr Motor Freight*, 365 U.S. 127 (1961); *United Mine Workers of America v. Pennington*, 381 U.S. 657 (1965); *Franchise Realty Interstate Corp. v. San Francisco Local Joint Executive Board of Culinary Workers, Bartenders and Hotel, Motel and Club Service Workers*, 1973 Trade Cases ¶ 74,513 (No. Calif. 1973). This rule is generally known as the Noerr-Pennington doctrine.

Concerted efforts to influence public officials to enforce state laws are exempt from anti-trust laws if they are bona fide and carried out by proper means, even though they may have an anti-competitive effect. *Semke v. Enid Automobile Dealers Assoc.*, 456 F.2d 1361 (1972).

In *Enid,* the Enid Automobile Dealers Association persuaded the executive director of the Oklahoma State Motor Vehicle Division to seek an injunction against an automobile dealer to restrain him from selling new cars without a license. In addition, the dealers association induced local news media to refuse to accept advertisements from the dealer, and refused to provide warranty service on cars purchased from him and to sell parts to him. The dealer brought an antitrust suit against the association. The jury awarded damages to the dealer and the association appealed. The Court of Appeals upheld the dealers' right to influence action against the dealer, but held that the dealer's failure to comply with Oklahoma's licensing law could not, by itself, be used as a defense to the antitrust action. Thus, the case was remanded for retrial with the instruction that only those damages arising from the dealers' concerted actions other than those related to obtaining official state action were to be tried.

Three types of lobbying may violate antitrust laws, despite Noerr-Pennington:

(a) "Sham lobbying," or lobbying pursued with the intent and effect to directly restrain trade. In *California Motor Transport Co. v. Trucking Unlimited,* 404 U.S. 508 (1972), a group of truckers who, through various tactics had allegedly gained sufficient control of the licensing process to frustrate the licensing of truckers and discourage potential applicants was ordered to stand trial for anti-trust violations.

(b) Lobbying directed at purely commercial governmental policies and activities. In *George R. Whitten, Jr. v. Paddock Pool Builders,* 424 F.2d 25 (1st Cir.), *cert. denied,* 400 U.S. 850 (1970), three affiliated corporations allegedly conspired to influence various public bodies to include specifications requiring the use of defendants' products in their solicitations for pool construction bids. The Court of Appeals declined to find the conduct protected under Noerr-Pennington, holding that the doctrine only protected attempts to influence policy decisions, not commercial activities by government.

(c) Lobbying which is directed to the "administrative-regulatory-judicial" sphere, rather than to the influencing of legislation.

III. ASSOCIATION SUBSTANTIVE ISSUES

A. Franchisee Associations and the Implied Duty of Good Faith Performance.

Franchise literature now abounds with references to the "implied duty of good faith and fair dealing," a concept codified in § 205 of the Restatement (Second) of Contracts, the Uniform Commercial Code and various franchise relationship statutes. However, insofar as relations with a franchisee association is concerned, analysis of implied good faith duties starts and generally ends with one basic principle: an implied duty of good faith and fair dealing is not an independent abstract principle; it does not direct contracting parties to "be nice"—much less to "love one another." It is a doctrine of *contract performance* which must find its origin in (and be limited by) the terms of the franchise contract. *See, e.g., Seaman's Direct Buying Service, Inc. v. Standard Oil of California,* 686 P.2d 1158, 1173 (1984); *Carlock v. The Pillsbury Co.,* 719 F. Supp. 791 (D. Minn. 1989); *Domed Stadium Hotel, Inc. v. Holiday Inns, Inc.,* 732 F.2d 480, 485 (5th Cir. 1984); *Patel v. Dunkin' Donuts of America,* 146 Ill. Ap. 3d 233, 496 N.E.2d 1159 (1986); *Aldeman Drugs v. Metropolitan Life Co.,* 161 Ill. App. 3d 783, 515 N.E.2d 689, 694 n. 1 (1st Dist. 1987); *Pappas Co., Inc. v. E. & J. Gallo Winery,* 801 F.2d 339 (9th Cir. 1986).

On the other hand, some franchise relationship statutes embody a different good faith standard; rather than referring to carrying out the terms of the relationship or specific franchise issues (such as renewal), they appear to mandate a general obligation to "deal with a franchisee" or "deal with each other" in "good faith." *See, e.g.,* Arkansas Franchise Practices Act, § 7; Hawaii Rev. Stat. § 482 E-6(1). Other statutes (see Part I.C., above) deal directly with a franchisor's obligation to refrain from acts which impair franchisees' right of association. Those provisions, however, do not appear by their terms to mandate affirmative action.

1. *Where the Franchise Contract Makes No Reference To Franchisee Associations.* Most (but not all) franchise agreements make no reference to an association of franchisees. Quite the opposite: the franchise agreement is typically a two-party, franchisor-franchisee document in which the interests of third parties are not considered, if not expressly disclaimed. Under such circumstances, it is difficult for a franchisee to argue that his or her contract implies a standard of performance between franchisor and a franchisee association.

Innovative franchisees, or their counsel, may nonetheless attempt to frame a contract-based good faith claim. In the first instance, that claim will rest on the assertion that franchises are expected to be issued to various parties in multiple serial transactions and that by referring to adherence by all franchisees to the tenets of the "System," commonality among franchisees is anticipated and encouraged or overtly required. But the fact remains that most agreements (which almost invariably do contain strong integration clauses) do not make this sense of relationship a matter of contract obligation. As a result, it is not possible to relate franchisor-association relationships to any standard of contract performance. Implication of a good faith obligation under these circumstances is not consistent with the doctrine as articulated in the Restatement, or case precedent.

Some franchise agreements may, however, go further. The "System" is sometimes defined to include the body of franchisees working together in concrete or metaphysical ways. If those references create a duty on the franchisee to engage in some inter-franchisee conduct, a basis for some type of implied duty is present. For example, if the franchise requires participation in a local franchisee advertising association, a franchisor effort to preclude that association from functioning effectively could be characterized as a breach of an implied good faith performance obligation. How far can this line of argument be pressed? The basis for implication is the notion that, given the contract terms themselves, the implied duty cannot be expanded beyond the contract reference; thus, in the example cited, any implied duty must relate to the association advertising function.

It would appear that the implied duty also cannot be one which is of a character that its omission from the express terms of the contract is logically seen as a deliberate decision by either franchisor or franchisee to omit the issue. For example, it would be difficult to assert that a contract provision requiring participation in a local advertising association implies an obligation that the franchisor is to bear the cost of operating the association. On the other hand, if a franchisor is contractually obliged to assist and counsel franchisees in matters relating to advertising, it is easy to see how this already-existing duty can be extended to the association, perhaps as a third party beneficiary, or an agent, of the franchisee. As in most dynamic areas of legal practice, the issue becomes one for careful line-drawing in light of legal precedent, the nuances of the language employed in the contract, and the considerations evidenced in a factual record developed by counsel in an effort to bring practical rationality to a court's attention.

As the foregoing discussion suggests, there is another route toward implied association rights. If the franchise gives an individual franchisee rights (subsidiary to the right to operate the franchised business), and/or if the franchisor has subsidiary performance obligations to the individual franchisee, may the franchisee direct that these rights be exercised by (or these obligations be discharged through) his or her franchisee association or provided to the franchisee within the organization? For example, if the franchisor is obligated to provide information as to new products or new marketing plans, can franchisees insist that the information be furnished to them at their association meeting (where it will be subject to group criticism) on pain of an implied good faith performance breach of contract claim? Put differently, does the franchisor's obligation to communicate imply a right on the part of the franchisee to specify (absent a contract provision speaking to the subject) when, where and how communication will take place? If the contract provides independent sourcing rights subject to franchisor consent, does a franchisee-owned purchasing co-op have any right to enforce a duty of commercial reasonableness if the franchisor arbitrarily withholds or delays consent?

Where the contract speaks to the subject (e.g., "as Franchisor shall determine"), the opportunity to imply a right in favor of an association is (or should be) foreclosed in light of the extensive precedent precluding implication of a good faith performance obligation where the contract has an express provision. Here, too, creative counsel can think of factual variations which may fall closer to either side of a sometimes elusive dividing line.

The franchise agreement often is not assignable. It would seem to follow, therefore, that rights to contract performance cannot be assigned as such to an association. If, however, a franchisee may appoint a general manager as an agent for certain matters without thereby "transferring" the franchise, why not appoint the franchisee association as agent for certain purposes? Would there be an implied good faith duty requiring the franchisor to recognize the association as the franchisee's agent? The franchisor's response is likely to rest on the individualized, one-on-one nature of the intended relationship (whether it be franchisor-franchisee or franchisor-designated individual manager). A more intricate argument would emphasize the franchisor's need to hold the individual franchisee responsible for performance; the franchisor did not enter into a contract in which its rights were subject to group discussion (much less group-based standards).

2. *Where the Franchise Contract Contains Explicit References to a Franchisee Association.* Some franchisors by-pass all of the preceding issues by signing franchise contracts which anticipate a relationship with a franchisee association or by entering into independent contracts with an association in its own right.

In these situations, a contract term does reference the association. As a result, that contract term must be performed in accordance with its terms and in accordance with the implied obligation of good faith and fair dealing which is generally accepted as a part of all contract provisions. Restatement (Second) of Contracts, § 205.

In the franchise association context, however, there may be considerable difficulty in applying the underlying principle that the implied duty of good faith and fair dealing prohibits parties from doing anything which will have the effect of destroying or injuring the right of the other party to receive the fruits of the contract or the reasonable expectations induced by the contract language. To the extent that the "reasonable expectations" of the parties is a factor, ordinarily one would look to related written materials and prior courses of conduct to assist in defining the limits of any such obligation. In general, franchisors do not develop such documents. Accordingly, it is particularly desirable for a franchisor whose contract incorporates specific references to franchisee associations to make certain that there is sufficient context within the franchise agreement to aid in defining the expectation of the parties. In addition, consideration should be given to use of the descriptive provisions of the Uniform Franchise Offering Circular and the development of collateral documents which will define (and limit) the franchisor/association relationship. Where such information has been prepared as part of the franchise transaction, it should provide an effective limit on the scope of good faith implications.

Where a franchisee association is party to a contract with the franchisor, the association must recognize that the implied duty of good faith performance is a two-way street; that is, it applies equally to both parties to the agreement. Of course, just as the doctrine cannot be used by a franchisee to contradict express contract terms or create new terms that are not encompassed within the express contract terms, it cannot be put to such use by a franchisor. Still, when a franchisee association and franchisor enter into contract relations, it would be useful for both sides to consider how the object of their agreement is expressed, since that expression (or a Court's sense of that expression) is the ultimate context for implication of good faith duties. For example, an association-franchisor contract should acknowledge the parties' object in preserving contract rights under franchise agreements, maintaining the confidentiality of proprietary information and the value of intellectual property rights, facilitating cooperation within the System and promoting the interbrand competitive effectiveness of the system. Association conduct which is inconsistent with these objections (for example, misuse of confidential information) can then potentially be challenged using the implied doctrine of good faith performance. There are no specific precedents to cite in support of such claims. The salient principle is simply that the implied doctrine of good faith performance can be used by *both* parties to the transaction regardless of which one is viewed as the "weaker" party and which as the "stronger" party.

B. Duty of Due Care.

A franchisor, like any person, owes a duty of due care to those with whom it interacts. An association may be the beneficiary of this duty either directly in relation to agreements it has with the franchisor, or derivatively as representative of its members, or as a third party beneficiary. Section 299A of the Restatement (Second) of Torts summarizes the duty in a commercial context (albeit in gender-specific terminology) as follows:

> Unless he represents that he has greater or less skill or knowledge, one who undertakes to render services in the practice of a profession or trade is required to exercise the skill and knowledge normally possessed by members of that profession or trade in good standing in similar communities.

This duty is a special expression of the definition in Section 299 of the basic principle of negligence in a commercial context:

> An act may be negligent if it is done without the competence which a reasonable man in the position of the actor would recognize as necessary to prevent it from creating an unreasonable risk of harm to another.

The comments to Section 299A relate that the section is applicable not only to doctors, lawyers, accountants and engineers (it is the source of the rule of "malpractice" by professionals) but also to ". . . others in the practice of a skilled trade . . ." such as pilots, plumbers, electricians and blacksmiths. There can be no doubt that a franchisor that holds itself out as having *any* skill or expertise, not just those claiming *special* skill or expertise, in various area of endeavor falls within the rule. Has ever a franchise been offered or sold without *some* assurance of the franchisor's prowess in training, marketing, or site selection, for example, or the utility of its name, operating systems or know-how? The focus under the Restatement rule is on the representations or undertakings made in fact by a particular franchisor in particular circumstances, not an abstract investigation of the duties of a franchisor as such, whatever they might be.

It also seems that, consistent with the principle of Section 299A, parties to a contract may define the nature and scope of their duty to one another by clearly delineating their undertakings. Comment c to § 299A.

At some outer extreme, however, common law contract principles of lack of consideration and unconscionability are likely to limit hyperactive drafting by a franchisor of its form contract in an attempt to escape the duty altogether, by eliminating or severely circumscribing its undertakings or its liability for negligence either in its contract or in its day to day administration of its system. Indeed, many form franchise contracts contain general indemnification clauses by which the franchisee indemnifies the franchisor against all consequences of the operation of the franchised business, which the franchisor probably intends to include consequences of *its* own negligence. Case law suggests, nevertheless, that franchisors can be held liable vicariously for the remote consequences of their actions in specifying or approving equipment, building designs or operating procedures for their franchises. *Singleton v. Dairy Queen,* 332 A.2d 160 (Del. Sup. Ct. 1975) (customer injured by glass door defect); *Papastathis v Beall,* 723 P.2d 97 (Ariz. App. 1986) (consumer killed by object falling from display rack); *Wise v. Kentucky Fried Chicken Corp.,* 555 F. Supp. 991 (D.N.H. 1983) (employee injured by pressure cooker); *Kosters v. Seven-Up Co.,* 595 F.2d 347 (6th Cir. 1979) (consumer injured by defective packaging).

If a franchisee-owned purchasing co-op had been involved in the procurement or distribution of these items, it could have both a liability exposure, and a duty of due care claim over against the franchisor which specified, and mandated use of, the instrumentality of harm.

Still, a substantial body of case law suggests that tort concepts cannot be used to recover for economic or expectancy losses as distinguished from personal injury or physical damage to tangible property. *Prosser and Keeton on Torts* at 92 (5th Ed. 1984). Legal malpractice cases deviate from this limitation, but may reflect a special and discrete class of cases. But some cases have extended the liability in tort of a party for economic losses suffered as a consequence of its negligence. *See, e.g., Invacare Corp. v. Sperry Corp.,* 612 F. Supp. 448 (N.O. Ohio 1984) (negligence in recommending a computer system and software package); *Wessell v. Erickson Landscaping Co.,* 711 P.2d 250 (Utah 1985) (negligence in executing a residential landscaping undertaking); *High v. McLean Financial Corp.,* 659 F. Supp. 1561 (D.D.C 1987) (negligent execution of undertaking to process a loan application); *Dunfee v. Baskin-Robbins, Inc.,* 720 P.2d 1148 (Mont. 1986) (franchisor's failure to process properly a franchisee's request for consent to relocate breached duty of good faith; recovery of damages for emotional distress and punitive damages allowed). *Dunfee,* while pleaded and tried on a contract-based claim of breach of the duty of good faith, might just as easily have gone off on a tort theory of breach of a duty of due care. (*Dunfee* was repudiated without being expressly overruled in *Story V. City of Bozeman,* 791 P.2d 767 (Mont. 1990)).

To illustrate the principle in a more traditional setting, if a plumber performs plumbing repairs in the shop of a small business which turn out to be performed in a manner that falls below the level of skill prevalent in the community (i.e., the pipe bursts due to poor workmanship), the plumber is clearly liable in tort for resulting property damage, and is probably liable as well for lost profits to his customer, the shop-owner, while the shop is closed for repairs.

By analogy, suppose a restaurant franchisor undertakes to introduce a new menu item, and in preparation to do so tests the product in company stores in three markets for 60 days. The test results are positive and the franchisor rolls out the product nationally. Franchisees who introduce the product have to invest $12,000 in new equipment in addition to training costs, incremental staffing expense and local advertising. The product is a flop in national distribution, and an independent expert is prepared to testify that more extensive testing would have predicted the failure and that most national franchisors customarily perform more extensive testing before rollout of a costly new menu item. Is the franchisor liable in tort, like the plumber, to franchisees who suffer economic losses from introducing the new item, under the rule of Sections 299 and 299A? If the association had approved or endorsed the rollout, would it have exposure, or a claim? Would a co-op that had an investment in inventory of the dud product have a claim? Would the local advertising co-op that spent thousands of dollars promoting the dud product have a claim?

Other sources of liability may exist for such losses—breach of contract (possibly through an implied warranty foundation under UCC 2-314 or 2-315), or breach of an implied duty of good faith (discussed in Part III.A., above). But the tort theory of breach of a duty of due care is not only the most direct access to redress, it also is the most dangerous to the franchisor because willful violation of the duty as distinguished from merely negligent breach could expose the franchisor to punitive damages. *Cf., Dunfee v. Baskin-Robbins. Inc.,* 720 P.2d 1148 (Mont. 1986) (repudiated in *Story v. City of Bozeman, supra*).

It is also worth noting that the rule of Section 299A is clearly bilateral. A franchis*ee* who ". . . undertakes to render services in the practice of a . . . trade is required to exercise the skill and knowledge normally possessed by members of that . . . trade. . .".

For a comprehensive treatment of this subject, *see Do Franchisors Owe a Duty of Competence?,* R. Joseph, Twelfth Annual Forum, ABA Forum on Franchising (ABA 1989), from which this section of this paper is digested.

C. Encroachment.

1. *Introduction.* "Encroachment" is a term which is usually used to refer to the placement of new outlets in the market area of an existing franchisee. It also describes situations in which the franchisor competes for business within the franchisee's market area to the alleged detriment of the franchisee. Encroachment is a turf fight. It reflects a clash of values as much as business expectations, and only very recently has it been addressed at all by the courts outside of a traditional common law breach of contract analysis.

Typically, the franchisor wants to retain complete discretion to exploit all opportunities for marketing its goods and services. Franchisees want to protect their investments. They expect the franchisor to follow a "hands off" policy regarding competitive activities which could reduce their revenues and profits. Charges of encroachment customarily arise when a franchisor establishes additional points or channels of distribution of products or services, under the same or a different brand as that used by the franchisee, which the franchisee perceives as competing with the franchisee's operations, threatening to or actually resulting in diversion of sales from the franchisee's business.

The franchisor in most instances regards its development activity as not merely justified, but necessary, to meet or forestall competitive incursion on the franchisor's overall distribution system, usually expressed in terms of a quest for market share. In other cases, the franchisor might seek to enhance the efficiency or profitability of the franchisor's own investment in its business enterprise by increasing the scale of activity it conducts. Sometimes, synergisms between the franchisor's franchise distribution system and some other secondary business activity is advanced as a justification.

Franchisees generally tend to object to what they regard as encroaching activities for one, or both, of two basic reasons: (i) the new activity threatens to divert sales from the franchisee's operation, eroding what may be a dangerously thin margin of profitability in a royalty and advertising fee-burdened business; or (ii) because the franchisee needs or wants to expand its own scale of activity and perceives the franchisor's development activity as depriving the franchisee of upside growth and expansion opportunities.

There are many reasons why franchisors engage in what franchisees consider encroachment. The franchisor may find company-owned stores more profitable and less troublesome than franchise operations. Some franchisees are not good candidates to whom the franchisor can entrust expansion due to financial or managerial limitations. Franchisors and franchisees may simply disagree on how many new stores are appropriate in a given market.

Expansion through the acquisition and/or conversion of a competitor's stores may be undertaken by the franchisor because it quickly creates additional market share. Sales through non-franchised retailers, national account sales, catalogue and other direct sales may be important components of the franchisor's profitability. Franchisees may consider these activities destructive to the franchise system, particularly since they are often excluded from participating in them under the terms of the franchise agreement. Franchisees may feel that distribution through other channels or ownership of competing chains undercuts the franchise system and violates the intent of the franchise agreement. Franchisors believe they should not be limited in the pursuit of these opportunities just because they sold franchises.

Where encroachment issues arise, it is only rarely the case that only one or a handful of franchisees are affected. System policy issues and economic impacts inherent in the activities lead inexorably to a collective reaction by franchisees, often through an association.

Outside of some special industry classifications where organized political power of dealer associations has resulted in direct statutory intervention in distribution practices (e.g., motor vehicle distribution governed by state and federal dealer day in court acts), distribution rights in franchising generally are a matter of private contract. In a handful of franchise registration states, state law or regulation which is largely redundant to existing common law remedies undertakes to provide some level of protection against encroaching activities. *See e.g.,* Minnesota Regulations, § 2860.440(c) adopted under § 14 of the Minnesota Franchise Act (M.S.A. § 80C.14) (franchisor may not compete with franchisee in an expressly granted area of exclusivity).

Where a franchisor intrudes into an exclusive area granted by the franchisee, an obvious breach of contract has occurred, remediable under ordinary common law contractual principles. *See e.g., Wellcraft Marine, Inc. v. Dauterive,* Bus. Fran. Guide (CCH) ¶ 8565 (La. Ct. App. 1986).

For franchisors who are hemmed in by franchisees' marketing rights, the choices are to repurchase those franchises obstructing the desired activity, terminate them unilaterally (perhaps justified by an "efficient breach" theory) with the probability of litigation, undertake the encroaching activity on the assumption that the benefits of the new business outweigh the potential liability, or negotiate a compromise with the franchisees.

What about franchisors who are not barred from pursuit of new marketing or expansion plans by express contract terms? Because it is possible for franchisors to act within the literal provisions of their franchises, and without punitive intent, but still do significant damage to the business expectancies and performance of their franchisees by engaging in dual distribution activities that are economically close enough to cause harm (if not to breach of an express term of a contract), franchisees have continued to sue when encroachment occurs of a magnitude that materially jeopardizes the franchisee's investment. Franchisees have used a variety of legal theories to attack encroachment. With some exceptions, courts have refused to grant relief to them, finding no legal basis for restricting the franchisor's competitive practices beyond those prohibitions expressly provided by contract. The theories franchisees generally rely upon in encroachment cases are set forth below. Many of the cases cited use of theories of fiduciary responsibility by the franchisor, or breach of the common law implied duty of good faith (§ 205, Restatement (Second) of Contracts), mostly unsuccessfully

2. Breach of Implied Covenant of Good Faith and Fair Dealing. Courts have universally rejected the notion that franchisors intrinsically incur a "fiduciary" obligation to their franchisees, a theory advanced primarily by Harold Brown, a noted franchise attorney from Boston (and a former member of the Governing Committee of the Forum on Franchising). *See, e.g., Boat & Motor Mart v. Sea Ray Boats, Inc.,* 825 F.2d 1285, 1292 (9th Cir. 1987); *Burger King Corp. v. Kellogg,* Bus. Fran. Guide (CCH) ¶9730 (S.D. Fla. 1990); *Rosenberg v. The Pillsbury Co.,* Bus. Fran. Guide (CCH) ¶ 9445 (S.D.N.Y. 1990); *Super Valu*

Stores, Inc. v. D-Mart Food Stores, Inc., 431 N.W.2d 721, Bus. Fran. Guide (CCH) ¶ 9255 (Wis. Ct. App. 1988). *See also Steve's Franchise Company,* 1985-1 Trade Cases (CCH) ¶ 66,421 (D Mass. 1984); *TLH Int'l v. Au Bon Pain Fran. Corp.,* Bus. Fran. Guide (CCH) ¶ 8787 (D. Mass. 1986); *Salinsky v. Perma Home Corp.,* 443 N.W.2d 1362, 1365 (1983). *Compare Arnott v. American Oil Co.,* 609 F.2d 873 (8th Cir. 1979) *with Bain v. Champlin Petroleum Co.,* 692 F.2d 48 (8th Cir. 1982).

The most frequently advanced basis for recovery in encroachment cases is breach of the implied covenant of good faith and fair dealing ("the covenant").[13] Properly understood, the duty of good faith does not, and cannot, add to, or subtract from, the explicit obligations of either party to a written contract. The duty of good faith, rather, is intended *only* to supplement the express terms of a contract in areas where either an undertaking was so fundamental that the parties did not think to express it, or the contract vests one party with discretion or power that is not specifically limited by the terms of the contract. In the latter case, the duty of good faith supplies a limit to the exercise of reserved discretion or authority to prevent oppression, or undue surprise. In some senses it is a contractual analog to the public sector doctrine of procedural due process.

The fundamental purpose of the covenant is to prevent one party to the contract from depriving the other of the basic benefit of the bargain. It may be thought of in economic terms as preventing a party to a contract from wrongfully recapturing economic opportunity foregone in the process of negotiating or entering into the contract. *See,* Comments to § 205, Restatement (Second) of Contracts; Official Comment to § 201, Uniform Franchise and Business Opportunities Act, Bus. Fran. Guide (CCH) ¶ 3600. The Restatement describes the implied covenant of good faith and fair dealing as being available only to supply a term which is reasonable under the circumstances and essential to a defining the parties' rights under the contract. Restatement (Second) of Contracts § 204. Under this authority, courts have usually declined to use the covenant to imply terms restricting the franchisor's right to compete or establish new franchisees in the franchisee's market area.

Claims for breach of the covenant based on encroachment usually fail for the simple reason that most franchise agreements do not prohibit franchisors from engaging in the activity underlying the claims and they usually reserve significant rights to the franchisor and grant limited, if any, marketing rights or exclusivity of territory to franchisees. The franchisee may contend that, regardless of these contract provisions, the covenant should prohibit the franchisor from taking any action which denies the franchisee the "fruits" of the franchise agreement or impedes the accomplishment of the agreement's purpose, and that, because the franchisee's profitability is an intended "fruit" or purpose of the agreement, the franchisor should be prohibited from encroachment where it will diminish the franchisees' profitability (at least beyond some *de minimis* threshold). This argument typically fails because franchise agreements normally do not assure the franchisee's prof-

---

[13] The implied covenant of good faith and fair dealing is a doctrine governed by state law. Under the law of some states, the covenant may give rise to both a contract and tort claim, and elements of the contract claim may vary greatly from the elements of the tort claim.

Although most breach of covenant claims brought by franchisees against franchisors to challenge encroachment are brought as contract claims, tort claims have been advanced. *Eichman v. Fotomat Corp.,* 880 F.2d 149, 169-170 (9th Cir. 1989) (unsuccessful tort claim for breach of covenant). *Cf. Photovest Corp. v. Fotomat Corp.,* 606 F.2d 704, 729-730 (7th Cir. 1979) (successful "tortious breach of contract" claim under Indiana law). Because the covenant usually provides a basis for only a contract claim, this paper will discuss breach of the covenant as a contract claim. *Story v. City of Bozeman,* 791 P.2d 767 (Mont. 1990).

itability and do not limit otherwise lawful competition from the franchisor. However, in at least four cases (discussed below) franchisees have been successful in advancing this argument.

Claims for breach of the covenant based upon the franchisor's distribution through other channels into the franchisee's market area have been unsuccessful where the franchise agreement expressly permitted the actions taken by the franchisor, regardless of whether those actions diminished the franchisee's profitability. For example, an ice cream store franchisor's parent company's mass distribution of pre-packaged ice cream products to non-franchisees under the same brand name did not breach the covenant where the franchise agreement expressly authorized the franchisor to distribute product "through any other distribution method which may from time to time be established." *Carlock v. Pillsbury Co.*, 719 F. Supp. 791, 817-819 (D. Minn. 1989).[14]

In *Carlock*, the court reached this conclusion notwithstanding evidence that the parent company of the franchisor recognized that mass distribution might make it difficult for the franchisee to remain competitive, that the parent focused on prepackaged distribution at the expense of franchise sales, and that the franchisor took ineffective measures to counter the effect of the distribution on franchisees. 719 F. Supp. at 817-818. The court found that the language in the franchise agreement gave the franchisor "the right to aggressively distribute the prepackaged pints, even though that distribution adversely affects retail sales by franchisees." 719 F. Supp. at 819.

Even where their franchise agreements expressly disclaim marketing rights and exclusivity of territory, franchisees have claimed that establishing additional outlets or dealers in their market areas is actionable as a breach of the covenant. These claims have usually failed under the reasoning that the covenant cannot be used to override or contradict express contract terms. *See Domed Stadium Hotel, Inc. v. Holiday Inns, Inc.*, 732 F.2d 480, 485 (5th Cir. 1984) (franchise agreement reserved right of franchisor to "construct and operate" hotels "at any place other than on the site licensed"); *Sparks Tune-Up, Inc. v. White*, Bus. Fran. Guide (CCH) ¶ 9411 (franchise agreement reserved franchisor's right to compete with franchisee "within or without" franchisee's marketing area and granted "non-exclusive" right to franchisee); *Super Valu Stores, Inc. v. D-Mart Food Stores, Inc.*, 146 Wis. 2d 568, 431 N.W.2d 721, 726 (Ct. App. 1988) (franchise agreement reserved franchisor's right to "choose and select" other franchisees and granted "non-exclusive" right to franchisee); *Patel v. Dunkin' Donuts of America, Inc.*, 146 Ill. App. 3d 233, 496 N.E.2d 1159, 1160-1161 (App. Ct. 1986) (franchise agreement granted franchisor right to establish new business at its own discretion and own terms); *C. Pappas Co. v. E. & J. Gallo Winery*, 610 F. Supp. 662, 663 (E.D. Cal. 1985) (distributor agreement granted distributor nonexclusive right), *aff'd without opinion*, 801 F.2d 399 (9th Cir. 1986). *See also Western Chance #2, Inc. v. KFC Corp.*, 734 F. Supp. 1529, 1540 (D. Ariz. 1990) (franchise agreement

---

[14] *See also Rosenberg v. Pillsbury Co.*, 718 F. Supp. 1146, 1147 (S.D.N.Y. 1989) (no breach of covenant by franchisor's direct distribution to non-franchised retailers where franchise agreement granted franchisor right to distribute product through any distribution method); *Computronics, Inc. v. Apple Computer, Inc.*, 600 F. Supp. 809, 813 (W.D. Wis. 1985) (no breach of covenant by direct sales to university which resold computers to students where contract reserved manufacturer's right to sell "to any customer").

required franchisor to negotiate in good faith before opening "new franchised outlet" but defined "outlet" to exclude company-owned franchises); *Fickling v. Burger King Corp.*, 843 F.2d 1386 (4th Cir. 1988) (*unpublished decision* available at Bus. Fran. Guide (CCH) ¶ 9099) (franchise agreement granted non-exclusive territory); *Pride v. Exxon Corp.*, 911 F.2d 251, 256-257 (9th Cir. 1990) (no breach of covenant where franchisor operated company-owned stores at time franchise agreement executed).

In denying franchisee relief against franchisor encroachment under the covenant, courts have emphasized the public policy favoring competition and discouraging restraints on trade. *See, e.g., Patel*, 496 N.E.2d at 1161. One court applying these rules described the franchisee's legal challenge to the franchisor's encroachment as seeking to imply a covenant not to compete in the franchisee's market. *Snyder v. Howard Johnson's Motor Lodges, Inc.*, 412 F. Supp. 724, 727 (S.D. Ill. 1976). The court declined to imply such a covenant, because the negotiations prior to executing the franchise agreement had concerned territory rights, exclusivity, and the right of first refusal. *Snyder*, 412 F. Supp. at 728.

A merger and integration clause in the franchise agreement also may be a barrier to a franchisee's claim that the covenant should be used to imply a contract term prohibiting the franchisor's encroachment. *See, e.g., Computronics, Inc. v. Apple Computer, Inc.*, 600 F. Supp. 809, 813 (W.D. Wis. 1985) (integration clause in distributorship agreement precluded implication of term prohibiting manufacturer's direct sales); *Carlock, supra* (integration clause renders unreasonable franchisee's reliance on earlier representations or understandings).

However, in a recent decision, summary judgment was denied to a franchisor on a franchisee's claim that the franchisor's decision to license a nearby existing restaurant breached the covenant, notwithstanding the express contract provisions. *Scheck v. Burger King Corp.*, 756 F. Supp. 543 (S.D. Fla. 1991). The franchise agreement, according to the court, declined to "grant or imply" to the franchisee "any area, market or territorial rights." 756 F. Supp. at 549. But the court held that this language did not "necessarily imply a wholly different right" to the franchisor to open other stores at will regardless of their effect on the franchisee's operation. 756 F. Supp. at 549. Noting that the franchisor had adopted specific policies on new franchise development against the "cannibalization" of existing franchisees, the court commented that "while [the franchisee] is not entitled to an exclusive territory, he is entitled to expect that [the franchisor] will not act to destroy the right of the franchisee to enjoy the fruits of the contract." 756 F. Supp. at 549. This is the essence of the duty of good faith.

A franchisee of photo processing kiosks also succeeded in its claim for breach of the covenant under a franchise agreement which granted no territory exclusivity when the franchisor placed company-owned stores in the franchisee's market areas with the result that the franchisee could not operate profitably. *Photovest Corp. v. Fotomat Corp.*, 606 F.2d 704, 727-729 (7th Cir. 1979), *cert. denied*, 445 US. 917 (1980). The court reasoned that because the covenant:

> imposes a duty on each party [to the contract] to do nothing to destroy the right of the other party to enjoy the fruits of the contract . . . the implied covenant prohibited actions by [the franchisor] that would preclude profitable operation of the franchise or coerce franchise owners to terminate their agreements on terms favorable to [the franchisor].

Photovest Corp., 606 F.2d at 728. Significantly, although the franchisor had represented to the franchisee that it would not place new stores within two miles of the franchisee's stores, and it had previously estimated that the fifteen stores being licensed to the franchisee represented the "saturation" level of the area (606 F.2d at 716), the franchisor proceeded to place thirteen more stores in the area, many of them within two miles of the franchisee's stores (606 F.2d at 717).[15]

In a decision from a federal bankruptcy court which did not discuss what the franchise agreement provided about marketing rights or exclusivity of territory, a franchisee's claim for breach of the covenant succeeded where the franchisor opened a company-owned store within the area the court deemed necessary to support the franchisee's store.[16] *In re Vylene Enters.,* 105 B. R. at 49.

A distributor's claim for breach of the covenant also succeeded where the supplier bid against the distributor for the business of one of the distributor's long-standing customers. *Conoco Inc. v. Inman Oil Co.,* 774 F.2d 895, 908-909 (8th Cir. 1985), *later proceeding* 815 F.2d 514 (8th Cir. 1987). Even though nothing in the contract forbade the supplier from competing with its distributors, the court found significant the numerous statements by the supplier in the distributorship agreement about the supplier's intent to promote the success of distributors, and the custom of oil suppliers within the area never to bid against their own distributors. 774 F.2d at 908-909.

Conoco and *Vylene* are the best established precedents for use of the duty of good faith outside of the egregious fact circumstances of *Photovest, supra. Scheck* is useful, in turn, to support a well pled, factually supported, claim, although its ultimate outcome remains highly uncertain.

3. *Encroachment as Monopolization.* Franchisees have also alleged the three offenses defined by Section 2 of the Sherman Act, monopolization,[17] attempted monopo-

---

[15] The court explained its holding saying that the franchisor's opening of the company-owned stores violated representations it had made to the franchisee. *Photovest Corp.,* 606 F.2d at 728. The court reasoned that it was implying a covenant requiring the franchisor to perform its representations in good faith, and it was not implying a covenant requiring the franchisor to do something it had not contemplated doing. *Photovest Corp.,* 606 F.2d at 728.

[16] However, the court's precise holding in *In re Vylene Enters.* was that the franchisee was allowed to terminate its franchise agreement (105 B. R. at 43); apparently the franchisee did not collect any money damages for breach of the covenant.

[17] The offense of monopolization has three elements: (1) the defendant's possession of "monopoly power" (2) in the relevant market coupled with (3) the willful acquisition or maintenance of that power. *United States v. Grinnell Corp.,* 384 U.S. 563, 570-571 (1966). "Monopoly power," defined as the power to control price or exclude competition (*United States v. E.I. du Pont de Nemours & Co.,* 351 U.S. 377, 391 (1956)) may be inferred from a finding of a "predominant" market share. *Grinnell,* 384 U.S. at 571. Typically, market share is assessed in terms of entry barriers, profit levels, market trends, identity of customers and competitors, pricing patterns, economies of scale and product differentiation. *See Metro Mobil CTS, Inc. v. New Vector Communications,* 892 F.2d 62 (9th Cir. 1989).

The third element, wilful acquisition or maintenance of monopoly power, distinguishes the offense of monopolization from the possession of monopoly power arising from circumstances like superiority of product, business acumen or historic accident. *Grinnell,* 384 U.S. at 571. Among the types of exclusionary acts commonly alleged to satisfy this element are predatory pricing, refusal to deal, and denial of access to an essential facility.

lization,[18] and conspiracy to monopolize,[19] in seeking a basis for recovery in encroachment cases. *See* 15 U.S.C. § 2. The major hurdle franchisees face in monopolization claims against the franchisor is the definition of the relevant market.[20]

A monopolization claim will probably fail if the franchisee claims the relevant market is the market for the franchisor's specific product. *Domed Stadium Hotel, Inc. v. Holiday Inns, Inc.*, 732 F.2d 480, 487-491 (5th Cir. 1984) (relevant product market hotel rooms generally, not Holiday Inn hotel rooms); *Carlock v. Pillsbury Co.*, 719 F. Supp. 791, 843 (D. Minn. 1989) (relevant market ice cream generally, not Haagen-Dazs ice cream). "The natural monopoly every manufacturer has in the production and sale of its own product cannot be the basis for antitrust liability." *Carlock,* 719 F. Supp. at 843.

A franchisee's claim of an attempt to monopolize against its franchisor's placement of company stores succeeded when the court accepted the franchisee's definition of the relevant market as "the drive-thru retail photo processing submarket in the Indianapolis metropolitan area." *Photovest Corp.*, 606 F.2d at 711-714 (7th Cir. 1979), *cert. denied,* 445 U.S. 917 (1980).[21]

---

[18] The offense of attempted monopolization has four elements: (1) the defendant's anticompetitive (exclusionary) conduct (2) undertaken with a specific intent to monopolize (*i.e.*, destroy competition in) (3) the relevant market, coupled with (4) evidence of a "dangerous probability of success." *Dimmit Agri Industries, Inc. v. CPC Int'l, Inc.*, 679 F.2d 516, 521 (5th Cir. 1982), *cert. denied,* 460 U.S. 1082 (1983). A showing of a dangerous probability of success oftentimes but not always turns on the defendant's market share. *See, e.g., Indiana Grocery Inc. v. Super Valu Stores, Inc.*, Bus. Fran. Guide (CCH) ¶ 68,388 (7th Cir. 1988). A gasoline supplier's "making a competitive offer to a competitor's customer" in itself does not constitute the anticompetitive conduct required for the offense of attempted monopolization. *Conoco Inc. v. Iman Oil Co., Inc.*, 774 F.2d 895, 906 (8th Cir. 1985).

[19] The offense of conspiracy to monopolize has five elements: (1) a conspiracy (combination or agreement), (2) an overt act in furtherance of the conspiracy, (3) specific intent to monopolize (4) in the relevant market, and (5) a showing a dangerous probability of success. *See, e.g., Bowen v. New York News, Inc.*, 552 F.2d 1242 (2d Cir. 1975). The offense is rare, perhaps because the plaintiff bears a lesser burden to establish a conspiracy offense under Section 1 of the Sherman Act.

[20] Courts use two tests to define the relevant market, "cross-elasticity of demand"—which involves identifying, from the user's point of view, all of the reasonable substitutes for a particular product or service, *see, e.g. Brown Shoe Co., Inc. v. United States*, 370 U.S. 294, 325 (1962)—or "elasticity of supply" (or "supply-side substitutability")—which involves identifying all of the suppliers or manufacturers capable of entering the market for a particular or service, *see, e.g., Twin City Sportservice, Inc. v. Charles O. Finley & Co.*, 512 F.2d 1264 (9th Cir. 1975). For example, in a franchisee's Section 1 Sherman Act case against a McDonald's franchisor, the relevant market was defined by the available substitutes comprised of "inexpensive food facilities." *Dunafon v. Delaware McDonald's Corp.*, 691 F. Supp. 1232, 1241-1242 (W.D. Mo. 1988). Although authority exists for finding a monopolization offense where the defendant possesses monopoly power in a portion of a relevant market (a "submarket") (*see, e.g., Int'l Boxing Club, Inc. v. United States*, 370 U.S. 294, 325 (1962)), the submarket must encompass more than merely the defendant's own product or service. *United States v. E.I. du Pont de Nemours & Co.*, 351 U.S. 377, 393 (1956); *Carlock v. The Pillsbury Co., supra.*

[21] The Seventh Circuit pointed to evidence that the price of drive-thru retail photo processing (the franchisor's service) was not cross-elastic with the price of retail photo processing generally, and to evidence that the public viewed the two services as separate markets, as evidence that the relevant market was the submarket of drive-thru retail photo processing, rather than the market of retail photo processing. 606 F.2d at 713-714.

The second obstacle to franchisees who bring monopolization claims against the franchisor is establishing standing, that is, "antitrust injury."[22] Antitrust injury requires a connection between the franchisee's loss or damages and the franchisor's conduct: "[A] drop in the franchisee's gross sales does not establish antitrust injury in the absence of a showing that the reduction in sales is the result of an antitrust injury." *Eichman,* 880 F.2d at 163 (9th Cir. 1989).[23] Practically speaking, standing requires that the plaintiff franchisee demonstrate that substantial barriers prevent entry to the relevant market, and that it has competed or attempted to compete vigorously in the market. *See U.S.F.L. v. N.F.L.,*1988-1 Trade Cas. ¶ 67,930 (2d Cir. 1988). This injury will usually be difficult for a franchisee to establish.

   4. *Unlawful Merger Claims Under Section 7 of the Clayton Act.* The offense defined by Section 7 of the Clayton Act, the direct or indirect acquisition of stock or purchase of assets "where in any line of commerce in any section of the country, the effect of such acquisition may be substantially to lessen competition, or to tend to create a monopoly"[24] (15 U.S.C. § 18),[25] has also been raised by franchisees in encroachment cases. Just as monopolization offenses require an identification of the "relevant market," a Section 7 Clayton Act offense requires an identification of the "line of commerce in any section of the country" in terms of subject matter and geographical area. *See Domed Stadium Hotel, Inc.,* 732 F.2d at 491. *First & First, Inc. v. Dunkin' Donuts,* Bus. Fran. Guide (CCH) ¶ 9595. The defendant's allegedly exclusionary conduct may affect a "submarket" (a portion of a relevant market), rather than the entire relevant market, if the submarket is a well-defined, separate economic entity. *See Brown Shoe Co.,* 370 U.S. at 325; *Photovest, supra.*

   Franchisees may raise Section 7 Clayton Act claims against the franchisor when the franchisor acquires stock or purchases the assets of a competitor of the franchisees, or

---

   [22] "Antitrust injury" is described as "injury of the type the antitrust laws were intended to prevent and that flows from that which makes defendants' acts unlawful." *Brunswick Pueblo Bowl-O-Mat, Inc.,* 429 U.S. 477, 489 (1977) (Clayton Act Section 4 claim).

   [23] In *Photovest Corp.,* in which the franchisee did succeed on an attempt to monopolize claim against the franchisor, the court found that the franchisor had engaged in predatory conduct—"saturating" the franchisee's market area with company-owned stores, concealing discounts available from (third party) film processors, marking up the price of film, escalating the franchisee's rent, etc., all for the purpose of reducing the profitability of the franchisee's stores—which gave rise to a "dangerous probability" that it would monopolize the market. 606 F.2d at 714-721. The court explicitly rejected the franchisor's reliance on the fact that the franchise agreement did not prohibit its opening of company-owned stores near the franchisee's stores, saying "a party's right to sue for antitrust violations is not dependent on the existence of a contract provision prohibiting the alleged anticompetitive behavior." 606 F.2d at 719.

   [24] A Section 7 Clayton Act claim has the following elements: (1) the acquisition of stock or purchase of share between two (or more) direct competitors (horizontal), or between supplier-customer or manufacturer-dealer (vertical) (2) within a relevant product market (3) which will result in an increase in market share or concentration (4) which in turn is likely to have an adverse effect on competition. *Domed Stadium Hotel, Inc.,* 732 F.2d at 492. The increase in market share may be such that the merger is "inherently suspect," or other data describing the market may indicate a likelihood that competition would be adversely affected. *Domed Stadium Hotel, Inc.,* 732 F.2d at 492.

   [25] A similar offense, oftentimes alleged alongside Section 7 of the Clayton Act, arises under the Federal Trade Commission Act, which prohibits "unfair methods of competition . . . and unfair or deceptive acts or practices." *See* 15 U.S.C. § 5(a). However, no private right to action exists for breach of this statute.

when the franchisor's stock or assets are acquired or purchased by a competitor.[26] As with the monopolization claims, demonstrating that the franchisor and the competitor combined have monopoly power in the relevant market (or submarket) may be impossible. The problem was articulated by one court as follows:

> Plaintiffs, for various reasons, do not want the proposed merger to take place and they have tried to define a relevant product market in which [the franchisor and its competitor-purchaser] were the principal participants and in which the proposed merger would seem, therefore, to eliminate substantial competition. We are not unsympathetic to their concerns, but [a]lleged market definitions that ignore obvious substitute products and suppliers are invalid. [*citations omitted.*] Market distinctions based solely on "price/quality" have routinely been rejected as "unrealistic" and "economically meaningless," particularly if the differences "are actually a *spectrum* of price and quality differences." [*citation omitted.*]

First & First, Inc., Bus. Fran. Guide (CCH) at ¶ 9595. In *First & First, Inc.*, in which Mr. Donut franchisees sought to enjoin Mr. Donut's acquisition by Dunkin' Donuts, the court rejected plaintiffs' identification of a relevant market consisting of "low-cost highly specialized prepared food franchises," as well as their identification of a relevant market consisting of a "cluster" of donut and coffee products.[27] Similarly, in *Domed Stadium Hotel, Inc.*, in which a Holiday Inn franchisee claimed that the franchisor's acquisition and conversion of a downtown New Orleans hotel would be likely to adversely affect competition, the court rejected the plaintiff's identification of a relevant market consisting of Holiday Inn hotel rooms. 732 F.2d at 487-489.

Even if franchisees succeed in identifying the relevant market, evidence that "prices are set by the individual franchisees" and that "the number of independent decision makers who set prices will be the same" after the proposed merger may be sufficient to defeat a Section 7 Clayton Act claim. *See First & First, Inc.*, Bus. Fran. Guide (CCH) at ¶ 9595.

5. *Price Discrimination Under the Robinson-Patman Act.* The Robinson-Patman Act proscribes direct or indirect sales of commodities "of like grade and quality" to two different purchasers on the same level of distribution at different prices, "where the effect of the discrimination may be substantially to lessen competition or tend to create a monopoly in any line of commerce, or to injure, destroy, or prevent competition with any person who either grants or knowingly receives the benefit of such discrimination." 15 U.S.C.

---

[26] Although most Section 7 Clayton Act cases are brought by the Federal Trade Commission or the Antitrust Division of the Department of Justice, franchisees may have standing to sue insofar as they are competitors of the merging entities, or insofar as they are targets of the proposed merger. As competitors, franchisees' standing turns on whether they can demonstrate that the proposed merger will result in predatory pricing. *Cargill, Inc. v. Monfort of Colorado*, 479 U.S. 104 (1986). As targets, franchisees' standing turns on whether they can demonstrate that they will lose "one of the vital elements of competition—the power of independent decision-making as to price and output." *Consolidated Gold Fields PLC v. Newmont Mining Corp.*, 871 F.2d 252 (2d Cir. 1989).

[27] As to the attempted definition of a franchise product market, the court noted:

> ". . . there was no testimony concerning franchises which was sufficient to allow us to infer the existence of a franchise product market. There are, of course, differences in things such as working conditions and initial cash outlays, nevertheless, we feel that most people go into business to make money and would usually pick the type of franchise which gave them the best return for the money." Bus. Fran. Guide (CCH) at ¶ 9595.

§ 13.[28] Were a franchisor to sell the same items at different prices to two different franchisees (whether in the same chain or in two different franchise systems owned by the franchisor), or to the franchisee and a non-franchisee competitor of the franchisee, a claim for unlawful price discrimination might arise.

However, no claim arises where the franchisee pays a price set by the franchisor and the franchisor's competitor pays a price set independently of the franchisor. The "common seller" requirement for an unlawful price discrimination claim is not met where the franchisor sells to franchisees at one price, and its parent corporation sells to an intermediate distributor at another price, where the distributor then sells to the franchisees' competitors at prices set independently of the franchisor. *Carlock,* 719 F. Supp. at 843-845 (common seller requirement for Robinson-Patman discrimination claim not met).[29]

The requirement for two sales is not met, and therefore no Robinson-Patman liability arises, where the franchisor transfers or sells to its company-owned stores. These intercompany transfers or sales are not "sales" for purposes of Robinson-Patman liability. *O'Byrne v. Cheker Oil Co.,* 727 F.2d 159, 164-165 (7th Cir. 1984) (gasoline distributor's supplying of product to company-owned stations not "sale" for purpose of price discrimination claim as between its sales to independent gas stations). *See also Ames v. Texaco, Inc.,* 568 F. Supp. 1317, 1322 (W.D. Mich. 1983). Thus, franchisors may lawfully transfer goods to company-owned stores on terms more favorable than those offered to dealers or franchisees. This rule would also apply to sales to a wholly-owned subsidiary of the franchisor, such as a competing chain, where the parent and the subsidiary are a single economic unit and do not deal with each other at arms' length. *See Russ' Kwik Car Wash, Inc. v. Marathon Petroleum Co.,* 772 F.2d 214, 217-221 (6th Cir. 1985).

6. *Other Causes of Action.* A franchisee's claim for breach of an oral contract for territory exclusivity, separate from the written franchise agreement, was defeated by application of the statute of frauds and the franchise agreement's integration clause, which in turn triggered the parol evidence rule. *Western Chance #2,* 734 F. Supp. at 1536-1539; *Fickling,* Bus. Fran. Guide (CCH) at ¶ 9099. *Cf. Carlock,* 719 F. Supp. at 814-815 (franchise agreement's integration clause triggered parol evidence rule to bar claims based on prior oral understandings).[30]

---

[28] The elements of a Robinson-Patman price discrimination claim are: (1) one seller (2) who sold a given commodity in interstate commerce (3) to two different purchasers at two different prices, (4) where the commodities sold were of like grade and quality, and (5) the effect of the price differential may be substantially to lessen competition. *Carlock,* 710 F. Supp. at 844. The last element requires a showing of effect on competition generally, not merely on the competitors of the alleged discriminator. *Carlock,* 719 F. Supp. at 846. *Cf. Conoco Inc.,* 774 F.2d at 901-902 (two elements to Robinson-Patman price discrimination claim, price discrimination and resulting injury to competition, where price discrimination is "difference in price between items of like grade and quality" and resulting injury "primary line," "secondary line" or "tertiary line").

[29] In *Carlock,* the franchisees' unlawful price discrimination claim failed, in the alternative, because they failed to present any evidence of the particular prices paid by the franchisees or the non-franchisees. 719 F. Supp. at 845. Without such evidence, the court could not assess the franchisees' contention that the royalties, franchise fees and promotion fees they pay comprise a cost which must be calculated into the price. 719 F. Supp. at 846.

[30] Similarly, in *Carlock,* franchisees' claims of fraud arising from the franchisor's alleged representations concerning the intended method of distribution of product to franchisees and non-franchisees was defeated where the alleged representations contradicted express language in the franchise agreement. 719 F. Supp. at 832-834.

A franchisee's claim for tortious interference with existing or prospective contract rights, arising from the franchisor's licensing of a competitor to operate near the franchisee, was defeated on the reasoning that the franchisor's action was a legitimate competitive action, not wrongful conduct such as fraud, misrepresentation, intimidation, or coercion, where the franchisor did not direct the new distributor to take any specific action in competition with the franchisee, and because the franchisee failed to demonstrate the existence of a particular prospective contract right. *See C. Pappas Co.,* 610 F. Supp. at 668-669. The court noted that "where no breach of contract is shown, the law recognizes a more extensive privilege to interfere with business relations than where a breach appears." 610 F. Supp. at 669.

Claims against a franchisor for tortious interference with existing or prospective contract rights arising from the franchisor's mass distribution of prepackaged product to nonfranchisees failed where the franchisees did not show that the franchisor acted with the intent of causing damage to the franchisees. *Rosenberg,* 718 F. Supp. at 1158. Because the franchise agreement expressly permitted the franchisor to take such action, "as a matter of law," the franchisor acted with "justifiable cause." 718 F. Supp. at 1158. *See also Conoco Inc.,* 774 F.2d at 906-908 (notwithstanding franchisee's showing of prospective contract rights and franchisor's knowledge of such rights, franchisor's interfering action justified where motivated by legitimate competitive purpose without wrongful means).

Finally, a franchisee's claim for tortious interference with prospective business advantage, arising from the franchisor's placement of company stores within the franchisee's market area, failed where the franchisee failed to demonstrate that its loss in sales was caused by the company store rather than a competitor's store. *Eichman,* 880 F.2d at 168.

Encroachment by direct sales to a customer in the dealer's market was held not to constitute conduct which can be said to "change the competitive circumstances of the dealership agreement" proscribed by the Wisconsin Fair Dealership Act (Wis. Stat. § 135.03), because the dealership agreement expressly allowed the conduct. *Computronics, Inc.,* 600 F. Supp. at 813. Similarly, that statute did not proscribe the franchisor's establishment of a new franchise in the franchisee's market, where the franchise agreement did not grant the franchisee any exclusive rights, on the reasoning that compliance with the express terms of the franchise agreement could not constitute a violation of the statute. *Super Valu,* 431 N.W.2d at 724-725.

In *Carlock,* the court rejected the franchisees' claim that various actions by the franchisor, including mass distribution of product to nonfranchisees, violated the Washington Franchise Investment Protection Act (Wash. Rev. Code Ann. § 19.100.180) because none of the actions fell within the statutory proscriptions. 719 F. Supp. at 852-853.

Claims of violations of state "little FTC Acts" have not fared well in encroachment cases, either because of the reluctance of courts to consider competitive activities permitted by contract to be "unfair or deceptive" or because the statutes were not applicable to the activity in question. For example, in *Fickling,* the court dismissed the little FTC Act claim summarily, on the ground that "no breach of contract, and, therefore, implicitly no fraudulent, unfair, or deceptive act on defendant's part in the formulation or execution of the contracts" had been found. *Fickling,* Bus. Fran. Guide (CCH) at ¶ 9099. And in *Carlock,* the franchisees were unsuccessful on their Colorado little FTC Act claim arising from the alleged price discrimination for the same reason that they were unsuccessful on their Robinson-Patman Act claim. 719 F. Supp. at 848.[31]

---

[31] However, the franchisees survived summary judgment on their little FTC Act claim that the franchisor fraudulently concealed the quality of the product sold to the franchisees. 719 F. Supp. at 849-852.

D. Retaliatory Termination for Associational Activity.

Although a franchisor may not lawfully impede the organization and utilization of a franchisee association, franchisors do nevertheless interfere from time to time with the activities of franchisee associations; sometimes to the extent of terminating or threatening termination of participants in retaliation for their collective activities.

Retaliatory termination of franchisees is analogous to the landlord's retaliatory eviction of tenants or an employer's discharge of an employee for advising the government of violations of law ("whistle blowers"). Retaliatory eviction has been prohibited by case law and legislation as contrary to public policy. Retaliatory termination offends those same principles, and should be treated similarly. An examination of retaliatory eviction law will lay the groundwork for this analogy.[32]

1. *Retaliatory Eviction.* In landlord-tenant law, retaliatory eviction occurs where the landlord, while possessing a legal right to evict, is improperly motivated to do so by a desire to retaliate against the tenant. The leading case is *Edwards v. Habib*, 397 F. 2d 687 (D.C. Cir. 1968), *cert. denied,* 393 U.S. 1016 (1969). In *Edwards v. Habib*, the tenant claimed that the landlord was evicting him because he had reported housing code violations to the city code-enforcement agency. The court allowed the retaliatory eviction defense after carefully analyzing three theories supporting it:

(a) *First Amendment and State Action.* The court first considered the argument that to permit the eviction would amount to state interference with the tenant's right to petition the government for redress. State action would be found in the use of the courts to enforce the eviction. This argument relies upon *Shelly v. Kraemer,* 334 U.S. 1 (1948), where the Supreme Court refused to enforce a private covenant restricting the sale of property to whites only. After some discussion, the *Edwards* court eventually passed on this theory.

The state action theory was accepted in the unreported opinion of *Tarver v. G. & C. Constr. Corp.*, No. 64 C 2945 (S.D.N.Y. Nov. 9, 1964), and later in *Hosey v. Club Van Courtlandt,* 299 F. Supp. 501 (S.D.N.Y. 1969). However, it has been rejected in *Fallis v. Dunbar,* 386 F. Supp. 1117 (N.D. Ohio 1974).

(b) *First Amendment and Private Action.* The second argument advanced in *Edwards* was that no state action need be found because the right to petition the government is protected against private action, as well. This argument is based on *In re Quarles & Butler,* 158 U.S. 532 (1895), where the Supreme Court held that "[t]he right of a citizen informing of a violation of law . . . does not depend upon any of the Amendments to the Constitution, but arises out of the creation and establishment by the Constitution itself of a national government, paramount and supreme within its sphere of action." *Id.* at 536. The *Edwards* court also rejected this theory.

(c) *Housing Code and Public Policy.* The next argument offered was that to permit retaliatory evictions would frustrate the effectiveness of the Housing Code as a means of upgrading the quality of housing, and as such would be contrary to public policy. The court cited the "appalling condition and shortage of housing in [the area], the expense of

---

[32] California retaliatory eviction law embodies principles and policies underlying retaliatory eviction laws of other states. Many states have similar statutes. *See, e.g.,* Ariz. Rev. Stat. Ann. §33-1381 (1973); D.C Code Ann. § 45-2552 (1990); Ill. Ann. Stat. ch. 80, para. 71 (Smith-Hurd 1991); N.Y. Real Prop. Law § 223-b (McKinney 1991). Thus, in this paper, we generalize from California law for purposes of example, only.

moving, the inequality of bargaining power between tenant and landlord, and the social and economic importance of assuring at least minimum standards in housing conditions" in holding that retaliatory eviction could not be tolerated.

The court in *Hosey v. Club Van Courtlandt,* 299 F. Supp. 501 (S.D.N.Y. 1969), adopted the first argument advanced in *Edwards* (state action). A tenant alleged that he was evicted for his attempts to organize fellow tenants to complain to public officials about health and building code violations. The court held that to permit the eviction would impinge upon the tenant's right to petition the government for redress. *Hosey* is generally cited for two propositions: (1) A state court may be required by the First and Fourteenth Amendments to allow the defense of retaliatory eviction; and (2) If state law clearly precludes this defense, federal courts may be used to enjoin such evictions.

In *Hernandez v. Stabach,* 145 Cal. App. 3d 309 (1983), the tenants alleged that the landlord had evicted them in retaliation for their organizing activities. The landlord had rented to families knowing they would overcrowd the apartments. After the tenants had formed an association and asserted the right to repair and deduct, the landlord sought to evict them for overcrowding. The appeals court upheld an injunction against their eviction, stating that the evidence showed both an unlawful business practice and retaliation prohibited by state statute.

In *McQueen v. Druker,* 317 F. Supp. 1122 (D. Mass. 1970), *aff'd* 438 F. 2d 781 (1st Cir. 1981), tenant organizing was held to be protected First Amendment activity. However, this notion was rejected in *Mullarkey v. Borglum,* 323 F. Supp. 1218, 1226 (S.D.N.Y. 1970). Nevertheless, the *Mullarkey* court allowed the tenant to proceed on a claim that the landlord and others conspired to interfere with the tenant's exercise of her rights, in violation of 42 U.S.C. 1985(2).

California Civil Code Section 1942.5(c) also protects the tenant from retaliation because he or she has "lawfully and peaceably exercised any rights under the law." *See Ackley v. Maple Woodman Assocs.,* (Ohio Ct. C. P., Mar. 21, 1979) 47 U.S.L.W. 2647 (freedom of speech and association); *Rich v. Schwab,* 162 Cal. App. 3d 739, 744 (1984) (freedom of political expression); *Barela v. Superior Court,* 30 Cal. 3d 244 (1981) (reporting crime by landlord); *Kemp v. Schultz,* 121 Cal. App. 3d Supp. 13 (1981) (complaint by tenant about tenantability of property). If "any rights" is understood to mean any lawful activity of the tenant, than this statute approaches a "good cause" requirement for eviction.

The logical extension of the public policy embodied in California Civil Code section 1942.5 is that tenants are protected from arbitrary treatment and termination. The Unruh Civil Rights Act, Cal. Civ. Code §§ 51-52 provides that "[a]ll persons . . . are free and equal, and no matter what their race, color, religion, ancestry, or national origin are entitled to the full and equal accommodations . . . in all business establishments. . . ."

In *In re Cox,* 3 Cal. 3d 205, 216 (1970), the California Supreme Court held that this language was intended by the legislature "to prohibit all arbitrary discrimination by business establishments." The Unruh Act has been applied to those who are in the business of renting apartments or houses. *Swann v. Burkett,* 209 Cal. App. 2d 685 (1962).

In *M & D Props. v. Lopez,* 13 Clearinghouse Rev. 310 (L.A. Mun. Ct., Nov. 7, 1978, No. 241-584) the court held that the Unruh Act requires a private landlord to show "good cause" in order to evict. In this case, the landlord had offered no evidence of his reasons for eviction. The court said that it was incumbent upon the landlord to show why the tenant must be evicted, due to the landlord's superior knowledge and the tenant's inability to access the landlord's reasons. *See also Stoumen v. Reilly,* 37 Cal. 2d 713, 716 (1951) (businesses covered by the Unruh Act have "no right to exclude or eject a patron 'except for good cause,' and if [done] so without good cause [it] is liable in damages").

2. *Retaliatory Termination.* By analogy, the doctrine of retaliatory termination would apply when the franchisor, while possessing a legal right to terminate, is improperly motivated to do so by a desire to retaliate against the franchisee. No published case specifically addresses the issue of a franchisor terminating a franchisee in retaliation for lawful exercise of rights. However, a strong argument for prohibiting such retaliation may be made from principles underlying the retaliatory eviction cases examined above.

Nine states offer statutory protection of a franchisee's right to associate. *See* Part I.C., above. These statutes provide franchisees with the right to organize and associate, and forbid franchisors from interfering with that right. Additionally, the right of franchisees to associate may be found in the First Amendment. *McAlpine v. AAMCO Automatic Transmissions, Inc.,* 461 F. Supp. 1232 (E.D. Mich. 1978). The antitrust laws may offer additional protections. *NAACP v. Claiborne Hardware,* 458 U.S. 886 (1982); *Missouri v. National Organization for Women (NOW),* 620 F.2d 1301 (8th Cir. 1980).

McAlpine held that franchisee organizing was protected First Amendment activity. It follows that franchisees may be protected under the first theory considered in *Edwards v. Habib,* and the theory accepted in *Hosey v. Club Van Courtlandt,* that a tenant engaged in Constitutionally-protected activity may not be evicted by the landlord for that activity. Similarly, the franchisor's attempted use of the courts to enforce the termination of a franchisee in response to protected activities may be impermissible use of "state action" to inhibit First Amendment activity.

Those states that have passed statutes explicitly granting the right of franchisees to associate have expressed their intention to protect such activity. Those states also have addressed the issue of inequality of bargaining power between a franchisor and its franchisees by expressly prohibiting franchisors from interfering with franchisee organizations. If retaliatory terminations were to be allowed, the policies embodied in those statutes would be severely inhibited.

Franchisors are prohibited from interfering with the franchisee's exercise of their right to collectively petition the government. The combination of franchisees to engage in this activity is exempted from antitrust scrutiny by the *Noerr-Pennington* doctrine. *Eastern Railroad President's Conference v. Noerr Motor Freight,* 365 U.S. 127 (1961); *United Mine Workers of America v. Pennington,* 381 U.S. 657 (1965). To permit the termination of franchisees in retaliation for their organizing for lobbying purposes would impinge upon the franchisees' right to petition the government. As the court found in *Hosey v. Club Van Courtlandt,* to enforce the termination of a franchisee for its participation in protected First Amendment activity would amount to illicit state action in the denial of those rights.

3. *Good Faith.* The requirements of good faith and fair dealing also establish a basis for the preclusion of retaliatory termination. "Every contract or duty [governed by the Uniform Commercial Code] imposes an obligation of good faith in its performance or enforcement." Uniform Commercial Code § 1-203; *accord* Restatement (Second) of Contracts § 205. This covenant of good faith is implied in every contract, including franchise agreements. *See C. Pappas Co., Inc. v. E. & J. Gallo Winery,* 610 F.Supp. 662, 666.

The trend in federal court rulings is to imply a good faith standard where the franchise agreement is silent or ambiguous. *Rosenberg v. The Pillsbury Co.,* 718 F. Supp. 1146 (S.D.N.Y. 1989); *see* Part III.C.2, above. The National Conference of Commissioners on Uniform State Laws has attempted to codify this trend by recognizing in its proposed Uniform Franchise and Business Opportunities Act that "A franchise . . . imposes on the parties a duty of good faith in its performance and enforcement." Uniform Franchise and Business Opportunities Act § 201. The comment to the Uniform Act states that "the section is intended to prevent arbitrary, malicious, or abusive conduct, or conduct that deprives the other contracting party of the benefit of the bargain, and to preserve the justifiable expectations of the parties to a franchise. . . ." The application of this duty of good faith would be restricted where it might "add to or override substantive provisions of" the franchise agreement.

The Model Franchise Investment Act (published by the North American Securities Administrators Association, Inc.) also recognizes that the parties to a franchise agreement are obligated to act in good faith to one another. The Act defines good faith as meaning "honesty in fact and observance of reasonable standards of fair dealing in the franchise relationship," and enumerates "good cause" standards for purposes of franchise termination and nonrenewal. Model Franchise Investment Act (July 17, 1989 draft).

A good faith requirement has been found to stem from the franchise relationship itself. In *Larese v. Creamland Dairies, Inc.,* 767 F.2d 716 (10th Cir. 1985), franchisee Larese brought suit against its franchisor Creamland Dairies, alleging that Creamland had unreasonably withheld its consent to an assignment of the franchise by Larese. Creamland based its withholding of consent upon a provision in the franchise agreement stating that Larese could not assign the franchise "without the prior written consent of [Creamland], any such unauthorized assignment . . . being null and without effect." Citing the unique relationship between a franchisor and its franchisee, the court found that the franchisor-franchisee relationship "requires that the parties deal with each other in good faith and in a commercially reasonable manner."

The *Larese* court held that a franchisor must act reasonably when a franchisee has decided to remove itself from the relationship. In light of the franchisee's investment of time and money into the franchise, by which the franchisor has benefitted, the reasonableness requirement cannot be considered "an excessive infringement of the franchisor's rights."

The uniqueness of the relationship has led some courts to impose a duty upon franchisors not to act unreasonably or arbitrarily in terminating a franchise. For example, in *Atlantic Richfield v. Razumic,* 480 Pa. 336, A.2d 736, the court held that a franchisor cannot arbitrarily terminate the franchise relationship, defeating the franchisee's reasonable expectations, and violating the franchisor's obligations toward the franchisee.

> [A]n Arco dealer such as Razumic can justifiably expect that his time, effort, and other investments promoting the goodwill of Arco will not be destroyed as a result of Arco's arbitrary decision to terminate their franchise relationship. Consistent with these reasonable expectations, and Arco's obligation to deal with its franchisees in good faith and in a commercially reasonable manner, Arco cannot arbitrarily sever its franchise relationship with Razumic. A contrary conclusion would allow Arco to reap the benefits of its franchisees' efforts in promoting the goodwill of its name without regard for the franchisees' interests. *Id.* at 742 (footnote omitted).

Similarly, in *Arnott v. American Oil Co.,* 609 F.2d 873 (8th Cir. 1979), the court found that a "fiduciary duty" was inherent in the franchisor-franchisee relationship (although the *content* of the duty was defined in identical terms to the duty of good faith. Arnott, an American Oil dealer, brought suit against American Oil claiming, *inter alia,* breach of American Oil's fiduciary duty in the termination of Arnott's lease without good cause. Citing *Atlantic,* the *Arnott* court held that:

> A franchisee . . . builds the goodwill of his own business and the goodwill of the franchisor. [citation omitted]. This facet of the relationship has led to the recognition that the franchise relationship imposes a duty upon franchisors not to act arbitrarily in terminating the franchise.

The Eighth Circuit later retreated from its characterization of the duty as "fiduciary." *Bain v. Champlin Oil Co.,* 692 F.2d 48 (8th Cir. 1982).

Accordingly, the reasonable expectations of franchisees will constrain franchisor activity in termination decisions. For example, a franchisor may not terminate a franchisee for associating with other franchisees for legitimate purposes. Such association, protected under many state statutes, would not constitute good cause for termination because the franchisee may reasonably expect such behavior to be protected. Termination under those circumstances would defeat the franchisee's reasonable expectations of the franchisee, and therefore violate the principles set forth in *Razumic. See also* Restatement (Second) of Contracts § 205.

The character of the franchise relationship requires that the franchisor act in good faith and in a commercially reasonable manner before terminating a franchise. As we have seen, public policy and California state law militates toward a "good cause" requirement for evictions. In the franchise context, public policy is moving toward a similar requirement, in that arbitrary action is forbidden, and good faith and fair dealing is demanded of the franchisor.

While motivation is an issue in retaliatory evictions, some courts have taken a different approach in the retaliatory termination context. In *Dayan v. McDonald's Corp.,* Bus. Fran. Guide (CCH) ¶ 8223 (Ill. App. Ct. 1984), the court found that Illinois common law prohibited termination of a franchise agreement without good cause, due to an implied covenant of good faith. However, if the franchisor has good cause to terminate, it need not possess a proper motive, in sharp contrast to the California retaliatory eviction cases.

> Where the franchisee is in substantial breach of the franchising agreement, particularly where the nature of the breach logically affects the interest of the franchisor in marketing its product, no legitimate expectations of the franchisee are violated by termination, regardless of what other motives the franchisor might have.

Id. at 14,691.

Accordingly, the court held that the implied covenant of good faith only requires that the franchisor have good cause for termination. As we have seen, courts will examine motive in the retaliatory eviction context. According to *Dayan,* courts will not look to motivation in the franchise termination context where "good cause" exists.

The right of franchisees to organize and associate is well-grounded. Because such activity is legitimate, protection should be afforded from franchisors who seek to frustrate these franchisee activities through terminations. Such protection may be found in the retaliatory eviction paradigm.

AUTHORSHIP

Part	*Author*
Introduction, I.A., II.D., E.	Mr. Aaron
I.B., II.A., B., E.	Ms. Blair
I.D., II.C., III.B., C.	Mr. Selden
I.C., II.G., III.A., D.	Mr. Shapiro
I.B., II.A., B., E.	Mr. Silberman
II.F., III.C.	Ms. Trice

Mr. Selden and Ms. Trice edited the manuscripts.

Bibliography**

1. *The Importance of Franchise Class Actions,* H.E. Kohn, Antitrust Law Journal 47:915, 1978.

2. *Dealing with Franchisee Associations,* Donald A. Mackay, presented at Annual Forum (Fourth) on Franchising, American Bar Association Forum on Franchising, 1979.

3. *Franchise Trade Associations,* Mark H. Rodman, presented at Annual Forum (Second) on Franchising, American Bar Association Forum on Franchising, 1979.

4. *Franchisee Organizations—Their Creation, Operation, and Effect on Franchising Relations,* M.P. Gordon, presented at Annual Franchise Law Seminar (Fourth), University of Missouri-Kansas City Law Center and Kansas City Bar Association, 1982.

5. *Franchisee Organizations—Their Creation, Operation, and Effect on Franchise Relations . . . A Franchisor's Perspective,* S.B. Early, presented at Annual Franchise Law Seminar (Fourth), University of Missouri-Kansas City Law Center and Kansas City Bar Association, 1982.

6. *Franchisee Trade Associations Workshop Outline,* Timothy H. Fine and Gerald T. Aaron, presented at Annual Forum (Seventh) on Franchising, American Bar Association Forum on Franchising, 1984.

7. *Franchisee Associations: Legal Issues that Will Shape Their Future,* C.E. Zwisler, III, presented at International Franchise Association Eighteenth Annual Legal Symposium, Washington, D.C., 1985.

8. *Outline of Practical Considerations in Dealing with Franchise Associations,* Michael R. Davis, presented at International Franchise Association Eighteenth Annual Legal Symposium, Washington, D.C., 1985.

9. *The Dynamics of Franchisee Associations,* G.T. Aaron, A.K. Blair, A.C. Selden, M.S. Shapiro, A.H. Silberman, and M.B. Trice, presented at Annual Forum (Fourteenth) on Franchising, American Bar Association Forum on Franchising, 1991.

10. *Challenging the Standing of Franchise Associations in Litigation,* P.J. Klarfeld and C.E. Lanzon, Franchise Legal Digest 1:14, International Franchise Association, Washington, D.C., Winter/Spring 1992.

11. *Dealing With a Franchisee Association: Legal Issues and Practical Problems,* Rodney R. Hatter, Roger F. Thomson, and Gil Thurm, presented at Annual Forum (Sixteenth) on Franchising, American Bar Association Forum on Franchising, 1993.

12. *Standing Issues Related to Franchisee Associations,* William B. Steele, III and A. Darby Dickerson, Franchise Law Journal 12:99, Spring 1993.

13. *Actions by Franchisee Associations: Antitrust and Other Legal Complications for Franchisors and Franchisees,* Erik B. Wulff, Franchise Law Journal 13:37, Fall 1993.

14. *Representing and Dealing with Franchisee Associations,* Mitchell S. Shapiro and Carl E. Zwisler, presented at Annual Forum (Eighteenth) on Franchising, American Bar Association Forum on Franchising, 1995.

15. *Counseling Franchisees,* Rupert M. Barkoff and Andrew C. Selden, Fundamentals of Franchising (1997).

**Portions of this Bibliography have been excerpted from the American Bar Association's *Franchise Law Bibliography* (2d. Ed. 1993).

CHAPTER 6

Termination, Nonrenewal, and Transfer

Lisa Pender Morse and Ronald T. Coleman, Jr.

Contents

Introduction: The Importance of Establishing and Following an Organized Compliance Program

A franchisor's ability to enforce its contractual rights and policies with respect to its franchisees depends, for both legal and practical reasons, upon the development of reasonable standards and procedures and upon the consistent enforcement of those standards and procedures throughout the franchise system. Developing and consistently following such a compliance program is particularly important in the areas of termination, nonrenewal, and transfer. Decisions in these areas impact who will be presenting the franchisor's concept and image to the public and how it will be presented. Moreover, decisions regarding termination, nonrenewal, and transfer most fundamentally impact the rights and interests of franchisees, and so these decisions therefore constitute the most fertile ground for disputes and litigation.

This chapter will provide guidelines to assist a franchisor in developing and implementing procedures regarding termination, nonrenewal, and transfer that are (1) consistent with the defined business objectives of the franchisor; (2) fair and reasonable in the context of the franchisor/franchisee relationship; (3) consistently applied to all similarly situated franchisees; and (4) most likely to avoid litigation concerning the franchisor's decisions in these areas or, if litigation occurs, best position the franchisor to prevail in any such dispute.

The development and implementation of a compliance program involves three fundamental steps. First, the franchisor must determine what issues are most important with respect to its particular business and franchise system, and it then must establish its policies and procedures in accordance with and in furtherance of these particular business objectives. Second, the franchisor must communicate its policies, procedures, and standards clearly and regularly to its own personnel as well as to all of its franchisees so that there can be no reasonable dispute over what the particular policy is and whether the franchisee was aware of that policy. Finally, the franchisor must diligently monitor and apply its policies, procedures, and standards consistently throughout its franchise system, particularly to similarly situated franchisees.

The obvious goal of such a compliance program is to further the business objectives of the franchise system while avoiding wherever possible disputes and franchisee litigation. If a franchisor finds itself in litigation, however, a well developed and properly implemented compliance program can serve as both a sword and a shield to protect the franchisor's legitimate business interests. For example, reasonable and consistently applied procedures leading up to the termination of a franchise can be powerful evidence in an injunction action by a franchisor against a franchisee who contests or otherwise refuses to acknowledge that termination. Evidence that a franchisor consistently followed not only the black-letter contractual requirements but also its reasonable policies and procedures can help defeat a franchisee's claim for wrongful termination under most contractual or tort theories. The ultimate goal of establishing and consistently following a reasonable compliance program in these areas is to show that, regardless of the legal standard that might be applied, the franchisor acted fairly, reasonably, and consistent with the parties' legitimate contractual expectations.

This chapter is intended to provide practical guidance for franchisors to use in establishing or evaluating their own compliance programs in the areas of termination, nonrenewal, and transfer. It deals first with termination, which is probably the most fertile ground for problems and disputes because termination often results in a forfeiture of the franchisee's rights and interests. It then addresses nonrenewal and transfer, respectively. Within each of these subjects, the contractual framework of the parties' relationship, potential statutory restrictions on the franchisor's rights, and common law issues relevant to these situations are each addressed. Although case law and statutes are discussed for illustrative purposes, this chapter is not intended to be an exhaustive legal analysis of these issues. An Appendix follows that summarizes key provisions in each state franchise relationship law dealing with termination and nonrenewal. Following this Appendix are certain checklists and exhibits which should be helpful in illustrating many of the issues discussed in this paper.

Termination

How Potential Termination Situations Typically Arise

Although potential termination situations can arise from a variety of circumstances, they typically arise from a relatively few common fact patterns. A franchisor's compliance program should anticipate these common scenarios, but should be flexible enough to deal with them differently as the particular circumstances might warrant.

Financial Difficulties of the Franchisee

The most straightforward circumstance leading to a potential termination is where the franchisee is in financial difficulty and therefore cannot or does not pay the required royalties, fees, or other monetary obligations to the franchisor on a timely basis. Virtually all franchise agreements give the franchisor the right to terminate for failure to pay fees, though most agreements include a notice and cure period for this type of default.

Before immediately exercising its rights under the contract, a franchisor generally should try to understand the reason for the franchisee's poor financial condition because the proper response may well depend upon how the franchisee got into that unfortunate situation in the first place. The franchisor's options in this circumstance range from a systemwide response, such as a reduced royalty rate for a limited period, where the reasons for the franchisee's problems are systemwide or market driven; to an individualized workout arrangement with the particular problem franchisee, which might involve taking a note for past amounts due (often in exchange for a release by the franchisee of all claims) and establishing a stringent payment schedule; to the more direct response of sending a notice of default and then terminating if the franchisee does not cure within the required time. The proper response by the franchisor obviously will depend upon the circumstances in a particular case.

Disgruntled Franchisee

Another common problem leading to a potential termination is where a disgruntled franchisee simply refuses to pay the royalties, fees, or other amounts due to the franchisor. This situation might arise where a franchisee is upset with a particular decision by the franchisor and decides to retaliate by refusing to pay fees. The situation can also arise in the context of a breakaway franchisee—a franchisee which, having learned the franchisor's business, seeks to leave the franchisor's system and set up a competing business at the same or a nearby location.

The situation of a franchisee that is not unable but rather unwilling to pay the required fees presents a clear case for immediate action by the franchisor under the default and termination of the franchise agreement.

Operational Problems

Potential termination situations also can arise for a variety of operational problems. Perhaps most commonly, a particular franchisee might not be complying or achieving operational standards set by the franchisor, such as quality or cleanliness, required hours of operation, or use of approved product. It is in the area of enforcement of systems standards that a well developed and consistently implemented compliance program is vitally important and can be most valuable. Again in this context, the franchisor must be able to understand and evaluate the reasons for the particular operational problems of the franchisee. Was the franchisee unaware of the particular standard involved? Was the franchisee aware of the standard but had difficulty effectively implementing it? Or, was the franchisee aware of the standard and simply chose to ignore it? Determining the cause of the problem is necessary to determine the franchisor's appropriate response.

How to Evaluate Potential Termination Situations

Once a potential default or termination situation arises, an effective compliance program should provide for a designated representative of the franchisor to analyze the reasons for the problem and for the franchisee's noncompliance. The franchisee that has legitimately tried to meet its contractual requirements but for some reason has fallen short logically should be dealt with differently than the franchisee that simply refuses to comply with its contractual obligations. In the former situation, the franchisor likely will want to make reasonable efforts to assist or counsel the franchisee regarding how to address and remedy the problems, be they financial or operational. In the latter situation, however, it might be more appropriate to take a more stern approach, advising the franchisee of the particular deficiencies noted and warning the franchisee that its failure to correct these deficiencies will result in prompt termination.

Regardless of the course of action chosen by the franchisor, it is critical that the franchisor communicate the standards or requirements involved, the deficiencies noted in the franchisee's performance, and the specific steps necessary for the franchisee to take in order to become in compliance. For example, in the case of a franchisee's failure to meet required quality, service, or other operational standards, the franchisor's notice should specify the particular standards involved and deficiencies noted, possibly by attaching a copy of the inspection report and relevant sections from the operations manual describing how to achieve compliance. These communications should be documented in writing and given in the precise manner specified in the franchise agreement. Where permissible under the agreement, notice should be communicated in an easily verified method, such as by facsimile, certified mail, or overnight delivery service. The franchisor's efforts to consult with and/or counsel the franchisee also should be documented, in the form of memos or letters by the appropriate franchise support personnel which are also provided to the franchisee. The goal of all of this is, first, to provide appropriate and effective assistance and/or warning to the franchisee to correct any deficiencies and, second, to provide a clear "paper trail" of the franchisor's reasonable efforts in the event the franchisor has to defend a subsequent termination decision.

If the franchisor's efforts to assist or to warn the franchisee do not result in sufficient compliance, the next step likely will be to consider termination. This is where most of the hard work needs to be done in establishing and implementing an appropriate compliance program for termination decisions. Because this issue involves both business and legal considerations, appropriate franchisor management personnel as well as counsel for the franchisor (whether inside or outside) should be actively involved at this stage.

On the business side, the franchisor might consider establishing a particular individual or committee to review and approve default and termination decisions. Considerations by this person or committee might include the nature of the franchisee's noncompliance, the nature of the franchisor's response (either assistance or fair warning), and the nature of the franchisee's effort to address and/or cure its deficiencies. This analysis also might include the negotiation of reasonable performance criteria to be met by the franchisee, and the franchisee's performance against those criteria.

In certain situations, it might also be appropriate or beneficial to involve a franchisee representative or franchisee committee in the decision-making process or as an advocate for the franchise community. This procedure is particularly appropriate where the enforcement of system standards is involved, because a poorly run or noncomplying franchised unit can have a serious negative impact on the goodwill of the franchisor's concept and therefore on the franchise system generally, a situation which other franchisees obviously have a strong interest in avoiding. Moreover, the involvement of a franchisee representative in the enforcement effort at this stage of the process can be a helpful fact for the franchisor in case it has to enforce or defend against a termination decision in court.

In addition, the establishment of a person or committee to review all default and termination decisions should help ensure that the franchisor's policies, procedures, and standards are applied consistently throughout the system and that similarly situated franchisees are treated in a consistent manner. Consistent, nondiscriminatory treatment of franchisees is required by law in some states,[1] and it also may be considered as a factor in the application of the implied covenant of good faith and fair dealing.[2] In addition, it is an important intangible factor in most types of termination disputes for the franchisor to be able to show that it acted fairly with respect to the challenged conduct.

Once the franchisor has decided that it would like to terminate a particular franchisee, the legal aspects of the compliance program come into play. The first, and most obvious, place to start is with the default and termination provisions of the franchise agreement, but that certainly is not the end of the inquiry. The franchisor also must examine any applicable statutory restrictions on its termination rights imposed by state franchise relationship laws or industry-specific statutes. Moreover, the franchisor must examine the course of dealings with the particular franchisee to make sure that its contractual rights have not been modified in any way by the conduct of its agents. Finally, the franchisor must consider potential bases for legal claims by the franchisee that might arise out of termination. These issues are addressed individually below.

Contractual Bases for Termination of a Franchise Agreement

Once a potential termination situation has arisen, the franchisor should look first to the franchise agreement to identify all potential bases for default and termination under that agreement. Most franchise agreements have specific sections addressing the types of franchisee conduct that will constitute a default, thereby potentially entitling the franchisor to terminate. Some contractual grounds might entitle the franchisor to terminate immediately, without notice or opportunity to cure, but the majority of these bases require the franchisor to give notice and allow for a cure period. The franchisor, of course, should strictly comply with the relevant default and termination provisions of its own agreement to make sure it accomplishes a valid termination.

Examples of conduct which, under many franchise agreements, authorize the franchisor immediately to terminate a franchisee include

1. filing of bankruptcy or becoming insolvent;
2. appointment of a receiver of the franchisee's assets or property;
3. abandonment of the franchise or cessation of the franchised business;
4. suit to foreclose on any lien or mortgage against the premises or equipment of the franchisee;
5. if the franchisee is convicted of or pleads guilty to a felony;
6. purporting to transfer its rights or interest in the franchise to a third party without the franchisor's consent;
7. intentionally underreporting sales or maintaining false records; or
8. operation of the franchised business in such a manner as to pose an immediate threat or danger to public health or safety.

These grounds for termination usually are straightforward and apparent, and thus generally are subject to reasonably definite verification by the franchisor.

A wide variety of other conduct may constitute a default under the franchise agreement which, if not cured, would authorize termination. Such conduct typically includes breach of or failure to perform other material provisions of the franchise agreement, including: payment of royalties, fees, and other amounts owed to the franchisor; compliance with the franchisor's operational standards as set forth either in the agreement itself or in an accompanying operations manual; or compliance with related legal obligations such as the lease for the franchised premises or other applicable laws and regulations. Most franchise agreements require the franchisor to provide written notice of a default and to allow the franchisee a specified time (often 30 days) within which to cure the specified default.

In addition to the relevant franchise agreement provisions, the franchisor should review its manuals and policies relating to the particular default issue to make sure the language of the agreement has not been modified or interpreted in a manner inconsistent with the purported basis for the default. If the franchisor has arguably modified any of its contractual requirements by policy or practice, such modification should be cured before attempting to default and terminate a franchisee on such grounds.

A written notice of default is the mechanism by which the franchisor should communicate its position to the franchisee. It is important for the franchisor to identify in a default letter all defaults that it might intend to use later as a basis for termination.[3] As a precaution, the franchisor should include a "non-waiver" sentence in its default letter. At a minimum, a notice of default should identify with specificity the following items:

1. The particular franchise agreement involved (especially in the case of multiunit franchisees)
2. The particular contractual provision or other standard that has been breached
3. A description of the acts or omissions that the franchisor contends constitute a breach of the agreement
4. The specific actions the franchisee must take to cure the default(s)
5. The time within which the franchisee must cure the default(s)
6. The method by which the franchisor will determine whether the franchisee has adequately cured the default(s) (that is, actual receipt of funds owed, follow-up inspection for violation of operational standards, and so on)

A notice of default should be reviewed by counsel for the franchisor before it is sent to make sure that it complies with all contractual and other legal requirements. Many franchisors choose to send notices of default and termination out under counsel's signature. Sample notices of default and termination for different types of defaults are attached as Exhibits 6-A, 6-B, and 6-C.

Once a notice of default has been sent, the franchisor should act diligently in following up to determine whether the default has been cured, whether there is basis to terminate, or whether to consider a work-out arrangement. A franchisor risks waiving its right to terminate if it fails to act promptly and the franchisee subsequently cures the default, even if it does so after the expiration of the cure period. Even if the franchisee continues to be in default, the franchisor also risks losing its entitlement to injunctive relief if it fails to act promptly to enforce the termination.

Once the franchisor has decided to terminate the franchisee, the franchisor should consider whether a voluntary termination, accompanied by either a closing of the franchised unit or transfer of the business to the franchisor or another franchisee, can be accomplished. A voluntary or acknowledged termination has the obvious benefit of avoiding an acrimonious and potentially expensive legal dispute. It also can benefit the franchisor by assuring an orderly transition during which the unit continues to operate, thereby avoiding the potential loss of customer goodwill from a unit closed due to a dispute. If the franchisee refuses to acknowledge the termination immediately, the franchisor might consider negotiating certain concessions such as forgiving of past due royalties, agreeing to pay for de-identification of the premises, waiving of noncompete provisions, or allowing the franchisee a reasonable time to sell the unit in order to induce the franchisee to cooperate. A franchisor should always document such a voluntary or acknowledged termination, although the specific terms will vary according to the particular agreement reached. Samples of different types of voluntary termination agreements are attached as Exhibits 6-D and 6-E.

Cross-default situations may also arise upon the default or termination of certain franchises, depending on the language of the particular franchise agreement at issue. If the franchisee operates multiple units, the franchise agreement for each unit may provide that a default or termination with respect to one of the units gives the franchisor the right to call a default or to terminate the agreements for the other franchised units. In addition, the termination of a franchise agreement might constitute grounds for terminating a related development agreement, sublease, or other contract with the franchisor. A franchisor should consider whether to invoke such cross-default provisions where that right exists.

In certain situations, however, a franchisor may decide that a workout arrangement and reinstatement rather than a termination are desirable. The reasons for this alternative to termination are varied. For example, the franchisor may wish to avoid negative public relations, avoid costly litigation, or avoid potentially risky claims by the franchisee. A workout option can generally be offered to troubled franchisees in exchange for compromises on amounts owed, confidentiality agreements, and/or general or specific releases of the franchisor. The specific terms of any workout agreement will vary depending on the nature of the franchisee's problems, the particular concessions sought by the franchisee, and the return consideration sought by the franchisor. A sample of one type of workout agreement is attached as Exhibit 6-F.

Once the franchisor has executed a termination, the franchisor should make sure to follow through on all of the post-termination provisions contained in the franchise agreement. Two of the most important of these obligations are de-identification of the former franchised unit (assuming that the franchisor is not taking possession of the property under a sublease or assignment) and ensuring the return of all trade secret and proprietary materials provided to the former franchisee. Franchise agreements, as well as federal trademark laws, provide that the former franchisee is responsible for de-identifying the unit once the franchise agreement is terminated and the franchisee no longer has the right to use the franchisor's marks and systems. It may be in the franchisor's best interest, however, to take such steps itself, either by agreement of the franchisee or pursuant to court order, so that the public does not develop a negative impression due to a closed or poorly run location still bearing the franchisor's name.

Ensuring the return of all trade secret and proprietary materials is equally important. The franchisor should immediately demand return of the operations manual, all bulletins or other communications regarding the franchisor's system, and all other proprietary documents or materials bearing the franchisor's name and marks. This step is important both to make sure that the former franchisee does not continue to operate its unit using the franchisor's proprietary system and to preserve whatever trade secret and other proprietary rights the franchisor might have with respect to this information and material. The franchisor should consider legal action to enforce these post-termination rights if the franchisee refuses to comply.

A related issue which arises upon termination in many franchise systems is the enforceability of noncompetition provisions in franchise agreements. This issue is an entire topic unto itself, and is the subject of an excellent monograph, *Covenants Against Competition in Franchise Agreements,* published by the American Bar Association Forum on Franchising in 1992 containing a state-by-state analysis of statutory and case law on this issue. It suffices here to say that the franchisor should first consider whether it desires to enforce any noncompetition provisions against the terminated franchisee, or whether it is willing to use those rights to bargain for voluntary termination or some other agreement to avoid a legal battle over the termination. If the franchisor desires to enforce a noncompetition provision, the franchisor should consult its own counsel to determine the enforceability of the particular contractual language under applicable law. State law varies greatly on this issue, and what is enforceable in one jurisdiction might not be enforceable in another.

Statutory Restrictions on the Right to Terminate

Although the franchisor must have a basis under the franchise agreement for defaulting and terminating a franchisee, the existence of such a contractual right is not the only factor a franchisor must consider in making a termination decision. Eighteen states and the District of Columbia have franchise relationship statutes on general applicability which impose varying degrees of restrictions upon a franchisor's right to terminate.[4] Some of these statutes impose a "good cause" requirement for termination, while others mandate the amount of notice the franchisor must give before terminating. Counsel for the franchisor must consider the applicability of such statutes before termination can be implemented. A summary of the key provisions of these statutes relating to termination is contained in the Appendix to this chapter.

In the case of a franchisor and franchisee located in different states, the first question that arises is which state's law applies. Most franchise agreements have choice of law clauses which purport to apply the laws of the franchisor's home state to the parties' relationship. If the franchisee is located in a state having a relationship law, however, a court (particularly one sitting in the franchisee's home state) might decline to enforce the choice of law clause on the grounds that the franchise relationship law of the franchisee's home represents a significant public policy which cannot be overridden by contract. *See, e.g., Wright-Moore Corp. v. Ricoh Corp.,* 908 F.2d 128, Bus. Franchise Guide (CCH) ¶ 9665 (7th Cir. 1990); *Instructional Sys., Inc. v. Computer Curriculum Corp.,* 614 A.2d 124, Bus. Franchise Guide (CCH) ¶ 10, 119 (N.J. 1992). Franchisors, however, have been successful in enforcing choice of law clauses in some instances. *See, e.g., Modern Computer Sys., Inc. v. Modern Baking Sys., Inc.* 871 F.2d 734, Bus. Franchise

Guide (CCH) ¶ 9354 (8th Cir. 1989); *TeleSave Merchandising Co. v. Consumers Distrib. Co.,* 814 F.2d 1120, Bus. Franchise Guide (CCH) ¶ 8819 (6th Cir. 1987). Counsel for the franchisor should analyze the relevant case law applying any potentially applicable state relationship statutes before implementing a contemplated termination.

Once it has been determined that a particular relationship law applies, the franchisor must measure its grounds for termination against any requirements of the applicable statute. Many of these relationship statutes define what is required as "good cause" to terminate.[5] The definition of "good cause" under most of these statutes includes a franchisee's failure to comply with material obligations under the franchise agreement, though many require that the franchisee first be given notice and an opportunity to cure. Some of these statutes also allow termination in other circumstances such as bankruptcy of the franchisee, abandonment of the franchised premises, or conduct that impairs the goodwill of the franchisor's name or mark.

A few of these state relationship laws do not define good cause, which makes the franchisor's termination analysis more uncertain. It usually is the case, however, that a franchisee's breach of a material provision of the franchise agreement which remains uncured after reasonable notice will be deemed to constitute good cause even under these statutes. Counsel for the franchisor should carefully analyze decisions under these statutes before implementing a termination, however, to make sure that the franchisor's reasons are considered to be legitimate.

Finally, counsel for franchisor should check to make sure that there are no industry-specific statutes which might apply even if there is no relationship statute of general applicability. Among the industries that typically have specific statutes regulating the relationship between franchisors and franchisees or manufacturers and dealers are the automobile industry, the petroleum industry, the farm equipment industry, and the alcoholic beverage industry. Virtually all of these industry-specific statutes regulate the circumstances under which the franchisor or manufacturer may terminate a franchisee or dealer.

Has the Contract Been Modified?—Examination of the Parties' Course of Dealings and Subsequent Performance

It is not enough that for the franchisor to determine that it has an apparent contractual basis for termination. Although such a contractual basis is necessary, it might not be sufficient if the franchisee can establish that the contractual provision relied upon by the franchisor has been modified or waived through the parties' previous course of dealings. Even if the franchise agreement contains an integral clause, the parol evidence rule generally will not bar evidence of the parties' course of dealings where such evidence is offered to assist in the interpretation of contractual language deemed to be vague or ambiguous. *See, e.g., Ponderosa Sys., Inc. v. Brandt,* 767 F.2d 668, Bus. Franchise Guide (CCH) ¶ 8413 (10th Cir. 1985) (evidence of promotional material admitted because it was "necessary to an understanding of the contract"); *Bert G. Gianelli Distrib. Co. v. Beck*

& Co.; 219 Cal. Rptr. 203, Bus. Franchise Guide (CCH) ¶ 8457 (Cal. Ct. App. 1985) (even where writing intended as final expression of parties' agreement, terms may be explained or supplemented by evidence of course of dealing). A franchisor thus should include as part of its compliance program for terminations a thorough review by legal counsel of the relevant files relating to the franchisee sought to be terminated to make sure that no "land mines" exist that might defeat its apparent contractual rights. Some of the relevant issues to look for are discussed below.

Waiver and estoppel concerns are paramount in this analysis. The franchisor should make sure that it has engaged in no conduct or communications that could reasonably be construed as having waived strict compliance with the particular contractual provision being relied upon for the termination. For example, if the franchisor has repeatedly accepted late royalty payments from a particular franchisee, the franchisor may be deemed to have waived the franchisee's noncompliance with that provision, at least for the moment, and thus not be able to terminate the franchisee immediately for that reason. *See, e.g., Sheldon v. Munford, Inc.*, 950 F.2d 403, Bus. Franchise Guide (CCH ¶ 9923 (7th Cir. 1991) (franchisor that had regularly allowed franchisee to be in arrears on royalty payments not allowed to terminate franchise for late payment). This problem can also arise in the standards context where the franchisor has tolerated noncompliance with operational standards, such as quality or cleanliness standards or required hours of operation, for an extended period of time. *See, e.g., Terry v. International Dairy Queen, Inc.*, 554 F. Supp. 1088, Bus. Franchise Guide (CCH) ¶ 8865 (N.D. Ind. 1983) (waiver can be implied where franchisor knows of franchisee's failure to meet standards but takes no action).

Even where the franchisor finds itself in this unfortunate situation, the franchisor can take steps to restore its contractual rights. The best procedure for doing so is to send a firm, clear notice in writing to the franchisee indicating that the franchisor will no longer tolerate deviations from the contractually required procedures and will in the future insist upon strict compliance with the terms of the contract. This type of communication is sometimes referred to as a "new day" letter. *See, e.g., Huang v. Holiday Inns, Inc.*, 594 F. Supp. 352, Bus. Franchise Guide (CCH) ¶ 8252 (C.D. Cal. 1984) (holding that franchisor's termination of franchisee for violation of quality standards was fair and reasonable where prior to termination franchisor implemented a new evaluation program designed to identify quality deficiencies and communicated this new program to all franchisees). Of course, a franchisor that has tolerated noncompliance must give the franchisee a period of time that is reasonable under the circumstances within which to correct its deficiencies and become in compliance under the contract.

Counsel for the franchisor should also review the relevant documents to confirm that no representative or agent of the franchisor has made any specific representations to the franchisee that might contradict the basis for the franchisor's termination decision. For example, if the franchisor is basing its termination upon the franchisee's failure to carry a required menu item, counsel for the franchisor should make sure that none of its franchise support representatives has told the franchisee that it need not do so for some reason. The franchisor should also make sure that none of its representatives has made any representations that might reasonably have induced the franchisee to incur significant new investment in the franchise business shortly prior to the proposed termination. Such representations could lead to a defense or counterclaim for fraudulent misrepresentation or recoupment.

In addition to the issues of waiver and estoppel concerning the franchisee which is the subject of the termination, the franchisor's conduct with respect to similarly situated franchisees also should be analyzed. Some state relationship statutes impose a requirement of nondiscriminatory treatment of similarly situated franchisees.[6] Even where not required by statute, the franchisor should be prepared as a practical matter to defend a termination by showing that it has acted fairly and reasonably with respect to the terminated franchisee. Thus, the franchisor should be prepared to show that it has treated similarly situated franchisees in generally the same way, or it should demonstrate a very good reason why it has not done so in a particular situation.

Another relevant factor to analyze includes evidence of the custom and practice in the industry with respect to the conduct providing the basis for termination. Evidence of custom and practice may in some cases be relevant and admissible in litigation to support a party's interpretation of what a particular provision of the contract means. *See, e.g., Bert G. Gianelli Distrib. Co. v. Beck & Co., supra; accord* UCC § 2-202 (even terms of written contract intended as final expression of party's agreement with respect to such terms may be "explained or supplemented . . . a course of dealing or usage of trade").

Finally, in addition to looking for potential land mines, counsel's analysis of the course of dealings and relevant documents should be done with an eye toward documenting the basis and broader justification for the termination as extensively as possible in the event the franchisee challenges the termination decision. Identifying a strong paper trail showing warnings and efforts to assist the franchisee allows the franchisor's decision-makers to have a higher degree of confidence in the termination decision. It can also be used in explaining and/or negotiating issues with respect to the termination with the franchisee or its counsel. Finally, in the event of litigation, developing this paper trail will greatly assist the franchisor in proving or defending the propriety of its conduct.

Analyze All Potential Bases for Claims by the Franchisee

Because the termination of a franchise is a serious matter with long-term consequences, the franchisor should assume that the terminated franchisee will attempt to challenge or reverse this decision by asserting all available legal claims it might have (or can try to create) against the franchisor. A franchisor should analyze and evaluate such potential claims to the extent possible prior to sending a notice of termination. This should include both a factual review by the relevant business and operational personnel as well as an analysis of the legal bases for any potential claims by the franchisor's counsel. The strength of any such potential claims by the franchisee might dictate that the franchisor pursue an alternative course at that time, such as negotiated performance criteria or a workout arrangement. Some of the more commonly asserted franchisee claims are discussed below.

The terminated franchisee might attempt to challenge the franchisor's basis for the termination and assert a claim for beach of contract or applicable relationship statute. The franchisor's wrongful termination of a franchisee can provide a basis for a breach of contract claim seeking either injunctive relief or damages for loss of the franchised business. *See, e.g., Cooper Distrib. Co. v. Amana Refrigeration, Inc.,* 63 F.3d 262, Bus. Franchise Guide (CCH) ¶ 10,743 (3d Cir. 1995) (affirming judgment for wrongful termination under New Jersey Franchise Practices Act though reversing and remanding damages award). Confirming the contractual and, if applicable, statutory bases for a termination, however, should already have been addressed as part of the steps outlined above.

The franchisor should also evaluate potential claims based on the implied covenant of good faith and fair dealing, which is usually deemed to be part of every contract. The implied covenant generally applies where one party is vested with discretion in performing a particular right or obligation under the contract. The doctrine operates to prevent that party from exercising its discretion in bad faith, arbitrarily, or for an improper purpose so as not to defeat the other party's reasonable expectations under the contract. *See, e.g., Taylor Equip., Inc., v. John Deere Co.,* 98 F.3d 1028, Bus. Franchise Guide (CCH) ¶ 11,045 (8th Cir. 1996); *Original Great Am. Chocolate Chip Cookie Co. v. River Valley Cookies,* 970 F.2d 273, Bus. Franchise Guide (CCH) ¶ 10,042 (7th Cir. 1992); *Dayan v. McDonald's Corp.,* 466 N.E. 2d 958, Bus. Franchise Guide (CCH) ¶ 8223 (Ill. App. Ct. 1984).

As a general rule, however, the implied covenant cannot override or negate express contractual terms, so courts generally give full effect to contractual provisions setting forth grounds for termination. *See, e.g., Davis v. Sears, Roebuck & Co.,* 873 F.2d 888, Bus. Franchise Guide (CCH) ¶ 9384 (6th Cir. 1989) (implied covenant held not to override language in contract allowing either party to terminate upon specified notice); *Grand Light & Supply Co. v. Honeywell, Inc.,* 771 F.2d 672 (2d Cir. 1985) (same). Further, good cause for termination generally will defeat a claim for breach of the implied covenant based on the franchisor's allegedly improper motive in taking the challenged action. *See Robertson v. McDonald's Corp.,* 147 F.3d 1301, 1309 (11th Cir. 1998); *In re Sizzler Restaurants Int'l.,* Bus. Franchise Guide (CCH) ¶ 11,408 (Bankr. C.D. Cal. 1998). The doctrine of good faith and fair dealing has been applied to a broad array of franchisor conduct (such as encroachment, advertising, and provision of franchise support services), and the law in this area is constantly evolving. Counsel for the franchisor therefore should be careful to analyze how this doctrine might be used in any aspect of the franchise relationship that might be open to challenge by the franchisee.

In addition to contract-based issues, the franchisor should look for potential common law tort claims such as fraud or tortious interference with business relations. Particularly in the context of a short-term franchisee that has not performed well financially, counsel for the franchisor should pay careful attention to potential fraudulent inducement claims based on alleged presale misrepresentations. A claim for tortious interference may be anticipated where the franchisor intends to take for itself the territory or group of customers previously served by the terminated franchisee.

Potential federal or state antitrust claims also must be considered. Generally, a franchisor acting unilaterally can terminate a franchise without violating the antitrust laws, but a franchisor may incur liability by terminating a franchisee pursuant to an agreement with other franchisees who have complained about price-cutting by the terminated franchisee. *See generally Monsanto Co. v. Spray-Rite Serv. Corp.,* 465 U.S. 752, Bus. Franchise Guide (CCH) ¶ 8141 (1984). Claims based upon illegal "tying" arrangements, preferred supplier programs, and horizontal price fixing also are potentially applicable in the franchise context.[7] Counsel for the franchisor must not overlook potentially applicable state antitrust statutes, which may provide different or additional remedies to those available under federal law.

Further, while there is no private right of action under the Federal Trade Commission Act,[8] state "little FTC Acts" or deceptive trade practices acts must be considered. Some state little FTC Acts provide that any violation of the federal Act constitutes a violation of the state counterpart. *See, e.g., Rodopoulos v. Sam Piki Enters., Inc.,* 570 So.2d 661, Bus. Franchise Guide (CCH) ¶ 9741 (Ala. 1990). *But see Symes v. Bahama Joe's, Inc.,* Bus. Franchise Guide (CCH) ¶ 9192 (D. Mass. 1988). Many states also have enacted versions of the Uniform Deceptive Trade Practices Act, and some, like the Texas statute, have been broadly construed to cover a wide range of allegedly "unfair" business conduct. *See* Tex. Bus. Code Ann. § 17.01 et seq. (West 1987 & Supp. 1997). These statutes often provide for enhanced damages for willful violations.

If a legal dispute over the termination cannot be avoided, the franchisor should consider what alternative dispute resolution (ADR) methods may be required by the franchise agreement, or may otherwise be desirable to explore in the particular circumstances. The franchisor should first determine whether the agreement contains an ADR clause requiring mediation or binding arbitration of a particular dispute. Although arbitration can sometimes be a faster and less expensive way to resolve the dispute than court litigation, that is not always the case. Moreover, franchisees often seek to avoid arbitration provisions on the theory that a judicial forum (particularly involving a jury trial) will be a more favorable place to prosecute or defend their claims. Franchisors are usually successful in enforcing agreements to arbitrate, even where the franchisee has filed suit first. *See, e.g., Southland Corp. v. Keating,* 465 U.S. 1 (1984); *Seymour v. Gloria Jean's Coffee Bean Franchising Corp.,* 7332 F.Supp. 988 (D. Minn. 1990). In short, a franchisor generally can enforce a contractual arbitration or other ADR process if it so desires and has not waived its right to do so.

Even if the franchise agreement does not require arbitration or some other form of ADR, a franchisor facing a legal dispute with a franchisee should always consider whether voluntary submission to some form of ADR is appropriate. Mediation is the most common, and often the most productive, ADR process used in avoiding or resolving franchise disputes. Indeed, many franchisors are part of the national Franchise Mediation Program, whereby they have committed to mediate most disputes whenever requested by their franchisees. Mediation is by its nature nonbinding, and the parties maintain complete control over whether or not to agree to any particular form of resolution. Mediation usually has very little downside to a franchisor facing a legal claim by a disgruntled franchisee; thus, mediation or some other form of ADR should always be considered by a franchisor and its counsel where termination is likely to be disputed or lead to other claims by the franchisee.

In conclusion, the goal of a compliance program for termination decisions should be first to confirm the validity of the grounds for termination and then to put the franchisor in the best position to defend, if necessary, those grounds or any other claims the franchisee might raise. The analysis described above should be undertaken with an eye toward whether an objective third party would conclude that the franchisor has acted "fairly" or "reasonably" before implementing a termination, which essentially constitutes a forfeiture of the franchisee's rights. Although "fairness" or "reasonableness" might not be the stated legal standard, assuring to the greatest extent possible that the franchisor's conduct meets the "fairness" standard will help ensure that termination decisions will be sound from both a business and legal perspective.

Nonrenewal

Differences between Nonrenewal and Termination

Most franchise agreements are contracts for a fixed term running from a few years to as many as twenty or more years. Much can change during the term of a franchise agreement, with respect to the franchisor's system, the franchisee's performance, and market or competitive conditions. The decision whether and on what terms to renew a franchise agreement, therefore, involves many facets and requires careful business and legal analysis.

Nonrenewal differs from termination—upon nonrenewal, the relationship is ended at the conclusion of the term specified in the contract for which the parties bargained. Nonrenewal usually occurs pursuant to express contractual language that the franchisee does not have an automatic right to renewal of the agreement. Termination, on the other hand, involves ending the relationship prior to the end of the bargained-for contract term and thus evokes a forfeiture of the franchisee's contractual rights. Because most franchise agreements specify that the franchisee does not have an automatic right to renew, the renewal decision generally allows for the exercise of business discretion by the franchisor and can be used by the franchisor to update its system with respect to image, method of operation, and competitive circumstances. Assuming that neither the franchise agreement nor any applicable statute requires renewal, the franchisor has greater flexibility in deciding whether a particular franchisee should be granted another franchise term than it does in deciding whether to end a franchise relationship before the contractual term expires.

The franchisor should begin thinking about its renewal options with respect to its franchisees long before particular franchise agreements begin to expire. This planning process has both "macro" and "micro" elements. From a "macro," or systemwide, perspective, the franchisor can decide whether any global changes are appropriate for its agreements or system operation, such as changes in royalty fees or providing for alternative methods of product distribution. From a "micro," or particular franchisee, perspective, the franchisor should continually monitor each franchisee's performance throughout the term of the agreement and decide upon what requirements, such as facility upgrades or operational changes, must be met before the franchisor agrees to renew a particular franchisee.

As discussed above with respect to termination decisions, it is often good practice for the franchisor to establish a centralized person or committee to review and approve renewal decisions. The factors this person or group might consider would be more business-oriented, such as current demographic patterns, current competitive circumstances, long-term business strategies for the franchised system, the franchisee's past performance, and how the particular franchisee fits with the franchisor's future plans for its system. As with termination decisions, the franchisor should make sure that its policies, procedures, and standards are applied consistently throughout the system and that similarly situated franchisees are treated in a consistent manner.

Although termination and nonrenewal are different in many ways, once the franchisor has decided that it does not want to renew a particular franchisee, it is appropriate for the franchisor to follow many of the same steps as part of its compliance program before finalizing and acting upon its decision. The place to start is, again, with the franchise agreement to determine what rights and obligations exist with respect to the renewal decision. As with termination, there are also statutory restrictions on the franchisor's nonrenewal rights which must be considered and complied with, where applicable. Further, the franchisor must consider certain common law issues as well as potential legal claims by the franchisee. These issues are discussed below.

Contractual Framework

The most fundamental question in any renewal decision is what rights, if any, the franchisee has under the franchise agreement for an additional term. Most franchise agreements do not grant the franchisee an automatic right to renew, although some contracts might call for renewal provided the franchisee meets certain specified criteria (such as minimum purchase or sale objectives). If the franchise agreement grants a right to renew, either generally or under certain circumstances, the franchisor obviously will have to honor that right absent some material default or failure by the franchisee to meet the required conditions. Failure to do so would subject the franchisor to potential liability for breach of contract.

Most franchise agreements grant the franchisor broad discretion to make renewal decisions. Agreements often, however, have time frames within which such decisions must be communicated to the franchisee—for example, a certain number of months or years prior to the expiration date. Such a notice requirement allows the franchisee to take appropriate steps to plan for the expiration of the franchise and wind down the relationship; it also gives the franchisor time to evaluate the need for and find a replacement franchisee if appropriate. If a franchise agreement contains a notice requirement, the franchisor must notify the franchisee within the contractually required time, or at least as soon thereafter as any disqualifying event might occur. *See, e.g., Burger King Corp. v. Agad,* 941 F. Supp. 1217, Bus. Franchise Guide (CCH) ¶ 11,159 (N.D. Ga. 1996) (rejecting breach of contract claim by franchisee where the franchisor gave notice of nonrenewal after general contractual notification date but promptly upon disqualifying events by franchisee).

Assuming the franchise agreement grants the franchisor discretion to make the renewal decision, the question then arises: What, if any, limits apply to the exercise of that discretion? Where the contract specifically addresses the extent of the franchisor's discretion, courts generally will respect and enforce the terms of the party's bargain. For example, if the agreement provides that the franchisor shall decide upon renewal in its sole and absolute discretion, with or without cause, the franchisor generally should be able to decide not to renew for any reason, or at least for any rational business reason.[9] However, where the franchise agreement provides that consent to renewal by the franchisor cannot be "unreasonably withheld" (or similar qualifying language), the franchisor generally must have a stronger business reason not to renew the particular franchisee. A material default under the franchise agreement most likely would meet this standard, though business reasons solely outside the control of the franchisee might not.

Whenever a franchise agreement grants discretionary rights to a franchisor in a renewal situation, the implied covenant of good faith and fair dealing comes into play, and counsel for the franchisor must carefully analyze its applicability in a particular situation. As discussed above, the implied covenant applies where one party is vested with discretion in exercising a particular right under the contract, and the doctrine operates to prevent that party from exercising its discretion in bad faith, arbitrarily, or from improper purpose so as not to defeat the other party's reasonable expectations under the contract. This doctrine has been applied to impose liability on a franchisor for refusal to renew a franchisee. *See In re Vylene Enters., Inc.,* 90 F.3d 1472, Bus. Franchise Guide (CCH) ¶ 10,981 (9th Cir. 1996).

Some courts construe the implied covenant to require that the franchisor's exercise of discretion must be reasonable under the circumstances, which can be an amorphous and uncertain standard. *See, e.g., Carvel Corp. v. Baker, supra* n.9; *Dayan v. McDonald's Corp.,* 466 N.E.2d 958, Bus. Franchise Guide (CCH) ¶ 8223 (Ill. App. Ct. 1984). Certainly, the franchisor should not act in subjective bad faith or with an improper motive in exercising its discretion upon renewal, for to do so would be contrary to the franchisee's reasonable expectations under the contract. In all events, this doctrine is highly fact-specific, and counsel for the franchisor should analyze how it has been interpreted in any applicable jurisdictions before making the final renewal decision.

Finally, the franchisor should be aware and take advantage of any specific rights that the franchise agreement might provide in connection with the renewal process. Many franchise agreements allow for the franchisor to require a new form of agreement upon renewal, as well as other modifications from the prior relationship such as upgrades to the franchisee's physical facility. The franchisor might also consider imposing other requirements on a case-by-case basis, where appropriate, for valid business reasons, such as requiring additional training for marginal operators or relocation of the franchised premises to enhance competitive positioning, In addition, if possible, the franchisor should require as part of the renewal application the execution of a release by the franchisee or at least require the franchisee to list all known claims it might have against the franchisor as of that time. Assuming that renewal is at the franchisor's option, and not a matter of right, the franchisor should use this process as an opportunity to update the relationship and provide both parties with a fresh start for the new franchise term.

Statutory Restrictions on Nonrenewal

As with termination, the franchise agreement is not the only source of rights and duties with respect to the renewal of a franchise. State franchise relationship laws may require a particular form and timing of notice of nonrenewal, and some states go so far as to require good cause in order for the franchisee not to renew the relationship. As discussed in the section regarding termination, the question of which state's law will apply to a particular nonrenewal situation is an important, and often dispositive, issue which must be carefully analyzed by counsel for the franchisor.

Most state relationship laws impose only minimum notice requirements for nonrenewal.[10] The length of these notice periods ranges from 60 days to one year. The franchisor must be careful to deal with a nonrenewal franchisee on the same terms and conditions during this notice period or risk liability under contract and/or statute. *See American Bus. Interiors, Inc. v. Haworth, Inc.,* 798 F.2d 1135, Bus. Franchise Guide (CCH) ¶8642 (8th Cir. 1986) (Refusal to provide product and pricing information to franchisee during notice period held to be violation of Missouri relationship law).

At the other end of this spectrum are relationship laws that prohibit the franchisor from not renewing a franchisee absent "good cause." Most of these statutes define "good cause" to be conduct imputable solely to the franchisee, such as failure to comply with a material provision of the franchise agreement.[11] Counsel for the franchisor should also review case law under all potentially applicable statutes to analyze any judicial gloss placed on these general definitions of "good cause."

In addition to notice and good cause restrictions, some relationship statutes impose other conditions in the nonrenewal context. For example, some states require that the franchisor repurchase the franchise or its assets where there is a noncompetition provision.[12] Other statutes prohibit the enforcement of noncompetition provisions altogether, at least in certain circumstances.[13] These divergent restrictions underscore the importance of careful review by counsel for the franchisor in connection with any nonrenewal decision. The Appendix to this chapter contains a summary of the key renewal provisions of state relationship laws of general applicability to franchising.

Finally, industry-specific statutes also frequently contain restrictions on non-renewal. These statutes can be even more onerous than general franchise relation-ship laws because contracts in the affected industries are often for shorter terms, therefore creating a greater perceived risk of franchisor abuse. Such industry-specific statutes must also be analyzed by franchisor counsel for implementing a nonrenewal decision.

Additional Legal Considerations

A franchisor who has decided that it does not want to renew a franchisee must carefully scrutinize its franchise files and other evidence of past dealings with the franchisee to make sure that its contractual rights have not been waived or modi-fied through the franchisor's conduct or representations. The same type of review discussed earlier with respect to termination decisions should be conducted by counsel for the franchisor to make sure that no such "land mines" exist.

One significant risk is the possibility of waiver based on the franchisor's fail-ure to insist upon compliance with particular requirements until the time of the renewal decision. Similarly, another risk includes estoppel based upon affirma-tive representations or failure to take action by the franchisor with respect to par-ticular issues. Of course, the franchisor should be sure to treat similarly situated franchisees consistently. Failure to do so may subject the franchisor to liability by statute in some states or under the implied covenant of good faith and fair dealing in other jurisdictions.

Analyze All Bases for Potential Claims by the Franchisee

Nonrenewal of a franchise may, like termination, be perceived as taking away the franchisee's business and livelihood; therefore, it can result in a major dispute and possibly litigation. A franchisor should evaluate all potential claims by the nonrenewed franchisee, both factually and legally, before implementing the non-renewal decision. Understanding the strength of any potential claims by the fran-chisee is crucial to inform the negotiating process in the event that a dispute arises. If there is any realistic possibility of exposure, the franchisor can consider whether to negotiate issues such as a buyout, consent to transfer to another fran-chisee, or a waiver of enforcement of noncompetes in order to resolve the dispute and avoid litigation.

The potential claims by a nonrenewed franchisee are generally the same as those discussed earlier with respect to termination. An analysis of contractual and statutory rights and duties should already have been performed prior to reach-ing this point, and the implied covenant of good faith and fair dealing should also be a part of that analysis. Potential tort claims such as fraud and tortious interference with business relations should also be analyzed. Counsel for the franchisor should also evaluate potential claims under federal or state antitrust statutes, state Little FTC Acts, deceptive trade practices acts, federal or state RICO statutes, and any other potentially applicable federal or state statutes. Franchisors also should consider any mandatory or appropriate voluntary ADR processes as a way to avoid or resolve legal disputes relating to a nonrenewal decision.

Finally, counsel for the franchisor should be aware that some states recognize the common law concept of recoupment, which provides that a franchisee whose agreement is not being renewed must be allowed a reasonable period of time to run its business in order to recoup its investment. *See, e.g., Sofa Gallery, Inc. v. Stratford Co.,* 872 F.2d 259, Bus. Franchise Guide (CCH) ¶ 9366 (8th Cir. 1989); *Schultz v. Onan Corp.,* 737 F.2d 339, Bus. Franchise Guide (CCH) ¶ 8189 (3d Cir. 1984). Sufficient notice of nonrenewal should avoid this issue, particularly in the case of a long-term franchise agreement where the franchisor can argue that the franchisee has already recouped its investment and obtained the benefit of its bargain.

Finally, the goal of a compliance program for nonrenewal decisions should be the same as it is for terminations—to confirm the validity of the franchisor's grounds for nonrenewal and then to put the franchisor in the best position to defend those grounds or any other claims that might be raised by the franchisee. The nonrenewal analysis should also be conducted with an eye toward whether an objective third party would conclude that the franchisor has acted "fairly" or "reasonably" in reaching and implementing the nonrenewal decision. Meeting the "fairness" or "reasonableness" test will help ensure that the nonrenewal decision both is in the best interest of the franchisor's system and will be upheld against any potential challenge.

Transfer

Reasons for Transfer Requests

The legal parameters of the relationship between a franchisor and a franchisee are defined by the franchise agreement and applicable law. The franchisor's initial decision to sell a franchise to a particular franchisee, however, is based on numerous criteria such as the personal characteristics of the franchisee, the franchisee's particular business skills, and the franchisee's financial capabilities. At the inception of the franchise relationship, the franchisor and franchisee envision entering into a long-term contractual relationship with one another for the mutual benefit of both parties. However, many foreseeable and unforeseeable events can occur which make the possibility of a long-term contractual relationship no longer desirable or feasible. Some of these events are discussed in the preceding sections on termination and nonrenewal. This section addresses issues surrounding the proposed transfer of a franchise agreement.

Transfer by the Franchisor

Most franchise agreements provide that a franchisor may transfer or assign a franchise agreement without the franchisee's consent. The granting of such broad authority to the franchisor is reasonable considering that during the term of any given franchise agreement, a franchisor may go through transactions such as corporate restructuring, refinancing, recapitalization, merger, buy-out, and so on, which will not materially affect what the franchisee bargained for when entering into the franchise agreement. It would be unduly burdensome and impractical to require the franchisor in most situations to obtain each franchisee's consent. Therefore, to avoid delaying and/or jeopardizing the franchisor's corporate actions designed for the benefit of the entire system, the franchise agreements generally provide that the franchisor may freely transfer or assign the franchise agreement.[14]

Transfer by the Franchisee

Whether out of disillusionment with the system, inability to manage and/or operate the franchise, necessity, retirement, and so on, franchisees request transfers of their franchise agreements for numerous reasons. The following outlines some examples of situations which constitute a "transfer" under most franchise agreements as well as reasons why franchisees might request to transfer their franchise agreements.

Transfer for the Convenience of Ownership

Frequently, an individual enters into a franchise agreement and subsequently seeks to transfer ownership of the franchise to a corporation for reasons such as minimizing the individual's potential liability to third parties. The franchisor, on the other hand, may be concerned that the franchise may be transferred to a "shell" corporation and may require proof that the proposed corporation is adequately funded. Some franchisors also require the individual to guarantee performance by the corporate entity of the obligations under the franchise agreement, including payment of all amounts owed.

Transfer as a Work-Out Option

A financially or operationally troubled franchisee may view a transfer of the franchise agreement as a last chance to salvage part of its initial and ongoing investment in a particular franchise. This option is usually preferable for a franchisor as well because it allows a franchisor to transition out a troubled franchisee without having to terminate a franchise agreement and risk incurring potential litigation costs. Another advantage to the franchisor is that a transfer under this scenario usually provides for the uninterrupted transition of the franchise business. Additionally, a transfer of the franchise agreement usually allows the franchisee to "save face" in an otherwise likely termination scenario.

Transfer as an Early Exit Option

A franchisee may desire to exit a system before the expiration of the franchise agreement term. The reasons for the premature departure vary and include, but are not limited to, a franchisee's illness, retirement, career changes, and so on. A transfer of the franchise agreement allows a franchisee to avoid breaching the franchise agreement, and provides the franchisee the opportunity to recoup some of its investment in the system. The franchisor benefits by acquiring a more engaged business partner and avoiding the business interruption that would otherwise be experienced should the franchisee merely walk away from the franchise agreement and cease operation of the franchise.

Transfer Due to Changes in the Effective Control of a Corporate Franchisee

Any change in the effective control of a corporate franchisee due to the sale of assets, shares, etc. can result in a transfer situation. Some franchise agreements define a transfer as the sale or transfer of a certain percentage or more of the shares of the corporate franchisee.

Transfer as a Business Strategy

Occasionally, a franchisee has entered into a franchise agreement that, for whatever reason, just does not make good business sense. It might be that the franchisee was undercapitalized for an additional franchise, or that an additional franchise spread the franchisee over too many markets. The transfer of the franchise agreement can be a viable business strategy in these instances for both the franchisee and the franchisor.

Transfer Due to Death or Disability

Most franchise agreements provide that upon the death or disability of a franchisee, the executor, the administrator, or personal representative of the franchisee may request to transfer the franchise agreement. Such requests often are allowed, provided that the transferee is qualified to operate the franchise or undergoes appropriate training.

Transfer Due to Offering by Franchisee

Much like changes in effective control, a public or private offering of stock may result in a transfer situation. Some franchise agreements require that franchisee pay a non-refundable fee to the franchisor to defray the franchisor's costs and expenses associated with reviewing the proposed offering.

Transfer to a Family Member(s)

Often a franchisee seeks to transfer a franchise agreement to a family member for purposes of estate planning, inheritance, or otherwise. Generally, the franchisor will reserve the right to request that the family member be capable of performing the duties and obligations of the original franchisee.

Transfers Due to Offers by Third Parties

A franchisee who receives an offer to sell its interest in the franchise to a third party may seek to transfer the franchise agreement. Frequently, franchisors will include a "right of first refusal" provision, or at least a review and approval requirement, in the franchise agreement to address these situations.

Contractual Framework

Most franchise agreements include the following contractual provisions (or some variation) relating to transfer rights:

Personal Relationships

Most franchise agreements acknowledge that the initial decision of the franchisor to sell a franchise to the original franchisee was based upon the personal characteristics of the franchisee, including the franchisee's business skill and financial capabilities. For example, the agreement might provide that "Franchisee and Franchisee's Principals understand and acknowledge that the right and duties set forth in this Agreement are personal to Franchisee and that the [Franchisor] has granted this franchise in reliance on the business skill, financial capacity, and personal character of Franchisee and Franchisee' Principals," or that "Licensor intends to rely upon the personal leadership and financial commitment of the Licensee to the business of the Unit, and may require the Licensee to retain absolute control over the decisions relating thereto." This type of provision is important to show that the franchisor is entitled to, and in fact does, exercise discretion to ensure that only properly qualified persons or entities are allowed to become franchisees.

Transfers Defined

Most franchise agreements provide a very broad definition of what constitutes a transfer of the franchise. For example, consider the following agreement provision:

> *Assignment.* (a) Licensee shall not sublicense, sell, assign, transfer, convey or encumber its rights and obligations hereunder or suffer or permit any such assignment, transfer or encumbrance to occur by operation of law without the prior express written consent of Licensor. In the event Licensee is a corporation, limited partnership, business trust, partnership or similar association, the shareholder, limited partners, beneficiaries, partners or investors, as the case may be, may not sell, assign or otherwise transfer their shares or interests in such corporation, limited partnership, business trust, partnership or similar association, without the prior written consent of Licensor. Furthermore, in the event that any shareholder or partner of Licensee (the "Shareholder") is a corporation, limited partnership, business trust, partnership or similar association, the interests of the shareholders, limited partners, trustees, beneficiaries, partners or investors, as the case may be, in such Shareholder, may not be sold, assigned or otherwise transferred, without the prior written consent of Licensor. In the event Licensee (or a Shareholder) is a corporation, all stock certificates of Licensee or Shareholder, as the case may be, shall have conspicuously endorsed upon them a legend in substantially the following form:

> "A transfer of this stock is subject to the terms and conditions of [Franchisor's] License Agreement dated the _____ day of _____, 19____."

Provisions addressing death and disability, third party offers, and so on, are usually set forth in separate provisions in the transfer section of a franchise agreement. Of course, such contractual definitions of a transfer also could be subject to the definition of and other restrictions imposed upon transfer by applicable state franchise relationship laws.

Transfer Subject to Franchisor's Prior Written Consent

One would be hard pressed to find a franchise agreement that does not provide that all transfers are subject to the franchisor's prior written consent. In fact, most franchise agreements provide that a transfer without the prior written consent of the franchisor is both invalid and grounds for the default or the immediate termination of the franchise agreement, using language such as: "[a]ny purported assignment or transfer, by operation of law or otherwise, not having the written consent of Franchisor, shall be null and void, and shall constitute a material breach of this Agreement, for which Franchisor may then terminate without opportunity to cure. . . ."

Most franchise agreements grant broad discretion to the franchisor to approve or refuse its consent to a transfer request. This broad discretion sometimes runs afoul of the statutory and common law restrictions on the franchisor's discretion to approve or disapprove a transfer. Further, some franchise agreements provide that the franchisor will not unreasonably withhold its consent to a transfer, which can also effectively limit the bases on which a franchisor can refuse a transfer request.

Some franchise agreements go even further and do not permit any assignment or transfer of the franchise agreement. Consider, for example, the following provision: "[t]he Unit Operator may not assign this Agreement to any person or entity, and the Unit Operator further may not assign his estate or interest in or sublet the Sites, or mortgage, pledge or otherwise encumber his interest in this Agreement or the Sites." These restrictions are also subject to applicable state relationship laws.

Conditions for Consent

Franchise agreements generally include the terms and conditions that must be met as a condition for franchisor's approval of a transfer. These terms and conditions serve to protect the franchisor's rights and interests by fully and finally concluding the relationship with its existing franchisee and setting the most appropriate terms for the relationship with its new franchisee. Some of the terms and conditions that might be required by the franchisor are set forth below.

1. The franchisee must be current on all accrued monetary obligations owed to the franchisor.
2. The transferee must execute the franchisor's then current form of franchise agreement, the term of which may expire on the date of the original franchise agreement or may include a new term.
3. The transferee must meet the franchisor's then current criteria for new franchisees, including capital and liquidity requirements.
4. The franchisee must agree to remain bound by the post-termination covenants of the franchise agreement.
5. The franchisee must sign a general release of the franchisor.

6. The transferee must agree to conduct facility upgrades, reimage require-
    ments, and/or renovations.
7. The transferee must complete the required training then in effect for
    new franchises and pay the training fee or other payment to reimburse
    the franchisor for its reasonable costs and fees associated with reviewing
    the request to transfer, including, but not limited to, legal and account-
    ing fees.
8. The franchisee must pay a transfer fee to the franchisor.
9. The transferee must be of good moral character and reputation and must
    have a business background satisfactory to the franchisor, including but
    not limited to a good credit rating.
10. The transferee must assume all the obligations of the franchisee under
    the franchise agreement.
11. The franchisor may require that the franchisee execute a written guar-
    antee of the transferee's obligations under the franchise agreement, which
    may be for the life of the franchise agreement or for a limited period of
    time.
12. The franchisee must not be in default of any of the material terms and
    conditions of the franchise agreement.

The franchisor should consider requiring that a franchisee seeking to transfer
the franchise agreement enter into some sort of formal agreement that contains the
terms and conditions that must be met to obtain the franchisor's approval. A sample Transfer and Release Agreement is attached as Exhibit G. These terms and conditions also are subject to the provisions of any applicable state relationship laws.

Miscellaneous Provisions

Some franchise agreements also include the following miscellaneous provisions
that address specific issues relating to transfers.

Non-Waiver   In order to avoid claims that the franchisor has granted its approval
of a transfer by accepting payment of royalty or other fees from the proposed transferee, some franchise agreements include express non-waiver provisions, such as:
"[a]cceptance by Franchisor of any royalty fee, advertising fee or any other amount
accruing hereunder from any third party, including, but not limited to, any proposed transferee, shall not constitute franchisor's approval of such party as a
transferee or the transfer of this Franchise Agreement to such party."

Right of First Refusal   Many franchise agreements provide that before a franchisee may accept a bona fide offer from a third party to purchase the franchisee's
interest in the franchise agreement, the franchisee must provide the franchisor with
a right of first refusal. For example, one franchisor's agreement provides as follows:

> *Right of First Refusal.* If Franchisee or any owner of an interest in Franchisee receives
> and desires to accept any bona fide offer to Transfer all or any part of his, her, or its
> Interest in this Agreement or in Franchisee, and the intended Transfer is not a gift to

a spouse or a direct descendant, Franchisee or the proposed transferor will submit to [franchisor] an executed copy of the agreement for Transfer (which will be conditioned on this right of first refusal). [Franchisor] may, within 30 days after receipt of a signed copy of the agreement and all necessary supporting documentation (including financial statements), send written notice to the transferor that [franchisor] (or a person designated by [franchisor]) intends to purchase the Interest which is proposed to be Transferred on the same terms and conditions (or, at [franchisor]'s election, the reasonable case equivalent, not including the value of any tax benefits, of any non-cash consideration) offered by the third party. Any material change in the terms of an agreement before closing will constitute a new agreement, subject to the same right of first refusal by [franchisor] (or its designee) as in the case of the initial agreement. [Franchisor]'s failure to exercise its right of first refusal will not constitute a waiver of any other provision of this Agreement, including any of the requirements of this Section 14 with respect to approval of the proposed transferee.

Deal Terms between Franchisee and Proposed Transferee Subject to Franchisor's Approval   In order to assure that a proposed transferee is not undercapitalized or otherwise financially disadvantaged at the outset, a franchise agreement may provide that the terms and conditions of the deal between the franchisee and the proposed transferee are subject to the franchisor's approval. For example, as a prerequisite to transfer, one franchisor's agreement provides as follows:

> We must not have disapproved the material terms and conditions of such transfer (including the price and terms of payment and the amount to be financed by the transferee in connection with such transfer, which shall not in any event exceed 75 percent of the purchase price of the assets or stock to be transferred) on the basis that they are so burdensome as to be likely, in our judgment, to adversely affect the transferee's operation of your [unit] or its compliance with its franchise agreements, any area development agreements and any other agreements being transferred.

Death or Disability of the Franchisee   The unfortunate death or disability of franchisee presents a unique transfer situation. Frequently, the death or disability of the franchisee is sudden and/or unexpected, thereby complicating the transfer dynamics. A franchise agreement ordinarily will provide a specified period of time within which the executor, administrator, or personal representative of the franchisee must transfer the franchisee's interest in the franchise agreement. Some franchise agreements provide that if the proposed transfer is to a descendent, heir, or legatee of the franchisee, the proposed transferee must be capable of performing the duties and obligations of the franchise agreement. In some instances, the franchise agreement will provide for the uninterrupted operation of the unit, such as the following:

> Until such transfer has been consummated in accordance with the provisions of this *Article XII,* Franchisor shall have the right, but not the obligation, to assume direct management control of the Restaurant on an interim basis, including, without limitation, installing representatives of Franchisor, at Franchisee's expense.

Statutory Restrictions on the Franchisor's Right to Approve or Disapprove a Transfer

Many of the same state relationship laws which impose restrictions on the franchisor's rights regarding termination and nonrenewal also impose certain limitations on the franchisor's right to approve or disapprove a transfer request. Ten states and the District of Columbia have included such restrictions on the franchisor's transfer rights in their franchise relationship statutes.[15] These statutes contain a variety of different provisions which a franchisor must comply with in processing a transfer request, ranging from the requirement of "good cause" for disapproval to merely requiring written notice of approval or disapproval within a specified period. As with termination and nonrenewal, counsel for the franchisor must be fully familiar with the requirements of these statutes and evaluate their applicability as part of its compliance program regarding transfers.

Two states, Hawaii and Michigan, contain explicit provisions prohibiting a franchisor from refusing to permit a transfer of ownership of a franchise except for good cause. Both of these statutes define good cause to include

1. Failure of a proposed transferee to meet any of the franchisor's reasonable qualifications or standards then in effect for franchisees;
2. The fact that a proposed transferee or affiliate is a competitor of the franchisor;
3. The unwillingness of the proposed transferee to agree in writing to comply with all lawful obligations imposed by the franchise; and
4. Failure of the transferor franchisee or proposed transferee to pay all sums owing to the franchisor and to cure any default under the franchise agreement or other agreements with the franchisor existing at the time of the proposed transfer.[16]

Both of these statutes provide that good cause is not limited to these factors, though a franchisor would put itself at significant risk in these states by rejecting a proposed transferee under circumstances where none of the statutory factors apply.

While they do not contain the words "good cause," the relationship laws of the District of Columbia, Minnesota, and Washington reach substantially the same result by requiring that the franchisor shall not "unreasonably withhold consent" to any transfer where the proposed transferee meets the current qualifications and standards required by the franchisor of its other franchisees. This more nebulous standard is subject to greater interpretation, and is somewhat analogous to the general commercial reasonableness standard applied by some courts to claims based on the implied covenant of good faith and fair dealing.[17] Some courts have construed the term "unreasonably" to require a legitimate business reason before the franchisor can disapprove a transfer. *Compare Town & Country Ford, Inc. v. For Motor Co.,* Bus. Franchise Guide (CCH) ¶ 8660 (N.D. Ga. June 7, 1985) (construing contract provision containing such language and holding that legitimate business reason existed where proposed transferee lacked requisite skills, experience, and financial resources), *aff'd mem.,* 800 F.2d 266 (11th Cir. 1986), *with Richter v. Dairy Queen,* 643 P.2d 508, Bus. Franchise Guide (CCH) ¶ 7809 (Ariz. Ct. App. 1982) (holding that franchisor's refusal to approve transfer was unreasonable where proposed transferees were experienced business persons qualified to operate franchise). Thus, as a practical matter, under these statutes a franchisor should have strong business reason, similar to the good cause factors referenced above, to support disapproval of a transfer request.

Further, the relationship statutes in California, Indiana, and Iowa expressly provide that the surviving spouse or heirs of a franchisee (or sometime the majority shareholder of the franchisee) must be allowed to continue operating the franchise for a reasonable time after the death of the franchisee, provided that the acquiring party meets the franchisor's then-current standards.

The relationship laws of Arkansas, Nebraska, and New Jersey are perhaps the least restrictive. These statutes require the franchisor to respond to a written request for a transfer within 60 days, and if not, approval is deemed granted. If the franchisor rejects the proposed transfer, the franchisor must state in writing the material reasons relating to the character, financial ability, or business experience of the proposed transferee that form the basis for the denial.

Finally, it should be noted that the Iowa statute is by far the most detailed and restrictive statute of any state. It incorporates to some degree each of the restrictions discussed above, including that the franchisor must approve a transferee which satisfies the reasonable current qualifications of the franchisor for its new franchisees. These qualifications must be based upon legitimate business reasons. The Iowa statute also includes a written notice requirement, an express nondiscrimination provision, and a limitation on enforcement of restrictive covenants. Significantly, the Iowa law defines a transfer as *not* including, among other things, succession of ownership upon death of a franchisee, incorporation of a franchisee, public offering or transfer to an employee stock ownership plan of less than a fifty percent (50 percent) interest in the franchise, and the granting of a security interest in the franchised business or assets under certain circumstances. Franchisors dealing with Iowa-based franchisees obviously must carefully review the provisions of this statute in evaluating any transfer request.

Common Law Restrictions on a Franchisor's Approval or Disapproval of a Transfer Request

Even in the absence of statutory restrictions, a franchisor must be aware of potential common law limitations on its discretion to approve or disapprove a transfer request. Where the franchise agreement requires that the franchisor must not unreasonably withhold its consent, the franchisor generally must have a legitimate business reason to disapprove a transfer. Courts have held the following to constitute legitimate business reasons to disapprove a proposed transferee.

1. Lack of business experience, *see Town & Country Ford, Inc. v. Ford Motor Co.,* Bus. Franchise Guide (CCH) ¶ 8660 (N.D. Ga. June 7, 1985)
2. Lack of adequate capitalization, *see Town & Country Ford, Inc., supra; In re Pioneer Ford Sales, Inc.,* 729 F.2d 27, Bus. Franchise Guide (CCH) ¶ 8132 (1st Cir. 1984)
3. Too many existing franchise locations to service adequately the prospective new location, *see Carter Equip. Co. v. John Deere Indus. Equip. Co.,* 681 F.2d 386, Bus. Franchise Guide (CCH) ¶ 7859 (5th Cir. 1982)

4. Poor performance by the prospective transferee in the same or similar business, *see In re Pioneer Ford Sales, Inc., supra; Philadelphia Fast Foods, Inc. v. Popeye's Famous Fried Chicken, Inc.,* 647 F. Supp. 216, Bus. Franchise Guide (CCH) ¶ 8584 (E.D. Pa. 1986)

5. Sale by the proposed transferee of a competitive product or service, *see Hawkins v. Holiday Inns, Inc.,* 634 F.2d 342, Bus. Franchise Guide (CCH) ¶ 7568 (6th Cir. 1980); *Rickel v. Schwinn Bicycle Co.,* 192 Cal. Rptr. 732, Bus. Franchise Guide (CCH) ¶ 8035 (Cal. Ct. App. 1983)

6. A proposed transferee's criminal record, *see Carrozza v. Webber Chevrolet Co.,* 1978-1 Trade Cases (CCH) ¶ 61,982 (D.R.I. 1978)

The implied covenant of good faith and fair dealing may also apply to restrict a franchisor's discretion in disapproving a proposed transfer. For example, in *Larese v. Creamland Dairies, Inc.,* 767 F.2d 716, Bus. Franchise Guide (CCH) ¶ 8398 (10th Cir. 1985), the court interpreted a provision in the franchise agreement requiring prior written consent of the area franchisor to mean that the franchisor may not withhold its consent unreasonably. *See also Davis v. Sears, Roebuck & Co.,* 873 F.2d 888, Bus. Franchise Guide (CCH) ¶ 9384 (6th Cir. 1989) (although Sears could refuse transfer where transferee failed to meet then existing standards, right to approve transfer must be exercised in good faith and Sears could not "feign dissatisfaction" to deprive plaintiff of best price for his business). As a practical matter, the existence of one or more legitimate business reasons listed above should be sufficient to support the reasonableness of a franchisor's decision to deny a proposed transfer.

Franchisees sometimes also attempt to assert claims for tortious interference with actual or prospective contractual relations in response to a franchisor's disapproval of a prospective transferee. These claims usually are unsuccessful, however, because to be unlawful the interference must be by "improper means," and the franchisor generally has a legal privilege to act to protect its own business interests. *See generally* Restatement (Second) of Torts § 766B; *James v. Whirlpool Corp.,* 806 F. Supp. 835 (E.D. Mo. 1992); *Town & Country Ford, Inc., supra.* Courts also have rejected tortious interference claims on the theory that, because the franchisor had the contractual right to approve any transfer request, the franchisor could not have been a "stranger" or third party to the actual or prospective contract between the franchisee and the proposed transferee. *See, e.g., Hall v. Burger King Corp.,* 912 F. Supp. 1509, Bus. Franchise Guide (CCH) ¶ 10,799 (S.D. Fla. 1995). Thus, if the franchisor has a legitimate business justification for disapproving the requested transfer, a tortious interference claim generally should not be successful.

Further, courts have generally held that a proposed transferee does *not* have standing to challenge a franchisor's refusal to approve a proposed transfer. *See, e.g., Superlease Rent-A-Car, Inc. v. Budget Rent-A-Car, Inc.,* Bus. Franchise Guide (CCH) ¶ 9368 (D.D.C. Apr. 13, 1989); *Genet Co. v. Anheuser-Busch, Inc.,* 498 So. 2d 683, Bus. Franchise Guide (CCH) ¶ 8778 (Fla. Dist. Ct. App. 1986). *But see Don Roses Oil Co. v. Lindsley,* 206 Cal. Rptr. 670, Bus. Franchise Guide (CCH) ¶ 8253 (Cal. Ct. App. 1984).

Finally, franchisors should take heart that, absent a contrary relationship statute, courts generally uphold reasonable contractual conditions and requirements relating to approval of transfers. For example, courts have upheld contractual provisions stating that the franchisor may withhold its consent to a transfer with or without cause. *See, e.g., C. Pappas Co. v. E&J Gallo Winery,* 610 F. Supp. 662, Bus. Franchise Guide (CCH) ¶ 8378 (C.D. Cal 1985), *aff'd,* 801 F.2d 399 (9th Cir. 1986). In addition, a franchisor may generally require the transferring franchisee to execute a general release of the franchisor as a condition to approval of the transfer. *See, e.g., Brock v. Entre Computer Ctrs., Inc.,* 933 F.2d 1253, Bus. Franchise Guide (CCH) ¶ 9831 (4th Cir. 1991). Where a relationship law might restrict the ability to require such a release, the franchisor should make sure that it does not release the transferring franchisee as part of approving the transaction. A franchisor also generally will be allowed to require the transferee to execute a new agreement in the franchisor's then current form, although some state relationship laws also may contain restrictions on this contractual right as well. Where it is not prohibited from doing so, a franchisor should take advantage of these and other reasonable terms and conditions in order to update and upgrade their franchise systems in connection with approving transfer requests.

Conclusion

Termination, nonrenewal, and transfer decisions often give rise to disputes and litigation within franchise systems. Where properly monitored and consistently enforced, policies and procedures addressing such issues will help minimize the risk of liability. To develop a solid compliance program, franchisors must identify their business objectives and establish policies and procedures accordingly; effectively communicate those policies and procedures throughout the system; and, finally, consistently monitor and enforce those standards throughout the franchise system. While it is important to remember that no system is immune to problems stemming from terminations, nonrenewals, and transfer decisions, franchisors who have developed a sound compliance program will reduce the risk of disputes and will be more likely to prevail in the event of litigation.

Notes

1. *See, e.g.,* Haw. Rev. Stat. § 482E-6(2)(C) (1993); Ind. Code Ann. § 23-2-2.7-2(5) (Michie 1985); Wash. Rev. Code Ann. 19.100.180(2)(c) (West Supp. 1997).

2. *See, e.g., Fiore v. McDonald's Corp.,* Bus. Franchise Guide (CCH) ¶ 10,876 (E.D.N.Y. Feb. 23, 1996) (denying motion to dismiss implied covenant claim where franchisee alleged that franchisor targeted franchisee's restaurants for repeated inspections).

3. Failure to list all alleged breaches in the notice letter might preclude the franchisor from later relying upon other reasons not set forth therein. *See, e.g., ABA Distribs., Inc. v. Adolph Coors Co.,* 542 F. Supp. 1272, Bus. Franchise Guide (CCH) ¶ 7872 (W.D. Mo. 1982).

4. These statutes are as follows: Ark. Code Ann. §§ 4-72-201 to 4-72-210 (Michie 1996); Cal. Bus. & Prof. Code §§ 20000 to 20043 (West 1997); Conn. Gen. Stat. Ann. §§ 42-133e to 42-133h (West 1992 & Supp. 1997); Del. Code Ann. tit. 6, §§ 2551 to 2556 (1993); D.C. Code Ann. §§ 29-1201 to 29-1208 (1996); Haw. Rev. Stat. §§ 482E-1 to 482E-12 (1993); Ill. Comp. Stat. Ann. 815/705-1 to 705-44 (West 1993 & Supp. 1997); Ind. Code Ann. §§ 23-2-2.7-1 to 23-2-2.7-7 (Michie 1995); Iowa Code Ann. §§ 523H.1 to 523H.17 (West Supp.

1997); La. Rev. Stat. Ann. tit. 23, §921(E) (West Supp. 1997) and tit. 12, § 1042 (West 1994); Mich. Comp. Laws §§ 445:1501 to 445:1546 (West 1989 & Supp. 1997); Minn. Stat. Ann. §§ 80C.01 to 80C.22 (West 1993 & Supp. 1997); Miss. Code Ann. § 75-24-53 (1991); Mo. Ann. Stat. §§ 407.400 to 407.420 (West 1990); Neb. Rev. Stat. §§ 87-401 to 87-410 (1994); N.J. Stat. Ann. §§ 56:10-1 to 56:10-12 (West 1989 & Supp. 1997); S.D. Codified Laws § 37-5A-51 (Michie 1994); Va. Code. Ann. §§ 13.1-557 to 13.1-574 (Michie 1993 & Supp. 1997); Wash. Rev. Code Ann. §§ 19.100.010 to 19.100.940 (West 1989 & Supp. 1997).

5. Those states having statutes that define "good cause" in some way include: Arkansas, California, Connecticut, District of Columbia, Hawaii, Illinois, Indiana, Iowa, Michigan, Minnesota, Nebraska, New Jersey, and Washington.

6. *See, e.g.,* statutes cited in note 1, *supra.*

7. *See generally Midwestern Waffles, Inc. v. Waffle House, Inc.,* 734 F.2d 705 (11th Cir. 1984) (tying claim); *Kentucky Fried Chicken Corp. v. Diversified Packaging Corp.,* 549 F.2d 368 (5th Cir. 1977) (preferred supplier program); *McCabe's Furniture, Inc. v. La-Z-Boy Chair Co.,* 798 F.2d 323 (8th Cir. 1986) (resale price maintenance claim).

8. *See, e.g., Days Inn of Am. Franchising, Inc. v. Windham,* 699 F. Supp. 1581, Bus. Franchise Guide (CCH) ¶ 9296 (N.D. Ga. 1988); *Akers v. Bonifasi,* 629 F. Supp. 1212, Bus. Franchise Guide (CCH) ¶ 8614 (M.D. Tenn. 1984).

9. *See, e.g., General Aviation, Inc. v. Cessna Aircraft Co.,* 915 F.2d 1038, Bus. Franchise Guide (CCH) ¶ 9698 (6th Cir. 1990) (rejecting challenge to nonrenewal where distributorship agreement expressly allowed for nonrenewal without cause); *accord Hubbard Chevrolet Co. v. General Motors Corp.,* 873 F.2d 873, Bus. Franchise Guide (CCH) ¶ 9402 (5th Cir. 1989) (reversing jury award to dealer holding that, where contract provided that franchisor had unrestricted authority to approve or disapprove franchise relocation for its own reasons, court could not "reevaluate the wisdom of the parties' decision to leave relocation decisions to GM"). *But cf. Carvel Corp. v. Baker,* No. 3:94CV1882 (AVC) (D. Conn. Decided July 22, 1997) (despite language in agreement that franchisor had sole discretion to sell through other distribution channels, franchisor had to exercise this discretion reasonably and in good faith).

10. States containing minimum notice requirements include: Arkansas (90 days), California (180 days), Connecticut (60 days), Delaware (90 days), District of Columbia (60 days), Illinois (6 months), Indiana (90 days), Iowa (6 months), Minnesota (180 days), Mississippi (90 days), Missouri (90 days), Nebraska (90 days), New Jersey (60 days), Washington (1 year), Wisconsin (90 days).

11. *See, e.g.,* N.J. Stat. Ann. § 56:10-5 (West 1989) ("failure by the franchisee to substantially comply with those requirements imposed upon him by the franchise agreement"); Wis. Stat. Ann. § 135.02(4)(a) (West Supp. 1996) ("[f]ailure . . . to comply substantially with essential and reasonable requirements").

12. *See, e.g.,* Mich. Comp. Laws Ann. § 445.1527 (West 1989).

13. *See, e.g.,* Iowa Code Ann. § 523H.8.1(b)(3) (West Supp. 1997).

14. Courts have held that franchisors generally have the legal right to transfer franchise agreements. *See generally Marc's Big Boy Corp. v. Marriott Corp.,* Bus. Franchise Guide (CCH) ¶ 9100 (E.D. Wis. 1988).

15. The statutes are as follows: Ark. Code Ann. § 4-72-205 (Michie 1996); Cal. Bus. & Prof. Code § 20027 (West 1997); Haw. Rev. Stat. § 482E-6(2)(i) (1993); Ind. Code Ann. §23-2-2.7-2(3) (Michie 1995); Iowa Code Ann. § 523H.5 (West Supp. 1997); Mich. Comp. Laws § 445.1527 (West 1989); Minn. Stat. Ann. § 80C.14(5) (West Supp. 1997); Neb. Rev. Stat. § 87-405 (1994); N.J. Stat. Ann. § 56:10-6 (West 1989); Wash. Rev. Code Ann. § 19.100.180 (West 1989 & Supp. 1997); D.C. Code Ann. § 29-1204 (1996).

16. *See, e.g.,* Haw.Rev.Stat. § 482e-6(92)(i) (1993); Mich. Comp. Laws § 445.1527(g) (1989).

17. *See, e.g., Dayan v. McDonalds' Corp.,* 466 N.E. 2D 958, Bus. Franchise Guide (CCH) ¶ 8223 (Ill. App. Ct. 1984).

Summary of State Franchise Relationship Laws Regarding Termination and Nonrenewal

[Editor's Note: This Appendix presents only a summary of the laws. In practice, reference to the actual statute is necessary, as these laws may be industry-specific, contain exceptions, have been modified, or be otherwise inapplicable to a particular transaction.]

ARKANSAS. Arkansas Franchise Practices Act
(Ark. Code Ann. §§4-72-201 to 4-72-210 (1987) (CCH Business Franchise Guide ¶ 4040)).

Termination—Good cause required.
> *Def'n of "good cause":*
>> (i)   Franchisee fails to comply substantially with nondiscriminatory standards imposed or sought to be imposed;
>> (ii)   Franchisee fails to act in good faith and commercially reasonable manner;
>> (iii)   Voluntary abandonment by Franchisee;
>> (iv)   Criminal conviction of Franchisee;
>> (v)   Franchisee impairment of trademark or trade name;
>> (vi)   Insolvency or bankruptcy of Franchisee;
>> (vii) Either party's loss of right to occupy franchise property; *OR*
>> (viii) Outstanding debt to Franchisor no paid within ten days of past due notice.

Nonrenewal—Franchisor must renew, unless:
>> (i)   Has good cause, *OR*
>> (ii) Refusal is in accordance with its current policies, practices, and standards that in their establishment, operation, or application are not arbitrary or capricious.

Notice
> *When Required*—90 days for termination or nonrenewal, including 30 days to cure before termination. If reason for termination or nonrenewal is repeated deficiencies within 12-month period giving rise to good cause, only 10 days' notice need be given.

> *When Not Required*—If reason for termination is "good cause" items (iii)–(viii) above.

Franchisee's Remedies
>> (i) *Treble Damages for Fraud*—If Franchisee is harmed by a misleading or fraudulent scheme, Franchisee may recover treble damages, reasonable attorney's fees, costs of litigation, and injunctive relief.

(ii)   *Actual Damages for other Violations*—For other harms to Franchisee due to Franchisor's violations, Franchisee may recover damages, including costs and attorney's fees and/or obtain injunctive relief.

(iii)   *Repurchase Obligation*—For termination without good cause, Franchisor must, at Franchisee's option, repurchase inventory, supplies, equipment, and furnishings purchased from Franchisor or supplier designated by Franchisor.

Other

Criminal Penalties—Fraud by Franchisor punishable as a "Class B" felony.

CALIFORNIA. California Franchise Relations Act
(Cal. Bus. & Prof. Code §§20000 to 20043 (1995) (CCH Business Franchise Guide ¶ 4050)).

Termination—Termination may be on either:

(i)   Good cause; OR

Def'n of "good cause"—Includes Franchisee's failure to comply with any lawful requirement of the Franchise Agreement, after being given notice thereof and a reasonable opportunity to cure.

(ii)   Reasonable grounds.

Def'n of "reasonable grounds"—If any of the following occur and is relevant to the franchise, Franchisor has "reasonable grounds" to give notice of immediate termination without a cure period: Franchisee insolvency, abandonment by Franchisee, mutual agreement, material misrepresentation or conduct by Franchisee that reflects unfavorably on franchise system, noncompliance with law following 10 days' notice, repeated noncompliance with Franchise Agreement, foreclosure on Franchisee or premises, criminal conviction, failure to pay franchise fees after five days' notice that overdue, or danger to public health or safety.

Nonrenewal—Franchisor must renew, *UNLESS* gives 180 days' notice *AND* one of the following:

(i)   Franchisee is permitted during 180 days' notice period, to sell to a purchaser that meets Franchisor's then-current requirements for granting new or renewal franchises;

(ii)   Refusal to renew is not for conversion of premises for operation by Franchisor *AND* noncompetition covenant is not enforced;

(iii)   Termination would be permitted under "good cause" or "reasonable grounds" above;

(iv)   Mutual agreement;

(v)   Franchisor is withdrawing from geographic market *AND* does not enforce noncompetition covenant *AND* refusal to renew is not for conversion of premises for operation by Franchisor *AND* if Franchisor owns interest in premises, it either offers Franchisee a right of first refusal on such interest or its assignee offers Franchisee a franchise on substantially similar terms; *OR*

(vi)   Franchisor offers renewal on substantially the same terms as it customarily offers renewal franchises (or new franchises if it is not then granting a significant number of renewals) *AND* Franchisor and Franchisee cannot agree on the terms of renewal *AND* Franchisor gives 30 days' notice that if its renewal offer is not accepted, the franchise will not be renewed.

Notice

Termination—Termination for good cause requires sufficient notice to give Franchisee a reasonable opportunity to cure. Termination on reasonable grounds may be immediate.

Nonrenewal—180 days.

Franchisee's Remedies

(i) *Repurchase Obligation*—For termination or nonrenewal in violation of law, Franchisor must offer to repurchase current inventory that required by Franchise Agreement or commercial practice.

(ii) *Other Rights*—Franchisee not precluded from exercising other legal rights.

Dispute Settlement

Arbitration—Agreements to arbitrate are enforceable as long as standards applied in arbitration are not less than required by California Franchise Relations Act and arbitrators chosen from list of an impartial body.

Venue—Provision in Franchise Agreement restricting venue to forum outside California is void.

CONNECTICUT. Franchise Act
(Conn. Gen. Stat. Ann. §§42-133e to 42-133h (1995) (CCH Business Franchise guide ¶ 4070)).

Termination—Requires either:

(i) Good cause;

Def'n of "good cause"—Includes Franchisee's failure to comply with material and reasonable obligations of Franchise Agreement.

(ii) Voluntary abandonment; OR

(iii) Criminal conviction of Franchisee.

Nonrenewal—Requires either:

(i) Good cause (as defined above);

(ii) Voluntary abandonment,

(iii) Criminal conviction of Franchisee; OR

(iv) If Franchisor leases premises to Franchisee, Franchisor may choose not to renew if either:

    (a) Franchisor sells or leases premises to other than an affiliate for any use;

    (b) Franchisor sells or leases the premises to an affiliate that will not use the premises for the franchise business;

    (c) Franchisor converts premises to a new use; OR

    (d) Franchisor's underlying lease is terminated.

Notice

When Required—With good cause, 60 days for termination or nonrenewal. If reason is voluntary abandonment, 30 days. In case of nonrenewal under item (iv) above, six months.

When Not Required—In event of criminal conviction of Franchisee, notice of termination or nonrenewal is effective immediately.

Note: Notice of termination or nonrenewal that also involves termination of lease to Franchisee must be served by sheriff or other third person and meet certain requirements of Connecticut law.

Franchisee's Remedies

(i) *Repurchase Obligation*—Regardless of reason for termination, Franchisor must, at option of Franchisee, repurchase inventory, supplies, equipment, and furnishings purchased from Franchisor or supplier designated by Franchisor. This remedy appears not to be available for nonrenewal.

(ii) Actual damages, including costs and attorneys' fees.

(iii) Injunctive relief.

Other

Duration—The original and any successive terms of all franchises must be for no less than 3 years.

DELAWARE. Delaware Franchise Security Law
(Del. Code Ann. Tit. 6 §§ 2551 to 2556 (1980) (CCH Business Franchise Guide ¶ 4080)).

Termination—May not be done unjustly.
Def'n of "unjustly"—"Without good cause" or "in bad faith" (neither of which are defined).

Nonrenewal—May not be done unjustly (as defined above).

Notice—90 days for termination or nonrenewal.

Franchisee's Remedies—If Franchisor threatens, attempts to, or actually unjustly terminates or fails to renew, Franchisor may seek:

(i) *Assets, Goodwill and Lost Profits*—Damages, including value of assets, lost goodwill, lost profits (at least 5 times profit in most recent fiscal year), and attorneys' fees.

(ii) Injunctive relief.

Other

Refusal to Deal—Franchisor may not "unjustly" refuse to deal with a Franchisee with whom it has been dealing for at least two years.

Rental of Real and Personal Property—Franchisor may not charge Franchisee rent for real or personal property that is unreasonable or excessive.

DISTRICT OF COLUMBIA. Franchising Act
(D.C. Code Ann. §§ 29-1201 to 29-1208 (1989) (CCH Business Franchise Guide ¶ 4510)).

Termination—Good cause required.
Def'n of "good cause"—Failure to comply substantially with requirements imposed by Franchise *OR* lack of good faith by Franchisee.

Nonrenewal—Good cause required (as defined above).

Notice

When Required—60 days for termination or nonrenewal, including 60 days to cure. If reason for termination is voluntary abandonment, 15 days.

> *Note:* Notice must set forth all reasons for termination or nonrenewal and a copy must be sent to Advisory Neighborhood Commission and Ward Councilmember 60 days prior to closing any store.

When Not Required—In event of criminal conviction of Franchisee, notice of termination or nonrenewal effective immediately.

Franchisee's Remedies
    (i)   Actual damages, including costs and attorneys' fees.
    (ii)   Injunctive relief.

HAWAII Franchise Investment Act
(Haw. Rev. Stat. §§ 482E-1 to 482E-12 (1988) (CCH Business Franchise Guide ¶¶ 3110 & 4110)).

Termination—Requires either:
    (i)   Good cause; OR

        Def'n of "good cause"—Includes failure of Franchisee to comply with lawful, material provision of Franchise Agreement, after given notice and a chance to cure.

    (ii)   In accordance with current nondiscriminatory terms and standards established by the Franchisor, after notice and a reasonable opportunity to cure.

Nonrenewal—Requires either:
    (i)   Good cause (as defined above); OR
    (ii)   In accordance with current nondiscriminatory terms and standards established by Franchisor.

Notice—Reasonable period of time to cure upon written notice of termination.

Franchisee's Remedies
    (i)   *Repurchase Obligation*—Upon termination or nonrenewal (even with good cause), Franchisor must, at Franchisee's option, repurchase inventory, supplies, equipment, and furnishings purchased from Franchisor or supplier designated by Franchisor.
    (ii)   *Goodwill upon Conversion*—If Franchisor refuses renewal in order to convert to Franchisor operation, Franchisee must also be compensated for goodwill.
    (iii) *Unfair Competition*—Violations concerning termination and nonrenewal entitle Franchisee to recovery under Hawaii unfair and competition and deceptive acts statute.

Other
    Non-Discrimination—Unreasonable discrimination between franchises is prohibited.

    Civil and Criminal Penalties—Violations subject to civil penalties of up to $100,000 and felony convictions resulting in *minimum* imprisonment of one year.

ILLINOIS. Franchise Disclosure Act
(Ill. Rev. Comp. Ch. 815, §§ 705/18 to 705/26 (1992) (CCH Business Franchise Guide ¶ 3130)).

Termination—Good cause required.
    Def'n of "good cause"—Includes failure to comply with lawful provisions of Franchise Agreement, after notice and 30 days to cure, *OR*, assignment for benefit of creditors, voluntary abandonment, criminal misconduct of Franchisee that impairs goodwill of Franchisor's name or mark, or repeated failure to comply with Franchise Agreement.

Nonrenewal—If Franchisor does not renew, it must compensate Franchisee for diminution in value of the franchise business, *UNLESS:*

> (i)   Noncompetition covenant is waived; *AND*
>
> (ii)   Franchisee is given at least six months' notice of nonrenewal.

Notice

> *When Required*
>
>> **Termination**—30 days' notice and chance to cure
>>
>> **Nonrenewal**—Six months' notice for nonrenewal (plus waiver of any noncompetition agreement) in order to avoid obligation to compensate Franchisee.
>
> *When Not Required*—No notice required if reason for termination is: assignment for benefit of creditors, voluntary abandonment, criminal conviction, or repeated failure to comply with Franchise Agreement.

Franchisee's Remedies

> (i)   *Nonrenewal Obligation*—See "Nonrenewal" above.
>
> (ii)   Actual damages, including costs and attorneys' fees.

Other

> *Non-Discrimination*—Unreasonable and material discrimination between franchises is prohibited.
>
> *Civil and Criminal Penalties*—Violations subject to civil penalties of up to $50,000 per violation.

INDIANA. Deceptive Franchise Practices Act
(Ind. Code Ann. §§23-2-2.7-1 to 23-2-2.7-7 (1985) (CCH Business Franchise Guide ¶ 4140)).

> *Termination*—Requires either:
>
>> (i)   Good cause; OR
>>
>>> *Def'n of "good cause"*—Includes material violation of the Franchise Agreement.
>>
>> (ii)   Bad faith on part of Franchisee.
>>
>>> *Note:* Impermissible to threaten termination in order to gain any agreement with Franchisee.
>
> *Nonrenewal*—Unless Franchise Agreement provides that it is not renewable or provides that Franchisee must meet certain conditions specified in Franchise Agreement in order to renew, not renewing requires either:
>
>> (i)   Good cause (as defined above); OR
>>
>> (ii)   Bad faith on part of Franchisee.
>>
>>> *Note:* Impermissible to threaten nonrenewal in order to gain any agreement with Franchisee.
>
> *Notice*—Unless otherwise provided in Franchise Agreement, 90 days for termination or nonrenewal.
>
> *Franchisee's Remedies*—Franchisee may recover damages or seek reformation of the Franchise Agreement.

Dispute Resolution—Not permissible for Franchise Agreement to limit litigation in any manner whatsoever.

Other

Non-Discrimination—Unfair discrimination between franchises is prohibited.

Non-Competition Covenants—Covenants not to compete after termination or nonrenewal must be for no more than three years *AND* not encompass as area greater than exclusive area granted in Franchise Agreement or reasonable area if no exclusive area was granted.

IOWA

(Iowa Code, Ch. 523H, §§ 523H.1 to 523H.17 (1995) (CCH Business Franchise Guide ¶ 4150)).

Termination—Requires either:
  (i)   Good cause;

> *Def'n of "good cause"*—A legitimate business reason, including failure to comply with any material lawful requirement of the Franchise Agreement, after notice and a reasonable opportunity to cure.

  (ii)   Bankruptcy or insolvency of Franchisee;
  (iii) Voluntary abandonment for at least five days;
  (iv)   Mutual agreement;
  (v)   Material misrepresentation by Franchisee;
  (vi)   Repeated material violations by Franchisee;
  (vii) Seizure of Franchisee's premises;
  (viii) Criminal conviction of Franchisee; *OR*
  (ix)   Endangerment to public health and safety.

Nonrenewal—In order not to renew, Franchisor must:
  (i)   Give at least six months' notice; AND
  (ii) One of the following:
    (a) Have good cause (as defined above);
    (b) Mutual agreement, with waiver of noncompetition covenant; *OR*
    (c) Franchisor completely withdraws from geographic market, with waiver of noncompetition covenant.

Notice

When Required

> **Termination**—For good cause termination, a reasonable period of time to cure (at least 30 days but not need to be more than 90 days).

> **Nonrenewal**—Six months' notice is required.

When Not Required—Notice, but no time to cure, is required if the reason for termination is items (ii)-(ix) of "Termination" above.

Franchisee's Remedies

  (i)   *Repurchase Obligation*—If Franchisee terminated or not renewed, Franchisor must offer to purchase franchise for fair market value (minus goodwill value of trademark), *UNLESS* either noncompetition covenant not enforced or Franchisee will continue in a business with a substantially similar marketing program.

(ii)   Actual damages, including costs and attorneys' and experts' fees.

(iii)   Injunctive relief.

Dispute Settlement—Franchise Agreement may not restrict forum to venue outside Iowa, but may provide for arbitration or mediation.

Other

Noncompetition Agreement—Franchisor cannot enforce a noncompetition covenant unless it offers in writing, no later than 10 days before expiration of the franchise, to purchase the assets of the franchised business for its fair market value as a going concern. After a transfer, Franchisor may not enforce noncompetition agreement against former Franchisee.

LOUISIANA

(La. Rev. Stat. Ann. Tit. 23, § 921(E) and Tit. 12, § 1042 (1991) (CCH Business Franchise Guide ¶ 4181)).

Note: No statute of general applicability to franchises.

Dispute Resolution—Unless otherwise provided by Franchise Agreement, disputes must be settled under Louisiana law in a forum in Louisiana.

Other

Noncompetition Agreements—Exception for franchises from Louisiana's general statutory prohibition against noncompetition agreements allows:

(i)   Franchisor to grant exclusive territory;

(ii)   Franchisee to agree to refrain from competing during Franchise Agreement and for 2 years after termination.

MICHIGAN. Franchise Investment Law Act

(Mich. Comp. Laws §§445.1527 &445.1535 (1989) (CCH Business Franchise Guide ¶¶ 4220 & 3220.34 & 35)).

Termination—Good cause required.

Def'n of "good cause"—Includes failure to comply with any lawful provision of Franchise Agreement, after being given notice and reasonable opportunity to cure.

Nonrenewal—If renewal terms generally available to other franchisees, Franchisor must offer such terms to Franchisee. If Franchisor does not renew for any reason, Franchisor must repurchase inventory, supplies, equipment, fixtures, and furnishings if:

(i)   Term of the Franchise Agreement is less than 5 years; *AND*

(ii)   (a)   noncompetition covenant prevents Franchisee from operating under a different name after nonrenewal; *OR*

(b)   less than 6 months notice given.

Notice

Termination—Must give notice and a reasonable opportunity to cure before terminating.

Nonrenewal—Six months' notice for nonrenewal (or no enforcement of noncompetition covenant), in order to avoid repurchase obligation.

Franchisee Remedies

(i)   *Repurchase Obligation*—See "Nonrenewal" above.

(ii) Restitution to Franchisee.

(iii) Injunctive relief.

Dispute Settlement—Franchise Agreement provision requiring litigation or arbitration to be conducted outside of Michigan is unenforceable.

MINNESOTA. Minnesota Franchise Act
(Minn. Stat. § 80C.14 (1993) and Minnesota Rules, Department of Commerce, § 2860.4400 (1989) (CCH Business Franchise Guide ¶¶ 3230 and 5230.31)).

Termination—Good cause required.

> *Def'n of "good cause"*—Includes failure to comply substantially with material and reasonable requirements imposed by Franchisor, including requirements concerning bankruptcy or insolvency, assignment for benefit of creditors, voluntary abandonment, criminal conviction or plea of guilty or no contest, or material impairment of Franchisor's mark or name.

Nonrenewal—Franchisor may not refuse to renew in order to convert to Franchisor operation. In order otherwise not to renew, Franchisor must either:

(i) Have good cause (as defined above); OR

(ii) (a) give at least 180 days' notice; AND

　　 (b) have given Franchisee sufficient time from the date of nonrenewal to enable Franchisee to recover fair market value of the franchise as a going concern.

Notice

> *When required*—90 days, including 60 days to cure, prior to termination or nonrenewal for good cause. One hundred eighty days prior to nonrenewal if not for good cause.

> *When Not Required*—Notice is effective immediately if reason for termination is for voluntary abandonment, criminal conviction, or failure to cure material impairment of goodwill, after being given at least 24 hours' notice.

Franchisee's Remedies

(i) Actual damages, including costs and attorneys' fees.

(ii) Injunctive relief.

Other

> *Civil and Criminal Penalties*—Violations subject to civil fines of up to $2,000 per violation and criminal penalties of up to $10,000 and/or five years' imprisonment.

> *Nondiscrimination*—Unreasonable discrimination between franchises is prohibited.

MISSISSIPPI. Pyramid Sales Scheme Act
(Miss. Code Ann. § 75-24-51 to 75-24-63 (1972) (CCH Business Franchise Guide ¶ 4240)).

Termination—No substantive requirement.

Nonrenewal—No substantive requirement.

Notice

> *When Required*—90 days for termination or nonrenewal.

> *When Not Required*—Notice period not required if reason for termination or nonrenewal is criminal misconduct, fraud, abandonment, bankruptcy, insolvency, or an insufficient funds check.

Franchisee's Remedies
  (i)   Damages resulting from not being given proper notice, including loss of goodwill and costs of suit.
  (ii) Equitable relief.

Other
Criminal Penalties—Violation of notice requirement is a misdemeanor punishable by a fine of not more than $500.00 and/or imprisonment of not more than 6 months.

MISSOURI. Pyramid Sales Scheme Act
(Mo. Rev. Stat. §§ 407.400 to 407.420 (1998) (CCH Business Franchise Guide ¶ 4250)).

Termination—No substantive requirement.

Nonrenewal—No substantive requirement.

Notice
When Required—90 days' notice for termination or nonrenewal.

When Not Required—Notice period not required if reason for termination or nonrenewal is criminal misconduct, fraud, abandonment, bankruptcy, insolvency, or an insufficient funds check.

Franchisee's Remedies
  (i)   Damages resulting from not being given proper notice, including lost goodwill and costs of suit.
  (ii) Equitable relief.

NEBRASKA. Franchise Practices Act
(Neb. Rev. Stat. §§ 87-401 to 87-410 (1993) (CCH Business Franchise Guide ¶ 4270)).

Note: Nebraska statute applies only if gross sales between Franchisor and Franchisee for 12 months preceding a suit exceeds $35,000.

Termination—Good cause required.
  Def'n of "good cause"—Limited to failure by the Franchisee to comply substantially with the requirements imposed upon it by the franchise.

Nonrenewal—Good cause (as defined above) required, UNLESS Franchise Agreement provides that franchise is not renewable or only renewable if Franchisee meets certain reasonable requirements.

Notice
When Required—60 days for termination or nonrenewal. If reason for termination or nonrenewal is voluntary abandonment, 15 days.

When Not Required—Notice effective immediately if the reason for termination or nonrenewal is criminal conviction, insolvency, default in payment, fraud, danger to public health and safety, or loss of right to occupy premises.

Franchisee's Remedies
  (i)   Damages, including costs and attorney's fees.
  (ii) Injunctive relief.

NEW JERSEY. Franchise Practices Act
(N.J. Rev. Stat. §§ 56:10-1 to 56:10-12 (1993) (CCH Business Franchise Guide ¶ 4300)).

> *Note:* New Jersey's statute applies only if gross sales between Franchisor and Franchisee for 12 months preceding a suit exceed $35,000.

> **Termination** Good cause required.
> > *Def'n of "good cause"*—Limited to failure of Franchise to substantially comply with requirements imposed by Franchisor.

> **Nonrenewal**—Good cause required (as defined above).

> **Notice**
> > *When Required*—60 days for termination or nonrenewal. If reason for termination or nonrenewal is voluntary abandonment, 15 days.

> > *When Not Required*—Notice effective immediately if reason for termination or nonrenewal is criminal conviction.

> **Franchisee's Remedies**
> > (i)   Damages, including costs and attorneys' fees.
> > (ii) Injunctive relief.

NORTH CAROLINA. General Statutes
(Chpt. 22B, Sec. 3 (1993) (CCH Business Franchise Guide ¶ 4330)).

> *Note:* No statute of general applicability to franchises.

> **Other**
> > *Dispute Settlement*—North Carolina has a statute of general application prohibiting contracts that require litigation or arbitration outside of North Carolina.

SOUTH DAKOTA
(S.D. Codified Laws § 37-5A-51 (1994) and undated Memorandum, Division of Securities (CCH Business Franchise Guide ¶¶ 3410.10 & 5410.01)).

> *Note:* Only substantive provision of statute is one prohibiting "unfair or inequitable practice" in contravention of rules published by Director of Division of Securities. No such rules published but Division has published a "Memorandum," which is summarized below.

> **Notice**—30 days' notice and opportunity to cure for termination.

> **Other**
> > *Liquidated Damages*—In accordance with South Dakota law (§ 53-9-5), liquidated damages provisions are unenforceable, unless it would be impractical or extremely difficult to fix actual damages.

> > *Covenants Not To Compete*—Noncompetition covenants in the Franchise Agreement must be accompanied (can be done in Addendum) by the following language:

> > > "Covenants not to compete upon termination or expiration of the Franchise Agreement are generally unenforceable in the State of South Dakota, except in certain instances as provided by law."

Arbitration—If the Franchise Agreement designates a site for any arbitration, the language below must be added (can be done in Addendum) (effect of the language is to allow the Franchisee to object to the site designated by Franchisor, and the American Arbitration Association to then determine the site):

> "In the event that either party shall make demand for arbitration, such arbitration shall be conducted in a mutually agreed upon site in accordance with Section 11 of the Commercial Arbitration Rules of the American Arbitration Association."

Governing Law—If the Franchise Agreement designates other than South Dakota law as the governing law, then the following language must be added (can be done in Addendum):

> "The law regarding franchise registration, employment, covenants not to compete, and other matters of local concern will be governed by the laws of the State of South Dakota; but as to contractual and all other matters, this agreement and all provisions of this instrument will be and remain subject to the application, construction, enforcement, and interpretation under the governing law of _____."

Venue—Provisions designating a venue outside South Dakota are void with respect to any cause of action which is otherwise enforceable in South Dakota.

VIRGINIA. Retail Franchising Act
(Va. Code Ann. §§ 13.1-557 to 13.1-574 (1979) (CCH Business Franchise Guide ¶ 3460)).

Termination—"Reasonable cause" required (but not defined).

Note: Franchisor also may not use undue influence to induce Franchisee to surrender any right given to it by the Franchise Agreement.

Franchisee's Remedies
(i)   Damages, including costs and attorneys' fees.
(ii)   Injunctive relief.

Dispute Resolution—Permissible to agree to binding arbitration.

Other
Civil and Criminal Penalties—Violations subject to civil penalties of up to $25,000. Violations can also be prosecuted criminally and are subject to the following:
(i)   Class 4 felony, if crime knowingly and willfully committed with intent to defraud Franchisee.
(ii)   Fine of $100 to $5000 and/or imprisonment of 30 days to one year, if knowingly committed.

WASHINGTON. Franchise Investment Protection Act
(Wash. Rev. Code §§ 19.100.180 to 19.100.190 (1991) (CCH Business Franchise Guide ¶ 4470)).

Termination—Good cause required.
Def'n of "good cause"—Includes failure to comply with lawful material provisions of Franchise Agreement, after given notice and a reasonable opportunity to cure. See repurchase obligation under "Franchisee's Remedies."

Nonrenewal—No substantive requirements except for repurchase obligation under "Franchisee's Remedies."

Notice
When Required

Termination—Notice and a reasonable opportunity to cure.

Nonrenewal—One year (plus no enforcement of non-compete covenant) in order to avoid obligation to compensate Franchisee for lost goodwill.

When Not Required—No notice required if reason for termination is violation of same provision in Franchise Agreement for fourth time in one year, insolvency, assignment for the benefit of creditors, voluntary abandonment, or criminal conviction or no contest or guilty plea.

Franchisee's Remedies
(i)   *Termination Repurchase Obligation*—For termination upon good cause, Franchisor must repurchase inventory and supplies.
(ii)   *Nonrenewal Repurchase Obligation*—If Franchisor does not renew, Franchisor must repurchase inventory, supplies, equipment and furnishings purchased from Franchisor. Franchisor must also compensate Franchisee for goodwill, *UNLESS:*
       (a) gives notice of one year; AND
       (b) waives noncompetition covenant.
(iii) *Unfair or Deceptive Acts*—Violations concerning termination and nonrenewal entitle Franchisee to recovery under Washington unfair or deceptive acts statutes.

Other
Discrimination—Unreasonable discrimination between Franchisees prohibited.

Civil and Criminal Penalties—Violations subject to civil penalties of up to $2,000 and, for willful violations, criminal penalties of up to $5,000 or imprisonment of up to 10 years.

WISCONSIN. Fair Dealership Law
(Wis. Stat. §§135.01 to 135.07 (1993-94) (CCH Business Franchise Guide ¶ 4490)).

Termination—Good cause required.
Def'n of "good cause"—Includes failure to comply substantially with essential, reasonable and nondiscriminatory requirements imposed by Franchisor *OR* bad faith by Franchisee.

Nonrenewal—Good cause required (as defined above).

Note: "Good cause" requirement also applies to "substantially chang[ing] the competitive circumstances" of the Franchise Agreement.

Notice
When Required—90 days, including 60 days to cure, for termination or nonrenewal. If reason for termination or nonrenewal is nonpayment of sums due, 10 days.

When Not Required—No notice required if reason for termination or nonrenewal is insolvency, assignment for the benefit of creditors, or bankruptcy.

Franchisee's Remedies

(i)   *Termination Repurchase Obligation*—Upon termination (even if for good cause), Franchisor must, at option of Franchisee, repurchase all merchandise with Franchisor's name or marks on it.

(ii)   *Damages*—For termination without good cause, Franchisor liable for damages, including costs and attorneys' fees.

(iii) Injunctive relief.

CHECKLIST NO. 6-1: Default and Termination

1.   Name of franchise

2.   Unit(s) involved

3.   Other units operated by or agreements with franchisee
    a. Franchisee's standing under other agreements
    b. Potential for cross-default/termination

4.   Franchisor's basis for default/termination
    a. Factual cause/event
    b. Specific contractual basis

5.   Communications with or efforts to counsel franchise regarding basis for default/termination
    a. Specific communications by franchisor
    b. Franchisee's response

6.   Whether franchisor/franchisee desires to try to negotiate workout arrangement to avoid termination

7.   Analysis of applicable statutory restrictions on termination

8.   Analysis of relevant course of dealings with franchisee

9.   Any inconsistency with treatment of other similarly situated franchisees and, if so, reasons for deviation

10.   Potential legal claims by franchisee

11.   Potential for obtaining negotiated, voluntary termination, and release by franchisee

12.   Internal approvals required for default/termination
    a. Business/operational approval
    b. Legal approval

13.   Required notice and cure period
    a. Written notice of default
    b. Follow-up by franchisor to determine if cured
    c. Written notice of termination

14.   Follow-up by franchisor to confirm compliance with post-termination obligations
    a. De-identification
    b. Return of all manuals and other proprietary materials
    c. Enforcement of noncompetition agreements

CHECKLIST NO. 6-2: Nonrenewal

1. Name of franchisee

2. Unit(s) involved

3. Other units operated by or agreements with franchisee

4. Franchisor's business decision whether it desires to renew franchisee
    a. Operational history
    b. Payment history
    c. Facility image status
    d. Facility location status
    e. Conditions for renewal (for example, release, facility upgrade, new agreement, additional training, and so on)

5. Franchisee's contractual rights regarding renewal
    a. Specific contractual basis
    b. Prerequisites for franchisee to obtain renewal
    c. Good cause for franchisor not to renew
    d. What form of agreement for renewal
    e. Ability of franchisor to impose conditions for renewal (see 4.3. above)
    f. Notice requirements regarding renewal

6. Analysis of applicable statutory restrictions on nonrenewal
    a. Good cause requirement
    b. Notice requirement
    c. Other conditions

7. Analysis of relevant course of dealings with franchisee

8. Any inconsistency with treatment of other similarly situated franchisees and, if so, reasons for deviation

9. Potential legal claims by franchisee

10. Potential for obtaining negotiated, voluntary nonrenewal, and release by franchisee

11. Internal approvals required for nonrenewal
    a. Business/operational approval
    b. Legal approval

12. Communication of required notice

13. Follow-up by franchisor to confirm compliance with post-termination obligations
    a. De-identification
    b. Return of all manuals and other proprietary materials
    c. Enforcement of noncompetition agreements

CHECKLIST NO. 6-3: Transfer

1. Name of franchisee

2. Unit(s) involved

3. Other units operated by or agreements with franchisee

4. Analysis of whether proposed transferee meets franchisor's current criteria
    a. Financial resources
    b. Operational experience
    c. Other business interests

5. Franchisor's business decision whether it desires to consent to transfer
    a. Is franchisee current on all obligations
    b. Conditions for consent to transfer (for example, release, facility upgrade, new agreement, and so on)
    c. Transfer fee

6. Franchisee's contractual rights regarding transfer
    a. Specific contractual provisions
    b. Prerequisites for franchisee to obtain consent
    c. Good cause for franchisor to refuse consent
    d. What form of agreement for transferee
    e. Ability of franchisor to impose conditions for consent (see 5.b above)

7. Analysis of applicable statutory restrictions regarding transfer
    a. Good cause requirement
    b. Notice requirement

8. Potential legal claims by franchisee and proposed transferee

9. Internal approvals required for transfer decisions
    a. Business/operational approval
    b. Legal approval

10. Communication of notice to franchisee and proposed transferee

11. Proper documentation of transfer transaction
    a. Conclusion of relationship with transferor franchisee (for example, payment of fees, release, noncompetition agreements, and so on)
    b. New franchisee relationship with transferee (for example, franchise agreement, guaranty, facility upgrade, and so on)

EXHIBIT 6-A: Notice of Termination for Financial Default

DATE

CERTIFIED MAIL XXX

Return Receipt Requested and U.S. Mail

Franchisee   Guarantors

XXX   XXX

XXX   XXX

Re: FRANCHISE AGREEMENT: XXX
FRANCHISEE: XXX
FRANCHISED RESTAURANT: *Unit No. XXX*
LOCATION: XXX
CONTRACT NO: XXX

NOTICE OF TERMINATION FOR FINANCIAL DEFAULT

Dear Franchisee and Guarantors:

On _____, Franchisee, entered into a Franchise Agreement for Unit No. XXX (hereinafter referred to as the "Franchise Agreement") with Franchisor. Further, on or about XXX Franchisee's principals, individually, executed a Guaranty and Subordination Agreement agreeing to be bound jointly and severally with Franchisee for any indebtedness and obligations to Franchisor arising under the Franchise Agreement.

Notice is hereby given that Franchisee is in DEFAULT under the terms and conditions of Paragraph XXX. ("Fees") of the above-referenced Franchise Agreement for failure to pay Royalty Fees, Advertising Fund Fees, Finance Charges and other financial obligations to the Franchisor, in the amounts set forth on **EXHIBIT "A"** which is attached hereto and incorporated herein by reference (hereinafter referred to as the "Financial Default").

Please be advised that this letter constitutes a formal "NOTICE OF TERMINATION" pursuant to Paragraph XXX. of the Franchise Agreement. In the event the foregoing Financial Default is not cured within ten (10) days of Franchisee's receipt of this Notice, the Franchise Agreement shall terminate without further notice, effective immediately upon the expiration of such ten (10) day period, or such longer period as applicable law may require.

Please be further advised that upon termination of the Franchise Agreement, Franchisee will be expected to comply with the provisions of Paragraph XXX. of the Franchise Agreement, which set forth the Franchisee's obligations upon termination. Franchisee's post-termination obligations include the following:

1. Franchisee must immediately cease and forever discontinue any and all operations at that location under the name of Franchisor or any name confusingly similar thereto;

2. Franchisee must immediately and forever cease to use any proprietary materials, information, equipment, procedures and techniques associated with the Franchisor's System, including any and all trademarks and service marks associated with this Company;

3. Franchisee must immediately de-image the restaurant premises to completely disassociate those premises from the Franchisor's System, including, without limitation, the removal of all signs bearing the Franchisor's name;

4. Franchisee must immediately surrender the Confidential Operations Manual, and all copies thereof, together with all records, files, instructions, correspondence and any and all other materials relating to the operation of the Franchised Restaurant; and

5. Franchisee must immediately pay any and all sums which are owed to this Company as a result of the operation of the Franchised Restaurant.

Franchisor waives no other defaults under the above-referenced Franchise Agreement and reserves all rights and remedies it may have under the Franchise Agreement or otherwise. Please feel free to contact me in the event you have any questions regarding this matter.

Sincerely,

FRANCHISOR

By: _____

EXHIBIT 6-B: Notice of Termination for Operational Default

CERTIFIED MAIL #XXX

Return Receipt Requested and

U.S. Mail

Franchisee

XXX

XXX

> RE: **FRANCHISE AGREEMENT DATED:** XXX
> **FRANCHISEE:** XXX
> **FRANCHISED RESTAURANT:**
> *Unit XXX* located at XXX
> **CONTRACT NO.:** XXX

NOTICE OF TERMINATION FOR OPERATIONAL DEFAULT

Dear Franchisee:

On_____, Franchisee entered into a certain Franchise Agreement for Unit No. XXX (hereinafter referred to as the "Franchise Agreement") with Franchisor.

On_____, Franchisor conducted operational assessments of Unit No. XXX (copies of the assessment forms are attached hereto as **EXHIBIT "A"**). Notice is hereby given that Franchisee is currently in DEFAULT under the terms and conditions of Paragraph XXX. ("Duties Of The Franchisee") of the above-referenced Franchise Agreement for failure to operate the Franchised Unit and/or maintain the premises of the Franchised Unit in conformity with Franchisor's standards and specifications for the operation of a restaurant (hereinafter referred to as the "Operational Default"). The foregoing Operational Default includes, but is not limited to, Franchisee's failure to maintain the premises, equipment, etc., in conformity with Franchisor's high standards and public image and failure to make repairs and replacement thereto.

Please be advised that this Notice constitutes a formal "NOTICE OF TERMINATION" pursuant to Paragraph XXX. ("Termination") of the Franchise Agreement. In the event the foregoing Operational Default is not cured within thirty (30) days of Franchisee's receipt of this Notice, or such longer period as applicable law may require, the Franchise Agreement shall terminate upon the expiration of the thirty (30) day period or such long period as applicable law may require.

Please be further advised that upon termination of the above-referenced Franchise Agreement, Franchisee will be expected to comply with the provisions of Paragraph XXX of the Franchise Agreement which set forth the Franchisee's obligations upon termination. Franchisee's post-termination obligations include the following:

1. Franchisee must immediately cease and forever discontinue any and all operations at that location shown on **EXHIBIT "A"** operating under the name of Franchisor or any name confusingly similar thereto;

2. Franchisee must immediately and forever cease to use any proprietary materials, information, equipment, procedures and techniques associated with the Franchisor's System, including any and all trademarks and service marks associated with this Company;

3. Franchisee must immediately de-image the restaurant premises to completely disassociate those premises from the Franchisor's System, including, without limitation, the removal of all signs bearing the Franchisor's name and logo;

4. Franchisee must immediately surrender the Confidential Operations Manual, and all copies thereof, together with all records, files, instructions, correspondence and any and all other materials relating to the operation of the Franchised Restaurant; and

5. Franchisee must immediately pay any and all sums which are owed to this Company as a result of the operation of the Franchised Restaurant.

Franchisor waives no other defaults under the above-referenced Franchise Agreement and reserves all rights and remedies it may have under the Franchise Agreement or otherwise.

Please feel free to contact me in the event you have any further questions regarding this matter.

Sincerely,

FRANCHISOR

By: _____

EXHIBIT 6-C: Notice of Termination

DATE

CERTIFIED/REGISTERED MAIL

RETURN RECEIPT REQUESTED

and U.S. Mail

Franchisee

XXX

XXX

Re: **FRANCHISE AGREEMENT DATED:** XXX
    FRANCHISEE: XXX
    FRANCHISED RESTAURANT:
    Unit No. XXX
    CONTRACT NO. XXX

NOTICE OF TERMINATION

Gentlemen:

On XXX, Franchisor, entered into a certain Franchise Agreement for Unit No. XXX at the above-referenced location (hereinafter referred to as the "Franchise Agreement for Unit No. XXX") with XXX Franchisee. Further, on or about XXX, by Guaranty and Subordination Agreement, Franchisee's principals, individually, agreed to be bound jointly and severally with Franchisee for any such indebtedness and obligations to Franchisor arising under the Franchise Agreement.

It has come to Franchisor's attention that the above-referenced Franchised Restaurant was permanently closed for business on XXX by Franchisee without the consent of Franchisor. Pursuant to Paragraph XXX ("Termination") of the Franchise Agreement, Franchisor hereby elects to terminate the Franchise Agreement and all rights granted thereunder, effective immediately upon Franchisee's receipt of this Notice of Termination.

POST-TERMINATION OBLIGATIONS OF FRANCHISEE

Accordingly, you must **IMMEDIATELY** comply with the post-termination provisions of Paragraph XXX of the Franchise Agreement, which include but are not limited to the following:

1. Franchisee must immediately cease and forever discontinue any and all operations at this location under the name of XXX or any name confusingly similar thereto;

2. Franchisee must immediately and forever cease to use any proprietary materials, information, equipment, procedures, and techniques associated with the XXX System, including any and all trademarks and service marks associated with this Company;

3. Franchisee must immediately de-image the restaurant premises to completely disassociate those premises from the XXX System, including, without limitation, the removal of all signs bearing the XXX name and logo;

4. Franchisee must immediately surrender the Confidential Operations Manual, and all copies thereof, together with all records, files, instructions, correspondence and any and all other materials relating to the operation of the Franchised Restaurant; and

5. Franchisee must immediately pay any and all sums which are owed to this Company as a result of the operation of the Franchised Restaurant. A Statement of Account for Franchised Restaurant No. XXX indicating a total amount due by Franchisee to Franchisor of $XXX, is attached hereto as **EXHIBIT "A"** and incorporated herein by reference.

Franchisor waives no other default under the above-referenced Franchise Agreement for and reserves all rights and remedies it may have under the Franchise Agreement or otherwise.

Please contact me to discuss the immediate de-identification of the premises formerly occupied by the Franchised Restaurant. In the event Franchisee fails to voluntarily comply with all post-termination obligations, the Franchisor will institute legal proceedings to enforce these obligations and seek all damages, costs and expenses, including reasonable attorney's fees incurred by Franchisor in seeking damages and/or in obtaining injunctive relief for the enforcement of the Post-Termination Obligations set forth in Paragraph XXX of the Franchise Agreement.

Please feel free to contact me in the event you have any further questions regarding this matter.

Sincerely,

FRANCHISOR

By: _____

EXHIBIT 6-D: Voluntary Termination of Franchise Agreement between [Franchisor] and [Franchisee]

Dated: _____, 1998

VOLUNTARY TERMINATION OF FRANCHISE AGREEMENT

THIS AGREEMENT is made this ____ day of ____, 1998, by and between _____ (hereinafter referred to as **"FRANCHISOR"**) and _____ (hereinafter referred to as **"LICENSEE"**).

RECITALS:

WHEREAS, FRANCHISOR and **LICENSEE** are parties to that certain Franchise Agreement dated _____ (hereinafter referred to as the "Franchise Agreement") pursuant to which **FRANCHISOR** granted **LICENSEE** the right to operate a [Name and Location of Unit] (hereinafter referred to as "Unit No. ___ or the "Franchised Unit"); and

WHEREAS, on _____, _____, [TITLE] of [LICENSEE] executed a Guaranty Agreement agreeing to be bound by all of the terms and conditions of the provisions of the Franchise Agreement for the Franchise Restaurant (hereinafter referred to as the **"GUARANTOR"**).

WHEREAS, FRANCHISOR, LICENSEE and **GUARANTOR** have determined that it would be in their mutual best interests and in the best interests of the [FRANCHISOR'S] System to terminate the Franchise Agreement and Guaranty Agreement as of the effective date of this agreement, upon the following terms and conditions:

AGREEMENT:

NOW THEREFORE, and in consideration of the terms, conditions, and covenants contained herein, and for the mutual benefit of the parties hereto, **FRANCHISOR, LICENSEE** and **GUARANTOR** hereby agree as follows:

1. *Termination.* **FRANCHISOR, LICENSEE** and **GUARANTOR** agree that upon execution of this Agreement, the aforesaid Franchise Agreement and Guaranty Agreement shall be terminated in its entirety, and all rights and obligations of the parties flowing from said Franchise Agreement and Guaranty Agreement shall immediately terminate and cease. **LICENSEE** and **GUARANTOR** agree to immediately pay one-half (1/2) of any and all sums which are owed to **FRANCHISOR** as a result of the operation of the Franchised Unit. A Statement of Account for the Franchised Unit indicating the total amount due by **LICENSEE** and **GUARANTOR** to **FRANCHISOR** of $ _____ is attached hereto as **EXHIBIT "A"** and incorporated herein by reference.

2. *Post-Termination Obligations.* **LICENSEE** and **GUARANTOR** acknowledge and agree that notwithstanding the terms of this Agreement, **LICENSEE** and **GUARANTOR** will continue to be bound by and will comply with all of the requirements of the Franchise Agreement, which, by their nature, are intended to survive the termination or expiration of said Franchise Agreement, including, but not limited to, the covenants against competition and against disclosure of confidential information as specified therein.

3. *General and Specific Releases Executed by **LICENSEE** and **GUARANTOR**.*

A. **LICENSEE** and **GUARANTOR,** as further consideration for the execution of this Agreement, on behalf of **LICENSEE** and **GUARANTOR** and **LICENSEE'S** and/or **GUARANTOR'S** heirs, executors, assigns, and agents, do hereby release, relieve, acquit and forever discharge [FRANCHISOR], and any and all of [FRANCHISOR'S] predecessors, successors, present and former officers, directors, affiliates, parent and subsidiary companies, shareholders, employees, agents and attorneys (collectively the "[FRANCHISOR] Released Parties"), of and from all claims, demands, actions, liabilities and causes of action and damages of whatever kind or nature, known or unknown, vested or contingent, suspected or unsuspected, dependent in any way on any fact or event occurring on or prior to the date of this Agreement, that **LICENSEE** and **GUARANTOR** has, or ever had against the [FRANCHISOR] Released Parties.

B. Without limiting the foregoing, **LICENSEE** and **GUARANTOR** specifically release and forever discharge the [FRANCHISOR] Released Parties of and from all claims, demands, actions, liabilities and causes of action of whatever kind or nature, known or unknown, vested or contingent, suspected or unsuspected, arising at any time, which **LICENSEE** and/or **GUARANTOR** have now, may have in the future, or ever had pertaining to, or arising from the Franchise Agreement and/or Guaranty Agreement.

4. By executing this Agreement, **LICENSEE, GUARANTOR** and **FRANCHISOR,** for themselves and their respective successors, represent and warrant that their representations herein are true and correct and that each of them has the right and authority to enter into and to accept the terms and conditions of this Agreement.

5. **LICENSEE** and **GUARANTOR** further acknowledge and represent that **LICENSEE** and/or **GUARANTOR** have not transferred or assigned the Franchise Agreement, any of the rights licensed therein, the Guaranty Agreement, or any claims, demands, or causes of action which they have or may have against **FRANCHISOR** under any or all of said Franchise Agreement and Guaranty Agreement. **LICENSEE** and **GUARANTOR** agree to defend, indemnify and hold **FRANCHISOR,** its officers, directors, employees and agents harmless from any claims of any such transferee or assigns.

6. **LICENSEE** and **GUARANTOR** shall cooperate fully with **FRANCHISOR** and do all things necessary, including execution of appropriate documents in forms satisfactory in all respects to counsel from **FRANCHISOR,** to satisfy **LICENSEE'S** and/or **GUARANTOR'S** obligations under this Agreement.

7. This Agreement represents the complete, integrated, and entire agreement between the parties, and shall not be modified except in writing signed by the parties.

8. This Agreement shall take effect upon its execution and dating by **FRANCHISOR,** and shall be governed by the laws of the State of _____, which laws shall be controlling in the event of any conflict of law.

9. The provisions of this Agreement are severable, and in the event that any of them are held void and unenforceable as a matter of law the remainder shall continue in full force and effect.

10. Each of the undersigned, if a corporation, hereby represents and warrants that, as of the date of execution of this Agreement, it is in good standing in the state of its incorporation, had the power to enter into this Agreement, has duly authorized the execution of this Agreement, and that such execution does not violate any other agreement to which it is a party.

[SIGNATURES ON FOLLOWING PAGE]

IN WITNESS WHEREOF, the parties hereto have duly executed, sealed and delivered this Agreement in duplicate on the day and year first above written;

WITNESS: **FRANCHISOR:**

By: _____

Its: _____

WITNESS: **LICENSEE:**

By: _____

Its: _____

GUARANTOR:

By: _____

[SIGNATURE PAGE OF VOLUNTARY TERMINATION]

EXHIBIT 6-E: Letter Agreement of Termination

[Date]

VIA FEDERAL EXPRESS
[Franchisee]

RE: **Former Unit Nos.** _____

Dear [Franchisee]:

On Friday October 25, 1996, [Franchisor] sent a Notice of Termination letter to you notifying you of the termination of the Franchise Agreements for the above referenced Units. On Tuesday, October 29, 1996, you telephoned me to inform me that you had received my October 25, 1996 Notice of Termination letter. During that telephone conversation you acknowledged that your account was once again past due and that you understood the October 25, 1996 Notice of Termination letter to be placing you on notice of the termination of the Franchise Agreements for the above referenced Units.

On or about December 17, 1996, [representative of Franchisor] received a letter from you requesting a reconsideration of the termination of the Franchise Agreements for the above-referenced Units. [Representative of Franchisor] has referred your letter to me for a response. Contrary to the statements in your recent letter, the Franchisee (*see* Exhibit "A") has been a chronic credit problem which resulted in the Franchisee being repeatedly placed in financial default. [Franchisor] repeatedly attempted to work with the Franchisee to resolve its payment problems, but to no avail. Prior to sending the October 25, 1996 Notice of Termination letter, various [Franchisor] personnel met with you in Atlanta, Georgia to discuss several outstanding financial and operational issues between the Franchisee and [Franchisor]. Time and time again, the Franchisee has failed to exhibit a willingness to be a true partner with [Franchisor] and as a result, [Franchisor] will not consider re-instating its Franchise Agreements. However, in the spirit of cooperation, [Franchisor] is prepared to reach the following agreement with you and the Franchisee:

  i.   By signing this Letter Agreement, Franchisee acknowledges that the Franchise Agreements for the above-referenced Units terminated effective October 29, 1996.
  ii. By signing this Letter Agreement, Franchisee and you, individually, acknowledge that the Promissory Note dated February 11, 1994 was accelerated on May 20, 1996. As of this date, Franchisee and you owe $_____ to [Franchisor]. (*See* Exhibit "B").
  iii. Contingent upon payment of all applicable fees as referenced below and agreement to the payment terms for the accelerated promissory note as set forth in Paragraph 6 below, Franchisee will be allowed to continue to operate the Units for a period not to exceed one hundred twenty (120) days in order to close the sale of the Units to a prospective purchaser(s) who is satisfactory to [Franchisor], provided that the Franchisee pay to [Franchisor] during such one hundred twenty (120) day period, all obligations that would otherwise have come due under the Franchise Agreements, including, but not limited to, royalties and advertising fund contributions (which past due amount currently totals $ _____) (see Exhibit

"C") and provided that the Franchisee is in full compliance with [Franchisor's] operational standards and insurance requirements from the date of this Letter Agreement and continuing throughout the one hundred twenty (120) day period. If requested by the Franchisee, [Franchisor] will provide Franchisee with assistance in attempting to sell the Units by way of providing the Franchisee with the names of any prospective purchaser(s) of which it may become aware.

iv.   In no event shall the payment or obligation of payment of such amounts or the permission to operate for the one hundred twenty (120) day period be construed to be a reinstatement of the Franchise Agreements.

v.   If Franchisee is unable to close the sale of the Units to a purchaser(s) satisfactory to [Franchisor] within the one hundred twenty (120) day period or Franchisee does not pay all obligations on a current basis, or if Franchisee fails to comply with [Franchisor's] operational standards and insurance requirements, Franchisee shall immediately, upon written notice from [Franchisor], de-identify the restaurants by removal of all signs utilizing the [Franchisor's] trademark or otherwise identifying the restaurants as [Franchisor's] Restaurants and will remove all other indicia that the restaurants are [Franchisor's] Restaurants, including any decor items, menu boards, trade dress, paper products or the like as more fully set forth in the post-termination provisions of the Franchise Agreements for the above-referenced Units.

vi.   From the date this Letter Agreement is executed by Franchisee and you, individually, until the close of the sale of the Units to a purchaser(s) satisfactory to [Franchisor], Franchisee and you shall continue to pay the current $____ monthly payment towards reducing the balance of the accelerated promissory note which currently totals $____. (*See* Exhibit "B"). Upon close of the sale of the Units to a purchaser(s) satisfactory to [Franchisor], [Franchisor] will agree to waive the interest on the principal amount of the accelerated promissory note (currently $____), the interest on the past due installments (currently $____) and the default payment portion of the accelerated promissory note ($____) which currently totals $____. (*See* Exhibit "B"). In exchange, Franchisee and/or you will pay the principal balance of the accelerated promissory note (which currently totals $____) out of the proceeds of any sale of the Units. Said numbers will be adjusted accordingly at the date of closing. If no sale is consummated at the end of the one hundred twenty (120) day period, [Franchisor] will waive the default payment portion of the accelerated promissory note ($____) and [Franchisor] will agree to issue a new promissory note for the principal amount of the promissory note plus all accrued interest, payable in ___ equal monthly installments, at prime plus 2.5%. Finally, if the Franchisee and/or you should become delinquent on any promissory note payment, then the default payment of $____ will be added to the promissory note balance and the promissory note will be immediately accelerated.

vii. By 5:00 p.m. E.S.T. on Friday, December 27, 1996, Franchisee must wire transfer to [Franchisor's] account or [Franchisor] must receive a cashier's check in the amount of all the past due fees which currently totals $_____ (as set forth in Paragraph 3 above and Exhibit "C"). [Franchisor's] wire transfer instructions are as follows:

Wire to: [wiring instructions]

viii.   Franchisee and you hereby relinquish all rights, interests and claims of whatever nature to, in or under the Franchise Agreements, the parties thereof and the relationships created thereby, and do hereby forever release and forever discharge [Franchisor], its predecessors, heirs, successors, representatives, assigns, agents, employees, attorneys, officers and directors, and each of them of and from any claims, debts, liabilities, demands, obligations, costs, expenses, actions and causes of action of every nature, character, and description, known or unknown, vested or contingent, which Franchisee and/or you now owns or holds, or had at any time heretofore owned or held, or may at any time own or hold against [Franchisor], arising pursuant to the Franchise Agreements or as a result of or arising out of the course of dealing prior to and including the date of this Letter Agreement.

This offer is final, not subject to further negotiation and is valid until 5:00 p.m. E.S.T. on Friday, December 27, 1996. If these terms are acceptable to you and the Franchisee, please sign and date this letter on the signature and date lines provided below and return to me via facsimile, by 5:00 p.m. E.S.T. on Friday, December 27, 1996 and return the original signed document to me via overnight mail.

If you have any questions regarding this matter, please do not hesitate to contact me.

Sincerely,

[Corporate Counsel]

SO AGREED:

_____
[Franchisee]

By: _____

Its: _____

_____
Date

_____
[Franchisee's Principal], Individually

_____
Date

EXHIBIT 6-F: Reinstatement of Franchise Agreement between [Franchisor] and [Licensee]

THIS REINSTATEMENT AGREEMENT (the "Reinstatement") is made this ____ day of _____ 1998, by and between _____ (hereinafter referred to as "Franchisor") and _____ (hereinafter referred to as "Licensee").

WHEREAS, Franchisor and Licensee entered into a Franchise Agreement dated _____ (hereinafter the "Franchise Agreement") for the operation of a _____ Unit located at _____ (hereinafter "Unit No. ___" or the "Franchised Unit"); and

WHEREAS, pursuant to a Notice of Termination letter dated _____ Franchisor terminated the Franchise Agreement due to Licensee's failure to pay Advertising Fund Fees, Service Fees and other financial obligations due to the Franchisor pursuant to the terms of the Franchise Agreement; and

WHEREAS, Licensee has requested that Franchisor reinstate the Franchise Agreement, subject to the terms and conditions hereof, and Franchisor has agreed to such request upon the terms and conditions set forth herein.

NOW THEREFORE, in consideration of the mutual covenants and conditions herein contained, and other good and valuable consideration, receipt of which is hereby acknowledged by each of the parties hereto, the parties agree as follows:

1. The Franchise Agreement which was terminated pursuant to the Notice of Termination letter dated _____ is hereby reinstated under the same terms and conditions as set forth therein, except as otherwise provided herein.

2. Licensee agrees that upon the reinstatement of the Franchise Agreement for Unit No. ___, all accrued monetary obligations owed to Franchisor, including, but not limited to, all obligations arising pursuant to the Franchise Agreement shall be paid in full or a satisfactory arrangement for payment of said fees must be made between Licensee and Franchisor.

3. This Reinstatement shall be attached to and become a part of the Franchise Agreement. The terms and conditions stated in this Reinstatement, to the extent they are inconsistent with the terms and conditions of the Franchise Agreement, shall prevail over the terms and conditions of the Franchise Agreement.

4. In further consideration of the obligations of the parties undertaken herein, Licensee hereby releases and forever discharges Franchisor and Franchisor's predecessors, successors, and its present and future representatives, assigns, agents, employees, officers and directors (hereinafter collectively referred to as "Designees"), and each of them, of and from any claims, debts, liabilities, demands, obligations, costs, expenses, actions and causes of action of every nature, character, and description, known or unknown, vested or contingent, which Licensee now owns or holds, or has at any time heretofore, owned or held, or may at any time own or hold against Franchisor, or its Designees (hereinafter collectively referred to as "Claims"). Notwithstanding the foregoing, nothing herein shall release the continuing obligations of Franchisor and Licensee which are set forth in this Reinstatement, and/or in the Franchise Agreement, the terms of which are hereby ratified by the parties hereto, and which shall remain in full force and effect, except as specifically amended herein.

5. As further consideration for the execution of this Agreement by Franchisor, Licensee does hereby forever discharge and release Franchisor, its predecessors, its successors and its present and former officers, directors, agents and employees from any and all claims, causes of action, obligations and liabilities arising prior to the date hereof, it being the intent of Licensee to grant in favor of the Franchisor a general release of any claims Licensee might have against Franchisor as a result of or arising out of their course of dealing through the effective date of this Agreement.

6. This Reinstatement and the documents referred to herein, constitute the entire, full and complete agreement between Franchisor and Licensee, concerning the subject matter hereof and supersede any and all prior agreements. No other representations have induced Licensee to execute this Reinstatement; and there are no representations, inducements, promises or agreements, oral or otherwise between the parties not embodied herein which are of any force or effect with reference to this Reinstatement or otherwise. No amendment, charge or variance from this Reinstatement shall be binding on either party unless executed in writing.

7. The parties hereto agree that this Agreement constitutes the full and complete understanding and agreement among the parties regarding the subject matter hereof, and no representations, agreements, warranties, or statements, oral or in writing, not contained therein, shall be of any force or effect against Franchisor and this Agreement shall not be modified, except in writing, signed by all parties. The parties intend for this Reinstatement to be construed and interpreted under the laws of the State of _____, without regard to its choice of law or conflict of law rules. All parties further waive any right to a jury trial and all defenses of personal jurisdiction and/or venue and agree that any litigation or other legal proceeding pertaining to or arising from the execution of this Agreement shall be brought in a court of competent jurisdiction within the State of _____.

8. Licensee acknowledges that it has received, read and understood this Reinstatement, that Franchisor has fully and adequately explained its provisions to Licensee's satisfaction, and that Franchisor has accorded Licensee ample time and opportunity to consult with advisors of its own choosing, including Licensee's attorneys, about the potential benefits and risks of entering into this Reinstatement.

9. The Franchise Agreement shall remain in full force and effect except as otherwise provided herein.

Licensee hereby agrees not to disclose the terms and/or conditions of this Reinstatement to any party, other than to Licensee's attorneys. Violation of this confidentiality provision shall be deemed a material default of the Franchise Agreement.

IN WITNESS WHEREOF, the parties hereto, intending to be legally bound hereby, have executed this Reinstatement, in duplicate on the day and year first above-written.

WITNESS: **FRANCHISOR:**

_____   By: _____

                               Its: _____

WITNESS: **LICENSEE:**

_____   By: _____

                               Its: _____

EXHIBIT 6-G: Transfer and Release Agreement

This **TRANSFER AND RELEASE AGREEMENT** (the "Agreement") is made and entered into on this _____ day of _____, 19___, by and among **Franchisor,** a XXX corporation, having its principal place of business at XXX, _____ a XXX corporation (hereinafter "Franchisee"); and _____, a XXX company (hereinafter "Transferee").

WITNESSETH:

WHEREAS, a Franchise Agreement dated _____ was executed by and between Franchisee and Franchisor for the operation of a franchised unit located at _____ (the "Franchised Restaurant"); and

WHEREAS, Franchisor has been notified of Franchisee's desire to transfer to Transferee all right, title and interest held by Franchisee, in and to the Franchise Agreement and, therefore, has requested that Franchisor consent to the transfer thereof to Transferee pursuant to Section ___ of said Franchise Agreement; and

WHEREAS, Franchisor is willing to grant its consent to the proposed transfer of the Franchise Agreement, subject to the terms and conditions set forth herein.

AGREEMENT:

NOW, THEREFORE, in consideration of the mutual covenants and conditions herein contained, and other good and valuable consideration, receipt of which is hereby acknowledged by each of the parties hereto, the parties agree as follows:

1. Franchisor hereby consents to and waives its right of first refusal in connection with the transfer by Franchisee to Transferee of all of Franchisee's right, title and interest in and to the Franchise Agreement. The foregoing consent and waiver is subject to and made in reliance upon the following terms, conditions, representations and warranties:

   A.   Franchisee and Transferee represent, warrant and agree that, subject to Franchisor's consent, Franchisee has transferred to Transferee all of Franchisee's right, title and interest in and to the Franchise Agreement, and that all legal actions necessary to effect such transfer have been accomplished.

   B.   Transferee must execute Franchisor's current form Franchise Agreement.

   C.   Payment by Franchisee to Franchisor, in a manner satisfactory to Franchisor, of all accrued monetary obligations, including, but not limited to, all obligations pursuant to the Franchise Agreement, and any Lease and/or Sublease Agreement.

   D.   Payment by Franchisee, in a manner satisfactory to Franchisor, of all other outstanding statements for equipment and/or merchandise purchased by Franchisee from Franchisor, or any other subsidiary or affiliate of Franchisor.

   E.   Franchisee and Transferee acknowledge and agree that all obligations owed by either of them to Franchisor, its subsidiaries and affiliates, must be resolved to Franchisor's satisfaction as a condition of Franchisor's execution of this Agreement.

   F.   Franchisee acknowledges and agrees that, notwithstanding the terms of this Agreement, Franchisee will comply with all of the requirements of the Franchise Agreement, which, by their nature, are intended to survive the termination or expiration of said Franchise Agreement, including, but not limited to, the covenants against competition and against disclosure of confidential information as specified therein.

G.   Transferee shall be and shall remain liable for all obligations under the Franchise Agreement and shall perform all unperformed or partially performed terms and conditions of said Franchise Agreement as though Transferee were the original Franchisee thereunder as of the effective date of this Agreement.

H.   For a period of thirty six (36) months from the date hereof, Franchisee, (hereinafter referred to as "Guarantor") shall remain liable, as guarantor, and hereby guaranties all performance, operations and financial obligations of the Transferee under the Franchise Agreement and the current form franchise agreement to be executed by Transferee. Guarantor acknowledges that, during the effective period of the guaranty, Franchisor may look first to Guarantor for all such unperformed obligations, without being required to first seek recourse against Transferee, the intention of this Paragraph being to render Guarantor and Transferee jointly and severally liable during the effective period of the guaranty. Guarantor shall execute the guaranty in the form attached hereto as Exhibit "1".

I.   Transferee must pay to Franchisor a _____ Transfer Fee which is due and payable upon execution of this Agreement.

J.   Transferee agrees to satisfy the work requirements for the repair and maintenance items listed on the Scope of Work Schedule attached hereto as Exhibit "2", and to complete such work in accordance with the time periods specified in the attached Exhibit "2". **Failure to complete such scope of work in accordance with the time periods specified in the attached Exhibit "2" will be considered a material default of the Franchise Agreement and may result in termination**.

2. As further consideration for the execution of this Agreement by Franchisor, Franchisee hereby relinquishes all rights, interests and claims of whatever nature to, in or under the Franchise Agreement, and the relationships created thereby, and does hereby forever discharge and release Franchisor, its predecessors, its successors and its present and former officers, directors, agents and employees from any and all claims, causes of action, obligations and liability arising from, under or out of the Franchise Agreement, or any other act or occurrence of any kind whatsoever, it being the intent of Franchisee to grant in favor of the Franchisor a general release of any claims Franchisee might have against Franchisor as a result of or arising out of their course of dealing through the effective date of this Agreement.

3. Franchisee and Transferee acknowledge and agree that, except for the preparation and execution of this Agreement, Franchisor has not participated in the transaction between them and, therefore, has no knowledge of, and does not attest to, the accuracy of any representations or warranties made by or between Franchisee and Transferee in connection with this transfer. Franchisor assumes no obligations in that regard.

4. All parties understand and acknowledge that Franchisor may, in the future, approve offerings and transfers under different terms, conditions and policies. Franchisor's consent and waiver in this instance shall not be relied upon in future transactions as indicative of Franchisor's position or the conditions which might be attached to future consents or waivers of its right of first refusal.

5. Franchisee and Transferee acknowledge and agree that Franchisor's execution of this Agreement, is not intended to provide, and shall not be construed as providing, Franchisor's consent with regard to a transfer of any right or interest under any other agreement not specifically identified herein. Such consent must be separately obtained.

6. If any material provision or restriction contained herein shall be declared void or unenforceable under applicable law, the parties agree that such provision or restriction will be stricken, and this Agreement will continue in full force and effect. Notwithstanding this Paragraph, however, the parties agree that, to the extent Franchisor suffers harm as a consequence of the striking of such provision or restriction, the other parties to this Agreement shall exercise best efforts to make Franchisor whole.

7. Franchisor and Transferee agree that, until further written notice has been provided in accordance with the terms of the current form franchise agreement to be executed by Transferee, the official mailing address of Transferee shall be _____.

8. The parties hereto agree that this Agreement constitutes, as of the date of execution by Franchisor, the complete understanding between the parties regarding the subject matter hereof, and no representation, agreement, warranties, or statement, oral or in writing, not contained herein, shall be of any force and effect against Franchisor and this Agreement shall not be modified, altered or amended except in writing signed by all parties. The parties intend for this Agreement to be construed and interpreted under the laws of the State of _____, without regard to its choice of law or conflict of law rules. All parties further waive rights to a jury trial and all defenses of personal jurisdiction and/or venue and agree that any litigation or other legal proceeding pertaining to or arising from the execution of this Agreement shall be brought in a court of competent jurisdiction within the State of _____.

IN WITNESS WHEREOF, this Agreement has been duly signed by the parties hereto as indicated and shall be effective as of the date it is executed by Franchisor.

WITNESS: **FRANCHISEE:**

                                                By: _____
_____

WITNESS: **TRANSFEREE:**

                                                By: _____
_____

WITNESS: **FRANCHISOR:**

                                                By: _____
_____

[SIGNATURE PAGE OF TRANSFER & RELEASE AGREEMENT]

EXHIBIT 6-G-1: Guaranty and Subordination

The Undersigned, for and in consideration of, and as an inducement to, the grant by **Franchisor** Franchisor of its consent to the transfer of franchise rights to _____ ("Transferee") for the operation of a restaurant at the location described in the Franchise Agreement establishing said rights, and other good and valuable consideration, receipt and sufficiency of which are hereby acknowledged, hereby guaranties payments of any and all indebtedness and performance of any and all obligations for which Transferee is now or may hereafter become responsible for a period of thirty six (36) months from the date of the Transfer and Release Agreement by and among Franchisor, _____ ("Franchisee") and Transferee. The Undersigned agrees to be bound by, and liable for the breach of, each and every provision (both monetary obligations and obligations to take or refrain from taking specific actions or to engage or refrain from engaging in specific activities) under and pursuant to a certain Franchise Agreement by and between Franchisor and Transferee dated _____, covering **Store No. XXX** located at _____.

The Undersigned hereby agrees to be bound jointly and severally with the Transferee for any such indebtedness and obligations to Franchisor arising under the Franchisee Agreement; and the Undersigned hereby waives (a) acceptance and notice of the acceptance of this Guaranty and Subordination, (b) notice of any and all indebtedness or obligations of Transferee to Franchisor, now existing or which may hereafter exist, (c) notice of default of payment, demand and diligence, and all other notices of any kind whatsoever, and (d) all legal and equitable defenses to which the undersigned might be entitled under the Franchise Agreement or under this Guaranty and Subordination.

The Undersigned also agrees that the written acknowledgment of the Transferee or the judgment of any court establishing the amount due from the Transferee shall be conclusive and binding on the Undersigned and the Undersigned's successors and assigns, and that any extension of time for payment shall not affect the Undersigned's liability hereunder.

The Undersigned agrees to pay reasonable attorney's fees and all costs incurred by Franchisor in attempting to collect, or in collecting, any sums owed by the Transferee, as described in the Franchise Agreement (unless attorney's fees and costs are included in the indebtedness of Transferee for which the Undersigned is liable thereunder), or owed by the Undersigned as a result of or in connection with this Guaranty and Subordination.

The undersigned understands that this Guaranty and Subordination is irrevocable and is independent of any and all other guarantees that may be made by any other parties with respect to the indebtedness or obligations covered hereby.

The Undersigned hereby subordinates to the rights of Franchisor any and all rights to repayment of loans, or any claims associated therewith, made by the Undersigned to Transferee, whether now existing or hereafter arising while this Guaranty and Subordination is in effect.

This Guaranty and Subordination is for the benefit of Franchisor, which may, without any notice whatsoever to anyone, sell, assign or transfer any part of the indebtedness guaranteed herein, and in that event, each and every successive assignee, transferee or holder of all or any part of the indebtedness shall have the right to enforce this Guaranty and Subordination, by suit or otherwise, for the benefit of such assignee, transferee or holder, as fully as though such assignee, transferee or holder were herein by name given such rights, powers and benefits; but Franchisor shall have an unimpaired right, prior and superior to that of any such assignee, transferee or holder, to enforce this Guaranty and Subordination for its benefit as to such much of said indebtedness that it has not sold, assigned or transferred.

The Undersigned acknowledge that, during the effective period of this Guaranty and Subordination, Franchisor may look first to the Undersigned for all such unperformed obligations, without being required to first seek recourse or exhaust all remedies against Transferee.

The foregoing is the entire agreement affecting the Undersigned's liability for the obligations described herein. The parties intend for this Guaranty and Subordination to be construed and interpreted under the laws of the State of _____, without regard to its choice of law or conflict of law rules. The parties further waive rights to a jury trial and all defenses of personal jurisdiction and/or venue and agree that any litigation or other legal proceeding pertaining to or arising from the execution of this Guaranty and Subordination shall be brought in a court of competent jurisdiction within the State of

_____.

EXECUTED in multiple originals this _____ day of _____, 19___.

WITNESS: GUARANTOR:

_____   _____

EXHIBIT 6-G-2: Scope of Work

[Work requests for repairs and maintenance, along with deadlines for completion of work, to be set forth here.]

Table of Cases

Index

About the Editors

Steven M. Goldman is Assistant General Counsel and head of the franchise practice group Marriott International, Inc., which franchises seven hotel brands worldwide. Prior to that he was Vice-President, Franchise Administration and General Counsel of the ITT Sheraton Franchise Division and Senior Litigation Counsel with Holiday Inn Worldwide. Mr. Goldman received a J.D., cum laude, from the University of Georgia in 1985, where he was an Articles Editor of the *Law Review,* and received a B.A., cum laude, from the University of Vermont in 1982, where he was Phi Beta Kappa. Mr. Goldman is a frequent speaker and author on franchise and hospitality law. He is a member of the Governing Committee of the American Bar Association Forum on Franchising, the immediate-past Director of the Forum's Corporate Counsel Division, and a member of the Editorial Board of Leader's Franchising and Business Law Alert.

H. Bret Lowell is a partner with Piper Marbury Rudnick & Wolfe, resident in the Washington, D.C., office. He concentrates his practice in the areas of domestic and international franchising and distribution law. Mr. Lowell serves as the Co-Chair of his firm's Franchise and Distribution Law Practice Group. He is the former Chair of the Governing Committee of the American Bar Association's Forum on Franchising. Mr. Lowell serves on several committees of the International Franchise Association, including the Legal/Legislative Committee, and is a member of the Advisory Board of the IFA's Counsel of Franchise Suppliers. He is a former editor of the *Franchise Law Journal* and has authored numerous books and articles on the subjects of franchising and distribution. Mr. Lowell is a frequent lecturer on franchise law issues. He received his J.D. degree from Georgetown University Law Center in 1978, and has been selected by his peers to appear in *The Best Lawyers in America.*

About the Contributors

Charles B. Cannon practices with the firm of Jenkens & Gilchrist in Dallas, Texas. He is a member of the firm's Franchise & Distribution Practice Group and concentrates his practice on the representation of franchisors in domestic and international transactions. Mr. Cannon was elected to the Governing Committee of the American Bar Association Forum on Franchising in 1994 and currently serves as Finance Officer. His major publications include "Practical Problems Associated with Buying or Selling a Franchise Company," *Mergers & Acquisitions of Franchise Companies* (ABA 1996), and "Dependence and Reliance: Keys to Unshackling Co-Branding Alliances from Federal Franchise Rule Compliance," *Franchise Law Journal* (Fall/Winter 1997). Mr. Cannon is also a member of the Franchise & Distribution Law Committee on the Texas State Bar Intellectual Property Law Section and an active participant in the Dallas Bar Association Franchise Law Section. Mr. Cannon received his B.A. from Texas Christian University and his LL.B. from Yale Law School.

Ronald T. Coleman, Jr., is a litigation partner in the law firm of Paul, Hastings, Janofsky & Walker, LLP, in Atlanta, Georgia. He focuses his practice on franchise and intellectual property litigation, as well as other types of trade regulation and commercial litigation. He has represented franchisors in a wide variety of matters, including cases on breach of franchise agreement, breach of implied duty of good faith and fair deal, fraud, violation of and constitutional challenge to state statutes, RICO and antitrust violations, and enforcement of terminations and trademark rights. Mr. Coleman received his A.B., cum laude, from Duke University and his J.D., with honors, from Duke University School of Law. He served as law clerk to the Hon. James C. Hill, U.S. Court of Appeals for the Eleventh Circuit in 1986-87. He is a member of the American Bar Association Sections of Litigation and Intellectual Property and the Forum on Franchising.

William A. Finkelstein is Intellectual Property Counsel of PepsiCo, Inc., whose divisions and subsidiaries have included Pepsi-Cola, Frito-Lay, Tropicana, Pizza Hut, Taco Bell, Kentucky Fried Chicken, Wilson Sporting Goods, and their respective worldwide businesses. He was President of the International Trademark Association (INTA) in 1985-86 and led the INTA task force on Alternative Dispute Resolution, which created the CPR/INTA ADR Program. He is the editor/author of *ADR in Trademark and Unfair Competition Disputes: A Practitioner's Guide.* Mr. Finkelstein served on the Governing Committee of the American Bar Association Forum on Franchising and has been active in the ABA Intellectual Property Section and the International Franchise Association. He is a graduate of the University of Virginia and Boston University School of Law, and received his L.L.M. in Trade Regulation from New York University School of Law.

Mark B. Forseth is Senior Counsel in the Franchise Development & Franchise Operations Section of the Marriott International Law Department. He supervises the company's franchise regulatory compliance for seven hotel brands in the United States and Canada and four hotel brands internationally, as well as responding to legal issues involving the development and operation of franchised hotels. Prior to joining Marriott, Mr. Forseth practiced with the Franchise & Distribution Law Group at Jenkens & Gilchrist and Locke, Purnell, Rain, Harrell for eight years. He has also been the Senior Franchise Examiner for the Maryland Division of Securities, responsible for enforcement of the Maryland Franchise Registration and Disclosure Law. Mr. Forseth is a member of the American Bar Association Forum on Franchising and International Law Section, the International Franchise Association, and the Maryland and Dallas Bar Associations.

Jerry Lovejoy is Division Counsel for McDonald's Corporation in Irvine, California. He has a broad background in general corporate law, including reviewing and drafting of contracts, various forms of commercial financing arrangements, real estate transactions, acquisitions, banking law, UCC transactions, antitrust law, franchise law, and products liability. Prior to joining McDonald's Corporation, he served as Vice President and General Counsel to Baskin Robbins, Inc.; Division Counsel to PepsiCo, Inc./Taco Bell Corp.; Second Vice President and Associate Counsel to Chase Manhattan Bank, NA; and an associate with Lord, Day & Lord in New York. Mr. Lovejoy received his B.A. from Dartmouth College, Phi Beta Kappa, summa cum laude, and his J.D. from Harvard Law School, where he was the recipient of the Earl Warren Scholarship and graduated in the top third of his class.

Donnell J. McCormack, Jr., maintains an office in private practice at Kilpatrick, Stockton in Atlanta, Georgia, where he represents clients in the franchise and hospitality industry, the home theatre and automation business, and the publishing industry. Previously, he was a partner at Kilpatrick, Stockton where he formed and managed a team to handle national litigation projects for Fortune 500 clients, worked on Y2K issues, and served as the interim general counsel for ITT Sheraton. Mr. McCormack is a member of the American Bar Association Forum on Franchising and Sections of Litigation and Antitrust, the International Association of Defense Counsel, and the Georgia, Tennessee, and Memphis Bar Associations. He attended the University of Tennessee–Knoxville, participated in the Rhodes at Oxford Program, University College, Oxford, England, and received his B.A. from Rhodes College. He received his J.D. from the University of Memphis School of Law, graduating in the top 15 percent of his class.

Ken R. Minami is Vice President and General Counsel for Allied Domecq Retailing International, the operating company for the Baskin Robbins, Dunkin' Donuts, and Togo's brands in all international markets, under the London-based Allied Domecq PLC umbrella. Previously, Mr. Minami served as Senior Corporate Counsel for Baskin Robbins USA, Co. and Allied Domecq Retailing USA. He has also worked in private practice in Century City, California, with the law firm of Tyre, Kamins, Katz & Granof. He is currently based in the Glendale office of ADRI and oversees legal affairs with respect to its brands in over 60 countries and a total of 3,551 international retail units. Mr. Minami is a member of the American Bar Association Forum on Franchising, the California State Bar Association, and the Los Angeles County Bar Association. He received his B.A. from the University of California at Los Angeles and his J.D. from Loyola Law School in Los Angeles.

Raymond L. Miolla, Jr., is a Region Vice President at Burger King Corporation, where he is responsible for the general management of Burger King Corp.'s 1,700 restaurants in the Western Region and its 500 franchisees. Previously, he worked in the legal department at Burger King Corp., where he ultimately served as the Assistant General Counsel responsible for all legal issues in the North American, Latin American, and the Asian/Pacific divisions. He worked extensively on franchising, finance, and joint venture matters in both domestic and international markets. Mr. Miolla also practiced at Hale & Dorr in Boston, Massachusetts, where he was a member of the Corporate and Commercial Law Departments. He received his B.A., magna cum laude, from Middlebury College and his J.D. from Boston University School of Law, where he served a term as Executive Editor of the *Annual Review of Banking Law.*

Lisa Pender Morse is Corporate Counsel—Franchise Dispute Resolution & Marketing and Assistant Secretary of AFC Enterprises, Inc., in Atlanta, Georgia. She is primarily responsible for all franchise dispute resolution issues, including domestic and international franchise litigation and intellectual property litigation, for all AFC concepts, which include Popeye's Chicken & Biscuits, Church's Chicken, Cinnabon, Seattle's Best Coffee, and Torrefazione Italia. Ms. Morse also provides legal counsel on a wide range of other transactional business activities for AFC and its concepts. She is a member of the American Bar Association Forum on Franchising and is President of the Board of Directors of the Corporate Counsel Section of the Atlanta Bar Association. Ms. Morse received her B.S. from Penn State and her J.D. from the University of Dayton.

Grover C. Outland, III, is General Counsel of ATL International, Inc., the nationwide franchisor of All Tune and Lube Centers. During his tenure with ATL International, the company's franchise network has grown from approximately 20 centers in relatively close proximity to its Maryland headquarters to over 300 franchisees in 35 states, the Caribbean, and Canada. Mr. Outland served as Chairman of the Franchise and Distribution Law Committee of the Maryland State Bar Association Business Law Section Council in 1997-99. He co-chaired the first-ever joint program sponsored by Virginia and Maryland franchise regulators and bar committees, MICPEL (Maryland Continuing Legal Education), and Virginia Continuing Legal Education to focus on franchise law and practice: "Understanding and Negotiating the Franchise Agreement." He serves on the Steering Committee of the Corporate Counsel Division of the American Bar Association Forum on Franchising. Mr. Outland is a graduate of the Virginia Military Institute and the University of Virginia Law School.

Andrew C. Selden is a shareholder and member of the Board of Directors of Briggs & Morgan, PA, in Minneapolis, Minnesota. He was chairman of the American Bar Association Forum on Franchising from 1985 to 1989 and a member of its governing committee from 1983 to 1989. Mr. Selden was the reporter of the Uniform Franchise and Business Opportunities Act promulgated by the National Conference of Commissioners on Uniform State Laws and is a member and former Chairman of the Industry Advisory Committee to the Franchise Regulation Committee of the North American Securities Administrators Association. He is an editorial representative for the International Bar Association Section on Business Law Committee on International Franchising. Mr. Selden has published articles on franchising in the *Franchise Law Journal,* the *Business Lawyer,* and the *IFA Franchise Legal Digest.*

Anthony M. Stiegler is a partner in the Litigation Department of Cooley, Godward, LLP, in San Diego, California. He focuses his practice on civil trials with an emphasis on intellectual property disputes, including copyright, trade secret, trademark, anti-counterfeiting, patent, unfair competition, unfair trade practices, and general commercial litigation. Recent cases include a five-week plaintiff's biotechnology patent infringement jury trial involving transcription-based assays resulting in an $18.5 million federal court jury verdict and permanent injunction on behalf of SIBIA Neurosciences, Inc. He is a former Vice President of the San Diego Chapter Federal Bar Association, as well as a former officer and founder of the Tulane University Alumni Association in San Diego. Mr. Stiegler was a law clerk to the Hon. Edward J. Schwartz, U.S. District Court, Southern District of California. He received his B.A. from Grinnell College in San Diego and his J.D. from Tulane University Law School, where he was Order of the Coif.

Sheri A. Young is Vice President, Associate General Counsel, and Assistant Secretary for Budget Group Inc., which owns various transportation and travel industry–related companies. Among her responsibilities, she provides legal advice on the full life cycle of franchise and other distribution relationships worldwide, including acquiring and selling franchise businesses, system development, and dispute resolution. Ms. Young previously practiced at Levin & Funkhouser, Ltd., and Arvey, Hodes, Costello & Burman in Chicago, Illinois. She has published a variety of articles, including "Evolution of Vicarious Liability as Applied to Franchise Law," and "Internal Dispute Resolution Techniques: A Review of What Works in Franchising." Ms. Young is a member of the American Bar Association Forum on Franchising and the International Section and of the American Bar Association Corporate Counsel Committee. She received her B.S. and J.D. from the University of Michigan at Ann Arbor, where she received the Xi Sigma Pi award and other scholastic awards.